Criminology and Criminal Policy Movements

Eugenio Raúl Zaffaroni
and
Edmundo Oliveira

UNIVERSITY PRESS OF AMERICA,® INC.
Lanham • Boulder • New York • Toronto • Plymouth, UK

University Press of America,® Inc.
4501 Forbes Boulevard
Suite 200
Lanham, Maryland 20706
UPA Acquisitions Department (301) 459-3366

10 Thornbury Road
Plymouth PL6 7PP
United Kingdom

Printed in the United States of America
British Library Cataloging in Publication Information Available

Library of Congress Control Number: 2012931662
ISBN: 978-0-7618-5852-2 (paperback : alk. paper)
eISBN: 978-0-7618-5853-9

∞™ The paper used in this publication meets the minimum requirements of American National Standard for Information Sciences—Permanence of Paper for Printed Library Materials, ANSI Z39.48-1992

Contents

Preface

History, Science, and Politics—Criminology's Foundations and Challenges

Emilio C. Viano, Professor, American University and Washington College of Law, Washington, D.C.

Crime in all its many manifestations, as defined by different societies, value systems, and interests, is very much on the mind of most people all over the world today. Street crimes, crimes against property, violent crimes, white collar crimes, domestic violence, child abuse, trafficking in persons, drug trafficking, sexual abuse and exploitation, the victimization of the elderly, and many other types of crime are very much part of today's panoply of social problems that concern billions of people, impact their lives, and influence politics and the law every day.

Most recently, terrorism has occupied center stage worldwide; spurred the enactment of countless laws and conventions; and absorbed a lion's share of available resources. Piracy, an ancient type of crime erroneously thought by some to be extinct, is resurfacing with considerable resilience and strength. It is noticeable especially because of the apparent inability and impotence of the worldwide community to fight it in a coherent and effective way. The so-called "war on terrorism" that has led to major conflicts in Iraq, Afghanistan, Somalia and other parts of the world from Ireland to Spain, France, the Philippines, some regions of China, and elsewhere has also called our attention to the possibility of state-planned and perpetrated crimes consisting most often of violations of human rights and humanitarian law norms.

The publication in the Spring of 2004 of the dramatic pictures of sexual humiliation and torture at Abu Ghraib prison near Baghdad revealed how some U.S. soldiers, intelligence officers, and private contractors mistreated Iraqi prisoners captured during and after the war. Similar abuses occurred elsewhere in Iraq, Afghanistan, Guantanamo Bay and other detention camps operated by the U.S. military, contractors or the CIA.

Government officials of high rank may have turned a blind eye, if not encouraged, the abuses. Only after the international outcry, the Americans have reluctantly agreed to provide protections customarily granted civilians and military combatants during a war to people detained in Iraq and Afghanistan. In other areas of the world, like for example the Congo, Somalia, Darfur, no such remedies are even minimally available.

Against this background of continuing conflict and war in the world, there is an increasing acceptance today of the norm and practice to prosecute persons accused of crimes of aggression, war crimes, and crimes against humanity before international criminal courts or tribunals. While this contemporary approach to justice administered after an armed conflict is becoming increasingly accepted, this type of tribunals that adhere to the rule of law and put justice before retribution, have been introduced only relatively recently.

The first example of modern international criminal tribunals came at the end of World War II when the Allied powers tried German officials at Nuremberg and Japanese officials at Tokyo for crimes committed during the war. However, the road to Nuremberg was hardly clear then, and the challenges and criticisms were many. The fact that there are now several active international courts, the International Criminal Tribunal for the Ex-Yugoslavia (I.C.T.Y.), the International Criminal Tribunal for Rwanda (I.C.T.R.), the International Criminal Court (I.C.C.), the Special Court for Sierra Leone and the Special Tribunal for Cambodia, is truly remarkable, given that the only two precedents came sixty years ago, and that the modern institutions follow a fifty-year Cold-War-induced inaction and silence on international criminal justice. As the modern tribunals have been organized and are operational, and the I.C.C. is functioning, these institutions have been and will continue to be challenged on grounds of legitimacy, fairness, legal establishment and criminal jurisdiction.

Another new and challenging form of crime is represented by cybercrime. The term "cybercrime" or "computer crime" was first introduced in the late 1990s as the use of the internet expanded dramatically, especially in North America. The so-called G-8 Group of countries[1] at a 1996 meeting in Lyon, France established a Task Force to study the emerging criminal problems connected to the growing use of the internet. This "Lyon group" used the "cybercrime" term to describe in a very imprecise way all crimes committed on the internet or through new networks of telecommunications sprouting up in part because of the lowering of telecommunications costs. With the input of the countries participating in the work of the Lyon group, the Council of Europe formulated the Cybercrime Convention presented for signature and ratification by Member States and other States on November 23, 2001. It includes an array of different computer related offenses in its substantive criminal law provisions.[2] For instance, one section on "computer-related offenses" is subdivided into articles on computer-related fraud and computer-related forgery. However, the Convention does not specifically define cybercrime. The challenge in defining "cyber or computer crime" arises partly because computers can serve many different roles in criminal activities.[3] They can be the "object" used to commit the crime, the "target" of the criminal activity, or tangential to the crime. Further, the widely different criminal conduct associated with computer crimes provides an endless list of activities that can be encompassed within the term "computer crime." For example, computer crimes can include crimes involving pornography, auction fraud, telecommunication fraud, copyright and piracy offenses, online extortion plots, identity fraud, hacking,[4] cyberterrorism, and cyberstalking. Many of these crimes are traditional offenses that are now being committed by using a computer and the internet.

The perpetrators, victims, and motives can also vary considerably in computer crimes. For example, one offender may be a young hacker intent upon demonstrating his or her abilities to break into a government or business security system. Then again, the offender may be a terrorist breaking into the same system for the purpose of destroying or disabling a government, a business or a military entity.

It should not be automatically assumed that criminal conduct that exploits cyberspace represents a totally new phenomenon, that is, "cybercrime." It may simply mean that perpetrators are using cyberspace to engage in conduct that has long been outlawed. The development of the telephone, radio and television, for example, all made it possible to perpetrate fraud in new and different ways, but fraud itself has been a crime for centuries. Thus, at the beginning there was considerable confusion. The term cyber or computer crime was being applied to old types of criminality like the distribution of pornographic material on the internet that was violating some, but not all, laws of different countries prohibiting unacceptable pornography and sexually oriented material exploiting children and women. The fact that the internet does not have frontiers facilitated the distribution of these materials at the international level, at times without leaving any traces of who the author was.

Another type of cybercrime is the illegal penetration of computer-based databanks and systems or computer piracy which in many countries was not yet a crime just a few years ago. One of the goals of the Cybercrime Convention was to establish uniform legal provisions that should be included in the laws of the countries signing and ratifying the treaty so that this new type of criminal activity can be fought against with better coordination and mutual assistance. Another area that has attracted a lot of attention, controversy and activity is internet gambling. There is no unified position of different countries on gambling. While attempts to outlaw internet gambling are often portrayed as measures to protect public morality and especially minors who might be able to access gambling through the internet and become addicted to it, many developed countries rely on the income of legal gambling, including state-run lotteries, to provide funds for the country's general budget and support tourism-based economies in gambling destinations. For these countries the introduction of virtual gambling competition was and is a major concern, probably mostly because of monopolistic financial considerations.[5] Before the Cybercrime Convention was produced, civil libertarians in the world were busy fighting domestic laws and policies that introduced the obligatory retention of data on citizens and the storage of data on the use of telecommunications and the internet on the part of citizens, justified by the need to investigate crimes and by the need to combat and prevent terrorism. The retention and storage of data on individuals was part of a package of controls introduced in the United States by the FBI around 1992 that deemed it necessary to fight crime on the "information superhighway" as the internet was described then.

During the 1990s internet activists, technical experts, and private enterprise did succeed in uniting to fight against the imposition of controls on cryptography, including depositing decoding keys with the government. Various governments wanted a copy of every decoding key so as to be ready to combat more easily criminal activity. Originally, cryptography was a field for military experts and national security but civilians steadily became more involved and cryptography became more and more publicly used. This confrontation lasted for several years. On the one hand it is true that management can cover up crimes, like drug trafficking, money laundering or fraud, through cryptography. On the other hand private companies have a legitimate interest and need to protect themselves from industrial espionage and criminal manipulations by using a strong system of cryptography.

Finally, the United States and other countries softened their position on this at about the same time that the Cybercrime Convention was being prepared. Regardless, during this time the climate between internet activists and the experts was marred by distrust because of the various actions by governments trying to block privacy and encryption on the internet. A major struggle for power began between governments that wanted to read everything that was transmitted over telecommunications networks, and especially the internet, and individuals, represented by civil liberties groups, who did not believe that the government was really protecting them. On the contrary, they thought that governments were attempting to take control at the beginning of this new era of information and create strict programs of surveillance that would proliferate and threaten citizens' civil and constitutional rights. This policy of governmental control has increased especially since September 11, 2001 ostensibly justified by the fight against terrorism. So, then, what is cyber or computer crime? But first, what is cyberspace? This word was coined by the science fiction writer William Gibson in 1982. It was applied to the internet by Howard Rheingold. It rapidly became a popular way to describe this new infrastructure of communications. But at times we forget that cyberspace does not exist. What exists is a network, servers and electronic machines. Internet communications are ephemeral, liable to easily disappear. There is a certain fragility in the relationship of an individual and his or her computer and e-mail programs. Who has not lost a document by forgetting to save it properly and regularly as the work progressed? Who has not lost e-mail messages and other documents because of a computer or program error and failure? But it is also true that a well-trained investigator with appropriate forensic tools can find and reconstruct practically everything. This is because, differently from the analogical world, the digital world leaves behind information on each bit and byte that was sent. For the common internet user, cyberspace provides a good description of this magical super-space in which data, information and messages are sent and received. However, it is not clear that the term "cybercrime" is necessarily useful or understood. Crimes occur in the real world and, generally, they involve real people and money. It is essential not to lose sight of this and to keep in perspective the more transient aspects of internet communications.

In reality, we have built a world where chips generate new information and send it around the world in electronic digital sequences. We are unable to detect and understand them without the help of computers and appropriate software. Regardless, this digital and parallel world does exist and the digital bits constitute a new type of evidence. The digital bits also represent a new type of risk for the individual since whoever knows how to falsify digital evidence can create a new digital person. This is an especially insidious type of crime, more subtle than others. It is becoming more and more frequent in the form of identity theft. This way the term "cybercrime" can be useful to describe and understand crime against the digital person.

The digital person is a model of a person created through the accumulation, recompilation, storage and analysis of data on that person. It is a very useful concept to understand the way in which the new networked world we live in, operates. The digital person is also a phenomenon potentially threatening, degrading and socially dangerous. The threat stems from the collection, monitoring and analysis of data collected on citizens and that allow monitoring persons through data. Keeping track of data is a means economically effective to exercise control on the behavior and habits of individuals, groups and societies. The digital person is subject to particular techniques of data collection and monitoring like comparisons, characterization and profiling done using appropriate software on a computer.

There has been considerable and maybe worrying progress in this area. The digital person is a model that helps us understand and appreciate the shadow that we project in the digital world of cyberspace. It is a model and representation of the public personality of an individual, based on data and maintained by means of transactions and that has been conceived and formulated to be used as a representation of the individual.

Bits are useful to identify individuals so that we can contact them through their email addresses or identify them as persons who are authorized to enter into certain transactions like paying bills on line, buy items, plan travel, etc. Through bits we can develop a composite of habits and a personality that are as real as the human being that exists behind them. Actually, governments and businesses rely on them to know their clients and have more confidence in electronic proof of identity and the digital person than in the corresponding real individuals. Of course, errors, hacking or security breaches in databanks demonstrate the fragility of placing too much faith in this digital reality. For instance phishing and pharming attacks and the illegal substitution of email addresses and websites to deceive unsuspecting users, seduce them to provide personal information and then defraud them, demonstrate how this trust can easily be misplaced. Fraudsters then use these data to convince business people, stores, vendors, governmental agencies and banks that they are the real person. There are also cases when fictitious but probable persons, with no "real" individual behind them, have been created by criminals using a composite of various data.

In the world of cyberspace, there could be an unlimited number of these fictitious models that operate there generally, even though not always, to deceive, swindle, and commit or combat crimes. Law enforcement personnel introduce themselves in chat rooms as very young persons to ensnare possible pedophiles and sex criminals. Singles looking for a mate create a profile of themselves to be posted on the internet that does not always correspond to reality, a measure at times justified by security concerns. Once one has come to know better some of the other people of the website or chat room, one can let his or her mask down and reveal his or her true self. This approach is especially dangerous when there is a pedophile or sex criminal at the other end of the conversation.

As we advance more and more towards a world where electronic control and monitoring of human beings is growing exponentially, we should ask ourselves: where are we going? Soon, identification chips embedded in the clothes, cars and many of the personal items we purchase every day and the identity cards that we carry with ourselves will communicate with data collection centers and provide considerable information on what we normally do. Transmitters incorporated into these items, thanks to nanotechnology, will follow our movements and inform relevant authorities, our employers, parents, friends, spouse and even our insurers.

If one correctly falsifies these footprints, a real human being could confront in court a digital person, very convincingly put together and beyond the control of the real person in question. Using biometry to connect these footprints with the individual whose identity has been stolen may help solve the situation or worsen it. Civil libertarians are concerned about the introduction and use of biometric identity machines in our daily lives also because they are known to generate false positives and false negatives.

There is no question that as the digital person—the *alter ego* of everyone of us in the eyes of government, business, and security—grows in social and economic importance, it attracts the attention of many, including criminals. What happens to us when we are forced to take extensive measures to protect our identity on a daily basis in some sort of "arms race" to combat the intrusion of the government and of delinquents? If we are obliged to distance ourselves from our "person" in order to meet the demands of constant vigilance against the threats that we face on a daily basis, what will this do to our perception of ourselves and of our relationship with others? Criminology is richly interwoven with sociology, psychology, criminal law and political science. The challenge posed by the rapid development of cyber identity, cyber and computer crime and related security measures, which no doubt will grow in technological sophistication and intrusiveness in the near future, is one, among others, that criminologists should seriously consider and address. Our perception of identity, of our place in society, of our importance and dignity is profoundly based on social relations, on how we are perceived by others and on the response that we receive from others. The definition of who we really are is becoming more and more blurred. It is increasingly digital, metaphysical, with an existence of its own, crafted, manipulated and controlled by others—the government, credit rating institutions, security agencies and so on. A complex panoply of new situations and crimes is rapidly unfolding. For criminology to be useful and relevant to society, it must redirect itself toward those new and developing phenomena that are deeply affecting our daily lives, and address the nature, types and impact of old crimes challenging us in new and very different ways. This requires bold and novel approaches, high intellectual energy and strong multidisciplinary knowledge and skills. There is no question that the criminal landscape has changed considerably since the first scientific attempts at understanding criminal behavior and how to prevent it. Considerably complex new challenges are facing criminology especially because of the massive technological revolution that is constantly ongoing and continuously demanding that we change our lives accordingly.

And it is here that this volume, *Criminology and Criminal Policy Movements*, comes in as a major contribution to provide much needed and timely analysis and new visions for addressing crime and the consequent criminal policies, ancient, perennial and ever changing phenomena that are now moving into the ethereal world of cyberspace. This volume offers an intellectual marathon, covering the major theories, policies, approaches, practices and techniques that have been or are introduced to tackle crime in society.

This is a collection of essays written by two distinguished Latin American criminologists, Eugenio Raùl Zaffaroni of Argentina and Edmundo Oliveira of Brazil.

The chapters authored by Eugenio R. Zaffaroni are mostly theoretical and policy-oriented in nature. They constitute a magnificent, intellectually challenging and satisfying journey into the depths of history, philosophy and legal theory to examine with brilliant insights and unerring analysis the roots, dynamics, prejudices and social forces that throughout the centuries have generated the notion, definition, classification, reaction to and punishment of crime.

Prof. Zaffaroni's work presented here is encyclopedic in nature, in the sense that it covers and addresses all the major schools of thought, all the more important theories, all the most important historical events, all the relevant legal approaches to crime and what to do with it. It is a rich, dense, chewy reading that requires intense concentration and attention to detail. It presupposes a deep craving for intellectually challenging and stimulating readings, a mind alert and open to collateral links to theories, laws, historical events, cultural tenets, and religious observances. Prof. Zaffaroni recounts and deftly analyzes events, people, encounters, theories, social movements, innovations, religious edicts and bloody revolutions from Paris to Rome to Mexico to various other countries and to periods of the history of Spain's colonization of South America.

There is no question that any attentive reader will derive not only great intellectual stimulation and satisfaction from reading Prof. Zaffaroni's chapters but also become finally able to comprehensively understand the historic, religious, cultural, economic and political dynamics that have impacted the definition of crime and deviance and society's response to them. Chapters like "Criminal Law and Social Protest" or "Seeking the Enemy: from *Satan* to *Cool* Criminal Law" or "Criminology and Psychiatry: The Trauma of the First Meeting" are major "tours de force" on the complexity, intricacy, and constantly evolving societal response to crime that takes into account the historical, religious, economic and social reality of different times and epochs. The chapter on Girardin, a forgotten French abolitionist of the Nineteenth Century, is a gem that delights at the same time that it instructs and enlightens.

Prof. Zaffaroni is a recognized authority and a true luminary in the fields of criminal law and criminology. It is a very positive development for both fields that his work is now reaching the English-reading world for even more diffusion, impact and recognition. His contributions will resonate in the academic and professional world and spur more debate, intellectual dialogue, research and pragmatic intervention.

The various chapters authored by Edmundo Oliveira focus on more concrete and operational matters while at the same time offering a solid theoretical foundation and keen political and historical analyses. Prof. Oliveira is not afraid to wade into very sensitive, delicate and hotly debated topics. "Crime and Heredity," "The Delinquent by Tendency," "Importance and Usefulness of the Criminological Exam" are some of the chapters in this book. These are very charged subjects that elicit strong reactions and heated discussions on both sides of the issue. Many scholars would rather steer clear of this "third-rail" type of subject matters. It is to the credit of Prof. Oliveira's superb scholarship, balanced approach, and pragmatic vision that he can deal with these topics in a positive, matter-of-fact and useful manner. These are not ideological chapters meant to advance a specific viewpoint with a slanted analysis and gerrymandering of the facts.

Prof. Oliveira approaches these sensitive areas with a keen sense of the complexity of the issues; an excellent command of the language that makes it possible for him to carefully calibrate the expression of his thoughts and appropriately address the issues; and with a steely discipline in avoiding any partisan advocacy and slanted points of view.

Prof. Oliveira must be truly commended for tackling these areas that are often "off limits" to criminologists in the United States and elsewhere because of political and ideological pressures that misconstrue the nature of the issues to be debated. His command of the historical foundations and evolution of the concepts, doctrines, purported scientific bases and centuries-old debates on these topics is impressive. One is offered a comprehensive view of how these issues originated, evolved and elicited support or rejection throughout the years and of how we can today rationally and dispassionately consider them for possible adoption and implementation. The issue of punishment and imprisonment is also of great relevance in the chapters contributed by Prof. Oliveira. Especially the chapters on the "Penitentiary Consensualism" movement and on "Criminology and Criminal Policy" are focused on themes that have attracted great interest and passionate reaction throughout time but especially today when the perceived insecurity in urban, suburban and also rural areas is stimulating lots of debate on what should be society's reaction to the accused and to the convict and on how we should proceed to institute crime prevention programs that really work. The chapter on "Technological Progress and Criminal Law in the Future" covers the Orwellian possibilities of video surveillance, electronic monitoring, computer and internet technologies while also showing in a balanced way how technology can be harnessed to strengthen a criminal policy that is respectful of human rights. No doubt some of his assertions and positions will elicit considerable reaction and debate. This is healthy and useful for an open discussion of delicate themes that often are avoided for fear of controversy and criticism.

This important volume makes available for the first time to the English-reading world the work of two prominent Latin American criminologists. Therefore it enriches the international criminology literature and substantially contributes to providing new and fresh approaches to the debate and solution of centuries-old problems. Its impact will be felt for a long time because of its originality, depth, rigorous analysis and novel ideas. This way this volume also helps create more solid and stronger contacts between South American criminologists and those of other areas of the world. No doubt this will enrich the criminological discourse worldwide; help to eventually generate a growing international consensus on how to tackle the perceived growth in crime and urban insecurity; facilitate vigorous exchanges and partnerships of a scholarly, policy and practical nature between "North and South"; and advance the status of criminology as a scholarly and scientific subject matter, growing and expanding its influence over policy-makers, decision-makers and people in the field implementing and executing crime control and crime prevention programs. For all these reasons this a major and original contribution to the world criminological literature whose impact will be felt for years to come in a positive, creative, and helpful way. It is a seminal work that will strengthen criminology's scientific and theoretical foundations and establish it as a serious discipline worthy of respect and influence.

Washington DC, January 1, 2013

NOTES

1. The G8 (or "Group of Eight") is a multilateral group consisting of the world's major industrial democracies: Canada, France, Germany, Italy, Japan, Russia, the United Kingdom, and the United States. While the European Union is not a member of the G8, EU representatives attend G8 meetings as "observers". The G8 address a wide range of international economic, political, and security issues.

2. The Convention on Cybercrime includes sections on "Offenses against the confidentiality, integrity and availability of computer data and systems," "Computer-related offenses," "Content-related offenses," and "Offenses related to infringements of copyright and related rights." Each of these categories also includes subsections.

3. Ellen S. Podgor, Computer Crime, in Encyclopedia of Crime & Justice 221-28 (Joshua Dressler, ed., 2nd ed. 2002); see also Scott Charney & Kent Alexander, Computer Crime, 45 Emory L.J. 931, 934 (1996) (discussing how computer can be "target of the offense," "tool of the offense," or "incidental to the offense"); Joe D. Whitley & William H. Jordan, Computer Crime, E-1 ABA White Collar Crime Inst. 21.01[1], at 21-3 to 21-6 (1999) (describing how computer can be "object, subject, or instrument of a crime").

4. The "hacker" who engages in the computer activity with a criminal intent to cause damage is often described as a "cracker." See Eric J. Sinrod & William P. Reilly, Cyber-crimes: A Practical Approach to the Application of Federal Computer Crime Laws, 16 Santa Clara Computer & High Tech. L.J. 177, 181-83 (2000).

5. Placing bets over the Internet has been effectively criminalized by the United States federal government to eliminate an activity pursued by up to 23 million Americans who wagered an estimated $6 billion in 2005. Attached to a port-security bill signed by President Bush on October 13, 2006, the Unlawful Internet Gambling Enforcement Act prohibits online gamblers from using credit cards, checks and electronic-fund transfers to place and settle bets.

Introduction

Eugenio Raúl Zaffaroni and
Edmundo Oliveira

Life is too brief to be small. Even so, one of the clearest realities of our time is the crisis in which humanity is struggling.

At the beginning of another millennium, the same technology that has led humanity to conquer the world has not yet provided a solution to the major problems that afflict the human spirit. And it never will, because they transcend the usual possibilities. People today know much about the universe, but have advanced little in knowledge of their origins and their destiny, although they have the marvels of science and it unreachable limits at their fingertips.

In fact, human nature is complex and opulent, polymorphous and impossible to be fitted in to a system of coordinates or in invariable schemes. No genius has yet appeared to teach us how to determine the abscissa of pain or the proportions in which suffering, passion, faith, ambition, fear, love and hate pierce the depths of the soul. No physical process has yet been invented to make one smile or to produce tears from chemical compounds in a laboratory.

Technology has given the First World countries comfort, well-being and abundance. That is all to the good, but not enough. It has not avoided an increase in violence, clashes between ethnic groups, genocide, proliferation of the drug trade, the machinery of corruption, unemployment, gangsters, increased misery among the poor, infant mortality and so many other evils, such as the unleashing of a hitherto unseen level of violence and insecurity.

Technology is advancing. With it, humanity can work less and consume more; however, what once sees on every side is that it is not up to meeting individual or collective challenges. The progress achieved did not avoid the chancre of Nazism; the breakdown of communism; it did not remove the quarrels between peoples of the Middle East, nor the humiliation of Czechoslovakia or the trampling of Hungary, drowned in blood for daring to have aspired to freedom; it has brought neither happiness nor peace. The war in Bosnia has shown, once again, the stupid and cruel side of humanity.

In short, technological evolution has not provided the human species with either happiness or peace, especially for the one billion and three hundred million persons living the role of main actors in the tragedy of absolute poverty.

Technology makes people lords of the universe, but they must also de lords of their own destiny. They must not be tied down by the machinery of cars they must drive, nor should they slay their creative capacities, their imaginations, their dreams.

In fact, a person today is faced with an option: someone who views satisfying appetites as the supreme good in life can abandon spiritual concerns and exclusively seek technical progress. However, such a one will have to grope and stumble around the world, exposed to distress of the spirit. On the other hand, one who aspires to self-realization in body and soul, and to sharpen all of one's talents, whose ambition is to go down to the source of existence to discover the meaning of life and to ascend to the heights of the ideal, cannot be contented with mere technology. One must raise one's sights above low horizons, remembering the words that Lessing put in the mouth of Philotas: "I am not a machine that needs to be perfected; I am a man who likes to laugh and to cry."

The modern world confronts Law with the need for reestablishing peace and security, without wounding justice, without violating fundamental human rights. We could live much better if we knew how to harmonize the rights of the individual with those of society, in the sense of preventing poverty and suffering from making equality before the law an illusion.

Harmonizing all of the values of the individual and society, and all instrumental and finalistic factors that mechanics cannot resolve, but that Law can, by grace of its social organization and legal discipline. Apart from this regulation of life in society, which is Law, there is neither security nor justice.

The constant shaking of the standards of justice is revealed, for example, in the current reality prevailing in penitentiaries, which is typically criminalizing in the context of an archaic system that serves to internalize the decayed values of prison life, and day by day encourages the evils that it theoretically proposes to avoid.

One component in this problematic scenario is the negative image that the population has of the Police, Justice and Legislative system, which it is in those institutions that the people ought to find necessary and useful partners in practicing respect for human rights, with effective protection and the promised wellbeing.

We have reached the Twenty-First Century without any country being able to show clearly that it has solved the problems of prisons, with prisons or without them.

It is true that one may find the occasional successful experiment here and there. However, on the whole, the worldwide scenario is poor, leading one to conclude that any penal establishment with a good degree of success, represents only an isle of grace in a sea of misfortune.

Leaving prison means finding the possibility of exchanging a process of death for one of life. That is why it is worthwhile do devote attention to the new penal alternatives that are appearing, especially for soft crimes, in the face of the general expectation for discovering or inauguration a new style of sentencing that will have the means to support a decisive movement for respecting and recognizing the human dimension of the immense legion of persons condemned by Criminal Justice. Modern penal reactions, especially community sentencing, should not be seen as legal clemency policy but as authentic formulas with of well-defined treatment, with a variety of procedures that are capable of giving an appropriate response to specific problems in areas of delinquency.

On the other hand, criminological theory over the last few decades has been oscillating between extremes: on one side there are calls for increasing the state exercise of punitive power as the only means of providing security, in the face of both urban and international rime; while other side highlights the need for reducing the exercise of punitive power because of the paradoxical effects that it produces. The first discourse enjoys great political success because of the publicity that social communications provides it, supported by the ratings obtained from its highly emotional impacts. In this way, political decisions become increasingly separate from the criminological academic discourse, which inevitably takes on markedly critical characteristics, including in conservative and traditional circles. Moreover, within criminology new epistemological winds are being announced that cannot help assuming their function of ideological criticism, both because serious crimes against humanity have been systematically ignored and because the reality of punitive power has gone overboard in violating the most elemental and historically consecrated guarantees.

The studies published here recover the historical roots of thinking that are currently in conflict with and critical of present-day tendencies.

The criminological theory over the last few decades has been oscillating between extremes: on one side there are calls for increasing the state exercise of punitive power as the only means of providing security, in the face of both urban and international rime; while other side highlights the need for reducing the exercise of punitive power because of the paradoxical effects that it produces.

Useful for academics, practitioners, professionals and students. this book will certainly contribute to a wider awareness in crime prevention and criminal justice to the exercise of citizenship without the sacrifice of the public welfare.

Chapter One

Seeking the Enemy

From Satan to Cool Criminal Law

Eugenio Raúl Zaffaroni

THE DIFFERENT ASPECTS OF PUNITIVE POWER

One cannot conceive of human beings apart from interactive relations (of cooperation or conflict), which proceed to create power structures that appear in small-scale societies (tribes, clans), extended to broader contexts (nations) and finally encompassed the globe. This process has advanced since the Fifteenth Century in the form of colonialism, since the Eighteenth as neocolonialism[1] and since the Twentieth as globalization,[2] with each moment preceded by an economic, political and social transformation known as a *revolution* (*mercantile*, Fourteenth/Fifteenth Centuries; *industrial*, Eighteenth century; and *technological*, Twentieth Century), all episodes in an expansive power process.[3]

The exercise of planetary-level power has always required a certain form of internal power for the dominant nations, since *one cannot dominate without first organizing in a dominant manner*. Thus Europe, to begin the process of globalizing power, needed to first reorder its societies into a form of higher hierarchization, very similar to a military organization (corporatization of societies),[4] through which it recovered an internal power that had been employed by the great conquering power (Rome) and had disappeared with its downfall[5]: *punitive power*.

This formidable instrument for social verticalization provided European societies with the ironclad economic and military organization (and ideological homogeneity[6]) that proved indispensable for the success of colonialist genocide. Neither would Rome have been able to conquer Europe, nor would the latter have been able to conquer America and Africa without the powerful internal verticalization derived from *confiscation of the victims* so as to neutralize dysfunctional elements. Furthermore, without such an instrument, it would not have been possible to control the colonized countries, where individual hierarchicized forms were assumed to turn them into immense concentration camps.

The *conquering armies are only the most visible expression of other much greater ones which are the colonizing societies or nations themselves*, corporatively structured, ordered into hierarchies and endowed with a unique ideology, which will not abide dissent. Those immense armies have armed themselves beginning with small controlling cells (families) commanded by an under-officer (*pater*). Submitting to him were the women, the elderly, the servants and slave, the children and domestic animals, all of them *biologically inferior* to the *pater*, who according to traditional civil law answered for damages caused by this subordinates. From this comes the importance given to controlling sexuality, to misogyny and homophobia as disciplining elements for those who, since the Middle Ages have dedicated more space to such themes than to regulation of property[7] in legal and manualistic texts,[8] that were obsessed with repressing all Dionysian expressions, which were considered diabolical.[9]

But *when one analyzes the phenomenon of expansion of planetary power from the perspective of its guiding verticalizing instrument, which is punitive power*, one normally confuses aspects that—although interacting—are not merely independent, but essentially different. One cannot understand an exercise of power that is constantly expanding if one confuses levels that correspond to the different agencies in its heterogeneous composition. To apprehend its reality, one must distinguish, at a minimum, three levels or perspectives:

a. One thing is the *real exercise of repression*, that is to say, *secondary criminalization* or individualization of persons on whom it falls, be this in the form of punishment, death or physical pain, legally or illegally imposed by executing agencies;
b. Another is what is prescribed by laws, in other words, *Primary criminalization* or repressive or penal legislation, which configures what *should be* produced by agencies that issue laws (parliaments, autocrats, etc), and that never completely coincides with the *is* of repression
c. And another, different from the first two, is what is theorized by authors of legitimating or critical discourses, that is to say, the *judicial-penal or ideological discourse*, which basically arises from ideology reproduction agencies (academies, universities, etc.).

d. To this one may add the publicity or *propaganda from the penal system*, which presents itself to the so-called *public opinion* as a protector or custodian, in this or in another world, acting through different agencies (ranging from sermons in churches, soapbox speeches in parks, harangues from village priests, etc., to sophisticated contemporary publicity, and involving the theater[10]).

It is only from the perspective of a whole that encompasses the four levels noted above that one perceives *the course of planetary power as a permanent search for the enemy*, without becoming entangled in the constant changes in analytical level, which is a trap that keeps one from understanding the phenomenon in its totality.[11] For it is from the perspective of this totality that one perceives that such corporatized societies have launched attacks on external and internal enemies; the external enemies were those destined to be dominated, while the internal ones were all those who weakened the hallucination of the moment, make up by the *emergency* of the moment.[12]

The question of the enemy was studied and discursively rationalized in the Nineteenth Century with Garofalo and in the Twentieth with Carl Schmitt,[13] *The search for and identification of enemies has been the permanent task of the punitive power throughout the last eight centuries*. The relation between corporatized societies, some to dominate and others to be dominated, could only be one of war, and that presupposes the existence of enemies. The delinquent is defined as the internal enemy, while the alien soldier is the external enemy.[14] The delinquent is a part of the *fifth column* that breaks down ideological homogeneity on the internal front. For those who define *power* as *power to define the enemy*, there is no possibility of using power to give validity to human rights, because they have no enemies, for they embrace all of humanity, and their use would be no more than a pretense for excluding those who violate them from humanity.[15] Long before Schmitt, it was correctly observed that *one who seeks the legal foundation of the sentence should also seek, if he has not found it, the legal foundation for war.*[16]

THE COLONIALIST AND NEOCOLONIALIST STAGES

The theocratic discourse presented colonialist discourse as a pious undertaking, but it killed internal dissidents, colonized rebels[17] and rebellious women.[18] The *enemy* of that undertaking was the devil.[19] Because Jesus is a victim of punitive power and not a warrior god, it invented a *warrior enemy*, the head of an army of demons, to legitimate its armies in the name of Christ.[20] That invention was built on top of European prejudice, which from ancient times had believed in the *maleficence* of witches,[21] admitted and ratified by academics of the period.[22]

The power legitimated by those discourses was exercised in the form of genocide (elimination of the majority of the American population, African slave trade,[23] destruction of pre-colonial cultures on both continents[24]). Its exercise set in motion an extractive economy that provided raw materials and means of payment,[25] which gave rise to modern capitalism, weakening the colonial powers and strengthening the neocolonialists.[26]

Power passed from Spain and Portugal to middle and northern Europe, the capitalist class raised itself up against the colonial nobility, and global power began to favor economic relations and relativize political dominion, largely replacing it with economic control. Punitive power played a central role in the internal structural changes in neocolonialist societies: to begin with, the new productive classes struggled to weaken such power exercised over them (with the discourse of penal liberalism, founded on contractualism and rationalism); but later on, the same classes revitalized it in order to contain the populations concentrated in the cities because of the wealth accumulated in them and to submit them to the training that would convert them into salaried workers.[27]

Prison became generalized,[28] police services were invented for controlling the *dangerous classes*,[29] and the penal spectacle was inverted: penalties ceased being public and judgments were shown on a previously determined stage,[30] although inquisitorial activities were retained with the figure of the police instructor.

Insubordinates and dissidents became biological inferiors,[31] the same as the colonized peoples,[32] and total institutions were dedicated for them. Subhuman status was assigned to women[33] and sexual minorities.[34] Medical doctors provided an academic discourse for the police[35]—a new institution lacking its own discourse[36]—and scientific dissemination in schools and the press operated as propaganda. Legislation invented *security measures*, in other words, *sentences that were not sentences*, to neutralize inferiors. Academics theorized that internal enemies were savages born by biological accident in the dominant societies.[37]

In the neocolonialist countries the total institutions took on the form of prisons and the repressive power served in fact to expel a goodly number of the enemies or dangerous European classes: those who were aggressive found themselves relegated to distant colonies[38] and those who were merely inconvenient were forced to emigrate.[39]

The punitive power played a crucial role at this stage of world history. The Roman Church had lost its discursive hegemony; the Reformation had paved the way for capitalism[40] accepting that the devil was the owner of this world and that only faith could save one in the next.[41] The philosophers and jurists discursively legitimated the reduction of punitive power over the new rising class, finally, the police and doctors, based on notions of permanent progress and on biological absurdities,[42] had provided a new hierarchizing discourse, that was clearly racist, paternalistic, organicist, misogynous, discriminatory, and whose final consequence was elimination of inferiors. Although one cannot blame the Nazi genocide on the discourse of danger—because no discourse in itself can produce genocide—it is also true that such a discourse made it possible to identify the enemies of the regime.

In summary, the seven centuries of uninterrupted punitive power prior to the Twentieth Century show us the main moments of its unlimited use: *colonialism*, with the discourse of *inquisition* (ecclesiastic or state[43]) and *neocolonialism*, with its *medical racism/police* discourse. Between the two, there was a drop in the struggle between those who were losing power and those who intended to assume it: this was the dominant moment in the *critical discourse for penal liberalism*. Thus, on the academic level, there arose *two discursive structures: authoritarian or inquisitorial and critical or liberal.*[44]

At a distance of five centuries, the legitimating texts conserve an identical authoritarian structure. On a real social plane, all evidence indicates that this alternation derives from a struggle amongst corporations to monopolize discourse on the criminal issue: the Dominicans held sway over the inquisition against the devil (Fourteenth Century), while the Jesuits reorganized it on a Spanish model against the heretics (Protestants) (Sixteenth Century)[45] and, thus, needed to delegitimize de Dominican corporation. That is why they were benevolent with the first critical discourse (Seventeenth Century).[46] Later on, the illuminists and liberals (corporation of philosophers and jurists) delegitimized the theocratic discourse with a new discourse, which responded to the critical structure that the Jesuits had inaugurated against the Dominicans.[47] When the industrialist class reached power, the doctors and police[48] provided it with a new authoritarian discourse that had the inquisitorial structure.

The penal discourse was degraded into direct police coercion (administrative) whenever it assumed an inquisitorial structure; it justified use of force to eliminate a supposed collective threat coming from very powerful enemies in a war that was to a large degree imaginary.[49] When it wanted to contain power (liberalism) it turned to civil law, where there are no enemies but only parties in conflict; civil law seeks reparation and not elimination of the vanquished. This equipped the penal discourse with a particular *avidity for assimilating elements from other discourses because it lacked elements of its own.*

PENAL AUTHORITARIANISM IN TWENTIETH CENTURY EUROPE: THE MYTHICAL FRONTALITY

The First World War (1914-1918) was uncommonly cruel, ushered in the first genocide in the last century,[50] made it plain that soldiers are only the visible advance of armies that encompass all wartime economies and changed the map of world power.[51] Europe on the wane, an ascendant United States[52] and the Soviet phenomenon[53] marked important changes in planetary and also internal power.

In Europe heroism was praised[54] and new authoritarianisms burst on the scene to assume various penal discourses of a biological nature: ranging from Marxism in Russia,[55] to idealism in Italy and to raw and brutal genocidal racism in Germany. Discourses in those regimes not only had an inquisitorial structure, but also the same ideology derived from the Nineteenth Century: *dangerousness* followed its *police/administrative* destiny, legitimating crimes to the extent that each autocrat wanted to forward his genocidal purposes, actually going far beyond the formal laws and the rationalizations—even the most aberrant ones—of his judicial and criminological scribes.

In effect: the dangerous were *parasites* to the Soviets, *subhuman* to the Nazis[56] and *enemies of the state* to the fascists,[57] and all were submitted to a *parallel penal system*, to inquisitory/police courts. It is obvious that the Nazis were the cruelest of all, but this does not exclude other atrocities or erase the fact that at heart all those systems had a common ideological penal base, which was *medical/police dangerousness* (racism) inherited from the Nineteenth Century.

In reality, such authoritarian structures carried out their repressive power in a genocidal matter, creating *subterranean* penal systems,[58] with disappearances, torture and police executions on individual and mass scales, with no legal basis whatsoever. The Holocaust had no legal basis even in Nazism, as had also been the case with the suffocating *Führerprinzip*.[59] This was also true of the elimination of Polish prisoners by Stalinism.[60] The infamous Night of the Long Knives was nothing more than the selective assassination of dissidents.[61]

The criminal laws in such authoritarian systems showed merely the visible face of the formal penal system and something of the parallel penal system, while underneath them a subterranean system operated, without law and without limits. However, if there were no limits to the punitive power *to whom should one show the law? To whom should one show the law with limited power when it was exercised without limits? Sociologically speaking, to whom should one show the law?* Laws were drafted by jurists, and they could not be directed to the autocrats who commissioned them through amanuenses. If the laws addressed them, it was not to limit their all-encompassing power, but instead *to please them.* All of the laws *for defense* and *protection* of the Nazi state[62] were directed to the *Führer* to please him, but also *to the public*, to *extol the virtues of a regime that intended to defend and protect them with such laws.*[63] Basically, then, *such authoritarian laws had two addressees: the autocrats, whom the scribes must please so as not to fall into disgrace, and the public, for whom they would serve as propaganda.* Only secondarily did they provide bureaucratic tools for suppressing *enemies*, who were the aliens or *hostiles.*[64]

The main characteristic of those laws was their *frontality.* This trait was described in courtly art by Julius Lange and Adolf Erman, who noted that the human figure or language or any manifestation, is directed towards an observer, whom one needs to please, in a respectful and servile manner. It is the same frontality of courtly theatre, which never turns the its back on the observer, which always focuses on the fact that what is happening is a fiction directed at the observer and not to another.[65] Frontality only disappeared with the rise of sophistic relativism and its pluralistic perspectives.[66]

The frontality of authoritarian criminal laws between the wars was part of a highly frontalist scene, which included monumental architecture with imposing neoclassical facades, colossal statues, immense parades and uniformed maches,[67] showy uniforms, medals, particularly ostentatious ceremonies, generalized histrionics and so on. *Frontality is characteristic of every manifestation of an autocratic regime and not only the autistic ones, which also means that its laws will be frontalist.*

Although those laws were directed to the autocrat and also to the public, they were not bifrontal, but had a single face: the autocrat was pleased with what served as propaganda for him, especially at a time in which the formidable power of propaganda was beginning to be clearly perceived.[68] That does not mean that those laws, because they were directed to the public, were democratic, since they responded to what from that time onward has been called *völkisch*, which should not be confused with *democratic*, nor with *popular* nor *populist.*

Strictly speaking, what was new was the name *völkisch*, but not the phenomenon in itself, a technique that has been used in manufacturing an enemy for centuries;[69] it consists of feeding and reinforcing the worst prejudices to publicly stimulate identification of the enemy of the moment. When one analyzes Nazism, this technique is particularly noteworthy, especially because it is intimately linked to the discourse that privileges the theory of the intended *plebiscitary democracy,* theorized by Carl Schmitt, associated with his concept of the political based on the *friend/enemy* distinction,[70] which he detailed during that period. Schmitt was able, like no one else, to lay bare the nature of power, designating its essence as the capacity for identifying and excluding the enemy, the stranger, the *hostiles.* Starting—as did Hobbes—with the assumption that the state is the only entity that can guarantee peace, he deduced that for this it is necessary to identify and exclude the enemy, without admitting that any third party is able to decide the conflict.[71] The Hobbesian connection of this reasoning is clear[72] and, although it is somewhat more distant, one cannot ignore the reference to Hegel, who excluded from judicial relations—and thus from a sentence with retributive limits—those who had not reached the moment of having a subjective spirit or self-consciousness. To maintain that one may only attribute judicial relevancy to those who are part of the judicial community, in other words, those who share certain common values, means excluding the strangers and submitting them to police measures.[73] From there to considering some or all of them as enemies is merely a step away.

At any rate, even though at this moment the discourse had reached its highest degree of sincerity, it was still a rationalization to justify a regime that exercised an unlimited repressive power, enabled by aberrant laws, or directly without any legal qualification, but, *with or without a quote from Schmitt and with greater or lesser elaboration, fell back on the recourse that has always been used to legitimize unlimited punitive power in any emergency: appealing to the hallucination of a war.*

Although *all identification of the enemy is based on a myth*[74], the frontality of between-the-war authoritarianism occurred in a coarse manner. The extreme Nazi brutality supplanted some of the more elaborate rationalizations, replacing them with cruder arguments; it preferred the fables of Rosenberg[75] to elaborations by Schmitt or Heidegger. In fascism different discourses seemed to coexist, and this did not perturb its disparate levels of elaboration,[76] and Stalinism directly eliminated those that might become a nuisance according to the autocrat's paranoia. The most grotesque myths won out because there is always an inverse relation between the degree of irrationality and brutality of the repressive power and the level of elaboration in the discourse used to legitimate[77] and also because myths are better suited to publicity demands.

Nevertheless, it is worth noting the presence of those myths, some of them very old—such as racial and blood myths,[78] others more nationalistic, the product of idealist traditions and the need for reinforcing recently unified states.[79] The ancient myths were partly combined with the old Spenserian racism, and, truth be said, although they were aberrant, one cannot deny—as is also the case with the old racism—their colorful inventiveness and depraved creativity, what one might call *the brilliance of their perversion.*

THE TWENTIETH CENTURY AT THE PERIPHERY OF GLOBAL POWER

Whereas the punitive or repressive power was the verticalizing instrument for colonialist and neocolonialist societies, it was employed in colonized societies to turn them into *immense concentration camps* for the natives (given that all were considered biological inferiors). The shameless Hitlerian slogan engraved above the gates of concentration camps was the synthesis of colonialist premises: the colonized were to work and submit themselves in order to learn to be free.[80] Because the *mestizos* were less domesticable that the pure natives,[81] miscegenation was discouraged (*apartheid*) and existing *mestizos* were considered *unbalanced* (moral degenerates).[82] The penal discourse treated the natives as unimputable (assimilating, in Lombrosian fashion[83] children and savages) and *mestizos* as potential *moral madmen*.[84] In this way it rationalized is exclusion and turned the most rebellious into enemies (*savages*, enemies of *civilization*, of *progress*, etc.).

The exercise of repressive power in the colonized countries was prolonged for many decades, supported by the oligarchic republics that kept their majorities under conditions analogous to servitude.[85] Justice exercised by landowners, private death penalties, murder of dissidents, massive repression, forced recruitment of *mestizos* for the armies, occupation police forces, arbitrariness and tortures, decapitations, imprisonment without trial, permanent states of exception and phenomena of incredible corruption, were all common in those immense concentration camps.[86]

While the punitive power in Latin America was exercised in this way, from the second half of the Nineteenth Century on legislators in the local oligarchies—proconsular groups linked to central interests—approved constitutions and criminal codes that were first liberal and later on based on dangerousness, the former copied from the United States[87] and the latter from continental Europe.[88]

THE LEGITIMATING EMERGENCIES OF THE LAST DECADES OF THE CENTURY

With the bloodiest civil war in the Latin American Twentieth Century—the Mexican Revolution[89]—the downfall of the old oligarchic republics began and the punitive power was transformed to the beat of old-style dictatorships[90] and political processes known as *populisms* that—in general—used it in a more prudent manner, although almost always under the aegis of police paternalism. The judicial-political discourses abandoned pure positivism and blended with German theories successively imported as techniques, with total disregard for their original political and social orientation.[91] Legislation underwent the influence of second-generation European codes,[92] such as the *Codice Rocco*.

Populisms were protectionist and nationalistic, unsympathetic towards United States administrations, who, by means of *coups d'états* caused set-backs for the incipient welfare states, which in some countries had achieved interesting levels by mid-century. Those regressions generated resistance and also some Marxist-inspired armed minority movements. With the pretext provided by the latter, the United States supported military regimes that practiced state terrorism with unusual cruelty, especially in the Southern Cone. To eliminate the last traces of populist policies, their definition of the enemy did not restrict itself to members of the armed minority groups, but in some cases physically extinguished a generation of current and potential leaders.

To this end they exercised a formidable and unlimited punitive power.[93] They established a parallel penal system that perverted the exceptional measures provided in the constitutions,[94] imposed thousands of sentences without trial and submitted civilians to military courts and commissions. But what set them apart was their setting up an *underground penal system* without precedents as to its cruelty, complexity, and highly calculated planning and execution, whose analogy with the *final solution* is undeniable. Using this apparatus they committed thousands of homicides, forced disappearances, torture and other physical abuses, kidnappings, sexual crimes, household invasions, damages and fires, intimidation, robberies, extortions, changes in civil status, and so on, without any normative base, including within their own *de facto* order.

The legitimating discourse for such atrocities was the so-called *national security doctrine*, inspired by the French coup plotters in Algeria[95] and disseminated among officers in the armed forces of the whole region through the *School of the Americas*, which the United States supported in Panama. Although somewhat more elaborate work was done,[96] it was explained in simplistic manuals, which began with a premise held in common with Trotskyism: the hallucination of a *permanent war*, waged between the Soviet Union and *the West*, in which each blow in a foreign zone of influence would be a battle.[97] The vision was of a *dirty war*, which, because it did not respect the rules of conventional warfare, required the violation of human rights and humanitarian law.[98] Despite this genuine atrocity, the criminal law discourse continued to be feed by the German theories, and no one theorized a national security criminal law, save for a few isolated exceptions.[99]

The U.S. administration also pressured those dictatorships to declare the *war on drugs,* in a first version that was closely linked to national security:

the drug dealer was an agent who wished to weaken Western society; the youth smoking marijuana was a *subversive*, and so on. As the fall of the *Berlin wall* drew new, a new enemy was needed to justify the hallucination of a new war and to maintain high levels of repression. To achieve this, the *war on drugs* was reinforced. During the 1980s, very similar *anti-drug laws* were passed throughout the region, forming a criminal legislation for exceptional cases analogous to what had already been employed against *terrorism* and *subversion*. These laws violated the principle of legality, multiplied texts following the North American legislative technique, assimilated participation and authorship, attempt, preparation and consummation, ignored the principle of offensiveness, violated the moral authority of the person and so on. Special courts were created for proceedings, inquisitorial elements were introduced, such as rewards for informers, training for spies and for *agents provocateurs,* anonymous witnesses, anonymous judges and inspectors, etc.[100] An aberrant authoritarian penal legislation was created, which few had the courage to denounce, under threat of being accused as participants and of covering up drug trafficking or of being imprisoned, in the best inquisitorial style, which actually happened to judges, magistrates, inspectors and academicians.

While the prisons became overpopulated with drug consumers (whom one would suppose to be the victims) and with the women who carried them (*mules*), parallel economies were created. Corruption of penal systems was formidable—including in the armed forces incorporated for police functions—the volume of trade to the United States grew incredibly and the price for the internal distribution process in that country remained high, placing into circulation something like five hundred billion dollars annually, which gives an idea of the recession that would be caused by its sudden drop. But it is certain that drugs have not been able to occupy the vacuum left by the fall of the Berlin Wall.

THE DAWN OF THE TWENTY-FIRST CENTURY: WHERE IS THE ENEMY?

With the arrival of globalization, capital changed its nature.[101] Its predominant speculative interests are guaranteed by a complex system of international agencies but are mainly supported by the Republican administration of the United States, a power that has been on the center stage since the First World War, after which a devastated Europe was left to its own devices by the Republicans who succeeded the idealistic president Wilson. During the 1920s the flow of capital to the United States also provoked an influx of immigrants, selected according to racist criteria[102] and Prohibition gave rise to strong market criminality organizations.[103] The terrible crisis of 1929 gave rise to the

New Deal; later occurrences highlighted the power of the United States in the world, not without a mythical component. The abrupt ending of the so-called *cold war* left it as the unquestioned hegemonic power.

Earlier on, the American penal system had been interesting in terms of some of its sentencing options that did not involve deprivation of freedom.[104] The odious presence of the death penalty seemed to be ending when in 1972 the Supreme Court declared it unconstitutional,[105] while imprisonment rates had been stable since the Nineteenth Century.[106] That situation has been changing since the end of the 1970s, when the imprisonment rate began to rise exponentially and the penal system became oversized,[107] keeping imprisoned and controlled (on *parole* and on *probation*) millions of persons and providing employment for other millions. As a hallmark of a service economy, the penal system has become a factor in reducing the unemployment rate.

The very high selectivity of repressive control in the United States is denied by the judges.[108] The death penalty has been reestablished, re-legitimized by the Republican judges nominated to the Supreme Court by that party's presidents, making it the only country in the Americas and Europe to apply it profusely,[109] condemned by the OAS for executing minors. Furthermore, penal legislation has been established that imposes a life sentence on those who have committed three or more crimes, which reestablished the definitive relegation of the *undesirables or enemies*, which violates the principle of rationality. On the procedural plane, judgment has become extraordinary, so that jury guarantees have been suppressed for people with scarce resources. *Bargaining* is little less than extortion against minorities and all low income segments. In this may the accusatory criminal proceedings are a mere fiction, since the decision lies in the hands of the accusation itself (the district attorney).

In contrast to productive capital, globalized capital is not managed by business people, but by administrators of *conglomerates*, who are technocrats charged with obtaining the highest profit in the shortest time, to prevent their investors from seeking out another more efficient technocrat. That is how such persons overcome their scruples, so much that their activity frequently enters into a zone that is little different that economic delinquency. This phenomenon has spawned inquisitorial legislation, with elements derived from the Middle Ages (spies, informers, secret proceedings, etc.) applicable to a nebulous set of infractions designated as *organized crime*, which has encouraged the rise of an incredible number of international instruments.[110] This is a *pseudo-concept* invented by the press, for which criminology has never achieved a legislatively adopted agreement to deal with heterogeneous hypotheses that cannot be confronted with the same measures. It definitely is equivalent to *market criminality*, which is enough to show the enormity of the universe covered.[111] The verification that the majority of such activities require complementary public corruption, has unleashed parallel witch-hunting campaigns, which, not because of bad luck, never find those responsible for the asset stripping of entire countries,[112] but motivate an enormous national and international bureaucracy and reached the heights of moral absurdity in the impeachment charges brought against a president of an extramarital sexual affair. Both *organized crime* and corruption[113] serve to enable punitive power state interference into any economic activity that is disagreeable to the group in power at the moment or that is useful to eliminate or defame competitors, without the limits or the constitutional guarantees for such interventions.

The United States does not answer to international courts, since it has not ratified the treaties that would leave it accountable. The former nation of Wilsonian multilateralism is today a champion of unilateralism and its isolationist policy is similar to that of the authoritarianisms that led to the collapse of the League of Nations. In terms of penal systems, the country that disseminated procedural guarantees today practices the most heartless inquisitional methods.

That context follows the idea that the new role of strongest power on the planet has required a reinforcement of its internal verticalism. The Republican penal discourse since 1980 has been simplistic: the politicians promise more sentences so as to provide more security; it is affirmed that delinquents do not deserve guarantees; hallucinations of a war (also *dirty*) on crime arise; it is claimed that delinquents violate human rights; some governors seek reelection surrounded by photographs of executed criminals whose death penalties they refuse to commute; a successful candidate for president closed his campaign showing a poster of a dead police officer; a mayor invested large amounts of funds in improving security services, cleaned up a large part of police corruption and governed at a time of full employment, but claimed that his success was based on *zero tolerance*[114] and delivers simplistic explanations to Latin American executives who pay him millions. On September 11, 2001, this penal system found an enemy in a certain organization. At the same time, it borrowed *prevention* from the legitimating penal discourse and tried to legitimate the war against Iraq as *preventive*. As never before seen, military and punitive power are nakedly united in a desperate search for the enemy.

This authoritarianism that is foreign to the American tradition signaled a cultural deterioration in its society, and a dangerous abandonment of the foundational values of its democracy in politics. It is characterized by its desperation in finding an enemy that will fill the vacuum left by the Soviet implosion. The multiplicity of candidates, the insufficiency of drugs and the excessive abstraction of *organized crime,* render them incapable of individualizing credible enemies beyond the delinquent on the streets. The lack of a preconceived background on which to manufacture a new enemy[115] can only be compensated for with a terrifying fact, and the attack in 2001 was foundational in individualizing a credible enemy. Although that enemy is dangerous, that does not legitimate repression of domestic dissidents—it does not replace common offenders—one cannot ignore that in the proliferation of candidates for the position of enemy there is also competition among federal agencies at play over stratospheric budgets.

THE LATIN AMERICAN *COOL* AUTHORITARIANISM

Because social communication is the most globalized form, the discourse of American authoritarianism is the most disseminated one around the globe. Its simplism is imitated throughout the planet by communicators avid for ratings, although its greatest success is in Latin America, given the region's institutional precariousness. Its worldwide diffusion is favored by its brevity and the emotional impact of its vindictive discourse, which are tailor-made for television, because of their high cost and the fact that the spectator is not disposed to think.

In the societies that are less favored by globalization, the principal problem lies in social exclusion, which cannot usually be controlled by direct repression, but is neutralized through broadening internal contradictions. The vindictive message is useful for reproducing conflicts among the excluded, since those who are criminalized, victimized and policed are recruited from this segment, and there is an inverse relation between the violence of the conflicts between them and their capacity for collation and protagonism.

In those same societies, the polarization of wealth that led to the globalized economy seriously weakened the middle classes, leaving them anomic.[116] That is why they clamor for norms, but do not know what norms. The are pathetically anomic, calling for norms and in their confusion end up taking refuge behind the simplistic authoritarian discourse of the North American model, which comes with the prestige of a society that they envy and admire. This is what will enable greater control over those same classes, which would otherwise again become suppliers of dissidents.

Given that the message is easily propagated, easy to spread overseas, profitable for social communication business leaders, effective in controlling the excluded, successful even among them and satisfactory for the decaying middle classes, it is not uncommon for politicians to make use of and even compete for it. Such politicians who intend to confront such a discourse will be disqualified and marginalized by their own parties, if they do not use it because of electoral calculations they will do so out of fear, and in that way the single discourse of the new authoritarianism triumphs.

The poverty of means for lawsuit proceedings, means that the police who are dependent on the executive are the true authorities in finding of facts or indictments. Police deterioration and corruption encourage by politicians who enable growing opportunities for illicit raising of funds degrade the effectiveness of security services, which, in a social scenario in which unemployment and anomie that generates exclusion increase the frequency of violent errors of conduct, result in a truly lethal combination: both primary and secondary prevention are degraded.

The discourse of North American authoritarianism is like that which is installed in the rest of the Americas, but its functionality is as different as the reality of repressive power. Whereas the United States turns it into an enterprise that employs millions of people, in other words that transfers resources social assistance to the penal systems and resolves an unemployment problem, the penal system in Latin America, far from providing jobs, serves to control those excluded from employment, becomes brutally violent and the police *autonomized and undergoing dissolution* lay siege to the political powers.[117]

The *cool* discourse inserts itself in this region in inverted penal systems, with prisons overcrowded by inmates not yet convicted,[118] where more than seventy percent of the penal population is in preventive custody in most cases serve out their sentences in that condition, if a conviction is finally handed down.[119] An increase in penal scales does not mean more sentences but more preventive imprisonments (because they impede prisoner releases), penitentiary law is to a large degree a utopia and the true guilty verdict is the act of prosecution: the final judgment operates as a review.

Furthermore, *Latin America is losing its police forces, and with them an elementary state support for civil society.* Autonomization, bans on union membership, militarization and greater levels of arbitrariness simply destroy police institutions through corruption. Systems of illegal fund collection are formed that are lost in the leadership of verticalized structures and whose preventive efficacy operates in an inverse relation to its unscrupulousness. The worst costs are fully paid by the lower ranks through degraded salaries, internal authoritarianism, very high risks, professional anomie, lack of information, lack of credibility among the public, social isolation and no conditions for a horizontal debate on their working conditions.

The Latin American authoritarian discourse participates in North American simplism and lacks any academic support, composed as it is of slogans or propaganda. Its irrationality is of such an order that it cannot even be legitimated through coarse myths—such as Rosenberg did for Nazism—but is reduced to a pure advertising campaign with predominant use of images. Its technique follows that of market research, which sells punitive power as merchandise. When it is confirmed that emotional promotion of vindictive impulses is commercially successful, techniques are perfected. News services and opinion makers are charged with disseminating them. The would-be *specialists* do not have serious empirical data available, but are simply opinionators who reiterate the single discourse.[120] *They sell the illusion that by approving laws that disproportionately focus on the few vulnerable and marginal persons who are individualized and by increasing police arbitrariness, they will directly or indirectly legitimate all manner of violence, including against those who object to the publicity discourse, they will achieve greater urban security against common crime.* Not only to the magnify insecurity, but in proclaiming the existence of a pretended impunity or generalized leniency, *the meta-message publicly incites the excluded to commit crime* ("do wrong because nothing will happen").

In the final analysis, it is a question of sending messages that are taken as true only because they have advertising success. The conviction that *a world in disarray can be organized through discipline imposed as repression* is imposed as a prejudice. No one knows who the enemy is, because they succeed each other without combining; instead of being defined photographically they are projected cinematographically, as a series of *constructs* of the mass media, especially television. *The state does not define them, but its authorities have found themselves besieged by successive impositions by the media, whose reproductive velocity is so dizzying that it impedes the holes that have provided space for critical discourses. There is no other corporation that intends to construct different enemies and that to do so must disarm the previous myths, but the same corporation that produces enemies discards them and replaces them.*

The succession of enemies increases the anguish and demands new enemies to remain calm, because if an appropriate scapegoat is not found, it will be empowered in a circular form. It is a case of a publicity apparatus that moves by itself, that has demanded autonomy and has returned autistic, which imposes a purely emotional propaganda that forbids denunciations and that, furthermore—and fundamentally—can only be described with the expression that the same media disseminate and that signals among the young that which is superficial and is in fashion, and that is used as a distraction: it is *cool.*[121] That is because *it is not assumed as a profound conviction, but as a fashion, to which one must give in, only so as not to be thought old-fashioned or out of place.*

Because the powerless state in those countries that are getting the worst part out of globalization cannot resolve serious social problems,[122] its politicians choose to simulate that they are solving them and know how to do so, and become *mannerists, affected*;[123] politics becomes a spectacle and the state itself becomes a spectacle.[124] The politicians—caught up in the competitive nature of their activity—stop seeking the best so as to concern themselves merely with what can better transmit their image and increase their electoral clientele.

That *cool* advertising authoritarianism has a vulgar frontality, but as it lacks a fixed enemy and also a myth, it is faded, it lacks the color of the between war period and the inventiveness of racist biologism, its histrionics are more pathetic, its creative poverty is formidable, it is orphaned of all *perverse brilliance*, but does have a horrid and depressing *perverse opacity*. There are no neoclassical monuments, rationalizing scientists, ostentatious parades, but it is poor, it functions because it is not very intelligent, it is elemental, does not think and promotes a strike against thinking,[125] because at the slightest whiff of a thought, it would implode.

As a whole, this *cool* authoritarian discourse of publicity communications operates with total autonomy from reality and its more serious conflictiveness. It is concerned with some acts of vengeance and ignores prevention and other massive unlawfulness. It ignores more victims than the ones it manipulates and dramatizes only the ones that it wants to be considered unique. As it lacks a myth, it also has no fixed direction. It is a war without enemies; the only enemy that is recognizes is the one that no authoritarianism can do without: those who confront its discourse.[126] Because of that, few are encouraged to contradict it and its authoritarianism is incredible: it is not a case of an authoritarian state that controls and censures the communications media, but communication converted into publicity in search of ratings. It has become autistic and imposes a discourse that it is forbidden to contradict, even the state itself, because the only fixed enemy that it has is one who depreciates repression, which is its product. It imposes itself on the state because it demands the alignment of politicians who must choose between joining in the publicity of repression (become *cool*) or be replaced by internal competitors from their own parties, who take advantage of their weak side if they show themselves to be *outdated* and *unpopular*, in other words, not *cool*.

In this scenario the politicians opt to get on this autistic bandwagon and approve criminal laws and procedures that are authoritarian and offend constitutional principles and guarantees, call for disproportionate sentences or those that cannot be fully served because they exceed a human lifespan, reiterate typifications and aggravating circumstances in capricious mazes, punish preparatory acts, dismantle criminal codes, approve criminal laws due to foreign pressures, introduce inquisitory institutions, regulate preventive prison as a sentence, and ultimately, confound the courts through *cool* modern penal legislation.

That legislation constitutes the saddest chapter in the current Latin American scenario, in which politicians intimidated by the threat of negative publicity provoke a major authoritarian legal chaos—incomprehensible and irrational—that has occurred in the history of out penal legislation since independence. This period will be identified as the most degraded time in penal history; its decadence cannot even be compared to the authoritarian legislation between the wars, which enacted frontalist laws for propaganda and the approval of their autocrats, because the current legislators do so only because they fear contrary publicity or because of opportunism. In other words, their conduct is not guided by ideological authoritarianism, but is simply *cool*, which seems more decadent from an institutional perspective. When the Latin American legislators—politicians—establish sentences lasting more than sixty years in their laws,[127] they are more pathetic than the Weimar Social Democrats who suppressed Jewish candidates from their lists for fear of losing votes.[128] The sign of *cool* authoritarian legislation in our days is its opacity, sadness, depression, mediocrity, lack of creativity, superficiality, disrespect for citizens: *it is simply decadence*. In it there is none of the brilliant frontality of ideological authoritarianism, but only the frontal opacity of the lack of ideas; it is absolutely *cool*.

The judges, for their part, also find themselves submitted to the *cool* publicity authoritarianism of the mass media. Every sentence that runs up against the single discourse runs the risk of being stigmatized and the judge, according to the circumstances, can end up in serious difficulties and even wind up being prosecuted or condemned, as has happened in various countries in the region. It matters little what the constitutions and international human rights laws say, if the judges cannot apply their provisions, under penalty of being denounced and persecuted by pressure from the communications media and by colleagues and politicians who take advantage of the opportunity to eliminate a bothersome judge, to get publicity, or simply to further their own careers or because of palace intrigues. The judges' vulnerability regarding the *cool* discourse is enormous.

RESPONSES OF THE JUDICIAL DISCOURSE TOWARDS *COOL* AUTHORITARIANISM

In light of the advance of cool authoritarianism, it is natural for the judges—disconcerted and threatened—to direct their gaze to the universities, that is to say, to ask for help from judicial penal doctrine. One can affirm that there is a general attitude of Latin American penal doctrine favoring defense of constitutional and international guarantees, in other words, that criminal law—understood as judicial-penal knowledge—fortunately reacts positively. However, as it is known, our criminal law is fed by continental European doctrine mainly German, either to follow in its footsteps or to debate with it,[129] and what is certain is that some discourses in that doctrine are worrisome,[130] especially because of their effects at this moment of *cool* penal in Latin America.

A detailed analysis of these theories and a *discussion* of their foundations would be the subject for another work, but we cannot neglect to mention here the only one that achieves a high degree of sincerity, by openly postulating the existence of an enemy and legitimating its identification.[131] From that perspective one directly assumes the need for distinguishing between *enemies* and *citizens*, to separate the treatment directed towards each. Hegelian roots are undeniable in this aspect, although Hobbesian roots are even more notable. The starting point seems to be diametrically opposed to the original liberal German conception, represented in the Nineteenth Century by Feuerbach,[132] who focused his criticism precisely on Hobbes.[133] Of all of the European theses of the last few centuries, this is the one that expresses itself with the greatest sincerity, but also with the greatest risks to our regional reality, in which historically, the definition of enemies has been brutal and the consequences genocidal. Furthermore, its Hegelian roots—as we have noted—involve a classification of citizens, presupposing that there are the included and the excluded, which is certainly no less alarming, taking into account the difficult situation through which our societies are passing.

In general, the responses that come from Europe seem to resign themselves—in a different measure—to accepting and assuming the search for the enemy and intend to save the guarantees of criminal law, at least for a part of it. We believe that such initiatives are particularly risky, given the brutal violence of our penal systems and the terrible role they are assuming in the region. It would be very negative for our judges to assume these positions, which would accomplish little in our context without the prudent limitation their authors see applied in the European context.

We do not believe that, in this hour, there is another solution than to maintain with greater firmness the principles of liberal criminal law, to oppose the *cool* criminal law of our margins. The path must be through strengthening judicial independence, respect for judges and their decisions, demanding institutional responsibility from our politicians and—free from any censorship—expanding freedom of expression so as to be able to confront the single discourse of *cool* authoritarianism using the same means. It is a time for struggle—which should not be confused with *war*—and one must not forget that law always seeks for peace by means of fighting against injustice: *the struggle is the means; peace is the end.*[134]

NOTES

1. Cf. Darcy Ribeiro, *O processo civilizatório, Estudos de antropologia da civilizaçao*, Petrópolis, 1987, pp. 129 and ss.

2. See the paper, *Globalization and las actuales orientaciones de la política criminal*, in "Nueva Doctrina Penal," 1999/A, reproduced in "Direito e Cidadania," Praia, República de Cabo Verde, año 3, nº 8, November 1999, February 2000.

3. Cf. Immanuel Wallerstein, *Utopística o las opciones históricas del siglo XXI*, México, 1998. Each one of those moments generated an understanding of the world and a legitimating and delegitimating discourse, with *integrados* and *apocalípticos* (Umberto Eco, *Apocalittici e integrati, Comunicazioni di massa e teorie della cultura di massa,* Bompiani, 1995), and equipped violent phenomena to an increasing extent, according to the increase of technological potential for control and destruction, until reaching the present, where it places the life of the whole planet at risk (Cf. Nicolas Skrotzky, *Guerres: crimes écologiques*, París, 1991).

4. See Ferdinand Tönnies, *Comunidad and sociedad*, Buenos Aires, 1947.

5. Especially because of German and is composition. See Eberhard Schmidt, *Einführung in die Geschichte der deutshcen Strafrechtspflege*, Göttingen, 1951, pp. 21 and ss.; Heinrich Siegel, *Deutsche Rechtsgeschichte*, Berlin, 1886, pp. 13 and ss.; Hugo Hoegel, *Geschichte des Österreichischen Strafrechtes in Verbindung einer Erleuterung seiner grundsätzlichen Bestimmungen*, Viena, 1904, pp. 3 and ss.; H. Rüping, *Grundriss der Strafrechtsgeschichte*, Manchen, 1991; regarding Roman criminal law: Albert Du Boys, *Histoire du Droit Criminel des peuples anciens depuis la formation des sociétés jusqua l'établissement du christianisme*, París, 1845, pp. 248 and ss.; R. Mommsen, *Römisches Strafrecht*, Berlin, 1899 (trad. castellana de Pedro Dorado, Madrid, s.f.).

6. "What do those who rise to power need today besides a good army, *aguardiente* and sausages? They need the text." (André Glucksmann, *Los maestros pensadores*, Barcelona, 1978, p. 43).

7. See the detailed investigation by James A. Brundage, *La ley, el sexo and la sociedad cristiana en la Europa Medieval*, México, 2000.

8. As proof one merely needs to see the 1st Part, question VI de H. Krämer/J. Sprenger, *Il martello delle streghe.*, Marsilio Ed., Venecia, 1995, pp. 85-96.

9. Cf. Norman O. Brown, *La vita contro la morte, Il significado psicoanalitico della storia*, Bompiani, 1986, pp. 183 and ss.

10. See the care taken with regulating it: on this, Valentino Rivalta, *Storia e sistema del diritto dei teatri secondo l'etica e i principii delle leggi canoniche e civili*, Bologna, 1886.

11. That happens when an observation on "a" is answered with an argument extracted from "c" or from "b" and vice-versa, in the thirty-two possible and disconcerting combinations.

12. On the concept of "emergency," Sergio Moccia, *La perenne emergenza*, Napoli, 2000.

13. See Joseph W. Bendersky, *Carl Schmitt teorico del Reich*, Bologna, 1989.

14. "In the eyes of the people, the codes, the procedures and even judicial power seem to have reached an agreement to protect the criminal from society, more than society from the criminal" (p. 15); "Through killing on the field of battle the nation defends itself from its foreign foes; through capital execution, from its domestic foes" (p.133) (R. Garofalo, *La criminología*, Trans. by Pedro Dorado Montero, Madrid, s.d.; pp. XXIII and 59 de la 2ª. Ed. Italiana, Torino, 1891).

15. Carl Schmitt, *El concepto de lo político*, México, 1985, p. 51.

16. Tobias Barreto, *Obras Completas, V Direito, Menores e loucos*, 1926, Sergipe, p. 151.

17. On resistance by the colonized, Richard Price (Comp.), *Sociedades cimarronas, Comunidades esclavas rebeldes en las Américas*, México, 1981; Daniel Valcárcel, *La rebelión de Túpac Amaru*, México, 1965; Ramiro Condarco Morales, *Zárate, el temible Willka, Historia de la rebelión indígena de 1899*, La Paz, 1965.

18. They were also occupied with diabolical pacts in the colony. See Fray Andrés de Olmos, *Tratado de hechicerías and sortilegios, 1553*, Edición de Georges Baudot, UNAM, México, 1990, p. 47.

19. See Alberto Cousté, *Biografia do diabo, O diabo como a sombra de Deus na história*, Rio de Jeneiro, 1997.

20. Cf. the complicated formation of that dynamic in Carlos Amadeu B. Byington, preface to the Brazilian edition of the *Malleus Maleficarum*, Ed. Rosa dos Tempos, Rio de Janeiro, 1991.

21. A broad investigation into those prejudices in Norman Cohn, *Los demonios familiares de Europa*, Madrid, 1980.

22. Cf. the voices "fascination" and "malefice," in Rossell Hope Robbins, *Enciclopedia de la brujería and demonología*, Madrid, 1988.

23. For all, Hubert Lechamps, *Storia della tratta dei negri*, Arnoldo Mondadori, 1971; Hugh Thomas, *La trata de esclavos. Historia del tráfico de seres humanos de 1440 a 1870*, Barcelona, 1998; Joseph E. Inikori, *La trata negrega del siglo XV al XIX*, Barcelona, 1981.

24. See Pierre Duviols,*La destrucción de las religiones antiguas durante la conquista and la colonia*, México, 1977; Angel M. Garibay K./Miguel León Portilla, *La visión de los vencidos*, México, 1961; Robert Jaulin, *El etnocidio a través de las Américas*, México, 1976.

25. See e.g., Walter Rodney, *De cómo Europa subdesarrolló a África*, México, 1982.

26. See Maurice Niveau, *Historia de los hechos económicos contemporáneos*, Barcelona, 1977.

27. See Melossi/Pavarini, *Carcere e fabbrica, Alle origine del sistema penitenziario*, Bologna, 1979.

28. See Michael Ignatieff, *Le origine del penitenziario*, Milano, 1982.

29. In France they were established by the Bourbons, but were greatly resisted in Great Britain. See the difficult English process in Sir Basil Thomson, *La historia de Scotland Yard*, Madrid, 1937.

30. A classic and masterful analysis of that transformation is found in Michel Foucault, *Surveiller et punir, Naissance de la prison*, París, 1975.

31. That was the ideology of all criminal positivism, but it reached its peak with Fructuoso Carpena (*Antropología Criminal*, Madrid, 1909, p. 15), who maintained that criminology was a branch of zoology.

32. Lombroso noted the similarity of the born criminal with the Mongoloid and Negroid (*L'uomo delincuente in rapporto all'antropologia, giurisprudenza e alle discipline carcerarie. Delincuente nato e pazzo morale*, 3ª. Ed., Torino, 1884, pp. 248 and 295). From ancient types human characteristics had been assigned to animals, and then humans were classified according to them. That was the task begun by physiognomists, starting with Giovan Battista della Porta, *Della fisonomia dell'uomo. Con illustrazioni dell'edizione del 1610*, Parma, 1988. In the Eighteenth Century, Johann Caspar Lavater / Georg Christoph Lichtenberg, *Lo specchio dell'anima. Pro e contro la fisiognomica. Un dibattito settecentesco*, a cura di Giovanni Gurisatti, Padova, 1991; also Lucia Rodler, *Il corpo specchio dell'anima. Teoria e storia della fisiognomica*, Bruno Mondadori, 2000. See a meticulous and intelligent development in Armelle Le Bras-Chopard, *El zoo de los filósofos. De la bestialización a la exclusión*, Taurus, Madrid, 2003.

33. The identification of the Jew with the feminine by the suicide Otto Weininger, led him to write his delirious book *Sesso e carattere*, Torino, 1922; on that foolishness: George L. Mosse, *Il razzismo in Europa dalle origine all'olocausto*, Laterza, 1992, p. 118.

34. On positivism and sexual minorities, Jorge Saléis, *Médicos, maleantes and maricas, Higiene, criminología and homosexualidad en la construcción de la Nación Argentina (Buenos Aires: 1871-1914)*, Bs.As., 1995. The adult man, white, "Aryan," strong and muscular was superior (Cf. George L. Mosse, *L'immagine dell'uomo. Lo stereotipo maschile nell'epoca moderna*, Torino, 1997), all the rest were considered inferior, weak, decadent, pathological or criminal: women, Jews, the colonized, Gypsies, the ill, the physical or mentally incapacitated, old people, children, political dissidents, sexual and religious minorities, etc.

35. Since the Sixteenth Century the doctors had tried to make use of the penal discourse: see Iean Wier, *Cinq Livres de l'imposture et de la tromperie des diables: des enchantements et sorcelleries*, París, 1569.

36. The most important book written by a Paris policeman showed the weakness of the discourse: H. A. Frégier, *Des classes dangereuses de la population dans les grandes villes*, Bruxelles, 1840.

37. Although that was the Lombrosian idea, such were also the political dissidents: Cesare Lombroso, *Gli anarchici*, Torino, 1894; Lombroso/Laschi, *Le crime politique et les révolutions*, París, 1892; and those considered supranormal were also suspicious (Lombroso, *L'uomo di genio in rapporto alla psichiatria, alla storia ed all'estetica*, Torino, 1894). Max Nordau followed him closely considering as degenerate all dangerously creative artists (*Degeneración*, Madrid, 1902). On this Daniel Dic, *Volti della degenerazione, una síndrome europea 1848-1918*, Firenze, 1999.

38. On the British deportation to Australia, Robert Hughes, *La costa fatídica*, Barcelona, 1989; on French deportation: Édouard Teisseire, *La transporation pénale et la relegation d'apres les Lois de 30. Mai 1854 et 27.Mai 1885*, París, 1893; C. O.

Barbaroux, *De la transportation*, París, 1857; H. Donnedieu de Vabres, *A Justiça penal hoje*, Sao Paulo, 1938, p. 102.

39. E.g., F. Devoto/G. Rosoli, *La inmigración italiana en la Argentina*, Bs. As., 1985.

40. It is also maintained that his preparation derives from Saint Augustine: León Rozitchner, *La Cosa and la Cruz. Cristianismo and capitalismo*, Bs. As., 1997.

41. Such was Luther's position, on it Norman O. Brown, op. cit.; the classic work of Max Weber, *Ética protestante*, Bs. As., 2004.

42. Fundamentally based on Herbert Spencer, *Principes de Sociologie*, París, 1883; *El universo social. Sociología general and descriptiva*, Spanish adaptation by Salvador Sanpere and Miquel, Barcelona, 1883.

43. One should not identify all inquisitory activities with the Roman or ecclesiastical inquisition, since witch-hunting was also broadly practiced by lay justice; for that matter, one should also not identify the Roman inquisition with the Spanish version. On this: a synthesis in Paolo Ceccoli, *L'Inquisizione Santa*, Colognola ai Colli, 1999; Martín Walter, *Historia de la Inquisición Española*, Madrid, 2001; Henry Kamen, *La Inquisición española*, Madrid, 1973.

44. See n. *Lectio Doctoralis* en la Universidad de Castilla-La Mancha, January 2004 (unpublished).

45. On that, Giovanni Romeo, *Inquisitori, esorcisti e streghe nell'Italia della Controriforma*, Firenze, 1990.

46. Friedrich von Spee, *Cautio Criminales ovvero Dei Processi contro le streghe*, Roma, 1986; see also, *Origen and evolución del discurso crítico en criminal law*, Bs. As., 2004.

47. Cf. Giovanni Romeo, op. cit.

48. Not without first disputes between doctors and judges over the heads of the guillotined, Cf. Pierre Darmon, *Médicos e assassinos na Belle Époque, A medicalizacao do crime*, Rio de Janeiro, 1991.

49. On direct coercion: Iñaki Agirreazkuenaga, *La coacción administrativa directa*, Madrid, 1990; also Otto Mayer, *Derecho Administrative Alemán*, Bs. As., 1950, T. II, pp. 3 and ss.

50. See Vahakn N. Dadrian, *The History of the Armenian Genocide, Ethnic Conflict from the Balkans to Anatolia to the Caucasus*, Providence/Oxford, 1997; on this and the other genocides from the Nineteenth Century: Yves Ternon, *L'État criminel. Las génocides au XXe. siècle*, París, 1995.

51. Marc Ferro, *La Gran Guerra (1914-1918)*, Bs. As., 1985; Basil H. Liddell Hart, *La Prima Guerra Mondiale*, Milano, 1999.

52. See Arthur Herman, *La idea de decadencia en la historia occidental*, Barcelona, 1998;

53. It was also interpreted as a result of genetic decadence: Lothrop Stoddard, *The Revolt against Civilization. The Menace of the Under-man*, London, 1923.

54. There were ample precedents in the cult of the hero, e.g., Thomas Carlyle, *On heroes, hero-worship and the heroic in history*, N. Cork, 1931; French translation: *Les héros le culte des héros et l'héroïque dans l'histoire*, París, 1914.

55. The dogmatic affirmation of Lamarck's thesis by Lyssenko as official biologist in Stalinism, implied that a new society would produce acquired characters that would be transmitted and generate different and better humans. On this dogma: Jean Rostand, *La herencia humana*, Bs. As., 1961, pp. 52-53.

56. See Michael Burleigh/Wolfgang Wippermann, *Lo Stato razziale, Germania 1933-1945*, Rizzoli, 1992; Francisco Muñoz Conde, *Edmund Mezger y derecho criminal de su tiempo. Estudios sobre criminal law del Nacionalsocialismo*, 4ª ed., Valencia, 2003.

57. Although Fascist racism was much less intense than the Nazi version, it certainly existed. Proof of this are publications such as: Paolo Orano, *Inchiesta sulla razza*, Roma, 1939; Julius Evola, *Il mito del sangue*, reed. 1978; an overall view in: Giorgio Israel/Pietro Nastasi, *Scienza e razza nell'Italia fascista*, Il Mulino, 1998.

58. On this concept, Lola Aniyar de Castro, *Derechos humanos, modelo integral de la ciencia penal, and sistema penal subterráneo*, in "Rev. del Colegio de Abogados Penalistas del Valle," Cali, 1985, pp. 301 and ss.

59. Carl Schmitt, *Staat, Bewegung, Volk: Die Dreigliederung der politischen Einheit*, Hamburg, 1933.

60. See Victor Zaslavsky, *La memoria storica nella Russia postsovietica: il bisogno di dimenticare e lo sforzo di ricordare*, in AA.VSee, "Storia, verità e giustizia, I crimini del XX secolo," a cura di Marcello Flores, Bruno Mondadori, Milano, 2001, pp. 222 and ss. (226).

61. On this Ian Kershaw, *Hitler 1889-1936*, Madrid, 2000, pp. 489 and ss.

62. See those high-sounding designations and laws in: Dalcke, *Strafrecht und Strafverfahren. Eine Sammlung der wichstigsten Gesetze des Strafrechts und des Strafverfahrens mit Erläuterungen*, Berlin, 1938.

63. One cannot deny that also, in the final analysis they served for dividing up the internal functions of power, to avoid in some measure the chaos caused in every authoritarian regime by competitive struggles between agency leaders and agencies.

64. On the sinister meaning of "foreigners" (*Fremde*) in Nazi legislation, Francisco Muñoz Conde, op. cit., pp. 170 and ss.; also Buleigh/Wippermann, especially chapter VI.

65. Cf. Arnold Hauser, *Historia social de la literatura and el arte*, Madrid, 1971, I, pp. 64 and ss.

66. Ibid, p. 129. It has been argued, with reason, that frontality, clearly manifested in ancient Egyptian art, is characteristic of autocracies, together with repudiation of nudity, which is only tolerated as a demonstration of the *healthy and superior man* in the muscular colossal marble statues common to all of them, suitable for sublimating homophilous tendencies that one wishes to control (Cf. Heinz-Dieter Schilling (herausg.). *Schwule und Faschismus*, Berlin, 1983). Hiding of nudity and death is hiding of equality (Arnold Hauser, op. cit., p. 101, con cita de Julius Lange), although clearly not only there.

67. See the impressive illustrations of: *Deutschland erwacht. Werden, Kampf und Sieg der NSDAP*, with texts by Wilfrid Bade and selection of photos by Heinrich Hoffmann, Berlin, 1933.

68. See the significant graphic work in Anthony Rhodes, *Propaganda. The Art of Persuation: World War II*, Pennsylvania, 1993.

69. Hitler himself had learned this from Karl Lueger, the anti-Semitic union leader from Vienna who he had heard as a young man, Cf. Joachim C. Fest, *Hitler, Il Führer e il nazismo*, Rizzoli, 1991, p. 46.

70. Carl Schmitt, *El concepto de lo político*, México, 1985.

71. On this, Julio Pinto, *Carl Schmitt and la reivindicación de la política*, La Plata, 2000, pp. 99 and ss.

72. This was the political philosopher most admired by Carl Schmitt (see, by this author: *El Leviatan en la doctrina del Estado de Thomas Hobbes*, México, 1997).

73. See Hegel, *Filosofía del Derecho*, Trans. by Juan Garzón Bates, México, 1985, p. 35.

74. That verificación throws the concept of *religious war* into a crisis, because it would lead to considering that all wars are *religious*. We do not believe that such a conclusion is correct, but it would demonstrate well that there are no true *religious wars,* but that all wars are mythic, or better still, that *all wars are idolatrous*.

75. Alfred Rosenberg, *El mito of the Twentieth Century. Una valoración de las luchas anímico-espirituales de las formas de nuestro tiempo*, Buenos Aires, 1976. This did nothing more than recycle Houston Stewart Chamberlain (*Die Grundlagen des neunzehnten Jahrhunderts*, Manchen, 1906) and Arthur de Gobineau (*Essai sur l'inégalité des races humaines*, París, 1967; Italian trans.: *Saggio sulla disuguaglianza delle razze umane*, Rizzoli, 1997).

76. See Emilio Gentile, *Le origine dell'ideologia fascista (1918-1925*), Bologna, 1996; on Giovanni Gentile, from different perspectives, Sergio Romano, *Giovanni Gentile. La filosofia al potere*, Milano, 1990; Ugo Spirito, *Giovanni Gentile*, Firenze, 1999.

77. Near to this, Georg Lukacs, *El asalto a la razón. La trayectoria del irracionalismo desde Schelling hasta Hitler*, México, 1983, p. 7.

78. See Léon Poliakov, *Il mito ariano. Saggio sulle origine del nazismo e dei nazionalismi*, Roma, 1999.

79. On the German and Italian penal Hegelians, n. *Tratado de Derecho Penal*, Bs. As., 1987, II, pp. 171-177.

80. That was the general meaning of the Latin American oligarchic order. The investigation by Leopoldo Zea is illustrative in that respect, *El positivismo en México: nacimiento, apogeo and decadencia*, México, 1984.

81. Hegel, *Lecciones on the filosofía de la historia universal*, Madrid, 1980, p. 171.

82. Thus, for example, Carlos Octavio Bunge, *Nuestra América. Ensayo de psicología social*, Bs. As., 1903.

83. And in a certain sense, also Freudianly: Rudiger Herren, *Freud und die Kriminologie, Einführung in die psychoanalytische Kriminologie*, Stuttgart, 1973.

84. E.g., Raimundo Nina Rodrigues, *Os africanos no Brasil, Revisao e prefácio de Homero Pires*, Sao Paulo, 1932; su inspiración era Dr. A. Corre, *Le crime en pays créoles (Esquisse d'ethnographie criminelle*), París, 1889.

85. See David Viñas, *Indios, ejército and frontera*, México, 1982.

86. See e.g., José C. Valadés, *El Porfirismo, Historia de un régimen*, UNAM, México, 1987.

87. See the comparative constitutional law at this period: F. R. Dareste, *Les constitutions modernes*, París, 1891; the American model was followed so closely that its commentators were translated: José Story, *El Poder Judicial of the United States. Su organización and atribuciones*, Buenos Aires, 1863.

88. On this, see the work, *Introduction a la codificación penal latinoamericana*, in Universidad de Salamanca, "Los Criminal codes Iberoamericanos," Bogotá, 1994. Those sources were quite incompatible, because the constitutions prescribed judicial control by Anglo Saxon constitutionality, whereas the codes were derived from the continental administrative tradition that entrusted all power to the state bureaucratic apparatus (Michel Fromont, *La justice constitutionelle dans le monde*, París, 1996; Louis Favoreu, *Los tribunales constitucionales*, Barcelona, 1994), which completely ignored that control, according to the Prussian and Napoleonic model. However, the academic, political and publicity contradictions mattered little, because the exercise of punitive power was in fact nothing more than the *instrument for internal disciplining of a concentration camp*, with limits only to the degree that it might affect some administrators and their families or aides.

89. See Alan Knight, *La Revolución Mexicana*, Mexico, 1996.

90. Perfectly depicted by the literature in works such as *Tirano Banderas* by Ramón del Valle Inclán, *El Señor Presidente* by Miguel Angel Asturias or *El otoño del patriarca* de Gabriel García Márquez.

91. On this, in the work *Política and dogmática jurídico penal*, in "Directo e democracia," Universidade Luterana do Brasil, Canoas (RS), vol. 3 n° 2, 2002.

92. See in the work, *Introduction*, cit.

93. See APDH, *La desaparición, Crimen contra la humanidad*, Bs. As., 1987; Maria Luisa Bartolomei, *Gross and Messive Violations of Human Rights in Argentina 1976-1983*, Lund, 1994.

94. See International Commission of Jurists, *States of Emergency, Their Impact on Human Rights*, 1983.

95. Equipo SELADOC, *Iglesia and seguridad nacional*, Salamanca, 1980; Joseph Comblin, *Le pouvoir militaire en Amerique Latine*, París, 1977 (translation: *Dos ensayos sobre seguridad nacional*, Sgo. de Chile, 1979).

96. Classics include: Golbery do Couto e Silva, *Planejamento estratégico*, Brasilia, 1981; Augusto Pinochet Ugarte, *Geopolítica*, Sgo. de Chile, 1984.

97. It was clear that this was nothing more than a discourse: the Argentine dictatorship did not hide its commercial ties with the Soviet Union, its main grain buyer during those years and a power that blocked denunciations in international forums.

98. The bishops made an acutely critical pronouncement in the so-called "Documento de Puebla," Buenos Aires, 1979, p. 67 (párrafo 49). A documented critique in: Hernán Montealegre, *La seguridad del Estado and human rights*, Santiago de Chile, 1979.

99. There were few judicial discourses: Mário Pessoa, *O direito da Segurança Nacional*, Rio de Janeiro, 1971; Carlos Horacio Domínguez, *La nueva guerra and*

el nuevo derecho, Ensayo para una estrategia jurídica antisubversiva, Bs. As, 1980; Fernando Bayardo Bengoa, *Los Derechos del Hombre and la defensa de la Nación*, Montevideo, 1979.

100. With greater detail, *La legislación antidroga latinoamericana: Sus componentes de criminal law autoritario*, in "Derecho Penal, Homenaje al Dr. Raúl Peña Cabrera," Lima, 1991, pp. 715 and ss.

101. Among others: Octavio Ianni, *A era do globalismo*, Rio de Janeiro, 1997; Hans-Peter Martin/Harald Schumann, *A armadilha da globalizaçao, O assalto à democracia e ao bem-estar social*, Sao Paulo, 1998; Richard Falk, *Globalization depredadora, Una crítica*, Madrid, 2002; Celso Furtado, *O capitalismo global*, Rio de Janeiro, 1998; Ulrich Beck, *Che cosa è la globalizzazione, Rischi e prospettive della società planetaria*, Roma, 1999; Zygmunt Bauman, *Globalizaçao: as conseqüências humanas*, Rio de Janeiro, 1999; Joseph E. Stiglitz, *El malestar en globalization*, Madrid, 2002; Heinz Dieterich, *Identidad nacional and globalization*, México D.F., 2000; Eric J. Hobsbawm, *Intervista sul nuovo secolo a cura di Antonio Polito*, Laterza, 2000; Bruno Amoroso, *L'apartheid globale. Globalizzazione. Marginalizzazione economica. Destabilizzazione politica*, Roma, 1999. See in the work, *Globalization and las actuales orientaciones de la política criminal*, in "Nueva Doctrina Penal," 1999/A, reproduced in "Direito e Cidadania," Praia, República de Cabo Verde, year 3, nº 8, November 1999, February 2000.

102. These criteria merited enthusiastic admiration from Adolf Hitler, *Mi lucha*, Sgo. De Chile, 1939, p. 126. There was an attempt to renew them in the last decade of the Twentieth Century: on that, John Sedgwinck, *Inside the Pioneer Fund*; Adam Millar, *Professors of Hate*, both in "The Bell Curve Debate," edited by Russell Jocoby and Noemí Glauberman, Times Books, 1995, pp. 144 and 162.

103. Hill Severn, *The End of the Roaring Twenties, Prohibition and Repeal*, N. York, 1969.

104. They have always aroused interest from comparativists: e.g., *La Probatios (Régime de la mise á l'épreuve) et les lemusres analogues*, Imprenta Administrativa, Melón, 1953. His influence on later European penology is clear: HEUNI, Norman Bishop, *Noncustodial alternatives in Europe*, Helsinski, 1988; Anton M. van Kalmthout/Peter J. P. Tak, *Sanctions-Systems in the member-States of the Council of Europe*, 1988.

105. Furman v. Georgia, en AA.VSee, *The death penalty in America, Current controversies*, edited by Hugo Adam Bedau, New York, 1997, p. 189; Marino Barbero Santos, *Pena de muerte (El ocaso de un mito)*, Buenos Aires, 1985, pp. 179 and ss.

106. See Nils Christie, *Crime control as industry, Towards Gulugs, western style*, 1993, p. 93.

107. Ibid.

108. McCleskey v. Kemp, en *The death penalty in America*, cit., p. 254.

109. Ibid, p. 10; José Sáez Capel, *Pena de muerte, Cuando el Estado asesina*, Buenos Aires, 1999.

110. See M. Cherif Bassiouni–Eduardo Vetere, *Organizad Crime. A Compilation of U.N. Documents 1975-1998*, N. York, 1998.

111. V in the work, *El crimen organizado, Una categoría frustrada*, in Hom. A Ricardo C. Núñez, Córdoba, 1995.

112. See for example, the works in José Octavio López Presa (Coord.), *Corrupción and cambio*, México, 1998.

113. It is unquestionable that corruption must be fought, but it is certain that it is absurd to intend to do this with the penal system, which is one of the areas most vulnerable to it, when everyone knows that corruption arises in a context of arbitrary power, and the only effective way of preventing it is by closing those spaces, by means of improved and constantly renewed institutional engineering.

114. On that, Charles Pollard, *Tolerancia cero ¿Y mañana qué?*, in "Milenio," Univ. de Gral. San Martín, año 2, n° 3, 1999, pp.17 and ss.

115. At that moment, belief in witches was founded on the prejudice of widespread European beliefs regarding them. Norman Cohn, *Los demonios familiares de Europa*, cit. As present there are numerous prejudices, but one is not allowed to build enemies on them. Undeniably, many social sectors maintain prejudices against women, Jews, blacks, Latinos, etc., but they are not allowed to use them to create enemies.

116. Both in the sense intended by Emile Durkheim (*Le suicide*, París, 1897), because the previous norms for access to wealth are no longer useful, and that of Robert Merton (*Teoría and estructura sociales*, México, 1984), because they socially lacked legitimate routes for that same access.

117. This corruption is combined with that of local party chiefs and provides financing for their interrnal elections, taints judicial powers and weakens political democracy at its base.

118. Cf. Carranza/Mora/Houed/Zaffaroni, *El preso sin condena in Latin America and el Caribe*, San José, 1983.

119. The regional situation in this aspect is no different from what Concepción Arenal described in Spain well over a century ago: *Estudios Penitenciarios*, Madrid, 1877.

120. It is interesting to note the similarity between publicity for the penal system as a product and advertising for toothpaste and pain-killers: in both it is common to present persons who act in the role of specialists. In other cases, it is the victims or their relatives who assume that role in the media, as if the justice of a claim for a solution were to spring miraculously from technical knowledge to decide solutions.

121. The multiple English meanings for the expression coincide in a meaning of superficial, unexciting, lukewarm, (*Webster's Encyclopedic Unabridged Dictionary of the English Language*, N. York, 1989, p. 321). The traditional Spanish translation is *tibio* (unexciting), *indiferente* (indifferent) (*Appleton's new English-Spanish Dictionary*, N. York, 1916, p. 115).

122. In some cases because their pride impedes them; in others because the urgencies of publicity demand production of sensational acts (what the politicians like to call "the time for politics," as opposed to "the times for technique") and in others, because budgetary limitations that are imposed internationally or transnationally on debtor countries prohibit.

123. On mannerism in pathology, Ludwig Binswanger, *Tres formas de la existencia frustrada*, Buenos Aires, 1072, pp. 127 and ss.

124. It is interesting how this phenomenon was perceived early on by Roger-Gérard Schwartzenberg, *O Estado espetáculo*, Rio de Janeiro, 1978.

125. "The last century saw the first systematic strikes in the factories. The next century will not end without the threat of a strike from the Noosphere" (Pierre Teilhard de Chardin, *El fenómeno humano*, Madrid, 1965, p. 277).

126. The First Question of the *Malleus Maleficarum*, in other words, the first one it deals with, is to consider as heretics and condemn those who deny or cast doubt upon the power of the devil and of witches, including those who do so because of ignorance this is intentional (trad. italiana, p. 40).

127. On the aporia of time in criminal law, Ana Messuti, *El tiempo como pena*, Bs. As., 2001.

128. On thes political stumblings in Weimar, Walter Laqueur, *La Repubblica di Weimar, 1918-1933: I mali oscuri della democrazia europea*, Milano, 1996.

129. See our work *Política and dogmática jurídico penal*, cit.

130. A solution is sought through a "right to intervention" that is different from criminal law, Winfrid Hassemer, *Crisis and características del moderno criminal law*, in "Actualidad Penal," nº 43, Madrid, 1993; also Hassemer-Muñoz Conde, *Introduction a la criminología*, Valencia, 2001; much more problematic is the proposal of a criminal law "at two speeds" of Jesús-Maria Silva Sánchez, *La expansión of criminal law, Aspectos de la política criminal en las sociedades postindustriales*, Madrid, 1999; on the so-called "symbolic criminal law" one may see the two works published in nº 1 of "Pena y Estado," Barcelona, 1991.

131. See Günther Jakobs-Manuel Cancio Meliá, *Derecho Penal del enemigo*, Madrid, 2003.

132. Gustav Radbruch, *Paul Johann Anselm Feuerbach, Ein Juristenleben*, Göttingen, 1969; Mario A. Cattaneo, *Anselm Feuerbach, filosofo e giurista liberale*, Milano, 1970; Eberhard Kipper, *Johann Paul Anselm Feuerbach, sein Leben als Denker, Gesetzgeber und Richter*, Darmstadt, 1969.

133. *Anti-Hobbes oder über die Grenzen der höchsten Gewalt uns das Zwangsrecht der Bürger gegen den Oberherrn*, Ital. trans. a cura di Mario A. Cattaneo, *Anti-Hobbes ovvero i limiti del potere supremo e il diritto coativo dei cittadini contro il sovrano*, Milano, 1972.

134. R. von Ihering, *La lucha por el derecho*, Trans. by Adolfo Posada and Biesca, Madrid, 1881, p. 3. On that concept see the works compiled by Agustín Squella, *Ihering and la lucha por el derecho*, "Revista de Ciencias Sociales," Universidad de Chile, Valparaiso, 1977.

Chapter Two

Criminology and Psychiatry

The Trauma of the First Meeting

Eugenio Raúl Zaffaroni

COMMUNICATING THE LACK OF COMMUNICATION

These reflections have the objecting of making it clear that criminology suffers from an *original birth trauma* and a *trauma of the first meeting*, which leads it to reject—or at least to mistrust—further and profitable contacts with psychiatry.

As a result, if one intends to establish a fruitful interdisciplinary base, one must first analyze this *trauma*, remember it with a certain precision, make clear its magnitude and its terrible consequences, meaning, remove it, and then, with the reservations derived from a painful experience, confront a new dialogue between both forms of knowledge. This continues to be indispensable, because it would be absurd to limit knowledge because of an old trauma, which it is clear that the link needs to be reestablished on very different bases, about which we can do more than to indicate their major lines with the mere objective of indicating the need for them.

We should note that the *trauma of the first meeting* is not small, and thus, the difficulty in removing it is also considerable. From such an original relation arose a racist, reactionary criminology, used to legitimate the destruction of all guarantees and limits in modern criminology, which provided arguments for serious de-articulating the rule of law. It is significant that one of its branches ended up legitimating genocide for the *different* and the *dissidents* in the Nazi concentration camps. Distrust and the resulting rejection, for their part, are not gratuitous or much less.

Nonetheless, it is clear that since that distressing experience, both criminology and the mental health sciences have traveled along paths that are radically different and diametrically opposed to the previous ones, that they have reached radical positions such as *radical* criminology and *anti-psychiatry.*

If criminology now intends to contribute useful knowledge to reduce the arbitrary exercise of punitive power, to diminish the pain that crime and punitive power produce, and, to definitively construct a world that is less violent, less unjust and more respectful of Human Rights, we believe that the moment has also arrived for demanding recognition of the importance of constructive and closer contacts.

We will begin, then, by looking at the course of relations between our knowledge and remembering the *trauma of the first encounter.*

PREHISTORY

Contrary to what theoreticians of etiological or traditional criminology usually affirm, it did not begin with authors at the end of the Nineteenth Century (Lombroso, Lacassagne, etc.), nor with the thinkers of penal illuminism (Beccaria, Feurbach, Carmignani, etc.), as maintained by criminologists of the social reaction paradigm. Criminology, with another name, but *as knowledge regarding criminalized and criminalizable evil,* as born with punitive power itself, that is, with the *demonologists* who were the first criminologists.[1] The power struggles over the discursive hegemony on the *criminal question* among criminologists and doctors are also very much prior to the delimitation of our disciplines as knowledge and especially their academic enshrinement.

The prehistory of the dispute goes back to the publication of a book by Jean Wier, in Basle in 1568,[2] in which he maintained that witches should not be punished by inquisitors, but turned over to the doctors, who disputed punitive power not only with the inquisitors but also with the courts and lay jailers.[3] Wier[4] thus rose up against the demonologist discourse.

One should also note that the institution for total psychiatric control, the *asylum* or *bedlam*, is much older than the prison as a penal sentence. Juan de Dios, founder of the *Fate-Bene-Fratelli* order, had an asylum built in 1540 in Granada and during the next century went over to France, to specialize in treatment of the mentally ill.[5] Contemporaneous with the appearance and spread of prison as a penalty, the asylum became laicized, going from a charitable entity to a tutelary entity, to contain those cases in which the threat of laws and counsel of the religious were considered insufficient.[6]

THE ORIGINS: MODERN PSYCHIATRY ILLUMINATES OFFICIAL CRIMINOLOGY

With industrialism, the urban concentration became obliged to gather the mentally infirm and violators of property into total state institutions, the *insane asylums and prisons*. The police were a new institution, charged with urban oversight and discipline, who lacked a discourse to encompass such duties. Through the work of psychiatrists dedicated to forensic medicine, the doctors offered their discourse to the police, and thus combined knowledge with power, leaving the hegemonic discourse to the jurists and philosophers and officializing etiological *criminology,* usually known as *positivism.*

This explains how criminology acquired its category of academic knowledge from the hands of the psychiatrists. The relative isolation of European countries determined parallel, though somewhat different courses.

The French case is highly illustrative of this process, because it is practically lineal. The lay transformation of the insane asylum occurs with the work of Phillipe Pinel (1745-1826),[7] even though much of his legend comes from the famous call for freeing the mentally ill from the prisons.[8] Strictly speaking, psychiatric regulations began with his teachings, although they were more concretely defined years after his death, through the work of his disciple, Jeán-Étienne Dominique Esquirol (1772-1840).[9] The French police lacked a discourse of their own. The most important essay in the police discourse was produced in 1838 by H.A. Frégier, an illustrious Parisian commissioner, responding to a contest called for by the College de France. In it he made the first reference to the *dangerous classes*, ten years before the famous *Communist manifesto*, but his inconsistency was clear, and he did not go beyond a series of observations, moral maxims and commonplaces.[10]

For their part, the psychiatrists had to deal daily with delinquents, with murderers, who provided occasions for public solemnities by trials that ended with the guillotine,[11] and, even more frequently, with urban marginalization of those who made up the *dangerous classes* in the terminology of the College de France. The idea soon arose that would encompass and explain both: *degeneration.*[12]

Degeneration was enunciated and enshrined by Bénédict Augustin Morel (1809-1873) in his famous *Traité des dégénerescences* in 1857.[13] For Morel, degeneration was the result of inheritance, in which inherited characters were combined with those incorporated from the environment, with Lamarck`s thesis of transmission of characters being admitted. Morel linked degenerative symptoms and signs and accentuated his interest in epilepsy, coining the expression *larval epilepsy*.

Morel's theses were followed by Valentin Magnan (1835-1916), who attributed degeneration to an imbalance between the higher and lower centers of the brain. His substantial difference with Morel lay in his refusal to admit a perfect type in the past, since for Magnan perfection was worked out through evolution and was in the future, which degeneration consisted in a reduction of the will, understood as being the capacity for struggling to survive and adapt. For Magnan degeneration was not the cause of rime, but crime was a political definition of what was socially harmful, and degeneration would provoke a difficulty in adapting to the issues of prohibition, so that in crime there would always be a component of social responsibility.[14] In this sense, there seems to be a prudent parallel with the thesis of Pedro Dorado Montero.[15]

The contrary position, which attributed criminality to degeneration and excluded all social responsibility in etiology, was set forth by Charles-Samson Féré (1852-1907),[16] working from radical Darwinism. He maintained a theory of social hierarchization based on the capacity of adaptation, which determined the social sedimentation of the degenerates, in other words, that society tended to be socially just for biological reasons. Social responsibility failed to operate for Féré in that the state had not sufficiently protected the non-degenerates, and because of that, should indemnify them.

These discourses fit in with selective police demands and soon, due to the forensic doctors, they jointly began to question the hegemonic power of the discourse on the criminal question with the jurists, reaching the ridiculous point of disputing over the heads of guillotined criminals.[17]

The most famous of the pioneers in officializing *criminal anthropology* (the first name for modern criminology) was Alexandre Lacassagne (1843-1924). From Morel he took the combination of inherited characters and those acquired and transmitted by inheritance and combined the phrenological theses of the German Gall with social stratification, maintaining that criminal etiology depended on modifications of the brain that could affect the occipital, frontal or parietal region, of alienated delinquents from upper classes.[18] Bertillon applied physical anthropology measurements for identification[19] and Topinard maintained that criminal anthropology is not a pure but an applied and practical science, while Manouvrier discussed the method that intended to distinguish the criminals from the non-criminals.[20]

Those French psychiatrists on the whole rejected Italian criminal anthropology, especially the thesis of the Lombrosian born criminal, but in their own way, with their psychiatric discourse, they legitimated police selection. Let us not forget that Morel, based on evolutionism, installed the theory of *apartheid*, postulating that it was inconvenient to have human interbreeding because it produced degeneration, meaning unbalanced human hybrids, a highly functional position at the time that he intended to confirm with the works of Corre.[21]

For its part, English psychiatry recognizes as its pioneering criminologist and anthropologist James-Cowles Prichard (1786-1848), who advanced important concepts for future developments: he was the first to precisely describe *moral insanity*, which soon became known as *psychopathy*; he published a book entitled *On the different forms of madness in its relations with justice*; and maintained that primitive man (Adam) was black.[22] As was the case with French psychiatry, Italian criminal anthropology was rejected in Great Britain and the United States. Nonetheless, the so-called *social darwinism*[23] was undeniable, above all because of the work of Spencer (1820-1903)[24] and the Lamarckian tradition, which had repercussions both in Lombroso and in the English school of *eugenesy* of Francis Galton (1822-1911) and K. Pearson (1857-1936).[25] The *racist* consequences of this thinking are clear, and moved from psychiatry to criminology and politics.

Henry Mauldsley (1835-1918), a prison doctor, apropos of the critique of English rules on imputability (*M'Naghten Rules*) discussed the absurd judicial concepts of his time and with that, claimed that crime should be treated as a medical question.[26] Charles Goring (1870-1919)[27] in his 1913 work was the one who faced Lombrosian theory with the greatest emphasis, conducting a study of 4,000 convicts to conclude that they did not present the characteristics defined by Lombroso, but—following the *eugenesic* line—he affirmed that the majority suffered from intellectual and physical deficiencies that he attributed to inheritance. Undoubtedly Goring clearly influenced the work of Henry Goddard (1866-1957) in the United States, famous for the *Kallikak family* case,[28] when he applied intelligence tests and concluded that there was a high incidence of hereditary mental weakness in juvenile criminality, and promoted preventive measures.[29]

In the German language, Franz-Josef Gall (1758-1828), born in Baden but whose activity was carried out first in Vienna and then in Paris, is undoubtedly the pioneer in studies of physical anthropology in criminal issues, although his field of action was much broader, encompassing the entire nervous system and its localizations. At any rate, by the middle of the Nineteenth Century, his *phrenology* had been all but forgotten in Europe[30] and a few decades later, German psychiatrists denied the Lombrosian concept of a born criminal, but insisted on looking for the constant variable and discovering the different forms of mental alienation that they presumed were determinants of criminal conduct.

This emphasis was followed by the line developed by Austrian psychiatrist Moritz Benedikt (1835-1920), who as a student of craniology was not able to establish physical differences among delinquents, but who was inclined to seek determinants in the so-called *step toward the act.* His idea of *secret life* or *second life* seems to have influenced Freud, but in criminology, beginning with the affirmation that a high percentage of the imprisoned were genuinely mentally ill and among the rest those on the borderline were predominant, the German-language psychiatrists pathologized practically every area of crime.

A very significant work was that of Gustav Achaffenburg (1866-1944)—*Crime and its repression*—which is practically a psychiatry for jurists and operators of the penal system,[31] preceded by the work if Richard von Krafft-Ebbing (1840-1902),[32] who quickly pathologized all non-conventional sexual activity, considering it *perversion* in his *Psycopathia sexualis* of 1866,[33] and was criticized for this by the Englishman Henry Havelock Ellis (1859-1839).[34]

It is curious to note that due to the work of scholars in judicial psychology, the etiological paradigm was partially broken, although without consequences later on, since it was not limited to the conduct of those being tried, but encompassed all protagonists in the process, including limitations of knowledge for judges, lawyers and witnesses. A classic work in this regard is that of the Austrian Hans Gross (1847-1914).[35] Another interesting curiosity was the thesis presented by Albrecht at the Rome congress in 1885; he affirmed that the normal person was a delinquent and the honest man was an abnormality.[36]

CRIMINOLOGY DEVELOPED HAND-IN-HAND WITH PSYCHIATRY

Criminology, officialized in this manner, with a letter of presentation valid worldwide through the extraordinary dissemination of the theories of Cesare Lombroso,[37] followed its course. It offered the world a discourse that allowed it to consider colonized peoples as inferiors, since the European criminals resembled them,[38] pathologized political dissidents,[39] reinforced the aesthetic prejudices of the criminal stereotype;[40] provided the basis for *dangerousness without crime*,[41] which made it possible to impose sentences on inconvenient people, in other words, in marginalized urban populations, known as *bad lives*,[42] rationalized elimination of so-called *social enemies*,[43] condemned innovators, calling them *geniuses* and noting the need for distrusting them,[44] promoted sterilization as a form of preventing crime through degeneration of the species,[45] encouraged reclusion of the mentally weak in gigantic establishments,[46] etc.

In summary, if it is true that European sociologists were advancing in their work,[47] psychiatry was converted into the dominant discourse on the criminal issue, neutralizing all of the limits established by criminal law in terms of illustration and modernity, while defending the most absolute social immobility and hiding social injustice while enshrining class hierarchization as a natural results of different biologically conditioned capacities. There were many variations to soften the blow, but they were not enough to undo the major premises.

North American criminological sociology was born during the period between the wars,[48] but the psychiatrists continued to dominate criminology in Europe, where sociology had suffered a sharp major decline, following a slightly less obstinate course, with a biological reductionism that was less accentuated, but followed an identical line.

The concept of constitution was initiated beginning with Dupré (1862-1921), with his theory of *perverse constitution,* combined later with contributions from endocrinology. A similar line guided the work of Nicola Pende (1880-1970)[49] in Italy, developed more broadly by his disciple Benigno Di Tullio with his classification of delinquents and especially with the definition of *constitutional delinquency,*[50] but even more widely disseminated were the works of Ernst Kretschmer (1888-1964), with their classification of body structures as leptosomatic, picnic and athletic, inclined respectively towards schizophrenia, manic-depressive psychosis and epilepsy.[51] Normal persons presented characteristics of abnormal ones; there was no neat dividing line, but degrees for classifying people as *schizomotics, cyclotimics* and so on. In the United States there was an attempt at making a new classification along the same lines.[52] To a greater or kisser degree, endocrinology contributed by reaffirming the pathologization of non-conventional sexuality;[53] from the *moral madman* the emphasis shifted to the concept of *psychopath,*[54] which, if arbitrarily handled could lead to very dangerous results as an obstacle to any penitentiary benefit or as the foundation for imposing a life or indeterminate sentence, and to which were added no less nebulous terms such as *sociopath and asocial.*[55]

It is altogether undeniable that the work of the Swiss Eugen Bleuler (1857-1940), through an article published in Aschaffenburg's *Treatise*, consecrated the nototaxia of *precocious* dementia later called *schizophrenia.*[56] And, with the systematization introduced by Emil Kraepelin (1857-1926),[57] order was brought to the classificatory chaos of psychiatric nototaxy, at the same time as the idea of *degeneration* was definitively abandoned.

THE *TRAUMA* OF GENOCIDE

Even though the period between wars was not very luminous for psychiatry or for the European criminology that continued under its tutelage, the first contacts with psychoanalysis produced an enormous initial bibliography dedicated to the theme.[58] Although of unequal quality and hastily prepared, as well as lacking a solid theoretical base, and with the growing distrust of biological and racist ideologies, a psychiatry with considerable psychological penetration began to appear, which culminated, many years later, in therapeutic prudence and an open criticism of institutionalization.

Nonetheless, that tendency began almost as an alternative, not very well defined and frequently contaminated by the dominant ideas, while the strong inertia of previous decades[59] followed its inexorably directed course towards genocide, because with the forms of totalitarianism during the period between the wars, it became shamelessly politicized and led to its ultimate and most inhuman consequences.

Lamarck`s thesis on the transmission of acquired characters applied to humanity led to an ineludible consequence: it was necessary to suppress inferiors or prevent them from reproducing in order to save *humanity* from their decadence.[60] There were multiple political uses of this ideological instrument: for some, the inferiors had caused the Russian revolution,[61] for others, it was necessary to neutralize them by means of the dictatorship of the proletariat in order to create the new man;[62] for some, the unilateral theories about the surrounding world were the product of materialist Marxism,[63] for others they were a product of the North American School.[64]

What is certain is that the inferiors needed to be neutralized, or, failing that, eliminated, to *defend society and save humanity* from irrevocable genetic decadence. The horrendous coronation of the first encounter was the imprisonment and annihilation of millions of people in the Nazi concentration camps, rationalized by jurists and doctors. Recent historical research has revealed the magnitude of the theoretical aberration and the degree of personal commitment achieved by criminologists who had been highly recognized and profusely cited in postwar years, such as Franz Exner and Edmund Mezger, the first a doctor and the second a jurist, who in 1944 designed legislation destined to lead to the disappearance of the *marginal* and *undesirables* in the concentration camps.[65]

The contradictions of the time led to many thinkers and scientists considered to be *progressives* in the political field not perceiving the aberrations fleshed out by the theses they defended in the criminological, psychiatric and penal. Biological positivism presented itself as a scientific response to medieval obscurantism, when in fact it allowed a renewal of the inquisition, by eliminating the limits imposed by modernity. The attempts to harmonize the incompatible were no more than rationalizations developed by those who were dumbfounded by the horror of the monsters they had helped to create.[66] To culminate, another line of biological inquiry ended up in experiments that were no less aberrant, leading to the practice of surgical interventions intended to modify behavior, such as the famous *lobotomy,* which enjoyed considerable prestige in the postwar years.[67]

The idea that criminology was a *dangerous science* began to take shape among the criminalists, who took refuge in an aseptic neokantism, although they were as contaminated as criminology itself, even to the point of sharing authors, since their greatest mentor during the period was Edmund Mezger himself, who published his terrible work of criminology during those years.[68] After the Second World War, everyone rejected the baneful consequences of the thesis that in some measure they had helped to support and diffuse, denied that their ideas had been necessary consequences of such a thesis, pointed to them as pure political deformations, and could not assume the responsibility for their own conceptual errors. Psychiatric criminology weakened and entered into open death throes. Psychiatry, which had enabled the first and traumatic encounter, also began a retreat, albeit more slowly. Its marked ideological character could not be hidden for very long and its excesses such as the killing of patients in Nazism and the grotesque Soviet manipulation[69] caused enormous horror.

The first encounter had been horrendous and was closed out with incoherent explanations and dissimulation. Even today it is necessary to delve into writings from that period to extract the original ideas, which are generally omitted or considered secondary and of lesser importance. One idea that was the product of this first encounter continues alive and in effect in laws, in jurisprudence and in periodicals: *dangerousness*. This is the most arbitrary ideological resource which still encumbers criminal law in our days, as a sad memento of the first encounter.

CRIMINOLOGY BECOMES INDEPENDENT OF PSYCHIATRY

The first and prolonged traumatic contact with criminology, with consequences as disastrous as those noted, and because of the fright it caused, led to a displacement of interest from criminology to North American sociology, in abandonment of the dying European psychiatric criminology.

In the 1960s criminology moved from the *etiological* paradigm to that of *social reaction.*[70] It is incorrect to interpret the move away from the *etiological* paradigm as abandonment of the study of *relations of connectivity and contemporaneity* regarding violent and conflictive behaviors. Understood correctly, the change of paradigm meant expansion of the fields in those phenomena (encompassing those of punitive power) and, furthermore, denunciation of a false analysis of those relations, as was done by the so-called *traditional or positivist (or neokantian) etiological paradigm*, which distorted the perception by doing without of violence and the reproductive effect of the punitive power itself and of the penal system.

Although it is necessary to abandon or redefine quite radically the word *etiology*, separate it from every medical connotation, from any mechanical causality (or also replace it) and deprive it of any pretension of having the correct *prognosis* in individual cases, the truth is that the social reduction paradigm correctly understood does not refuse to ask itself about the *why* of certain conducts (especially violent and lethal ones). Rather, in the first place, it *expands the horizon of the included conducts, incorporating those of the operators of the penal system and,* as a consequence, rectifies the explanations of the *positivist or neokantian etiology.*[71] This proved to be false precisely because of the narrowness of the universe included and the dogmatic presupposition that the penal system and the exercise of punitive power operate legitimately, a conclusion reached through the simple expedient of omitting its analysis, passing over its character as a very important confluent factor that in many cases is determinant and replicable, as well as the criminal actions of its own operators.

Stated another way, *the paradigm of social reaction does not renounce etiology, but, taking the word with due reservations, can affirm that by expanding the universe of conducts covered and including in it those of the ones themselves the operators and responsible for punitive power (penal system), denounces and rectifies the false etiologies that omitted them and, as a result, did not take into account their highly determinant and reproducing confluent character.*

As a result of the special attention that punitive social control has merited since the Sixties, at least for the most important criminological sector, it became a central component of criminological knowledge, and of the patent falsity of the etiology arbitrarily selected beforehand; the so-called *clinical criminology* has fallen out of favor. It has apparently remained anchored in the old paradigm of the false etiology, without a precise place within the criminology of social reaction.

At times one has the impression that it is antiquated and reactionary to refer to the individual aspects of violent behavior in the field of criminology, or, in the best case scenario, it is considered an area that should be left to other specialists, but is no longer in the realm of criminological knowledge.

It is not possible to forget that this is also a result of the fact that *criminological discourse has ceased to belong to health professionals and moved into the realm of sociologists.* That transference of hegemonic discourse, which had been produced in the United States as the result of the primordial importance that country had acquired in sociological studies after the First World

War,[72] was produced in Europe later on and as a consequence of the traumatic shock of the first encounter with psychiatry, which exposed the false positivist etiology and laid bare its profoundly conservative and racist ideology.

THE PERSPECTIVE OF A FRUITFUL REENCOUNTER

The *labeling approach,* symbolic interactionism, phenomenology, ethno methodology, and others, cast light upon the falsity of the premises on which sentencing and all penal theorization[73] is supposed to be founded; *criminal and radical* criminology incurred excesses but left a track that keeps later expositions from being ingenuous or simplistic;[74] *antipsychiatry* in some ways was its equivalent in the psychiatric field,[75] but made the repressive nature of the insane asylum irreversibly clear;[76] the thinking of Foucault[77] contributed towards clarifying the nature of *psychiatric power.* In this manner, much water has gone under the bridge since the first and traumatic encounter, since neither criminology nor psychiatry are the same today; there are highly plural views in both camps.

It is true that a biological criminology survives,[78] and it is also certain that there is no lack of an *administrative and pragmatic* criminology for a sort of *Reaganesque* criminology that *rediscovers* the importance of studying identical twins and other similar *novelties*,[79] that there is no lack of pseudoscientific reappearances of racism,[80] that some hasty consequences of genetic research intend to invigorate a *sociobiology* that smacks suspiciously of reductionism, similar to a psychiatrist excessively enamored of drugs and the *chemical lifejacket* on occasion leads people to forget the prudent lessons left by the horrors of the past. One cannot deny that in both fields, there are dangerous regressions.

Nonetheless, the progressive and prudent tendencies that one finds in both camps cannot mutually ignore or mistrust each other to the point of rejecting all contact, when they have important spheres of applied knowledge that they cannot elude and that they can only successfully confront by working together. It would be unpardonable to waste the river of knowledge of human health, whose importance is undeniable for clarifying conflictive and violent human behavior, which we now know for certain is not reduced to something easily controlled.

The trauma of the first encounter must be overcome because it demands the need for providing treatment for the imprisoned population, for reversing or neutralizing the regressive consequences of jail, for stimulating positive self-perception and avoiding the consequences of fixing roles. There is also the need for assisting the victims not only of the crime, but also of multiple violence by the penal system itself, of compensating and avoiding deterioration of its agents, meaning the police personnel, the penitentiary personnel, the judges, the lawyers, the judicial personnel, the family conflicts and the institutions that generate violence. Criminology needs to eliminate its prejudices towards psychiatry in order to analyze the role played by pathology in all of this violent conflict, for if it is quite certain that it would be absurd to pathologize all violence, one may also not ignore that on many occasions psychic pathology has a determinant or predisposing incidence.

Furthermore, if a contribution is unquestionably needed for the criminology of social reaction, it lies in the irreversible admission of the criminalizing and victimizing selectivity of the punitive power. In analyzing that selectivity, one must not be allowed to ignore the individual and especially the pathological factors that contribute towards configuring vulnerability nor the mechanisms that lead to assuming negative stereotypes, which are both criminalizing and bureaucratizing as well as policizing and victimizing.

The dramatic situation of Latin American penal systems and the repressive, authoritarian and imprisoning systems that one observes in the world, impede criminology from wanting to exhaust itself with theoretical musings, passing over its concrete applications to the suppositions of violence, including the responsibility it has in the training function of agents and operators of the penal system, who must not be left ignorant of the disciplines of mental health as they seek to find effective solutions for facing the conflictive situations in which they must intervene.

NOTES

1. About these, the selection of: Abbiati-Agnoletto-Lazzati, *La stregoneria. Diavoli, streghe, inquisitori dal Trecento al Settecento*, Milano, 2003.

2. Jean Wier, *Cinq livres de l'imposture et de la tromperie des diables: des enchantements et sorcelleries*, Paris, 1569.

3. The power of the courts and inquisitors was strongly defended by Jean Bodin, in *De la demonomanie de sorciers*, Paris, 1587, in which he dedicated an extensive refutation of the work of Wier (pages 238 to 276). It is interesting to remember that Freud was impressed when he noted that the practices attributed to demons by their worshippers were identical to childhood accounts by his patients. About this: Amand Danet, *L'inquisiteur e ses sorciéres,* in Henry Institoris (Kraemer)/Jacques Sprenger, *Le Marteau des Sorciérres. Malleus Maleficarum,* Paris, 1990, p.53.

4. He may be cited as Vier or Weyer lo que se atribuyó a que *Wier* significaría *reservoir* en francés and *piscinarius* en latín (así, Victor Moliner, *La vie et les travaux de Jean Bodin sur sa Démonomanie des sociers et sur les procés pour sorcellerie au seiziéme et au dix-septiéme siécle*, Montpellier, 1867, p. 21 nota2). Strictly speaking,

la explicación no es muy clara, porque haría referencia a estanques o piscinas, although la palabra *Wier* no aparece en los modernos diccionarios alemanes.

5. Mario Calzigna *La malattia morale. Alle origini della psichiatria moderna*, Venecia, 1988, p.31; enunciates the hypothesis that ayslum for the mentally ill derives from Arab culture.

6. Ibid, p. 30.

7. Regarding Pinel, Klaus Dörner, *Ciudadanos and locos, Historia social de la Psiquiatría*, Madrid, 1974, p. 185.

8. See Jacques Postel and Claude Quétel, *Nueva historia de la psiquiatría*, México, 2000, p. 608.

9. *Des maladies mentales considérées sous les rapports médical, hygiénique et médico-legal*, París, 1838.

10. Cfr. Zaffaroni, E. R., *Las clases peligrosas: el fracaso de un discurso policial prepositivista*, en "El penalista liberal, Homenaje a Manuel de Rivacoba and Rivacoba," Buenos Aires, 2004.

11. The compilations of "great trials" enjoyed large success throughout Europe: *Causes célébres étrangers*, published in a series by Panckoucke, París, 1827, translated from several languages by an anonymous society of jurists and people of letters; José Vicente and Caravantes, *Anales dramáticos del crimen, Causas célebres, españolas and extranjeras, estractadas de los originales and traducidas, bajo la dirección de . . .* , Madrid, 1858; the tradition continued in the XX century: Henri-Robert, *Les grands procés de l'histoire*, París, 1924.

12. A general overview in: Daniel Pick, *Volti della degenerazione, Una síndrome europea 1848-1918*, Firenze, 1999.

13. Also his *Traité des maladies mentales*, París, 1860.

14. See Magnan et M. Legrain, *Les dégénérés (état mental et síndromes épisodiques)*, París, 1895.

15. Pedro Dorado, *El derecho protector de los criminales*, Madrid, 1916.

16. Féré's work was published in 1888, see Ch. Féré, *Degeneración and criminalidad*, traducción de Anselmo González, Madrid, 1903.

17. Cfr. Pierre Darmon, *Médicos e assassinos na belle époque, A medicalização do crime*, Rio de Janeiro, 1991.

18. Proceedings of the various congresses of criminal anthropology. His admiration for Gallat the Rome congress of 1885.

19. Alphonse Bertillon, *Sur le fonctionnement du service des signalements anthropométriques*, in "Archives de l'Anthropologie criminelle et des sciences pénales," III, París, 1888, p. 138; by the same, *De l'identification par les signalements anthropométriques*, idem, T. I, 1886, p. 193. Regarding Bertillon and his time, Jürgen Thorwald, *El siglo de la investigación criminal*, Barcelona, 1966. He is famous for failing as a psychiatric expert in the Dreyfus Affair: Jean-Denis Verdín, *O Caso Dreyfus*, Sao Paulo, 1995.

20. At the 2nd congress of criminal anthropology, 1889.

21. Corre, A., *L'Ethnographie criminelle*, París, s.d.; *Le crime en pays créoles (Esquisse d'ethnographie criminelle)*, Lyon-París, 1889.

22. Cfr. Marvin Harris, *El desarrollo de la teoría antropológica. Historia de las teorías de la cultura*, Madrid, 1 983, p. 82.

23. About this, Don Martindale, *The Nature and Types of Sociological Theory*, Boston, 1960, pp. 162 and following.; Friedrich Jonas, *Storia della Sociologia*, Roma, 1989, I, p. 263.

24. Perhaps it would be more correct to speak of a *biological Spencerianism*, given Spencer's well-known influence on Darwin, and furthermore, because Charles Darwin never intended to mechanically transfer his concepts to society. On this, see Marvin Harris, op. cit., pp. 91 and following.

25. Regarding Galton and Pearson, Martindale, op. et loc. cit.

26. H. Maudsley, *El crimen y locura, versión castellana de la última edición inglesa por* Francisco Lombardía and Sánchez, Valencia, s.d.; *Physiologie de l'esprit, traduit de l'anglais par* Alexandre Herzen, París, 1879.

27. Charles Goring, *The English Convict, a statistical study*, 1913 (republished New Jersey, 1972).

28. Goddard's work is entitled *Human Efficiency and Levels of Intelligence*, New York, 1920. The genealogical investigation of the Kallikak does not seem to have been serious; obfuscated for having shown the antidemocratic political consequences of its thesis, it maintained that it would be terrifying if the masses had power in their hands, but that in practice, it was always a few million who made use of power. More about this, more broadly, Stephan: Chorover, *Del Génesis al genocidio*, Madrid, 1986, p. 70.

29. These assume openly racist characteristics that were approvingly accepted by known Nazi authors, such as Exner, who affirmed that adaptation to North American civilization was a task for which the Negroes "did not have the capacity" (Franz Exner, *Biología criminal en sus rasgos fundamentales*, Barcelona, 1957, p. 80), reproducing North American theses that ressurrected the *apartheid* of Morel during the time of struggles for civil rights, especially Henry E. Garret, *General Psychology*, New York, 1955, p. 65, cit. by Chorover, op. cit., p. 70.

30. Cfr. Postel-Quétel, op. cit., p. 642.

31. G. Aschaffenburg, *Das Verbrechen und seine Bekämpfung*, Heidelberg, 1903; Portuguese translation by S. Goncalves Lisboa, Lisbon, 1904

32. Krafft-Ebing, *La responsabilité criminelle et la capacité civile dans les états de trouble intellectuel*. París, 1875.

33. It is fair to note, nonetheless, that he seriously criticized punishment for it.

34. See the much broader perspective of Havelock Ellis in the introduction to Calverton/Schmalhausen, *El sexo en la civilization*, Madrid, 1930.

35. Gross' work is from 1898 and the first English translation from 1910 (cfr. Debuyst/Digneffe/Pires, op.cit., p. 197), but it is curious that there is a Spanish translation in two volumes that is much earlier: *Manual del Juez para uso de los jueces de instrucción y municipales, jefes políticos, alcaldes, escribanos, oficiales, agentes de policía, etc., por el Dr. Hanns* (sic.) *Gross, de Graz. Traducción del alemán por Máximo de Arredondo, Juez de primera instancia and secretario auxiliar del tribunal*, México, 1901.

36. The informant at that congress synthesizes his thoughts in the "Archives": "Extracting his arguments from anatomical and pathological anomalies, such as harelips, supernumerary incisors, bifid canine roots, enormous apophysis of the mandible in men, and the major development of the orbital angle, Albrecht, by means of ingenious reasoning, concluded that man does not descend from monkey, for the excellent reason that he himself is a monkey, and an inferior monkey. Coming to the question of criminal anthropology, he concluded that the criminal man is normal, and the honest man, who controls his passions is a phenomenon, an inferior being among the most inferior monkeys. As these theories were presented calmly and with a serious tone, I believe that the members of the congress began to look at each other, soon reacted and began to warmly applaud, without taking the very spirited professor very seriously" ("Archives de l'Anthropologie criminelle et des sciences pénales," I, 1886, p. 286). We are unaware of works along this line, as has been pointed out by Christian Debuyst in Debuyst-Digneffe-Pires, *Histoire des savoirs sur le crime et la peine*, Montreal, 1998, II, p. 467, note 66.

37. The Lombrosian bibliography is enormous. Among works in recent decades: Renzo Villa, *Il deviante e i suoi segni. Lombroso e la nascita dell'antropologia criminale*, Milano, 1985; Luigi Guarnieri, *L'atlante criminale. Vita scriteriata di Cesase Lombroso*, Milano, 2000; Carlos María Landecho, *La tipificación lombrosiana de delincuentes*, Madrid, 2004.

38. "In general, the majority among the born delinquents have wing ears, abundant hair, sparse beard, marked frontal sinuses, enormous mandibles, square and emergent jaw, frequent gesticulation, to sum up, a similar type to the negroid and sometimes to the mongoloid" (Lombroso, Cesare, *L'uomo delinquente*, Torino, 1884, p. 248).

39. C. Lombroso, *Gli anarchici*, Torino, 1894; C. Lombroso / R. Laschi, *Le crime politique et les révolutions*, París, 1892; Benito Mario Andrade, *Estudio de antropología criminal espiritualista*, Madrid, 1899, pp. 203 and ss. The leaders of mass movements were seen in the same manner: Gustavo Le Bon, *La psicología política and la defensa social*, Madrid, 1912; del mismo, *Psicología das multidoes*, Rio de Janeiro, 1954; Scipio Sighele, *I delitti della folla*, Torino, 1910; J.M. Ramos Mejía, *Las multitudes argentinas*, Buenos Aires, 1912: On criminalization of multitudes and leaders, Jaap van Ginneken, *Folla, psicologia e politica*, Roma 1989.

40. M. L. Patrizi, *Preliminari d'un indirizzo antropológico (bio-psicologico) nella critica e storia dell'arte figurativa*, en *Dopo Lombroso*, Milano, 1916; Alfredo Nicéforo, *Criminali e degenerati dell'Inferno Dantesco*, Torino, 1898; Enrico Ferri, *Les criminels dans l'art et la littérature*, París, 1902; *I delinquenti nell'arte ed altre conferenze e saggi di scienza ed arte*, Torino, 1926.

41. Mariano Ruiz-Funes, *La peligrosidad y sus experiencias legales*, La Habana, 1948.

42. Salillas, Rafael, *El delinquente español. Hampa (Antropología picaresca)*, Madrid, 1898; Nicéforo, Alfredo–Sighele, Scipio, *La mala vida en Roma*, Madrid, 1901; Bernaldo de Quirós, Constancio, *La mala vida en Madrid. Estudio psicosociológico con dibujos and fotografías al natural*, Madrid, 1901 (reed. Madrid, 1998); Bembo, Max, *La mala vida en Barcelona*, Barcelona, 1912; Gómez, Eusebio, *La mala vida en Buenos Aires*, Buenos Aires, 1908 (with prologue by José Ingenieros).

There is an interesting literary recompilation by Ernesto Ferrero with a prologue by Leonardo Sciascia, *Storie nere di fine secolo. La mala Italia*, Milano, 1973.

43. R. Garofalo, *La Criminología*, trans. by Pedro Dorado Montero, Madrid, s.d., p. 7, 11, 14 and 15; Franz von Liszt, *La idea de fin en criminal law*, Valparaíso, 1984, p. 120.

44. Lombroso, *L'uomo di genio in rapporto alla psichiatria, alla storia ed all'estetica*, Torino, 1894; Max Nordau followed him closely and considred all dangerously creative artists as degenerates (*Degeneración*, Madrid, 1902).

45. Cfr. The information from Mariano Ruiz-Funes on sterilization laws in the United States, Switzerland, Denmark, Canada, Sweden, Norway, Finland, Estonia, Latvia and Germany (*La peligrosidad*, cit., pp. 510 and sgts.).

46. Degeneration could be prevented with campaings against social illnesses. For example, Louis Rénon, *Les maladies populaires. Maladies vénériennes, alcoolisme, tuberculose*, París, 1907; later on in Argentina: Francisco De Veyga, *Degeneración y degenerados. Miseria, vicio y delito*, Buenos Aires, 1938; regarding this period and its ideology: Ruth Harris, *Assassinato e loucura. Medicina, leis e sociedade no "fin de siécle,"* Rio de Janeiro, 1993, pp. 81 and following.

47. Without a doubt North American sociology, and later the resulting sociological criminality received and continued lines that had been drawn by European sociology, which had faded with the Great War (1914-1918), especially that of Durkheim (1858-1917), Max Weber (1864-1920) and Georg Simmel (1858-1918). About that, George Ritzer, *Teoría sociológica contemporánea*, México, 1998; Patrick Baert, *La teoría social en el siglo XX*, Madrid, 2001; Jeffrey C. Alexander, *Las teorías sociológicas desde la Segunda Guerra Mundial*, Barcelona, 1990.

48. Martín Bulmer, *The Chicago School of Sociology*, Chicago University Press, 1984.

49. Nicola Pende, *Trabajos recientes sobre endocrinología and psicología criminal*, Madrid, 1932; also, *La ciencia moderna de la persona humana*, Buenos Aires, 1949; *¿A dónde vas, hombre? Problemas humanos de nuestro tiempo*, Buenos Aires, 1958; his Spanish translator, Mariano Ruiz-Funes, had published *Endocrinología y criminalidad*, Madrid, 1929. The discussion on imputations of racism and antisemitism, is in Giorgio Israel/Pietro Nastasi, *Scienza e razza nell'Italia fascista*, Bologna, 1998.

50. Benigno Di Tullio, *Manuale di Antropología e psicología criminale applicata alla pedagogía emendativa, alla polizia ed al diritto penale e penitenciario*, with preface by Silvio Ottolenghi, Roma, 1931; *Tratado de Antropología Criminal*, Buenos Aires, 1950.

51. Ernst Kretschmer, *Körperaubau und Charakter, Untersuchungen zum Konstitutionsproblem und zur Lehre von den Temperamenten*, Berlin, 1925; *Manuel théorique et pratique de Psychologie Médicale*, París, 1927.

52. Sheldon and Eleonore Glueck, *Nuove frontiere della criminología*, Milano, 1971; Sheldon Glueck, *Crime and Correction, Selected Papers*, Massachussets, 1952; W.H. Sheldon, S. S. Stevens, W. B. Tucker, *Les variétés de la constitution physique de l'homme*, París, 1950; W. H. Sheldon, S. S. Stevens, *Les variétés du temperament. Une psychologie des différences constitutionneles*, París, 1951.

53. Gregorio Marañón, *La evolución de la sexualidad y los estados intersexuales*, Madrid, 1930; Luis Jiménez de Asúa, *Libertad de amar and derecho a morir. Ensayos de un criminalista sobre eugenesia, eutanasia, endocrinología*, Santander, 1929.

54. Kurt Schenider, *Las personalidades psicopáticas*, Madrid, 1962.

55. Göbbels, Hans, *Los asociales. Esencia y concepto de la asocialidad*, Madrid, 1955.

56. Eugen Bleuler, *Demencia precoz, El grupo de las esquizofrenias*, Bs. As., 1960.

57. Cfr. Postel-Quétel, op. cit., p. 664.

58. A broad bibliography from the period in: Quintiliano Saldaña, *Nueva Criminología*, Madrid, 1936, pp. 248 and following. The most disseminated works from this period are: Franz Alexander-Hugo Staub, *Der Verbrecher und seiner Richter*, Wien, 1929 (spanish translation, *El delinquente y sus jueces desde el punto de vista psicoanalítico*, Madrid, 1935); Theodor Reik, *Der unbekannte Mörder, Von der Tat zum Täter*, 1932 (*Psicoanálisis del crimen, El asesino desconocido*, Buenos Aires, 1965). In Spanish, for example, Cesar Camargo Marín, *El psicoanálisis en la doctrina y en la práctica judicial*, Madrid, 1931; Luis Jiménez de Asúa, *Psicoanálisis criminal*, Madrid, 1935.

59. As seen, for example, in the singular importance assigned to investigation into the criminal behavior of identical twins univitelinos: Lange, *Verbrechen als Schicksal: Studien an kriminellen Zwillingen*, 1929; F. Stumpfl, *Die Ursprünge des Vebrechens*, 1936; Carlo Ferrio, *Gemelli*, en Eugenio Florian-Alfredo Nicéforo-Nicola Pende, *Dizionario di Criminología*, Milano, 1943, I, p. 400.

60. From a broader perspective, Arthur Herman, *La idea de decadencia en la historia occidental*, Barcelona, 1998.

61. Lothrop Stoddard, *The Revolt against Civilization. The menace of the underman*, London, 1923.

62. Such were the biological ideas of Lyssenko, with the so-called "Mitchurin school," which led to the loss of several harvests for Stalinism. See in Jean Rostand, *La herencia Humana*, Buenos Aires, 1961, pp. 52.

63. Vierstein, quoted by Edmundo Mezger, *Kriminalpolitik aus kriminologischer Grundlagen* (1933), translated as *Criminología*, Madrid, 1942, p. 158.

64. For this, see the prologue to Exner, Franz, op. cit., p. 6.

65. New light on this project has been shed by the painstaking investigation of Francisco Muñoz Conde, *Edmund Mezger y derecho criminal de su tiempo. Estudios sobre criminal law en el nacionalsocialismo*, Valencia, 2003; this project and the concrete proposal by Mezger are also dealt with by Michael Burleigh/Wolfgang Wippermann, *Lo Stato razziale, Germania 1933-1945*, Rizzoli, 1992, p. 158.

66. Perhaps the greatest effort in this regard is the quoted but not highly esteemed work of the exiled Spanish Republican professor, Mariano Ruiz-Funes, *La peligrosidad y sus experiencias legales*, La Habana, 1948, where the autor strives to make dangerousness compatible with the principles of a state of law.

67. See Egas Moniz, *Confidencias de um investigador científico*, Lisboa, 1949. At the end of the book one may see the enormous number of lobotomized patients, according to information from the Lisbon congress of 1948.

68. Edmund Mezger, *Criminología*, translated by José Arturo Rodríguez Muñoz, Madrid, 1942 (the original title is: *Kriminalpolitik auf kriminologischer Grundlagen*), his prologue begins with the following words: "The mighty political and spiritual revolution of the liberating movement in Germany has placed state life in this country on a new cultural basis. The new totalitarian State has risen by building on the basic principles of people and race."

69. On this, see Elizabeth Antébi, *I fabbricanti di pazzia*, Milano, 1979.

70. Among others, Alessandro Baratta, *Criminología critica e critica del diritto penale*, Bologna, 1982, p. 83.

71. Strictly speaking one may speak of a "positivist-neokantian" paradigm, since whereas positivism corresponds to an integrated model of penal sciences, the second splits it up, separating criminal law as a science from the culture of criminology as a natural science, exactly in order to save the positivist etiological paradigm (regarding integrated and split up systems, Baratta, Alessandro, op.cit., pp. 41-42).

72. Cfr. Massimo Pavarini, *Introduzione a . . . La Crimnologia*, Firenze, 1980, p. 42.

73. See George B. Vold, Thomas J. Bernard, Jeffrey B. Snipes, *Theoretical Criminology*, New York, 1998, p. 219; on its deligitimating potential: Alessandro Baratta, *Criminologia e dogmatica penale. Passato e futuro del modello integrato di scienza penalistica*, in "La questione criminale, 1979, 2, p. 147.

74. *Radical Criminology, The coming Crisis*, edited by James A, Inciardi, Londres, 1980; Ian Taylor-Paul Walton-Jock Young, *The new Criminology, For a social theory of deviance*, Londres, 1973; G. B. Traverso–A. Verde, *Criminologia critica. Delinquenza e controllo sociale nel modo di produzione capitalistico*, Padova, 1981; an important balance in: Elena Larrauri, *La herencia de la criminología crítica*, Madrid, 1992.

75. See R. Angelergues and others, *La Antipsiquiatría*, Siglo XXI, México, 1975;Thomas S. SAS, *Legge, libertá e psichiatria*, Milano, 1984; from the same author, *Ideología e doenca mental, Ensaios sobre a desumanizacao psiquiátrica* do homem, Rio de Janeiro, 1977; R.D. Laing, *O eu e os outros*, Rio de Janeiro, 1978; from the same author, *O eu dividido*, Rio de Janeiro, 1978; R. D. Laing–D. G. Cooper, *Razao e violencia*, Rio de Janeiro, 1976.

76 Franco Basaglia, *La institución negada, Informe de un hospital psiquiátrico*, Bs. As., 1972; Romano Canosa, *Storia del manicomio in Italia dall'unitá a oggi*, Milano, 1979.

77. Michel Foucault, *El poder psiquiátrico, Curso en el Collége de France*, Bs. As., 2005.

78. Hans J. Eysenck and Gisli H. Gudjonsson, *The causes and cures of criminality*, New York, 1991.

79. James Q. Wilson and Richard J. Herrnstein, Crime and Human Nature, New York, 1985 (on the cover appears an antiscientific subtitle of astonishing arrogance: *The definitive study of the causes of crime.*)

80. See *The Bell Curve Debate, History, Documents, Opinions*, edited by Russell Jacoby and Naomi Glauberman, New York, 1995.

Chapter Three

Criminal Law and Social Protest

Eugenio Raúl Zaffaroni

DELIMITING THE PHENOMENON

In recent decades and as a consequence of a crisis in the *social* state model (the *Welfare State*), which is suffering around the world because of the impositions of growing planetary economic authoritarianism built around globalization (and sometimes confused with it), there have been public protests and demands for rights that assume different forms that generate conflicting situations of varying intensity.[1] In our midst protests and public manifestations expressed through creating obstacles to vehicle traffic have been especially noteworthy.[2]

Although some might consider this a new phenomenon, the demand for rights through non-institutional means and at the fringes of legality[3] is far from being something new.[4]

On the one hand, one may affirm that it is an aspiration to every state of law to achieve institutions that are so perfect that it is not necessary for anyone to resort to non-institutional means to obtain satisfaction for their complaints; on the other hand, the same aspiration seems to be held by all citizens who demand rights that are really or supposedly not satisfied. But both in historical reality and the present, the states of law are not perfect and have not achieved the level of the ideal model that guides them, so that neither the state nor the citizens are able to see realized the aspiration to have all demands channeled via institutional routes.

On the other hand, in general, the citizens also do not intend to opt for non-institutional routes to obtain the rights they are demanding, but they choose them only to enable institutional functioning. That is, they definitely *demand that the institutions operate according to their expressed purposes*.

In Argentina especially, the constitutionalists and the non-governmental organizations that are working in this area, have used the term *right to social protest* for activities exercised for that purpose of making demands,[5] while they call the phenomenon of repressing it *criminalization of social protest*. These terms are quite appropriate; moreover, although recent, they are already consecrated in use and individualize the issue quite well.

A different denomination may also be justified, since although certainly at certain points it overlaps with other forms of demand known in the country and around the world, it is quite distinct from them and it is also necessary to differentiate them in order to appropriately delimit the field of analysis.

In principle, one must clearly distinguish the *right to resist the usurper*, explicitly recognized by the National Constitution for all citizens,[6] because the protest is carried out in the framework of a state of law with legitimately elected authorities.

Nor is it a case of the *right to resist the sovereign*, which would take us back to the contractual debate between Hobbes and Locke, since it is exercised to remove the oppressor—as it is understood—one who has ceased to be sovereign through betraying his or her mandate and has become an oppressor,[7] meaning that resistance to the sovereign is definitively a *right to revolution*. The social protest current in our midst does not seek to overthrow any government. Not even in some very exceptional case—which has led to federal intervention—does it propose to ignore the state of law, but to provoke functioning of its federal institutions so that they are the ones that replace the local government. Even for those who profoundly sympathize with Hobbes it would not be appropriate to invoke him to criminalize social protest, since one may not argue he intends in any manner to reintroduce the *bellum omnium contra omnes*.

Even though on occasions such a right may overlap with some manifestations of the so-called *civil disobedience*, whose most notable representatives would be Thoreau, Gandhi and Luther King,[8] the fact is that it does not identify—or does not yet identify—with it altogether.

In civil disobedience, the protagonists confront the state by disobeying and by generally accepting the consequences, because those become the banner and publicity for the injustices that they suffer. Not always—nor much less—do social protests seek to face the consequences so as to make injustices clear, but instead they pursue solutions to conflicts by means of intervention by the same authorities. Protest itself is the form of calling attention of the public and the authorities regarding the conflict or the needs for which satisfaction is being demanded.

Civil disobedience involves strongly disciplined *tactics of non-violence.* Among its principles it is essential not only not to use violence, but to exercise extreme care so that *nothing may be maliciously interpreted or projected publicly as the use of violence,* and to quickly and carefully exclude any uncontrolled person or someone who is a *provocateur* or infiltrated in the ranks. When that rule is not observed so rigorously, *non-violence* combines with some sporadic more or less violent act, or one appearing to be so, giving rise to *civil resistance*, which may have occasional success, but is not the appropriate form for movements with a greater reach over time.

Regarding the way in which social protest is developed in our midst, one may say that it is moving from *resistance* to *disobedience,* even though its progressive movement—and on occasions its identification with disobedience—keeps one from bringing in the assumption and introjections of all of its techniques and rules on the part of all of the protagonists.

It is natural that, in a country whose official history has always glorified violent actions and that, for many years has not experienced the needs produced by the violation of basic social rights, because the welfare state has achieved a respectable degree of development (certainly inferior to that of industrialized countries, but coming close to it at certain periods), there is no profound conviction of the power of *non-violence* and much less, certainly, of a practice of internalized non-violence, with the degree of organization and discipline that it would demand.[9]

At any rate, it is certain that Argentine social protest, outside of isolated acts, generally does not assume violent forms, and, even more, one might say that there is an inverse relation between violence and organization (less violence the more organized the protest is), which is explicable, since otherwise the organizers would be employing a tactic that strategically would end up being suicidal.

It is natural that, where the *culture of non-violence* has not been sufficiently extended, the first expressions of social protest are inorganic, and may later on suffer intervention by overly emotional people, not to mention that, when it is expressed massively and with poor organization, they can also notoriously suffer from *tactical infiltration* by provocateurs oriented towards justifying repression. As the protest assumes more organic forms, it is also known that it progressively refines its tactics and carefully distances itself from other occasional manifestations that use violence and expresses lament for inorganic breakdowns that are alien to it and run the risk of contaminating its own struggle.

But it is certain that for the time being the more or less organized social process is not completely familiar with *the tactics of non-violence* and, as a result, incurs episodes in which errors conspire against its own purposes, since they neutralize the publicity that is being sought. At any rate, it is necessary to specify that those few contradictions—such as frequently happen with demands for social rights—are often extremely magnified by those who which to delegitimize those demands and argue for indiscriminate repression of any social protest. This in spite of the fact that the magnitude of such violence practiced by the demonstrators is not even remotely comparable to the degree of violence that *historically* has been inflicted on those who protest, which, as is publicly and widely known, has translated into multiple homicides and all manner of arbitrariness and ill-treatment.

However, unfortunately, all movements must build their own experience, which is not always susceptible to being replaced by the advice or experience of others—or of the protagonists of other demands—so that, almost inevitably, their own survival is conditional on their assuming the tactics that around the world have been common in *civil disobedience* or they will end up dissolving due to their own errors. *Given that the needs do not disappear as rapidly as desirable, the space for protest will continue to be open, and certainly the organizations that do not assume a progressive identification with civil disobedience will dissolve, while those who advance until they achieve such identification will go forward.*

However, the legal problems for which the protests demand solutions continue to be open and it will be necessary to go more in depth in analyzing the legal area, where there are no simplistic solutions, due to the multiple situations that occur, especially during the time when the transition in question is taking place.

Although within the constitutional law area several voices have been raised calling for recognition of the right to protest, there have been almost no answers so far from dogmatic criminal law. There is a considerable complexity of hypotheses and case and we cannot cover them all in this brief work, but we believe it is necessary to remember the categories of the theory of crime and position them in relation to the problem, in order to orient the focus on particular cases, without falling into casuistry and only to highlight the need for more particularized investigation. We will simply limit ourselves to pointing out those themes that require reflection according to the traditional categories of the theory of crime.

We do not doubt the existence of a right to protest and in that sense we are in harmony with work by the constitutionalists.[10] Nonetheless, with this elementary recognition we advance very little, especially when immediately the shopworn argument is invoked that there are no absolute rights and with this everything falls into a nebulous terrain that opens up a huge space for arbitrariness.[11] It is clear that not anyone who suffers an injustice can stop traffic on a street or highway, and even less that someone can damage another's property or commit even greater infractions. If this obvious truth is going to be expressed as the so-called non-existence of absolute rights, this seems to us to be a technically deficient expression: the correct course of action would be to say that although every person who suffers an injustice has the right to protest, that does not enable that person to always exercise it in the same way and same manner. For an obviety does not satisfy any elementary legal rigor for solving particular cases, when what one is asking exactly about exactly the extent and for to which it is legally admissible to exercise the right of protest, according to the particularities of the case.

NON-INSTITUTIONAL PROTEST

The recognition of the right to social protest will depend upon the answer one gives to the question as to *whether a state of law should accept demands for change through non-institutional routes.*

It must be understand that one must answer in the negative in the case of a perfect state of law: when there are institutional routes for demanding rights, it is not admissible to opt for non-institutional ones. But it is certain that there are no perfect states of law, and that none of the historical or real states of law make available to their inhabitants, in equal measure, all of the institutional and effective means to achieve effective use of all rights.

The third consideration of the Universal Declaration of Human Rights states that it is *essential that human rights be protected by a regime of Law, in order for man not to be compelled to take the supreme recourse of rebellion against tyranny and oppression.* If there is a *regime of Law*, as called for by the Declaration, there is no appropriate rebellion against tyranny and oppression, but one also supposes that such state will be as perfect as possible in terms of effective functioning of its institutions as providers of fundamental rights, so that men and women will not feel themselves compelled to rebel, given the presupposition of a framework for a state of law, but that they will be able to make use of non-institutional protests.

The right to protest not only exists, but is expressly recognized by the National Constitution and by international and regional Human Rights treaties, since it is necessarily implicit in the right to freedom of thought, of conscience and of religion (article 18 of the Universal Declaration of Human Rights), of opinion and expression (article 19) and to freedom of meeting and peaceful association (article 20). These provisions impose on all states the duty of respecting the right to dissent and publicly demand rights, and, obviously, not only to reserve them inwardly, but to publicly express their dissent t and demands. No one can argue judicially that freedom for meetings is only recognized for expressing consent. Furthermore, there is recognition not only of the right to protest, but to the right to demand rights before the courts (article 8).

The problem comes when rights are demanded that are enshrined in the so-called article "14bis"of the National Constitution and in the *International Pact for Economic, Social and Cultural Rights,* which are part of the so-called *second generation* rights or those found in social constitutionalism that originated in the Mexican Constitution of 1917[12] and in the Weimar Constitution of 1919.[13] These do not consist of omissions on the part of the state, but in positive actions and obligations for action, and when institutional routes consisting of public manifestation, the call for large-scale measures, petitions to authorities and court cases themselves end up ineffective in facing the reiterated and continuous omission of the state, in other words, which are not able to obtain effective measures, or at least to obtain them in timely fashion, impeding irreversible effects or interrupting their progression. Those are the situations in which, that which has generically been called the *right to protest* raises questions for criminal law, because as long as it remains within institutional routes the questions it can raise are not real but merely apparent, given that *a constitutional and international right regularly exercise can never constitute a crime.*

INSTITUTIONAL PROTEST IS ALWAYS ATYPICAL

Public order begins with recognition of the dignity of human beings and the freedom of expression inherent to it. It would be of little use to recognize that humans had the dignity of personhood, as beings endowed with conscience, it they were not allowed to express their freedom of conscience. There is thus a general basis for freedom from which one subtracts merely a few types of conduct previously identified in criminal laws through legal types, which, in the case of not being supported by any special permission (cause of justification), constitute unjust or criminal acts. The protest that is maintained within institutional boundaries is nothing more than the regular exercise of constitutional and international rights, and as a result, can never be a subject for criminal classification, meaning that legally prohibiting it is inconceivable. These suppositions are excluded from the first specifically penal category of the stratified crime theory, meaning the same type of conduct.

It makes no sense for someone to ask in these cases if one is talking of conduct justified by the regular exercise of a right provided for in the general formula for justification found in article 34 of the Penal Code, because such actions cannot be covered by penal types. Both the National Constitution and international treaties prohibit states from banning such conduct, so that, even though some penal types, merely at the level of exegetical analysis, can cover such conduct; an elementary dogmatic analysis will discard typicity.

As a result, the exercise of the right to petition authorities, the public manifestation to do so, the public that gathers to do so, regardless of how much inconvenience their numbers cause, how their march interrupts circulation of vehicles or pedestrians, how they create disturbing noises, drop pamphlets that dirty the sidewalk and so on, is a legitimate right within the strict institutional framework. It is clear that such supposed inconvenience, noise, dirtiness or interruption of circulation is produced as a necessary consequence (a number of persons gathered or moving causes interruptions) or usual consequence (using drums, setting of small fireworks, throwing pamphlets, etc) of the number of participants and the need to exteriorize the demand and during the time reasonably necessary for exteriorizing it (walk down streets, stop and listen to speeches, sing, etc.).

It is lamentable that some intend to comb through criminal and contravention codes in order to look for types and how to flexibilize them with the object of holding back such conduct, which belongs to the sphere of exercising citizen liberty. *The square, the square belongs to the people, as the sky belongs to the condor,* wrote Castro Alves, the antislavery poet of romanticism in Brazil.[14]

THE NON-INSTITUTIONAL PROTEST IS NOT ALWAYS TYPICAL

The circumstances in which the limits of institutional protest are exceeded do not become converted automatically into characteristic conduct. When the protest goes beyond institutional limits, meaning that it exceeds a reasonably necessary time for expression (camping or deciding to spend the night in a square), they do not interrupt street activity due to the mere effect of number of people but because of actions intended to disrupt; small groups prolong their shouting after the protest has finished, they reiterate the shouts on transportation used to return home, etc. In such cases one penetrates a field that can be anti-judicial or illicit, but that is not necessarily criminal, because only a small part of anti-judicial conduct is classified as criminal. In effect: staying and spending the night on a square is not anti-judicial conduct. Bothersome unnecessary noises once the protest has concluded can be anti-judicial, but are not criminally classified, although they may constitute a misdemeanor.

This is the field in which the greatest emphasis is dedicated with the intent of flexibilizing criminal classifications or limiting oneself to pure exegetical analysis in order for those who wish to criminalize them to classify occurrences of transgressions in non-institutional protest. This is certainly the area in which criminal law should react with the greatest care. Penal classification is a purely legal exercise, restrictively interpreted, that does not agree to mere proof of elements of the objective legal classification. No one doubts that the end of a sporting event (football match) may be accompanied by bothersome shouts by spectators as they return home, but one is not fishing for classifications of transgressions in order to incriminate them, because such is the usual consequence of an act encouraged by the state. Although it is true that protest is not an activity encouraged by the state, it is an elemental constitutional and international right, whose consequences cannot even be classified as contraventions in those cases.

However, there may be other situations in which a contravention classification may be more or less unquestionable, such as when a street is interrupted by an action that is not the necessary result of a march by protesters or of their meeting because of their number, even though it does not correspond to that without intending a criminal classification. With regard to protest, whenever codes are combed through in search of criminal classifications and these are then flexibilized, of necessity there is a trampling of the principles by which criminal law seeks to contain punitive power through a strict interpretation of the dogmatic principles that must be applied in interpreting any criminal classification.

Leaving aside the fact that it is not possible to omit application of the principles of strict legality and restrictive interpretation, which are the result of the discontinuous nature of criminal legislation or of classification, one may also not pass over or deny the principles of offensiveness, insignificance or proportionality.

The case of traffic interruption or disturbance is the issue that has appeared most frequently in judicial practice, considering that interrupting of any street or impeding the departure of any form of collective transportation are actions classified in article 194 of the penal code.[15] It is a case of extensive interpretation of a criminal classification, for if article 194 had exclusion of creating a *common danger*, it is not correct to consider this identical to exclusion of *any danger*. Article 194 is for a type of danger and not a mere type of infringement of the right to circulate without disturbance. If that had been the meaning of the classification, the text would have excluded *all danger* and not only *common danger*.

Disturbances to circulation are the subjects of national, provincial or municipal regulation, depending on the nature of the route, and finally, punishments will be the subject of legislation on infractions at the various levels (if railroads or national highways they can be a case of federal violations, which do not exist; if they are provincial, provincial contraventions apply; if streets, there are municipal ordinances). The only possibility of interpreting article 194 in a constitutional manner is to understand that it is a conduct that through impediment, nuisance or disturbance place in danger judicial assets outside of the hypothesis of *common danger.*

The classification is not exhausted with the mere proof of the extremes demanded by the type of legal objective, but it is also necessary to assess if this objective classification results in something *offensive* (through lesion or through danger) to a judicial asset (and is also imputable as the author's own act, which is not in question in the case). Forgetting that premise (not requiring danger) or presuming danger (meaning to say, consider it as certain when it has not been produced) violates the *principle of offensiveness* enshrined together with the principle of reservation in article 19 of the National Constitution,[16] or is an invasion of federal contraventional jurisdiction or of provincial and municipal rules.

Another principle that must not be forgotten is the Roman maxim *minima non curat Praetor,* translated today as the *principle of insignificance*: insignificant or trivial affectations are not sufficient to complement the principle of offensiveness, as it is understood that that the transgressions should affect the judicial assets with a certain relevance, and issues that are more or less trivial or that do not have an elemental proportion with the magnitude of the threatening sentence cannot be applied. In other words: the judicial consequence of the transgression, meaning the sentence, indicates by its magnitude that it requires a respectable degree of affecting the judicial asset, which does not complement the harm or represent an insignificant danger.

That is a question that not only should be dismissed when it is a case of interruptions or hindrances to communication routes, but also included in other penal classifications. For example, extortion constitutes a multi-offensive classification that affects both property and liberty, but the magnitude of the harm to liberty must present a certain gravity in the content of the evil that threatens. It is not the same thing to threaten with a public protest as to place an explosive or cause a fire and less with a death threat, and one must also admit that the protest does not correspond to institutional requirements in all of its characteristics. The magnitude of the *intimidation* required by the type of extortion does not occur with any harm or eventual loss of assets. On the other hand, in the current law the analyses of the types of extortion that might be valid in the original text of the Penal Code do not apply, as the sentence currently applied to simple extortion (which is not less than imprisonment or reclusion for five to ten years) reveals that intimidation demands a quite considerable degree of seriousness.

In the classic example from the manual, one cannot consider as deprivation of liberty the act of the person responsible for public transportation that does not stop the vehicle at a stop requested by the passenger and allows the passenger to get off at the next stop, even though some national sentence has found otherwise. In the cases of protest fustigation can constitute a contravention, but in no way could it be classified as one of the actions found in Article 141 of the Penal Code.

There are a number of other difficulties with other penal classifications that one can appeal to in the combing for classifications that some carry out on those occasions. In every manifestation of public protest *the people* are invoked. There is practically no protester who has not petitioned in the name of the people. Nonetheless, not every manifestation can be considered as sedition, according to subsection 1 of article 230 of the Penal Code,[17] because it is not enough to petition in the name of the people, but also, according to the conjunction demanded by the Constitution and Code, it is necessary to *attribute to oneself their rights,* which no manifestation, protest or demand does, however much it intends to express itself in the people's name, something that is nothing more than a universally employed rhetorical resource. A different interpretation would criminalize not only social protest, but also any meeting that is called, and demand greater repression that in fact—judging by its disastrous results in penal legislation—intends to intimidate the true and authentic representatives of the people.

No lesser problems are brought with the classification of article 239[18] of the Penal Code in the variable of *disobedience*—not so much of *resistance—to a public employee in the legitimate exercise of his functions,* whose classification must be meticulously reduced to avoid falling directly into unconstitutionality. Disobedience to a public employee may bring about administrative and perhaps contraventional sanctions and one might think this appropriate, but only in cases where it causes harm to other judicial assets of a certain magnitude and in very specific and serious cases, but not every disobedience to an employee in the exercise of his functions, as legitimate as they may by, may constitute a transgression. That is because the extent of this classification would achieve an unprecedented level that is incompatible with the state of law: it would be a transgression to refuse to show a driver's license to a traffic agent, to hand over documentation to police who were requiring it, to pay a tax or fee upon official demand, to disobey an order not to place posters or to stop smoking in a public place, etc. Obviously, each one of those actions has legal consequences, but they could not be classified under article 239 of the Penal Code.

Something similar happens regarding defense of a crime in article 213 of the Penal Code.[19] In certain forms of civil resistance, including those carried out by those who follow the line begun in the XIX by the famous Thoreau[20] in the United States, legal and penal consequences of such acts are accepted exactly as a form of protest and social criticism. Any expression of admiration or support for the attitude of those persons would be incriminated, when in fact it is nothing more than manifestation of social criticism. It would be a different case if one were providing an apologia for crimes of another nature, such as sex crimes, family violence, multiple and serial murders, genocide and so on. The classification of article 123 is another that needs to be interpreted restrictively in order to make it compatible with the Constitution and the international treaties on Human Rights.

The risk is no less that, as social protest becomes more organized and perfected, it will seek to include participants in those organizations in the classification of illicit association, which is another figure raising serious constitutional problems that are not sufficiently resolved.[21]

The classification of illicit association was profusely employed against labor demands when strikes were considered crimes in the struggles of European governments against the Social Democrats. Through inertia this has remained in modern legislation with relatively low sentences. Due to specific reforms during moments of political and social violence, the sentences have been increased to the current extremes and have not return to the traditional levels, even though the circumstances were overcome decades ago. This is a classification that extends to acts that are clearly preparatory, that is, quite previous to the attempt and do not even consider desistance: someone who agrees with other persons to commit simple thefts (proposes the organization of petty criminals or robbers of small articles in stores), is punished with the equivalent to the sum of the minimum sentences for thirty thefts, even if after the meeting none of the participants do anything in the future. The Republican principle indicates that this classification—and with the due reservations—could only be harmonized with the Constitution in the case of associations proposing to commit very serious crimes, such as the massive and indiscriminate destruction of judicial assets, not to mention that it is debatable whether a crime could be configured merely with an agreement and no later activity.

These examples serve to demonstrate that it is necessary for criminal law, in its function of judicial contention against the pressures of a police state, to keep a watchful eye on attempts for force criminal classifications not only in the cases where social protest is maintained within institutional channels, but also when it overflows such boundaries, and penetrates environments of illegality that can emerge from infraction against the administrative or contraventional order.

PROTEST THAT MANIFESTS ITSELF IN CLASSIFIED CONDUCT AND ITS JUSTIFICATION

So far we have occupied ourselves with protest that does not incur a penal classification (prohibition), even though it exceeds the institutional framework and may incur other illegal acts. Nonetheless, protest can involve classifications, such as crimes with not insignificant damages, harm, resistance to authority, etc.

Naturally, we will discard from this analysis those cases in which the protest is only a pretense for committing more serious crimes. Although that does not seem to be the characteristic of the dominant social protest, it would not present any problem to have a penal solution for someone who merely takes advantage of the protest to commit a homicide, a violation or a robbery. We will thus limit ourselves to the crimes that may be committed during the course and due to the protest itself, of which those previously mentioned (damages, harm and resistance) seem to be the most frequent.

In these suppositions one must analyze if the characteristic conduct is supported by a cause that justifies it. To do this one may not appeal to the formula of a legitimate exercise of a right more than as a general definition of all of the justifying causes, because the legal formula of article 34 is nothing more than a remission to all the judicial order, in order to determine if anything in a particular provision allows the performance of the characteristic action. The constitutional right to protest does not enter into that formula in the Penal Code, as it is what directly guarantees the atypical nature to which we have referred beforehand. The cases that need to be investigated regarding justification are exactly those that had fallen within the typical characterization. In those suppositions, as a general rule, one should ask in each case if it can fit within the framework of legitimate defense of in the state of justifying necessity.

It is not possible to consider here all of the hypothetical cases or to reiterate the development of the theory of justification, without only insisting on the necessity, in each case, of analyzing if the characteristic conduct is not supported by some of those justifications.

As for participants in social protests who do not fit into the needs or in conduct justified by legitimate defense, one should observe that those justifications also cover them when they really operate according to the circumstances of the case, for one who cooperates with someone who acts with justification, is also supported by the cause of justification being dealt with, and in the case of legitimate defense, the legitimate defense of third parties is especially regulated.

This last case presents the particularity that, in case the person attacked had sufficiently provoked the aggressor, the third party could equally defend him or her legitimately, subject to the condition of not having participated in the provocation. This is important in the cases of violent repression of public protests or meetings: someone who defends one of the protesters who is physically attacked after insulting or provoking in another manner is acting legitimately, even if the protester was not supported by that cause of justification by virtue of the previous provocation.

The state of necessity also presents interesting and complicated problems in connection to particular cases. First of all, the evil caused must be less than the one desired to be avoided, so that it must be a case of a protest calling for a fundamental right. No one has the right to any characteristic conduct when demanding vacation, for example, but the right to food and health, according to the circumstances, may provide such a right, in other words, according to the seriousness and nearness of the evil one wishes to avoid. It cannot be a case of remote or hypothetical ills, but only those that are relatively close and urgent.

Secondly, there must not be another appropriate route, that is, one that is reasonably usable, to neutralize the threatened harm. The appropriateness of the alternative route for demands cannot be merely formal or hypothetical, but it must be a case of a real and effective appropriateness. No one may commit harmful conduct to obtain foods, if it is possible to call on the authority for to provide them within a reasonable timeframe.

Furthermore, the characteristic conduct must be conducive to that result, either because it is less harmful and more appropriate for attracting public attention, because there are no means of doing it by another means, because the communications media have not paid attention to the demand, because the authorities do not wish to repair the need, etc. If in a community elementary needs for food and sanitation are not met, if human lives are in danger, if contamination of drinking water is not prevented or detained or malnutrition is on the verge of causing irreversible damages, if the community is isolated and the authorities do not respond to petitions, it would not be permissible to destroy the city hall, but it would be justifiable to call the attention of the public and authorities by cutting off traffic on a road, even if this lasts for a considerable time and causes some danger to property and business. It is a case of the least offensive measure that falls into people's hands in order to call attention to their needs in an extreme situation.

The question has been raised many times on the state of necessity created by privation that is general. As a rule, needs found to have been generalized do not enable a state of necessity, but in a country with considerable necessities, it will always be necessary to establish what is the average standard for satisfying social necessities, and thus to meet that standard to establish the nature of the needs. It is almost inevitable that immediately after an earthquake there will be needs and nothing will give people the right to carry out characteristic conduct while attempts are being made in a reasonable time and with urgency in the case, given that this is a question of suffering being borne my all inhabitants in the region or place.

Notwithstanding the above, in the framework of general neediness situations of particular necessities may arise. If, in the example of the earthquake, no one, because of the fact of being left homeless, has the right to occupy a hospital, one cannot deny that if a child is at the point of dying of thirst or hunger, it may take possession of liquids or foods that it finds in the ruins of a store.

It is thus not possible to exhaust herein all the hypotheses that may at some point justify social protest that leads to characteristic conduct; however, the considerations presented above are enough to illustrate the difficulty of the question.

PROTEST THAT MANIFESTS ITSELF IN ILLICIT ACTIONS AND CULPABILITY

When the conduct is characteristic and anti-judicial, in other words, when it constitutes an illicit or criminal act, there still remain the problems where social protest presents culpability. When that is understood in the normative traditional sense of judgment of reproach or reproachability, this presents problems that lead to the need for understanding illegality and excusable necessity.

In principle, when the protest adopts the form of an unjust act because the justification of need is excluded since there are viable and really appropriate institutional routes for satisfying needs, a mistaken prohibition may operate, if those routes were really unknown by the protagonists of the protest or if they believed they did not have within their reach the means for forwarding their demands or did not believe they would be effective for reasons grounded in previous experiences.

Given that such protests may be massive, such a lack of knowledge does not have to be general, but there may be an error of invincible prohibition with respect to some or the majority of the people that participate in it, while others may fall into a vincible error, because they know the available and effective institutional means. That means that it is not possible to equally criminalize all of those who participate in the protest, only that culpability must be evaluated for each person to the extent that such a person can individually understand the illicit nature of their behavior and its penal relevance. Let us remember that the law (article 34 of the Penal Code) demands that the agent shall have had the possibility of understanding the *criminality* of his or her act and not its mere illegality or antijuridical nature: for Argentine law it is not enough for the agent to believe he or she is committing a contravention or fault when in reality she or he is committing a criminal offence.

As to excusable necessity, the hypotheses are more remote, and do not seem to share characteristics with the cases of social protest known in our midst, even though one may not discard the possibility on a situation that will fit with exculpation. Those who in the face of the total inaction of authorities and absolute public indifference, with the looming loss of harvests due to the lack of water, with irrigation water supplies interrupted by arbitrary acts or lack of attention, channel water that is not theirs to save what is the only means of livelihood for them and their families, threatened by misery and hunger, in that case are affecting another's property rights to save their own. It is a case of judicial assets of a similar entity, and thus, no justification is measured, but there is an excusable necessity, without prejudice to the need to make restitution to the affected property owner.

Everything said about culpability needs to be complemented, including in the case where the crime is completed, with an appropriate quantification, not only based on traditional culpability, but on culpability due to vulnerability, in other words, that it will be necessary to measure the effort that the person has made to reach the concrete situation of vulnerability that, in the case of social protests is usually minimal, given the special attention of the authorities in some of these cases.

In others, to contrary, the attention by the authorities favors the errors of invincible prohibition. This is because the social demands are, at heart, political or government problems, which means that with a certain frequency they are met by the political authorities themselves, who resolve them on occasions *in situ*. It is conceivable that when an executive or legislative authority helps a place and resolves the conflict (a meeting is held, a protest is called off, etc.), the participants do not have the capacity to understand the antijudiciality of their conduct, because the state itself is contributing to resolving the conflict. Moreover, in the case of interrupted routes or concentrations of people, the state is usually present to guarantee the physical integrity of the participants. This would seem to give the impression that the police are taking care of the intended delinquents. To a lay opinion, it is incomprehensible that the state will on the one hand try and resolve the conflict and take care of the complainants, and, on the other hand intend to criminalize them. In such circumstances, it is very difficult to pretend that there is a demandable possibility of understanding the criminality.

SOME POLITICAL REFLECTIONS

What was pointed out in the previous paragraph indicates that the substance of the matter being confronted in criminal law at this point is a question of an eminently political nature. No one can deny that realizing Human Rights for a second generation is of that nature. Leaving the problem in this environment to deal with it in criminal law is the most radical and definitive means of leaving it without a solution. Whenever one extracts a question from its *natural* environment and assigns it an *artificial* nature (such as penal) one guarantees that the problem will not be resolved. *This indicates that the best contribution towards solving conflicts of a social nature that criminal law can make is to maximize its means of reducing and containing punitive power, reserving it solely for very extreme situations of intolerable violence and for those who take advantage of protests solely to commit wrongdoing. In that way, criminal law preserves itself, returns the problem to its nature and assigns responsibility for the solution to state agencies that are not only have constitutional standing to do so, but that also have the judicial duty to provide the solutions that we have known from the beginning cannot be provided by punitive power.*

In terms of distributing legal authority and powers, it is obvious that to want to criminalize social protest in order to solve the complaints that it forwards, is to demand from judicial powers a solution that is the responsibility of strictly political state powers, and thus, any omission in the effort by criminal law for containment will be not only inconvenient, but also unconstitutional from the perspective of separation and independence of the powers of the state.

NOTES

1. Since the European *antiglobalization* manifestations there have been much more specific and articulated organizations, such as in Brazil. On this: Bernardo Mancano Fernández, *MST formacao e territorializacao em Sao Paulo*, Sao Paulo, 1999; José Carlos Garcia, *De sem.rosto a cidadao*, Rio de Janeiro, 1999; Roseli Salete Caldart, *Pedagogía do Movimento Sem Terra*, Petrópolis, 2000.

2. On this, CELS, *El Estado frente a la protesta social 1996-2002*, Buenos Aires, 2003.

3. See for instance, AAVV, Sobre la resistencia a las violaciones de human rights, Trabajos debatidos en la reunión de expertos celebrada en Freetown, Sierra Leona, del 3 al 7 de marzo de 1981, Serbal/UNESCO, Barcelona, 1984.

4. It is not possible to forget the marked tendency of the Nineteenth Century to criminalize the leaders of mass movements, considered degenerates: Cesare Lombroso,

Gli anarchici, Torino, 1894; Lombroso/Laschi, Le crime politique et les révolutions, París, 1892; Benito Mario Andrade, Estudio de antropología criminal espiritualista, Madrid, 1899, pp. 203 and ss.; Gustavo Le Bon, La psicología política and la defensa social, Madrid, 1912; from the same author, Psicología das multidoes, Rio de Janeiro, 1954; Scipio Sighele, I delitti della folla, Torino, 1910; J.M. Ramos Mejía, Las multitudes argentinas, Buenos Aires, 1912. In general, on criminalization of multitudes and leaders, Jaap van Ginneken, Folla, psicologia e politica, Roma 1989.

5. See Raúl Gustavo Ferreira, *La Constitución vulnerable. Crisis argentina and tensión interpretativa*, Buenos Aires, 2003, pp. 23 and following.

6. Article 36, 4th paragraph, of the Argentine National Constitution: *All citizens have the right to resist those who carry out the acts of force listed in this article.*

7. In that perspective, Feuerbach, P. J. A., *Anti-Hobbes oder über die Grenzen der höchsten Gewalt und das Zwangsrecht der Bürger gegen den Oberherrn*, Giessen, 1797.

8. See María José Falcón and Tella, *La desobediencia civil*, Madrid, 2000.

9. On non-violence in general, Michael N. Nagler, *Per un futuro nonviolento*, Milano, 2005; nevertheless, there are clear examples of non-violence in Argentina, such as the *Madres and la Abuelas de Plaza de Mayo*.

10. For all of them, Roberto Gargarella, *El derecho de protesta, El primer derecho*, Buenos Aires, 2005; Raúl Gustavo Ferreira, *La Constitución vulnerable*, cit.

11. That seems to be the route taken by some court decisions.

12. UNAM, *Constitución Política of the United States Mexicanos Comentada*, Rectoría, Instituto de Investigaciones Jurídicas, México, 1985; James Frank Smith, *Derecho Constitucional Comparado México-United States*, UNAM, México, 1990.

13. René Brunet, *La Constitution Allemande du 11 Aout 1919*, París, 1921.

4. Cf. Jorge Amado, *A.B.C. de Castro Alves*, Sao Paulo, s.d., p. 53.

15. *Anyone who, without creating a situation of common danger, impedes, bothers or complicates the normal function of land, water or air transportation and the public services for providing water, energy and energetic substances, shall be repressed by imprisonment of from three months to two years.* In the sense of classification, Sala 1, C.N.Cas.Penal, JA, 2002-IV, p. 375 and our note, in the same, p. 384.

16. *The private actions of men that in no way offend the public order and morality, nor harm a third party, are solely reserved to God and exempt from the authority of judges. No inhabitant of the Nation shall be obliged to do what the law does not command, nor deprived of what it does not prohibit.*

7. *Repression by imprisonment of from one to four years shall apply to: 1) The individuals of an armed service or gathering of persons, who attribute to themselves the rights of the people and petition in their name (article 22 of the National Constitution).* Article 22 of the National Constitution states: *The people do not deliberate or govern, except for through their representatives and authorities created by this Constitution. Every armed service or gathering of persons who attribute to themselves the rights of the people and petition in their name, commit the crime of sedition.*

18. *Repression by imprisonment from fifteen days to one year shall apply to one who resists or disobeys a public employee in the legitimate exercise of his functions*

or to the person who provides assistance for a request made by that person by virtue of a legal obligation.

19. *Repression by imprisonment of from one month to one year shall apply to one who publicly and by any means defends a crime or someone convicted of a crime.*

20. Henry D. Thoreau, *Desobediencia civil y otros escritos*, Madrid, 1994.

21. *Repression by imprisonment or reclusion of from one to ten years shall apply to one who takes part in an association or band of three or more persons destined to commit crimes for the sole fact of being a member of the association. For the leaders or organizers the minimum sentence shall be five years of prison or reclusion.*

Chapter Four

Organized Crime

A Frustrated Category

Eugenio Raúl Zaffaroni

INTRODUCTION

Organized crime is a denomination applied to an uncertain number of criminal phenomena by various specialists, by the mass media, by novelists, by politicians and by the operators of the penal system (specifically police, but also judges and penitentiary administrators, each one with his or her own objectives).

To facilitate understanding of the problem a basic understanding is required: it is necessary to point out that this is not the same thing as explaining the intention of pointing out certain phenomena that have the name of organized crime, that is, the explanation of categorization and the explanation of the phenomena that one intends to categorize.

We shall concern ourselves here with the first, since, as we have explained beginning with the title, we believe it is a failed enterprise, not requiring a false categorization, which, because it does not achieve its objectives, hinders understanding of the phenomena in the scientific field.

PLURALITY OF AGENTS AND ORGANIZED CRIME

The plurality of agents has drawn the attention of penalists and criminologists in every epoch and in different ways. Thus, in Nineteenth Century Europe, particularly after the Paris Commune, a considerable literature was produced regarding crime by the multitudes, which led to various assessments of the multitudes[1] and of the criminal liability of their leaders or conductors.[2]

On issues that are closer to the ones that now occupy us, and certainly linked to prohibition of unionizing for workers, the judicial–penal concept of illicit association or association of wrongdoers or association for delinquency became generalized. Today it is a conventional classification in penal codes in the continental European tradition, whose constitutionality can be questioned, but have little to do with the category of organized crime as is the intention today, among other things, because the latter is a product of the North American tradition. Nor do the traditional qualifiers of some penal types when committed in bands, gangs or by three or more agents link to this concept. In the case of assaults by bands in unpopulated places and banditry in general, there is also an ancient criminological literature,[3] as there is for political wrongdoing committed by organizations,[4] some of which we would consider terrorists today, such as the concern of the positivists with anarchism,[5] but a superficial analysis will suffice to show that all of this area is alien to what today we seek to understand as organized crime.

Organized crime as an attempt at categorization is a phenomenon of our century and it does little good for authors to lose themselves in discovering is supposed historical precedents, including remote ones, as they will contradict their own categorical premises. It is absolutely useless to seek organized crime in antiquity, in the Middle Ages, in Asia or in China, in piracy, etc.,[6] because this does do more than to indicate that one has forgotten one or more of the characters on which one intends to found the category, such as the business structure and, particularly, the illegal market.

If we restrict ourselves to those characteristics, it is clear that when one speaks of organized crime, one is not referring to any plurality of agents nor to any illicit organization, but to a distinct phenomenon, which is unconceivable in the pre-capitalist world, where there were neither companies nor markets in the form we know today. To return to those ancient delinquent organizations would be to do no more than to mention previous forms of plurality of criminal agents or associations that are not useful to focus on the intended concept one is seeking.

Accepting that all attempts at characterization start with the phenomenon of plural agents, but that this, because of its broadness does not serve for this purpose, we shall mention the different paths that have been attempted.

AN OVERVIEW OF CONCEPTUALIZATIONS

There are many authors who sincerely admit the lack of definition, and attribute this to the dominance of a “popular” conception, warning that criminologists are not in agreement and that the boundary between organized crime and white collar crime is not clear because of the lack of definition of the former.[7] In the field of politics there is also no definition; the advisory committee to the United States government concluded in 1976 that "we do not believe that there is a sufficiently broad definition, which will satisfy the needs of very different individuals and groups that can use it as a means for developing an effort to control organized crime."[8]

On the legal level the situation is not much different, as the Racketeer and Corrupt Organizations act, known as "RICO," and which constitutes chapter 96 of the Federal Criminal Code and Rules, as the specific legal instrument for fighting organized crime in the United States, contains a very extensive list of illegal activities, but no categorization.[9] In Germany the situation is not much different, because they sincerely not their enormous deficit in theoretical concepts and empirical basis.[10] Brazil legally incorporated the concept that goes back to the traditional illicit association,[11] which is notoriously insufficient, but that does no more than to reveal the lack of a more adequate definition.

Within an environment that is strange, criminology has received the task of categorizing organized crime, marked by a reference to the illegal market, because since prohibition of alcohol and even before, the North American public has associated it with the illegal market, in other words, with "the prohibition of prohibited goods and services."[12] This pre-scientific limit to the supposed concept is actually useful, because it at least leaves outside of its scope activities which, would otherwise lead to an even greater confusion, as would be the case of including terrorism, bands of robbers, urban vandals and so on.

Nonetheless, that pre-scientific limit opens up a debate about the reach of attempts at categorization, as to whether the focus should be on type of organization or type of criminal activity, with some maintaining that the correct attitude is to correlate both types.[13]

Over the last decade there have been many authors occupied with those difficulties. Among them we shall cite two, who have performed a balance of the conceptual attempts at a theoretical level. Hagan reviewed definitions of organized crime by comparing thirteen authors and finding a consensus among them on the following points: a) it involves a permanent enterprise that operates rationally to obtain benefits by means of illicit activities; b) it sustains its action through real or fictitious violence; c) it implies corruption of public employees. As to the other characteristics, such as service monopoly, secret codes and closed status of the ground, he found very little doctrinal consensus.[14] Maltz, for his part, did not go much farther, because his comparison led only to broadening the scope of multiple enterprises, but he denies the necessity of involvement in illicit business, organization on a Mafia paradigm and the sophistication of that paradigm.[15] Bynum considers that those contributions clarify the question, although he also recognizes the ambiguity and lack of consensus surrounding the theme.[16]

POWER IMPOSES AN IMPOSSIBLE MISSION ON CRIMINOLOGY

The criminologist's discomfiture is not unwarranted, but derives from the fact that they are seeking a category that will satisfy politicians, police forces and, above all, the news media, and to a point, fiction authors.

Organized crime is not a criminological concept, but a task that power has imposed on criminologists. There are authors who expressly recognize that there are four conceptual sources for organized crime: police, criminological, the "penitents" and the economists (to those we would add that of the politicians, based on the various *ad hoc* committees). However, the criminologists and the economists (and the politicians) work with data provided by the police and the penitents, so that "this monopoly of data has given the police a preeminent power in developing policies and strategies regarding organized crime."[17] The police agencies do not allow the scientists to access their data.[18]

"Apart from sex and domestic struggles, there is not theme that provides greater entertainment than organized crime," as proved by the success of the Untouchables and the Godfather as well as the *ad hoc* hearings in the United States Congress.[19] This is linked to the conspiratorial sense in which the phenomenon has been interpreted within the Mafia paradigm. With the generalizing of the idea of a grand Mafia conspiracy at the national level in the United States, with a secret and highly sophisticated organization, it began to exert the fascination characteristic of all conspiracies. The attraction of conspiratorial versions is partly explained in that it always produces a discharge of anxiety when one knows whom to attribute the root of the evil, while one also admires those who can retain a secret without weaknesses, as they seem to acquire an enormous power of domination.[20] The sadly famous "Protocols" are a deplorable proof of this public fascination,[21] which in literature is dealt with masterfully in "The Pendulum of Foucault."[22]

As is natural, everything that attracts the public eye moves politicians to use it for clientelist purposes and the police to devote preferential attention to it. In that way, the police end up handing over sources for policy preparations and the politicians provide documents for the police to work with.[23] Various commissions and committees of the U.S. congress fit into this feedback system, such as the one presided over by Senator Kefauver in 1951, the McLellan Committee in 1962 and the 1967 Commission. The political revenue from such undertakings has been no less significant. Thomas Dewey, twice nominated as the Republican presidential candidate in the United States, gained his fame by prosecuting Lucky Luciano, while Estes Kefauver achieved recognition with his committee that almost won him the Democratic presidential nomination in 1952.[24]

As is clear, criminology had very little to do with this attempt at conceptualization, other than receiving a task from those in power. Regrettably, it was unable to fulfill it, although not lacking in good will, because "organized crime and the illegal markets have been largely a source of myths and the truth is less entertaining.[25]

Criminologists did not occupy themselves much with this theme until the Twentieth Century. As one would logically expect, the first important works appeared from the "Chicago School"[26] and Sunderland considered that it grew in unity and in opposition to society as a result of the state's weakness.[27] Much later it would be Cressey who took on the task of preparing the official version of organized crime.[28] Even though criminology was born closely linked to power and so greatly permeated by it that one would could say it was a "suspicious" science, in this case, it did not reach the point of founding the official conspiracy thesis, because it was too much informed by sociology to tolerate such as degree of servility and partiality. Thus, operating side by side were the non-systematic use of the police, the politicians, the media and fiction, and on the other hand criminological disconcertment: one could hardly construct a category based on a conspiratorial idea with little credibility.

THE POLITICAL FUNCTIONALITY OF THE CONSPIRACY VERSION

The idea that organized crime is a conspiracy at the national level in the United States, aside from exercising the usual popular attraction of all conspiracy theories and of being readily believable by the lay audience, was also driven by the criminals themselves and in that way appeared as more powerful and worthy of admiration (especially if in moments of crisis they adopt Robin Hood attributes of appear as social defenders or benefactors). This fulfilled a dual purpose in the years of its growing postwar recognition: a) on the one hand, its political recognition in that period (Kefauver Committee in 1951), in the midst of the cold war, it served to compare organized crime with authoritarian and totalitarian regimes; b) on the other hand, it attributed an anti-national conspiracy to foreign ethnic groups with foreign connections, in other words, to blame the evil on a foreign conspiracy. Although the first function disappeared with the circumstance that gave rise to it, the second has remained until the present, with some variants in terms of the ethnic groups involved.

The idea of conspiracy with a totalitarian structure, analogous to Communism or Nazism is expressed in reports from Kefauver and is continued in the Oyster Bay conferences, called by the governor of New York, Nelson Rockefeller, during the 1960s,[29] which noted the great power and centralization, a small directing group and even a paramilitary structure in organized crime. As Cressey affirmed,[30] this was ideal for the Maccarthy era.[31] Thus, belief in the centralized control of markets is the heart of the official policy doctrine in this area.[32]

That version has lost political importance in our days, but during its time it accompanied and was complemented by the idea of a foreign conspiracy: both communism and crime were foreign conspiracies that were an attack on democracy and the American way of life.[33] That function had the political advantage of citing the evil outside of American society. It is true that it is almost as grotesque in scientific terms as it is useful in political terms, for there were several authors who from the beginning pointed out that organized crime should be considered an American product and not a foreign conspiracy.[34] It was Bell, for example, who in 1953 through a route close to Mertonian functionalism, noted that it should be understood as an innovative route for ethnic minorities to gain access to power.[35] In some way, in that explanation one may see a parallel with the self-realized prophecy of Jews in Europe: their social space was first reduced and they were next criticized for doing the only thing that that their reduced social space allowed them to do, which at the same time reinforced the arguments for reducing their space.[36]

Although the official version—which some criminologists call "orthodox"—has no serious factual support, since to the present all researchers not the insufficiency of empirical research,[37] it has been the object of a criminological version by Cressy,[38] which was considered the most coherent along its line, although admittedly it did not present any supporting data.[39]

We cannot forget to observe, incidentally, that attributing organized crime to the ethnic groups that immigrated to the United States fit very well with the entire racist immigration policy in effect in the period between the wars, which was praised by Hitler himself in *Mein Kampf*[40] and that is experiencing a resurgence in our days,[41] financially supported to a certain extent by the same foundations that upheld racism in those years.[42]

THE CRIMINOLOGICAL INCONSISTENCY OF THE *MAFIOSO* PARADIGM

No one in criminology doubted the existence of the Mafia or Mafias in the United States, but instead what one could legitimately call the Mafioso paradigm as an approach to organized crime, meaning: a) the affirmation that those organizations had a structure that was so sophisticated, centralized, hierarchical, national and so on, meaning so strongly conspiratorial, that it could be compared with Bolshevism or National Socialism; b) that it responded to phenomena from outside of American society, and fundamentally, to cultural or biological determinants from immigrant groups; and c) that the Mafia model with those characteristics could be transported to all criminality linked with the illegal market for goods or services.

In reality, that paradigm lacked serious supporting empirical data,[43] notwithstanding all of the documents and authors speaking of the "*capos*" and "*capo de tutti capo*" and that had been adopted and disseminated by the Kefauver committee (1951), by the Oyster Bay conferences, by the committee on Law Enforcement and Administration of Justice of 1967, by J. Edgar Hoover, by the 1976 commission, etc.[44] This is the description of organized crime which, formed during the postwar period, has since then influenced public attitudes in that country and is introduced as an ideological substrate in the criminology manuals.[45]

The principal source for feeding that paradigm are the testimonies of the "penitents," one of which, that of Joseph Valachi before the Mclellann Senate Committee in 1963 had major repercussions, since the contributions of data from the Kefauver Committee were minimal.[46] However, many authors seriously criticized him, especially because very few criminal prosecutions were initiated because of the data provided, while others observed that his testimony was almost concurrent with other versions appearing in the press and from police.[47] In 1969 efforts were made to strengthen this testimony with some magnetophonic recordings taken clandestinely at the offices of a famous *Mafioso* (De Cavalcante).[48]

Such untrustworthy data cannot seriously inform a paradigm intended to conceptually cover organized crime in its entirety, if by that one understands all criminality linked to the illicit market. Later empirical research has shown that the FBI has not been able to provide any evidence for its usual affirmation that illegal gambling is the major source of political and economic support for the Mafia, that in both gambling and usury (typical activities in the intended category) in very few circumstances is it possible to use violence to suppress competitions and that, in general, the Mafia is less centrally coordinated than legend and popular ideology would have us believe.[49]

In this regard one must note the extremely important conclusions by Reuter, for whom the press and the police provide each other with feedback in a way that sustains the Mafia's reputation. "Because organized crime is broadly treated in the daily newspapers as entertainment, they provide information on the delinquent bands known to the readers, which raises the Mafia. The penal agencies, understandable desirous of calling the attention of the press to their activities, are driven to prefer the Mafia to other less known bands. In this way, the Mafia's preeminence increases."[50] To that author, the mafia is the "visible hand" in the illegal market, but he also considered that there was an "invisible hand" operating, which were the personal interests and technology that shape the markets for legal goods and services and there is often a tension between the two hands in the illegal markets. He concludes that in the three markets investigated in his work (racetrack betting, lotteries and loan sharking) it is not true that they are monopolized or centrally controlled, with the "invisible hand" emerging victorious, considering that there are theoretical arguments that allow one to suppose that this is typical of all of the criminality in the illegal market.[51] "To summarize," he adds, "the orthodoxy has a weak foundation. Affirmations about the Mafia dominating the markets and the importance of the Mafia's power are not based upon any effort at systematic academic or official verification. The academic literature has provided some isolated *ex-post* support, but the theory has never been well-developed nor submitted to rigorous verification. The best available documents cast serious doubts upon the entire orthodoxy."[52]

In addition to everything that has been pointed out, the inescapable political functionality of the aforementioned paradigm is much more than significant; all authors agree that organized crime existed in the United States previous to the Volstead Act of 1920, and the allied 18th Amendment to the Constitution, or the "dry law," "prohibition" or the "noble experiment,"[53] but did not have the characteristics and the volume it acquired from that point onward.[54] One must not forget that the Mafia paradigm arose with this experience and only became officially consolidated during the second postwar period (during the so-called "cold war"). This paradigm has continued without important changes up to the present, and, additionally, until very recent times there has not been a change in the Italian or Italian–American stereotype, enriched with detailed stories of the Mafia and its families and homicides.[55] The focus was on the Sicilian mafia, the Neapolitan Camorra and the Calabrian "onorata societa," meaning all immigration from Southern Italy (which is the predominant Italian immigration to the United States[56]), in other words, one of the most numerous Latin or non-Puritan minorities, a part of the tavern culture, against whom the anti-alcohol propaganda of the first postwar period was directed,[57] the same as would later happen with the war on drugs in the United States, always publicly linked with some particular immigrant group.

ORGANIZED OR DISORGANIZED CRIME?

The activities that criminologists generally consider to be manifestations of organized crime are things such as extortion and other attacks on freedom of work by unions, all forms of illegal gambling, usury, drug traffic, political corruption, white slave and foreign human traffic, and, most recently, electronic crimes.[58]

We have seen that, with varying field methodologies (participant observer, interviews, opinion polls), it has become clear in the United States that these activities are usually organized in a sub-cultural and local manner, and that they do not have the rigid or bureaucratic organization widely depicted by the politicians, the police and fiction authors.[59] Nonetheless, the United States Chamber of Commerce seems to be taking the exact opposite position, when it affirms that organized crime is a national power, operating with impunity and free of all constitutional limits, and asking if is not the fifth Estate.[60]

Between these two antagonistic positions, there seems to be nothing in common, in principle, but when one looks deeper there is actually something linking them below the surface: by going deeper on the first, one may find the reason for the second. In effect, the second complains against what seems to be unfair or advantageous competition and is not much different in tone from complaints by formal against formal commerce in many Latin American cities.

The class of activities that many attempt to categorize as organized crime are linked to the market and, in that sense, the approximations of economists and criminologists who point out the economic aspect are clearer than those that move away from this position or underestimate it. One should not think that such approximations fit into Marxist theorizing regarding such phenomena, since, although it is true that Marxist have indeed given thought to the issue and from their perspective consider organized crime as an ally of the establishment and a contributor to maintaining proletarian subordination,[61] the great majority of economic approaches to organized crime do not fit into that theoretical framework.

A sizable number of those who focus on this question by favoring the economic perspective consider that it is a case of activities that imply a continuation of illegal commercial practices from the Nineteenth Century (the so-called "robber barons"), who infiltrated and flourished in industries with excessive competition, penetrating small sectors of the economy, where disorder and instability rule. Organized crime goes about neutralizing or destroying competition through threats and political corruption, and with that brings economic stability through a monopoly or oligopoly that disciplines the market, that is even territorially distributed.[62]

In that manner, organized crime would be the set of illicit activities that operate in the market, disciplining it when legal or state activities do not do so. In more precise terms, its economic function would be to cover the areas of savage capitalism that remain in a disciplined market.

Along a similar line and in a certain manner complementary to that explanation moves what we could call the business paradigm, close to sociological functionalism. Starting from the supposition that any business organizes itself to obtain benefits, Smith maintains the theory of a business spectrum at whose opposite extremes would be found legal and illegal activities, but the differences would preferentially be issues of degree and not of quality. He concludes that any explanation such as conspiracy or ethnicity, if it has any relevance to the interpretation of organized crime, will always be subordinated to the theory of the enterprise.[63] Bynum[64] is entirely correct in observing that this focus can be traced to Merton, who maintains that it is not possible to distinguish economically between organized crime and political corruption in legal businesses.[65]

It is certain, whether because undisciplined areas exist in the market, or because they are created on the grounds that prohibition interferes with raising income disproportionately, spaces are opened which, as in any market, are occupied by businesses, in an activity that appears in the form of a spectrum—as Smith has well described—at whose extremes are legal and illegal activities. However, they appear so confused and dispersed that it is very difficult to distinguish the shades or degrees that incline to one or the other extreme. This leaves thousands of questions without answers. At what point of the capital flow is the money black or at what point does it begin being white? Does a lawful business that occasionally launders money practice organized crime? Is the activity of a lawful business that massively employs immigrants so as to pay lower salaries organized crime? Is a gang of kidnappers organized crime? Does a bank that occasionally takes money with no concern for its origin fit in this category?

In summary, one has the feeling that, at least from the economic angle, that organized crime is a phenomenon of a disorganized and undisciplined market, which is open to the disciplining that a lawful, or unlawful or more or less lawful business produces. It is obvious that such openings or gaps in disciplining the market are very different, and are furthermore quite unstable and variable, for because every market is dynamic, there are spaces that close and others that open. Hence, it is impossible to conceptualize and the attempts are frustrated; moreover, the spaces themselves cannot be suppressed, as that would mean halting the market dynamics, in short, making it disappear.

Undoubtedly there are Mafias and gangs, which perform legal and illegal activities, but there is no concept that can encompass the entire set of unlawful activities that are able to take advantage of indiscipline in the market, and which, in general, appear as indissolubly mixed or blended with lawful activities.

Thus, the attempts being made at categorization cannot be completed, because they are a pretension of fitting market dynamics into a criminological concept. The enterprise becomes even more unreachable when one seeks to find a category that can be transferred to criminal law.

Consequently, there is a set of economic activities and phenomena, among which some are very clearly criminal, but there is no category capable of covering all of them in the criminological and much less the legal field.

It is natural for the question to have been raised in the United States in a priority manner and that it appeared during the period between the wars and that the political tendencies have tried to categorize it during the second postwar period. This is because the war of 1914–1918 had consequences that the European politicians had never imagined. They believed they were going to carry out a relatively brief war, but did not imagine that technology would lead them into a conflict in which the winner would be the one who could consume its industrial potential for the longest time.[66] That is why in Europe, the victors, in practice, gained very little, having been left almost as destroyed as the vanquished, and the United States was left in a privileged position, attracting an enormous mass of capital and of immigration from those who did not see achievable and secure conditions in a Europe destroyed by a war whose consequences they had not even imagined. That was the environment that allowed the United States to implement a racist immigration policy in the midst of a genuine festival of concentrating capital and speculation that ended with the Great Depression in 1929.[67] The disorder in this market and its interference with the 18th Amendment ("Dry Law") provided the ideal conditions for penetration by illegal activities mixed with legal ones and, as usual in that country, politicians arose who saw an open route to clientelism and gained fame with their famous "wars" through the penal system, as well as police agencies who adopted their mottoes and discourses, and criminologists who allowed themselves to be swept along by public opinion that was infused by the Mafia stereotype, and also, with a certain narcissism that comes to those who feel that they own the key to solving all of the problems that are caused by indiscipline in the world's largest market.

After the Depression and the New Deal, with the United States finding itself after the Second World War as the most powerful country in the world, unlawful activities in the market had acquired different characteristics and volumes appropriate to the new economic situation, while the politicians continued gaining their clientele with the same methods, and as a result, the phenomenon allowed the rise of some in the same way that the Cold War gave Maccarthy the opportunity to place in check the Truman administration and Eisenhower's first term.

THE EXTENSION OF A FRUSTRATED CATEGORY

The frustrated category of organized crime, associated to the Mafia stereotype, extended itself around the world long before the present. Any more or less serious manifestation of criminal organization, especially if it involved foreigners, brought forth the frustrate category in the most unusual places. The penal reform approved by the Argentine senate in 1933 responded to it, to the point of implanting the death penalty through electrocution.[68]

Nonetheless, one cannot deny that the massive exportation of that category from the United States has occurred in much more recent times and as a result of the so-called market globalization. Whatever opinion one may have regarding the nature, scope and perspectives of this phenomenon, one cannot deny that the circulation of goods and services across borders has acquired a hitherto unknown flexibility, that the fall of so-called "real socialism" and advances in technology, the regional markets, the rise of newly industrialized nations in the Far East and the indisputable presence of Japan as a world power, have extraordinarily favored it.

It is natural that as the world market globalizes in this fashion, it has not been limited in exporting its undisciplined environments, but it enables new and previously unsuspected spaces for indiscipline, quickly taken advantage of by business activities, lawful or unlawful. It is clear that this has generated genuine complementary economies that are partly unlawful, but in general, one may affirm that, given the volume of illegal activity blended with legal activities, we find before us a new, hitherto unknown form for accumulating capital: dirty money derived from illegal business and tax evasion, traffic in forbidden goods and services, financial speculation and so on. It seems that the market grows without goods, at least in its traditional aspect.

In light of the disorder that globalization causes and that is characteristic of the market, added to the prohibitive interferences and the characteristics that it assumes at the periphery of global power, where greater or more manifestation is the norm, it was natural that there would also be an export of the technology for control, or at least an attempt to do so. It is a case of repetition of a law: when a social problem is transferred, it is followed by transference of the ideology of control. The massive population transplant, especially from Southern Europe to the Southern Cone of America,[69] from 1880–1914, with the transference of anarchism, socialism and the protests for social demands, led to the racist European criminological positivism,[70] particularly the Italian variety[71] being rapidly called form by the governing elites who assumed it as their own.[72]

The political operators at the periphery of power have no qualms about assuming the discourse of organized crime as their own, among other things because they consider it harmless to limit their arbitrary power. They base that belief on the following: a) it is so displaced from its genetic context that its incapacity for control is obvious even for those who are less alert; b) their trust, with reason, in the way in which they control all power and their unlimited capacity to corrupt any institution and in the capacity of their scribes to rationalize this; c) in no lesser measure, in their own ignorance of the problem, which for peripheral political operators is always secondary and only deserves their intention when they must implement some clientelist maneuver or neutralize some problem that would discredit them.

In this manner, the covering discourse of the frustrated category of organized crime extends itself around the world, is recognized by politicians from all latitudes, is translated into criminal laws, is disseminated by the mass media, gives rises to new stereotypes and so on.

AN INTERVENTIONIST CRIMINAL DISCOURSE IN A MARKET ECONOMY

The discourse that incorporates organized crime is not as inoffensive as may be believed by the majority of political operators in countries at the periphery of world power, at least in terms of its economic consequences. It would be too simplistic to believe that its total ineffectiveness regarding obvious functions leaves it with latent functions, those that it does not seem to regard seriously, since it limits itself to discussing the first.

In principle, it is a question of a frustrated category, in other words, an attempt at categorization that ends up in a diffused notion. When this is in the framework of punitive intervention, a supplementary quota is added to the selective arbitrariness of those interventions.

In these conditions, prohibitions interfere in the market, generating a disproportionate growth in income from what is prohibited (services or goods) and this is translated into a rare protectionism, because it is protectionism based on the criteria of penal and not economic selectivity. From the economic point of view that protectionism is completely irrational and its arbitrariness can be totally dysfunctional.

On the other hand, punitive intervention is always arbitrary (selective) but, since legal and illegal appear inseparably mixed, a nebulous notion as the guiding idea for intervention does nothing but add greater arbitrariness to the chosen penal intervention, which, in some manner is demanded in the form of abstention (non-investment due to the perspective of insecurity) or in the demand of some income disproportionate from the size of the investment, as the price of insecurity.

Punitive selectivity is not entirely arbitrary, because it is generally guided by the standards of penal vulnerability of the candidates for criminalization, which in this case are the weaker companies, who are easier prey for extortion. With that, the penal system, more corrupt at the periphery, interjects itself in the market as monopolizer of the Mafia-type activity extorting the business leaders who are more vulnerable because of their weakness, and who in time, due to the difficulty of competing with large corporations and the added cost of extortionate protection, end up being excluded from the market. In this way, the penal system is converted into a factor of economic concentration, that does not necessarily mean exclusion of illegal activities from the market, but merely their concentration together with the legal ones.

All of this is said, in addition to the fact that in competition between large corporations, the penal system can also enter, as it is always used to entering, as a factor at play in the struggles for hegemonic power, leading to the loss of covering for those who lose out in such a fight: the rare cases in which the penal system falls on someone invulnerable happen because that someone lost invulnerability in a hegemonic struggle with another competitor of almost equal power.

In summary, and contrary to what one might usually believe, punitive intervention in the market is a phenomenon that introduces itself in all the changing and unstable openings of indiscipline that open up, without a guiding category and without ceasing to intervene as well in legal activities. It ends up being a set of measures for irrational protectionism or selected arbitrariness, which with excessive frequency empower the illicit activities themselves. Corruption (particularly in peripheral countries) destroys competitiveness in the weaker business leaders and eliminates them from the market and may take part as a decisive element in struggles among the stronger. Few forms of interventionism can be more negative for a market economy.

This supposed remedy for activities that threaten competition is nothing less than one of the strongest threats the market may face, much more irrational and destructive than the thoughtless and wrongheaded protectionist measures that at least are debatable in economic terms, while the penal interventions, as a general rule, hide their economic character under the discourse of ethical absolutism.[73]

CRIMINALIZATION BY MEANS OF A FRUSTRATED CATEGORY: AUTHORITARIAN PENAL LAW

The transport of a frustrated category to the field of penal law is nothing more than criminalization that appeals to an idea that is diffuse, undefined, lacking in real limits, and thus, a violation of the principle of legality, that is, the first and fundamental characteristic of liberal penal law or law with guarantees.

Even though in terms of scientific logic the failure in characterization should determine that it would be no more than an attempt in the criminological field, political logic operates in another manner and, thus organized crime made its entry into penal legislation, with the predictable consequence that elements of authoritarian penal law were introduced. The failed concept in criminology was taken to legislation to allow penal and procedural measures that were extraordinary and incompatible with liberal guarantees.

It is not our intention here to review the tortuous path of penal and procedural legislation managed with a basis on this categorization that failed in the scientific field and succeeded in the political field. We will limit ourselves to pointing out the major legislative principles that have adopted it in the legislative projects that call for adopting it both penally and procedurally.

In Penal Matters

a. The impunity of hidden agents and the so-called "penitents" constitutes a serious injury to State ethics, in other words, the principle that forms an essential part of the state of law; the state may not make use of immoral measures to avoid impunity.

One should not confuse state action that tends towards discovering and convicting a guilty party with the effort it should extend to save a human life or another important judicial asset that is being attacked or that is in imminent peril of aggression. In the latter case we find ourselves with a police and non-penal measure[74] and the judicial assets that are in collision are the life and physical integrity of an innocent person and the administration of justice, and the inclination must always be towards the former because of the well-known weight of judicial assets (or weighing of evils) of the state of necessity. That concrete threat that leads to police action has nothing to do with the injury already suffered or with the danger of new injury in case the author of the other carries out a new analogous conduct. That is the substantial difference between penal coercion and police coercion, which is often overlooked when rationalizing the use of immoral means by the state or the penal system.

Confusing both situations the state authorizes its employees to commit violations, sometimes with a scope and extension that are even more inadmissible or scandalous, giving rise to ambiguous situations in which it is possible that cases of corruption are overlooked by invoking a state of necessity or something similar.

As for the so-called “penitent,” this has nothing to do with the traditional giving up of an attempt. This classical “bridge of gold”—as Von Lizst[75] called it—takes place before consummation, while the penitent performs an action after it. On the other hand—and this is more determinant—the one who is desisting must be the true penitent, since his or her desistance must be completely voluntary and free, while the false “penitent” is nothing more than a delinquent negotiation a benefit in exchange for information, in other words, an informer. The state is making use of cooperation from a delinquent, bought at the price of his or her impunity, to “do justice,” which liberal criminal law as repudiated since the time of Beccaria.[76]

There is nothing in terms of common penal law and according to the principles governing quantification of sentencing that allows mitigation of the sentence with a benefit for a delinquent because of information provided, nor does it mean a better prognosis for conduct of the person. From the ethical point of view, such an act by an informer is not an element that improves judgment regarding a previous behavior, and it general, it further degrades the person.

b. The sentencing system (mandatory sentencing) of recent American law or the high minimum penalties of written law from the continental European tradition, often appealed to in the cases covered in this failed category, harm the principles of rationality, proportionality and humanity in sentencing, while at the same time intending to reduce judges to the role of simple computing machines that lack any evaluative capacity.

The system of fixed sentences disappeared during the Nineteenth Century, after having been established in codes such as those of revolutionary France[77] and the Empire of Brazil,[78] but reappeared at the end of the Twentieth Century, either due to the effects of the American fixed sentences, faulted as being unconstitutional by several American federal judges,[79] and to very high minimum sentences in some Latin American laws, which, however, no one has dared to challenge as unconstitutional.[80]

In no less violation of the most elementary rationality are the absurd maximum sentences, which go beyond forty and fifty years of prison. These are really lacking in seriousness, since no one can believe with any good sense that prisons should become asylums for the elderly with the passing of years. It is only in the United States, where they are attempting a penal policy that is on its way to a total catastrophe and brag about having a million and a half prisoners,[81] that something so absurd is believed; in the rest of the world we know that within forty or fifty years governments will have other more important concerns and the jails will have perhaps been supplanted by control technologies that are cheaper, albeit no less dangerous.[82]

Also no less dangerous than what was presented above is to appeal to the usual "label fraud" and change the name of sentences, calling them "security measures" or something else: it is not a case of returning to the old stratagem consisting in violating all of the limits in liberal criminal law through the old recourse of calling the sentence by another name, thus allowing its retroactive application, as well as disproportion, irrationality, cruelty, etc., as is the frequent intent with those laws and projects.

c. There are many ways of violating legality without abandoning the traditional forms of doing so in criminal law in the Continental European tradition, but, in a different twist, the exportation of the nebulous idea of organized crime has desired to bring into our laws one of the most well-known, criticized and clear mines of violating it known to Anglo-Saxon criminal law, the concept of conspiracy.[83] Contrary to what is scientifically correct, in other words, to adopt the institutions of another tradition that serve to improve our own, the ones adapted are capable of worsening it.

Conspiracy is one of the most diffused and disputable concepts in Anglo-Saxon criminal law. English legal historians have determined that it was born centuries ago as an independent law for false accusations and that it was soon extended to all crimes, as the rule of law or legality was extended. In other words, as the ability of courts to create new categories of crime was being reduced, through the empire of law, conspiracy was being extended, as a judicial resource for violating it.

In effect: some crimes were clearly determined by common law and others by statute law (by laws of parliament), without the courts being able to broaden the catalogue of either, they appealed to a supposed diffuse criminal type, in which one could arbitrarily introduce any action imaginable and define it in an original manner: agreement to do an unlawful act or a lawful act by unlawful means.[84] To complete the panorama of uncertainty, one should clarify that the word "unlawful" is not understood only as illicit, but also as "immoral."

This has nothing to do with illicit association in Continental law, because it is enough that there be a proposition directed to a person, even though it is not admitted; because it is sufficient to propose one single crime in particular; and because the measure can be lawful. This curious formula has been used not infrequently to pursue labor unions and certain political forces, and its history has not been at all praiseworthy in terms of the service it has provided to public freedoms.[85]

Besides the introduction of conspiracy, the general tendency to criminalize preparatory acts that are atypical from the point of view of traditional formulations of an attempt are no less serious.

In Issues of Criminal Proceedings

a. In almost all laws that are founded on the idea of organized crime the preventive capacities of the police are expanded, which leads to a serious detriment to the principle of judiciality and as one of the most appropriate forms for rapidly extending the use of torture and occasions for corruption.

b. At the same time there is a tendency to limit the right to defense in various forms, with one of the most usual ones being secret proceedings, extended indeterminately, incommunicado status for the accused, prohibition or difficulty in communicating with the defense counsel, secrecy related to the identity of judges, inspectors, witnesses and so on.

c. The conspiratorial character attributed to organized crime almost always leads to restriction of the principle of public criminal proceedings.

d. Generous authorization is given for intercepting correspondence, telephone calls and other communications, in a way that seriously affects reserve and privacy.

e. Without a doubt, all such proceedings are accompanied by limitations to prison release, so that the principle or presumption of innocence is inverted.

f. Evidence of a doubtful nature is admitted, among others, which presented by the famous undercover agents and informers, which is not resolved by the pretension that they should be accompanied by objective evidence. In our law the informants are not witnesses, so that they are free to falsify facts.

g. In expanding the diffuse concept of organized crime around the world, it is not uncommonly accompanied by rules that establish special jurisdictions, sometimes special commissions of a very doubtful judicial nature, violations of the principle of the judge designated by law before the fact, etc.

In general, one may affirm that transforming into law a frustrated criminological category invented by American criminologist under pressure by politicians, police corporations and the mass media, has no other effect than to harm legality in criminal law in multiple ways, and prosecution in criminal procedural law, which is explainable, because these in reality are the two faces of liberal criminal law.[86] Authoritarian or anti-liberal criminal law have had their characteristics established for many centuries, especially through foundational works such as the Inquisitor's manual,[87] and it is exactly this that we are seeing every time that in a case such as this liberal criminal law is broken.

Every time phenomena such as these are produced in history, they appear in the framework of a war against a cosmic or almost cosmic enemy, who personifies evil itself. American politicians have a great propensity towards political clientelism in this way, so that this is not the first time they have undertaken a war against a social problem or one of an economic nature by means of criminal law—and, regrettably, it will not be the last—with the usual result that they have lost all such wars[88] and endangered their democratic institutions, without mentioning the sorry and negative example that such fables provide for the world, given the reproductive capacity of what goes on in that country.

CONCLUSIONS

a. No one doubts the real existence of illicit associations, societies existing to commit transgressions, gangs or bands.

b. In every market economy undisciplined sectors appear and disappear, as the result of their own dynamics, which are occupied by businesses, the same as in disciplined sectors, but those businesses very few times are illicit associations, given that in most cases they combine lawful and unlawful activities in different measures.

c. Outside of the cases of genuinely illicit associations there is no clear or even approximate limit that would allow one to distinguish between a "legal" company and an "illegal" one, because they always combine activities and in fact it is very rare for a "lawful" business not to incur some illegal activity. The attempt to categorize illicit activity as "organized crime" has failed on the scientific level, since the only thing that it has been able to prove is the existence of a market phenomenon.

d. The "Mafia myth" extended to all illegal activities on the market is a scientifically false conspiracy theory, maintained by the media, fiction, political clientelism and the police, which criminology has made efforts to elaborate but was unable to do so, although it had found favor with many criminologists.

e. The pretension of taking the "mafia myth" to criminal law implies a totally arbitrary interference in the market economy, which may lead to economically catastrophic effects: economic concentration, elimination of small and medium-sized businesses, corruption in corporations due to concentration of legal activity, excessive protectionism, irrational alterations in some goods and services with a resulting increase in legal activity because of absurd profitability.

f. At the penal judicial level this punitive penal intervention based on a false and unlimited concept implies a serious setback to liberal criminal law and the resulting establishment of authoritarian (inquisitorial) criminal law, injuring constitutional and international guarantees and encouraging corruption in agencies of the penal system.

NOTES

1. See for example the different assessments of multitudes by authors such as H. Tainé, Les origines de la France contemporaine, La Révolution, tomo I, París, 1878; G. Tarde, Essais et mélanges so-cio-logiques, Lyon–París, 1900; Scipio Sighele, I delitti della folla, Torino, 1910; G. Le Bon, Psychologie des foules, París, 1895. About this period, in general, Jaap Van Ginneken, Folla, psicología e política, Roma, 1991.

2. In general, almost all authors from the period seek punishment for the leaders, in whom they seek to find degenerative signs. For example, C. Lombroso–R. Laschi, Le crime politique et les révolutions par rapport au droit, à l'antropologie criminelle et à la science du gouvernemente, París, 1892, especialmente el tomo II: Pascual Rossi, Los sugestionadores and la muchedumbre, Barcelona, 1906; la primera edición de La folla delinquente de Sighele, Torino, 1891.

3. In Spanish one may recall the pioneering work of Constancio Bernardo De Quiróz in Spain, soon extended to Mexico; in Portuguese Chrysolito Chaves De Gusmao, O banditismo e associações para delinquir, Río de Janeiro, 1914.

4. All sorts of organizations are mentioned, including the political ones, and among them there is frequent reference to the *Carbonari*. On these: Indro Montanelli, L'Italia giacobina e carbonaria (1789–1831), Rizzoli, Milano, 1978.

5. E.g., C. Lombroso, Gli anachici, Torino, 1894.

6. E.g., August Bequai, Organized Crime, The Fifth State, Lexington Books, 1979, page 9.

7. Timothy S. Bynum, Controversies in the Study of Organized Crime, in "Organized Crime in America: Concepts and Controversies," edited by T. S. Bynum, New York, 1987, page 4.

8. National Advisory Committee on Crime Justice Standards and Goals, Report on the Task Force on Organized Crime, Washington, 1976.

9. 1993 Edition, Federal Criminal Code and Rules, as amended to February 1, 1993, St. Paul, Minn., West Publishing Co., page 665.

10. Cf. Marion Bögel, Strukturen und Systemanalyse der organisierten Kriminalität in Deutschland, Berlín, 1994.

11. Thus, law 9.034 of May 3, 1995. "Deals with the use of operational means for the prevention and repression of actions practiced by criminal organizations."

12. Peter Reuter, Disorganized Crime. The Economics of the Visible Hand, The MIT Press, 1983.

13. Michael Maltz, Toward Defining Organized Crime, in "The Politics and the Economics of Organized Crime" edited by H. Alexander and G. Caiden, Lexington Books, 1985, page 21.

14. Frank Hagan, The organized Crime Continuum: A Further Specification of a New Conceptual Model, en "Criminal Justice Review," 1983.

15. Maltz, op. cit.

16. Bynum, op. cit. page 7.

17. Bequai, op. cit., page 2.

18. Reuter, op. cit., page 8.

19. Ibid, page 9.

20. Cf. Jean Chevalier–Alain Geevrabt, Dizionario dei Simboli, Bib. Univ. Rizzoli, 1986, T. II, page 3545.

21. See Norman Cohn. El mito de la conspiración mundial. Los Protocolos de los Sabios de Sión, Madrid, 1983; George L. Mosse, Il razzismo in Europa, Dalle origine all'Olocausto, Laterza, 1992, page 127.

22. Umberto Eco, Il pendolo di Foucault, Bompiani, Milano, 1988.

23. Reuter, op. cit., page 8.

24. Ibid, page 7.

25. Ibid, page 5.

26. The field work with the diaries of John Landesco Organized Crime in Chicago, 1929 (reprinted by Chicago University Press in 1968), fits into the first tradition of this class of work by the Chicago school. About it, in general, Martin Bulmer, The Chicago School of Sociology, Institutionalization, Diversity, and the Rise of Sociological Research, The University of Chicago Press, 1984, especially pages. 101–102. A selection of readings including texts from the period with a different tendency, in Gus Tyler, Organized Crime in America, A Book of Readings, The University of Michigan Press, 1962.

27. Edwin H. Sutherland, Criminology, Lippincott Co., 1978, page 270.

28. Donald R. Cressey, Theft of the Nation: The Structure and Operations of Organized Crime in America, New York, 1969.

29. Cf. Bequai, op. cit., page 3.

30. Cressey, op. cit., page 314.

31. See Richard H. Rovere, El Senador Joe MacCarthy, FCE, México, 1987.

32. Cf. Reuter, op. cit., page 9.

33. Cf. Bynum, op. cit., page 7.

34. Cf. Reuter, op. cit., page 3.

35. Daniel Bell, Crime as an American Way of Life, in "Antioch Review," June, 1953.

36. This self-fulfilling prophecy is illustrated in highly documented fashion in the classic work of León Poliakov, Historia del antisemitismo, Raíces. Buenos Aires, 1989.

37. The same is recognized for Germany by Marion Bögel en op. cit.

38. Cressey, op. cit.

39. Cf. Reuter, op. cit., page 9.

40. Adolfo Hitler, Mi Lucha, Sgo. de Chile, December 1939, page 126: "There they refuse to accept the immigration of elements that are harmful from the social health point of view and absolutely prohibit the naturalization of certain and specified races, thus taking some timid steps towards a way of looking at things that looks very much like the concept of a National State."

41. We refer to the best-seller by Richard J. Herrnstein and Charles Murray, The Bell Curve, Intelligence and Class Structure in American Life, New York, 1994.

42. See John Sedgwick. Inside the Pioneer Fund; Adam Miller, Professors of Hate; both in "The Bell Curve Debate. History, Documents, Opinions," edited by Rusell Jacoby and Naomi Glauberman, Times Books, 1995, pages 144 and 162.

43. Bequai, op. cit., p. 7.

44. See Francisianni–Elizabeth Reuss Ianni, A Family Business: Kinship and Social Control in Organized Crime, New York, 1972; President's Commission on Law Enforcement and Administration of Justice, The Challenge of Crime in a Free Society, Washington, 1967.

45. Cf. John Galliher–James Cain, Citation Support for the Mafia Myth in Criminology Textbooks, in "American Sociologist," 1974.

46. Jay Albanese, Organized Crime in America, Cincinnati, 1985.

47. Cf. Bynum, op. cit., page 6; Reuter, op. cit., page 9.

48. Cf. Bequai, op. cit., page 4.

49. Cf. Reuter, op. cit., pages 3–4.

50. Ibid, page 4.

51. Ibid, page 7.

52. Ibid, page 10.

53. Regarding this period, Bill Severn, The End of the Roaring Twenties, Prohibition and Repeal, New York, 1969.

54. Cf. Bequai, op. cit., page 34.

55. E.g., the story recounted by Bequai, op. cit. page 12.

56. See Ercole Sori. Las causas económicas de la inmigración italiana entre los siglos XIX and XX, en Devoto–Rosoli, "La inmigración italiana en la Argentina," Buenos Aires, 1985, p. 15.

57. Cf. Joseph R. Gusfield, El paso morágal: el proceso simbólico en las designaciones públicas de la desviación, in "Estigmatización and Conducta Desviada," recopilación de Rosa del Olmo, Universidad del Zulia, s. d. pág 73.

58. Cf. Joseph R. Gusfield, El paso morágal: el proceso simbólico en las designaciones públicas de la desviación, in "Estigmatización and Conducta Desviada," recopilación de Rosa del Olmo, Universidad del Zulia, s. d. pág 73.

59. Thus Albanese, op. cit.; Anneslise Anderson, The Business of Organized Crime, Stanford, 1979; Howard Abadinsly, Organized Crime, Boston, 1981.

60. Cit. by Bequai, op. cit.

61. William J. Chambliss Functional and Conflict Theories of Crime, in "Whose Law, What Order," edited by Chambliss–Mankoff, New York, 1976, page 8; of the same, Exploring Criminology, Macmillan, New York, 1988, page 86.

62. Cf. Bequai, op. cit., page 6.

63. Dwight Smith, Paragons, pariahs and Pirates: A Spectrum Based Theory of Enterprise, in "Crime and Delinquency," 1980, page 358.

64. Bynum, op. cit., page 8.

65. Robert K. Merton, Teoría y estructura sociales: A Spectrum Based Theory of Enterprise, in "Crime and Delinquency," 1980, page 358.

66. See Marc Ferro, La Gran Guerra (1914–1918), Buenos Aires, 1985.

67. Cf. Maurice Niveau, Historia de los hechos económicos contemporáneos, Barcelona, 1977.

68. See José Peco, La reforma penal en el Senado de 1933, Buenos Aires, 1936.

69. See Devoto–Rosoli, op. cit.

70. In general, all of criminological positivism operated within the racist paradigm of the period, particularly in the version of Herbert Spencer (Principes de Sociologie, Trans. by M. E. Cazelles, París, 1883).

71. The racism of Italian positivism is notorious, especially in La Criminología by Rafael Garofalo (translation by P. Dorado, Madrid, s.f.).

72. One may see the early Argentine positivist production: Luis Maria Drago. Los hombes de presa, 2ª ed. Buenos Aires, 1888: the bibliography indicated by Hugo Vezetti, La locura en la Argentina, Buenos Aires, 1983.

73. A recent critique of ethical fundamentalism in Douglas N. Husak, Drugs and Rights, Cambridge University Press, 1992.

74. Regarding this, Iñaki Agirreazkuenaga, La coacción administrativa directa, Civitas, Madrid, 1990.

75. FRANK VON LISZT, Lehrbuch des Deutschen Strafrechts, Berlín, 1891, page 216.

76. See Opere diverse del Marchese Cesare Beccaria Bonesana, Patrizio milanese, Parte Prima, Prima Edizione Napoletana, Napoli, 1770, I, page 117; Dei delitti e delle pene, a cura di Franco Venturi, Einaudi, 1981, page 89; Trans. by Laplaza, Buenos Aires, 1955, page 188.

77. Code Pénal. Des 25 Septembre–6 Octobre 1791.

78. Approved in 1831, see, by De Josino Do Nascimento E Silva, Código Criminal do Império do Brasil, Río de Janeiro, 1863; Code Criminel de l'Empire du Brésil, Trans. by Victor Fouchr, París, 1834.

79. On that: G. M. Weitekamp–Scania Herberger, Amerikanische Strafrechtspolitik auf dem Weg in die Katastrophe, in "Neue Kriminalpolitik," 1995, book 2.

80. The Argentine Supreme Court had found for the unconstitutionality of the minimum sentence for armed automobile theft, which is higher than the minimum for simple homicide. Later on, with another composition, it changed its criteria with an argument that implies that it is renouncing the power to control constitutionality of sentences, which is lamentable.

81. Cf. Weitwkamp–Herberger, op. cit.; Marc Mauer, The Fragility of Criminal Justice Reform, in "Social Justice," 25 nº 3; Nils Cristie, Crime Control as Industry, Towards Gulags Western Style? Roytledge, 1993.

82. See Diego Manuel Luzón Peña, Control electrónico and sanciones alternativas a la prisión, in "VIII Jornadas Penitencias Andaluzas," Sevilla, 1994.

83. Law 24.424 introduced in Argentina the term "confabulación," which is a poor translation of conspiracy, although, given the form in which was legislated, it is clear that the person presenting the law did not know what it was about.

84. Cf. Smith and Hogan, Criminal Law, London, 1992, page 269.

85. Elisabetta Grande, Accordo criminoso e "conspiracy." Tipicitá e stretta legalitá nell'analisi comparata, CEDAM, 1993.

86. This is admirably expanded by Luigi Ferrajoli, Diritto e Ragione. Teoria del garantismo penale, Laterza, 1989.

87. Malleus Maleficarum Translated with an Introduction, Bibliography and Notes by the Rev. Montagne Summers, Londres, 1951.

88. Cf. Weitekamp–Herberger, op. cit., in "Kriminalpolitik," 1995.

Chapter Five

Is a Non-Authoritarian Enemy Criminal Law Possible?

Eugenio Raúl Zaffaroni

THE MOST RECENT PROPOSAL FOR A CRIMINAL LAW OF THE ENEMY

The current interest in enemy criminal law has brought forth a proposal by Günther Jakobs, formulated in a brief work[1] that has given rise to criticism,[2] to which are added discussions as to its constructions in the purely dogmatic field.[3] Those debates make it necessary to take precautions, since, especially in terms of enemy criminal law, one walks along the edge of the offense, which is never scientific or illuminating. Therefore, we do not wish to qualify the proposal and still less to disqualify it without sufficient analysis.

If we have not misunderstand what Jakobs is proposing, we believe he is setting forth *the possibility of a non-authoritarian enemy criminal law. While it is true that all authoritarian criminal laws are also "for the enemy," the reverse might not be exactly so.* We believe that Jakobs does not achieve this objective and the demonstration of that hypothesis is the purpose of this chapter, in the conviction that, scientifically speaking, affirming that a theory has not achieved its objective does not imply any disparagement whatsoever. Nor do we link Jakobs' theory of crime with his proposal for enemy criminal law, beyond the methodological objections that we formulate at the end of these pages, that is, his tendency towards sacralization and legitimization as a result of use of data.

POLARIZATION IN CURRENT CRIMINAL LAW

Jakobs affirms that punitive power fulfills the symbolic function of reaffirming the validity of the norm—his well-known theory of the sentence—in criminal law for the *citizen*, while in criminal law the *enemy* operates as a mere impediment. Nonetheless, he maintains that both functions always make themselves present; therefore, regarding the terrorist, the contention serves to reaffirm the norm's validity, and in the common thief, that reaffirmation, although it translates into a privation of freedom, means an impediment to repeating the behavior during time in prison. The professor from Bonn complains that the contemporary doctrine does not handle that polarity.

Strictly speaking, we believe that doctrine in all ages has dealt with solving this question, which is not at all new. Except for some extreme positions, for practically two centuries—not to go farther back—there have been abundant attempts to combine *neutralization*,[4] in other words, in different terminologies, criminal law for *culpability* (of the act, of sentences, looking at the *past,* etc.) with criminal law for *dangerousness* (of the *author*, of *measures*, looking at the *future*, etc.). At the base of all of those denominations is found the polarity to which Jakobs referred, and one can maintain that it is the central and never resolved problem of all theories that legitimate punitive power. Decidedly, with one name or the other, we believe that it is the result of criminal law's eternal lack of its own discourse regarding the sentence, which it sometimes legitimates with elements of administrative law (restraining) and other times with elements of private law (retribution). Ratification of the validity of the norm is no more than a metafunction (or parafunction) of all legitimate coercion by the state: a civil penalty, for example, fulfills a restitutive or reparative function, but one cannot deny that at the same time it ratifies the validity of a norm and has preventive effects.

AN UNCOMMON PHILOSOPHICAL POLARIZATION

Jakobs affirms that the distinction between a criminal law for a citizen and another for an enemy should be understood using a philosophical key. For him, it is based on contractualism and he maintains that Rousseau and Fichte defended extreme conditions, by considering that every delinquent was an enemy. As a counterpart to those authors he presents a position that he considers more prudent, that of Hobbes, who distinguished the common delinquent from the enemy, and was followed in this regard by Kant. Thus, there would be a philosophical polarization between Rousseau/Fichte as extremists on the one hand, and Hobbes/Kant on the other hand, as moderates.

Along the lines of Hobbes and Kant, someone who remains out of the contract—and so in a state of nature—represents a danger, his or her presence is a threat, and thus, Kant affirmed that anyone could require such a person to enter the contract. This is consistent with the idea of the human being permanently at war in a natural state. If that anthropological conception is true, if the natural state of the human being is *war of all against all*, and the only guarantee of peace is the state, someone who remains out of the contract is a savage at war—an enemy—and someone who intends to rise up against the sovereign is also an enemy, because with this the *bellum,* the chaos of total war is reestablished.

Remaining within the contract as *citizens* and as *persons* would be lawbreakers who do not threaten the state as sole guarantor of the peace, meaning that common thieves, for example; instead, those who represented such a threat would be *enemies* and mere *individuals.* Someone who robbed a bank to spend the money on prostitutes and alcohol would be a citizen; someone who did so to aid resistance to the state would be an enemy.

If it is true that this is the consequence of adopting the theses of Hobbes and Kant, it is not certain that the opposing thesis would be that of Rousseau and Fichte. Regardless of the fact that it is doubtful that those authors maintain that every delinquent is an enemy,[5] it is not for nothing that no historian of philosophy places Hobbes against Rousseau and Fichte, but that all do so for Locke,[6] representing the two traditional versions of the state: *absolutist with Hobbes and liberal with Locke.*

This theoretical polarization of the Seventeenth Century state was reproduced in the Eighteenth Century in a German version with Feuerbach's objections to the Kantian theses on the idea. It is not a lesser philosophical error to omit every reference to the Locke/Feuerbach line, as it the liberal conception of the state had not existed. At least one may affirm that this is not the usual contraposition and we definitely believe that this is the key to the failure of the enterprise that Jakobs proposes.

THE HOBBES/LOCKE CONFRONTATION

Although no one can consider Hobbes as a positivist, he was undoubtedly an important forerunner to that movement. All of his construction is based on causality and on a certain mechanicism. His anthropological conception is very particular; humans develop their faculties through their desire for power.[7] He considers that competition, mistrust and the desire for war are the causes of disputes, which in the natural state determine a state of permanent war.[8] In that state there are no rights, since each one has what he or she can obtain and conserve; nor are there moral judgments. It is a brutal state, of which he affirms that there are examples in America. To put an end to that state, humans achieve the social contract, through which they deliver all power to the sovereign, who is not part of the contract, because it is agreed upon between the subjects.[9] Because of that—for Hobbes—the sovereign cannot violate the contract, which is established because of feat (of others or of the sovereign). As that sovereignty is the only thing that can contain war, it cannot be partial: sovereignty must be total. The subject can hardly retain any rights, because before sovereignty there were no rights, or to put it better, there is the right to do everything that power allows each one to do, which is precisely what the subjects hand over in the contract and it is inconceivable for them to claim anything.

For Hobbes, resistance to the sovereign's power is inadmissible, because that would mean reintroducing the *bellum omnium contra omnes,* the *war of all against all,* and precisely because of that, those who resist the power of the sovereign cannot be punished, but only submitted to forced containment because they are not delinquents but enemies. *Once cannot consider as punishment the harm inflicted on someone who is a declared enemy. Because that enemy has never been subjected to the law, he cannot transgress it. Either he was subject to it and declares that he is no longer, denying, as a result, the possibility of transgressing it. Therefore, all of the harm that can be caused must be understood as acts of hostility. In a situation of declared hostility it is legitimate to inflict any sort of damages. One can thus conclude, thus, that if by acts or words, knowingly and deliberately, a subject should deny the authority of the representative of the State, whatever may be the penalty called for in case of treason, the representative may legitimately make him suffer as he sees fit. In denying subjection, he has denied the penalties called for by law. As a consequence, he must suffer as an enemy of the State, meaning according to the will of the representative. The penalties are established in the law for subjects, not for enemies, as is the case of those who, having become subjects by their own acts, rebel and deny the power of the sovereign by their own will.*[10]

It is clear, then, that the enemy for Hobbes is the one who resists the power of the state, because in that way, war is reintroduced. However serious a crime may be, its author is not an enemy, but one who resists the sovereign is the enemy, as an *outsider* or *foreigner*, or one who goes back to being one through leaving the contract with an act of resistance.

The thinking that opposes Hobbes' idea of an absolute state is that of Locke, for whom in the natural state there is a natural law, and therefore there are rights.[11] Locke's contractualist metaphor is much more realistic than that of Hobbes. For Locke it is implicit that civil society predates the state, which some take to presuppose two contracts. What is certain is that once civil society is constituted, the majority decide the state contract, and hence, cannot assign all rights, but only those necessary for conserving those rights. The legitimate resistance that overthrows a sovereign, to Locke, does not dissolve civil society, although that is the effect that Hobbes attributes to it. *For Locke, a critic of absolute monarchy, someone who carries out an act of legitimate resistance demanding respect for rights previous to the state contract, is a citizen exercising rights; to Hobbes, a defender of the absolute state, such a one is an enemy who needs to be repressed and contained with unlimited force, without even respecting the boundaries of the sentence, because such a one has ceased to be a subject. Someone who, to Locke, is exercising the right of resistance to oppression, is for Hobbes an enemy worse than a criminal. For Locke, the sovereign who abuses power loses the condition of sovereignty and becomes simple another person; for Hobbes it is the subject who resists abuse of power by the sovereign who loses subjecthood and begins to be an enemy.*

THE KANT/FEUERBACH CONFRONTATION

In support of his thesis Jakobs cites Kant, and strenuously insists on a note by him in the second section of his treatise *Perpetual Peace: a Philosophical Sketch* published in 1795.[12] In that note, Kant affirms that there may be peoples or humans in a natural state, whose very anarchical presence represents a danger, and in those conditions there is the right to obligate them to enter the contract. Anyone can force those who insist on remaining outside of the contract to come under it, because that is the only way to guarantee peace. In that sense, Kant was following the tradition of Hobbes, and along identical lines was denying the right to resist oppression, because for that philosopher, destruction of the state represented loss of the external guarantee of the categorical imperative, and thus, the return to the natural state and resulting restoration of war of all against all.[13]

Feuerbach's response to Kant was not long in coming and in 1798, he published his *Anti-Hobbes*,[14] which was, strictly speaking, an *Anti-Kant*.[15] This was not a merely speculative dispute, for in the question of the right to resist oppression lay the question of attitudes towards the French Revolution. Feuerbach defended rights prior to the contract. He affirmed that rights also existed in the natural state, e.g., blacks sold as slaves had a prior right to freedom, although they could not exercise it because they had been impeded in doing so by force.

To Feuerbach, the sovereign is part of the contract, and because of it he is given the right to choose the means to carry out his ends. Dissident regarding those choices—politics—cannot establish any right to resistance, which only appears when the sovereign acts against civil society and intends to return it to the state of nature. By deviating from the purposes assigned by the contract to sovereignty, it is understood that the so sovereign loses his character as such, and thus, resistance is not to the sovereign but to a particular person with power. There is no right to resistance to the sovereign, but to one who has ceased to be one by departing from the ends that the contract assigns for exercising sovereignty. By not admitting that resistance, one would fall into the contradiction of maintaining that the contract imposes the duty of obeying someone who wishes to destroy society.

That also explains Feuerbach's liberal jusnaturalism: there is not only a practical moral reason, but also a practical judicial reason, which indicates that there may be an exercise of rights that are prior to the state contract.[16] While the first indicates a moral duty, the second indicates the judicial space as a subjective right in society, independent of the will of the sovereign.

We also believe that it is clearly demonstrated that the question of the enemy does not involve contraposition of Rousseau/Fichte with Hobbes/Kant, still less because the first were radicalized and the second moderate, but in the discussion on the absolute state and the liberal state, between Hobbes and Locke first, and then between Kant and Feuerbach, where the key lies in the right of resistance to oppression, which the defenders of the absolute state not only deny, but assign the character of enemy to those who intend to exercise it.

HOBBESIANISM IN THE PAST CENTURY: CARL SCHMITT

The Hobbesian thesis was also developed in the last century with particular sagacity, reaching its highest level in the thought of Carl Schmitt,[17] whose most specific writing in this regard is found in a work from before he joined Nazism,[18] published in 1927 and reprinted several times since then, including after the war: *Der Begriff des Politischen.*[19] In it Schmitt asks about the distinction of substance that he makes about the essence of the political, in other words, that which is equivalent to *good and evil* in morality, to *beauty and ugliness* in aesthetics, to *profitable and unprofitable* in economics, for if this essence is not achieved, the political would lack autonomy. His answer is that *the specific political distinction to which it is possible to refer the political actions and motives is the distinction of* friend *and* enemy.[20]

He affirms that such a distinction indicates the *extreme degree of intensity of a union or a separation, of an association or dissociation,* which has no reason to appeal to the other distinctions or to base itself on them. Thus, regardless of whether good or bad, beautiful or ugly, *the enemy is simply the other, the foreigner,*[21] *and it is enough for him to be existentially, in a particularly intensive sense, someone else or foreign, so that in an extreme case it will be possible to have conflicts with him that cannot be decided either through a system of pre-established norms or through the intervention of a third party who is uncommitted and thus impartial.*[22] In the case of the extreme conflict, it is the politician who *decides if the otherness of the stranger in the concretely existing conflict means the denial of his modes of existence and if because of this it is necessary to defend oneself and fight, to preserve one's own, peculiar mode of life.*[23]

Schmitt does not intend that it is desirable or undesirable for humans to group themselves into friends and enemies, but that they accept the data of the reality, and he does not intend for any aggressor to be an enemy, the same as Hobbes. As such, he distinguishes between the *inimicus* and the *hostis*;[24] the true enemy would be the *hostis*, with whom the possibility of war would always be raised, as the absolute negation of the other or the extreme realization of hostility.[25] If the world were to have a single government and all possibilities of war had been cancelled, for Schmitt, politics would have ceased; it would be a world without politics. If in that world the pacifists had the strength to confront the wars, so to speak, making war on war, they would be confirming the essence of the political. As for humanity, he affirms that, as such *one cannot have any war, since one does not have enemies, at least on this planet. The concept of humanity excludes that of the enemy, given that the enemy also does not cease being human, and this does not present any specific difference.*[26] He thus affirms, citing Proudhon, that *whoever speaks of humanity, wishes to deceive.* He affirms that a war in the name of humanity would lead to extreme inhumanity, thereby discrediting the *League of Nations* and the Wilsonian discourse.

Schmitt affirms that even the bourgeois and constitutional state, notwithstanding all of the limitations imposed on it by its Constitution, can do no less than recognize that when it needs to defend the Constitution itself, the fight is carried on outside of it and outside of the law, purely by force of arms.[27]

The concept of the political as the power of defining the *hostis* links Schmitt to theology and to the political thinking that he refuses to describe as *pessimistic*. Just as all theologians affirm that because of original sin humans are not good,[28] this fact is also recognized in political thinking whose clearest is considered to be that of Hobbes, emphatically maintaining that his *bellum* was *no fearful and unbalanced fantasy,* but *the elementary presupposition of a specifically political system of thought.*[29]

Starting from a similar anthropological perspective he not only denounces liberalism but the denial of politics, but also directly denies the historical existence and even the possibility of a liberal policy, reducing it to a simple *liberal critique of politics.* He indignantly notes that *what liberalism saves from the State and politics is reduced to the guarantees of conditions of freedom and the elimination of disturbances to freedom.*[30]

There are several revealing observations in Schmitt for a criminal law of the enemy. In principle, it is important to note that his theory is not constructed faced with a concrete enemy, but he elaborates it at a more abstract level than all of the others, and because of that, mentioning him is unavoidable. On that abstract plane he maintains that politics should always have an enemy, meaning that *if there is none, in order for there to be politics, an enemy must be constructed or found, which seems to be historically confirmed as to punitive power, which spends eight hundred years seeking enemies when it intends to free itself of all limits, meaning that Schmitt's affirmation is true in the sense that the authoritarian state—not all politics—will always require an enemy.*

If political liberalism does not exist, penal liberalism would be merely the critique of authoritarian criminal law and also would not exist; the only criminal law would be authoritarian. The history of criminal law would be made up of a succession of discourses to legitimate emergencies, liberal criminal law would be merely a succession of discourses critical of the previous ones, and thus a mere historical illusion. Still less would there be limits to repressive power when it was a case of defending the Constitution itself, since that defense would be carried out outside of that. Hence, in other works he expressly rejects the function of custody of the Constitution assigned to judges and unleashes a polemic with Kelsen.[31] With the constitutional system in peril, it would be the end of all of the guarantees and limits, with which the Constitution itself would provide the most perfect argument for its annihilation.[32]

The synthesis of the Schmittian thesis could be that outside of the authoritarian state, always constructed in the face of an enemy, there are no politics. From that one may deduce that set against authoritarian criminal law there would be no liberal criminal law, but simply a liberal critique of the former. It would be enough to involve the need to defend the Constitution against an enemy for all of the liberal limits to punitive power to immediately cease. Given that there can be no politics without an enemy, the Constitution would be a pipe dream, because the constitutional state could not eliminate politics and, thus, it would also have enemies, against whom it could not defend itself within the Constitution itself.

THE PENAL REFLEX OF THE ENEMY DURING THE LAST CENTURY: EDMUND MEZGER

The prehistory of criminal law of the enemy may go back to Plato,[33] who developed for the first time in Western thought the idea that the wrongdoer is inferior due to his incapacity to rise to the world of pure ideas, and when that condition is irreversible, he should be eliminated. Leaping many centuries, the first theorization about the enemy in penal scholarship—albeit very crudely—is due to Rafael Garofalo, who affirmed that penal science has as its object defense against the *natural enemies of society*[34] and that indulgence by judges was no more than *the triumph of logic achieved at the expense of social security and morality.*[35] *In the eyes of the people the codes, the proceedings and even Judicial Power, seem to have reached an agreement to protect the criminal against society, better than society against the criminal.*[36] Garofalo defined the enemy through the *recta ratio* of *those civilized peoples, of the superior races of humanity, with an exception made for those degenerate tribes that represent evildoers in society.*[37] As a faithful follower of Spencer,[38] he affirmed that society needed to produce an equivalent to Darwin's natural selection,[39] and thus, the enemies needed to be eliminated, which he justified with the sharp remark that *through a slaughter on the battlefield the nation defends itself against its external enemies; through a capital execution, against its interior enemies.*[40]

But leaving aside such crudities, it is unquestionable that the most refined elaboration comes from the Twentieth Century and seems in good measure to be the penal reflection of Schmitt's theories, a task carried out by Mezger, who was the best-known German Neo-Kantian criminalist in the Spanish-speaking world.[41] His thesis on *culpability due to conducting life* is a clear manifestation of the author's criminal law: those who conduct themselves as enemies gradually reduce their scope of decisions, and thus, their crime; if it was not reproachable *in acto*, it was *in causa*, which corresponds to reproaching them for all of the choices of their existence that have culminated in that act. The offense is not reproached, but the construction of the personality that this offense expresses, in the form of an existential *action libera in causa.* Hence, he is coherent in affirming that the stranger the act is to the personality of the agent, the less reproachable it is, and vice-versa.[42]

Mezgerian idealism directly sought the enemy personality to neutralize it. Mezger participated with Franz Exner in preparing the project on *strangers to the community (Gemeinschaftsfremde),* destined to be eliminated in the concentration camps and who were certainly the same persons who, according to the positivists, incurred the status of dangerousness without wrongdoing.[43]

Mezger wavered between the concept of *enmity towards law (Rechtsfeindlichkeit)* and *blindness towards law (Rechtsblindheit),* in other worlds, between considering as an enemy one who *felt* in a manner contrary to the state that was regenerating racially with Nazism, meaning, purifying itself in order to reestablish the hegemony of the superior race,[44] or one who *did not see* that regeneration. This meant he oscillated between Garofalo and Plato and used both terms successively. For Mezger *enmity towards law* supplied the effective knowledge of the anti-judiciality of the crime: *The judicial blindness of the author refers to an attitude that is not in agreement with the* healthy intuition *of the public regarding the just and the unjust, so that, under normal conditions, one should not excuse, but, to the contrary, configure the foundation for punishment.*[45] Not only should one stress the reference to *the healthy intuition of the people* (a Nazi formula of the analogy, which Mezger also participated actively in introducing into legislation[46]), but—as has been correctly noted—the examples used to illustrate the concept are terrifying: the *outrages against the race* (sexual relations between Germans and Jews, punished by death), abortion and sodomy.[47]

All of Mezger's construction is based on the idea of an *enemy of the law* who, in reality is an enemy of the values imposed by an omnipotent state, and who is not any offender, but one who shows with his or her life conduct (*Lebensfürhrung*) a personality that is incompatible with those values that make up a racially purified superior race (settled on *soil* and *race*). The *stranger to the community* was one who *because of his personality or form of conducting his life, especially due to his extraordinary defects in understanding or of character will be incapable of fulfilling with this own forces the minimal demands of the community of the people.*[48] From that definition and from the precise definition that follow in this distressing text, one deduces that the strangers were not the authors of serious crimes, but of those who bothered people, those who disturbed the peace, those who did not work, the drunkards, those who made up the positivist *evil life.* For them Mezger proposes the extension of police law, not of criminal law.

The idea that the *stranger* should be submitted to administrative law and not criminal law may be found in Hegel. Given that every judicial relation presupposes freedom of the will, someone without self-awareness cannot enter into that relation, since *the field of law is the spiritual, and its precise place and starting point is the will, which is free, so that liberty constitutes its substance and determination; and the system of Law is the kingdom of freedom realize realized, the world of the spirit expressed by itself, as in a second nature.*"[49] From that starting point, it is easy to affirm that the *stranger* is not *self-conscious*, and because of that does not share that *second nature*, which is judicial; from that there is just one step to convert such a person into an enemy as one who is *refractory*. It is fair to recognize that Hegel himself did not go that route, but his pejorative expressive regarding colonized cultures allow one to infer it.[50]

It is clear that for Mezger—and perhaps for Hegel, or at least for some Hegelians—the *strangers* or *enemies* are excluded from criminal law and administrative treatment is reserved for them. It is a matter of perspectives to establish if they propose two criminal laws (ordinary or common and for *strangers*) or if it is a question of a single criminal law and the rest is police law, but *it is certain that the punitive power of the state is split in two: one for common people and the other for the strangers, who are the enemies.*

THE FRUSTRATION OF THE ASPIRATION FOR A NON-AUTHORITARIAN ENEMY CRIMINAL LAW

We have seen the development that the thesis of the enemy has had from its Hobbesian starting point to its development in the following centuries: denial of the right to resistance in Kant, policy reformulation in Schmitt and the repressive pathology of Mezger. It is appropriate to ask if Jakobs' intent in going back to Hobbes and Kant offers a development that will guarantee a different and non-authoritarian line.

In principle, Jakobs starts by recognizing a reality, which is the legislation of *fighting* that is spreading around the world in these days: war or struggle against organized crime, serious crimes, sexual criminality, corruption, drugs, economic criminality, terrorism, etc. In each country one might recognized laws analogous to those that Jakobs mentions in Germany and some much less cautious. Faced with that reality, he proposes to assume and separate this criminal law of *fighting,* meaning of the *enemy*, from criminal law for the *citizen*. The professor from Bonn alleges that *a clearly delimited criminal law for the enemy is less dangerous, from the perspective of a State of Law, than mingling* all *of criminal law with fragments of regulations that should be in a criminal law of the enemy.*[51] In that way, he tries to separately package this punitive power with its intended containment to save at least part of criminal law, which would remain faithful to traditional liberal criminal law. The proposal gives the impression that, faced with the advance of criminal law of the enemy, he resigns himself and assumes it as reality, intending only to isolate it in order to set a limit.

In principle, it is not possible to ignore the fact that the various forms of authoritarianism take advantage of laws for *fighting, protecting and defending,* meaning the frontalist[52] laws that intended to set up a criminal law of the enemy.[53] The circumstance that laws of this nature are currently being propagated is also an unquestionable fact. Nonetheless, as for resigned acceptance of reality it is worth remembering the objection that Rousseau formulated to the method of Grotius: *Grotius denies*—he said—*that the human powers have been established for the benefit of the governed, citing slavery as an example. His constant manner of reasoning is to always establish the fact as the source of the law.*[54] In effect: the circumstance that there have been slaves, in other words, that the governments have not been established for the benefit of the governed, does not indicate that one should not establish things that way nor that it is not desirable; likewise, the circumstances in which authoritarian laws are propagated does not oblige us to legitimate them.

A second consideration is that separation of both *criminal laws* is impracticable, since Jakobs himself recognizes that it is a question of a polarity and that a component of enemy criminal law exists even in the more common sentences. In the best case, one could only separate the very notorious, obvious or declared suppositions, meaning that separation would depend upon a question of degree that would not guarantee one would avoid contamination. On the other hand, authoritarian criminal law has always been installed as *exceptional* and soon become *commonplace.*

Accepting—merely *ad argumentandum*—the possibility of keeping the so-called enemy criminal law or containment law separate, one should ask who defines its extent, in other words, *who decides who the enemies are*. The answer does not seem very different from that of Schmitt, except that the latter postulates it as a proper and exclusive function of politics and Jakobs limits himself to recognizing it as a reality. That possibility of unlimited political definition of the enemy eliminates every guarantee that it will not reach the extremes that Mezger rationalized during his days. Jakobs undoubtedly does not have that in mind, but in his proposal these delirious extensive pathologies do not crash against any safe dike.

To admit—as Jakobs does—the legitimacy of a war to persecute delinquents, at the cost of the lives of innocents who suffer the consequences of those attacks, in a direct reference to the Iraq war, opens up the way for unlimited international anarchy and implies a serious historical retrogression: the First World War also had a crime as a pretext (the assassination of the Austrian archduke and his wife). Not to mention the fact that transporting the same criteria to supposed internal or civil wars gives rise to the famous *dirty war*, which was the discourse for legitimating state terrorism in the name of national during the 1970s.

It should be noted that every state of law recognizes the possibility of an eventual need for exercising coercive power as mere contention, but they have constitutionally limited the state of siege, of blockade or of exception, provided for in the constitutions with the appropriate precautions. It was exactly through ignoring those precautions that there were abuses absurdly beyond limits of those few provisions to try and legitimate the *dirty wars* outside of criminal law. In other words, there was the pretext that major sentences depriving persons of freedom decided by the dictators were administrative detentions enabled by exceptional or emergency dispositions. However, neither outside nor inside criminal law is there any constitutional authorization to exert pure containment power, so that the limited constitutional provisions for the states of exception correctly understood, meaning within the strict limits and conditions established in the supreme texts cannot be invoked in such cases.

Nor is the difference that Jakobs establishes regarding international criminal law clear. That author affirms that such law has a marked character of enemy criminal law, and that it exercises punitive power not to reaffirm the validity of the norm but to establish its validity. We believe we understand that he refers to the cases in which international courts condemn in the absence of action by national courts, meaning that the sentences imposed by international courts would have the objective of establishing the internal validity of the norm and not of ratifying it. Independently of Jakobs' theory of the sentence itself, we believe that such an opinion derives from the thesis of *double law,* since from the perspective of *single law* the norm is valid and if it is not applied by national judges, an international court will apply it, or, according to the universal principle, any court in the world. No validity is established with this, but a norm valid in both international and internal law is applied.

CONSEQUENCES OF THE SACRALIZATION OF THE DYNAMICS OF PUNITIVE POWER

Parmenides and Heraclitus mark the eternal pendulum of thought regarding the being of all things, but also of each thing. Although we insist that we do not consider his thesis on enemy criminal law as necessarily linked to its dogmatic construction, it is possible to observe that in all of Jakobs' theorizations there are two methodological characteristics that throw a negative weight on this theme: (a) One is his tendency to enshrine or immobilize a Parmenidic search for security. One may clearly observe this in his sacralizing of social roles as a criterion of objective imputation. The roles lose all of their dynamism, and become as if photographed as if subsuming did not capture the images cinematographically but instantaneously. (b) Another is his tendency to assume the facts by considering them legitimating due to the mere fact of their being.

The characteristics determine—on the one hand—that Jakobs assume the reality of authoritarian laws as a mere datum and not question the supposed necessity for an intended enemy criminal law, and on the other hand, that he ignore the dynamics of power in a state of law, dealing with statically resolving a question of dialectical nature. The state of law always encapsulates a state of police,[55] and the pressures of the latter sometimes translate into authoritarian laws, with science having the function of knowing criminal law in order to be able to contain or neutralize such laws. In that way, every real or historical state of law makes use of judicial power programmed by knowledge of criminal law in order to contain the police state that remains in its breast in a relation involving tension.

To intend to compartmentalize forces that permanently interact in a contrary fashion when one of them tends to expands its limits and the other constitutes precisely its containment leads to an error of perception whose results may be tragic, for *while it tends to free from all containment the pressures of the police state, it leaves the judicial power of containment of the state of law without a function.* That is the greatest risk of a *Parmenidic* vision of punitive power, which generates a perceptive distortion that makes it possible to legitimate the power of the police state and neutralize the containment function of the state of law.

NOTES

1. He formulates a brief reference to the them in *La ciencia de derecho penal ante las exigencias del presente*, Trans. by Teresa Manso Porto, in "Revista Peruana de Ciencias Penales," año VII-VIII edición especial nº 12, and especially in *Bürgerstrafrecht und Feindstrafrecht*, en HRRS, March 2004, Spanish translation in Günther Jakobs/Manuel Cancio Meliá, *Derecho Penal del enemigo*, Cuadernos Civitas, Madrid, 2003.

2. Among many, Albin Eser, en Eser/Hassemer/Burkhardt, *La ciencia of criminal law ante el nuevo milenio* (Francisco Muñoz Conde, coordinador), Valencia, 2004, p. 472.

3. Also, among many, Lúcio Antônio Chamon Junior, *Do giro finalista ao funcionalismo penal, Embates de perspectivas dogmáticas decadentes*, Porto Alegre, 2004. From this title and the criticism pointed out in the previous note one concludes that the debates are proceeding in a tone that somewhat excedes that which is habitual in our discipline.

4. Not to question the general or idealist preventive theory that deals with the sentence, but either of these theories can be combined with sentences that each one singularly contains.

5. It seems better to maintain that only murderers are enemies, but not every delinquent. At least in Rousseau that seems deducible in Chapter V of Book II that Jakobs

cites, without mentioning the contradictions in Rousseau himself, who in Chapter IV of Book I affirms that *a State may not have as an enemy anything but another State, and not men, siince one cannot set up relations between things of diverse natures.* In fact, he states that without a declaration of war *there are no enemies, but only bandoliers.*

6. Cf., for example, Wilhelm Windelband, *Historia de la filosofía, La filosofía del iluminismo*, México, 1948, pp. 60 and ss.; Alfred Verdross, *La filosofía del derecho del mundo occidental, Visión panorámica de sus fundamentos and principales problemas*, México, 1962, pp.179 and ss.; Frederick Copleston, *Historia de la filosofía*, Barcelona, 1983, vol. V, pp. 122 and ss.; M. Federico Sciacca, *Historia de la filosofía*, Barcelona, 1966, pp. 335 and ss.; Émile Bréhier, *Historia de la filosofía*, Bs. As., T.II, pp. 617 and ss.; N. Abbagnano, *Historia de la filosofía*, Bacelona, 1973, II, pp. 185 and ss.

7. *Leviathan*, 1, 8, 10.

8. Ibid, 1, 13.

9. Ibid, 1, 18.

10. Ibid, 2, 28.

11. John Locke, *Ensayo sobre el gobierno civil*, 2, 6.

12. *Zum ewigen Frieden*, en *Werkausgabe, herausgegeben von W. Weischedel*, Frankfurt, 1977, T. XI, p. 203.

13. *Werkausgabe* VIII, *Die Metaphysik der Sitten*, p. 756.

14. *Anti-Hobbes oder über die Grenzen der höchsten Gewalt und das Zwangsrecht der Bürger gegen den Oberherrn*, Erfurt, 1798.

15. The reference to Kant in chapter 1 is unquestionable 1. Also, the note in which he expressly cites Kant criticizing his position regarding changing of the constitution. (chap. 3). He takes care to respectfully separate Kant from Hobbes regarding the inviolabity of the sovereing in chap. 6. It is clear that Feuerbach was twenty-three years old when he wrote *Anti-Hobbes* and could not openly confront the prestige of the old and respected Kant.

16. See Erik Wolf, *Grosse Rechsdenker*, Tübingen, 1951, p. 543; also the investigation by Mario A. Cattaneo, *Anselm Feuerbach, filosofo e giurista liberale*, Milano, 1970.

17. Regarding Schmitt's Hobbesianism, Matthias Kaufmann, *¿Derecho sin reglas?*, Barcelona, 1989, p. 126.

18. Although Schmitt was the *Kronjurist* of the *Dritte Reich* (Cf. Joseph W. Bendersky, *Carl Schmitt teorico del Reich*, Bologna, 1989), his reference regarding the question of the enemy is noted without meaning any pejorative intention, since Schmitt's ideas were taken up by many critics of the bourgeois liberal state with different political persuasions and including some who openly opposed to his politics. In that sense one may see the presentation by José Arico to *El concepto de lo politico* that we cite; also Luciano Albanese, *Schmitt*, Editori Laterza, 1996, p. 7; Julio Pinto, *Carl Schmitt y reivindicación de la política*, La Plata, 2000, p. 179.

19. Carl Schmitt, *El concepto de lo político*, Ediciones Folios, México, 1985.

20. Schmitt, p. 23.

21. We respect the translation that we have cited, but it should be observed that the word Schmitt uses is *Fremde*, *stranger*, in other words, the same that Mezger would soon use, Cf. infra n° 5.

22. Schmitt, p. 23.
23. Ibidem.
24. Ibid, p. 25.
25. Ibid, p. 30.
26. Ibid, p. 51.
27. In that regard he cites Lorenz von Stein, p. 44. That is linked to his proposal about the custody of the Constitution: Carlo Schmitt, *Il custode della Costituzione*, Giuffré, Milano, 1988.
28. The fall of the Ancien Régime is attributed to the illusion of human goodness, in that it was unable to perceive the menace of its hated French Revolution.
29. *El concepto de lo político*, cit., p. 61.
30. Ibid, p. 68.
31. See Schmitt,*Der Hüter der Verfassung*, 1929; Italian trans., *Il custode della Costituzione*, cit.; Spanish version, *La defensa de la Constitución*, Madrid, 1983; Hans Kelsen, *¿Quién debe ser el defensor de la Constitución?*, Madrid, 1995.
32. This Schmitt intended to save by making a hierarchy of constitutional norms, which one may observe in his concept of the constitution as a plurality of laws: Schmitt, *Teoría de la Constitución*, Madrid, 1992, p. 37.
33. *Las Leys*, IX (Platón, "Obras Completas", Bib. Ameba, Bs. As., 1967, T. IV, p. 95 and ss.).
34. R. Garofalo, *La criminología*, Trans. by Pedro Dorado Montero, Madrid, s.d., p. 7, 11, 14 and 15.
35. Ibid, p. 11.
36. Ibid, p. 15.
37. Ibid, p. 102.
38. He considered him "the greatest of the contemporary philosophers," idem, p. 97.
39. Ibid, p. 326. That proposal was taken up again by Nazism: Helmut Nicolai, *Die rassengesetzliche Rechtslehre, Grundzüge e. nazionalsozialist. Rechtsphilosophie*, München, 1932.
40. Ibid, p. 133; p. 59 de la 2ª Italian ed., Torino, 1891.
41. It is true, by the way, that liberal Neo-Kantions such as Max Ernst Mayer and Hellmuth von Weber were not translated. Gustav Radbruch himself—as was the case with M.E. Mayer—was translated by legal philosphers, but not by the penalists.
42. We have presented criticism of these theses in *Teoría del delito*, Bs. As., 1973, pp. 534-541 and in *Manual de Derecho Penal*, Bs. As., 1977, pp. 446-448. Bettiol defended his position from a different angle, from a philosophical perspective and without the particular meaning of Mezger, Cf. his response to our criticism in Giuseppe Bettiol, *Gli ultimi scritti 1980-1982 e la lezione di congedo 6.See82*, CEDAM, Padova, 1984, p. 13.
43. New light is being shed on this draft project through a detailed investigation by Francisco Muñoz Conde, *Edmund Mezger y derecho criminal de su tiempo. Estudios sobre criminal law en el nacionalsocialismo*, Valencia, 2003; this project and the concrete proposal by Mezger are also examined by Michael Burleigh/Wolfgang Wippermann, *Lo Stato razziale, Germania 1933-1945*, Rizzoli, 1992, p. 158.

44. He expresses this clearly in the first and last chapters of this *Criminología*, Editorial Revista de Derecho Privado, Madrid, s.d., pp. 3 and 284.

45. Mezger, E., *Rechtsirrtum und Rechtsblindheit*, in "Probleme der Strafrechtserneuerung, Fest. f. Kohlrausch", Berlin, 1944, pp. 180-198 (p. 197-198).

46. On his participation in the reform, Muñoz Conde, op. cit., p. 85.

47. Cf. Muñoz Conde, op. cit., p. 145.

48. Muñoz Conde, op. cit., p. 193.

49. Hegel, *Filosofía del derecho*, México, 1985, pp. 31-32.

50. Hegel, *Lecciones sobre la filosofía de la historia universal*, Madrid, 1980, pp. 169, 177, 183, 215, 354, 596, 657.

51. Jakobs, op.cit., 4ª conclusion in the summary.

52. On the concept of "frontality" in court and authoritarian art, Arnold Hauser, *Historia social de la literatura and el arte*, Madrid, 1969, I, pp. 64-66.

53. See e.g., las *strafrechtliche Nebengesetze* of the National Socialism that Dalcke reproduces, *Strafrecht und Strafverfahren*, Berlin, 1938, pp. 385 and ss.

54. Rousseau, *Contrato social*, I, 2.

55. Cf. Merkl, A., *Teoría general del derecho administrative*, México, 1980, pp. 325 and ss.

Chapter Six

Girardin

Abolitionism between the Second Empire and the Third French Republic

Eugenio Raúl Zaffaroni

VARIABLES OF PUNITIVE POWER

When one speaks today of *penal abolitionism* to indicate the set of movements that intend to abolish punitive power, it is common to mention as forerunners the anarchists and socialists of the Nineteenth and even the Eighteenth Centuries, but there is no mention of the very valuable contribution of an author who was not affiliated to those political currents but, to the contrary, was closer to conservative positions, to the point of being considered an opportunist to some degree. This was Èmile de Girardin, who wrote a quite singular abolitionist book in 1868 and published it in 1871.[1]

Girardin was a French journalist who was born in Paris in 1806 and died in the same city in 1881. He wrote several works for the theater, including one in collaboration with Alexandre Dumas (h). In 1836 he founded *La Presse,* which was the first large circulation and low-price daily, which he supported at Thiers until 1846.[2] The modern mass-circulation press was inaugurated precisely with the daily founded by Girardin, who thanks to small advertisements and publicity, was sold at half the price of the other dailies. He was thus the initiator of the modern press, which raised serious polemics in the journalistic world. Armand Carrel, founder of the *National* in 1830 and converted to militant republicanism, considered himself offended because a journalist had converted daily journalism into a commercial issue, and due to that, challenged Girardin to a duel, losing his life in that encounter.[3]

Girardin was a deputy in 1834 and in 1849 a member of the legislative assembly. He was expelled after the *coup d'état* of December 2, 1851 and on his return to France went back to publishing *La Presse* and founded the daily *La liberté,* through which he rose in defense of the liberal empire, to soon support the Thiers government in *Le Moniteur universel* and *Le petit Journal* and next attack Mac-Mahon and De Broglie in *La France.* He was married to a famous writer: Delphine Gay (1804-1855).

His abolitionist book of 1871 is cited very rarely. Matteoti refers to it as one of the few works to not only de-legitimate aggravation due to relapse, but to dare to directly deny the right to punish.[4] We believe that it is worthwhile to dust off this old book, because in highlighting the abolitionist position of someone who has no ties to anarchical and utopian thought one disarms the myth that de-legitimization of punitive power is an issue only for authors with those tendencies in the Nineteenth Century and Nordic Europeans in the second half of the Twentieth Century. With Girardin we find ourselves before a French politician, a singularly successful journalist, who supports abolition with arguments that today may seem someone curious, but that on the other hand are simply the thoughts of a liberal astounded by the devastating panorama presented by the structural characteristics of the exercise of penal repression. On the book's cover, under the title appears an engraving of a crucifix, which is explained in the text, when Jesus Christ is considered as the most notable victim of the power that de-legitimates and MENTA as useless in its pages.

Since the book was published, more than one hundred and thirty years ago, only the variable circumstances of punitive power have changed, but its structural traits continued unaltered—it could not be any other way—and in its regard, the author's observations conserve all of their validity and are sometimes notably fresh and current.

The exposition is quite coherent and opens with a reflection on liberty that occupies almost the entire preface. He remembers an old polemic from 1850, in which he maintained that between the freedom to *say anything* and the freedom to *do anything* there is an enormous difference, because *saying has nothing to do with doing.* He expresses that he immediately had major doubts in this regard and twenty years later—when he was writing the book—he became convinced that freedom is one and indivisible. *If the freedom to think implies the freedom to say, the freedom to say implies the freedom to do. Should I then admit the freedom to do evil? And why should I not admit it, if after having admitted the freedom to think evil, I admit the freedom to speak evil? But then, in what does society DEVIENE?*[5] That is the question I have thought about for twenty years, to conclude that *freedom is unique and indivisible and that when one wants to divide it, freedom ceases and arbitrariness appears.*[6]

He affirms that he reached that conclusion as the result of what today we would call cultural relativism and that in his words he considers the testimony of history: what is forbidden in one country is not forbidden in another; that which one religion sanctifies another condemns; that which under one name is a crime ceases to be so with a change in name. And he adds that the last happens with homicides and with the collective robberies known under the name of *war. Do the individual homicides and robberies perchance make more blood run than the collective ones for which triumphant arches are raised?* He maintains that if war and conquest did not exist, it would certainly be maintained that they were incompatible with the state of society, meaning that, if society exists with similar impunity, would it also exist with that of homicide and of individual robbery.[7] Society without war *would not lose manpower with military service, taxes would greatly reduce, public debt would be quickly amortized and society would be the kingdom of science, of liberty, of the production of wealth, instead of being that of violence, oppression, destruction and misery.*[8] When war and conquest close their schools of death and robbery, the general wellbeing would make crimes of homicide and robbery on an individual level completely rare.

He makes the notoriously up-to-date statement that *no one wants to rob when he can make more with his work that he would make with robbery. If robbery was not punished, someone who robbed with impunity could also be robbed with impunity. What, then, would be the advantage of robbing?*[9] If robbery ceased feeding homicides, they would be reduced to a few cases of derangement.[10]

He reaffirms that the three freedoms (of thinking, speaking and doing) are inseparable, because the freedom to think is unable to do that without that of speaking, which is necessary to demonstrate error, and that is inconceivable without the freedom to doing and verify the inconsequence. *The act is necessary to verify the world, as that is to verify the thought.*[11] That liberty is indispensable for people to learn how to think well, and *one who thinks well does not act badly: no one pretends that 2 plus 2 will be 5, when they know it will be 4. In that way man is made in the image of civilization. We should not punish a man without instructing him.*[12] It is through the transformation of society that man will be transformed. What will this transformation be? He answers that it will be *that which logic prescribes, so that the kingdom of indivisible freedom may be the kingdom of human reason.*[13] He asks if that transformation will be carried out violently and with a coup or scientifically and progressively, and responds by inclining towards the latter alternative, which today would be defined as *reformist.* Girardin is not an unreflective utopian, but perceives the long road ahead, resignedly observing that the justice of an idea is independent of the means for applying it: that steam is a force is one thing, but finding someone who will invent the boiler and not become discouraged by the explosions and failures is another. Defending the idea that man, the brother of man, does not have the right to sentence him, that society does not have the right to employ the barbaric methods that it uses and that there are better ways to contain the idiot and the madman, implies provoking a first reaction of incredulity, which will give way to reflection that will generate objections, which, for their part, will engender the solutions.[14] *And when society lives without jail keepers and executioners, with fewer homicides and robbers, it will seem as is their existence today without slaves or servants, considering that for centuries it was maintained that such would be absolutely impossible.*[15] Consequently, he maintains that he is publishing his book without the least hope of watching the triumph of his ideas, but hopes to appeal to meditation by thinkers and to the controversy of journalists about the most important question of his time, which is the foundation of liberty.[16] With a certain degree of omnipotence he trusts that the sole power of the truth of his idea will regenerate the world after his death. Since he represents a relatively conservative point of view, he makes it clear that he is not criticizing for the sake of criticizing, that he never criticizes an existing institution without thinking about what should substitute it, that if he questions the legitimacy of the right to punish, he does so to substitute a defective wheel in the social apparatus with another that is simpler and stronger. He wishes to do with freedom what Watt and Fulton did with steam; they were not the discoverers, but simply the ones harnessing its strength.[17] *Freedom has won the right to think and shortly later won the speak and print what it thinks, but it is incomplete, because for fullness it lacks the right to do, with no other limit than reason exercised through reason.*[18] He closes Aristotelically regarding the reform that he is proposing: *neither timidity nor temerity.*[19]

In the first chapter (*On penal servitude*) he demonstrates that the sentence is an evil aftertaste of slavery. *The corporal punishments, the afflictive punishments, are the last link in the long and heavy chain of slavery, why is exactly why they are called "penal servitude."*[20] Girardin is not precisely timid, since he makes it plain that with this work he is continuing the work of Beccaria, who had fallen short in limiting penal servitude, so that now it is he who is responsible for perfecting its de-legitimization, now against all penal servitude. *The penalty has a civil origin. In Rome the free citizen who had challenged the law's severity was declared a slave of the sentence, "servus poenae." That slavery stripped him of his inviolability.*[21] With that recourse, the Roman punitive power applied slave sentences to citizens. In France the assimilation of the noble with the servant for the same purposes was progressively produced.

Girardin cites Du Boys[22] to reaffirm that the origin of the sentence was to satisfy a desire for vengeance. He said that vengeance follows composition, recognizing that the latter has a pacifying effect and that it amounts to a reconciliation, that the medieval asylum was an imitation of the Greek and Roman asylum and that *the rigor of the sentence increases with the spirit of domination.*[23] He makes a lengthy case against the dissuasive effect of the atrocity of tortures, showing with historical data that where the laws have been harsher, crimes have multiplied. He establishes periods, affirming that there was a period in which there was not punishment in Europe and everything was private vengeance, a second moment in which punishments were cruel and a third in which they became milder, which would be that of Beccaria. He proposes a fourth, in which the sentences should disappear. It is interesting to note that this division into periods generally coincides with what was used by criminological positivism a few years later, especially by Ferri, and repeated up to the present (private vengeance, public vengeance, humanization, and for the Ferrian positivists, *the scientific period,* which Girardin replaces with disappearance.

He observes that Beccaria defends the right to punish in the name of utility, and affirms that in the same vein (more than that of justice) he will have to deny it.[24] He maintains that corporal punishment is the greatest obstacle that civilization has encountered in its progress,[25] to the point of citing the critique of slavery formulated by Montesquieu and affirming that it is completely valid for penal servitude. He thus concludes that the punishment cannot be justified through its legitimacy or through its utility.[26]

LEGITIMACY OF THE RIGHT TO PUNISH

In the second chapter (*On the legitimacy of the right to punish*) he makes use of the arguments that de-legitimize punishment. *Outside to the narrow boundary of legitimate offense—he affirms—society does not recognize that one man has the right to punish another. If man does not have the right to punish, by what right does society have it? If society has received it from God, let it start by demonstrating the existence of God and then prove that he has delegated that right to it. If society in itself does not have it, given the form in which it exercises it, how can it legitimate having it for use? If this use has not been more than a long and cruel abuse, more useful for barbarity and oppression that for civilization and liberty, on what will it base its legitimacy? Nothing testifies to such legitimacy, but everything confirms this abuse. There is not one page in history that has not been stained by blood.*[27] *What is history but the bloody martyrology of countless victims sacrificed by ignorance, superstition, tyranny, cruelty, iniquity, armed with the right to punish.* He adds that to deny these doubts it would be necessary to resurrect from their tombs the *guilty immortals,* at whose head is Jesus Christ. He vehemently rejects the social contract argument (Beccaria, Hobbes, Locke, Vattel)[28] and also that the right to punish derives from legitimate defense (Blackstone, Romagnosi, Carmigani),[29] as well as the thesis of social defense (Beccaria, Rossi), affirming that society defends itself by improving things and not appealing to reproducing violence.[30] To the reactionary thesis—which even so is not omitted from the unexpressed thoughts of many respectable persons in our days—of Leibnitz and Joseph de Maistre, who deduce the legitimacy of expiation, he answers, among other things, that moral deformities exist in nature in the same way as physical ones, but asks how the state can want expiation when it glorifies in the name of conquest the same things it punishes in individuals. If required military service is no more than required instruction in murder under penalty of the firing squad for those who refuse, war is the school of all crimes and all excesses. *Killing a man and stealing his money is a criminal act punished by justice. Killing five hundred thousand men and stealing the soil on which they were born is a glorious act immortalized by history*[31]. *If crime is punished in individuals, no one punishes the crimes committed by state against state or people against people, there is no expiation in that regard. With what authority can society demand expiation if it is guiltier itself?* The only expiation he admits is that of reparation, which for robbery is restitution, but *the freedom that is taken from the thief does not restore the money to the victim, nor does the life that is taken from the murderer restore the life of the victim.*[32] To Guizot and Cousin, who maintain that legitimacy derives from justice, he answers that for that justice would need to be single and universal and not local as is now the case, where what is a crime in one country is not in another. *What can one say about justice that burns heretics and wizards? What can one think of justice that punishes thinkers in the same way as it does thieves? What shall one call justice that has condemned, tortured, killed, crucified, burned, broke on the wheel, quartered, imprisoned or exiled the greatest philosophers, the most celebrated writers, the most illustrious wise men?*[33] *Justice is an expression of society, but that is not the expression of humanity. To say that punishment is a form of justice is nonsense, since a society's justice may be the form of human iniquity and a mask for barbarism.*[34] He next turns to the Kantian tallion, considering it a poor argument for a philosopher of Kant's caliber, and denies its legitimacy, also based on the arbitrariness of social laws.[35] As a result of this tour of the legitimating theses, he concludes for the illegitimacy of law to punish, and thus moves to asking about its usefulness.

In the third chapter (*On the usefulness of the right to punish*) he puts forth the opinion that punishments have no utility at all, with the curious affirmation—to which he will return more specifically on various occasions—that the only penalty that would really be useful would be the death penalty. Because of that, he maintains that Maistre was right and not Beccaria, who falls into a series of contradictions. *Logically, it is Beccaria, the death penalty critic who is wrong, and it is Joseph the Maistre, apologist for the hangman, who is right. Beccaria is inconsequent, since all of his proposals contradict each other: but de Maistre is an imposter, for supposing a God who does not exist, a creator God burning with impatience, punishing his creature with uncontrolled fury.*[36] *I do not accept either the penalty according to Beccaria or the double penalty according to de Maistre. I say double, because the condemnation pronounced by a God who judges men after death, if it accumulates with condemnation of the man judged by man, constitutes a pleonasm that violates the principle of "no bis in idem." Someone who affirms the innocence of the hangman denies the existence of God; one who affirms the existence of God denies the innocence of the hangman. The same guilty party cannot be justly punished two times for the same fault, the first time before his death and the second time after it. Joseph de Maistre is not a Christian but a pagan.*[37]

This deals with the situation of social stigmatization that weighs on people who have been freed to de-consecrate the efficacy of sentences that deprive them of freedom and highlights the paradox that the only punishment with a real negative special preventive effect would be death. If one cannot prove the usefulness of the punishment *with society having usurped the name of justice to disarm man, has the time not arrived in which man will disarm society in the deserved name of science?*[38]

In the fourth chapter (*The penal scale*) Girardin reviews the punishments in the Code Napoleón[39] and cites authors who criticize its useless complexity. For the purposes of analysis, he reclassifies them into five categories: punishments of deprivation of life, liberty, homeland, civil and family rights and of a sum of money.[40] In the fifth chapter (*One deprivation of life*), he insists in his curious affirmation concerning the death penalty, clarifying that he is against it, but that before it is suppressed the penalty of deprivation of freedom should be suppressed, meaning that abolitionism would rise on the penal scale instead of descending.[41] He maintains that the advantages of the death penalty are that it does not pervert, deprave, corrupt the enormous staff needed for execution, does not increase crime and so on. As to its irreparable character, he considers that the forced labor sentence that sickens and kills is also not reparable.[42] He highlights the contradiction between considering the life of an innocent as so valuable and having no problem in allowing states to destroy innocents so easily due to a small conflict over territory. Although he observes that the death penalty has been abolished in several countries and that its application is less and less frequent in France, he concludes that he is opposed to all corporal punishment and not only the death penalty, and that he would maintain the latter temporarily for murderers exclusively after the disappearance of the remaining sentences and until the total extinction of the punitive power.[43]

In the sixth chapter (*On deprivation of freedom*), he analyzes the complicated system of sentences depriving freedom in the Code Napoleón and formulates a critique of each one of them, beginning with a life sentence at forced labor, which he considers to be penal servitude *par excellence.*[44] He holds forth at length against the sentence of deportation, showing not only its failure in the French case but also in Australia,[45] which seems to be a reiterated them in the penal literature of his time, given the primitive confidence in that punishment as a penal substitute.[46] Regarding the temporary forced labor sentence, he says that he understands it less than lifetime sentences. He maintains that prisons are a higher school for crime, so that society is incredibly contradictory in maintaining a penal echelon system that encourages crime instead of containing it.[47] As for imprisonment, which was a sentence in which the condemned was shut up in a *maison de force* for five to ten years, he says that it is the prison preparatory school.[48] He goes on at length about the consequences of prison, about the regime, about the never resolved issue of the freed prisoners who relapse as a result of their social stigmatization,[49] and concludes that a sentence depriving one of freedom is nothing more than a death sentence slowly executed, so that its disappearance is necessary.[50]

In the seventh chapter (*On deprivation of one's country*) he criticizes the deportation sentence with the sagacious observation that if France can send its wrongdoers outside of its territory, it should have the duty of receiving foreigners on its soil.[51] It would not be remiss to remember that during Girardin's time Argentina was sending delinquents to Paraguay. In the eighth chapter (*On the deprivation of civic, civil and family rights*) he maintains that depriving persons of the condition of citizenship is indefensible and that such penalties are unnecessary, as publicity could easily fulfill the same function.[52] He occupies the ninth chapter (*On deprivation of a sum of money*) with the question of fines and reparation of damages. Regarding the first, he notes its inequity, and as for reimbursement, he recalls with admiration the old English provisions that required reparation in common with the delinquent's origin.[53]

The tenth chapter (*On the abuse of the sentence*) may be the most interesting one in the book, since it demonstrates that whenever there has been punitive power there has been of abuse of it, meaning that abuse is a structural and not conjunctional note in the exercise of punitive power. *If it is characteristic for man to generally abuse all things, it is fair to recognize that society, which has attributed to itself the right to punish, has at no time and in no country shown itself more prudent than that.*[54] He is not referring here to the ferocity of the sentences, in other words, to their magnitude, but to the acts submitted to it. The history of religious intolerance alone would fill volumes, for which reason he limits himself to citing some isolated examples, beginning with the Mosaic Law. He records that death was the punishment for killing a vulture in Egypt, for sacrilege in Athens (the case of Socrates), in Rome, for Vestals who allowed the flame to die and for Christians, especially under the decree of Diocletian, who were submitted to the punishment for high treason, meaning being burnt alive (*vivicomburium*) or handed over to the beasts (*damnatio ad bestias*). He next records the punishments for blasphemies and other sacrileges and heresies, Torquemada, the punishments of Jews for marrying non-Jews or for being served by non-Jewish servants, and the expulsion of Jews from Spain. He follows with examples and concludes that *even when the abuse of punishments did not have this incomplete numbering as an irrefutable testimony, it would be absolutely confirmed by all the sufferings inflicted on countless martyrs of their faith and of their opinion.*[55] He then moves to persecution of witchcraft and sorcery, which dates back to the Mosaic law itself (*Maleficos non patieris vivere*, the Exodus states), continues with the Greeks, in Rome with the Cornelia law and others, then moves on to medieval and modern Europe, to end with the punishments imposed on those who made attempts on the lives of monarchs through sorcery.[56] He continues by reviewing the ridiculous definitions of the crimes of *lèse majesté,* from imperial Rome until England.[57] *How many punishments and sufferings have not been caused by Slavery, without which Plato affirmed that society could not subsist.* He remembers the Spartan and Athenian laws; regarding the latter he notes that the testimony of slaves was not valid and to compensate for that failing there was recourse to torture; the *quaestio* answered by the slave under torture was valid,[58] which would also be the case in Rome. He quickly moves to the punitive powers of the *pater familiae,* the sanctions against unmarried persons and the sentences against prostitutes, condemned to death by Saint Louis in case of relapse.[59] As for gambling, he points out that it is the greatest proof of the impotence of sentences in containing human passions.[60] He records the penalty for illegal hunting, the penalties for suicides, the penalties for using tobacco in Russia, Turkey and Persia,[61] those for contraband, and regarding the latter, he reproduces a phrase from Blanqui that is quite contemporary: *Citizens owe no taxes except to the state. When you require a man to by a shirt or a sheet under the aegis of prohibition, you impose on him a task to the benefit of a manufacturer who provides him nothing in exchange.*[62] For those who believe that the severity of punishments will contain those who falsify revenue stamps, let them remember the terrible punishments threatened in the Seventeenth and Eighteenth Centuries, as well as those for contraband.[63] He also refers to the atrocious penalties for other conduct: the duel; for those who do not declare to which party they belong; for calumny; for staging a theater play; to losing the instrument used to commit the crime;

to executions of *murderous* bulls in 1313 and 1499; to excommunication of caterpillars in 1516; to Gaspar Bailly, who in the Sixteenth Century published a book on proceedings against animals[64] and the proper defense technique. He notes that failing to become an informer, *which honors a man*, has in every time and country been the subject of very serious punishment.[65] Thus it was in France, including in the Code Napoléon until 1832, for those who did not denounce crimes of lèse majesté and plots. He records the prohibitions in the Convention for emigrants,[66] the sumptuary laws (sanctions for the number of servants or animals and for eating certain foods, using certain clothes, building a new bedroom in a house, etc.). He recalls that the first German printers who took books to Paris were condemned as witches and saved themselves by fleeing[67] and the no less interesting ban on teaching any logic that was not Aristotelian,[68] restored in dictatorial Argentina. He concludes in the following manner: *After having read these very incomplete principles, how could one not agree that the annals of criminal punishment testify less of the ignorance and perversity of peoples than of the stupidity and cruelty of the governors. But they also prove that greater than the arbitrariness of the punishment is its impotence.*[69]

After rejecting as absurd the so-called specific sentences, such as cutting off the hand of a thief or a blasphemer's tongue, etc. (eleventh chapter, *On specificity in sentencing*),[70] he begins the next chapter (*On penal elimination*) with an observation that is fully relevant today: *What characterizes penal progress, much more than mitigating the sentences, is the successive impunity for acts that were considered crimes or wrongdoing, as well as their more exact, more precise determining, more founded on the truth, in other words, their definitive elimination.*[71] According to that criterion the current tendencies in penal legislation around the world would be clearly regressive, as is noted by authors who still maintain liberal lines of thinking.

Girardin relates that the annals of more civilized countries abound in extreme and cruel punishments for witchcraft and sorcery, as well as for people who believed they had the freedom to think and to express themselves, and more recently the so-called press crimes. He asks who would be to blame for those condemnations, the condemned or the judges, and concludes that *it is time to finally emerge from the penal labyrinth in which society has left humanity lost for centuries.*[72] He affirms that to do so it should start by eliminating the crimes that exist only in the imagination of ignorant peoples and backward legislators; in the second place, the numerous and unnecessary distinctions in the penal scale should be cancelled. In this way, he states, there will be a reduction in the number of wrongdoers that repression has produced and that penitentiary experience testifies to, because *punishment has never corrected others who would have been corrected without it, because of the return of their absent conscience;*[73] instead, he maintains that punishment has often impeded correction. *Repression*—he affirms—*is a pillow on which society has slept for too long. If it delays in awakening, it will be swallowed by the revolution that is undermining the soil on which we have carelessly built or dwellings, an implacable revolution, which we can only escape through a radical reform, one of whose first steps must be penal reform. They are blind who do not see that the prisons that tranquilize us are the headquarters for our threat. What is the first act of the victorious crowds? Is it not freeing the detained, bringing them into the ranks and sometimes making them chiefs? Having nothing to lose, they risk everything: there is no excess, it has been seen, which will detain them.*[74] He roundly affirms that the time for *legal repression* has ended and the time has arrived for *penal elimination*. That elimination will not be excessively hasty or excessively radical. Until the day for the definitive abolition of all corporal punishment, of all of the different penalties of penal publicity and of the proportional fine for the fortune certified by the tax transformed into insurance, there should be no more than one crime, homicide, and a single sentence, death.[75] He continues by demonstrating how various criminalized conflicts could be resolved without punishment; although some of his solutions are simplistic, others make sense, broadly speaking: one prevents corruption of public employees through an effective control that will make it almost impossible; if illegal arrests are still possible, it is the fault of society. As for robbery, he reasons that after persecution of heretics was abandoned in France the number of Protestants diminished, the same as happened with witches and sorcerers, and finally, he observes that when the punitive power is interrupted violently after each revolution, far from increasing, homicides and robberies diminish.[76]

He maintains something that seems to occur in our daily reality: *a society offers more security when it has fewer criminal laws*[77] and even though he does not believe that the punitive power can disappear very rapidly, he at any rate believes that one should ponder the major faults that produce punishment, which are people who are freed and recidivists.[78] Girardin did not perceive that the penal system provokes reproduction because it needs a clientele to feed itself, but he hit the nail on the head regarding the phenomenon of client reproduction. In the words of his time, given that the problem of freed prisoners has no solution, he follows Montesquieu in affirming that a good state should dedicate more time to preventing crime than to punishing it, thus concluding that all corporal punishment should disappear,[79] except that of death, whose disappearance he reserved for the end, because if was not reproducing.

In the thirteenth chapter, (*On attenuation of sentences*) he says that *attenuating sentences, their short duration, can seduce those who believe they have the power to correct the guilty, but it is an illusion that will not be shared and that will be rejected by those who have a firm conviction based on in-depth study that the sentences, whatever they are, pervert the condemned instead of correcting them.*[80] He cites several authors who make it clear that the moral state of France in the era of cruel sentences was not superior to that of their own time.[81] Although he does believe that attenuated sentences are positive from the point of view of humanity, society and morals as a real penal progress, it should still not be thought that they are more effective than cruel sentences, meaning that he concludes that neither is effective.[82] The great problem that Girardin poses for punitive intervention is what sociology in the Twentieth Century called *secondary deviation:* his great problem is the freed prisoner, whom he calls the *soldier of all revolutions*,[83] who represents a greater threat on leaving prison than on entering, which he reaffirms with numerous opinions. *If it is certain that freedom leads to recidivism, if it is true that corporate punishment is converted into a school for perversion and revolution, in order for it to cease being a school for cruelty and tyranny, we must curb it.*[84]

After concluding the de-legitimating critique of punitive power in the *first book* of his work, Girardin dedicates the *second book* to construction, meaning to imagining society without corporal punishment. The first chapter of this second book (*On penal publicity*) is dedicated to demonstrating how social sanctions can adequately replace formal sentences with much less artificiality and greater benefit. *Human freedom and corporal punishment are two terms that exclude each other; but if there is a radical incompatibility between indivisible liberty and legal penalty, there is not between indivisible liberty and penal publicity.*[85] Publicity is the necessary presupposition for social sanctions, the true natural penalties, to work. There are many social acts—says Girardin—that are punished through contempt, hatred, misery, ruin and lack of consideration, and that are not brought to the judges' attention. In other words, he proposes publicity that will free conflicts so as to face social sanctions. *The penalty that I propose is not some invented penalty, it has nothing arbitrary about it, it is the inherent consequence of the action itself, it is this action that is the body's shadow, it is what should be, it is publicity, no more, no less. As gravity is a law, publicity is as well. Publicity is to the social order what light is to the physical order.*[86]

As to the inevitable objection that without a formal penalty there would be an increase in crime, he maintains firmly and very modernly that criminality and punishment are two independent terms,[87] which he proves with abundant data from his time. The independence of the two variables is thus not a new ascertainment at all, even though it is always denied by judicial penal discourse.

In order to orchestrate publicity, Girardin proposed a *life record*, which was a sort of letter that citizens should carry, in which would be recorded the entire course of their existence and condemnations would be noted. It was a sort of record of repeated debtors that was quite impracticable in its time. The book includes a detachable page with the model, albeit an ingenuous one, which the author imagined for receiving the data. He supposes that he will be accused of trying to bring back branding and defends himself by saying that this would be a mark transformed by society and that it would exclude barbarity. He asks wrong there would be in persons who had blotted their life record receiving a corresponding social sanction. He cites Montesquieu and Rousseau in supporting the efficacy of his proposal and ends by asking: *and giving as the only answer to crime committed that of crime recorded, what will society do?* And he responds that the subject will *be reproached by his family, his community and his birthplace, all of them, and cannot elude this reproach any more than he can elude his shadow*[88]. He recognizes that in some manner he is proposing reestablishment of the sentence of voluntary exile, in other words, of exclusion from society. The only acts that he temporarily leaves out of his proposal for publicly marking faults in a record system and leaving them freed for social sanctions were homicides, for which he proposes to temporarily maintain the death penalty until it could disappear, taking into account that its frequency was on the wane in France.

In this aspect, Girardin's position was extremely interesting, since starting with a reality of penal scales that was crowned by the death sentence for murder, he was against having abolition begin with the death penalty and inverted his proposal, meaning that he first opposed eliminating corporal punishments and shortly after that eliminating the death penalty. He expresses himself in a manner that criminology would later recover and present as innovative with the sociological critique of the total institutions of the 1960s, and he expresses himself in the following manner on the transitory moment before disappearance of the death penalty. *Experience proves that every penitentiary system, whatever it may be, demoralizes the guardians, making them cruel and tyrannical without moralizing the detainees, who it leaves cynical and hypocritical. This is evidently not yet the society without corporal punishment, but it undoubtedly will be a great step forward until the society of the year 1900, until a society in which there will no longer be any penalty save for penal publicity and where pecuniary penalties replace legal and corporal penalties. Of all of the sources of depravation, the coarsest will have been suppressed; of all of the schools of tyranny and cruelty, to most dangerous ones will have been closed.*[89]

In the second chapter of this second book (*Society without corporate punishment*) Girardin deals with showing how a society in which sentencing has disappeared should be reorganized. *If I have accumulated evidence that, whether they are aggravated or attenuated, the penalties in effect are all equally important, whether they propose to amend the condemned or to intimidate him, the consequence that logic will extract is that we must seek a way that is different from what society has followed for so many years, obstinately marching against the flow of humanity.*[90] According to Girardin, society's mistake—that constant repetition has establish as a truth beyond question—is thinking that concentrating a group of persons considered dangerous due to their perverse natures will neutralize them, when in fact it has done no more than to increase the danger and reproduce it. He maintains that one should do the exact opposite, in other words, distribute them so that they lose themselves in the immensely superior totality of the population. To do this they should be placed under the surveillance of their pecuniarily responsible family, but above all, that of their birth commune (*comuna materna*). It seems incredible, but in 1871 he defines the function of the welfare state, except that it is in the hands of the municipality. He prophetically foretells its failure in the hands of a centralizing state, which he considers to be an obstacle that complicates everything, and revalues the function of the municipality. *Let there be treatment of the condemned, the freed men, the alienated, the abandoned children, those invalidated for work or laborers deprived of work due to causes beyond their will, let all of those and other social problems be treated. There is nothing which, after the family, the normal commune cannot resolve.*[91] He clarifies that in this regard the idea of the *phalanstère* is fruitful, but specifies farther on that he does not join in the utopian socialist conception in that regard, but demands that the commune assume its real municipal function and nothing else.[92] He hammers away against state centralization and maintains that the centralized state is a state condemned to forced labor.[93] That is why he defends a free commune in a free state, in which they would be the links in a chain (which would be the state). He calculates that in France this would require about five thousand communes. He uses numbers to show how to resolve the penitentiary problem, since each commune would be responsible for a handful of prisoners, totaling no more than ten.[94] With this, the evils of penal concentration and overpopulation would end. He rejects the idea of a halfway house (*patronato*) after freedom and demands that this stage intervene before prison and it its place, and not after the evil has been done and is difficult to remedy.[95] He resolves the financial question of the communal welfare state that he proposes through a reform of the civil code, which makes the *comuna materna* the heir of a child of all of its inhabitants, as a form of compensation for all of the new tasks in which it invests.[96] In that manner he proposes to attack the root of what causes robberies and homicides, preventing them before they are born: it is a question of *suppressing ignorance and misery at the source.*[97] *If that idea were false it would not be true that the criminality that falls to the blows of the courts and police would be more rare among those who know how to read and write than among those who do not, among those who reason that those who do not reason, among those who have wellbeing than those who do not.*[98] He continues by defining in detail the ideal of a welfare state, maintaining that with technical and administrative advances by the state and the economy it is inconceivable that there be a single illiterate adult, a single inhabitant not insured against all contingencies, without the certainty that the means that allow one access to wellbeing, among them hard work and probity demand less effort. *As work becomes less burdensome robbery will become rarer*[99] and as robbery rarefies the risks of homicide will diminish.

Girardin considers that a society without corporal punishments must educate for solidarity and cease to train the military for killing, and as it educates for values it should educate for honesty. He does not propose banning alcohol, but instead affirms that by giving people the opportunity of going to a café they will stop going to a bar, roundly maintaining that *the increase in wellbeing will raise the level of morality.*[100]

He maintains that once a principle is enunciated one must have enough courage to extract all of its consequences, without neglecting any. That defect he observes in those who defend *in any means a corporate penalty, as expiation or as retribution, as intimidation or correction, who admit it halfway, who admit it without full rigor, an inconsistency that is condemned by the uncertainty of their hesitation, in both the old and the new world.*[101]

He compares the risks of war and conquest with homicides and robberies with the statistical probabilities of being a victim of an individual act and considers that the first are much greater.[102] Metaphorically, he considers society to be a besieged and isolated city, which might reach the point of practicing cannibalism, but as that ceases to be necessary it disappears; in the same way he believes that robberies and homicides will disappear, as civilization has made cannibalism disappear, and thus *civilization will take the place of barbarism.* He maintains that society has the task of de-habituating humans from homicide and robbery[103] and to achieve that proposes: extinguishing war, investing the budget for war in education to move away from general ignorance, eliminating inveterate and inherited misery, establishing pecuniary liability for relatives in the same degree in which they qualify for an inheritance, pecuniary responsibility for the *comuna materna* to the defect of the family, compensated by the inheritance of a child. He also proposes to free the state regarding crimes and wrongdoing, with liability being placed on the families and the communes, transforming the obligatory tax into an insurance premium that will cover all social risks, to substitute the passport with a life record or general and special social security insurance policy. He defends establishing social welfare through retaining one-hundredth per hour of work, collected and deposited by the employer, offering mutual and real estate credits and replacing all existing sentences by a fine, interdiction or death, until these can also be made to disappear.[104]

Regarding penal slavery he insists: *The extreme difficulty—or impossibility—of reintegrating freed prisoners into a society that has rejected them without pity, that has struck them, branded them, jailed them, tossed them into perpetual misery and obstructing their capacity to rise again, . . . that impossibility is the sovereign condemnation to penal servitude.*[105] It is obvious that what he calls *penal servitude* is the result of the reproductive function of the penal system. Of it, he affirms that *the slavery of corporal punishment cannot continue. Everything one could say of it will be as false as what Aristotle said when he declared that there could not be a society without the slavery of its time.*[106] Nonetheless, the ancient slavery and feudal servitude disappeared without taking society with them, for which reason he is fully confident in a society without corporal punishments, which will be a very dynamic society capable of saving itself from a modern revolution, which would be achieved not by weapons but by votes. He states that just as it is too late to cry "fire!" when the flames are already devouring everything, it would be too late to cry "let us have at ignorance and misery!" when the freed prisoners, recidivists and others have destroyed everything driven by ignorance and misery.[107]

Girardin asks: *Can society subsist without the right to punish? In other terms, can it substitute the culture of man for man for that of punishment of man by man, which is only possible when man dominates man?*[108] To achieve that he proposes to suppress military training, stopping half a million men marching with weapons in hand and trained to respond to the cry of "fire" by killing their someone, maintaining only the gendarmerie, substituting bodily recruitment with intellectual recruitment, the spirit of rivalry with that of reciprocity, armed peace with assured peace, nationalism with rationalism, the old international politics with inter-communal politics.[109]

Girardin was firmly convinced that punitive power would disappear, as had other things that at his time seemed to be consubstantial with society itself. *Neither paternal power, nor marital, nor domestic nor public power, not the same penalty are today what they were during the epochs I have just finished summarily remembering, and what today seem to us incredible atrocities were at the time considered just sentences and legitimate necessities by men such as Cicero and Tacitus, and by judges such as Paul and Ulpianus.*[110] Farther on he remembers Fachninei's critique of Beccaria's book[111] and in the response by Muyard de Vouglans in 1780 to that author's critique of torture,[112] and laconically observes that nine years after that work, the revolution broke out. He remembers the derogation of torture in 1780 and the later efforts to eradicate all of its manifestations and revise the ordinances of 1670,[113] which brought for rejection from the judges (the so-called parliaments). He concludes with the following paragraph: *Torture, quartering, and all manner of torments without which it seemed society could not exist, have disappeared. Today molten lead and boiling oil are no longer poured on the patient's wounds, and society subsists, nonetheless, as it will continue to do so after prison, reclusion, detention, life and temporary sentences at hard labor, deportation, and finally, in the first year of the next century, the death penalty.*[114]

In the third chapter, finally, the author appeals to controversy. He recognizes his limitations, considers the possibility of overcoming wars, laments that Bismarck unleashed the war on France, paints the Paris Commune as a lamentable act that even burned all of Paris, and, finally, calls for a controversy to debate the idea that he has launched in his book.

We find ourselves faced with an author who can be considered a forerunner of the welfare state, who in 1868—before the Paris Commune and horrified after it—adopts what he calls a *reformist* path and predicts that the future welfare state, managed by municipalities and not by national states, would make corporal punishments disappear and with that crime would drop. Although this did not happen as quickly as Girardin intended (according to his timeline sentences could disappear more or less rapidly and the remnant death penalty would disappear in 1901), more than one hundred and thirty years later one cannot deny that one part of his forecast has come to pass: the welfare state has arrived in some regions of the planet, although it has not spread to the rest. Where it has arrived, the welfare state has made the death penalty disappear and the remaining corporal punishments have been greatly reduced. For all that, punitive power has not totally disappeared, but now, the welfare state itself is tending to shrink and disappear with the resulting new expansive tendency of punitive power, which is recovering the characteristics that Girardin had considered overcome by the limiting liberalism of Becarria.

Girardin's work is the work of an authentic abolitionist and also of a politician. He is not a utopian or an old-style revolutionary, but a progressive liberal who dreams of a welfare state or a municipalized state that provides for needs. The virtue of his work is that it clearly de-legitimates punitive power, with the same arguments that almost one hundred and fifty years later continue to be undeniable. His tactics of having prison disappear first and after that the death penalty is that of a politician: he would conserve for this penalty for awhile for crimes that cause great alarm (he was the first mass circulation journalist). His error consists of not warning us of what Foucault noted a century later: maintaining the penal system is not interesting because it prevents nothing, but for the form of power that it exerts and that translates into surveillance for the whole population. The question that remains is the following: today, when electronic technology allows us to carry out the publicity that Girardin called for in a much less ingenuous and much more effective manner, one should ask if that means of control and surveillance will not tend to replace the penal system, and also if that control would not be much more repressive than punitive control itself, and if the two would not achieve symbiosis and increase the levels of repression. It is suggestive that one of the most debated rights in our day is the right to privacy in light of the incredible advance of publicity.

NOTES

1. Èmile de Girardin, *Du droit de punir*, París, Henri Plon, 10, rue Garancière, 1871, 440 pages.
2. Guy Antonetti, *Histoire contemporaine politique et sociale*, París, 1986, p. 239.
3. Ibid, p. 260; also: Pierre Pellicier, *Emile de Girardin*, París, 1985.
4. Giacomo Matteotti, *La recidiva, Saggio di revisione critica con dati statistici*, Milano, 1910, p. 240.
5. Girardin, op.cit., p. 3.
6. Ibid, p. 5.
7. Ibidem.
8. Ibid, p. 6.
9. Ibidem.
10. Ibid, p. 7.
11. Ibid, p. 8.
12. Ibid, p. 9.
13. Ibid, p. 10.
14. Ibid, p. 12.
15. Ibidem.
16. Ibid, p. 13.
17. Ibid, p. 14.
18. Ibid, p. 12.
19. Ibid, p. 16.
20. Ibid, p. 19.
21. Ibid, p. 20.
22. Albert Du Boys, *Histoire du Droit Criminel des peuples anciens despuis la formation des sociétés jusqu'a l'etablissement du Christianisme*, París, 1845.
23. Ibid, p. 24.
24. Ibid, p. 30.
25. Ibid, p. 31.

26. Ibid, p. 31.
27. Ibid, p. 32.
28. Ibid, p. 34.
29. Ibid, p. 36.
30. Ibid, p. 40.
31. Ibid, p. 41.
32. Ibid, p. 42.
33. Ibid, p. 43.
34. Ibid, p. 44.
35. Ibid, p. 46.
36. Ibid, p. 51.
37. Ibid, p. 52.
38. Ibid, p. 57.
39. Ibid, pp. 58-59.
40. Ibid, p. 61.
41. Ibid, p. 63.
42. Ibid, p. 65.
43. Ibid, p. 75.
44. Ibid, p. 82.
45. Ibid, p. 113.
46. See for example, in 1875, the work of Concepción Arenal, *Las colonias penales de la Australia and la pena de deportación*, published in her *Obras Completas*, Madrid, 1895, Tomo X.
47. Girardin, op.cit., p. 114.
48. Ibid, p. 117.
49. Very often on this issue he cites Charles Lucas, who was one of the highest authorities of his time on the subject and who continued to be during later years: by the same author, *La récidive et le projet de rélégation des récidivistes, extrait du compte-rendu de l'Académie des Sciences morales et politiques*, 1883; idem, 1879.
50. Ibid, p. 157.
51. Ibid, p. 160.
52. Ibid, p. 164.
53. Ibid, p. 173.
54. Ibid, p. 174.
55. Ibid, p. 191.
56. Ibid, p. 204.
57. Ibid, p. 206.
58. Ibid, p. 208.
59. Ibid, p. 216.
60. Ibid, p. 217.
61. Ibid, p. 220.
62. Ibid, p. 221.
63. Ibid, p. 222.
64. Ibid, p. 227.

65. Ibid, p. 226.
66. Ibid, p. 228.
67. Ibid, p. 235
68. Ibidem.
69. Ibid, p. 236.
70. Ibid, p. 241.
71. Ibid, p. 242.
72. Ibid, p. 244.
73. Ibid, p. 245.
74. Ibid, p. 246.
75. Ibid, p. 250.
76. Ibid, p. 251.
77. Ibidem.
78. Ibid, p. 254.
79. Ibid, p. 255.
80. Ibid, pp. 256-260.
81. Ibid, p. 260.
82. Ibid, p. 261.
83. Ibid, p. 272.
84. Ibid, p. 275.
85. Ibid, p. 285.
86. Ibid, p. 280.
87. Ibid, p. 299.
88. Ibid, p. 318.
89. Ibid, p. 320.
90. Ibid, p. 322.
91. Ibid, p. 324.
92. Ibidem.
93. Ibid, pp. 326 and following.
94. Ibid, p. 335.
95. Ibid, p. 336.
96. Ibid, p. 338.
97. Ibid, p. 339.
98. Ibidem.
99. Ibid, p. 341.
100. Ibid, p. 343.
101. Ibid, p. 344.
102. Ibid, p. 349.
103. Ibid, pp. 351-355.
104. Ibid, p. 361.
105. Ibidem.
106. Ibid, p. 362.
107. Ibid, p. 367.
108. Ibid, p. 369.

109. Ibid, p. 377.

110. See Cesare Beccaria, *Dei delitti e delle pene, con una raccolta di lettere e documenti relativi alla nascita dell'opera e alla sua fortuna nell'Europa del Settecento*, A cura di Franco Venturi, Giulio Einaudi Editore, 1981, p. 164.

111. He is referring to a later edition of the well-known work of Pierre-François Muyard de Vouglanns, *Institutes au Droit Criminel, ou Principes Géneraux sur ces matieres, suivant le droit civil, canonique, et la jurisprudence du Royaume: avec un traité particulier des crimes*, París, 1757.

112. Regarding them: *Nouveau Commentaire sur l'Ordonnance Criminelle du mois d'Août 1670*, Parìs, 1769.

113. Ibid, p. 387.

114. Ibidem.

Chapter Seven

Globalization and the Current Orientations in Criminal Policy

Eugenio Raúl Zaffaroni

Proportion is not always respected by Roman laws and they punish with death the majority of expiated crimes. This disorder was born because of corruption in customs and in the state. In Rome's better days they maintained the proportion of sentencing more exactly, but having lost virtue, extinguished the love of public welfare, neglected public education, and, thus corrupted customs, there was a growth in crimes that always were multiplied because of vices. Sentences that at one time contained the virtuous citizens could certainly not contain corrupt men. No other remedy could be offered then for public disorders than to increase the sentences, given that they could not or would not adopt the true remedy, which was the reestablishment of the ancient system and the return to good customs. Thus, the blood that at one time expiated the more atrocious crimes was now spilled to punish less severe offenses.

The cruelty of sentences became a principle of criminal legislation when terror was supposed to freeze the spirits.

With exacerbation of the penalties a distinction was also born between them according to the diverse condition of the citizens, so that the harsher or lighter sentence did not correspond to the greater or lesser atrocity of the crime, but to the nobility or plebeian status of the delinquent.

At the same time that the more serious penalties were being established they became more arbitrary, either because judicial arbitrariness was the necessary consequence of political arbitrariness, or because of the lack of an exact penal code.

Francesco Mario Pagano
Principi del Codice Penale
Opera postuma, Milan, 1803, p. 58.

INTRODUCTION

It is fair to recognize that globalization has considerably altered the *center-periphery* paradigm, with a tendency to present it in other terms that—at least for the moment—one cannot exactly predict. We believe that, both for those of us for are habituated to thinking about this paradigm, however much we may be aware of that transformation, habit makes it impossible for us to completely eliminate it from our horizon of understanding, which perhaps could be done more easily by colleagues from other latitudes. Given that it is not clear how it is being modified, we do not know if this is a limitation of knowledge of the globalization phenomenon or an advantage. At any rate, it is a warning that we believe needs to be formulated.

There is—we know that much—a limitation of knowledge for anyone who takes up the theme, that one may not remove from prior consideration, whatever may be the paradigm used for analysis. It consists of the almost infinite edges that demand enormous precision. It would be simplistic to hide the difficulty by a partial approach to presenting it and limiting it to the aspects that we believe we understand, hiding the rest of our profound ignorance in a discrete omission. That would be an intellectual disloyalty, and would furthermore conspire against a vision of the hole. We will not try to hide our doubts or the enormous gaps nor will we avoid the effort at synthesis that is required to maintain the vision of the whole problem, even at the risk that—because they are a synthesis—making some affirmations that may become cryptic. Anything is better than simplifications that introduce falsification.

GLOBALIZATION AS A FACT OF POWER AND THE SINGLE THOUGHT AS A LEGITIMATING DISCOURSE

Marching directly to the theme, it is a question of establishing a *relation* between one *phenomenon of general power and another that is particular, each with its respective discourses and ideologies.* The general phenomenon is *globalization.* But *globalization* is an *ambiguous expression,* because it is employed both to designate the *fact of power itself* and the *ideology that intends to legitimate it.* It is vital not to confuse both concepts, and thus we prefer to call *globalization* the *fact of power in itself* and to use the *single thought of globalism* (Beck) or *market fundamentalism* (Soros) to describe the legitimating ideology. In that understanding, *globalization* is not a discourse, but nothing less than a *new movement in planetary power.* It is a reality of power that has arrived and that, like the previous ones, is not reversible. *The mercantile revolution and colonialism* (Fifteenth and Sixteenth Centuries), *the industrial revolution and colonialism* (Eighteenth and Nineteenth centuries) *and the technological revolution and globalization* (Twentieth Century), *are three moments of planetary power.* There is no lack of people maintaining that globalization is the totality of that process of planetarizing power (Wallerstein), as it would not be conceivable without the previous stages, but it is preferable to reserve the designation for the current stage, without prejudice to recognizing that—like every phenomenon of power—it has a historical gestation. As happened with the previous moments, there is a change in the perspective on the world in the sense of a *new significant mark for all things,* and also like them, it arrives accompanied by a legitimating discourse (*theological supremacy* in colonialism, *racist evolutionism* in neocolonialism, the *single thought* in globalizations). That is why globalization is not the market fundamentalism of von Haydeck and Friedman: that is merely the ideology of some of its interpreters, who assume a legitimating function for the advantages that the protagonists obtain by—for the moment—seeming to achieve the upper hand. Just as with colonialism, the recognition of the irreversible fact that Cortés conquered Mexico does not imply assuming the attitude of la Malinche, in globalization the *single thought* or *globalism* would be nothing more than *malinchism* facing a new fact of power.

The preceding moments of power produced horrors. Dispensing with—so as not to move too far from—those caused by colonialism, it is unquestionable that industrialism caused the neocolonial genocides, the frightful exploitation of the periphery by the center, but also democracy, the republic, revolutionary ideas as the awareness of human rights, meaning all of the depreciated ideology of modernity, which is nothing more than humanist thought. In Brazil, the sugarcane plantation slaves were turned into famished freedmen in the cities; in Mexico the Indians were transformed into peasant servants of the absentee landholders, in Europe the peasants became the urban pariahs described by Dickens and Zola or our immigrant grandparents. Savage capitalism led to crisis and that to disciplined capitalism and the welfare state in some parts of the planet and also to the world wars, the Holocaust and the bureaucratic single-party dictatorships. And the penal system was immensely cruel and bloody in the period of urban concentration, but also the liberal reaction imposed limits that medical police racism (dangerousness positivism) and the totalitarian and authoritarian states proceeded to eliminate. In other words, formal punitive control had an entire class of alternatives in the industrial and neocolonial era. One cannot escape the fact that *globalization opens up analogous perspectives.* There is no absolute evil, but absolute good is also not of this world; thus, we do not believe that penalists should assume attitudes that are either *apocalyptic* or *integrated,* but only—and nothing less—*critical* ones, which is not easy in light of the paradigm shift which, as in previous cases, tends to alter the meaning of all things and *leaves us without categories of thought to allow us to come closer to understanding reality.*

CHARACTERISTICS OF THE NEW PLANETARY POWER

One may summarize the principal characteristics of this new moment of planetary power in the following way: A) The technological revolution is, first of all, communicational: the speed of communication has increased to limits that were unthinkable a few years ago. B) There has been a reduction in the economic regulating power of all states, although in different measure, invoking the need for favoring a worldwide market. C) There has been an acceleration in concentration of capital, with an obvious predominance of the financial sector. D) Capital is displaced at zero cost, to where the profits are greatest, generally at the cost of reducing expenses by cutting personnel and lower taxes. E) Political power competes to attract that capital, meaning also that politicians compete to reduce its power, especially in peripheral countries. F) The use of salary, employment and taxation as variables for adjustment, leads to growing unemployment and deteriorating salaries, while lower tax revenues allow fewer social investments. G) As a result of all of the previous points the states have lost their capacity to mediate between capital and labor. H) The labor unions lack the power to protest against the situation. I) Financial speculation is adopting forms that make the line between lawful and unlawful increasingly murky. J) The tax havens for capital of unlawful origin are known to all and no one can block their action. K) The tax system is inverted, compensating for lower taxes on capital with higher taxes on consumption, which falls more heavily on those with less income.

The principal consequence of this phenomenon of power is to generate a broad and growing sector that is excluded from the economy. The *exploiter-exploited relation* has been replaced by one of *included-excluded non-relation.* The specialized bibliography—especially German and European in general—frequently speaks of *Brazilianization* as a generalization for a model with 20% included and 80% excluded (*20 to 80 society*), which leads to a society where isolated *ghettoes of wealth* are fortified in a sea of poverty. In a model like that there is scarcely any space for the middle classes. The *excluded* are not the *exploited*: the latter are necessary for the system; the former are too much, their very existence is unnecessary and bothersome, they are socially *disposable.*

The main political consequence of globalization is the impotence of national political power in the face of globalized economics. That can be explained in that the first world politicians in the 1980s ceded their power, renounced its exercise and with that freed economic forces that in concentrating themselves supranationally cannot be controlled or regulated. This means that *there is a globalized economic model, but there is no global society nor are there strong international organizations and much less a global state.* Single thought, in legitimating that situation becomes—in a certain sense—an *anarchical ideology,* as with every anarchism, it is definitely a radicalized jusnaturalism. In effect, *market fundamentalism radicalizes the dogma of market equilibrium and makes it absolute by rendering the state unnecessary.*

THE GENERAL IDEOLOGICAL DISCONCERTMENT

A different moment of planetary power changes the world understood as the set of meanings or the *why* of all beings, so that it makes the previous key to understanding incomprehensible. Eduardo Galeano has rightly observed that Alice, in order to get to the inside out world today, would not need to go through the looking glass, because sticking her head out of the window would suffice. However, we can only add that it is difficult to endure the harsh spectacle that the window shows, and also that one feels unbearable impotence at not being able to understand such a spectacle. In this emergency, unfortunately, there is often an attitude of taking the mirror for the window, with the illusion that all is in order. That confusion is an unconscious escape mechanism that is called *denial* but that assumes the form of *autism* and—as an escape mechanism—is the current response to the *absurdity*, which is the superlative expression of the structural *disparity* between reality and norm, between being and should be, not judicial—which would be less of a problem—but also ethical. No one can bear the spectacle in which all values—including those of human life itself—are converted into market values, without being able to explain it, without categories for thought that will allow one to think and act on this reality to overcome or transform it.

Those categories do not exist: we are faced with a world that can be described but not explain, except for some commonplace statements, because the *integrated* invoke David Ricardo and Charles Darwin, which the *apocalyptic* call on the utopian Marx. They intend to explain the Twenty-First Century with ideologies from the Eighteenth and Nineteenth. The anguish of the window makes us stick our head out of it without categories of thought that will allow us to explain what we see. That explains the autism, the preference for the looking glass in which everything appears backward, and thus, in apparent order.

When we look out to window through the discourses of the penal system, the spectacle seems even more unbearable because it is more absurd. To the emotional load of the observer as a participant of that reality is added that of the specialist, and this transcends any human capacity for tolerating the incomprehensible. We see market criminality at a macroeconomic scale without any containment of its revenues in well-known, agreed-upon and safe tax havens. State prohibitions only serve to increase the income from a thousand forbidden trades. The world seems to lack a rudder: each character, however powerful he or she may seem to be, appears to be like a disposable microchip in an enormous electronic device: *they cannot stop doing what they are doing, under penalty of being immediately replaced.* Theorists of this system celebrate it under the name of *autopoiesis*, and say that because of it there is no use in making speeches warning about the risks of social cataclysms, of the total crisis of the financial system or of global warming, in the case of a pile of microchips inserted in the device or of offering it to a large number of people smiling into the looking glasses. Some intelligent conservatives are starting to discover that Marx's romantic utopias were a sign of the times, soon used by pamphleteers, but that he also wrote something about the concentration of capital that is worth reading, at the same time as other beneficiaries of the system are realizing that if they cannot control it they will be dragged along with its downfall.

THE DISCONCERTMENT OF PENAL SYSTEM IDEOLOGIES

The general ideological disconcertment is more severe in penal systems discourses, criminological or criminal policy, considering that those have not always had a thinking content, if one understands *thought* in the original sense. There have been high points, such as those derived from the *penal illuminism* of the second half of the Eighteenth Century or first half of the XIX, and moments of profound decadence, such as during foundations of the inquisition (Fifteenth Century) or of its resurgence in the positivist dangerousness or medical police ideology. The irregular progress of the level of though in the penal discourse indicates the sharpening of dangers in the disconcertment in that area, the greater risk of autism, the lower level of preparation and training so as to bear the anguish of the lack of categories of thought.

A very brief *criminological consideration* would be useful in order to appreciate the magnitude and the causes for the disconcertment in current penal system discourses. First of all, *globalization has definitively buried the old paradigm of etiological simplistic.* A simple example that is so pedestrian and b anal that it would not even deserve the slightest journalistic consideration demonstrates the almost infinite complexity of the problem: *in any Latin American city a teenager threatens another with a firearm to steal his or her tennis shoes.* This insignificant fact is enough for communication and for the penal system itself, to show the falsifying impracticability of any simplistic statement:

1st—The object of the robbery was made in Asia by enslaved children.

2nd—The motive for the robbery is not the need for survival, but that its object is elevated to a status symbol amongst adolescents because of worldwide advertising.

3rd—The enslaved Asian production replaces the work of the robber's father or mother, fired in the country by the same company to reduce production costs.

4th—The father of the robbery victim, as a middle class person, can buy those shoes for his children because we obtains greater income from his modest invested savings.

5th—He will be happy when those reduced savings allow him a higher income.

6th—That income will increase because the accumulated capital of all of the savers will be invested in more profitable undertakings.

7th—Those undertakings will increase income through reducing jobs and in places where there are lower taxes.

8th The higher the small income of the father of the victim is, the fewer will be the opportunities for future work for the victim of the robbery and the greater will be the chances of the middle class saver of having grandchildren whose parents are unemployed.

9th—Lower taxes will reduce social investment and the grandchildren will have even fewer opportunities for health and education than the robber.

10th—It is not rare for the father of the victim to call for the death penalty, fewer guarantees and direct police measures (homicides) and to vote for politicians who call for such actions.

11th—Those politicians end up diverting scarce social investments towards clientelism (corruption) and reducing even more the chances for the saver's grandchildren.

12th—The more arbitrary police will be more corrupt and will allow more contraband and black market opportunities for guns that can reach more adolescents.

13th—Greater corruption in the penal system will determine that its own executive agencies will become cogs in the criminal organization or in the administrator of its own crime-friendly zones.

14th—That will increase the chances of victimization through kidnapping of the savers themselves and the resulting loss of their capital. The old *criminological causality* is entering an enormous crisis.

That complexity in the sphere of social since has an immediate consequence in judicial penal thinking: it becomes extremely difficult to reference criminal law with criminal policy objectives (as some contemporary thinkers, e.g., Roxin, intend) without taking into account this overwhelming complexity. That is why it is not strange that some may choose to leave aside those references and prefer to focus on deductive constructions of a more or less Kantian or Hegelian type, whether through radicalization of systemic thought in sociology (Jakobs) or a direct assumption of the idealist ethic (Köhler) or even—which is even worse—by a return to the technique of the commentators and post-commentators, who systematized without reference to any political function for sentencing. This regression is not odd, since one may observe that the *single thought* or market fundamentalism and idealist retributionism have the same origin (in the thinking of the Eighteenth Century) and share the same distorted anthropological image: the single thought converts into dogma that which is an ideal, meaning that it gives as reality a guiding *should be*, which is equilibrium in the markets. That supposes that human conducts are always governed by reason, which presupposes that humans always act rationally. Idealist retributionism does the same; it presupposes that a human, before breaking the law, makes a rational calculation of costs and benefits. That leads to the conclusion that increasing the costs (the sentence) reduces lawbreaking. The dogma of rationality of human action as the common basis for single thought (or market fundamentalism) and penal retribution, is clearly manifested in works and theories such as those of Ludwig von Mises, who for many years based his construction on the concept of action on Welzelian finalism.

It seems a lie that, with such weak foundations both economic power and the penal system are legitimated, against all evidence, including personal or introspective evidence. It is no use observing that the markets do not tend towards equilibrium but to immediate and unlimited competition or to herd behaviors that are hard to explain, that there are runs, panics and other phenomena that have nothing rational about them, or that humans kill each other in uncountable wars around the planet; it is useless to remember economic history or psychoanalysis, faced with dogmatic deductivists whose autism ignores the inspired warning of Martin Buber: *human beings are not rational, but they can learn to be so.* When one confuses should be with being, rationalist idealism is distorted to the point of radical irrationalism, since *there is no worse irrationalism than considering human rationality as done,* with the resulting wreckage of any stimulus for struggling for it, every time one does not fight to achieve a natural fact.

MACROECONOMIC WRONGDOING: PLANETARY POWER

Industrialism created racist anthropology to legitimize neocolonialism, in other words, the planetary power system, so much so that it invented sociology (beginning with criminology with Quetelet, Guerry, etc.) to legitimate internal social control. Globalization—at least for the moment—is less creative, because, as has been seen, it resorts to ideologies from past centuries; it does not invent *sciences* but instead appeals to myths. In summary, those are *the natural equilibrium of markets* at the planetary level and *the preventive efficacy of punitive power* at the national level (or what is worse: the absolute need for reaffirming the norm, as an extreme of idealistic romantic irrationalism). One should not consider this decadence strange, because it is known that the more irrational the exercise of power is, the lower is the level of discursive rationality that it intends to legitimate. In this regard, one should not confuse rationality with elaborateness of the discourse; a discourse can be elaborated with great sophistication, but if it rests upon a false base, it will be no more than a better systematized delirium, and it is obvious that deliriums do not become rational that way.

The reality of planetary power is to contradictory in comparison with the immediately preceding moments of world power, or at least they were lived in that manner. What were previously crimes against the national economy, such as hoarding, artificial changes in markets, use of confidential information, tax evasion, monopolies and oligopolies, and conduct that borders on national classifications of less sophisticated crimes, such as extortions and swindles, are now lawful conduct in the world economy. In the absence of a regulating or criminalizing power at the international level, these activities are carried out with impunity, with the particularity that there are committed at macroeconomic proportions, meaning that astronomical sums are involved. A review of the most elemental bibliography on the subject will be enough to find descriptions of activities and observed that recourse to ancient criminal methods is incessantly incremented, because even if some operators wish to do without them, the competition will employ them and eliminate them from the market. In that manner, the so-called organized crime—a quite debatable concept, which we employ here only *brevitatis causa*—is becoming the rule and day by day the states have fewer possibilities for containing it, because they themselves are victims of its extortions.

The most serious ecological crimes are committed by the economic power itself, which has been planetarized through globalization. None can detain the accelerated destruction of planetary living conditions. The Rio UNCED 1992 conference demonstrates this, not having gone beyond expressions of good will. Economic power is in the hands of persons who have no alternative but to seek for greater income in less time, because otherwise they will lose their clientele who are seeking such income and will move to other operators. One of the greatest costs of that profitability is the progressive and unlimited degradation of the environment. The operators themselves try to calm opinions by hiring *scientists* who underestimate the effects of uncontrolled depredation, while species disappear, desertification advances, the forests shrivel, the ozone layer diminishes and the average temperature of the planet and frequency of climate catastrophes increase.

In summary, in the planetary order one may affirm the clear effect of *generalized anomie* as an objective datum. Reality never coincides with the norm, because should be is a being that is not, or at least is not yet. But when the reality is triggered with regard to the rule it becomes nonsense, and prescribes a being that will never be and the norm ends up cancelled because it is useless and is destined to be wasted. The perspective of this anomic power process, projected without containment into the future translates into: a) a growing dominion by economic crime that tends to take control of the worldwide economy, given the impotence of national states and international agencies (every day economic activities at the global level will assume a greater similarity to Mafia-type criminal practice); b) a marked decline in the environment, which announces production of serious changes in the biosphere; c) in the progressive loss of power of the national states and their political operators.

THE DETERIORATION OF POLITICAL POWER: NATIONAL POWER

The growing impotence of national political power to resolve social problems derived from the exclusion and degradation of social services (including public safety) is undeniable. This is a phenomenon that political operators try to minimize, but its dimensions do not allow concealment or dissimulation. In this context, the emergence of communications is producing a completely novel profile for politicians. These are people who speak as if they had power, launch their concise slogans in front of the cameras, dissimulate their impotence as best they can and promise that which they know they have no power to do. In summary, faced with the impossibility of transforming reality, they assume unauthentic attitudes and their conduct is not motivated by their real effects but by those that cause their communications projection. They exhaust their acting capacities, there is growing public opinion mistrust with such profiles and the entire political activity is discredited. Political mannerisms are too notorious; they lack the *grace du naturel* of other times. Someone who does not appear on the screen is not part of the show, and thus is outside of politics and the virtual world in which it is developing. Undoubtedly political activity is competitive and proselytizing in its essence, which is why it always has a communications or showtime aspect, but with globalization, it exhausts itself in what should not be more than one aspect of the activity. It is transformed into pure communications without content, which in the medium term is perceived by the public, who watches it as a reiterative and not very interesting spectacle, carried out by non-authentic and untrustworthy persons. The *Weimar syndrome* assumes planetary dimensions. It is not possible to think of a *rational criminal policy* where there are no *rational politics*, but only total degradation to a poor spectacle that ends up being a *state spectacle. The criminal policy of a spectacle state can be nothing else but a spectacle.*

Through communications the phenomenon of *virtuality* appears and replaces reality: the extreme idealism which led to a certain current of thought that wrongly interpreted phenomenology, which believed that it could change everything merely by changing the significant messages, but which ignored the fact that phenomenology respected and did not deny the materiality of the world (*Welstoff*), seems to be the tacit rule of the moment among politicians almost the world over. Just as the majority of transactions with financial capital are realized upon *maturity,* meaning on future money that does not exist—which also generates virtual capital—politicians issue messages for a virtual reality in which power is symbolized. Certainly the messages are not always inoffensive symbolic acts, but are also wars, such as in the Balkans, with which they understand that they are symbolizing the re-empowerment of the strength they lost to globalized capital, meaning that they symbolically reaffirm their hegemony as lords of war and peace.

The profile of the politician as a spectacle is highly susceptible to corruption. Traditional corruption has been obscured by *macroeconomic corruption* as a criminological novelty not yet sufficiently detected because it presents its clearest manifestations in peripheral countries. Macroeconomic corruption is distinguished from the traditional form in which there is support for the destruction of the state and even the market itself. For directed, closed and centralized markets there were corresponding models of state management, where corruption took place in the area of hiring; for open markets there are corresponding models of regulating states, without which the market cannot function, because no one will defend it. *Macroeconomic corruption occurs where the managing state is dismantled, but the regulating state is not set up—or is neutralized—meaning that under the pretext of globalizing the market, the customs systems, the central banks, tax collection are entities regulating privatized public services are all annulled.* The sphere of corruption that is opened up with such maneuvers acquires a volume that recognizes no precedents. To support it secondary politicians appear, who have been called *backstage politicians.*

The *anticorruption* discourse is also globalized, but it is not totally clear if its meaning is unequivocal and that it does not enclose a contradiction and perhaps a dialectic. At least up to a few years ago, it was clear that the policy of the central countries was to exploit corruption in the peripheral ones. In the current search for higher profits or for slave labor and lower tax burdens, capital is moving to countries that are not states of law (or are so purely *pro forma*), and are thus highly corrupt. In them, the higher profits due to lower salaries and tax burdens are partly lost with the costs of corruption, meaning that there is a sort of illicit taxation that ends up being dysfunctional. The risk of globalized corruption is that it extends its previously peripheral practices to the central countries; containing it or reducing its demands can only be achieved by empowering the state of law, but states of law are not compatible with a population that is around 80% excluded. The integrated optimists suppose that this can be achieved through major growth in *entertainment,* which seems quite absurd, as well as hypocritical.

THE CRIMINAL SPECTACLE OF THE POLITICAL SPECTACLE

People *are able to tolerate injustice, but they cannot tolerate despair.* Having projects and seeking to project oneself us part of the human essence. There is no existence without a project. Exclusion is despair, frustrates all projects, closes all possibilities, empowers all social conflicts (whatever their nature) and errors of conduct. Industrial civilization has generated a work culture that led it to define identity through work; exclusion and unemployment not only create a crisis for survival but also for identity, and are thus the sources for the most absurd conduct. The exploited person had an identity and also a place: the excluder and everything he symbolized. The excluded person does not have an target and also a role: he is simply any excluded person, without considering the errors of conduct that lead him to deny a target for the excluded people themselves. The social tissue is weakened by not having an *included-excluded* social relation, relations themselves are destroyed and not only those of cooperation, but if any are strengthened they are those of conflict; with indifference and lack of knowledge space is opened up for a progressive process of mistrust, wariness, fear, panic and paranoia. Social exclusion becomes acute through the deterioration of social investment and its resulting services: health, education and welfare. Structural violence can do no less than generate violent responses.

It is thus unquestionable that *exclusion—not poverty—generates higher levels of social violence,* because in itself it is structural violence. In light of this there are no rational responses for the politics of spectacle; quite the contrary, among the deteriorated social services, that of security services is noteworthy. The absence of a response to exclusion makes any primary prevention illusory, but the deterioration of security services and their participation in the so-called *organized* crime and in corruption (which is its true consort), also degrades secondary prevention. Since time immemorial, at the periphery of world power the public security service has been entrusted to militarized and underfunded police forces. With precarious salaries and equipment, they lack the professional consciousness that can only grow with unionization, which is also the most important vaccine against corruption. To compensate for their work conditions, police are allowed a quota of illicit financial collection (usually gambling and prostitution), which is shared inequitably: the verticalized pyramid-shaped power translates into a sharing of illicit collection that is exactly inverse, meaning an inverted pyramid. In that way there is an exchange of governability for enclosed corruption.

But globalization has thrown this traditional exchange mechanism into a terminal crisis: *the destruction of the regulating state and the worldwide traffic impede any demarcation for to consented corruption, because they penetrate all existing illegal traffic, especially drugs, arms and persons.* The deteriorated service itself introduces one of the main enablers of violence; the peripheral countries are flooded with weapons introduced through organized contraband, while the police end up participating in the most horrendous crimes. The rich are *ghettoized*, security services are privatized, there is in creasing selectivity in victimization, there is an accentuated contradiction and violent conflicts between the police, the criminalized and the victimized—all selected from amongst the most dispossessed levels of societies—who definitively *are functional to the extent that they hinder their own understanding, coalitions and political protagonism.*

The powerless politicians have no response, but their show must go on. Any irresponsible person can all for vengeance in the mass media, which are open to the most ridiculous discourses. And *the showtime politicians produce penal laws, which are cheaper and provide them with publicity for a day.* For a few minutes on television they demand the handing over of the lives, liberty, honor and possessions of their own fellow citizens, many of whom—one should note- applaud the handing over of their own writes in exchange for the illusion of a badly defined slogan. *Zero tolerance, heavy hand* and other slogans mean only greater police arbitrariness. The politicians become even more powerless, because with corruption as the base *autonomous and corporate police power* are reinforced, and with them the ineffectiveness of prevention, the extortionate capacity of corporations that are increasingly committed to illicit traffic and a new empowerment for the same problem. There is almost no difference between the attitudes of political forces that follow traditional ideological tendencies: *conservatives and progressives, reactionaries and liberals share the same rules.* The *progressives and liberals seek to neutralize the imputations from conservatives and reactionaries, with even more repressive laws than the ones the latter had approved. Right and left* lose their meaning in terms of their traditional definitions; perhaps Bobbio's proposal was not a mere definition, but a complete reconsideration: *left and progressivism, in globalization, would seem to be a symbol of the fight against the discrimination and exclusion that it presupposes.* We will return to that later. In synthesis: a) the population ends up caught between fear of the police and aggression on the streets; b) the politicians are discredited because of their poor performance and worse spectacles; c) the parties lack representativeness, their moral authority destroyed by corruption; d) penal legislation is tied to pre-modernism; e) law is despised as useless; f) the middle classes are ready to identify anyone different as the enemy; g) the *extra-system* demagogues lie in wait. The *Weimar* syndrome is not a pure coincidence, only *Weimar* was in Germany and *the current situation is expanding from the periphery to the entire world.*

At a strictly legislative level, penal laws have assumed the function of reaffirming the virtual power of the impotent and powerless politicians, directed to the population with the intent of re-normalizing situations that cannot be resolved at the level of read deeds. The intent is to regulate that which no power can regulate and prepare an economical penal legislation that will not be applicable in practice, because it would produce an immediate displacement of capital that political power is not in a condition to avoid. They wish to regulate the market by creating crimes when there is no effective regulating power, so that they do no more than to make illicit services and objects more expensive. They *administratize* penal legislation before the ineffectiveness of administrative legislation, which in reality is a *banalization* of criminal law, which is consider useful for achieving any object. They reduce procedural guarantees and restore medieval institutions, such as informants and anonymous witnesses, judges and inspectors. Never before has penal legislation encompassed such a broad range of conduct as it does now: every day there are fewer administrative misdeeds that are not criminal at the same time (as crimes or as contraventions). The classification no longer selects some illicit acts from the framework of illegality, but seems to select those that that it excludes from its space, and tends to be a continuous system of penal prohibitions with non-penal exception. The material for preparing symbolic legislative messages is being exhausted.

THE CENTER OF THE MARGIN: THE PROCESS OF LEVELING

We have insensibly been describing peripheral realities and warning of their extension into the central world. As we said at the beginning, we do not know exactly in what form and with what characters this projection will definitively occur, but there is no doubt that the *center-periphery* relationship is clearly changing. Up till a few years ago we spoke of a *criminology from the margin* and of a *marginal realism* in criminal law. The *margin* was our Latin America; the *center* was the north. We believed that to face the criminological critique from the north, we should attempt our own *marginal* form. The dizzying dynamism of globalization tends to change the position of the *margin* and leave us without a *center*. Today ever-growing *margins* are beginning to appear in the old centers: that is why people increasingly use the term *Brazilianization* to describe the phenomenon that is rapidly becoming universal: the formation of isolated ghettoes of the included in a human sea of the excluded.

Perhaps the most victimizing target of globalization are the labor sectors in the old center, where *there are more who have more to lose;* there is no longer full employment in the old central countries and the objective seems to be to have their salaries complete with those from Malaysia and Thailand. Marginalization is becoming globalized and the *exploiter-exploited* dialectic is also being replaced by a pure division between included and excluded, before which even the limits of the bronze law do not exist, exactly because for the system, the best result is to have the excluded disappear. Countries that try to mitigate this process with welfare measures see the results in their falling behind in the race for *growth*: their GNP does not grow or grows at a slower rate than that of countries that ignore the consequences of social exclusion.

THE IMMEDIATE PERSPECTIVES OF PUNITIVE POWER, FROM DISCOURSES OF THE PENAL SYSTEM AND HUMAN RIGHTS

It is as evident as it is inevitable—at least in the short term—that human rights will deteriorate. There are no signs that allow one to predict a rapid or immediate reaction in the contrary direction. With the disempowerment or subordination of politics, globalization has generated two symmetric and opposing symmetries: *regionalization* and *fragmentation*. Faced with the political spectacle, xenophobic *outsiders* instigate fragmentation and attribute all ills to regionalization and to the newly arrived. It is not possible to have the Yugoslavian horror on the one hand, when states break up and sectarian groups declared demented independence or when in Mexico and Brazil, albeit with inverted poles, some pit northern states against the southern ones. We live in a cruel reality of racism, ethnic wars and Xenophobia. Buchanan, Le Pen, Haider, Bossi or Peters are real and are as present as Yugoslavia, Africa and the nuclear experiences of India and Pakistan. None of those perspectives is encouraging for a not very irrational exercise of punitive power.

The judicial penal discourse could raise a light resistance and contribute a more realistic vision, but the marked tendency to flee to idealism (or to systems closed by another methodological route) and share the anthropological perspective of single thought do not prognosticate any great efficiency in containment. The theoretical constructions of penal law in the form of closed systems (not fed with data from reality and deduced solely from the function that the constructor arbitrarily assigns to the sentence) warn of what scientists see as the risk of artificial intelligence in robotics in the future and call the *risks of feedback* that drive the system *insane*. In reality, a *closed and deduced system, placed in judicial hands to resolve all cases, is nothing more than the program for a complicated—and perhaps not so complicated—robot for manufacturing sentences.*

The closed or robotic system of penal law tends to include and rationalize the legislation produced in disorderly fashion by the politicians of the spectacle state in its growing and incessant production of messages of virtual power. They reach the point of maintaining that theorization should be functional to such messages, because otherwise it would b e excluded from the system. That is why there are those who resignedly offer themselves with a good will to be at the service of such messages, and, even more, to train future generations of jurists so that they will only learn how to do the same. Thus, there is no lack of an intended penal theory that insists on the mere symbolic effect of the penal law and assumes it, prepared according to the demands of the theatrical politicians, ignoring the fact that penal law is translated into secondary criminalization in a way that is selective for the most vulnerable. Centuries-old theories are renewed without awareness of their origins, which are actually often ignored: a) the principle of lesivity is renounced, no longer with crimes of abstract or fictitious danger, but with the thesis that there are *accumulative* misdeeds, meaning that they do not affect anyone, but if we all practiced them they would affect everyone: that was the argument used by Feuerbach two hundred years ago to rationalize punishment for sodomy. b) The old rationalizations of Sprenger and Kramer from the *Malleus Maleficarum* of 1484 or Eymerich from the *Inquisitor's Manual* of 1376 are brought back to legitimate illicit evidence introduced in extraordinary criminal proceedings and which—as happened before—tend to become ordinary. c) It is maintained that there should be a *two-speed criminal law:* one with greater guarantees for the weak and another with fewer guarantees for the strong, ignoring the fact that in the latter will do nothing else except reach the less powerful, the non-powerful who aspire to power, and those who have lost out to others even more powerful, and that it will also become ordinary in time. d) It is recognized that criminal law for the powerful would be applied more exceptionally, which is why it is proposed to compensate impunity with a greater penalty for those few cases where it applies; it is forgotten that this rule was proposed by Bentham and refuted by Carmigani as lacking any logic. Its practical translation that it will be a greater penalty will be applied to the less powerful who are caught so that people will believe in its efficacy. e) It is also maintained that the lower the gravity that a penalty has, the less will be the guarantees that should surround its imposition. It is forgotten that day-to-day configuring power—which is more important than punitive power—is managed with lower penalties and to misdemeanors, while harsher penalties—including the death penalty—have very little configurative importance, given that the majority of the population abstain from similar crimes. On the other hand, it is reasonable to deduce the result of a proposal that intends to reduce the guarantees for sentencing for the powerful, the less powerful and the powerless, but also for light sentences—which the powerful do not incur—and also those that are imposed due to emergencies, meaning for everyone.

POSSIBLE PERSPECTIVES

At any rate, it is not a question of despairing and leaving the window and choosing the looking-glass. There various penal discourses in the Eighteenth Century from both the *practical* scholars and the post-commentators as well as those of Beccaria, Verri, Howard and Sonnenfels: while the first made efforts at reasonably explaining the cases in which torture is imposed and carried out, the second wished to abolish it. It is unquestionable that globalization will give rise to penal judicial discourses that are equally disparate and encountered, when not surprising. A planetary power process is always extremely complex and contradictory, and, in the withdrawal of its conflicts, it leaves space for discourses of incompatible power. Among the penalists there have always been those who showed a preference for the post-commentators and who inclined towards Beccaria, Verri and Sonnenfels, The important point will be how the various discourses will play out in the dynamics of the power process called *globalization,* whose beginning we are now seeing.

In reality, globalization is disconcerting, because the first thing it places in doubt is nothing less than knowledge itself; it requires us to think with humility, without pretensions to omnipotence, in a very prudent manner. That seems to be the only way to extract some conclusions and provide a few explanations. It also requires us to control our emotions, to contain the impact produced by a world completely different from what we are used to, and thus, to overcome the pessimism of the *anomic* and apocalyptic as well as the optimism of the *autistic* and the integrated. From that modest interrogation, perhaps one can infer some of the future of the globalizing process and deduce some lines of behavior regarding it, in the condition of preferentially asking *what we see*, without becoming disillusioned by not being able to explain things totally. After all, technology has accustomed us to using devices whose purpose we understand, but not how they work, much less how they are built.

If what we are witnessing now through the window is another moment of power, we must presuppose that, like the previous ones, it has limits. A device in which everyone is a microchip cannot be so perfect and in fact is not. Extortion only reaches as far as the limits of fear; when one has nothing to lose, fear ceases and blackmail fails. The deregulation of everything, meaning, the minimization of political power to optimize profits, also has limits; when there is no regulating power nothing can be regulated, nothing is lawful or unlawful. Market crime also cannot be regulated. All activities are converted into *organized crime* (with the due reservations regarding the meaning of that expression). In macroeconomic terms, the uncontrolled speculation at every moment places the entire machine on the brink of disaster, globalized unlawfulness corrupts the entire structure of power and transforms it into a dysfunctional search for profit, the monopoly destroys the market, unemployment destroys the capacity for consumption. One may think that something will happen with ingenuity, even if after some disaster. The very operators of the globalized economy are starting to demand regulations. They are aware of the risk, even though the showtime politicians are the only ones who do not seem to notice; they have become so accustomed to doing nothing serious that they confuse the projection of their pantomimes shadows with action. This is a modality that was previously reserved for the periphery, but is not observed with concern in the central countries. The failure is with the media-hungry politicians, who are incapable of confessing their limitations and presenting them clearly to public opinion, and that perhaps—which is even more serious—are even not aware of them. While, some financial operators are beginning to warn of the danger, the showtime politicians are the international bureaucracies obstinately insist on their virtual reality, confusing the mirror with the window. However, the voices of alarm indicate that least not all of the operators are suicidal.

At the level of internal punitive social control in each state, the empowerment of autonomous authority for police corporations cannot be made infinite, because as they become autonomous they venture into crime, displacing or competing with other powers and even leading *coups d'état*. However impotent and incompetent the showtime politicians may be, at some point they perceive the growing risk they are running, at least in the central countries. One may think that they retain some vestiges of class conservation instinct. However, it is also true that in Weimar they never woke up to the risk.

But the safest thing one can affirm regarding the future—perhaps the only thing—is that thousands of millions of excluded persons to not stand looking into mirrors until they disappear. Globalization has many dimensions and contradictions, but perhaps the most notorious occurs with communications, with whose technological revolution it maintains a link that is almost identification. Competition lowers costs rapidly in the communications are. At the end of the Nineteenth Century, the freed Brazilian slaves, the Mexican *campesinos* and the English mine children were not aware of each other's existence. Globalization will not be able to avoid the formation of a globalized civil society and its own technological revolution will drive it, despite all of the obstacles people may wish to raise. On the other hand, the newly excluded—the middle class—will learn how to survive from the formerly exploited and will provide them with the entertainment that they lacked. At the margins—old and new, meaning at the old periphery and the exclusion of the metropoles in the old central countries—no one will be quiet for very long, and they will not always be driven by the errors that feed prejudices and discriminator or that meekly offer their cheek to repression.

THE MEANING OF ACTION

Although it will not be easy and will require a path full of contradictions and misunderstanding, the dialectic between included and excluded is as inevitable as the catastrophe of the model if no organizing regulation is achieved. The social fabric will be rebuilt, and even if it will be on a basis that we cannot even imagine, alternative cultures and responses will arise, because *the excluded also have an imagination* and have something that the included lack: *time.* It is not possible for a human to *not exist* without ceasing to be human. When the paths for existence are abruptly closed (the projects) others open up and humans continue existing. That is know by the same ideologues of the excluding society, and thus, they propose entertainment for the remaining 80%, meaning to invent a virtual reality for their projects of virtual existence, stripping them of humanity. But they forget that a human being will also not be content solely with existing in non-authenticity, in the impersonal entertainment of the *das man* and in idle chatter. At least, in the lifetime of every person there are critical moments when that is not enough. The program for entertaining the leftover 80% is nothing less than a project for transmuting humans into something different, which for the moments seems to be nothing but the obese eating high-calorie fatty foods, sitting on sofas with eyes glued to television screens vertiginously showing scenes of violent hyperactivity.

If the ideology of this first moment of globalization is exclusion of the 20 and 80 society, it is necessary not to abjure globalization as a phenomenon, but to *accommodate oneself to its dimensions and inside it provide an opposing ideology and action, in favor of a inclusive and non-discriminatory global society.* It will not be possible to leave this negative stage of globalization by appealing to the revolutionary methods of neocolonialism or industrialism. At the moment of planetary power for globalization one does not transform reality by taking *the winter palace*, not because of ethical reasons or other arguments against violence, but simply because *there is no winter palace.* There is little one can do to transform globalized reality by using national political power, due to its deterioration and subordinate role. The most desirable asset because of its transforming effect is *knowledge. Power is exercised by those who have knowledge and information.* If it occurs that the included 20% do not exercise a monopoly of knowledge, it will be removed, or at least there will be a dispute for power. This should therefore be the area to dispute, no matter how cyclopean the enterprise may seem to be and how absurd compare to the categories of industrialism's political thought and action, in which we are coached.

The immediate objective for driving the new dialectic between excluded and included is the *guarantee of minimal conditions for food, health and education* for the excluded. However weak the states may be, that objective can be achieved, by availing ourselves of the secondary and tertiary structures (provinces and municipalities) that are well administered. With the survival of the excluded thus assured, the necessary education for making use of information and providing that information will be enabled by globalization itself, with its growing and contradictory lowering of communication costs. The included lack the time for taking advantage of all of the *non-garbage information* that they receive, while the excluded have time to spare. *If knowledge is power, it is necessary to take control of knowledge.* Controlling this power will allow a) *competition with the included,* b) *its differential and countercultural employment regarding the excluded,* c) *the appearance of globalized cultures according to new and reactive norms for utilizing knowledge.*

From those new and alternative globalized cultures will emerge new forms of thinking and knowledge, means of reworking knowledge itself and for opening the way to a new knowledge that will not be one of *dominus,* that will not be the knowledge of the inquisitorial interrogator, *knowledge to be able to hold sway,* knowledge that asks but is not prepared to listen, but a knowledge in dialogue with *everything that is in the world.* Just as the knowledge acquired by *fighting* (of the warrior) gave way to that acquired by *interrogation* (of the lord, the *dominus*), it will be necessary to move from it to *dialogue* (of the *frater*). Only an alternative culture of the excluded can achieve this knowledge, in light of the planetary survival crisis that is the final development of the inquisitorial interrogation knowledge of the *dominus.*

It is not clear who can call up a coalition of the excluded from around the world to fight for this knowledge, aware of the power it implies. Certainly such a call would not sound strange to the feminist movements, since they represent half of subordinated humanity, as they learn to flee from the traps that patriarchal society has for them so that they will be dedicated to sending messages in penal laws and thus join in with its spectacle politics. As with any struggle, the coherence of the coalition will guarantee its effectiveness and allow it to confront any violence with the most effective peaceful or nonviolent means. It is true that even though there is no call to arms, it is no less certain that the *dominant and growing exclusion, added to the minimal conditions for survival, time and information,* are components that cannot help but to produce a competitive and confrontational dynamic between the excluded and the included, who have the virtual money but lack the *time* and cannot digest the information.

It would seem that the true global society would need to start to configure itself by taking ownership of the knowledge of the different excluded groups. Its effectiveness in transformation will depend upon its capacity for coalition, but when outside of the *wealth ghettoes,* in the *pueblos jóvenes, favelas* and *villas miseria* one can produce theses with the same materials as those found at Harvard or Heidelberg, the dialectic of globalization will be fully functional.

The struggle for knowledge is indispensable for avoiding a *consecration of discrimination,* a sort of *self-fulfilling prophecy of racism.* The dialectic place in movement by the excluded, aided by those who do not wish to be totally excluded, is the main hope for the cyclopean task of stimulating the new African leaders, for incorporating into the coalition of the excluded the forgotten peoples of the entire planet, before the knowledge of genetics makes it possible to enshrine biological differences and transform discrimination into real genetic privileges.

THE PENAL KNOWLEDGE OF GLOBALIZATION

Progressive penal, criminological and criminal policy thinking in globalization will have the task of *attempting to contain the punitive power that wishes to devastate the alternative cultures of the excluded* and who—certainly—will not spare its efforts in doing so. It must be assumed that this punitive power will assume new forms, because penal control in a short time will totally change its appearance. It is already technically possible to replace prisons with electronic control of behavior, which is much cheaper, and thus applicable to a larger number of persons. The powers of observation and surveillance have increased considerable, but in a few years will reach levels never before imagined. Intelligent houses and buildings will be a major technological advance, which will undoubtedly bring many conveniences to the included, but will also mean the end of privacy and every building will be a potential prison. The role for progressive penal thinking will be together with human rights non-governmental organizations engaged in preservation of alternatives that arise outside of the ghettoes of inclusion, On this side will be the colleagues, who are descendants of Beccaria, Verri and Sonnenfels, Howard, Feuerbach and Carmignani, and who will engage themselves in an increasingly committed task of preparing judicial penal discourses that will preserve social spaces for the alternative cultures of the excluded in the new globalized society. Unfortunately, there will be no lack of discourses with delayed explanations, which Francesco Carrara depreciated as *la schifosa scienza.* That will be inevitable, as it has been in the previous moments of planetary power, and especially in the immediately preceding one.

From what we seen from the window, we are sure that something will change: a) before the entire world economy is converted into a large Mafia-type organization and shatters with the first victims being its own operators, b) before the police corporations become bands of assassins that depose governments and usurp political power, c) before the 80% excluded population of the world disappears, d) before the Le Pens, Buchanans, Haiders and one thousand insane Hitlers—or even more insane—take over the governments, and e) before the globalizing tendency of *Brazilianization* is replaced by the tendency towards *Yugoslavization.* Obviously we must watch from the window to discover what will change, in order to contribute towards thinking about and driving such change, in order to minimize the obstacles that may be found in such a change. *Nothing is produced alone but is everyone's responsibility.*

The penal system will follow the alternatives of those *before* and perhaps—also and unfortunately—of some afterwards, with its moments of *absurdity* and others of mere *disparity.* And the judicial, criminological and criminal policy will legitimate or de-legitimate the absurdities, and as a result some authors will wish to cultivate the *schifosa scienza* or the true penal science. The previous experience indicates that no one remembers the earlier times, except as a curiosity.

The only truly painful thing is that—according to all previous experience—the path to a global society, the coalition of the excluded and the struggle for ownership of knowledge will not be linear. These are civilizing paths that have always been plagued by marches and countermarches, contradictions and distractions, dead ends and failed experiments. All of history teaches us that many penal and criminological discourses have started out with enthusiasm and gotten lost in twists and detours, and the sad thing is that in all this many fall dead.[1] Let it be said with the sincerity of an *active and non-ingenuous optimist,* meaning someone who does not confuse the looking glass with the window and tells what he sees from the window without selling gratuitous optimism, under the penalty of adding to the globalized spectacle in a *malinchista* attitude.[2]

NOTES

1. It is impossible to cite all of the bibliography that supports the multiple themes related to globalization and to its penal effects. Merely as an indication of the information paths traveled in this text, we mention the following texts: Hans-Peter Martin–Harald Schumann, *Die Globalisierungsfalle*, Hamburg, 1996; Ulrich Beck, *Che cos'è la globalizzazione. Rischi e prospettive della società planetaria*, Roma, 1999; Ignacio Ramonet, *Un mundo sin rumbo, Crisis de fin de siglo*, Madrid, 1997; Hans Magnus Enzenberger, *Guerra civil*, Sao Paulo, 1995; Noam Chomsky, *Habla de América Latina*, Buenos Aires, 1998; Octavio Ianni, *A era do globalismo*, Rio de Janeiro, 1997; Ernesto López, *Globalización and democracia*, Buenos Aires, 1998; Sapelli, Giulio, *Cleptocracia, El mecanismo único de corrupción entre economía and política*, Buenos Aires, 1998; Vincenzo Ruggiero, *Economie sporche, L'impresa criminale in Europa*, Torino, 1996; del mismo, *Delitti dei deboli e dei potenti. Ezercizi di anticriminologia*, Torino, 1999; Camera dei Deputati, *La lotta alla corruzione*, Bari, 1998; Eduardo

Galeano, *Patas arriba, La escuela del mundo al revés*, Montevideo, 1998; George Soros, *La crisis del capitalismo global, La sociedad abierta en peligro*, Buenos Aires, 1999; Eric J. Hobsbawm, *Il secolo breve, 1914-1991: l'era dei grandi cataclismi*, Milano, 1995; Luigi Ferrajoli, *La sovranità nel mondo moderno*, Roma, 1997; Javier Tusell, *La revolution posdemocrática*, Oviedo, 1997; Roger-Gérard Schwartzenberg, *O Estado espetáculo*, Sao Paulo, 1978; Noam Chomsky-Heinz Dieterich, *La sociedad global, Educación, mercado and democracia*, Santiago de Chile, 1996; Emir Sader (Organizador), *O mundo depois da queda*, Rio de Janeiro, 1995; Jeremy Rifkin, *El fin del trabajo, Nuevas tecnologías contra puestos de trabajo, el nacimiento de una nueva era,* Buenos Aires, 1997; Josef Thesing - Wilhelm Hofmeister, *Medios de comunicación, democracia and poder*, Buenos Aires, 1995; Carlos Alonso Zaldívar, *Variaciones sobre un mundo en cambio*, Madrid, 1996; Viviane Forrester, *El horror económico*, Buenos Aires, 1997; Héctor Horacio Dalmau, *El país de los ríos muertos*, Buenos Aires, 1995; Walter Laqueur, *La Repubblica di Weimar*, Milano, 1974; Anthony King, *Global Cities*, London, 1991; José Maria Simonetti, *El ocaso de la virtud*, Buenos Aires, 1998; Ludwig von Mises, *Epistemological Problems of Economics*, New York, 1981; Michel Foucault, *El saber and las formas jurídicas*, Barcelona, 1980; Marion Bögel, *Strukturen und Systemanalyse der organizierten Kriminalität in Deutschland*, Berlin, 1994; Moccia, Sergio, *La perenne emergenza, Tendenzie autoritarie nel sistema penale*, Napoli, 1997; Piero Rocchini, *La neurosis del poder*, Madrid, 1993; Lester Thurow, *Cabeça a cabeça, A batalha econômica entre Japao, Europa e United States*, Rio de Janeiro, 1993; Samuel P. Huntington, *El choque de civilizaciones and la reconfiguración del orden mundial*, Barcelona, 1997; Ralf Dahrendorf, *O conflito social moderno*, Rio de Janeiro, 1992; Scott Lash-John Urry, *The end of organized capitalism*, Madison, 1987; Immanuel Wallerstein, *Utopística o las opciones históricas of the Twenty-First Century*, México, 1998; Michio Kaku, *Visiones. Cómo la ciencia revolucionará la materia, la vida and la mente en the Twenty-First Century*, Madrid, 1998; Norberto Bobbio, *Derecha e izquierda*, Madrid, 1995; Lee M. Silver, *Vuelta al Edén, Más allá de la clonación en un mundo felíz*, Madrid, 1998; Celso Furtado, *O capitalismo global*, Rio de Janeiro, 1998.

2. An updated bibliography is found in: Katja Franko Aas, Globalization and Crime, London, 2007.

Chapter Eight

The "Dangerous Classes"

The Failure of a Pre-positivist Police Discourse

Eugenio Raúl Zaffaroni

HISTORICAL DISCOURSES

Rivacoba's admiration for penal and liberal illuminism meant that his conversation frequently gravitated towards that theme. He preferred the summits of thought of penal discourse, and avoided the moments of its police and racist decadence. For my part, I more frequently venture into those low places, not out of morbid curiosity, but to try and understand their discursive structure in order to better neutralize their sadly sinister effectiveness. Rivacoba's fine sensitivity towards anti-liberal discourses rapidly exhausted his patience and kept him from accompanying me on those incursions into the deteriorated suburbs of penal thought. That is why I do not remember—despite a dialogue of more than thirty years having discussed with Rivacoba the police origin of positivism nor can I affirm that he totally shared that opinion. However, without a doubt I know that he held in high esteem the efforts of others to dismantle the effectiveness of authoritarian discourses, especially when they consisted in paths through arid heights his scarce patience did not allow him to travel. That is why I consider that this excursion through the origins of positivism will allow me to discharge the police of an ideological stigma that they do not deserve: their contribution to positivist hegemony was enormous but corporate, not ideological. Positivist racism is a discourse completely provided by its associated corporation, that is, the medical ideology of its time.

Positivism returned to its inquisitorial discourse, especially in Central Europe,[1] breaking the branches of that tree, which in its medieval origin covered the armies of demons with the foliage of uncountable signs of degeneration or the biological infrahumanity of racist evolutionism, as ingenuous as it was coarse. When in the middle of the Nineteenth Century the European bourgeoisie took power, the liberal discourse ceased to be functional for its interests; it needed another one, which would legitimate its hegemony, but at the same time would consolidate the new agency that had arisen with the industrial revolution: the police. Every time that it lacked its own discourse, it was provided by the medical corporation, with the result being the medical-police discourse of positivism. In the struggle between corporations for ownership of the criminal question,[2] the discursive hegemony in criminological knowledge, which had heretofore been held by corporations of jurists and philosophers, passed to doctors and policemen. Positivism was preceded by previous medical discourses, but those had not arrived at the appropriate moment; the physiognomists and phrenologists[3] essayed their theories too early. Hegemony arrived when its discourse was assumed by the police corporation; that was the opportunity for Lombroso and Lacassagne.[4]

This chapter has the objective of verifying and ratifying that the police corporation needed the medical discourse because it had not been able to elaborate its own, despite trying to do so. *I demonstrate here that the attempt at a discourse by the police corporation before positivism was not successful due to the structural weakness of the product, its resulting contradictions, and, to a large part ended up dysfunctional for legitimating unlimited police repression. If the doctors had owned discourses but had lacked the power to achieve hegemony, the police corporations had power but had not achieved an appropriate discourse; it is curious that its scarcity of elements was such that, to a large degree, the attempt was almost illuminist and a social critique.*

The work analyzed here is that of H.A. Frégier, police chief of the Seine zone, published in 1840,[5] but written at least two years earlier. It is a very original document, with opinions that are sometimes surprising. It is little known, but was cited in parliamentary debates in 1888, in the closing days of imperial Brazil.[6] For the first time the expression *dangerous classes* was used,[7] but not in Frégier's work, but as the title that the Acádemie de Sciences Morales et Politiques had used for the contest in which the author presented his prize-winning book, in the following terms: *Investigate, according to positive principles, what are the elements that make up in Paris or in any large city, that part of the population that forms a dangerous class due to its vices, its ignorance and its misery: indicate the means that can be employed by the administration, the rich, the accommodated, the intelligent workmen and laborers, to improve this dangerous and depraved class.* The Academy presupposed that the dangerous and depraved class was made up of workmen who were neither intelligent nor hardworking, characteristics derived from vices, ignorance and misery. The author expressly answers that he will also focus on the literate dangerous class, due to the role that intelligence plays in depravation.

The work is divided into four parts: statistics, living habits, measures for avoiding expansion of vice and remedies.[8] Strictly speaking, the scheme is simple: the later positivist terms would be *description* (quantification and characteristics) and *prevention* (primary and secondary).

The discourse is based on exclusively moral points of view: *vice is the cause of all ills.* Although it is a police work, its theoretical framework is the moralizing psychiatry of that time period,[9] founded on the confidence that material progress entails moral progress. That is why he affirms that vice is *inherent to human nature,* so much that the virtuous person is nothing more than a less vicious being. The vice of the rich deprive charity of what they hand over to their passions, while for the poor man it deprives his family. Despite the moralizing tone of the work as a whole, the author is surprising in his insistence on the principle of offensiveness. *Where there is no offense or harm, penal action has nothing to do: that is the line that separates the domain of civil law from that of moral law. Nonetheless, it is no less certain that the lack of morality is the source of wrongdoing, which is why a good governor should pay attention to it.*[10]

While vices affect all social classes, for Frégier those of wealthy classes are not as dangerous, because they dissipate that which they have in excess and offer fewer cases of criminality. *The poor and vicious classes, it happens, have always been and continue being the greatest producers of all sorts of wrongdoers. That is why they are more properly called dangerous classes. A vicious individual of that class is always a source of feat, even if the vice is not accompanied by perversity. The moment such a one ceases to work because of his vice, he becomes an enemy of society.*[11] He distinguishes the idle class from that of working laborers, even though some of latter share the vices of the former. The most suspicious part of the dangerous class are the convicts and freed prisoners; the latter form the most depraved and fearsome sector of the dangerous population. He notes that there are those who combine a lawful activity with evildoing, who are generally form honest homes, which they have abandoned to seek refuge in large cities. From this class and the upper class come the swindlers with fine manners who operate in the casinos and the gallant salons. Obviously, he does not forget the women: *The women, albeit in smaller numbers, play an important role as the first cause or the instrument in all sorts of attacks that afflict society: they are recruited from all ranks of the social hierarchy and cover all forms of depravity: the prostitute, the flatterer, the accomplice of the swindler and the thief.*[12]

He distinguishes between vice from perversity, but since the first moves towards the second, one cannot separate them, and he thus ends up including both in the concept of dangerous classes, although he excludes activists in popular seditions, because he considers them as emerging from extraordinary moments and only wants to occupy himself with what is permanent.[13]

Because the poor and vicious part of the working class is the one that most contributes to crime, he begins by numerically assessing the industrial population, which he considers as being made up of workmen, working women, apprentices and junkmen. It is interesting to note that police control of this segment was a failure due to disorganization, since Frégier complains that he had never been able to make the legal system of saving accounts effective for workers. He calculates the number at 75,000, but soon, based on other data from the lodgings controlled by the police, especially the so-called furnished houses, estimates it at 78,000 for the low season and 105,000 for the high season, with one third being single,[14] some 40,000 working women married or cohabiting and another 20,000 single women. Thinking that every working family has two apprentices, he establishes their number at 100,000, so that he reaches a total number of workmen, working women and apprentices at 235,000 in the low season and 265,000 in the high season.[15]

He clarifies that the portion of these who launch into vice could in no way be completely controlled by the police. He frequently invokes the distinction between morality and law in that respect: *Our society, although strongly advanced, could probably not support preventive measures by the police that had the objective of focusing, in cabarets and other places of that nature, on drunkards and gamblers, to deprive them of the means of freeing themselves from their vicious habits,* which he contrasts with the United States, where he affirms that *they do not distinguish between laws and morality*.[16] His estimate of the number of the vicious, presented without a greater empirical basis, is quite high, since he assigns to it a third: 35,000 workmen and 20,000 working women. Without a reasonable explanation he calculates that, as there are degrees of vice, half of the vicious workmen and two-thirds of the working women should be considered as the number of the most depraved.[17]

The *idle class* is the antechamber of all that is most abject, corrupt and dangerous for society. It is made up of gamblers, public women (prostitutes), their lovers and pimps, ruffians, brothel madams, vagrants, swindlers, crooks, male and female thieves and their accessories. He affirms that *the dominant vices in the individuals designated here are indolence, gambling, intemperance, libertinage and in general all low and immoral passions.*[18] They live in a state of continuous excitation that hastens them into crime. The different unlawful activities combine with each other and one person can do several simultaneously, which he uses as a pretext to explain the imprecision in the data he is managing; since a thief can be at the same time a pimp and a prostitute a swindler, it is not possible to make exact statistics available. He classifies the public women into *registered* prostitutes (3800), who may be free (two-thirds of them inhabit furnished rooms or rent unfurnished ones) or be in houses of tolerance (one-third), or *non-registered or rebellious,* who are the ones who make up clandestine prostitution (4,000). He counts the number of lovers and pimps at 7,800.[19]

As for the vagrant, he affirms that *this is the type who originates all potential for evil, being found in every place where illicit or criminal industries are performed,*[20] estimating their number at 1,500. He next analyzes lodgings for the dangerous classes, from the most miserable boarding rooms to those who are able to find private houses with good references from their neighbors. He complains that *the kindness of our customs, the humanity of our laws and the extreme discretion of landlords all conspire in favor of impunity.*[21] He concludes that the total of the dangerous class in Paris is 63,000 individuals of *all sexes and ages.*[22]

As a good policeman concerned with order, he does not neglect to note the scarce public interest in statistics and suggests the form for elaborating them for better knowledge and control. He proposes a census of workers by profession and registration of industries, from the business leader to the apprentice, as part of the desire for disciplined control from which he is not free. To calculate the total of unknown delinquents (which would soon be called the *obscure number*), he proposes comparing the data from detention sheets with the number of denunciations, even though he clarifies that it would be an error to suppose that every denunciation means a different wrongdoer, because the same person can commit several crimes.[23]

CUSTOMS, HABITS AND LIFESTYLES

He then moves to focus on the customs, habits and lifestyles of the vicious and dangerous classes, beginning with the vicious portion of the working classes. He recognizes that the working classes have gifts of virtues, especially of solidarity in facing need and disease, even though these are the product of primitivism: *Their moral qualities are derived from primitive human virtues and they practice them with a zeal and simplicity that are worthy of praise from all people of good will.* He bucolically describes the relations of the employer with the worker and of the worker with his companions. He recognizes that extramarital children are raised as legitimate and that the workers hand over almost all of their wages to their wives, even though some do so by halves and others keep it and the wife maintains herself with her own wages.[24] *The cabaret is the place of rest and recreation for the worker.* He goes there to complain about mistreatment, about humiliations, and family conflicts, although he does not always become drunk from drinking alcohol. A worker asked about his custom of frequenting a *cabaret* will say that it is due to weakness of character or pride. Even owners of small factories share this custom. He considers that the bosses should impose a certain discipline in that regard. He describes in a somber tone the indigence brought about by wastefulness in the *cabaret* and the condition in which one returns to his wife. In a small number of cases he recognizes that passion for wine absorbs all other passions, describing the wife and children spying on the husband as he leaves on payday in order to try and save the wages, *but wine wins out and the brute ends up in the cabaret in Bacchic orgies*.[25] But not all women are good models: there are those who give themselves over to vice and return home Monday morning almost drunk, giving a bad example that corrupts the children. He attributes to certain workers who live in common-law relationships the practice of swapping wives. They defraud their providers and there are cases in which they are served dinners and do not pay for them.[26]

He ponders the virtues of *the honest daughters of workers, good daughters, who only go out on festival days with their parents, and later on are good wives. Those who work in workshops or stores require greater care from their parents, their voluntary relations with colleagues have nothing worth criticizing, while they maintain principles of prudence and decency. But if it is the case of a workshop where decency is not the norm and insolent comments by gathered workers are allow, they cast in doubt the moral principles of new female workers*.[27] He criticizes parents who retain all of their daughters' wages, keeping them from being able to wear clothing in keeping with their condition and causing an aversion to the household that leads to a breakdown in relations. Female workers are divided into employees in shops and in factories. The former have superior education and manners. Vice operates in both, but is more refined in the first case. Factories are the antechambers of corruption, since the women's wages are low and when they have a family they need someone to support them, which they generally find in marriage or as concubines, although some *go from disillusionment to disillusionment and fall into prostitution*.[28] Others find themselves loaded down with children and abandoned by their lovers. Workers in the spinning mills find themselves obliged to take their children to work and live in an insane mixture of ages and sexes, with no one taking care of morality. From the age of twelve children are placed as apprentices, which takes a load off of their mothers, but that means that they go to their courses at school after ten or twelve hours of work. Working women in factories are often impregnated very young, by workers who ignore the plight of the children. Nor is it strange to find drunkenness among female factory workers.[29]

Frégier dedicates special attention to the junkmen, who have to work at least three shifts to earn the minimum wage. He reports that they live in miserable and unsanitary conditions, that they store the items they pick out in their own homes, that they get drunk the same as the other workers, but instead of wine they prefer rum.[30]

He then moves on to consider the customs of the vicious portion of the accommodated classes, although the title does not seem to fit the contents with total precision. He refers in principle to those employed as clerks or copyists who, since typewriting did not exist at the time, offered their services on the street on inside the Palace of Justice. He affirms that among them are found *scholars fired from their studies, officers expelled from the army, former prisoners, children of repudiated families, who make up the dregs of society. The main vices of the depraved class of copyist are drunkenness, gluttony, gambling and idleness.* These are people who because of gluttony consume what they make in food, so that nothing is left to spend on clothes or for sleeping anywhere but in revolting places.[31] He paints the lives of students in positive colors, but then dedicates attention to their disorderly behavior with women and gambling, and there is a shopworn reference to *the Jews who exploit them.*[32] He describes the cases of students who fool their parents with their supposed studies, but who are visited by them and punished by having their funds totally cut off. He affirms that the students most inclined to do this are those in their first year, corrupted by others on finding themselves alone and uncontrolled in the city. A minority of students are swept along and end up doing petty thefts in restaurants and other minor infractions. At any rate, he notes that they should be viewed benignly and clarifies that he does not intend to raise himself up as a censor of the morals of a class to which he has the honor of belonging.[33]

He affirms that the employees in commerce have more solidarity that the students. They suffer through a harsher apprenticeship in which they make less and are always tempted to steal from their boss, who will only notice because they talk and news of inappropriate spending reaches his ears. He affirms that flattering women seduce employees in the shops and that the public balls are the most scandalous.[34]

The author introduces himself in the treatment of the *customs of the dangerous classes and the causes of their depravation and misdeeds,* describing the neighborhoods, homes and boarding houses where the wrongdoers spend the night and explains the organization of the Paris police. The dangerous class prefers to concentrate in certain districts, because of their central position. He notes that the *Cité* district has a particularly sinister aspect, which contrasts with the neighboring monuments. The streets are narrow (eight feet) and harbor small shops, and meeting places for prostitution and bandits. He mentions other neighborhoods where brothels and bars abound: *Saint Jacques, Sainte Antoine, Palais Royal, Saint Denis, St. Martín des Champs, St. Thomas d'Aquin, Porte St. Martin, les Invalides, Arsenal, Hôtel du Ville, Observatoire* and the *Temple* neighborhood, one of the most infected. *The houses of prostitution are a source of infection, the rooms lead to corridors without light or air, there is dirt everywhere, only a few have beds or cots.*[35]

Entering the theme, he starts with the gamblers, whom he describes as persons in whom the need to gamble absorbs other needs. These being people from the needy classes, since the only occupy themselves with their need for gambling, they are destined to end up as thieves or vagrants. On the other hand, the passion for gambling is shared by almost all delinquents, because of the strong emotion that it provides. Frégier does not miss a chance with this argument to excuse the police's difficulty *in fully recovering the booty from robberies and thefts. The prisoners have are not ashamed of gambling over anything, including the bread that they need to survive.* He closes by reporting the case of a prisoner who, in the infirmary, gambled the food and drink he needed to recover his strength and who ended up dying of starvation.[36]

The author spends considerable time on the theme of prostitution. He affirms that it is an ill that extends throughout the world and that in Paris it has been regulated, in contrast with the prohibitionist policy of the old kings, and he considers it the saner solution.[37] He complains of a refractory clandestine prostitution, which refuses to register with the police and which severely effects morality, without giving any reason for the without giving any reason for the registered woman to suppose she will not be affected. He affirms that such the registered person undergoes stricter surveillance by the police, she tends not to commit crimes. The women register voluntarily or are registered because of their position, even though *registration does not mean authorization for prostitution.* If she is of age and the authorities can *prove good sentiments,* they do everything possible to *return her to her family.* If she was not born in Paris, to continue she may elect to sign in the *registry of infamy*[38] or if *after the first offense she had been far from her family.* At any rate *the authorities use great circumspection: it is probable that they will reject the registration and to avoid here falling into clandestine prostitution they will return her to her place of origin.* In any case, the authority requires a birth certificate from the mayor and through it consults the family, who *always will be informed that the woman is on the brink of the abyss.* Care is even greater in the case of minors, and they are interned in the Convent of the Ladies of Saint Michael for a period of one to six months, and if, despite this rigor they do not mend their ways, only then is it resolved to register them, once it has been verified that the *woman is totally dominated by vice.* She is made to sign (or make an X on) a document in which she commits herself to observing the health rules; he maintains that this is very important, since the woman represents a sort of agreement with the administration.[39]

He calculates the ages of the women following research by Parent-Duchatelet in 1831, in which the numbers rise from age 14 to 28 and decline from 28 to 40, and from that point drop abruptly, so that there are none aged 50. He observes a high percentage of women who are relatives, which he takes as proof of corruption in certain families and of the *moral contagion* of prostitution in the poor classes.[40] He makes a classist analysis of prostitution, noting that there is a small number of free prostitutes who live in luxury, charge high fees, have powerful lovers; these are followed by those from the middle class, whose clients are law students and young lawyers. He concludes that the poor ones are the most corrupt and that class differences promote refusals between them, who sometimes need to share hospitals and jails. In the prisons their correspondence is controlled by the police, but he complains about powerful lovers who speak up for them, which in his opinion proves the corruption of the elevated classes.[41] He expresses a certain admiration for the love of prostitutes for their pimps (*soutneurs*), who provide them with protection from police inspectors, with whom they sometimes have violent resistance and encounters.

He classifies the brothels into public and passageway houses. The owners are known as *maitresses* of *dames de maison*, a term that substitutes others that sound offensive.[42]

NOTES

1. Kraemer and Sprenger: *El martillo de las brujas*, Span. trans. by Miguel Jiménez Monteserín, Madrid, 1976; *Malleus Maleficarum*, English trans. By Montague Summers, London, 1928 (reprint, 1951); *O Martelo das feiticeiras*, Trans. by Paulo Froes, Rio de Janeiro, 1991; *Il martello delle streghe*, Trans. by Buia-Caetani-Castelli-La Via-Mori-Perrella, Venecia, 1977; *Der Hexenhammer*, Ger. Trans. By J. W. R. Schmidt, Berlin, 1920 (three volumes); *Malleus maleficarum*, Lugduni, MDCXX (that edition is part of three volumes that compile other treatises on the theme; I owe the copy to the kindness of Prof. Fernando Perez Álvarez, of the Universidad de Salamanca).

2. On that, Zaffaroni, E.R., *La criminologia como curso*, in "Política criminal, Derechos Humanos and sistemas jurídicos en the Twenty-First Century," vol. de hom. al Prof. Dr. Pedro R. David, Buenos Aires, 2001, pp. 925 and ss.

3. Della Porta, Giovan Battista, *Della fisonomia dell'uomo, con illustrazioni dell'edizione del 1610*, Parma, 1988; Lavater, Johann Caspar, *La physiognomonie ou l'art de connaitre les hommes d'apres les traits de leur physionomie, publié par*

Gustave Havard, París, s.d.; Lavater, Johann Caspar/Lichtenberg, Georg Christoph, *Lo specchio dell'anima Pro e contro la fisiognomica, un dibattito settecentesco a cura di Giovanni Gurisatti,* Padova, 1991; Courtine, Jean-Jacques/Haroche, Claudine, *Storia del viso. Esprimere e tacere le emozioni (XVI a XIX secolo)*, Palermo, 1992; Kassner, Rudolf, *Fondamenti della fisiognomica, Il carattere delle cose,* Vicenza, 1957; Cerchiari, G. Luigi, *Fisiognomia e mimica*, Milano, 1990; Getrevi, Paolo, *Le scritture del volto, Fisiognomica e modelli culturali dal Medievo ad oggi*, Milano, 1991; Kris, Ernst, *La smorfia della follia, i busti fisiognomici di Franz Xaver Messerschmidt*, Padova, 1993; Magli, Patrizia, *Il volto e l'anima*, Milano, 1995; Rodler, Lucia, *I silenzi mimici del volto. Studi sulla tradizione fisiognomica italiana tra Cinque e Seicento*, Pisa, 1991; Giufredi, Maurizio, *Fisiognomica, arte e psicologia tra Ottocento e Novecento. In appendice Saggio di fisiognomica di Rodolphe Töpffler*, Bologna, 2001; Niceforo, Alfredo, *La fisiognomica nell'arte e nella scienza*, Firenze, 1952.

4. Among the immense biography on them, the latest studies, for example: Guarnieri, Luigi, *L'atlante criminale. Vita scriteriata di Cesare Lombroso*, Milano, 2000; Villa, Renzo, *Il deviante e i suoi segni, Lombroso e la nascita dell'antropologia criminale*, Milano, 1985; on Lacassagne, Debuist, Charles, in Debuist/Digneffe/Pires, *Histoire des savoirs sur le crime et la peine*, Quebec, 1998, pp. 343 and ss.

5. *Des classes dangereuses de la population dans les grandes villes et des moyens de les rendre meilleures. Ouvrage recompensé en 1838 par l'Institut de France* (Académie des Sciences Morales et Politiques). Par H.A. Frégier, Chef de Boureau a la Préfecture de la Seine. Bruxelles. Meline, Cans et Compagnie, Librairie, imprimerie et fonderie, 1840.

6. Chalhoub, Sidney, *Cidade Febril. Cortiços e epidemias na Corte Imperial*, Sao Paulo, 1996, p. 20.

7. Chalhoub (ibidem) also attributes it during the 1840s to the English writer Mary Carpenter, but at the same time recognizes its partial use, and for the reasons presented here, it is also clear that employment of the expression by the French Academy was earlier.

8. Frégier, p. 16.

9. Cf. See e.g., Sauze, Alfred, *De l'imprisonnement cellulaire: de sa double influence sur la santé physique et morale des détenus*; and *Études médico-psychologiques sur la folie*, Paris, 1862, p. 165; historically, Galzigna, Mario, *La malattia morale. Alle origini della psichiatria moderna*, Venezia, 1988.

10. Frégier, p. 9.

11. Ibid, p. 11.

12. Ibid, p. 13.

13. Ibid, p. 15.

14. Ibid, p. 24.

15. Ibid, p. 25.

16. Ibid, p. 27.

17. Ibid, p. 29.

18. Ibid, p. 37.

19. Ibid, pp. 39/40.

20. Ibid, p. 40.

21. Ibid, p. 44.
22. Ibid, p. 45.
23. Ibid, pp. 47/51.
24. Ibid, p. 58.
25. Ibid, pp. 61/65.
26. Ibid, pp. 66/67.
27. Ibid, pp. 69/70.
28. Ibid, p. 73.
29. Ibid, p. 76.
30. Ibid, p. 80.
31. Ibid, p. 83.
32. Ibid, p. 88.
33. Ibid, pp. 89/91.
34. Ibid, p. 94.
35. Ibid, pp. 95/100.
36. Ibid, pp. 105/107.
37. Ibid, p. 108.
38. Ibid, p. 110.
39. Ibid, p. 112.
40. Ibid, p. 114.
41. Ibid, p. 117.
42. Ibid, p. 120.

Chapter Nine

The Legitimation of Penal Control over the "Strangers"

Eugenio Raúl Zaffaroni

AN OLD IDEA IN A NEW OVERVIEW

In *theorizing criminal policy* higher levels of repression are always defended for the more serious crimes, including in the more radicalized positions.[1] Furthermore, a different repression has almost always been theorized for the *non-harmful* (to the police) and another for the *harmful*, with the others being the target of measures for segregation or elimination that are disproportionate to the gravity of the infractions committed. As a result, it is nothing new for *plural penal repression* to be theorized: on the one hand for the *sinister (Kill them!)* and for the *insane and bothersome (Get them out of here!)*, and, on the other hand, for the *occasional (People more like us, who made a mistake).*

This is no different from what Günther Jakobs has proposed more recently,[2] with the idea of a special class of sinister criminals that would be the terrorists. Except for his sincerity and precision—in the use of the qualification of enemies—the proposal is not new. One can consider that it is the *banal conduct of a penalist* impressed by acts of unusual gravity.

Nonetheless, this proposal has unleashed an intense debate with an unusual tone.[3] Why has an idea older than penalism—it goes back to the Greeks—produced a scandal? We would be underestimating the intelligence of our critics if we thought that they followed only the sincere terminology used by Jakobs.

Our hypothesis starts with the presupposition that all conduct is or is not banal according to the context and the circumstances. We understand what the Professor from Bonn has said in words much clearer than many others have said before with greater confusion, but at a different moment. At this stage power is at a planetary level and threatening with a global dictatorship; the technological potential for information control may spell the end of all intimacy; the use of this controlling potential would not be limited to investigating terrorist, as all historical experience teaches. Massive communication, of formidable technical power, is thrown into a *völkisch* and vindictive propaganda without precedents; the planetary power manufactures enemies in series. Thus, however much it is dressed up as judicial, the unusual reaction is political, because *the question that is placed is—and always has been—of that nature.* The proof of that is that Jakobs himself relies on Hobbes, and thus, in the central point of *sovereignty,* a clear question of *political science* and, precisely, the new globalizing overview is characterized by a profound political change.

The crimes of mass and indiscriminate destruction of September 11, March 11 and July 7[4] are expressions of brutal violence that make up crimes of *lesse humanité,* but which respond to other violence and thus we could keep on going backwards. It is not necessary to fall into the extreme of dogmatically maintaining that all violence must be answered with non-violence, to verify that *never has a conflict been definitively resolved by violence,* unless one confuses a *definitive* solution with a *final* solution (genocide). Those that did not end in genocide were resolved by *negotiation*, which belongs to the field of *politics*. But globalization has impoverished politics until it has reduced it to its minimum expressions. The current structural decisions in practice assume the pre-modern form defined by Carl Schmitt, meaning the mere power of marking out the enemy.[5] This is delineated on two fronts: that of Human Rights and negotiation on the one hand, whose most important bastion is found in Europe and in the academic field of almost the entire world (including the United States), and, on the other, one of a violent solution that crushes Human Rights and ends in genocide. The awareness of this disjunction is greater in places where there the experiences of state terrorism remain in the collective memory (Europe and Latin America), not so in the United States, where there are other repressive abuses, but whose population has never suffered from state terrorism.

In this context we would propose admitting that a *criminal law of the enemy* cease to be the banal conduct of the penalists, who almost always have postulated it, to recover its true nature, which is political. And as such, it becomes intolerable, because what up till yesterday was banal today may be read as a *type of desertion in the world political dispute.*

One should clarify that Jakob's proposal is one of the most absolute good faith, for when he proposes distinguishing one penal law for the *citizen* and another for the *enemy,* he does so imagining that both function in a state of law, as many other authors have done previously. Furthermore, he assumes a real phenomenon, which is the repressing of penal legislation, in a mixture of tactical withdrawal and resignation, seeking to impede the extension of the phenomenon to all of criminal law.

Admitting that the question is political, our hypothesis is that in this camp it will be intolerable to have the judicial category of *enemy* or *foreigner* in ordinary law (penal and/or administrative) in the framework of a state of law, and thus it has always been, even though theorized with other names. We intend to demonstrate that this can only be admitted if one opts for a model of an absolute state, as was postulated by Carl Schmitt.

FIRST CONCEPTUAL PRECISIONS

Abused words become equivocal and in judicial language the wear and tear is more serious, exactly because it demands precision. Thus, it does not seem tolerable to have the semantic deterioration of the expression *criminal law.*

From any discourse, including a technical one, one can extract phrases such as these: (a) *Criminal law cannot combat poverty.* (b) *Criminal law does not punish that conduct.* (c) *Criminal law does not analyze that theme.* One same grammatical subject but with three different semantic subjects: phrase (a) denotes the punitive power of the state as a real, sociological datum; phrase (b) has penal legislation as its subject and phrase (c) indicates that theoreticians and doctrinalists have omitted themselves.[6] To sharpen the basic instrument of the word, we will successively call the subject of phrase (a) *punitive power,* that of phrase (b) *penal legislation* and we will reserve the term *criminal law* for the penal judicial doctrine (knowledge or science of penal law) of phrase (c).

Whereas *criminal law* (as a science) is the work of jurists (penalists), the *real exercise of punitive power* is the work of executive agencies of the state and *penal legislation* is produced by the appropriate policy agencies. *Criminal law* (the knowledge of jurists) is not destined for exercising punitive power, which is practiced by the state executive agencies, but for programming its containment, which should be performed by judges and their jurisprudence. *Liberal criminal law is destined for judicially containing the punitive power of the state,*[7] without which the state of law disappears and the *police state* prevails. The latter does not disappear, but always remains more or less encapsulated by the historical states of law, struggling to exceed its limits,[8] in a *constant dialectical relation.*

The Enemy in the Exercise of Punitive Power

Punitive power reappeared in European societies eight centuries ago, as an instrument of corporate social verticalization of the national states. The Church as the central power reaffirmed itself with its punitive power, first launched against dissidents (Cathars), soon after that against witches and later on against Protestants. The first *enemy* was the witches, who made a pact with Satan, the head of an army of demons, an invention built on prejudice against the *maleficent*[9] and women's inferiority, reinforcing the hierarchical regulation of sexuality, consolidated together with punitive power.[10] That corporative organization enabled the colonizing enterprise into America and Africa, which set in motion an extractive economy for raw materials and means of payment[11], giving rise to modern capitalism, which ended up weakening the colonizing powers and strengthening the neocolonizers,[12] displacing world hegemony from Spain and Portugal to the central and northern European powers.

Throughout this long course of events repression was always exercised in a different manner, depending on whether its recipients were *peers* or *strangers*. The peers always deserved more consideration, save for when they were political dissidents, in which case they were treated as *strangers*. The treatment for *strangers* distinguished between *severe offenders* (those who were directly enemies), *bothersome* (indirect enemies: with their conduct they challenged the vertical order) and *simply inferior* (potential enemies due to lack of discipline). The *severe offenders* (serious crimes or dissidents) were eliminated by killing them; the *bothersome* were eliminated through forced incorporation into the armies[13] or for the production of energy for movement (sentences rowing in the galleys). The *simply inferior* were exploited (Indians, servants and blacks) and submitted to exemplary elimination by death in cases of resistance or strongly controlled (women and children; the elderly did not count because of their low numbers).

This panorama was maintained until the Industrial Revolution, which gave way to changes that did not erase differentiated control, but attenuated it (sometimes more discursively than in reality). Nonetheless, once the new hegemonic class was settled in power, it reaffirmed the *duality of penal treatments:* although it maintained the guarantees for the *peers*, few changes were introduced for the *strangers*. Although the death penalty was reduced to *serious crimes* (murder) and to *dissidents* (e.g., the Paris Commune), those were killed, and ceased to be a problem. The *bothersome* were eliminated, being placed in prisons with high mortality rates,[14] submitted to interminable judgments,[15] or even deported (especially by Great Britain and France,[16] but also in Argentina[17]), in other words, although prison replaced death in many places, it was a death penalty by chance in the large cities, as was the case with the deportation sentence that replaced the *levies* and the galleys, which had become unsustainable because of the technification of war and introduction of steamships.

During the last century, the duality of punitive power was maintained, and there were quite differentiated models. We believe that the following different exercises of punitive power demonstrate the attempted models: (a) the authoritarian European model between the wars; (b) the democratic European model currently dominant in the European Union; (c) the current North American model; (d) the Latin American national security model and (e) the dominant current Latin American model.

In the between-war authoritarianism (Nazism, Fascism, Stalinism) there was a clear distinction between the *strangers and dissidents* and the *peers.* The *dissidents* were submitted to special police tribunals or executed without trial. The *severe criminals* were also physically eliminated. The *bothersome,* called *strangers to the community* in Nazism and *parasites* in Stalinism, were also destined for eliminatory concentration camps. The *peers* were treated according to the penal legislation that was the focus of the manuals of the period.

In the European countries, the *strangers* are also not treated as *peers*. Almost all legislations recognize *security measures* for *strangers*, which replace to old relegation sentences for those who seem to conduct their lives in an undesirable manner. The serious criminals receive major sentences, although not to the point of elimination. The *dissidents* are treated with greater consideration, due to tolerance and social pluralism. Although the diversity of repression has not totally disappeared, the division between *serious criminals, dissidents* and *strangers* on the one hand and *peers* on the other has been largely attenuated.

The repression set up in the United States in the last few decades—and which departs from its previous tradition—configures a pre-modern model carried out with high technology and unlimited financial resources. Differential repression is accentuated as in the preindustrial models: the *serious criminals* are eliminated through death or life sentences; the *strangers and dissidents* are submitted to elimination through very long sentences or undetermined ones (*three strikes out*); the dominant prison population, in an absurdly high number, belongs to African-American or Latin American minorities and sentencing is done through forcing negotiation. The *peers* are treated with the penal legislation explained in the manuals. The anti-terrorist penal legislation (*Patriot Act*) cancels constitutional guarantees. *It is the only country in the Americans that continues to freely apply the death penalty*[18] *and maintains a prison population that can be counted in the millions*, sustained by a vindictive *völkisch* publicity that extends around the globe, while it is beginning to legalize a parallel penal system for terrorists.

Labels have been applied on very different stereotypes, according to the emergency invoked, in other words, the quality of being a *stranger* has been handed out with notorious *arbitrariness.* Stated in other terms: *Who always individualized the enemy or the stranger? Those currently in power. How did they do so? As they saw fit. To whom was the label applied? To those who confronted or bothered them, really, imaginarily or potentially.*

The Latin American national security dictatorships applied eliminatory sentences for the *serious criminals* (life imprisonment, to a much lesser degree the formal death penalty), eliminatory measures for the *bothersome* or police executions without trial, but they established two penal systems for the *dissidents:* a *parallel penal system* that eliminated them through unlimited administrative detentions (invoking the *state of siege* or *war*), and another *underground penal system,* which proceeded with direct elimination by death and forced disappearance, without any trial.[19]

Currently, Latin American repression of *serious crimes* is done with lifetime imprisonment. The *bothersome* continue to be eliminated through administrative measures, disproportionate sentences (for recidivists) and imprisonment in jails where there are recognizably very high rates of violence, mortality and morbidity, in other words, with a high probability of physical elimination, while police and para-police executions without trial have not disappeared. The *dissidents* are tolerated for the most part, even though repression of social protest is on the rise. The *peers* usually enjoy the benefits and guarantees found in the manuals, especially of remaining at liberty during trials, which in practice is almost a pardon, given that around three fourths of the penal population is not condemned.

With this review we verify that, (a) on the one hand, there have always been different forms for controlling the *peers* and the *strangers*, (b) on the other, the more open, egalitarian and tolerant a society is, the more the differences between repressive treatment for *peers* and *strangers* are attenuated, as happens in the European Union countries. Moreover, one is encouraged with this being the case, considering that every other position is a *attempt to undermine the power of the state.*[20]

THE PENAL JUDICIAL KNOWLEDGE OF THE ENEMY

The prehistory of *criminal law of the enemy* may go back to Protagoras and Plato. The latter developed for the first time in Western thought the idea that the wrongdoer is inferior due to his incapacity to rise to the world of pure ideas, and when that condition is irreversible, he should be eliminated.[21] Protagoras maintained a general and special preventive theory of the sentence, but also postulated a *differential penal law:* incorrigibles were to be excluded from society.[22]

However, since the reestablishment of punitive power eight centuries ago, every theory of plurality of penal laws has been based on *emergencies*, meaning threats to the survival of civilization itself that assumed the character of *wars,* and thus, *reduced criminal law to administrative law and penalties to direct coercion.*[23] The first emergency was theorized by medieval criminologists called *demonologists,* coming from the Dominican order and summarized in the famous *Malleus Maleficarum*,[24] the first integrated model of criminological etiology, criminal law, penal process and criminalistics.[25] The inquisitorial procedure used torture to force denunciations of other suspects, in a manner reproducible *ad infinitum*. Its advantages for power rapidly extended to the lay tribunals, where it was applied even more extensively than in the ecclesiastical courts. The judges/police/inquisitors considered themselves immune to the evils of the devil. The etiology of evil (witchcraft) corresponded to a *theocratic/biological* discourse founded on the inferiority of women (more vulnerable to evil temptation) due to genetic weakness (derived from the man's curved rib), and they found physical signs of that inferiority (marks of the devil), disguised torture with neutral terminology, and so on.[26] The worst enemies were those who denied the existence or the power of witches, because they considered that witchcraft was a more serious crime than original sin.

With modernity, theorizations based on theocratic/biological discourses were cast aside. There was a return to Platonic idealism and a tendency to leave the *stranger* outside of criminal law to free him or her for police measures (administrative law), especially in dealing with those who were *bothersome* or *undisciplined (potentially dangerous)*. This could be theorized by resorting to Hegel, because given that every judicial relation presupposes freedom of the will, someone without *self-awareness* cannot enter into that relation, for *the field of law is the spiritual, and its precise place and starting point is the will, which is free, so that liberty constitutes its substance and determination; and the system of Law is the kingdom of freedom realize realized, the world of the spirit expressed by itself, as in a second nature.*[27] Because the *stranger* is not *self-aware*, and does not share that *second nature*, such a person cannot be submitted to a penalty, because he or she does not act with judicial relevance and cannot commit a crime, but only represent a menace, like an animal escaped from a zoo. From that there is just one step to convert such a person into an enemy as one who is *refractory*. It is fair to recognize that Hegel himself did not go that route, but his pejorative expressive regarding colonized cultures allow one to infer it.[28]

With the open return to inquisitorial behavior operated by *criminological positivism, all criminal law was theorized as administrative law and all sentences as measures of direct coercion against dangers. The inquisitorial principle definitively puts an end to criminal law and dissolves it into administrative law.* Four centuries after the *Malleus*, criminological positivism, with the same integrated scheme of etiological criminology, criminal law and penal and criminalistic procedure, has blatantly returned to the inquisitorial system. The *stranger,* both as a serious criminal and as a dissident,[29] returned to being biologically inferior, not because of gender as in the case of witches,[30] but because of pathology or belonging to an insufficiently evolved race (such a colonized person born by chance in Europe[31]) or due to being a *degenerate* (involuntary product of a superior race[32]). The law disappeared, replaced by administrative measures for direct coercion destined for containing the dangers that the offenders presented to society. Judges assumed police roles (as in the *Malleus*), and, obviously, the *strangers* (recognizable due to the stereotype) were much more dangerous than the *peers*, and, given their unchangeable inferiority, the only thing to do was eliminate them. The theoretical presentation cancelled the old differential treatment of the Hegelian matrix, the *peers* were also submitted to police measures, but it was the ones directed towards the *strangers* that were eliminatory.

The crudest expressions of that *dangerousness* belong to Rafael Garofalo, who affirmed that penal science has as its object defense against the *natural enemies of society*[33] and that indulgence by judges was no more than *the triumph of logic achieved at the expense of social security and morality.*[34] *In the eyes of the people*—he wrote, in what seems to be the best tone of the vindictive publicity of the early Twenty-First Century—*the codes, the proceedings and even Judicial Power, seem to have reached an agreement to protect the criminal against society, better than society against the criminal.*[35] As a follower of Spencer,[36] he affirmed that society needed to produce an equivalent to Darwin's natural selection,[37] and thus, the enemies needed to be eliminated, which he justified with the sharp remark that *through a slaughter on the battlefield the nation defends itself against its external enemies; through a capital execution, against its interior enemies.*[38]

The *enemies* were not limited to the *serious criminals,* but encompassed the *bothersome* as well (petty thieves, prostitutes, homosexuals, drunks, vagrants, gamblers, etc.), characterized as *dangerous classes*,[39] soon baptized as those of *evil life* and made the objects of literature with pretensions to field work.[40] Sentences without crimes were destined for them (unlimited police detention measures[41]).

In the most juridical variant of positivism, Franz von Liszt proposed imposing re-socializing penalties for the *peers* who made relatively small mistakes and merely intimidating sentences for occasional offenders (*very much peers*). However, for those who were incorrigible (the true *strangers*, encompassing the categories of serious and bothersome criminals), given the impossibility of killing or deporting them, he opted for imposing eliminatory sentences: *Society*—he wrote—*must protect itself from the irrecoverable, and because we cannot behead or hang them, and deporting them is not an option for us, we have no other choice than to deprive them of freedom for life (in their case, for an indeterminate period).*[42] This last category was complicated to the extent that the doctrine hearkened back to idealism, and thus, upon taking up again the scheme that can be traced back to Hegel, his disciple Karl Stooss replaced it with administrative police measures,[43] inventing what are now known as *security measures.*[44] From Stooss' Swiss project one criminal law is theorized for *peers* and another for *strangers*, with the first destining retributive sentences and the second providing *measures* that have one foot in penal law and the other in direct administrative coercion, since they answer to *positivist dangerousness.* They are definitively sentences without the limits or guarantees of the sentence, which is why from the outset *the lie of the labels* was denounced.[45]

The combination of this breakaway criminal law, which allows an idealist development for the *peers* (persons) and a determinist one for the *strangers* (dangerous beings), was carried out in two ways: the *vicariant* system and the *two-way system.* In both, measures are imposed on those who are decidedly *strangers*, but in the cases in which one cannot totally assure that quality for the subject, in the *vicariant* system the judge is authorized to replace the measure with a sentence, while in the *two-way* system the sentence is imposed as well as the measure. This latter criterion, undoubtedly more authoritarian, was adopted in 1930 by the *codice Rocco.* There can be no doubt that the indeterminate detention measures of the texts that follow the Fascist code are destined for eliminating *enemies* (*serious* criminals on the one hand and *bothersome* on the other, called *habitual professionals*, etc.)

The most extreme elaboration of the theme of differential treatment of the *stranger* or *enemy* was carried out by Edmund Mezger[46] participated with Franz Exner in preparing the project on *strangers to the community (Gemeinschaftsfremde),* destined to be eliminated in the concentration camps and who were certainly the same persons who, according to the positivists, incurred the status of dangerousness without wrongdoing.[47]

Mezger indistinctly used the concepts of *enmity towards law (Rechtsfeindlichkeit)* and *blindness towards law (Rechtsblindheit),* referring to *an attitude that is not in agreement with* the healthy intuition of the people *regarding the just and the unjust, so that under normal conditions, they should not apologize, but quite the contrary, set the basis for punishment.*[48] The terrifying examples of that enmity were the *outrages against the race* (sexual relations between Germans and Jews, punished by death), abortion and sodomy.[49] The *stranger to the community* was one who *because of his personality or form of conducting his life, especially due to his extraordinary defects in understanding or of character will be incapable of fulfilling with this own forces the minimal demands of the community of the people.*[50] From that definition one deduces that the *strangers* were the *bothersome* of the positivist *evil life.*

THE ENEMY, STRANGER OR *HOSTIS* IN POLITICAL THEORY

Traditional criminal law has limited itself to discussing it differentiated penal treatment of *enemies* or *strangers,* destined to neutralize the danger that they represent, is a subject for criminal law itself or for administrative law (police) and to deciding the entity that is to carry out such neutralization (from the *security measures* of Stooss to genocidal elimination by Mezger). With this it *presupposed the political admissibility of* the category of *stranger* derived from Roman law, where the *foreigner*, the *stranger,* the *enemy,* the *hostis,* was one who absolutely lacked rights, who was *outside of the community.*[51] The maximum penalty was expulsion from the community, *exile,* exactly because it left the subject in the situation of *foreigner, stranger, enemy,* deprived of every right.[52]

However much we qualify the idea, when we distinguish between *citizens* (persons) and *enemies* (non-persons), we are referring to humans who are deprived of certain individual rights.[53] The political question, that is, the kernel of the question, consists in determining *if it is politically and judicially admissible to have an updated version of the concept of "hostis" from Roman law.*

The current debate regarding enemy criminal law proposed by Jakobs makes reference to other explanations of current repressiveness, such as symbolic criminal law, the expansion of criminal law, criminal law at various speeds, etc., and there is criticism of the author's thesis that maintains that it is a case of introducing a criminal law of the author.[54] But what is certain is that the only form of admitting a *really limited* enemy criminal law would be through an extreme penal law of the author, in other words, limited to a group of persons actually identifiable due to physical characteristics, because otherwise, what is being discussed is not if one can treat some *strangers* in a differentiated manner, but if the *state of law can limit the guarantees and laws of all citizens.* This is so, because in permitting intervention in private communications one affects everyone's intimacy. By limiting procedural guarantees one places everyone at risk of being unduly prosecuted and even condemned for terrorism. By typifying equivocated preparatory acts one threatens everyone with sentences for conduct that in most cases is harmless (buying precursor chemicals to pay a house or fertilize a garden, take money to legally buy a property, carry fingernail clippers on an airplane, joke about some security measure, omit declaring a bank transfer, etc.). In other words, the supposedly novel anticipation of typification follows the almost two-thousand year old path of the *lex Julia* against crimes of lèse majesté, which was expanded to the point of punishing possession and manufacture of purple cloth, because it implied the risk of a preparation for magnicide.[55]

The discussion is thus clearly political; first if the Roman category of *enemy* or *hostis* is admissible in a state of law, and second, *if based on it one can limit the rights and guarantees of all inhabitants.* These political questions are not independent, because if one rejects using *hostis* to refer to an ethnically differentiated group, admitting its use will mean limiting citizen liberty. That means that differentiated penal treatment of the *hostis* implies *an injury to the limits on the state regarding the citizen, meaning that it is a more repressive treatment for everyone, which is much more compatible with an absolute state than with a state of law.*

Jakobs perceives the political nature of the question, but moves it towards a debatable polarizing dilemma; he depicts as radical positions those of Rousseau and Fichte, for whom all delinquents would be enemies, and those of Hobbes and Kant as moderate, for whom only some would be. In philosophy the current practice is not to oppose thinkers in this way,[56] but Hobbes is usually opposed to Locke. Moreover, the positions of Rousseau and Fichte are not so radical.

In principle, Rousseau is contradictory; he seems to refer only to murderers and not to any delinquent, and furthermore, he only admits depriving of life one who cannot be maintained without danger, and, if that were not enough, in the same book he admits that a state can only have as an enemy another state, never a person.[57] In the case of Fichte, we believe that a more careful reading will allow us to understand that although he is not proposing an enemy criminal law, he maintains that those should be the domain of administrative law, considering as such only murderers, incorrigibles and traitors, for whom he reserves noting less than the death penalty as an eliminatory administrative measure.[58] Here, perhaps, one may find the first reference to the famous Stalinist phrase, which was that the death penalty was not a penalty, but the maximum measure for social defense.

The true confrontation in political thinking is produced between Hobbes and Locke. Starting with the idea that humans develop their faculties because of their desire for power,[59] Hobbes understands that competition, mistrust and the desire for war are the causes of disputes, that in a state of nature determine a state of permanent war,[60] in which there are no rights, since each one has what he or she can obtain and conserve, nor are there moral judgments. To put an end to that state, humans achieve the social contract, through which they deliver all power to the sovereign, who is not part of the contract, because it is agreed upon between the subjects.[61] As that sovereignty is the only thing that can contain war, it cannot be partial: sovereignty must be total. The subject can hardly retain any rights, because before sovereignty there were no rights.

For Hobbes, resistance to the sovereign's power is inadmissible, because that would mean reintroducing the *bellum omnium contra omnes,* the *war of all against all,* and precisely because of that, those who resist the power of the sovereign cannot be punished, but only submitted to forced containment because they are not delinquents but enemies,[62] who, with their resistance reintroduce war. However serious a crime may be, its author is not an enemy, but someone who resists the sovereign is an enemy, because he or she returns to being a *stranger* or *foreigner* by leaving the contract through an act of resistance.

The thinking that opposes Hobbes' idea of an absolute state is that of Locke, for whom in the natural state there is a natural law, and therefore there are rights.[63] Locke's contractualist metaphor is much more realistic than that of Hobbes. For Locke it is implicit that civil society predates the state, which some take to presuppose two contracts. What is certain is that once civil society is constituted, the majority decide the state contract, and hence, cannot assign all rights, but only those necessary for conserving those rights. The legitimate resistance that overthrows a sovereign, to Locke, does not dissolve civil society, although that is the effect that Hobbes attributes to it. *For Locke, a critic of absolute monarchy, someone who carries out an act of legitimate resistance demanding respect for rights previous to the state contract, is a citizen exercising rights; to Hobbles, a defender of the absolute state, such a one is an enemy who needs to be repressed and contained with unlimited force, without even respecting the boundaries of the sentence, because such a one has ceased to be a subject. Someone who, to Locke, is exercising the right of resistance to oppression, is for Hobbes an enemy worse than a criminal. For Locke, the sovereign who abuses power loses the condition of sovereignty and becomes simple another person; for Hobbes it is the subject who resists abuse of power by the sovereign who loses his condition and begins to be an enemy.*

In support of his thesis Jakobs cites Kant, and especially emphasizes a note by him in the second section of his treatise *Perpetual Peace: a Philosophical Sketch* published in 1795.[64] In that note, Kant affirms that there may be peoples or humans in a natural state, whose very anarchical presence represents a danger, and in those conditions there is the right to obligate them to enter the contract. Anyone can force those who insist on remaining outside of the contract to come under it, because that is the only way to guarantee peace. In that sense, Kant was following the tradition of Hobbes, and along identical lines was denying the right to resist oppression, because for that philosopher, destruction of the state represented loss of the external guarantee of the categorical imperative, and thus, the return to the natural state and resulting restoration of war of all against all.[65]

Along the same lines as Locke, Feuerbach responded to Kant in 1798, he publishing his *Anti-Hobbes*,[66] which was, strictly speaking, an *Anti-Kant*.[67] Feuerbach defended rights prior to the contract. He affirmed that rights also existed in the natural state, e.g., blacks sold as slaves had a prior right to freedom, although they could not exercise it because they had been impeded in doing so by force. To Feuerbach, the sovereign is part of the contract, and because of it he is given the right to choose the means to carry out his ends. Dissident regarding those choices—politics—cannot establish any right to resistance, which only appears when the sovereign acts against civil society and intends to return it to the state of nature. By deviating from the purposes assigned by the contract to sovereignty, it is understood that the so sovereign loses his character as such, and thus, resistance is not to the sovereign but to a particular person with power. There is no right to resistance to the sovereign, but to one who has ceased to be one by departing from the ends that the contract assigns for exercising sovereignty. By not admitting that resistance, one would fall into the contradiction of maintaining that the contract imposes the duty of obeying someone who wishes to destroy society.

That also explains Feuerbach's liberal jusnaturalism: there is not only a practical moral reason, but also a practical judicial reason, which indicates that there may be an exercise of rights that are prior to the state contract.[68] While the first indicates a moral duty, the second indicates the judicial space as a subjective right in society, independent of the will of the sovereign.

We also believe that it is clearly demonstrated that the question of the enemy does not involve contraposition of Rousseau/Fichte with Hobbes/Kant, still less because the first were radicalized and the second moderate, but in the discussion on the absolute state and the liberal state, between Hobbes and Locke first, and then between Kant and Feuerbach, where the key lies in the right of resistance to oppression, which the defenders of the absolute state not only deny, but assign the character of enemy to those who intend to exercise it.

Hobbes' thesis presents two important contradictions that can be summarized in one, which has not gone unnoticed by subsequent scholars. The first was pointed out by *liberal criticism,* in other words our Anselm von Feuerbach, and which we have just mentioned; if it is the sovereign himself who reintroduces *bellum omnium contra omnes*, it is absurd for citizens to passively stand by and watch the social destruction. In that sense his state is *excessively absolute.* But in another sense, Hobbes' state is *not very absolute* and in this sense also falls into another contradiction that has been pointed out by *authoritarian critics.* Hobbes was writing at the time of the influence of religious wars and was thinking of *inner conviction.* He distinguished between *private* and *public;* his "Leviathan" *reached to the boundaries of the private* but did not enter it. As to the question of faith in miracles,[69] the sovereign decides which miracles are to be believed, but *this refers to public worship, not to inner conviction.* Faith is an intimate question, its profession is public, and in the first instance Leviathan does not enter.

Carl Schmitt, the most penetrating reactionary theoretician of the past century, warned in 1938 that *this turned out to be the mortal germ that destroyed the powerful Leviathan from inside and killed the mortal god. Already a few years after its publication*—he adds referring to Spinoza—*the gaze of the first liberal Jew fell on the barely visible crack.*[70] Schmitt then begins raving that practically all of the distinctions between morality and law—the most precious achievement of European civilization[71]—from Christian Thomasius forward, and including Kant—are Jewish subterfuges to *erode and undermine the power of the state as the best means for paralyzing foreign peoples and for emancipating the Jewish people themselves.*[72] But the Nazi ravings must not cloud the truth of the contradiction pointed out: *if the sovereign cannot intrude into inner conviction, when he does so there is no other alternative but to recognize the birth of the right to resist the sovereign.* Moreover, one might think that in doing so one reintroduces religious war and with it the *bellum omnium contra omnes* and—in a curious paradox—the contradiction indicated by absolutism would coincide with that of liberalism, because in such a case the sovereign would lose legitimacy, and cease to be sovereign for violating his function, however much Hobbes considers this foreign to the contract. Schmitt perceives that Feuerbach's thesis could be maintained by Hobbes himself, but minimizes that, considering Feuerbach little more than a petulant youth and avoiding answering the issue through the recourse of criticizing the theory of psychological coercion,[73] which is certainly the least fortunate among the brilliant Feuerbach's theses, forgetting that contradiction of a thought is not answered by another contradiction of the thought of the critic.

But Schmitt's political criticism of Hobbes, despite having been an heir to his thought,[74] is accurate from the authoritarian point of view, and, furthermore, is a necessary starting point for all of his conception of the *enemy*, he being the only one to consistently develop it to its final consequences.[75] Their brutality does not gainsay their consistency; quite the contrary, we believe that it is exactly Schmitt's formidable consistency that demonstrates that *the thesis of the enemy in the field of political science ends up necessarily with his conclusions.*

The Hobbesian enemy could not be one limited to acting as such, to outwardly resisting the sovereign, but to be coherent with the thesis of the absolute state, the enemy had to be someone who with his thought or faith resisted the path imposed by the sovereign. If obedience needed to be outward and inward, enmity could also be both outward and inward disobedience.

From that point on, the dilemma is clear: for liberalism there are only offenders (*peers*); for absolutism not only are there offenders or delinquents (*peers*), but also enemies in war (*strangers*). The function of liberal policy would be to guarantee peace among the citizens (*all peers*), punishing offenders according to the seriousness of the violation. The function of absolutist policy would also be to guarantee peace among the citizens (*peers*), but in order to do this it would be necessary to neutralize the enemies (*strangers*) with war and punishment of offenders would become a less important question. Without neutralizing the enemies (*strangers*) with war there could be no peace among citizens (*peers*); if the state loses the war it cannot guarantee its interior peace, and the state always has enemies (*strangers*) that make war against it and against those for whom there is no other remedy save answering them with war. When facing an enemy in war there is no limit imposed by *humanity,* because it has not enemies. He might have endorsed the elegant affirmation of Joseph de Maistre—another coherent and forerunning reactionary—when he said that *there is no such thing as a "man" in the world; in my life I have seen Frenchmen, Italians, Russians, etc., but as regards "man," I declare that never in my life have I found him and if he exists, he is unknown to me.*[76] Hence Schmitt affirms that all invocation of *humanity* is false and can be suspected of manipulation, because any limit to the power of the sovereign against the enemy puts an end to the very concept of the enemy, weakens the state and keeps it from guaranteeing peace among the citizens. The Roman idea of the enemy, of the *hostis*, does not admit half measures, not even the limit of inner conviction imposed by Hobbes, because it opens up the path of resistance to the sovereign and with that impedes the exercise of sovereignty in *war.*

The reasoning that admits a distinction between *citizens and enemies* must presuppose a *war* (for without it there are no *enemies*) and one that is practically permanent, since exceptional wars are the province of military and wartime law and not criminal law or ordinary administration. Starting from that premise, one must conclude, as does Schmitt, that the essence of politics, that is, what is equivalent to *good and evil* in morality, to *beautiful and ugly* in aesthetics, to *profitable and unprofitable* in economics (for if it does not find this essence, the political will lack autonomy) consists in the *friend/enemy* distinction: *the specific political distinction to which it is possible to refer political actions and motives is the distinction between* friend *and* enemy.[77] That is coherent, for if one admits a permanent war, the essential function of politics could be nothing else than being occupied with it.

The crowning point of Schmitt's thinking, in pointing out the essence of politics in this way is that *there is no liberal politics, but only liberal criticism of politics.* As a result, liberal criminal law would be nothing more than a critique of authoritarian criminal law (of the enemy), in other words, a succession of discourses that criticized the succession of discourses of enemy criminal law, but in reality it would be an illusion. One must recognize its merit in being *the most formidable and coherent unprejudiced effort to deny the dialectic between the police state and the state of law, intending to reduce the latter to a bothersome and hollow disturbing illusion and assigning reality only to the former.*

Schmitt affirms that this line of *friend/enemy* distinction indicates the *extreme degree of intensity of a union or a separation, of an association or dissociation,* which has no reason to appeal to the other distinctions or to base itself on them. Thus, regardless of whether good or bad, beautiful or ugly, *the enemy is simply the other, the foreigner,*[78] *and it is enough for him to be existentially, in a particularly intensive sense, someone else or foreign, so that in an extreme case it will be possible to have conflicts with him that cannot be decided either through a system of pre-established norms or through the intervention of a third party who is uncommitted and thus impartial.*[79]

Who decides which group or groups are the enemies. Schmitt's response can be no other: the politician, in other words, the sovereign. In the case of the extreme conflict, it is the politician who *decides if the otherness of the stranger in the concretely existing conflict means the denial of his modes of existence and if because of this it is necessary to defend oneself and fight, to preserve one's own, peculiar mode of life.*[80]

This means that in emergencies, the power to defend the Constitution corresponds to the executive and not to the judiciary, considered by Schmitt to be a bureaucratic power, useful in times of normality but not in an emergency.[81] Thus, when it is a case of defending the Constitution, the sovereign is enabled to cancel all limits and guarantees, without any control by the judiciary, which he explains by maintaining that the Constitution is a set of laws and that some have priority over others; the republican principle, for example, is a priority, and thus, to save it, one may suspend all guarantees and rights.[82]

The Roman concept of the *hostis* can only be coherently maintained through a line of thought that leads to the political consequences pointed out by Schmitt. One may argue that even war has limitation, which is undoubtedly right. But when one speaks of the *hostis* as the enemy introduced in "normal" or "permanent" criminal or administrative law, we are not referring to war under Geneva law. To the contrary, we are introducing a *spurious or private concept of permanent war,* of *irregular war,* which Schmitt also did not ignore. With that idea of the *hostis*, as an enemy in an irregular and permanent war, one ends up with the *dirty war* of the national security doctrine, according to which one should not respect the rules of regular war in an irregular one.[83] This has its roots in the French action in Algeria and in Schmitt's own theorizing, which does not focus on it in vain, intending to find its first manifestations in the Spanish resistance to the Napoleonic invasion and vindicating General Raoul Salan.[84] To do this, he arbitrarily interpreted Clausewitz's famous thesis, confusing the political moment with the military moment. Clausewitz indicated the continuity, but did not confuse them; Schmitt confuses them with the irregular war of his *partisan.* The continuity is real, but they continue to be two moments, and, in the political moment, there cease to be *enemies* and there begin to be *offenders.* The *power of war* (against *enemies*) of the war moment begins to be *punitive power* (against *offenders*) in the political moment. Schmitt confuses them to allow enemies to subsist in the political moment; his *war* does not cease, but is permanent.

The intention of introducing the *enemy* or *hostis* in ordinary criminal or administrative law in a clarified or limited form does not invalidate the affirmative that the only coherent introduction of the concept is that of Carl Schmitt, exactly because in it resides the contradiction that Schmitt pointed out in Hobbes: if we admit the existence of the *enemy,* but place limits on singling out such a person, we cannot deny that when the defining power exceeds those limits a right to resistance appears for the citizen who is arbitrarily singled out as an enemy. With that, we weaken the state in war, which is inadmissible.

It will obviously be argued that there exists a state of law and that it has institutions and controls that impede the arbitrary singling out of enemies. That is true, but *in limiting the rights of everyone in order to be able to effectively individualize the enemies, one narrows the possibilities of defense for citizens before those same organisms, since by definition were are neutralizing—or at least weakening—the controls of the state of law.*

On the other hand, the concept of *enemy* or *hostis* provides for the sovereign and for mass publicity an argument that de-legitimates institutions and controls and allows them to stigmatize them as obstacles, antipatriotic, useless and blind bureaucrats, ideologues covering up enemies, useful idiots and, definitively, traitors in wartime. Almost all Latin American *coups d'état* have rationalized their crime by invoking the need to defend the Constitution that they themselves have violated or annihilated. *Thus, the judicial admission of the concept of the enemy in law that is not strictly of war is, logically and historically, the germ or the first symptom of the authoritarian destruction of the state of law.*

SOME CONCLUSIONS

We have traced the history of punitive power and criminal law and we end up with the basic political question. We can formulate some concluding reflections, even though the question has no conclusion, because it is a *formidable political problem.*

1. To begin with, the proposal by the Professor from Bonn is not new in theorizing criminal policy, since it has been maintained long before and is almost reiterative.
2. The reaction it provokes—not to mention the sincerity with which it is expounded—is the product of the current situation of world power, which makes it much more dangerous because it may facilitate the bath to regression in carrying out a universal program of Human Rights.
3. The punitive power of penal legislation in every period has distinguished between *peers* and *strangers,* meaning that there has always been a category of offenders for those to be eliminated: first by death or by deportation and galleys, later by lifetime prison sentences and indeterminate segregation sentences and, finally, security measures have been invented for neutralizing *strangers.*
4. Criminal law has had more than its fill of theorizing the difference between *corrigible* and *incorrigible, peers* and *strangers*, to the point of openly confessing that it invented the security measures because it can neither apply the death penalty nor deport.
5. Given that the *strangers* cannot be individualized through physical features, the question is not limited to reducing the guarantees and freedoms for terrorists and other sinister sorts, but the question to clarify is if one can limit the freedoms and guarantees for citizens in order to more effectively individualize the enemies, including assuming the risk of considering some citizen as an enemy.
6. The discussion as to whether *strangers* should be penal or administrative presupposes the political admission of the category of *enemies,* which is something that must be discussed with total clarity.
7. If besides *citizens* there are also *enemies,* that is because there is war, and in that case one cannot admit any resistance to the sovereign and thus, one cannot place limitations on the individualization and containment of enemies.

8. Any limitation to pointing out and containing the enemy means recognizing the right to resistance, and if there are enemies and permanent war, the only possible model for a state is an absolute state.
9. If one admits the existence of *enemies* and *war* in a permanent form, the limitations of a state of law are an obstacle to effectively neutralizing them.
10. When one confuses military and political movements the war becomes permanent and the limitations on extraordinary war disappear, giving way to the thesis of the *dirty war.*
11. It is not possible to avoid that consequence without clearly distinguishing the political moment (in which one can only have *violating* citizens) and the military moment (in which the *enemies* appear).
12. The admission of the judicial category of the *enemy* in ordinary law (penal and/or administrative) introduces the seed of the destruction of the state of law, because its limiting and controlling institutions become an obstacle for eliminatory effectiveness: *one who is a hindrance in the war is a traitor.*

NOTES

1. Émile de Girardin, the abolitionist during the later years of the second empire, maintained that the death penalty was the last one that should disappear (*Du droit de punir*, París, 1871).

2. A brief reference to the theme is formulated in *La ciencia of criminal law ante las exigencias del presente*, Trans. by Teresa Manso Porto, in "Revista Peruana de Ciencias Penales," año VII-VIII edición especial nº 12, and especially in *Bürgerstrafrecht und Feindstrafrecht*, en HRRS, March 2004, Spanish trans. in Günther Jakobs/Manuel Cancio Meliá, *Derecho Penal del Enemigo*, Cuadernos Civitas, Madrid, 2003.

3. Among many, Albin Eser, in Eser/Hassemer/Burkhardt, *La ciencia of criminal law ante el nuevo milenio* (Francisco Muñoz Conde, coordinador), Valencia, 2004, p. 472. Also among many, Lúcio Antônio Chamon Junior, *Do giro finalista ao funcionalismo penal, Embates de perspectivas dogmáticas decadentes*, Porto Alegre, 2004.

4. We refer to *crimes of massive and indiscriminate destruction* and not to *terrorism*, which is a judicially nebulous term.

5. Infra, n° 5.

6. The equivocations are not exhausted with this, since we could also add another that uses the same grammatical subject to designate the jurisprudence of penal or constitutional courts, for example, and we could think of another that with the same expression places the reflex of punitive power in the public imagination.

7. This counterposition may go back to Franz von Liszt; on it, Claus Roxin, *Kriminalpolitik und Strafrechtssystem*, p. 2.

8. Merkl, A., *Teoría general del derecho administrative*, México, pp. 325 and ss.

9. A broad investigation on these prejudices in Norman Cohn, *Los demonios familiares de Europa*, Madrid, 1980. See the terms "fascinación" and "maleficia," in Rossell Hope Robbins, *Enciclopedia de la brujería and demonología*, Madrid, 1988.

10. And to a large degree in effect until the present. About that, the detailed investigation by James A. Brundage, *La ley, el sexo and la sociedad cristiana en la Europa Medieval*, México, 2000.

11. See e.g., Walter Rodney, *De cómo Europa subdesarrolló a África*, México, 1982.

12. See Maurice Niveau, *Historia de los hechos económicos contemporáneos*, Barcelona, 1977.

13. This was imposed administratively through the *leyes de leva*, these being the first *security measures* in colonial times and after independence.

14. On the mortality in Spanish prisons, Rafael Salillas, *La vida penal en España*, Madrid, 1888, p. 54 and ss.; in France, Pedro Kropotkine, *Las prisiones*, Trans. by La Juventud Literaria, Bs. As., s.d. (1900 *circa*); Michel Bourdet-Pléville, *Galeotes, forzados and penados*, Barcelona, 1963, pp. 101 and ss.; Jacques-Guy Petit, *Ces peines obscures, La prison pénale en France 1780-1875*, Par´s, 1990.

15. Formally in preventive prisons, about which Concepción Arenal wrote in 1877: "Imposing on a man a serious penalty, such as deprivation of liberty, a blot on this honor, as is having been in jail, and this without having proven that he is guilty, with the probability that he is innocent, is something that says much about justice" (*Estudios Penitenciarios*, Madrid, 1877, p. 12).

16. On the English deportation to Australia, Robert Hughes, *La costa fatídica*, Barcelona, 1989; on French deportation: Édouard Teisseire, *La transporation pénale et la relegation d'apres les Lois de 30. Mai 1854 et 27.Mai 1885*, París, 1893; C. O. Barbaroux, *De la transportation*, París, 1857; Michel Bourdet-Pléville, *Galeotes, forzados and penados*, cit.; H. Donnedieu de Vabres, *A Justiça penal hoje*, Sao Paulo, 1938, p. 102. Against the opinión of Concepción Arenal, Salillas proposed it for Spain, *La vida penal en España*, cit.

17. See C. Muratgia, *Director, Presidio and cárcel de reincidentes. Tierra del Fuego. Antecedentes*, Bs. As., s.d., (1910 *circa*); also *Ushuaia 1884-1984. Cien años de una ciudad argentina*, editado por la Municipalidad de Ushuaia bajo la dirección de Arnoldo Canclini, 1984.

18. See Hugo Adam Bedau, *The Death Penalty in America. Current Controversies*, New York, 1998.

19. On the concepts of underground and parallel penal systems, Lola Aniyar de Castro, *Derechos humanos, modelo integral de la ciencia penal, and sistema penal subterráneo*, in "Rev. del Colegio de Abogados Penalistas del Valle," Cali, 1985, pp. 301 and ss.

20. Carl Schmitt, *El Leviatán en la teoría del estado de Thomas Hobbes, Sentido and fracaso de un símbolo político*, México, 1997, p. 117.

21. *Las Leyes*, IX (Platón, "Obras Completas," Bib. Ameba, Bs. As., 1967, T. IV, p. 95 and ss.)

22. Platón, *Protágoras*; on this, Alfred Verdross, *La filosofía del derecho del mundo occidental*, México, 1962, p. 35.

23. Police power in the old administrative terminology.

24. See Abbiati-Agnoletto-Lazzati, *La stregoneria. Diavoli, streghe, inquisitori dal Trecento al Settecento*, Milano, 2003.

25. H. Krämer–J.Sprenger, *El martillo de las brujas para golpear a las brujas con poderosa masa*, traducción de Miguel Jiménez Monteserín, Valladolid, 2004; *Il martello delle streghe*, Venecia, 1995.

26. Those characteristics were detailed by the first organic critic of the *Malleus*, Friedrich von Spee, en 1631, *I processi contro le streghe (Cautio criminalis)*, Roma, 2004.

27. Hegel, *Filosofía del derecho*, México, 1985, pp. 31-32.

28. Hegel, *Lecciones on the filosofía de la historia universal*, Madrid, 1980, pp. 169, 177, 183, 215, 354, 596, 657.

29. On the dissidents, Cesare Lombroso, *Gli anarchici*, Torino, 1894; Lombroso/ Laschi, *Le crime politique et les révolutions*, París, 1892; Benito Mario Andrade, *Estudio de antropología criminal espiritualista*, Madrid, 1899, pp. 203 and ss.; and the supranormal were also considered suspicious (Lombroso, *L'uomo di genio in rapporto alla psichiatria, alla storia ed all'estetica*, Torino, 1894). Max Nordau followed this closely considering all dangerously creative artists as degenerates (*Degeneración*, Madrid, 1902). Leaders of mass movements were considered in the same manner: Gustavo Le Bon, *La psicología política and la defensa social*, Madrid, 1912; by the same, *Psicología das multidoes*, Rio de Janeiro, 1954; Scipio Sighele, *I delitti della folla*, Torino, 1910; J.M. Ramos Mejía, *Las multitudes argentinas*, Buenos Aires, 1912: On the criminalization of multitudes and leaders, Jaap van Ginneken, *Folla, psicologia e politica*, Roma 1989.

30. Although women continued to be inferior in intelligence and, as such, with tendencies towards prostitution, as "equivalent" to crime: Cesare Lombroso-Guglielmo Ferrero, *La donna delinquente, la prostituta e la donna normale*, Torino, 1915; also regarding prostitution, Paul Kovalevsky, *La Psychologie criminelle*, París, 1903, I, pp. 181 and ss.

31. Lombroso notes the similarity between the born criminal and a Mongoloid or Negroid (*L'uomo delincuente in rapporto all'antropologia, giurisprudenza e alle discipline carcerarie. Delincuente nato e pazzo morale*, 3ª. Ed., Torino, 1884, pp. 248 and 295). Since ancient times human characteristics had been assigned to animals, to thus classify humans according to them. That was the task begun by physiognomists, beginning with Giovan Battista della Porta, *Della fisonomia dell'uomo. Con illustrazioni dell'edizione del 1610*, Parma, 1988. Para el siglo XVIII, Johann Caspar Lavater / Georg Christoph Lichtenberg, *Lo specchio dell'anima. Pro e contro la fisiognomica. Un dibattito settecentesco*, a cura di Giovanni Gurisatti, Padova, 1991; also Lucia Rodler, *Il corpo specchio dell'anima. Teoria e storia della fisiognomica*, Bruno Mondadori, 2000. Un meticuloso e inteligente desarrollo en Armelle Le Bras-Chopard, *El zoo de los filósofos. De la bestialización a la exclusion*, Taurus, Madrid, 2003.

32. On this Daniel Dic, *Volti della degenerazione, una síndrome europea 1848-1918*, Firenze, 1999.

33. R. Garofalo, *La criminología*, Trans. by Pedro Dorado Montero, Madrid, s.d., p. 7, 11, 14 and 15.

34. Ibid, p. 11.

35. Ibid, p. 15. Garofalo defined the enemy through the *recta ratio* of *those civilized peoples, of the superior races of humanity, with an exception made for those degenerate tribes that represent evildoers in society* (Ibid, p. 102).

36. He considered him "the greatest of contemporary philosophers," ibid, p. 97.

37. Ibid, p. 326. That proposal was taken up again by Nazism: Helmut Nicolai, *Die rassengesetzliche Rechtslehre, Grundzüge e. nazionalsozialist. Rechtsphilosophie*, München, 1932.

38. Garofalo, *Criminología*, p. 133; p. 59 de la 2ª ed. italiana, Torino, 1891.

39. The most important book, written by a Paris policemen, although showing the shortcomings of the discourse, at the same time reflected the importance assigned to the problem: H. A. Frégier, *Des classes dangereuses de la population dans les grandes villes*, Bruxelles, 1840.

40. In reality, they followed in the tradition of Frégier, mixing police information with prejudices and moral concepts: Salillas, Rafael, *El delincuente español. Hampa (Antropología picaresca),* Madrid, 1898; Nicéforo, Alfredo—Sighele, Scipio, *La mala vide en Roma*, Madrid, 1901; Bernaldo de Quirós, Constancio, *La mala vida en Madrid. Estudio psicosociológico con dibujos and fotografías al natural*, Madrid, 1901 (reed. Madrid, 1998); Bembo, Max, *La mala vida en Barcelona*, Barcelona, 1912; Gómez, Eusebio, *La mala vida en Buenos Aires*, Buenos Aires, 1908 (con prólogo de José Ingenieros). There is an interesting literary compilation by Ernesto Ferrero with a prologue by Leonardo Sciascia, *Storie nere di fine secolo. La mala Italia*, Milano, 1973; on the differential treatment in Rio de Janeiro, Lená Medeiros de Menezes, *Os indesejáveis: desclassificados da Modernidade. Protesto, crime e expulsao na Capital Federal (1890-1930)*, Rio de Janeiro, 1996.

41. The definition by Ingenieros is supremely illustrative regarding the *enemies* identified as strangers: *It is a foreign and hostile horde within their own terrain, bold in their lurking, open in their proceedings, untiring in the treacherous proceeding of its tragic programs* (Prólogo a Gómez, p. 6).

42. See Franz von Liszt, *La idea de fin en criminal law*, Valparaíso, 1984, p. 120.

43. First invented for the unimputable: *Vorentwurf zu einem Schweizerischen StGB, Allg. Teil, Im Autrages des Bundesrates ausgearbeitet von Carl Stooss. Avant-Projet de Code Pénal Suisse, Partie Générale, Traduit par mission du Département Fédéral de Justice et Police par Alfred Gautier*, Basel und Genf, Verlag von Georg & Co., 1893, pages 10 and 11.

44. On this, see the very particularized analysis by Enzo Musco, *La misura di sicurezza detentiva, Profili storici e costituzionali*, Milano, 1978.

45. An expression of Ed. Kohlrausch, *Sicherungshaft. Eine Besinnung auf den Streitstand*, en ZStW, 44 (1924), pages 21-34.

46. He was the Neokantian penalist most disseminated in the Spanish language, which did not see translations of liberal Neokantians such as Max Ernst Mayer and Hellmuth von Weber. Gustav Radbruch himself—as was the case of M.E. Mayer—was translated by legal philosophers, but not by penalists.

47. New light is being shed on this draft project through a detailed investigation by Francisco Muñoz Conde, *Edmund Mezger y derecho criminal de su tiempo. Estudios*

sobre criminal law en el nacionalsocialismo, Valencia, 2003; this project and the concrete proposal by Mezger are also examined by Michael Burleigh/Wolfgang Wippermann, *Lo Stato razziale, Germania 1933-1945*, Rizzoli, 1992, p. 158.

48. Mezger, E., *Rechtsirrtum und Rechtsblindheit*, in "Probleme der Strafrechtserneuerung, Fest. f. Kohlrausch," Berlin, 1944, pp. 180-198 (p. 197-198). The *healthy intuition of the people* was the Nazi formula with which the analogy was introduced, a reform in which Mezger also participated (Cf. Muñoz Conde, op.cit., p. 85).

49. Cf. Muñoz Conde, op. cit., p. 145.

50. Muñoz Conde, op. cit., p. 193.

51. *Foreigner* and *enemy* meant *hostis*, which came from the Sanskrit root *ghas*, *to eat* (from whence comes *hostelry*). *Hostire* is to *kill* and *hostia* is *victim*. On this: R. von Ihering, *L'esprit du Droit Romain dans les diverses phases de son développement*, París, 1877, tomo I, p. 228.

52. Cf. Albert Du Boys, *Histoire du Droit Criminel des Peuples Anciens*, París, 1845, p. 245.

53. This becomes much more problematic in Jakobs' proposal, since, starting with his normativism he affirms that the enemy should not be considered as a *person*. Strictly speaking, he is in fact also sincere here, since every criminal law that theorizes by admitting that some human beings *are dangerous* and only because of that must be segregated and eliminated, *reifies* them, ceases to consider them *persons,* and thus violates article 1 of the Universal Declaration of Human Rights. In this sense, Jakobs' proposal should not scandalize us, but every todo criminal law of the enemy should, in other words, every tradition that excludes *strangers* from sentencing and eliminates them as dangerous. It is posible that Jakobs merely intended to postúlate that the enemies have fewer individual rights than citizens, but this is not made clear in his writing. On the polemic that the expression has aroused: Luis Gracia Martín, *Consideraciones críticas sobre el actualmente denominado "criminal law of the enemy,"* "Revista electrónica de Ciencia Penal and Criminología," 7-2-2005.

54. Cancio Meliá, Manuel, en Jakobs-Cancio Meliá, *Derecho penal del enemigo*, cit., pp. 65 and ss.

55. Cf. Teodoro Mommsen, *El derecho penal romano*, Trans. by P. Dorado, Madrid, s.d., II, p. 63; also Mariano Ruiz Funes, *Evolución del delito político*, México, 1944, p. 18.

56. Cf., for example, Wilhelm Windelband, *Historia de la filosofía, La filosofía del iluminismo*, México, 1948, pp. 60 and ss.; Alfred Verdross, *La filosofía del derecho del mundo occidental, Visión panorámica de sus fundamentos and principales problemas*, México, 1962, pp.179 and ss.; Frederick Copleston, *Historia de la filosofía*, Barcelona, 1983, vol. V, pp. 122 and ss.; M. Federico Sciacca, *Historia de la filosofía*, Barcelona, 1966, pp. 335 and ss.; Émile Bréhier, *Historia de la filosofía*, Bs. As., T.II, pp. 617 and ss.; N. Abbagnano, *Historia de la filosofía*, Barcelona, 1973, II, pp. 185 and ss.

57. The text to which Jakobs refers is in chapter V of book II: "every wrongdoer, in attacking social law, because of his misdeeds is a rebel and a traitor to his country, ceases to be a member of it by violating its laws and makes war on it. Therefore, conservation of the State is incompatible with his own; it is necessary for one of the two to

perish, and when the guilty party is executed, it is more as an enemy than as a citizen. The procedure and the sentence are the proof and the declaration that he has broken the social contract, and as a result, is no longer a member of the State" (page 37). Nevertheless, he adds: "There is no evil man who could not be made a good man for something. There is no right to put to death, not even as an example, except for one who cannot be maintained without danger" (page 38). In chapter IV of Book I he affirms that "a State may not have as an enemy anything but another State, and not men, since one cannot set up relations between things of diverse natures." In fact, he specifies that "without a declaration of war there are no enemies, but only bandoliers." (page13) (Jean-Jacques Rousseau, *El contrato social*, Trans. by Consuelo Berges, Madrid, 1973).

58. He reasons by thesis and antithesis, and although in his thesis he maintains that every delinquent becomes an enemy, based on the *rebus sic stantibus* clause, in other words, that the offender loses all rights in violating the contract. In his antithesis he asserts the emergence of a new contract, which is one of *expiation*. To the extent that it is able to protect public safety (general prevention and dissuasion), it establishes the right to demand punishment. Only when expiation is insufficient does Fichte accept exclusion from society, but based on a new contract (one of *amendment*) the person can claim the right to improve; it is a case of temporal exclusion. Only if the subject does not amend or in case of murder does Fichte allow for definitive exclusion. He leaves only murderers, incorrigibles and traitors irremediably out of the contract. For them Fichte reserves the death penalty, but without any tallion foundation (he believes that tallion is a theocratic theory), but as a measure of administrative security that the state should carry out merely as an administrator (J. G. Fichte, *Fondement du droit naturel selon les principes de la doctrine de la science (1796-1797),* PUF, París, 1998, págs. 269-293).

59. *Leviathan*, 1, 8, 10.

60. Ibid, 1, 13.

61. Ibid, 1, 18.

62. Once cannot consider as punishment the harm inflicted on someone who is a declared enemy. Because that enemy has never been subjected to the law, he cannot transgress it. Either he was subject to it and declares that he is no longer, denying, as a result, the possibility of transgressing it. Therefore, all of the harm that can be caused must be understood as acts of hostility. In a situation of declared hostility it is legitimate to inflict any sort of damages. One can thus conclude, thus, that if by acts or words, knowingly and deliberately, a subject should deny the authority of the representative of the State, whatever may be the penalty called for in case of treason, the representative may legitimately make him suffer as he sees fit. In denying subjection, he has denied the penalties called for by law. As a consequence, he must suffer as an enemy of the State, meaning according to the will of the representative. The penalties are established in the law for subjects, not for enemies, as is the case of those who, having become subjects by their own acts, rebel and deny the power of the sovereign by their own will (ibid, 2, 28).

63. John Locke, *Ensayo sobre el gobierno civil*, 2, 6.

64. *Zum ewigen Frieden*, en *Werkausgabe, herausgegeben von W. Weischedel*, Frankfurt, 1977, T. XI, p. 203.

65. *Werkausgabe* VIII, *Die Metaphysik der Sitten*, p. 756.

66. *Anti-Hobbes oder über die Grenzen der höchsten Gewalt und das Zwangsrecht der Bürger gegen den Oberherrn*, Erfurt, 1798.

67. The reference to Kant in chapter 1 is unquestionable 1. Also, the note in which he expressly cites Kant criticizing his position regarding changing of the constitution. (chap. 3). He takes care to respectfully separate Kant from Hobbes regarding the inviolabity of the sovereing in chap. 6. It is clear that Feuerbach was twenty-three years old when he wrote *Anti-Hobbes* and could not openly confront the prestige of the old and respected Kant.

68. See Erik Wolf, *Grosse Rechsdenker*, Tübingen, 1951, p. 543; also the investigation by Mario A. Cattaneo, *Anselm Feuerbach, filosofo e giurista liberale*, Milano, 1970.

69. Leviatán, capítulo 37.

70. Carl Schmitt, *El Leviatán*, cit., p. 111.

71. This has been enshrined in the Argentine Constitution since 1853 in its article 19 with an admirable formula: *The private actions of men that in no way offend the public order and morality, nor harm a third party, are solely reserved to God and exempt from the authority of judges. No inhabitant of the Nation shall be obliged to do what the law does not command, nor deprived of what it does not prohibit.*

72. Ibid, p. 117.

73. Ibid, p. 138.

74. On Schmitt's Hobbesianism, Matthias Kaufmann, *¿Derecho sin reglas?*, Barcelona, 1989, p. 126.

75. Although Schmitt was the *Kronjurist* of the *Dritte Reich* (Cf. Joseph W. Bendersky, *Carl Schmitt teorico del Reich*, Bologna, 1989), his reference regarding the question of the enemy is noted without meaning any pejorative intention, since Schmitt's ideas were taken up by many critics of the bourgeois liberal state with different political persuasions and including some openly opposed to his politics. In that sense one may see the prsentation by José Arico to *El concepto de lo político* that we cite; also Luciano Albanese, *Schmitt*, Editori Laterza, 1996, p. 7; Julio Pinto, *Carl Schmitt y reivindicación de la política*, La Plata, 2000, p. 179.

76. Cit. by Stephen Holmes, *The Anatomy of Antiliberalism*, Harvard University Press, Cambridge/London, 1993, p. 14. Schmitt affirms regarding humanity that, as such, *one cannot have any war, since one does not have enemies, at least on this planet. The concept of humanity excludes that of the enemy, given that the enemy also does not cease being human, and this does not present any specific difference* (Carl Schmitt, *El concepto de lo político*, Ediciones Folios, México, 1985, p. 51).

77. Schmitt, *El concepto de lo político*, p. 23.

78. We respect the translation that we have cited, but it should be observed that the word Schmitt uses is *Fremde*, *stranger*, in other words, the same that Mezger would soon use, Cf. infra n° 5.

79. Schmitt, p. 23.

80. Ibidem.

81. That was with polemical basis with Kelsen: Schmitt,*Der Hüter der Verfassung*, 1929; Italian trans., *Il custode della Costituzione*, cit.; Spanish version, *La*

defensa de la Constitución, Madrid, 1983; Hans Kelsen, *¿Quién debe ser el defensor de la Constitución?*, Madrid, 1995.

82. On the constitution as a plurality of laws, Schmitt, *Teoría de la Constitución*, Madrid, 1992, p. 37. With this argument he legitimated the right of the German executive to suspend guarantees and to imprison legislators and political opponents during the death throes of Weimar: on that, Bendersky, op. cit.

83. On the critique of the so-called national security doctrine of Lati American dictatorships: "Documento de Puebla," Buenos Aires, 1979, p. 67 (paragraph 49); Hernán Montealegre, *La seguridad del Estado and human rights*, Santiago de Chile, 1979; Equipo SELADOC, *Iglesia and seguridad nacional*, Salamanca, 1980; Joseph Comblin, *Le pouvoir militaire en Amerique Latine*, París, 1977 (translation: *Dos ensayos sobre seguridad nacional*, Sgo. de Chile, 1979). The classical ideologists are: Gobery do Couto e Silva, *Planejamento estratégico*, Brasilia, 1981; Augusto Pinochet Ugarte, *Geopolítica*, Sgo. de Chile, 1984. There have been few judicial discources: Mário Pessoa, *O direito da Segurança Nacional*, Rio de Janeiro, 1971; Carlos Horacio Domínguez, *La nueva guerra and el nuevo derecho, Ensayo para una estrategia jurídica antisubversiva*, Bs. As, 1980; in criminal law, Fernando Bayardo Bengoa, *Los Derechos del Hombre and la defensa de la Nación*, Montevideo, 1979.

84. He did this at a conference given in Spain many years after the fall of German Nazism: *Theorie des Partisanen. Schwischenbemerkung zum Begriff des Politischen* (Italian tran.: *Teoria del partigiano. Integrazione al concetto del político*, Milano, 2005). He also affirmed in passing *that Spain knew how to defend itself, with a war of national liberatio, from being swallowed up by international communism* (p. 79 of the Italian translation).

Chapter Ten

The Path of Criminology

Eugenio Raúl Zaffaroni

CRIMINOLOGICAL KNOWLEDGE AS A PATH

The *Divine Comedy* is a singular poem, because in it Dante Alighieri summarized all of the knowledge of his time and culturally closed out the Middle Ages. To do so, he chose the tale of a journey or path: he starts by relating that he lost himself in a *savage wood,* on Good Friday in 1300, and seen met Virgil, the Latin poet who guided him through Hell and Purgatory, until he quietly moves away and Beatrice appears, who guides him through Paradise, where Virgil could not enter because he is a pagan. It is curious that seven centuries later, the best way of showing knowledge about the punitive power that arose in Dante's time, is also imposed in the form of a journey or path. There is no better way to introduce oneself into the labyrinths of criminology. It is not good to limit oneself to showing the dust, which at the end of the road has stuck to one's clothes; that would only be proof of having made the journey. But if one intends to show the path, it would also be dangerous guide who invited one to travel it without any warning, with the careless pride of an expert, because this will demonstrate ignorance of the difficulties of the path. It is preferable for one to chose modesty and warn of the risks. For in *criminology*, the risk is always lurking, given that it is—exactly—*the knowledge and art of clarifying discursive dangers.*

Criminology is the *path* of *discourses* regarding the *criminal question*. As with a path through a wood, landscapes fall behind and one is enchanted by new sights that appear, but *the previous scenes do not disappear because of that;* we simply stop looking at them, to the point that on all too many occasions, we return to the same point without recognizing it. Even though it is much more terrestrial, it reminds one of Dante's path through hell and purgatory. In criminology there is always the temptation of the panther, the lion and the she-wolf, who blocked Dante at the beginning of his course (who symbolize lust, pride and earthly power—*Inferno, Canto I*). However, his guide will never be a Virgil: he sent Beatriz and from his lips the Divine Poet know that she would be his guide through paradise. However, a good guide in the paths of criminology knows that, along the path, Beatriz and paradise are merely mirages. The guide also knows that at the end of purgatory he or she must withdraw in silence, *a la inglesa*—as Virgil did—and, perhaps, it would be appropriate to remind the reader that when Dante was lamenting the disappearance of the Latin poet, he was reprimanded not to suffer because of it, and warned that it was fitting for him to reserve his pain for another wound (*Purgatorio, Canto XXX*). In effect, if after that he attentively followed the course, *he would have forever lost his good conscience.* Someone has spoken correctly and precisely of the *bad conscience a good criminologist* (Pavarini). That will not be the fault of the guide, but of the one who chose to walk through the wood that is *selva selvaggia e aspera e forte che nel pensier rinnova la paura!*

THE PATH OF ADMINISTERING FEARS

Perhaps the idea of election is not totally true, because generally one who decides to traverse the path of criminology does not do so entirely voluntarily. But when one chooses it without a bureaucratic or circumstantial impulse, one does so because one feels lost in a web of contradictory discourses, and is pressured by fear of victimization of oneself and others, both from robbers and from the arbitrary power of a police state. The driving force for the discourses and the tangle between them is always *fear*: some manipulate it, others suffer from it, but both tangle themselves in it, even if they do not know this. At some moments, it seems as if reason is suspended. Everything seems to depend on *sensitivity to fear*, as to what one fears the most: if criminal aggression or the arbitrariness of power. The old *fear of chaos,* of pillage and of death as a result of the war of all against all (invoked by Hobbes to justify absolutism in the Seventeenth Century and by Kant to deny the right to resistance against despotism in the Eighteenth), against the *fear of the omnipotent state,* of arbitrary power, of death as the result of police and political torture.

However, behind those nearby fears, there is another which is not much examined: the fear of cultural instability. In the course of criminology, the meaning of too many things changes. Solid institutions and those with very clear ends are blurred in a close analysis of the distance between what they do and what they say they do, of their effects, of their genealogy. A sizable part of the world, which seems orderly, ceases to be so. One does not fall into another world, but there is considerable change in the world we know and the one where we freely move. It is no small thing to fear losing a cultural world that, although not always comfortable, is at least known. That may be the greatest disconcertment that the path of criminology may cause, and also the greatest source or resistance that it generates. In dealing with those themes, it is not rare for some to opine that there are things that it is better not to know, but what is certain is that once they are known they cannot be ignored. If at the end of the journey, when the guide disappears, the reader suffers that disconcertment, it is because he or she has begun to understand what criminology is.[1]

But not all of these fears have always existed. And fear suspends reason, leading to paralysis. The terrified subject can neither think nor move (is like the *earth*), suffers a semblance of death, relives the experience of the primal clay, is *dumbfounded* (returns to *nothing*), confuses the signal with signs, the drawing with the drawn, the name with the thing (Sartre). And one who exercises power knows it: power is exerted by administering fears, stimulating them by magnifying dangers, or lessening them by underestimating them. And the greatest sensitivity to fears does not depend only on personalities, on the paths of life, on the experiences of each one, on their conscious and unconscious reasons, but also varies according to social circumstances, and, especially on one's own construction of reality by means of communication. But in fear lies the key to the permanence of all criminological discourses created throughout history, because: a) fear of pain and of a violent death always accompany people; b) and this fear travels along all of history, being polarized according to whether its production is considered nearer or more probable by barbarism, which is imagined as the product of total *disorder* or of the *order* of the totalitarian state.

DEFINITION AS AN AUTHORITARIAN TAUTOLOGY

To try and be a little more concrete—and perhaps a little less cryptic—the best thing to do is show the route of the journey. That is what is usually done in introducing a course: one provides a definition, which serves to establish the horizon for projection or the epistemological boundaries (of what is of interest, and thus, of what is not of interest), the method with which one operates, etc. In honor of that tradition, one may provide a definition, saying, for example, that *criminology is the critical analysis of knowledge that is not strictly judicial about the criminal question, so as to reduce the levels of violence linked to it.*[2]

If, according to tradition, the next step were to move forward with the exegesis of this definition, we would be doing nothing more than to smuggle an act of authority that, with good reason, could be classified as arbitrary. In criminology, from the beginning we should mistrust all acts of power, because *this is knowledge so linked to power that it sometimes identifies totally with it.* We can never accept without criticism someone putting markers around a set of entities and declares that it is a scientific boundary. They may have a reason for doing so, but we must always demand that they exhibit it.

But to exhibit the reason for the definition it would be necessary to develop everything it contained, since every definition, if it is true, is *tautological* (covers everything defined). Thus, the definition can only be well understood at the end of the journey; in other words, the journey must be the verification of the non-arbitrary nature of the definition. But in that demonstration (or unveiling) it is necessary to proceed through successive approximating steps. In general, these steps are followed in a course according to a *logical preference,* which establishes what elements should be considered before others. The particularity of criminology is that the best approximation for defining it is one that replaces *logical preference* with *chronological priority,* with *chronological order,* in other words, with its path in time. A first approximation according to that order, can show the path to follow and the reasons leading one to prioritize it.

THE *WISE* CRIMINOLOGIST AND THE *NAÏVE* CRIMINOLOGIST

Dante became lost in the *selva selvaggia*, and it would be good to start by ascertaining that it is the wood in which the person who accepts our hand in the path of criminology has gotten lost. We think that someone who grants us this confidence is an urban inhabitant, who was previously called *bourgeois*, or inhabitant of a burgh, an expression that has now fallen into disuse because after Marx it acquired a pejorative connotation. As does any urban inhabitant who receives news and talks with congeners at the dawn of the Twenty-First Century, this person becomes informed about any serious crime and reads and hears the opinions of the others. One affirms that the agent of the crime is mentally ill; another says that such persons need to be killed; others that they must be segregated forever; others that an eye for an eye must be applied; others affirm that the cause of it all is the destruction of the family and traditional values; others that it is all due to social injustice. If the author has not been identified, others affirm that it is due to excessive procedural guarantees, while others say that it is necessary to have more rigorous control and sometimes to apply some form of violence and even torture. The disconcerted urban inhabitant questions the *wise criminologist* and this person, takes any one of these opinions as his or her own, and develops it down to its ultimate consequences. If the urban inhabitant is not very curious, he or she will be satisfied with the unfolding of cleverness, which makes it possible to exhibit reasoned developments of consequences that he or she had never imagined, and will also be astounded at the enormous amount of bibliographical material that the wise man expounds and quotes. But if this inhabitant is bold enough to question another *wise criminologist,* he or she will see that the second takes ownership of a different opinion than the previous one, and also develops it until its ultimate consequences. And he or she can seek out a third and a fourth, and they will do nothing else but increase disconcertment.

Thus the urban inhabitant will go allow until encountering a *naïve criminologist,* who perhaps will say that there are many questions that have no right answer, but assuredly the mentally ill criminal is from the *alienism* of the second half of the Nineteenth Century, that the death of the offender is prerevolutionary expiationism of the Eighteenth or *Garofalian neutralization* of the early Twentieth, that perpetual segregation is European colonial *relegation* from the Eighteenth and Nineteenth Centuries, that the eye for the eye is Eighteenth Century *contractualism*, that social disorganization is from *North American sociology* of the early Twentieth Century, that the excessive guarantees are something from *positivist dangerousness* of the end of the Nineteenth and that torture is a method from the Twelfth and following centuries.

CRIMINOLOGY HAS BEEN ACCUMULATING DISCOURSES FOR FIVE CENTURIES

The *naïve criminologist* may not have explained very much, but however lacking in sagacity the urban inhabitant may be, he or she cannot help but compare that situation with any other from daily life and will perceive the difference; it would be madness if, commenting on the need for a trip, his or her colleagues engaged in a passionate discussion in which each one defended the best means of travel as being everything from a primitive canoe to a jet engine, or, if it were a case of sending a message, proposed everything from drums, smoke signals and messengers to electronic mail. It would be much more serious if in medical seminars some doctors defended Galen's theory of humors and others favored the conclusions of genetics, investigated with powerful computers. The *naïve criminologist* will show the worried urban inhabitant that criminology is not a paleontological museum, but a genuine zoo in which all species are conserved alive. It is very strange to find such a formidable coetaneity of the non-coetaneous (Mannheim), and thus, an explanation of that particularity. It also seems reasonable that, given the co-existence of discourses for several centuries, one will begin to seek an explanation, following the chronological order of the discourses and clarifying the reasons for that succession. Through inquiring into this journey, the reason for its survival and force will be revealed.

THE DISCOURSES AS STRUGGLES BETWEEN CORPORATIONS

We already know that the trees in the wood are criminology's multiple and contradictory, intertwined and non-coetaneous discourses (or the *criminologies* of the *wise criminologists*). We have also delineated the nature of the path that will allow us to move across them. We are in conditions for taking forward a second and closer step, starting be asking from whence these discourses come (how are they born? From branches or from seeds?), and, from that, how did they arise in each period and if they hearken back to an original speech.

If the urban inhabitant were to verify the origin of each one of the contradictory discourses, meaning if he or she were to be beyond a somewhat inorganic repetition by ordinary people, kit would be possible to see that one discourse was prepared at a certain moment by a doctor, others by jurists, others by police, others by sociologists and others by academicians. He or she will not be long in discovering that the doctors, jurists, police, sociologists and academicians were specially trained people, who formed separate, hierarchical and verticalized groupings, which exert a certain power, and that generally behave according to interests that correspond to that power: these are the *professional corporations*. The contradictory discourses come, then, from professional corporations that compete amongst themselves, but who also have struggles for power in their own midst, so that all of those fights translate into competing and contradictory discourses. *All of the contradictory discourses were produced by members of powerful corporations at some moment, to oppose other corporations or to discuss the hegemony at the top of the corporation itself.* All of the corporations have their *wise* criminologists, who produce their discourses, and who do not limit themselves in exercising power outwardly, but also reproduce themselves, raising their own chicks, that is to saw, training and domesticating their own new members.

With this we will have come a little closer to the nature of the trees in the wood, but it remains for us to ask *why* and *how* the wood itself came to be. As for the *why*, the *wise* criminologist will respond that it is because humans are curious by nature, and their refined curiosity is *science*, which advances driven by the urge for knowledge. This would not seem to be the appropriate answer, given that in criminology, more than an advance, there is an accumulation; no discourse disappears but they are repeated and, sometimes, something new is added or two or more existing discourses are combined. It seems to be a wood whose trees are immortal, and limit themselves to changing their foliage. The *naïve* scientist will give a different answer: simply smiling and affirming that *up till now, humans have always sought power.* He or she will not attribute this to any *nature*, a question to be referred to the philosophers, but will be content to not that, at least during the centuries recorded by history that has been the case. The answer to the second question—*how* the wood came to be—is complicated, but less problematic than the first. It is not a question of getting lost in the reasons that drive the search for power, but of explaining why exercise of power itself has been developed by agencies and corporations, which throw speeches into hegemonic struggles between themselves and amongst themselves.

The role of the guide is to seek clues, saving the lost inhabitant from becoming entrapped in the discursive jungle. To do this, he or she must favor certain strong and original trunks, which can be used for orientation. It is not necessarily to totally rely on one of them, but to at least recognize its bark and use it as a reference. In this sense there are the indispensable elements contributed by Michel Foucault during the 1970s, which are the means by which that author interpreted: a) the appearance of punitive power in Twelfth and Thirteenth Century Europe, and b) the transformation of the state and of punitive power in the Eighteenth Century.

THE MIDDLE AGES ARE NOT OVER

As for the appearance of punitive power, it is necessary to point out that the affirmation that it has always existed is false. Humanity walked the planet for thousands of years, without knowing punitive power. It appeared at different historical moments and soon disappeared. Its installation in an irreversible manner to this date, dates from the European Twelfth and Thirteenth Centuries. Up till that time, punitive power did not dominate in the way that we know it today.[3] When one German harmed another, the aggressor took refuge in a temple (ecclesiastical asylum) to avoid vengeance, and there remained, while the chieftains of the respective clans gathered the reparation that the offending clan owed to the injured clan (*Wergild*), under threat that, if it were not resolved, war would be declared (*Blutrache* or *blood vengeance*). Another method for solving conflict was to resolve the question through a judge, who solved with direct intervention from God in person, meaning with *trials* from God or ordeals. The judge, in fact, was a sort of sports referee, who saw only to the transparency and equality of the contestants, to allow God to express the truth. The most common ordeal was judicial contest, fight or combat, a duel between the parties or their representatives: the winner was the one possessing the truth.

CONFISCATION FROM THE VICTIMS

All of that changed when one fine day the lords began to *confiscate the victims.* The clan chiefs ceased collecting reparations and the judges left behind their role as sports referees, because one of the parties (the victim) was substituted by the lord (state or political power). The lord began to select conflicts and, when they occurred, would set apart the victims, affirming *I am the victim*. That is how *political power* came to also be *punitive power* and to decide the conflicts, without relying on the victim for anything, so that until today victims have disappeared from the penal scenario. It is true that now one hears some discourses and timid steps are being carried out to take them into account for something, but this is nothing more than a palliative to the confiscation, that is, a means of attenuating its excesses, and is in no way a restitution of the confiscated right. The day in which punitive power seriously restores the victim, will become another model for solving conflicts, but it will cease being the punitive power, because it will lose its structural character, which is confiscation of the victim.

THE ABDUCTION OF GOD

Starting with that confiscation; a) the penal procedure (or judgment) ceased to be a procedure for resolving a conflict between the parties, and became an act of power by a delegate of the lord or sovereign. Because one of the parties—the victim—has left the proceedings, the sentence does not attend to his or her interests, but the interests of power. b) The penal judge has ceased to be a referee, who guaranteed objectivity and balance between the parties, and become an employee, who decides according to the sovereign's interests. c) Because it was now no longer a judgment between parties, one should no longer established whose side God was on, because it was assumed by default that he was always on the side of power. It was thus assumed that it would make no sense to call him to a judgment, because it was presupposed that he was already there, represented by the judge. It is quite clear that not only had the victim been confiscated, but also God.

This last item, in other words, the certainty that *God always assists the judge,* determined that the proof of God would disappear, that the method of establishing the truth of the facts would no longer be a duel, a combat, but that it would involve *a violent interrogation*: the truth is provided by the defendant or the accused, responding to the *violent interrogation* (the *inquisition* or *inquisition*) of the judge. The interrogation was *violent,* because if the defendant did not wish to confess, he or she was *tortured* until being made to talk, and if this did not happen, the silence was also a confession (it was considered that it was his or her own evil that provided the strength for resistance).

VIOLENT INTERROGATION AS A SCIENTIFIC METHOD

The punitive power's method for obtaining truth was not limited to penal procedure, but over time became a method to obtain any truth that was not religious, meaning that it gradually evolved *from the penal process to the scientific method.* Up to that moment, scientific truth was also being obtained through a struggle: in alchemy, there was a struggle with nature; in astrology, the subject sought to rip from the stars their cosmic secret that regulated everything; even in philosophy advances came through the *questions*, which was a fight involving cross-questioning between opponents. When the move was made from alchemy and astrology to chemistry and astronomy, knowledge was also accumulated through violent interrogation: since then objects that one wishes to know have been interrogated, and when the object does not respond or does not give an answer about itself that is of interest, if possible, it is violated, through an *experiment.*

Since that moment, knowledge has ceased to advance through struggling with nature and things, to begin doing so through interrogating things or beings, with questions that are also violent and may reach the point of torture (*the experiment:* from the opening of cadavers until vivisection, including the Nazi doctors and exposure of thousands of persons to radiation).

This knowledge through violent interrogation is to *know to be able.* Even though this new formula was expressed in 1620 in a work by Francis Bacon (in the *Novum Organum*), the idea that *it is necessary to know about things in order to be able to dominate them* (it is only possible to dominate nature by submitting to its laws) is of the for learning through interrogation or inquisitorially. Thus, *knowledge for power* is accumulated by asking the entities, according to the power that one wishes to exert over them. The *subject* of knowledge (scientific) places him or herself in the position of *inquisitor*, is always on a higher level than the *object* or being under interrogation, has God on his or her side, is an envoy of God for learning, is the Lord (*dominus*) who asks *in order to be able.*

THE KNOWLEDGE OF THE LORDS

One does not interrogate scientifically through mere curiosity, but to obtain some result, that will allow one to exert a power over the object being interrogated: if one studies a cow, one does so to find how to make it provide more milk; if one interrogates the soil it is to know how to achieve better harvests; if one interrogates the sky, it is to predict the rains. One does not ask anything, except for what is of interest for the power objective that motivates the investigator. For the subject interrogating—or the one financing the investigation—the only thing of interest are the answers that serve his or her purposes and the rest are ignored, because they do not matter, nor is he or she prepared to hear them, since he or she only wants to and can hear what is of interest, to receive the information that is functional for the power being sought. It is a lordly knowledge, only the lords no longer obtain their power by warring amongst themselves with primitive weapons, but by accumulating knowledge that will aid them in dominating nature and other humans, who, because they have less knowledge, are inferior.

Therefore, knowledge through questioning and torture of violence (interrogation and experiment), as a knowledge of the *lord* (*lordly,* of a *dominus,* virile, patriarchal), has a paradoxical effect, which is that of *crushing the lord himself.* It is not easy to understand this, because for hundreds of years we have been accustomed to this lordly knowledge, despite which we continue asking about its negative effects, without being able to understand what they are obeying. We have seen that this knowledge has undesired effects; it ends up being used to kill or to destroy; the knowledge that one acquires by asking in order to improve, is employed and ends up harming other things.

KNOWLEDGE SUBJECT TO THE LORDS

Nonetheless, the reason for this effect of lordly knowledge is no secret: the *subject* interrogates the *object* to dominate it; it formulates the questions that serves or that it believes that serve for that purpose, but the interrogated entity does not know and answers in the only way that it can, that is, with its entire *being* (beings can only respond with their being: the cow with its complete *cowness*, the rock with its complete *rockness*). But the subject is not prepared to listen to the answer, given with all its beingness by the violently interrogated being, because it is only prepared to listen to what it needs or believes in needs in order to dominate. That is how the unheard part of all the answers accumulates on the subjects and crushes them. No different is the phenomenon that is summarized by stating that *technology dominates humans.* The etymology explains this very well: an *object* is what is thrown (*projected*) against, it is the violently interrogated being that throws itself against the interrogator with all of its beingness; the interrogator is *subjected* (thrown or *projected* down), becoming *subjected* by the accumulated beingness answers, which it is not equipped to hear. That is the consequence of the knowledge of *dominus,* which is lordly, patriarchal.

IS IT POSSIBLE TO OVERCOME KNOWLEDGE THROUGH VIOLENT INQUISITION?

One may thing of overcoming the knowledge of the *dominus* with the knowledge of a *brother,* not only of humans but with all of the other entities, as a third stage or form of knowing: from truth through *struggle* one moves to that obtained with *interrogation,* and it is possible that this may move to another that has arisen through *dialogue*. If one can conceive of a dynamic that, just as the *duel* moved to the *inquisition,* from there it move to the *dialogus,* that is, from the knowledge of the competitor to that of the inquisitor and from that to the *frater.* But that dynamic will demand a total shift in to current paradigm of knowledge, which leads to biological hierarchization of society and confiscation of the victim, as a means of corporative verticalization of said victim. Imagine a society with the knowledge of a *frater* and not of a *dominus,* it would mean at the same time imagining it with little or no punitive power, without discrimination and without wars. The *wise criminologist* will say that this is an unattainable utopia; the *naïve criminologist* will remember that all realizations start out as utopias. But *naïve* means asking about the principle without accepting anything as a given, and, in that sense, naiveté is the opposite of foolishness. Because of this, he or she will not neglect to warn that such a proposal implies the removal of structures of power settled across many centuries and that, furthermore, they are not only exteriors but that we also introject them as part of the psychological team that has conditioned us, when we produce as subjects that we know, so that we think within the channels that we have imposed, and from which it is not easy to escape.

It is not possible to ignore that these three main beams have been perfectly articulated for eight centuries, because they are three indispensable elements of the same structure. Patriarchal power controls more than half of the population: the women, the children and the elderly, and in other periods the slaves, servants and serfs. The punitive power for that reason is preferentially entrusted with controlling young men and adults, in other words, *with controlling the controllers.* Instrumental knowledge is power at the of service of the controllers and of the controllers of the controllers. The basic articulation is maintained, although the relations of power have become complicated in a thousand ways over the course of eight centuries, in class struggles, corporate and group struggles, the autonomization of the power elites, colonialism, neocolonialism, ethnic and cultural hegemonies, and so on. However, in all of those complexities, the same basic scheme has continued to operate, which is inserted in different manners in other relations, which exclude from power and socially marginalized dissidents, immigrants, sexual, ethnic and cultural minorities, persons with special needs, the physically and mentally inform, needy urban inhabitants, the unemployed, those under psychiatric treatment, people with chemical dependencies, the obese, and others.

DISCRIMINATION AS A STRUCTURAL PRODUCT

As the *subjects* of knowledge (the scientists) assume the position of *inquisitor*, just as the latter did, they assume a position higher that the *object,* or being, and from that hierarchical perspective violently begin interrogation, presupposing that they have God on their side, are God's envoys to learn, that they are the lord (*dominus*) who asks *to be able.* They can switch God and replace him with an impersonal entity (*progress*) or with their own idealization (*humanity, class, nation, race*), but there is always a God to legitimate their interrogating violence, who will guarantee their hierarchical superiority. That being the case, it is natural that when the *object* is another human, the lordly knowledge presupposes, through its own methodical structure, a hierarchy: the human *object* will always be inferior to the human *subject.* There is no dialogue, but only violent interrogation. The hierarchical discrimination among humans is, thus, a *structural product of the means of learning through violent interrogation,* in the same way as is the depredation of nature and the extermination of the *inferior* and the *different.*

THE FIRST PRIVATIZATION OF SECURITY

The first task that punitive power and *inquisitorial* knowledge proposed for themselves resulted in the corporatization of society, in other words, the overall predominance of the hierarchical model of the *Gesellschaft* (corporate) over the horizontal *Gemeinschaft* (community or traditional) model. Within that corporation, it was necessary to reaffirm and strengthen the *patriarchal hierarchical structure*, meaning, to reinforce the subordination of half of the population, as an indispensable chapter in its corporate social and verticalizing discipline. The *first privatization of security* (of police services and punitive justice) and the most massive one occurred with the appearance of modern punitive power itself, when the lord (state) delegated to its adult free men (*superiors*) control over women. The European inquisition directed its power against *dangerous* or *fallen women,* reaffirming the power of men, by freeing them from any women who might reveal themselves against them, meaning those who did not resign themselves to being simply submissive wives and mothers.

It was necessary to discipline society, *eliminating anarchical pagan or dysfunctional elements,* and replacing them by the guiding components of corporate political hierarchy and, most especially, sexually discipline society, particularly the women who—as is known—are the transmitters of culture. Their control and subordination were key elements for eliminating the dysfunctional pagan elements considered a drag on society. *The inquisition did not subordinate the woman, who was already in that state, but merely reaffirmed her subordinate condition and uprooted any attempt at reaction.* On may say that in this respect it was the criminological discourse that provided cover for the most successful enterprise in punitive control in history, to judge by the later silence on the theme. Discourses are not only significant for what they say, but also for when they are silent, meaning that they are not only important for what they show but also for what they hide, and their authors not only express the limitations of their knowledge by describing what they see or believe they see, but also by what they do not see. The enterprise of privatizing security for women was singularly successful, because the criminological discourse was to spend almost five hundred years without mentioning again the theme of women; *for the next five centuries, criminology concerned itself only with men.*

INQUISITION: THE STATE AS ADMINISTRATOR OF DEATH

In this context we see appearing the first modern criminological discourse, organic, carefully prepared, explaining the causes of evil, the forms in which it appears, its symptoms and the means for combating it. This was the discourse of the first major agency for punitive social control: the inquisition. In the

Fifteenth Century it recapitulated all of its prior experience and struck out at women, in a magnificent manual of extraordinary coherence and highly refined theoretical elaboration (the *Malleus Maleficarum* or *Hammer of Witches,* 1484). This was the first and inevitable theoretical product of punitive power; it first exerted itself and then explained and discursively legitimated its actions, in an increasingly refined manner, until achieving the degree or expositive coherence that this first work of modern criminology presents, and which undoubtedly constitutes its foundational theoretical moment.

The first criminological discourse was that of the inquisitors.[4] The authors of the *Malleus* were two inquisitors. But who were the inquisitors? It has been said that they were judges and that is true; but they were also police, and that is true; one could say that they also were sanitation doctors or meteorologists and agronomists, and that would be true. One could say they were jurists and legislators, and that would also be true. It would be no less accurate to affirm that they played the roles of theologians and philosophers. Strictly speaking, the inquisitors were the operators of a major punitive agency, that *decided the life or death of people* and that accumulated the functions that were later shared amongst many agencies. In practical terms, *it was the mother agency or common trunk, branching off from which were all of the other specialized agencies, which exert the power of social control.*

When, five hundred years later, in the middle of the Twentieth Century, Talcott Parsons—the sociologist of North American systemic functionalism—considered that *social control* was only the function that agencies operated when the process of socialization had failed and deviant conduct appeared, without realizing it, he described the function of the inquisition quite well. When patriarchy failed in its task of domesticating the woman to be only a submissive female and mother, and she manifested deviant conduct because she was seeking malignant superhuman allies in order to exercise another class of power, then the punitive social control of the inquisition came into play. The only difference consists in Parsons having theorized in this way the functioning of a set of agencies, while the authors of the *Malleus* theorized only that of their own and only mother agency.

The essential functions of the inquisition were gradually divided. The inquisition and its method were not the exclusive remit of the authorities or ecclesiastical power. The inquisitorial process and torture were forms of punitive power exercised by all political power, which attributed to itself the right to life or death over people. But *the right to life or death*—due to obvious natural limits—only meant the possibility of *killing or allowing to live,* meaning, *to cause to die or leave alive* someone or anyone. That is why—as far as possible—suicide was punished, because *causing to die* was a divine or royal privilege; the suicide was usurping the power of God or of the lord.

THE BUREAUCRACIES: THE STATE THAT ADMINISTERS LIFE

This idea of the *state* as the *administrator of death* was gradually replaced by that of the state as the *administrator of life*. Foucault situates this change in the Eighteenth Century; perhaps he might have placed it somewhat earlier, but what is certain is that at some moment, there was a shift from the power of *causing to die or letting live,* to that of *causing to live or letting die.* The state began a favorable focus on the life of its subjects, not of each life in particular, but the life of a new collective subject, which is made up of its subjects as a *public* subject. The state took on the role of administering the distinct aspects of the life of this collective subject in all its complexity, planning according to rules for *large numbers* and producing *massive effects* on their health, education, social discipline, children and labor.

As this *move from administering the death of individuals to that of the life of the public* was being carried out, it became necessary to distribute the functions that the inquisition had assumed in the Fifteenth Century among specialized agencies. The inquisition could assume them all, because it is *much simpler to administer death than life:* the task of killing or allowing to life can be done by a single agency that retains all of the power or a major part of it, but when it is a case of organizing the life of the *public,* the question becomes extremely complicated and, the more the lord wants to regulate the life of his subjects, the more specialization he will require from his collaborators to attend to all of the aspects he intends to cover.

THE CORPORATIONS DIVIDE UP LIFE

The lord (the state) saw the need for creating bureaucracies, meaning specialized institutions in the different areas of life that it intended to regulate or administer. But those bureaucracies become autonomous and begin to exert their own power, competing with each other for budget shares, prestige, political power, obtaining private funds, parliamentary support and etc. A struggle begins between corporations to hegemonize the power of the state, or, at least, to obtain the best privileges possible, both for the bureaucracy and for those who have the specialized training needed for it. Normally, persons with this specialized training group themselves corporatively, that is, in an institutionalized and hierarchical manner, giving way to a plurality of professional corporations that dispute power among themselves and also carry out major internal power disputes.

As is natural, the autonomized corporate power is exercised, aided by specialized knowledge that translates into *scientific discourses*. Each corporation develops a specialized knowledge that it expresses in discourses according to its own and peculiar specific dialect. Those scientific discourses produced in their respective dialogues not only differ between the corporations, but the same corporation can accommodate a plurality of discourses, which reflect the internal hegemonic struggle. A closer look at any discipline will reveal the *battle of the schools* in its midst, which are largely incomprehensible to the *extraneus.* Depending on the circumstances, those corporations dispute spheres of reality, and the inclusion of an area inside the epistemological limits of their discourses means expansion of their power. Because of that, they mark out a greater territory of reality, and the inclusion of an area within the epistemological boundaries of their discourses means the corporate appropriation of that territory, and thus, a larger slice of power.

THE CORPORATIONS TEACH ONE NOT TO SEE

Reality is a continuous whole; in reality there are no fissures or solutions for continuity. Nor is anything immovable, but—from Heraclitus to quantum physics—we know that everything flows and in continually changing. However, the discourse by corporations has no other recourse but to fragment that reality in a more or less arbitrary manner and, at the same time immobilize the piece of reality that it has appropriated. Its comprehension is always distorted by fragmentation and immobility. Its operators learn and train themselves, and train their own apprentices so they may acquire particular skill in observing some entities and some of their aspects, but at the same time they are training and training their apprentices to not see other entities and other aspects of the same entities.

Just as throughout evolution, certain animals have developed organs that allowed them to perceive the presence of food and of dangers and enabled them to take the former and flee from the latter, this same development impedes them from seeing others when they are outside of their habitat or natural environment, or when that environment is altered, those trained in their corporations acquire perception skills and agility for certain stimuli and, sometimes, slowness towards others. Their training for skill is also always training for slowness. The difference lies in the fact that such slowness is not phylogenetically conditioned, and thus can be employed for the internal hegemonic structure of the corporation itself. Some of its members glance over at other corporations, make an attempt at taking control of another field, change the markers and manifest a new skill in facing the old dominators of the corporation. To the degree that this school is considered necessary by the corporation, they will replace the previously hegemonic entities with their renewed arsenal of skills and slowness. These are the *scientific revolutions, paradigm shifts or epistemological outbursts,* which drive the so-called *progress of science.*

THE CORPORATE LINK WITH BROAD SOCIAL POWER

These autonomized bureaucratic powers organized in the form of corporations, with their own knowledge expressed in discourses through peculiar dialects that are poorly understood by the common people, have greater or lesser luck in the hegemonic struggle. This depends on various factors and also—as always happens in power struggles, particularly in the short term—on imponderables. Imponderables by definition cannot be categorized. At any rate, when it is a case of power that demands a certain meaning over more prolonged periods, the imponderables tend to lose their importance and factors that are susceptible to a certain cataloguing predominate, given that they perform the mechanics of accumulating power. Basically, the power of a corporation increases, to the extent that its discourse is functional to political and economic power. That depends on a) factors that derive from the corporation itself and b) others that derive from political and economic power.

Those that derive from the corporation correspond to a) the *availability of a discourse that is functional,* but in the absence of that, the degree of ductility that a corporation has in elaborating a functional discourse counts. In the latter case, that ductility is facilitated by the prior existence of elements incorporated into training its members and due to the greater conviction of those elements on their part, which is to say that their members can modify their discourses and offer a new one with available elements and in those that they create. Should conviction relating to those elements be low, it may be compensated by the lack of scruples in incorporating others because of their conjunctural functionality, but that is usually difficult, because it demands a conspiratorial attitude and an ethical renunciation that is very complicated, although not impossible. b) That the discourse of a corporation is functional does not mean only that it *coincides with the interests of broader social power,* but also that *it is credible in the cultural framework:* not every esoteric discourse achieves hegemony, but only those that are capable of being transmitted to the *opinion* of those who decide or have weight in deciding and are accepted by them, so that there is a certain consensus produced. In every epoch there have been absurd effects at criminological discourses, that have been totally ignored by those in power, exactly because their lack of institutional focus has left them useless and even discredited. Discourses also lose hegemony when, because they stay outside of the changing cultural framework, they cease to be credible. The same dynamic of power that is reflected in knowledge makes the foundations of hegemonic discourses lose credibility and leads to their becoming caricatures. The theocratic discourse was unable to maintain hegemony in a cultural world in which there was more and more appeal to reason and it was clear that it was nothing more than a caricature of a theological discourse. The later discourse that intended to deduce everything from reason was unable to maintain hegemony when it because very evident that it had fallen into a caricature of rationality, by means of rationalization derived from gratuitous intuition. The medical discourse was unable to maintain its effectiveness when it became clear that there was no verification and that it was a caricature of science, resulting from an intuitive and unverifiable affirmation about the nature of society. c) No less important is the negotiating capacity of a corporation, which is crucial for reducing conflicts with political and economic power and for establishing a more or less stable *status quo;* there is generally a promotion or designation of power and functions to the members of the corporation, and other compensations that are typically established and negotiated.

As for the factors that contribute to increasing the power of a corporation and that do not stem from it, but from hegemonic political and economic power, one must take into account the degree of rationality in such powers in the exercise of authority. The greater this share is, the more a power discourse with a greater level of elaboration will be functional for it, and provide greater legitimating solidity. Otherwise, it will be necessary to make use of quite despicable discourses in its formulation, which can only be provided by those at the fringes of professional corporations, who also use that power by throwing it into internecine struggles inside the corporation. Generally in those cases, the struggle for power is starkly exposed and drops its weak legitimating cover. That does not mean that they are incapable of effective control for some time, but preferably based on power, which is exercised too crudely for the socio-cultural context.

CORPORATE HEGEMONY AND MERCENARISM

What has been presented above explains that there are two phenomena that must be carefully distinguished: a) one is the *hegemony of a discourse and of a corporation with its respective bureaucratic agencies, in a certain historical moment,* that occurs when, without a particularly skilled effort, the agency has available a dominant discourse that coincides with the interests of broader social power and that fits within the cultural framework of this moment. Because of this it is functional with the juncture of power with a certain degree of rationality, which is what assumes a particular interest in the course of criminology and of social sciences in general. b) the other is a phenomenon of *intellectual marginality or mercenarism,* which occurs when in the face of excessively irrational power, someone at the fringes of the corporation maintains a discourse of inferior quality that is circumstantially functional, or when some subordinates prepare discourses of very low quality, to place them at the service of political or economic power.

The second class of phenomena obviously are not lacking in the course of Criminology, but are anecdotic and, in reality should be considered less as discourses—because they easily fall apart under analysis—and more as part of the conflictiveness that the criminological discourses themselves attempt to explain. We will have occasion to mention several of them. In their circumstances they are often dangerous, but seen at a distance are curious and somewhat ridiculous, except for their tragic effects. If the guide stops to look at some of them along the path of criminology, it is not only to entertain the traveler with curiosities or to be amused at the absurdities, but because it is necessary for us to learn to distinguish them, in Criminology, as is the case with any other discipline.[5] In the final analysis, a traditional psychiatrist may argue to infinity with a psychoanalyst, a functionalist sociologist may do the same with a conflictivist, and a judicial positivist may do so with a jusnaturalist. The specialists know—as does the public—that if the debate is along the lines of *Bleuler-Freud, Lukmann-Dahrendorf* or *Bobbio-Welzel*, that it will always worthwhile to follow it. But they also know that this cannot be confused with the irresponsible acts of intellectual delinquents, and thus, it is indispensable to learn how to detect the latter and carefully distinguish them from the first. The intimate relation between knowledge and power—undeniable—does not mean that everyone who makes a scientific discourse is a mercenary or an intellectual delinquent, however mistaken he or she may be and however useful the discourse may be for power, very much despite the fact that the latter also exist and it will be necessary to know how to identify them and distinguish them.

THE CORPORATE DISPUTE FOR OWNERSHIP

Beginning in the Eighteenth Century, when the appearance of corporations and their autonomization began to become increasingly manifest, with their resulting hegemonic struggle and the fighting in their midst, the criminal issue began to have a very contested environment. It is extremely interesting to observed how the discourses of different corporations were hegemonic, and how they gave way to discourses from other corporations. Obviously, even if the criminological discourse of one corporation ceases to be hegemonic, because political and economic power has privileged another one that is more useful for the new situation of power, the corporation that had prepared the previous discourse will not cease to exist, or to continue preparing new discourses, but those will simply not have the primacy nor be privileged by the political and economic power of the moment.

Furthermore, when a corporation loses hegemony (or when it does not achieve it) in the sphere of criminology it may develop discourses that are not always incompatible with those of the hegemonic agency, but—although those discourses will appear in it—also others will appear that tend to be compatible with the new hegemonic discourse, meaning that one part of the corporation adjusts itself to the new demands of the dominating discourse in power. It is clear that the penal judicial discourse adapted itself to the biological discourse when it lost its hegemony and that became dominant. Every authoritarian penal law on dangerousness proves this conclusively.

All of this explains why the trees in the wood do not die, never wither, but only renew their foliage. The corporations lose hegemony, cease to receive official favor as authors of criminological discourses, extend their struggles to other fields, but do not abandon what has already been marked out in the criminal sphere. They maintain some of their cultivators who constantly renew their discourses and continue offering them to the public sector, which is now more reluctant to give a hearing to someone from that corporation, but may occasionally make use of them. No corporation abandons the field of battle for ownership of *crime*, and their renewed discourses remain alive.

Because of everything that has been pointed out, *one must not confuse this path of Criminology with a history of the discipline*. History involves recording past events that are projected in their consequences and in the present, but this path refers to events from the past that continue to be directly present. No one believes that the guide who conducts us along this path of criminology takes us through the corridors and rooms of a museum of dead theories, but that he or should be ready to tread the paths through a forest of living and constantly renewed discourses, produced by corporations that fight amongst themselves to gain hegemony, under the support of negotiations with larger social powers. The middle ages have not even finished in criminology, and its discourse continues to be as relevant as ever, only one needs to know the true discursive trunks and not be impressed by the change in tones of the leaves. Here it is not a case of losing sight of the forest for the trees, but of looking incorrectly at the trees and believing that they are different. It is not easy to learn to travel through a forest where the trees are blended.

THE MAJOR STAGES OF HEGEMONY

The course of this dispute has long periods and lesser conjunctural episodes that are not worth spending much time on. During the major periods—which are the important ones—the stages of discursive hegemony accompany the major chapters of political and economic global power, which have adopted certain discourses and discarded others. Over the last five hundred years one can identify the following stages of world power: a) the *mercantile revolution* (Fifteenth Century), which exercised planetary power in the form of *colonialism* (Fifteenth to Eighteenth Centuries); b) the *industrial revolution* (Eighteenth Century), which exercised planetary power in the form of *neocolonialism* (Eighteenth to Twentieth Centuries), with a *1st stage of the rise of the bourgeoisie* (Eighteenth Century to the mid-Nineteenth Century and a *2nd stage of the bourgeoisie placed in power* (Nineteenth Century till the end of the Twentieth); c) The *technological revolution* (end of the Twentieth Century to present), that exerts its planetary power as *globalization.*

The dynamic began in the Fifteenth Century. Punitive power served to corporatize, hierarchize and militarize society, meaning to discipline it to allow colonialist expansion into other societies. That was the European phenomenon that gave rise to the *mercantile revolution of the Fifteenth Century* and to *colonialism* as an exercise of planetary power. *The colony was a sort of total institution at a massive level; it was the institutionalized abduction of many millions of human beings, even the majority of the population of the planet. At least two continents (America and Africa) were transformed into total institutions, with immense concentration and extermination.* It was the stage of large voyages (called *voyages of discovery* by the colonizers, of the first submission of America and Africa, of the hegemony of the maritime powers and the legitimating discourse for transnational and national power, with a *discourse in a theocratic package*, according to the cultural framework of the moment. It was the foundational stage of criminology, with the *Malleus* as the discourse for the inquisitors, prior to the net division of the corporations and the competition between them.

However, throughout the colonialist centuries (Fifteenth to Eighteenth), the corporations were emerging and achieving autonomy; they began to elaborate their own discourses and, finally in the Eighteenth Century the *industrial revolution emerged and ushered in the stage of neocolonialism* (until the middle of the Twentieth Century), those power began to grant hegemony to the *discourse of the jurists and philosophers of the Enlightenment.* The hegemony of the criminological discourse of jurists and philosophers lasted until the settlement of the bourgeoisie in social power, with its decline beginning in the mid-Nineteenth Century. The *bourgeoisie,* meaning the industrialist, commercial and banking class that was concentrated in the *burghs* or cities (the so-called urban concentration of industrialism that would characterize industrial civilization from this moment forward), needed this discourse in its struggle for power with the nobility, because it was vital to reduce and limit the exercise of punitive power that the nobles had available. But when the bourgeoisie achieved hegemony and settled into power in the central countries, it was no longer interested in limiting the exercise of punitive power and fell out with the jurists and philosophers who elaborated discourse to limit it.

When this fact took shape, a new agency arose in some countries, while in others—where it already existed—it gained new strength and roles: the *police.* But the police do not have their own criminological discourse and thus, the police criminological discourse was elaborated by the doctors in alliance with the police and against the judges, jurists and philosophers. The hegemonic criminological discourse was—beginning in the mid-Nineteenth Century—the medical-police discourse, of a biological nature, which, with various nuances maintained its dominance until the Twentieth Century and still survives today in a sizable portion of European and Latin American criminology. Neocolonialism strengthened the economic links between the center and the periphery and legitimated all of its power with a racist biological discourse; it rationalized internal power with criminology and planetary power with anthropology, both supported by the medical corporation. *Neocolonialism was a sort of work camp for millions of people.*

A third moment began when the biological discourse began losing credit, because the cultural framework was changing, especially because European totalitarianisms took ownership of the discourse with singular and tragic coherence, and the very complex and dynamic societies began to ask questions about the phenomena in a collective and non-individual fashion. In that circumstance it became very clear that conflictivity is modified by social conditions and the critics of power took advantage of this fact and highlighted it. The sociologists who had hitherto been silenced by the biologic reductionism of their discipline and who, to survive, needed to accommodate their discourses with biology, broke free of that and began to perfect their own particular dialogue, to elaborate and offer discourses as the authentic product of their own corporation. This process appeared with the first crisis of capitalism (1890) and in a few years demanded hegemony in the United States and was soon extended to the rest of criminology, even though in some countries it continued to run in close competition with its predecessor, now conveniently renewed. There were also important attempts to incorporate the criminal question on the part of psychologists, but they were never hegemonic. Even less important were the attempts of some economists, although they were not lacking.

THE CURRENT DEFICIENCY IN DISCURSIVE HEGEMONY

Finally, we reach the confusing end of the Twentieth Century and beginning of the Twenty-First, in which there is no hegemonic discourse from the point of view of the wider society, even though the sociological discourse maintains hegemony at the level of academic power. This is because the broader social power is at a difficult stage of transition, and is not very predictable. Political and economic power have had close cooperative relations as well as conflict, but in the 1980s, the politicians directly renounced control of economic power, which has become transnationalized as never before eluding all political control for the first time. Globalized economic power always imposes itself on national political powers, without there being an international power capable of containing it. In that way, economic conduct criminalized in the national states (artificial market changes) goes unpunished at the global economic level. The national states—and with them the power of the politicians—suffered a terrible loss of the attributes of so-called *sovereignty,* basically of taxing power (globalized capital demands lower taxes, under penalty of moving to another state) and the punitive power (it cannot repress the extortionate and speculative maneuvers of that same capital).

The reduced national political power cannot resolve the growing conflictivity that generates the conditions imposed by globalized economic power, which exclude large portions of the population from production (unemployment, underemployment) and that reduce their domestic product in direct relation to the deterioration of social investments (education, health, welfare).[6] In other words: it would seem that the enterprise of administering life has been abandoned, even though because of that—for the moment—the administration of death has not been resumed. In a certain sense, following the Foucaultian terminology, one may say that the old *cause to die or leave alive* of the old inquisitorial regime has given way to the modern *cause to live or let die* of the industrial revolution, to now end up in a *let live and die* of the current stage of the technological revolution. The police agencies take advantage of the growing conflictivity to exert greater autonomous power, freeing themselves from controls and finally, manifesting a tendency to monopolize all of the wrongdoing in the illicit market. When faced with any attempt at control, they intimidate by using the threat of ungovernability against the weakened national political powers, which, for their part, are besieged by the demagoguery of the operators *outside of the system* with their extremist authoritarian ideology. In this emergency, the operators of political agencies of the *status quo*, faced with the threat of those *outside of the system,* take measures with communicative effects that demonstrate their firm resolve of containing the conflictivity, generally ceding power to the police agents. Meanwhile, the progressive political operators, generally accused of being *soft* on crime, go about showing the opposite by ceding even more power to the police agencies.

In summary, the technological revolution of the Twentieth Century opens up the path to a new stage of worldwide power (*globalizations*), in which traditionally criminalized behavior tends to be monopolized by the economic power and by the national police agencies themselves. The economic power tends assume exclusive control over criminality in the transnational market, while criminality in the local market (traffic in unlawful objects, persons and services) tends to be concentrated in the police agencies who confront the political powers that are weakened and in a process of permanently ceding their attributions.[7] This *process of decadence in political power,* which only succeeds in spasms of ceding its own power, is incapable of adopting any discourse that is rational or appears to be so. The sociological discourse, including the etiological one, is functionally inadequate, because it lays bare the incoherence of the political powers weakened by their impotence in regulating economic power and in controlling the increasing autonomizaton of the corporations. Even less can they assume a coherent discourse when they engage in appealing to short-range solutions and communicative effects, which reduce their power even more. Thus, one cannot speak in our days of a hegemonic discourse with such a hierarchy, other than the appeal to erratic and disconcerting remnants of speeches from the past, separated from any context and generally deformed. There is no hegemonic criminological discourse, favored and assumed by the political power, because there is no configurating political power, but only deteriorated political powers dealing with halting their fall. The suicide of political powers cannot assume any coherent discourse as hegemonic, because it does not have hegemonic power. For its part, the economic power does not need a similar discourse, because it is being exercised for the first time without any mediation by the political power. In the era of technological revolution, up till now the important thing for political power has not been to assume an academically coherent discourse, but to issue discourses tailored to media communications that have a tranquillizing (normalizing) effect, even though in practice they produce paradoxical effects. A political power that cannot reduce the violence that its impotence generates, only succeeds in issuing incoherent discourses, provided that—by means of simplistic social communications—they have normalizing results. More than a discourse, it requires a libretto for its show, because it itself and the state itself end up assuming the character of a show.

The path of criminology has passed through these three hegemonies and reached the unpredictable transition of the present, in a process where the corporations, beginning with the industrial revolution, have been increasingly appealing to the mediation of another social actor, as its importance increased: the agencies of *social communications.* At this moment the devaluated political power appeals to those agencies, which have assumed a central importance, given that the political power—incapable of providing real solutions—makes efforts to communicate false solutions that will mask its permanent renunciation of power. The struggle is waged on the communications stage, through which a virtual reality is constructed, which each day is more separated from the facts. It is not possible to conceive of any discourse that will be functional for this form of renouncing power, because the discourses have always been functional for exercising power and not renouncing it. All of that explains the reason why we speak of a moment of unpredictable transition, because it seems to be excessively unstable and its projection into the future in these conditions is not viable for a prolonged period.

The critical review of all of these discourses and their relations with power, when they were hegemonic—and before and after that—and their relations with broader power, with their corresponding cultural context, in their case, with the agencies of social communications, is the task of theoretical criminology, from which should be extracted the elements necessary for reducing the violence of the conflict generated around the issue of crime. This first vision of the path followed by criminology, comes close to what is often called a definition, but without imposing it as an arbitrary act, but by advancing in demonstrating it. The question of what criminology is can only be responded by journeying along its curious accumulation of perspectives and discourses, of hegemony and falls, of struggles between corporations and the fickleness of broader social power, until reaching its current crisis, which is not the crisis of criminology, but that of the power that divides up hegemonies.

NOTES

1. A supremely illustrative view can be found in: Jorge de Figueiredo Dias and Manuel da Costa Andrade, Criminologia: o Homem Delinquente e a Sociedade Criminógena. Coimbra, Coimbra Editora, 1984.

2. That characteristic explains it very well: Alessandro Barata, Criminologia Critica e Critica del Diritto Penale, Bologna, Cedam, 1982.

3. See: Claus Roxin, Problemas Básicos of Criminal Law, Madrid, Reus, 1976.

4. On classic Criminology: Massimo Pavarini, Introduzione a la Criminologia, Firenze, Edizione Universitaria,1980; Hans Schneider, kriminologie, Berlin, Gruyter, 1987.

5. A quite complete overview of contemporary Criminology may be found in: Roger Hopkins Burke, An Introduction to Criminological Theory, Cullompton, Willan Publishing, 2003.

6. Allen Steinberg, The Transformation of Criminal Justice, North Carolina, University of North Carolina, 1989.

7. Katja Franko Aas, Globalization and Crime, London, Sage Publications, 2007.

Chapter Eleven

Can Criminal Law Really Contribute to the Prevention of Crimes against Humanity?

Eugenio Raúl Zaffaroni

States mass crimes have such a huge unlawful content that they seriously limit the juridical power of containment of criminal law. The unpunished mass criminal is in practice subject to a *Friedlossigkeit* or loss of peace, he is excluded from the juridical community, and any damage caused to him is practically unpunished, because criminal law is incapable of condemning the person who executes it. International efforts to submit the criminal to a process are legitimated because they redeem him/her from the status of *hostis*, ratifying that for the law he/she continues being a person, in spite of the terrible magnitude of the committed crime.

This is the maximum contribution and the legitimation of international criminal law: it would avoid a degrading act of barbarism for the mass crime victims themselves, and would avoid falling within the enemy's criminal law; moreover, it would just be the opposite by avoiding the return to the *hostis*, which is the 'de facto' situation in which the unpunished mass criminal is. But international punitive power does not prevent state mass homicides, the true prevention of mass homicides that criminological knowledge can provide, shall be through the exercise of criticism and the frontal rejection of the *values neutralization techniques*, finely prepared by theorists, and roughly by public or mediatic inducement to revenge.

STRUCTURING PUNITIVE POWER

Punitive power is always structurally biased. Intentional mass homicides committed from state power have been a recurrent phenomenon during the last century (see Ternon 1995). International law interweaves with criminal law so as to punish them. The outcome is the authorization to exercise a punitive power that cannot lose its structural selective character, which brings along similarly valid criticisms for such exercise at internal level, like almost all criminology of social reaction has seen (for all Baratta 1982). Some sad procedural parodies contribute to discredit international juridical efforts (e.g., the judicial parody and outrageous execution of Sadam Hussein).

Although the clear objective pursues an incipient world citizenship (Ambos 2005: 62) guaranteeing punishment for those who brutally injure it from the state power (Werle 2005: 81; Mettraux 2005: 5; Huet/Koering-Joulin 1994: 104), the risks that threaten that difficult path are well known.

For this reason it is criticized from two opposite positions. Therefore, it is convenient to differentiate—at least—two critical approaches: (a) On one hand, those who fear that the structurally biased of punitive power may favour world hegemony of some powers. (b) On the other hand, those who fear that it may become an obstacle for the pretended defence needs of these powers against its *enemies.*[1] In common terms, one could commonly say that there are *criticisms from the left and from the right,* with some casual crossings in their arguments.

The gestation of world citizenship is not linear. Notwithstanding the fact of acknowledging hegemonic disputes, the truth is that the idea of a world citizenship is praiseworthy.[2] Although it is true that what has been done evidences some flaws (about the difficult road covered from First World War until today, among many: La Rosa 2003: 11 and following), it is worth mentioning that no institution was born perfect nor did it develop in the linear and rational way in which jurists prefer, but according to political vicissitudes.[3]

International punishment can avoid a chaotic application of the universal principle. Taking into account what was stated above, we are not fully *apocalyptic* and, *in principle, we believe that internationalization of punishment can be positive in practice, in what concerns the arrangement of the universal principle*, according to which any state can judge the authors of crimes against humanity if this was not done in accordance with territoriality. Although this is an old principle,[4] its application in modern times becomes complicated and can derive in chaotic situations. Therefore, an important practical solution for these cases would be an international competent court.

Criminal law does not know which the purpose of the penalty is. But besides what has been stated, this punishment may offer another advantage that, in our opinion, is the one that definitely grants it legitimacy.

In order to explain this second positive aspect, it is necessary to state that we start with the premise of denying the legitimacy of all the so-called *positive theories of punishment,* because they respond to primary intuitions with which the *purpose, sense or essence of punishment is revealed* to the theorist, and from there on he infers the whole theory of criminal law.[5] Therefore, the positive theories on punishment carefully separate what *is* from what *should be*,[6] because social science demonstrates that punishment in the world—in reality—never *is* how theorists state it *should be.*

Although it is true that the '*is' does not determine the 'should be',* it is not possible to deny that *it limits it,* because a '*should be' that cannot become an 'is',* far from being the expression of a juridical value, is an absurdity. And the truth is that punishment, in most cases, cannot be what any of the theories pretend it *should be,* for which reason today the tendency is to abandon *preventivism* to return to a simple Hegelian reaffirmation of the validity of the rule (Jakobs 1999). In short, it is verifiable that criminal theory knows little about the function of punishment and uses multiple idealist constructions with an intuitionist basis.

THE RESULTS OF PUNITIVE POWER

Mass homicides are committed by punitive power. Beyond any doubt, it is also verifiable that when the state's punitive power gets out of control, the rule of law disappears and its place is occupied by the state of police[7] and, besides, that *mass crimes are committed by this same uncontrolled punitive power,* that is to say, that *the same punitive power agencies commit the most serious crimes when they operate without containment.*[8]

Therefore, the criminal doctrine of the rule of law can well cease legitimating punishment and sincerely admit it does not know what its function is,[9] because it knows it must rationally contain the use of punitive power as far as its juridical control counter power to preserve the rule of law and avoid mass crimes[10] allows it to. At political times, criminal law would be the equivalent to humanitarian law at war times: both would be useful to contain a *factum* as far as their limited juridical power of containment allows them to (Zaffaroni 1993: 383 and following).

What makes international criminal law legitimate? If internationalized punitive power loses control, it would turn into an hegemonic instrument of some sort of planetary police state, which seems to be what left-wing critics want to avoid and right-wing critics try to provoke. In the face of this risk, it is advisable to ask oneself if internationalized punitive power, within less irrational limits, could be legitimated by some positive contribution—even a limited one—to the gradual evolution towards a better international coexistence.

Mass criminals lose peace. Mass crimes have such a huge unlawful content that they seriously limit the juridical power of containment of criminal law. The unpunished mass criminal is in practice subject to a *Friedlossigkeit* or loss of peace, he is excluded from the juridical community, and any damage caused to him is practically unpunished, because criminal law is incapable of condemning the person who executes it. Theorists do not admit this, but when it has occurred[11] executors have remained unpunished. This data from the real world obeys to the fact that criminal law loses its ethical strength to contain, being it of little importance if it pulls through inventing an incompetence[12] or an unconcluded state of war.[13] These pretexts conceal a civilizing regression, because, in fact, we return to a declaration of Roman *hostis* (von Jhering 1877: 228) which deprives the subject from his condition of being a *person*, member of the human community, which is undoubtedly an extreme version of the *criminal law of the enemy.*[14]

International criminal law redeems him as a person. International efforts to submit the criminal to a process are legitimated because they redeem him/her from the status of *hostis*, ratifying *that for the law he/she continues being a person, in spite of the terrible magnitude of the committed crime.*

This is the *maximum contribution and the legitimation of international criminal law:* it would avoid a degrading act of barbarism for the mass crime victims themselves, and would avoid falling within the enemy's criminal law; moreover, it would just be the opposite by avoiding the return to the *hostis*, which is the 'de facto' situation in which the unpunished mass criminal is.[15]

But international punitive power does not prevent state mass homicides. By what has been previously stated, it is evident that we do not accept the supposedly preventive function of international punitive power in what concerns future mass crimes. Its legitimacy, provided it remains within limited channels, lies in the reestablishment of the criminal's personality, according to the juridical–humanist basic principle that states that *every human being is a person.*

Is it possible to prevent mass crimes? But if international punitive power does not prevent mass crimes, but it is criminal law the one in charge of limiting it so that it does not drift towards a reproductive planetary hegemony in that dimension of the state of police (and turns itself into active subject of mass crimes), it is necessary to ask oneself if there is any way explorable for law to prevent those crimes. To accomplish this, it is necessary to examine the deep roots of those crimes, where we reach the *Kernel.*

We move towards a much more complex field where idealist answers of traditional criminal law are not sufficient, and where criminology omits,[16] and where narcissism—that has trained us to respond to the most varied conflict with punitive power[17]—must collect its colourful sails, if it does not wish to sink in the storm. Although the field may be tremendously difficult, we must explore it, *without any pretension of reaching any conclusive truth, but with the most absolute certainty as to the need of going through it.* We must explore a spot of depths we are not used to in criminal doctrine and criminology.

Revenge has an enormous political efficiency. Punitive power—with its structural selectivity—criminalizes a few persons and uses them to project itself as neutralizer of social evil which, as in the case of madness, appears as irrational.[18] It presents itself as the rational power that confines irrationality in prisons and mental hospitals. Thus adorned, it directs revenge impulses, which provides a wonderful political efficiency, currently verified when mass communication glorifies[19] the moral promoter[20] of revenge to neutralize limits to punitive power (i.e., for the benefit of the authoritarian state).[21] The political efficiency of vindictive speech does not explain itself through contextual circumstances, because it remains unchanged throughout the history of state and even *pre-state* punitive power.

Punitive power always tends to mass homicide. Since the moment that in the Eleventh and Twelfth Centuries, punitive power reappeared in Europe, its tendency to become uncontrolled has been a constant under the pretext of fighting against enemies that generate emergencies that are an imminent threat to humanity,[22] and in almost all of them, their agents have committed mass crimes against humanity.[23]

PARANOIA AND THE CREATION OF ENEMIES

Enemies are created by agencies and are destroyed by disputes between them. The enemy is created by a moral promoter agency that hegemonizes punitive speech and mass criminal power until another agency disputes this, starting by denying the enemy's danger, to create another one, as the true or new threat that generates another emergency.[24]

Between one agency's declining hegemony and the ascent of the next one (at the moment of the discursive criticism), a gap opens through which the critical speech of punitive power secularly advances—criminal law of containment or reduction[25]—as well as the resulting rule of law in the political field. The first one is usually called *authoritarian criminal law* and the second one, *liberal criminal law,* although these denominations belong to centuries much later to the beginning of this pendular movement.

In spite of the fact that uncontrolled punitive power always renews the same discursive structure,[26] its content wholly varies according to the chosen enemy, although it invariably reduces all criminal law to direct coercion (administrative law), because one is supposedly fighting against an on-going harmful process.[27]

On the other hand, criminal law of containment, has also had since its origins the same discursive structure,[28] only that—unlike the inquisitorial—its contents do not change, but increase and improve themselves with the successive experiences of criticism to absolutist impulses, while it borrows elements from civil law (punishment as payment for a guilt, crime as a breach of contract).

When punitive power gets out of control, the phenomenon it generates does not exhaust itself in criminal theory—and far from this—it *directly passes on to political theory,* because there arises the police, authoritarian or totalitarian state, with a tendency to absolutism.[29]

The creation of the enemy has the form of a paranoid delusion. Although it is risky to go from individual pathology to collective phenomena, an entity's hypertrophy until erecting it into an enemy and the illusion of emergency, are signs equivalent to paranoid delusion. Modern state always presents a *paranoid tendency* (Hillman 1991: 78) that reaches *paranoid psychosis* when it proclaims emergency, being it then a mad state that suffers a very serious error of meaning (Hillman 1991: 83). The basic idea invades the whole; it is a victim and an instrument of fear, because it believes that all evils come from the enemy, source of the emergency. When delusion is reduced, the state recovers reason and accumulates experience to contain delusion, the result of which is the set of guarantees of constitutional and international law, which starts generating a culture that gradually becomes regional and planetary (Häberle 1997).

Paranoia has been positively theorized as essence of politics. Historical verification of the collar of delusions that from the Twelfth Century up to these times has claimed millions of lives committing the worst crimes, has yielded the aberrant result that an *amoral political thesis* presents the perennial need to create—or identify—enemies, making the essence of politics itself lie in that, and discrediting constitutional culture as a mere *criticism of politics* (Schmitt 1932). To summarize, for this thesis, politics would be the art of building the absolute state, and criticism of the absolute state and the constitutional culture derived from it, would be mere words that weaken state power, which would make the state vulnerable and weak: democracies would be weak structures; the true strong and consolidated state would be the absolute one, the only one capable of annihilating its enemies.

The amorality of this thesis is such that it does not need to *naturalistically* qualify the enemy; the latter is not marked by anything. It is simply the one whom the politician chooses as such.[30] The only strong state would be the delirious, and hence, the absolute one (Schmitt 1938), because—as every delusion—it does not admit any *correction.*

It is an amoral thesis that exploits psychosis. As amoral[31] this theorization may be, the truth is that it is founded on a secular historical verification: relapse into state delusion. But its amorality lies in the fact that it pretends the political exploitation of delusion that, as it accepts it as normal, does not question its causes or nature. No psychotic asks himself about the causes of his madness when—due to his psychosis—he does not admit it, or, what is even worse, no psychopath does so although he admits it, when he decides to politically exploit it.

It is an amoral political resource, but why is it used and how can one explain its millennial efficiency? What leads punitive power to lose control and what leads the state to become absolute, paranoid, to eliminate limitations to its powers, and to annihilate a human mass that the state itself identifies as its enemy? Certainly, individualization of an enemy by the state directs discomfort and revenge; it is evident that blaming a group for all evils and recommending its destruction so as to make it stop, is a very strong political resource, tremendously amoral, but very efficient.

Given its efficiency, there are people who perceive it as a simple *means to accumulate power,* which is still an obviousness that does not explain (a) why a human group obtains such an accumulation of power until it reaches absolute power, nor does it explain (b) the reason for this resource's great political efficiency, which repeats itself without being worn out throughout thousands of years, in spite of the verification that it always ends in a mass crime.

These two questions are the key to any serious attempt of prevention: the reason for *motivation* and the *efficiency.* We start walking on slippery ground but one we must inevitably walk through, and we shall see that both issues are intimately related.

What leads to the indefinite search for power? Capitalism? The impulse of death? Dominant civilization has been criticized from psychology, as being the impeller of an indefinite amount of wealth, in such amounts that thousands of very long-lived lives would not be able to consume, assigning this to a *civilizing pathology,* detected through corrections made to the Freudian theory of its creator's last years.[32] The idea of human history as a *history of neurosis* (Brown 1964: 262) was original at that time, and this would be due to the incapacity to incorporate death, because by radically separating it from life, it causes an indomitable ambivalence. It is not only the indefinite search for goods, but for power, which is also true for the accumulation of knowledge as power, because the search for indefinite power through science also definitely results in the accumulation of goods. With this, modern society presents morbid characteristics not in what concerns knowledge itself, but as regards the schemes that rule the search for knowledge, the purpose of which is to dominate objects (Brown 1964: 267, remembers that this had been stated by Freud; years after, Foucault goes deep into this). Although this psychologist criticism is half a century old the conclusion that the goal of a non-morbid science would not be the domination of nature but the union with it, is very up-to-date (Brown 1964: 268).

Capitalism, the stimulator of indefinite accumulation, would be the expression of this civilizing neurosis, which by setting the accumulation of wealth as its goal leads to the denial of thc Eros, to the sublimation of the body: wealth is not the means but the end in itself,[33] with which the triumph of the death instinct advances.

Indefinite accumulation supports itself in linear time, which also supports revenge. The mentioned conclusions do not differ much from those pointed out from other theoretical frames. Every indefinite accumulation of power assumes a temporal environment which is also indefinite, and which corresponds to the idea of linear time—in the form of an arrow—that exceeds individual existence and does not return. No wonder it has been observed that the idea of revenge is also based on that same idea of time: revenge is always revenge against time (Nietzsche 1883: 409), because one cannot makc what happened not to have happened. Therefore, the linear idea of time is an assumption both of indefinite accumulation of power and of revenge. However, a necessary assumption is not sufficient explanation.

Science that accumulates power is an aristocratic knowledge that does not think. It has been observed that *science does not think* when it looks for power. In the knowledge to *dominate*, the interrogated entity is an *object*, and the interrogator a *subject* that *questions him* to more and better dominate him.[34] The relationship between the interrogator and the interrogated in this knowledge of *dominus* is asymmetrical, because the interrogated is always in a lower level.[35] This has a double effect: (a) On one hand, the interrogator does not expect the answer with all the importance of the interrogated entity (which is the only one the entity can give: the human being with its *humanity*, and the rock with its *quality of stone*), but only in the part that is useful for it *to dominate*. As it cannot assimilate them, the remains of the entities' answers accumulate; the entity *objects to it* (goes against it) and *subjects it* (pushes it downwards).[36] This accumulation of inassimilable answers ends up *subjecting it* and makes this technique lose human control. (b) Besides, when the interrogated entity is another human being, the asymmetry of aristocratic knowledge places the interrogator in a superior level, and, therefore, the knowledge of *dominus* essentially hierarchizes human beings, which allows the rationalization of colonial mass crimes and of every other arbitrary identification of enemies, which are always considered humanly inferior or sub-human (*Untermenschen* or *Unmenschen*).[37]

But mass homicides are prior to this and to the state itself. But the observation of the civilizing neurosis as well as of revenge and the feudal accumulation of knowledge, all supported by revenge, although they convincingly explain a lot, seem to rest in events of the last millennium. However, mass homicides are much previous to this, and do not limit themselves to our dominating, modern, and pre-modern civilization. Mass crimes appear covered by religious visions, are as old as religion, and as religion, are *pre-state* or committed by societies with organizations completely different from modern ones and very different from each other.

Neither do we know how to make the weight of revenge stop. When we nowadays read the abolitionists[38] we smile with the superiority of him who lacks an answer, because we have not reached the bottom of the question. We know that what they propose is impossible or almost impossible, but we do not know why. We stammer because we do not dare to look for the answer. We direct revengeful violence in the criminal justice system, but remain silent when punitive power breaks the barriers of juridical containment of criminal law and bursts into mass homicides, the authors of which are none other than those whom the discourse assigns the function of preventing them. We know that revengeful violence is previous to the state, that its origin is related to religion, that no matter how modernity has encouraged it—and it has undoubtedly done so—it has not generated it, but we cannot eliminate it and we do not know why. We know that the hard search for an unlimited power generates mass homicide violence, that the knowledge of *dominus* strengthens it and threatens planet life, that the exploitation of revenge destroys our juridical culture and leads to the absolute state and mass homicide, but we cannot neutralize its instigation nor move to a non-morbid or *frater* or *non-dominus* science; we cannot move from asymmetrical *inquisitio* to symmetrical *dialogues.*[39]

PUNITIVE POWER, BIOLOGY AND ETHNOLOGY

Is it a biological determinism? It could be said that the persistency and antiquity of the phenomenon could be due to biological reasons, that is to say, to something non-mutable in human biology, to a genetic flaw that leads it to violence and self-destruction.

Although this thesis is unverifiable, it cannot be denied that it underlies in Hobbes and in many who follow his line, who were able to observe mass death with a somewhat amoral indifference,[40] because it was limited to a considerable number of persons. But for some time now it has been seen that technological advance—*science does not think*—today considers the possibility of a catastrophe that may affect the whole species, and not through a war, but due to the production system itself that seeks to accumulate goods and does not stop even in the face of catastrophes with huge consequences (Boff 2002) with the risk of total annihilation. The current perspective of mass homicide includes the possibility of extinction of life in the planet; a biologist even thought that the *cephalopods* or molluscs in the bottom of the sea could replace human beings—after many millions of years of evolution.

The festive, lethal, amoral and irresponsible glorification of paranoia, and the thesis of its inevitability mean today—just to clearly say it—the proximity of mass homicides much greater than the past ones and the not distant extinction of the species. It may be stated that over the past years it has been the theologists (Boff 2003; Küng 2004) who have moved away from every religious and ecclesiastical exclusivism to draw attention over the risk in the search for a basic ecumenical coincidence of brotherhood of (and with) living beings.

There is no evidence that violence and revenge are a biological fatalism. The truth is that there is no evidence of this biological fate of the species. Many are the behaviours that were historically considered conditioned or *natural,* when they were a product of culture, and very frequently it was pretended that they were *natural* institutions or cultural standards as a resource of power. If there were times when slavery or the superiority or inferiority of human races were considered *natural*—and not by authors lacking intelligence[41]—one cannot avoid been suspicious that the fate of the creation of enemies and the subsequent mass crimes are also a *politically naturalized* cultural product.

If the process goes back to pre-history it is necessary to appeal to ethnology. The only verified fact is that since immemorial times enemies are invented and sacrificed; that afterwards a new enemy is invented and a new sacrifice occurs; that this is clearer and dramatically notorious as modern civilization becomes planetary and technology advances, and each new sacrifice implies new mass homicides, in the form of genocide or war crimes with *collateral effects* or under other euphemisms.

Not being there any evidence that this is a biological predestination, one may ask oneself about its deep origin in culture. The greatest and most brilliant intuition of the past century in this sense seems to have been Freud's when in *Totem und Tabu* he theorized on society's origin (Freud 1974: 287), with which he focused the true location of the problem in ethnology. *Freudism* watched this intuition with certain mistrust and the ethnological verification defects weakened it.[42] On the other hand, taking the issue back to ethnology always makes one think that we are going too far behind.

We can now ask ourselves the same question: Aren't we going too far behind if we pretend to explore in ethnology when we try to prevent modern times mass homicides? The narrowness of the criminal or criminological discourse we are used to, causes us vertigo when we take a look at that depth, but it seems there is no other resource when we clear up the contextual anecdotic data and we observe the unceasing succession of enemies, emergencies and mass homicide violence as far as we can look back into history, and we verify that it goes back to pre-history and tragedy, always related there to religion.

We cannot become excited believing that a phenomenon that only shows circumstantial new characteristics is new. Only the illusion that we are living something entirely new encourages the criticism that states we are unnecessarily going back too far, which is thoughtlessly stimulated by the difficulty of venturing up to the ethnological root of the phenomenon, but we cannot deny that although what is new is important in many senses, it does not alter the essence of the phenomenon. The novelty is the discursive garment, the greater technical-homicidal potential, the perpetration by those who for some centuries now have invented themselves as those formally in charge of avoiding or penalizing them, the acceleration in the production of enemies, and—what is most important—that its indefinite continuity makes it possible to foresee planetary destruction. But we know that with or without this information *the structure of the enemy creation process, of directing evil and revenge so as to end up in sacrifice,* has been exactly the same since before history, where it always appears related to religion, and there is nothing to prove that this is unchangeable due to biological predestination. To prevent the phenomenon there is no other way than to grasp its essence and, for this purpose, we must follow Freud up to ethnology, that is to say, beyond history.

From criminal law and criminology we are very limited, but we must do it. We cannot but observe the extreme limitation of criminological discourse in the face of this urgent need, nor the narrowness of criminology that practically omits treatment of mass crimes[43] and, therefore, how little trained we are to go up to where we should. However, it is impossible to avoid this responsibility if we wish to contribute something to the prevention of facts so serious that they imply an irreversible limit situation for all human beings.[44]

PUNITIVE POWER AND SACRIFICE

Freud's explanation is insufficient, because it is not a fact of the past, but a fact that repeats itself. Although it is possible to follow Freud up to ethnology, today it does not seem adequate to move there following his steps. Little does his hypothesis explain to us about the *Urvater* homicide as foundational (Freud 1974: 426), because its explanation is static, sacrifice occurs once and for all and leaves society founded (Girard 2005: 280). For this reason, we believe that in the field of ethnology, it is René Girard's investigations the ones that provide us with a dynamic explanation, the ones that can guide us in the road towards that we are looking for, as far as they suggest the improvement of the Freudian hypothesis, getting rid of the *terrible father,* of the identity of the victim of the sacrifice, stressing that the important fact is not that identity but its suitability to direct the function of revenge assigned to it and which it really performs (Girard 2005: 294).

Sacrificial victims are very varied, although not everyone can be one. Girard emphasizes that this function is assigned to very different sacrificial victims, who are such due to their suitability to act as channels in different societies, without this role being determined by a previous *ontological identification.* It must be stated that by the end of the Nineteenth Century, criminology pretended the *ontological identification* of the sacrificial victim (Lombroso 1884; Garofalo: 1891: 59)—of the enemy—but in the Twentieth Century, political theory, with a greater penetration, admitted that identification was purely political, although it did not establish the political power's identification limits, because *although there is no ontological identification, there is an ontological limit for that power, that is determined by each society's specific conditions.*

An expiatory victim cannot be anyone, but only that who is strange but not completely different (Girard 1978: 93), and which for that reason can personify all the evils of society, all its members' violence, without analysing if it is guilty or innocent (Girard 2005: 17). Definitely, the guilt or innocence of the expiatory victim does not decide its capacity of directing revenge: the primitive is not concerned about guilt, because he fears that by appealing to it he may encourage violence, for that reason he is only concerned with the victim's channelling suitability (Girard 2005: 40). Although for us this is a sign of cultural inferiority and the under-estimation of the subjective element of the infringement belongs to a savage criminal law, something similar is recommended by the political theory that encourages the state's absolutist paranoia, but because it wants to have its hands free to better direct and encourage revenge. Anyhow, everyone will believe the victim's guilt has been verified when after killing him, peace and order return (Girard 1978: 72).

The victim becomes miraculous. The struggle for the same objects gives rise to tensions that lead to collective violence that destroys coexistence: blood is shed demanding more blood—revenge—in an escalade (*essential violence)* that only ceases when it is directed through the expiatory victim, whose sacrifice results miraculous, because it immediately stops destructive violence. This causes an inversion in the assessment of the victim who from being the personification of evil turns to be an agent of goodness. Hence, worship of the victim is ritually perpetuated and becomes sacred. The intimate relationship between the circle of revenge—identification of enemies—and religion,[45] answers to this.

The criminal justice system plays the role of directing revenge. Modern society's judicial criminal justice system tries to rationally direct revenge, which moves from private revenge to public revenge (Girard 2005: 32).[46] Whereas religion tries to avoid revenge or to deviate it over a secondary object, the criminal justice system pretends to make it rational.[47] *Behind the practical and at the same time mythical difference, it is necessary to affirm the "no" difference, the positive identity of revenge, of sacrifice and of judicial penalty, precisely because these three phenomena are at all times the same that always, in the case of a crisis, tend to relapse in the same undifferentiated violence* (Girard 2005: 43-44).

Capitalism accelerates violence, but does not create it. Improvement of the Freudian ethnological thesis by Girard is very rich for criminal law and, although it is not possible to exhaust it now,[48] the very brief mentioned notes make it possible to formulate certain considerations to approach the answer to the question posed.

In theory, if *essential violence* results from the desire for the same objects, when society encourages competition and their infinite accumulation supported in a temporal arrow that is also infinite, social crisis in which collective violence and revenge explode are also accelerated. This reaffirms that the circle of revenge (the production of successive enemies and emergencies that sacrifice numerous human groups) is not a phenomenon generated by capitalism, in spite of encouraging and accelerating it, with the consumption society and the concentration and polarization of wealth. This acceleration explains the already mentioned speed with which enemies currently change, whose position lasts very little and some are also even outlined as manipulation attempts of the violence directing mechanism, without fully turning it into operation.

The overwhelmed criminal justice system pretends to recover its legitimacy by executing revenge. If religion tries to deviate revenge and the criminal justice system tries to manipulate it, what is true is that when one reaches critical times—when demystification neutralizes the deviation from revenge or the capacity of criminal direction is surpassed—modern society repeats the process, with the special feature that agencies of the criminal justice system itself execute revenge over the expiatory victim without any rationality, and, besides, assign that channelling role to a human group or mass.

Truly, the modern invention of the criminal justice system is almost diabolic, because although Girard does not observe this, it is not only a manipulating means of revenge but also—and according to circumstances—a very powerful means for its execution. When social tensions and collective violence (with its *blood that claims for blood*) exceed the manipulating capacity of the criminal justice system and this is surpassed, it is discredited, because it loses the confidence of being capable of directing violence. Punitive power agencies launch themselves to retaining or recovering their channelling legitimacy (which is equivalent to their power), for which purpose they assume the leadership of executing sacrificial revenge, under the pretension of capitalizing the merit of the restoration of peace. It is true that the inversion of the victim's assessment—which ends up capturing the merit of the cessation of violence—reverses the effect of the homicidal impulse and the same agents of the punitive power become future sacrificial victims. Anyhow, this explains why the rule is that the criminal justice system itself commits homicides and not another state system. This process is independent from violence being ascribed to power or that the latter encourages it to more rapidly sacrifice the expiatory victim and restore the pretended peace; this is contextual information of every process repetition, that is not essential.

Colonial genocides are resources to avoid the outburst of violence in colonizing societies. This analysis would explain mass crimes during the past century—such as the Holocaust or the Armenian genocide—but at first sight, the repetition of the expiatory sacrifice would not be sufficient to explain colonialist mass crimes (Ferro 2005; Ferro 2000), such as the Iberian colonialism (Jaulin 1976; Gerbi 1978), slave trade (Hugh 1998) or the most recent one of Leopold II in the Belgian Congo. However, it is not correct to rule out the application of the same theoretical frame, although with a different mechanism.

There are two ways of preventing the outburst of collective violence in the dispute for the same object: to reduce demand by discouraging it, or to increase the offer, by increasing the objects. In both cases, there will be less conflict. Today it would be impossible to pretend to increase offer by means of the indefinite increase of production and consumption levels, because we would destroy the planet, but in times of colonialism and of neo-colonialism, the most efficient way to increase objects was the subjugation of other complete societies to force their inhabitants to provide goods, precious metals (means of payment or currency) or elements with which to elaborate the objects of dispute.[49] This was colonialism, at the expense of which colonialist societies pretended to reduce their internal conflicts, although due to their internal conditions (excessive centralization of wealth, difficulty to become dynamic, excessive verticalization, etc.) not all of them achieved this.

Colonies are gigantic jails or concentration camps for inferior beings. Although it may seem that this has nothing to do with punitive power, in truth this subjugation was achieved through the extension of punitive power to another complete society, which had to be submitted to this power by reason of its inferiority and of the danger that because of this, it supposedly represented for the *civilized,* for they were enemies because they were foreigners—strangers—who for not being similar were dangerous inferior beings. Colonialist power was punitive, because *a colony is a prison for containment and forced labour, that is to say, a gigantic concentration camp* where prisoners were deprived (colonized)[50] from their culture, language, religion and traditions. European prisons confined their inferior natives (similar to their colonized), while colonies confined foreign natives because all of them were dangerous inferior beings (savages) that threatened them with their mere existence.[51]

The sacrificer must invent a new enemy to avoid becoming the next sacrificial victim. The thesis of the sacrifice of the expiatory victim also explains why an international criminal justice system will have little preventive strength in the face of mass homicides. When revenge is directed towards the expiatory victim, and the latter is sacrificed, peace and order are restored, but the victim starts gaining a sacred capacity, its ambivalence arises: from the personification of evil it changes to the personification of goodness, the mythical component is introduced, the sacrificer himself starts being a candidate to become an expiatory victim, which is somehow the fate of the hero (Girard 2005: 126) and, on occasions, of the autocrat—of the king (Girard 2005: 150)—and the new contradictions that reintroduce violence will be directed towards him, for which reason the political theory of the absolute state advises him to create a new enemy, something that is not always achieved.[52] The only thing that international criminal law can then do is to limit or contain the new wave of revenge, as we stated when pointing out its source of legitimacy.

Primary prevention of mass homicides is strange to the field of criminal sciences. But the problem of prevention remains unsolved. Deviation of revenge through myths and the restraints of the criminal justice system are not sufficient when society's violent conflicts are beyond the limits of the channel through which revenge circulates, with which it is clear that both only provide palliatives or postponements, but do not solve the problem, they do not interrupt the chain that dates back to basic violence.

In spite of acknowledging that every preventive resource is good, in spite of being a palliative, or if it only provides a shift in time, the truth is that if basic violence is not attacked, it will not be possible to avoid its explosion sooner or later, and with it, revenge and its well known process of sacrifice of the expiatory victim.

In order to attack basic violence, it is essential to decelerate the appetite for the same objects and reduce the social level of competitivity. This would be what is usually called *primary prevention* applied to mass homicides. Criminal theorists are not the ones in charge of projecting a future, more supportive and less competitive society, at least in what concerns our specific function and knowledge, although we can warn politicians and managers of the transnational economic power, who seem absorbed in fighting over the best cabin in the *Titanic* while they speed up towards the iceberg, about its need.

THE WAY FORWARD

Secondary prevention demands the inversion of current criminal policies prevailing in the world. But we are concerned with the so-called *secondary prevention.* Everything we may do to reduce conflict or its effects, will be healthy. Criminal policy applied throughout the world, inspired by United States republican administrations over the last decades,[53] who repudiating their own tradition[54] constantly extend criminalizing programming and each time authorize more punitive power to direct revenge, does not realize that if the limits of the criminal justice system are exceeded, its reversal occurs, because when it is surpassed, from being a channelling element it becomes an executioner of revenge itself so as to maintain or recover its power and, therefore, the sacrifice of the expiatory victim.

Functionalist thought here faces a strong dilemma, because if it remains in its usual ascertainment and its corresponding assessment jump, it would reach the conclusion that the overflow of the channelling capacity of the criminal justice system that leads to sacrifice is *functional* to stop violence, for which reason it would agree with the amoral thesis of the absolute state; only that under present circumstances the suicidal thesis of the supposed functionality of a catastrophe that compromises the whole species, would be undefendable. It seems that deeper functionalism has no other way than incorporating new values and accepting the malfunctioning of the repetition of sacrifice ad infinitum.

Therefore, an adequate secondary prevention of conflict would consist in exhausting the possibility of the models of effective solutions of conflicts (as the repairing, restoring, therapeutical and conciliating models, among others), limiting the application of the punitive model to those few cases when these are absolutely inadmissible.

Current direction leads to new mass homicides. On the other hand, a realistic policy, truly concerned about the solution of social problems, cannot continue pretending that punitive power is the one in charge of solving them, when primary prevention must be social, and secondary prevention should be oriented towards a reasonable—and demandable—reduction of damages.[55] Direction of these conflicts towards punitive power is a hypocritical way of leaving them unsolved,[56] fostering social tensions.

This means that criminal policy that prevails in the world needs an urgent turn on the opposite direction to become a factor that may break the high level of conflict. Disintegration caused by conflict can be neutralized in two ways: encouraging efficient models of conflict solution, which would strengthen social cohesion, or else sacrificing the expiatory victim, that is to say, with mass homicide.[57] To avoid the latter, it is obvious that the alternative must be encouraged.

It will not be simple to bring about this turn, because present world seems to follow the amoral indications of the absolutist political theory, that stimulated state paranoia: the discursive pretence of fighting against terrorism these days, supposing there is a *war,* only legitimates the alleged *war* of the Islam, with which not only they do not fight against terrorism but they also fall within a shared paranoia or delirium à deux.[58]

The old amoral formula did not work. But the old amoral political formula does not yield the expected results, because to create the new foreign enemy far from its own frontiers, a real war was created outside and an economic recession within, which announces an increase of tensions, that means that it resulted in a perverse manipulation of the revenge process, the consequences of which are still unimaginable. The old amoral political formula did not establish economy's limits and its strict application instead of reducing tensions seems to generate other new ones, running the risk that some of its promoters may become the new sacrificial victims.

This phenomenon is not new—in essence—because old colonialism many times frustrated its objective of reducing internal tensions as a consequence of metropolitan economy's failure to adapt itself to the abundance of desirable objects, as it occurred with Spanish colonialism that did not know how to capitalize results through industrialization and ended losing its colonial hegemony, which moved to the hands of European central and northern powers. Although now—following an old formula[59] and the experience of the previous century (Mammarella 1986)—it was believed that a war would strengthen economy, apparently it depressed it (or was insufficient to avoid the announced depression). It is a failure of an attempt to avoid violence by creating external violence, which would show the need of correcting the amoral formula: *when one appeals to the creation of an external enemy (because it is inferior) violence directs itself provided the internal conditions make it possible to take advantage of its benefits; if not, external mass homicide results useless and even negative.*

There are few alternatives provided by criminal doctrine. In the face of the current criminal political tendency that, if it is not interrupted, leads to the commission of new mass homicides, criminal doctrine faces three logical variables: (a) to discredit the dominant policy; (b) to legitimate and stimulate it; and (c) to try to reach a compromise with it. The second variable is the option for the absolute state typical of amoral politics, that today does not deserve greater attention, because it seems a forbidden road.[60]

The third one is the most frequent one, although with a curious duality: it is formally rejected when it is made express, but it is accepted and daily put into practice. Its express formulation gave place to a discussion which was at times scandalous and confirmed the expression *criminal law of the enemy*

(Jakobs 2004). But truly, what is called *criminal law of the enemy* is a current practice, in a greater or lesser extent, in almost the whole world and especially in Latin America, where its preferred instrument is *temporary detention pending trial* used as the main form of punishment and almost the only one.[61] Considering that the only express theoretical formulation—besides general contempt—is unfeasible because it is based upon a static vision that ignores the dynamics inherent to punitive power,[62] the truth is that compromise with the dominant criminal policy is degraded to a practice without theoretical support. It seems something more of a compromise of agencies that a theoretical position: juridical agencies—conscious or not—assign power due to the fear of being devastated by executive agencies and by the publicity of the apparatus of power, similarly to politicians besieged by the *völkisch*[63] and revengeful sole speech of mass media.

Ethical and cultural compromise. From a compromised attitude, it is objected that criminological knowledge can do nothing in front of the decisions of power, for which it is better to take shelter in the supposedly pragmatic compromise. This objection under-estimates the power of the speech, that is precisely the one that jurists must not give in. With discourse one exercises power—dictators always knew so—although it is not the same power owned by the executive agencies of the criminal justice system, but without discourse, these become discredited, and in the end, power without discourse, although it may cause serious damage before falling apart, does not last very long. If criminal law massively deprives it from discourse, public inducement to revenge would be reduced to what it is: pure mediatic publicity, with the limitations proper to any product's publicity.

Real criminal prevention consists in denouncing the neutralization techniques of mass homicides. Individualization of enemies, that is to say, the state's paranoid outbreak, nourishes itself from discourses that rationalize expiatory sacrifice, expanding the causes of justification and exoneration of criminal law in a different way, but always based on what criminology of the past mid-century called *neutralization techniques* (Sykes and Matza 1957). When criminologists of those times exposed these techniques, they did so based on simplistic discursive resources that were at the time used by *rebels without a cause* to minimize, justify or excuse their vandalism; but neutralization techniques in mass crimes are theorized at high political level—even by academic or reproduction agencies—and are glorified through the social communication media. This has not been observed by criminology because it has not been concerned with these crimes,[64] because in order to do so, it should abandon its pretended and impossible ideological neutrality.

In fact: criminal sciences have no other option than getting rid of their incredible aseptic pretension if they seriously pretend to approach the issue of the most serious crimes, because they can only do so by criticizing ideologies,[65] so as to be able to discover those which true nature is that of neutralization of mass homicides or their preparation by means of revengeful speeches, even penal and criminological. If the *criminal law of the enemy* legitimates the typification of preparatory acts, penal and criminological knowledge must correct this by advancing their criticism to preparatory acts of mass homicides, such as is the preparation of their *neutralization technique*.[66]

It is amazing that we still do not clearly see that *we are in a revival of the ideology of national security now at world level*,[67] when we have been living its regional experience for over half a century, and that we tolerate that with identical simple plans they may undermine the states of law. That is the true preventive function that criminal juridical knowledge must and can perform in what concerns mass homicides.

International criminal law may offer palliatives or possible pragmatic benefits, may avoid the restoration of the *Friedlossigkeit*, but the true prevention of mass homicides that criminal juridical knowledge can provide, shall be through the exercise of criticism and the frontal rejection of the *values neutralization techniques,* finely prepared by theorists, and roughly by public or mediatic inducement to revenge. If we do not do so, our knowledge will fall within another thinking drainage[68] and for some time it will be *another science that does not think.*

NOTES

1. This seems to be the Republican policy of the United States of America, denying the ratification of any treaty that may limit its interventions or control its actions.

2. The most extreme theoretical rejection to this idea belongs to Carl Schmitt, because from the perspective of his identification of the political with the paranoia of the absolute state, this would imply the abdication of sovereignty (waiver to arbitrarily elect the enemy). The people who reject this—according to Schmitt—will disappear due to their weakness (see Schmitt 1932). According to this thesis, the assumption of the international commitment to punish the terrorism of state, mass murders and war crimes, implies a sign of weakness of the state that assumes it and announces its disappearance.

3. It is sufficient to think, for example, about the appearance and advance of the democratic representation or in the consecration of the fundamental rights. On the vicissitudes of vote in Great Britain, generally quoted as the cradle of political rights, one can see Schama 2002; the criticism to universal and secret vote in Argentina in the discriminatory publications of the then national senator Benjamín Villafañe, see Villafañe 1936 and Villafañe 1937. Social rights were incorporated to constitutional law in the Mexican Constitution of 1917 or *Carta de Querétaro*, in the middle of the

worst Latin American civil war of the Twentieth Century, and in the Constitution of Weimar, finally destroyed by Nazism.

4. The Argentine Constitution recognizes this since 1853 (section 102, current section 118), specially very ancient treaties consecrate it, as the one of International Criminal Law of Montevideo, 1889. Its records go back to the United States of America during the end of the Eighteenth Century. A doctrinaire reference can be seen in the famous *Derecho de Gentes* of Vattel (See Vattel 2004: 155-6).

5. "The starting point of all idealist systems is the immediate intuition of the absolute and unconditional" (cf. Rivacoba 1963: 29).

6. It works by assigning the first one to a "natural" science and the second one to a "cultural" one, according to the neo-Kantian philosophic assumptions: see Rickert 1965.

7. The inquisitive model, where all procedural functions are concentrated in the "court," because it is not impartial but always acts for "the good," makes them stop being judges and start being policemen. In a modern sense the inquisitors were not judges, as neither were the members of the "special" political courts, as the Nazi *Volksgericht.* The courts of absolute states are always police courts, administrative entities because of their dependence and partiality. A police state—sociologically speaking—is a state where the police agencies operate without limitations, as Gestapo, KGB or the intelligence service of any dictatorship. In the best of cases these "courts" would be mere internal controls of the administration. Those who exercised judicial power in Latin American dictatorships were not judges, although the constitutional regimes were forced to recognize the value of their judgments due to elemental public order reasons.

8. It is true that many of these crimes are attributed to military forces, but it is also true that, beyond the cases that are authentic war crimes, these forces have committed them by operating materially police functions and not war ones.

9. Because of this we propose a criminal law based in a negative or "agnostic" theory of punishment (See Zaffaroni, Alagia and Slokar 2000: 35).

10. As long as the judicial power planned by criminal law contains the punitive power, the rule of law operates better; when this one gives away containment space, the rule of law is deteriorated. *In extenso* see Zaffaroni 1989. This explains the fragility of the rule of law and criminal law that is proper to it, which Wolfgang Naucke makes reference to (See Naucke 2000).

11. It can be objected that it has happened in few cases. Beyond the pretended "tyrannicide," that is to say, when the criminal has lost power, in many cases the revengeful execution has not taken place because the victims themselves or their blood relatives chose the legal ways, but it must be observed that they do this, precisely, so they do not fall in the denial of the condition of person of the criminal, what would place them in their same ethical level and would not only delegitimize the fight for legal punishment, but would make the criminals "sacred," offering themselves as candidates for future sacrifice victims.

12. The young Armenian who executed Talât in Berlin, the direct responsible of the Armenian genocide, was acquitted by a German court due to transitory unindictability (See Dacrian 1997: 288-9).

13. In the case of the execution of Mussolini, it was closed with the argument that the marionette republic of Salò had not subscribed the armistice and it was an act of war. The truth is that if the marionette republic ever existed, it no longer did, because its governors were escaping to Switzerland. The General Attorney of Milan's decision not to proceed due to this reason (Bianchi 1977: 473).

14. Leaving the mass criminal unpunished and released to any private revenge is much worse than what is proposed by the actual version of "criminal law of the enemy," that only proposes security measures.

15. Against what was affirmed by G. Jakobs, who pretends that international criminal law is criminal law of the enemy, its—main and possibly only—virtue is precisely to rescue the mass criminal from a real situation of "criminal law of the enemy" raised to the extreme.

16. It is curious that being the crimes that have caused more deaths in the last century, there is a suspicious silence of criminology about them, very well pointed out by Morrison 2006.

17. To such point it is true that the concept of juridical interest, developed by criminal liberalism as requirement of offensiveness or harmfulness, suffers the effects of a curious alchemy, because the "injured juridical interest" turns to be a "tutelary juridical interest," giving as true that the criminal rule "protects" it, when nothing verifies that this goal is actually achieved: the only verifiable thing is that criminal rule prohibits a conduct that may affect it.

18. When dealing with this issue, one cannot forget the contributions made by Michel Foucault (Foucault 2003).

19. On the concept of "glorification" and its relevance through communication mass media, see Agamben 2007.

20. The concept of the *moralpromoter* goes back to Malinowski 1956; a new phenomenon is the creation of the *victim/hero*: see Eliacheff and Soulez Larivière 2007.

21. This success is once again verified with the present revengeful advertising trend and the consent of the populations that demand greater controls and more punitive power, satisfied by irresponsible and frightened politicians that advance in an accelerated road of destruction of the rule of law, through a revival of authoritarian and totalitarian criminal laws. This experience is almost planetary, that is to say, it is not exclusive of any country or region, and is simultaneous to last century's market fundamentalism, that brought about social exclusion and the stop of development. The leaders of such fundamentalism are today the main promoters of revengeful publicity.

22. Since reappearance of punitive power, the main emergency invented when it was necessary to strengthen the central power of the Church was the heresy of the Cathars and Albigenses (Mestre 1995), and, immediately, witchcraft, that is to say, the identification of the demon as the enemy which, as it was unreachable, fell upon women who came to an agreement with it. Since about eight centuries ago, emergencies—and enemies—were successively changing each time faster: the degeneration of races, syphilis, alcohol, drugs, international communism, and others, up to reaching terrorism in present times. Each of these enemies existed in reality and sometimes were a danger (witches were persecuted since Roman times, at least) but emergency

erects it in the sole evil that justifies any degree of repression. In the individual level, delusions almost always have a minimum real basis.

23. Although here we only deal with mass homicides, these have not been the only crimes against humanity committed in the emergencies generated through the creation of enemies. The handicapped, the ill, the mentally ill, the blind, the dumb, homosexuals, indians, have been the scapegoats, the victims—among other things—of many thousands of forced or illegal sterilizations. We can mention the aberrations committed against degeneration as enemy of the race (Black 2003).

24. This dynamic operates since the origins of current punitive power. The Roman Inquisition against witchcraft was organized by the Dominicans and then deteriorated. The manual that encloses and summarizes the experience against witches is the *Malleus Maleficarum*, of 1487. When in the Sixteenth Century it was reorganized—based on the Spanish model—against the reformed, it was placed under control of the Jesuits, who discredited the speech of emergency against witches.

25. The first critical discourse published in a work especially devoted to this job (because he had been preceded by other Jesuits in general theological works) appeared in 1631 and belonged to the Jesuit Friedrich Spee (Spee 2003).

26. The structural elements of inquisitorial discourse recognizable in manuals of the Fifteenth Century, and even before, remain unaltered: severe punishment against those who doubt of the dangerous condition of the enemy and emergency, enemy's human inferiority, agency's immunity to evil, prejudiced signs of evil, euphemistic language at the time of declaring punishment, agency's exclusivity in the recognition of evil, etc. These elements clearly appear in the *Malleus*, which is a late work, published almost by the end of the persecution of witches, but which summarizes the inquisitorial experience of two centuries.

27. The difference between punitive power and direct administrative coercion is broken; every violence to ruin the enemy becomes legitimate by means of necessity or of legitimate defence. This was the legitimating discourse of torture proper of the ideology of national security in the south of America thirty years ago, and today's speech in the north: once the difference between punitive power and direct coercion has been annulled, it is the same to twist an individual's arm or to slap his face to grasp the key to disarm a bomb tied to a bay's cradle, than to organize and plan the subjugation to pain of a gang's member so as to destroy it.

28. In Spee's mentioned work, one can see the critical elements to punitive power that have been in force up to now: indifference of the political authority in front of the agencies' abuses, their corruption and extortions; disinformation of the population; aboulia and repetition of prejudice by the theorists; concealing euphemisms to apply tortures; condemnation of innocent people; selectivity due to vulnerability; perverse interpretation of victimization signs; allocation of special powers of resistance to the victim; reproduction of the system, etc.

29. More than a relationship between criminal and constitutional law, in the rule of law there exists a reciprocal dependency, because when constitutional law does not provide criminal law with its containment principles, criminal law loses its main function, and when it does not comply with its containment function, constitutional law loses its effect.

30. Schmitt sees in this the essence itself of sovereign power: "Sovereign is he who decides over the state of exception," that is to say, whoever has the power of choosing the enemy (Schmitt 2005: 23).

3. Minimization of responsibility as the intellectual participant of the author of this thesis, may have been sincere, because it is not possible to demonstrate that it has "caused" anything, because it limited itself to legitimizing what was being committed, although in the facts this has been true. See his defensive arguments in the early post-war in Schmitt 2006.

32. We refer to Freud's thesis on "Eros" and "Thanatos."

33. In page 339 (Brown 1964: 339) it reproduces the following paragraph from Keynes: *When the accumulation of wealth stops having great social importance, there will be great changes in the moral code. We will be able to free ourselves from many pseudo-moral principles that have obsessed us for two hundred years, with which we have raised some of the most unpleasant human qualities to the place of the highest virtues. We will be able to allow ourselves the audacity of giving the motivation of money its fair value. Love for money in terms of possession, different from the love for money as a means for enjoyment and for the reality of life, shall be recognized as it is, a morbidity which, in a certain sense, is unpleasant, one of those semi-criminal tendencies, semi-pathological, that with a shudder are derived to specialists in mental illnesses.*

34. According to Foucault, the interrogatory (the *inquisitio*) as a form of access to procedural truth, that replaced the fight (*disputatio*) of the ordeal of combat or duel, extended itself as a model to all wisdom and generated what we here call the *dominus* (Foucault 1980).

35. It is the position that corresponds in this scheme to the entity to be dominated. Foucault's thesis on the extension of the *inquisitio* as a scientific model may not be shared, but the truth is that the change of scientific paradigm is temporarily near and the cruelty which knowledge submits the "object" to is highly significant.

36. It may be stated that etymology here is significant: *ob and sub* give a clear idea of the relationship.

37. Generally this is identified with racism, but hierarchization of human beings is not reduced to racism nor does it always have a pseudo-biological origin or fundament. Discrimination of women, the elderly, homosexuals, the mentally ill, is not always related to racism. Division into castes, for instance, usually has—as is the case of India—a supposedly spiritual rationalization: the good ones reincarnate themselves into the superior caste.

38. We refer—for example—to Louk Hulsman, Nils Christe and Thomas Mathiesen (Hulsman and Bernat de Celis 1982; Cohen 1989).

39. It would be the form of knowledge that would learn how to listen to the entity in a horizontal and symmetrical way. This knowledge is the only one that would guarantee the preservation of planetary life. It is true that the difficulty for this *dialogus* was intensified by two marked Medieval tendencies with respect to the animal: one radically separated the animal from the human being, while the other one humanized it to the point of submitting it to process and punishment, that is to say that none recognized its condition (on this Pastoureau 2006: 27 and following).

40. In the same line of biological determinism, we could place Herbert Spencer's catastrophic cosmo-vision, which was the one that nourished neo-colonialist racism and positivist criminology and criminal law, until culminating in the legitimation of racist totalitarism of Nazism (thus, Grispigni and Mezger 1942).

4. Lack of intelligence may not be attributed to Aristotle or Thomas Aquinas. However, see the efforts thought needed to make to demonstrate the aberration of slavery; (on this see Brion Davis 2001).

42. In anthropology, it was the Boasian culturalists who in principle rejected Freud's conceptions, but even the investigators who followed his steps, such as the Hungarian Géza Róheim abandoned the idea of the phylogenetic memory of essential parricide, the same as the further synthesis of Kardiner (on this Harris 1983: 370).

43. Only during the last years interdisciplinary works have been published, such as Raffin 2006.

44. Besides, we have extensively nourished the speech supporting the disposition of our criminal and criminologist knowledge towards the opening to other disciplines, using expressions such as *interdisciplinarity, transdisciplinarity,* etc.; the time has come to demonstrate this.

45. It is possible to think that the circle is not always completed when the originary experience is repeated, because not always does the victim have the conditions to become sacred; however, experience indicates that there are many cases when this happens, as is evidenced by the multiple sanctification of delinquents—generally decorated with Robin Hood conditions—who make "miracles" happen in Latin America.

46. Girard notes that the expression "public revenge" is not common, although it is used by those who pretend to see in the criminal justice system a "civilizing evolution," especially positivists of social Darwinism and even earlier ones, as the followers of Comte. Besides the hollowness of the fundament of the "retribution," there are few doubts as to the reality of criminal execution, even in developed countries; in this sense, Pratt 2006.

47. If our system seems more rational to us, truly this is because it is more closely made up with the principle of revenge. The insistence as to the punishment of the guilty has no other meanings. Instead of endeavouring to avoid revenge, to moderate, to evade or deviate it towards a secondary object, as all procedures that are really religious do, the judicial system rationalizes revenge, is capable of sub-dividing it and limiting as it best fits it; it makes with it a limitedly efficient curing technique, and, secondarily, of violence prevention (Girard 2005: 40-41).

48. His thesis presents an attraction that greatly exceeds our subject's interest. One can see the implications found by Vattimo 1999; also Girard and Vattimo 2006.

49. On the role of colonialism in the Industrial Revolution see Cole 1963.

50. Similarity between colonized and true born criminals was sustained by Cesare Lombroso, who described the latter as bearer of Mongoloid and Africanoid characteristics (Lombroso 1884: 248 and 295).

51. Kant writes—it is commonly admitted that no one can harass another person, unless the latter has attacked the former. This is very precise when both live in the civil and legal status. Because for the mere fact of having entered in the civil status,

every one gives all the others the necessary guarantees; and it is the sovereign authority the one that, having power over all of them, serves as an efficient instrument for all those guarantees. But man—or the people—who is in the state of nature, does not provide me with those guarantees, and even hurts me due to the mere fact of being in that state of nature; in effect, he is besides me, and although he does not actively harass me, the anarchy of his status is a perpetual threat for me. I can force him to enter with me into a common ordinary status or to part from my side (Kant 1977: 203).

52. In repetitions, a victim is not always consecrated. Frequently, the power chooses one that lacks the necessary conditions. It is clear that the mechanism is known by those who hold power and many times manipulate it, but not always find the ideal candidate for the sacrificial victim.

53. Since the eighties, the United States' criminal justice system has been hugely expanded, being the country that has achieved the highest imprisonment level, what it always uses as exchange token to adjust its rate of employment (it removes prisoners from the market and demands services to maintain the criminal justice system).

54. The present US criminal justice system has nothing to do with its tradition prior to the eighties of the past century, where it presented stable imprisonment indexes since half a century before.

55. Such are the cases of toxic substances and abortion. Faced to both problems, punitive solutions have failed, events increase their frequency and their terrible social and individual effects do not diminish, while everybody feels satisfied with absurd criminal laws that are indifferent to the deathful reality. Prohibition in what concerns toxic substances has generated an unbelievable profit derived from the distribution service, through which a national and international criminality has been organized which has caused the death of a high number of persons, being it time to ask oneself what causes more death, if the prohibition or the toxic substance. In the case of abortion, the rule is impunity, through which millions are performed with the indifference of the criminal justice systems, that do nothing—nor do the states—to try to reduce that number.

56. Those dead through violence generated by the traffic of toxic substances and their distribution, and the number of deaths of foetus seem not to matter the criminal justice systems nor the politicians who show their concern supporting criminal laws with paradoxal effects.

57. This would be "functional" in a sense analogous to the one in which Émile Durkheim considered criminality.

58. When the "enemy" assumes a paranoid attitude, as is the case of the "Holy War" of some authors of indiscriminate mass destruction crimes, power is offered the ideal pretext to nourish its own paranoia, that is to say, to re-invent another "war," which definitely ends strengthening the "enemy's" paranoia and even legitimating his speech. How did the Inquisition explain its extermination in the name of Christ, who died in an instrument of torture of the criminal justice system of his times? Christ is not a warrior, but just the opposite. Simply, a bellicose enemy (Satan) was invented in front of a powerful army (of devils and she devils) that declared war, and where he made use of all sort of dirty tricks. Satan was the rebel head who did not respect the

rules of the gentlemen's war; he was Schmitt's "partisan" in the Middle Ages and in a fight against Christ.

59. Bodin seems to advise making extreme war so as to avoid the civil war. This is how he interpreted Rome's history: "*But after the Romans partly subjected the people of Italy, and partly confederating with them, and seeing that they could not live in the city without civil dissension, they found out that for their Republic's security it was good to look for, and even invent, new enemies, ordering triumphs, degrees and prizes for the brave captains*" (Bodin 1992: 904).

60. In the academic field, there are no serious theorists that support this. We are not very sure if there aren't others who share it, but today it would not be possible to express this with Carl Schmitt's amoral sincerity, because the dominant juridical culture does not tolerate this, and whoever does so would immediately be marginated. It is possible to notice that sometimes, in political publicity, some significant incoherent clippings may be found.

61. Criminal law of the enemy argues "depersonalizing" the enemies and, therefore, not to submit them to punishments measured according to guilt, but to "contain" them so as to neutralize their danger. It is no other than the repetition of the "security measures" for the multi-reoffenders, usual ones, etc., known since Karl Stooss, that is to say, punishment without guilt according to Kohlrausch's known thesis ("the lie of labels"). Well then, since almost 70% of Latin American prisoners are in temporary detention pending trial and usually serve their term during this period, it is very evident that this operates as a punishment without guilt, in advance to formal judgement.

62. The review of this thesis was made in Zaffaroni 2006.

63. The expression "*völkisch*" is often translated as *populism*. Its most accurate translation would be "*populacherismo*", because it implies a serious underestimation of the people through the exploitation and deepening of society's most serious prejudices. *Populism* is a political current that offers highs and lows, but that in Latin America has enabled the possibility of incorporating important and wide sectors of population to society. There existed populisms that employed *völkisch* techniques, and they were also used by other political currents with the aspect of a greater ideological coherence.

64. Maybe one of the factors of this omission has been, precisely, the need to resign to its pretended "assessing" or "ideological" neutrality.

65. It may be stated that by "ideology" we understand a certain system of ideas, without associating the expression to negative assessments nor concealments. In each case, it will be the ideological critic the one who will express if the ideology is rational, paranoid or concealing.

66. Ideologies of racial superiority, of hierarchization of human beings, of national security, of destruction of the limits of the state of law, that legitimate torture, etc.

67. National security ideology's characteristic is to invent "wars," under the pretext of being "anomalous wars," that is to say, "dirty wars," and, therefore, not subject to the laws of war among "gentlemen" (which would be the only ones obliged to respect the Geneva Convention) nor to criminal law due to their being wars. That is to say that, due to their being "wars" and "dirty" wars they remain within a hollow

space outside law, free from limiting rules. The thesis of the "dirty war" was prepared by French commanders in Indochina and Algeria, and then spread to the United States and Argentina (See Robin 2005); the hardest critic to this policy was written by Jean Paul Sartre, in the famous prologue to Fanon 1965; the finest theorization of this genocidal policy belongs to Carl Schmitt in a veiled defence of the chief Raoul Salam, head of the terrorist organization OAS, in a conference in 1962 in Spain: in Schmitt 2005).

68. We believe that the thinking contents of juridical–criminal knowledge have suffered alternatives: from the high level achieved in the Nineteenth Century, it started falling by the end of that century until reaching its almost complete drainage, which ended in some shameful legitimating of the worst crimes of the Twentieth Century, to reappear in post-war times.

Chapter Twelve

Crime and Heredity

Edmundo Oliveira

The will is the basis for measuring a person's degree of culpability. If that will is free, the crime should be imputed to him or her (the agent is capable, imputable); if the will is compromised by disease, retardation or incomplete mental development, the agent, depending on the concrete case, will be declared as having reduced imputability or be declared unimputable.

But the capable person suffers the influence of factors that, if they do not actually determine the person, weight to a greater or lesser degree upon the individual's power of self-determination.

In this chapter we will highlight the importance of heredity and the factors related to the genetic makeup of a human being.

HEREDITY

Darwin confessed his admiration of the facts of heredity and lamented that the laws that controlled it were not known.[1] But exactly in 1859, when the English scholar published his *Origin of Species by means of Natural Selection* the monk Johann Mendel (his religious name was Gregory Mendel) was performing his experiments on plant hybridization and heredity among plants and reaching some conclusions that would allow him to formulate the famous laws that bear his name.[2] To better understand them, we will summarize the research path followed by him and by other geneticists later on. Mendel began by observing the modest pea, but today we also have experiments on animal species and observations regarding humans available.

The study of heredity can be made taking into account any characteristic (e.g., color) of a plant, an animal, a human.

If we cross a white rooster with a dark chicken (or vice-versa), we will obtain chicks with bluish plumage (the chicken known as "Andaluzian." The color blue intermediates between white and black (characters that Mendel called *antagonists and Bateson aleomorphs*). If, later on, we cross a rooster with an "Andalusian" hen, that is, hybrids, we will have white, black and blue chicks, in the proportion of 1/4, 1/4 and 1/2, respectively. Thus, for example, for every twenty chicks, five will be white, five black and ten bluish. If we next mate white with white or black with black, the chicks will be white or black like the parents. But crossing blue with blue will produce 1/4 white, 1/4 black and 1/2 bluish. The whites and the blacks are pure breeds; the blues are hybrids or bastards.[3]

One may perform the same experiment with plants that produce flowers of various colors. If we pour the pollen of a red flower on the granulous body placed on the pistil part (stigma) of the white flower, we will obtain pink-colored flowers, that is, intermediate between white and red. But if we place the pollen from a pink flower on the stigma of another pink one (both hybrids), we will obtain red, white and pink flowers in a proportion of 1/4, 1/4 and 1/2.

The characteristics of the parents do not mix. They order themselves as cards in a deck. And just as those have greater or lesser value, among organisms there are some that have more value than others, they are *dominant.* But those of less value do not disappear; they stay as if hidden inside the offspring, as *recessives.* Furthermore, as Bateson notes, there are *intermediate* characteristics that are now dominant and later recessive.[4]

Specifically among animals and among humans, it happens that from the union of the male and female sexual cells (gametes) a new cell (zygote) arises. From the crossing of pure and varied breeds (e.g., white and black) a new intermediate breed creature may arise (heterozygotic), as in the case of the Andalusian chicken, or the breed of one of the parents (all white, all black) (homozygotic).[5]

Mendel's first law affirms that the hybrid inherits the dominant characteristic, which evidently only occurs in the second of the hypotheses mentioned above (homozygotic).

Mendel`s second law (Law of segregation or disjunction of characters) may be enunciated in the following manner: in crossing individuals from the first generation of hybrids, one-fourth of the offspring will monozygotic dominants, meaning with the characteristics of one of the parents; half will be no heterozygotic dominants, meaning an intermediate breed; one-fourth will have recessive characteristics, meaning those that had been hidden under the dominant characteristics.

Finally, the third law (Law of independence of characters) states that in producing poli-hybrids, meaning in breeding individuals that differ in carious characteristics—such as one being white, another black, one fat, one thin, one an alcoholic, the—each one is transmitted entirely depending on the others, so that the offspring can inherit some from the father and others from the mother.[6]

Later studies revealed that the parents' characteristics are transferred to the children through segments in which the cell nucleus chromatin is divided during karyokinesis, that is, during cell division, which starts with the nucleus.[7] Those segments receive the name of *chromosomes* and are in a constant number for each animal. In the fruit-fly (drosophila) there are 8 chromosomes; in the grasshopper, 12; in the celenterate known as *cebola*, 16; in the frog, 24; in the earthworm, 32; in the cat, 40; in humans, 48; in the dog, 78, and so on. Chromosomes are distributed in pairs in the fertilized cell (zygote) and in all of the cells of the organism (diploid disposition of chromosomes). In genetics we must consider the chromosome as a group of *particles* that transmits characteristics, in other words, as *genes*. In the primitive sense the word *gene* designates the hypothetical element of Mendelian inheritance, that is, the inheritable factors, such as shape, skin color, sexual structure in plants, hair and iris color in humans, talent for a given art or science, nose shape, longevity and so on.[8]

Taking into account that the fruit-fly (*Drosophila melanogaster,* meaning that which likes the dew—*drosophila*—and has a black belly—*melanogaster*) is an animal with a low number of chromosomes, some biologists from the school of the American Morgan, such as Bridges and Guyénot gave made important and illustrative experiments.[9]

The chromosomes in drosophila are easily observed because of their characteristic shape: two are simple points; two are stick-shaped; two are curved and have their concavity facing one side while two are curved and have their concavity facing the other side.

To observe the relations between metabolism and the sex life, Jennings preferred the Paramecium Infusorian.[10] Currently biologists work more with the Ascaphora Neurospora.

Today it is known that each human creature results from the fusion of a cell from the father and one from the mother. Before uniting, the sex cells divide, so that each part keeps half of its chromosomes. And the cell resulting from this union has the same number of chromosomes as any human cell. Those of the mother are the same and are called X chromosomes; those of the father are different and are called X and Y. In the female body there are no Y chromosomes.

At the moment of fertilization, the fertilizing cells move towards the ovule. If the cell that arrives first carries the X, a female is created; if it carries a Y, a male appears.

Fritz Kahn has appropriately shown that the power the gene has to transmit characteristics[11] encounters opposition at some points:

1. In the same way that a single man and woman give up part of their freedom with marriage, the father's and mother's genes also offer resistance to each other. The child's chromosomes are made up of half of the father's chromosome and half of the mother's. That is why in science they are called "copulatives." To illustrate, a woman who carries an X chromosome for hemophilia or myopia may or may not transmit that characteristic. A child that inherits it may transmit it; one who does not receive it will not transfer it;
2. Heredity properties are always manifested in a group. Thus, it is known that every child born with six fingers has black hair. That happens because the two genes are part of the same lamina. Every rat born deprived of the sense of being able to walk in a straight line and which walks in a spiral pattern has white fur. Every white male blue-eyed cat is deaf;
3. Throughout life genes change, are transformed. In the embryo growth genes predominate. In children the sexual genes are recessive; in puberty they become dominant and the growth genes reduce their strength. During senescence the sexual genes return to being recessive and those that had been recessive increase their strength;
4. The fourth factor that limits the gene's power is the environment. Farther along we will deal with the influence of the environment on personality and on the genesis of crime. For now, we will deal only with the influence of surroundings on genes. It is known that coloring in a butterfly depends on the season of the year in which it was born. Also among plants, sprouts change color when the temperature varies. Fish, in which sexual genes are definitively dominant or recessive as in the higher animals, change their sex when environmental conditions are modified.[12] In the same way, in the human species a recessive gene can, under favorable conditions, become dominant, come to the surface and change the entire psychosomatic structure. It is common to see a genuinely healthy person be transformed right after a traumatic occurrence. The dominant gene is weakened, the recessive comes to the surface and predominates.[13]

Mendel's discoveries were ignored for more than a quarter of a century (35 years), especially because they were contrary to Darwin's teachings. Fortunately, the titles of his works were introduced in a bibliography, and in the last year of the Nineteenth Century, that is, in 1900, three researchers sought to learn about them. They then verified that Mendel had anticipated the conclusions that they themselves had reached. Their names were Hugo de Vries, C. Correns and Tschermak. Researching in different places and entirely independent of each other, they reached the same results.

Hugo de Vries took the first step forward by describing the phenomenon of *mutation.* Two years publication of de Vries' book *Theory of Mutation, Die Mutationstheorie,* in 1906 professor Wilhelm Johansen, of Copenhagen, brought a new contribution to the study of this phenomenon. Up until that period, the scientific dogma was that "Nature does not make leaps." The affirmation that *natura non facit saltus* had been in fact repeated by major thinkers,[14] such as Linnaeus (*Philosophia Botanica,* chap. XXVIII) and Leibniz (*Novos Ensaios,* VI, 6). Darwin himself relied on this teaching in defending a slow evolution, without revolution. De Vries observed the spontaneous appearance of a new species of the flower *Oenothera lamarckiana.* He then provoked the appearance of new species and obtained them. He himself was not able to explain the origin of the transformation. Today it is known that it is caused by a detour (as if there had been a shove) in the structure of the giant molecules of chromatin, which is the substance controlling heredity.[15]

THE PROGRESS OF GENETIC MANIPULATION

For many centuries science considered the phenomenon of life as an impenetrable mystery, whose secret belonged to nature with absolute exclusivity. But scientists ended up learning to take part in the work of nature, by stealing a portion of that secret.

In fact, recent decades have seen prodigious discoveries in the area of *Biotechnology* and have marked the beginning of a new area full of impressive genetic experiments involving manipulation of genetic material.[16]

By *genetic manipulation* we mean all deliberate interference in the heredity of persons or populations. At present, three types of such manipulation are recognized: 1. *Euphenic engineering;* 2. *Genetic engineering;* 3. *Eugenic engineering.*[17]

To better understand the difference between those types it is good to remember that each individual has a genetic heritage, represented by a set of genes, particles made up of DNA (deoxyribonucleic acid). This *genotype* or *genome* heritage manifests itself through a great number of characteristics, be they morphological (color of skin, hair, eyes, body shape, type of nose, etc.) or physiological (the reactions that keep the individual functioning). Those characteristics, taken as a whole, form the *phenotype* or *phenome.* They are fundamentally determined by the genes, even though the environment can modify them, without such modifications generally having repercussions on the genome or being transmitted from parents to offspring. Broadly speaking, we can say that the phenotype is the expression of the genotype.

Through *euphenic engineering,* we seek to modify or control the expression of genes, but without modifying them. In *genetic engineering* we seek to alter the genes themselves, eliminating or modifying the bad ones, with the objective of obtaining an individual who functions better. In *eugenic engineering* we seek to improve a population by means of selecting and recombinating the genes existing in it.

At the current stage of fantastic scientific evolution, the scientists responsible for the genetic revolution obviously seem destined for the same immortality reserved, for example, for the founders of nuclear physics. At the beginning of the 1950s, for having unveiled the double helix structure of DNA, geneticists Francis Crick, James Watson and Maurice Wilkins, of Cambridge University, became world famous. One should also note that the American Barbara McClintock received the Nobel Prize in Medicine in 1983 thanks to her discoveries in genetic manipulation.

With automated machines, the scientists, after having been able to transfer genes from the natural environment, are learning to manufacture in laboratories genes that are outside of the basic building blocks of life, with the objective of replacing the defective or absent ones, seeking to manufacture protective vaccines against viruses or anomalies of genetic origin that affect the human species.

By learning to manipulate the secrets of genes, humans are gradually becoming the guarantors of their own biophysical evolution. We need only remember that we already owe to Biotechnology the discovery of interferon as the great hope in fighting viral diseases and certain types of cancer.[18] It is also because of this fantastic progress that recent court decisions in various American states have found doctors liable for not warning parents about the risk of bearing abnormal children.

For such reasons, medical care with pregnant women in the more developed countries has begun large-scale use of *genetic counseling* to substitute the eugenics campaigns.[19] *Genetic counseling* has the purpose of supplying the parents of a child diagnosed with a problem with all known implications of the anomaly with possible indications for treatment, as well as offering the family useful orientations for future decisions to be taken. To determine the type of possible inherited diseases, geneticists first of all perform a family *heredogram*, meaning the family history related to the disorder. They then proceed to make an estimate through exams, to then make the parents ware of the risks, encouraging adoption of preventive and therapeutic attitudes according to the concrete case, with a view to success in the family planning to be adopted in light of the risks.[20]

There are two procedures not often employed, *amniocentesis* or *spectrophotometry* consists of introducing a needle into a women's abdomen to extract some of the amniotic fluid that surrounds the fetus inside the mother's womb. It has the advantage of detecting organic implications and serious diseases, such as Down's syndrome and metabolic disturbances (Saucher's syndrome). To proceed, for example, with a blood transfusion in intrauterine life affected by profound anemia, the doctors, after examining the amniotic fluid, employ ultrasonography to visualize the exact place where they need to inject the new blood, which goes through a needle inserted into the mother's abdomen until it reaches the child's abdomen.[21]

With more sophisticated technology, although it is also a delicate procedure that can cause damage to the patient or the fetus, the application of *fetoscopy*[22] is being developed in the United States, a process by which doctors can clearly see the fetus inside the uterus. *Fetoscopy* makes it possible to examine the entire fetus, providing certainty of normality or discovering serious defects that were not detected by amniocentesis, such as anomalies caused by blood cell diseases.[23]

In 1970, Indian scientist Gobind Khorana working at the University of Wisconsin, was able to synthesize an artificial gene in a test tube, which, placed in contact with a natural cell, duplicated and reproduced itself. That is how science was able to obtain artificial life in the laboratory using organic compounds, undoubtedly a highly important step towards the long-dreamed intention of developing human life in the laboratory. The geneticists view with optimism the possibility that the biological world will come to be dominated by humans, in the same sense as, after having discovered the intimate nature of matter, they dominate the inanimate world through atomic physics.[24]

Dr. Khorana's discovering has sparked serious debates in the scientific world, especially because to the expectations with biotechnological advances, which, for some scientists, may reach the point of control over humanity through producing humans in series.

For Gobind Khorana the correction of a single gene, for the purpose of curing a hereditary failing is possible and is near. The great interest in his research, besides deciphering the harmful aspects of the genetic code, is directed towards the *possibility of curing or controlling the aggressive characters of individuals,* a fact that will be possible in the future, if humans continue giving the necessary vote of confidence to the rhythm of actions in Genetic engineering, Euphenic Engineering and Eugenic Engineering.

In our understanding, much more useful than trying to create human beings artificially, would be greater technical depth in processes to remedy some genetic defects in people. Even with the positive result of fertilizing an egg in the laboratory, how will genetic duplication be possible, if interiorizing environmental stimuli and the manner of acting and reacting for each person is so highly personalized?

In parallel, the *test-tube fertilization* method, perfected in the United Kingdom by Dr. Patrick Steptoe,[25] found its strongest defense as a solution for the problem of female sterility, but at the same time the specialists themselves are becoming concerned with the fact that genetic manipulation may produce serious risks for the general population, with unpredictable and perhaps disastrous results. Already in October 1976, the 16th Plenary Assembly of the International Council of Scientific Associations, gathering in Washington, approved the creation of an International Committee of Scientists to oversee work in genetic manipulation in the sixty-five countries that make up the Association. The participants in the assembly recognized the potential benefits of the experiments, but did not hide their concern regarding the appearance of lethal microorganisms for warlike applications, with the appearance of abnormal beings and with the possibility of a cancer-causing gene that would inevitably bring distress to the worldwide community.

IMPORTANCE FOR CRIMINOLOGY

From everything that has been observed up to the present one may conclude that the fundamental law of genetics is this: that living beings generate similar beings. The resemblance manifests itself in the *essential* characters of the parents, but also includes many accidental characteristics, such as facial features, tone of voice, body language, manner of walking and so on. The dissimilarities result from accidents in the embryonic period, from incidental factors (in mutation) and from atavism (*atavus* means grandfather). Fritz Kahn says, with a certain humor, that "we are more children of our grandparents than of our parents,"[26] but to be exact, we need to distinguish the various degrees of heredity. In the first, the offspring reproduce characteristics of their parents. Beginning with the second degree, a reversion to ancestral characteristics occurs (atavism). That explains why a hereditary disease, a particular disposition, a deficiency may not be transmitted from parents to children and then reappear in a subsequent generation (a phenomenon known as Mendelization). Mendel's great merit consisted exactly in continuing the crossings and in observing successive generations. First-degree heredity stabilizes families; the others perpetuate the species, excepting a mutation that leads to the rise of a new species. Heredity does not create; it limits itself to conserving. Atavism makes averageness return; the descendants of a genius can be—and generally are—mediocre.

The important thing for Criminology is the conclusion by specialists that heredity, besides its direct link with physical characteristics, has implications for psychological and moral tendencies during development of the complex human behavior. It is this theme, particularly, that occupies Genetic Psychology today.[27]

There is thus no inherited *predestination* towards crime. There can, indeed, be a *predisposition*. The genetic element alone is not decisive. Personality is a function of several factors, only one of which is heredity. "Criminal families" are only so because of the contaminating environment in which their members live.[28]

Exner is correct in affirming that "the personality of a human being is made up of the inherited and the experienced."[29] The inherited disposition, in the words of Middendorff, establishes only a "travel plan for life."[30] Lombroso and his followers maintained that there is a causal relationship between inheritance and crime. The same occurred in Nazi Germany. Mezger, in a short work on *Crime as destiny* (*Verbrechen als Schicksal*), informs us of a school of thought in Japan along the same lines.[31] That orientation is flatly rejected by American criminologists.[32] Humans live in an inherited atmosphere, but they can clean or pollute the spiritual air that they found at their birthplace. They can even sublimate tendencies and purge their negative inclinations, through artistic or literary production. An athlete exhausted by daily physical exercises loses aggressiveness that way. Goethe rid himself of a suicidal inclination by pouring it into a literary personage, Werther. And Werther Karl May, whose works of fiction were so widely disseminated in Brazil, practiced several small swindles as a young man. In prison he began to write books about the Orient and about American Indians, and in them he unloaded his criminal inclinations. One should note that justice always triumphs in his narrations.[33]

THE XYY CONSTITUTION AND PREVENTION OF DELINQUENCY

In 1968, researcher Robert Stock produced an interesting work in the United States, on the much discussed XYY chromosome constitution and its reflexes on anti-social conduct. In *The XYY and The Criminal,* he affirmed that "boys born with XYY chromosomes (the normal is XY) seem to have an uncommon inclination to become delinquents of tall stature, foolish and with faces marked by pimples."[34]

Robert Stock mentions the experiments of Dr. James Hamilton, head of the Downstate Medical College in Brooklyn. In tests of a genetic nature, James Hamilton placed hundreds of trios of small fish called killifish in glass tanks, full of water at a constant temperature of 27 degrees centigrade. Each trio was made up of a normal female, a normal male and a rare type of super-male killifish whose cells contained a double dose of the Y chromosome, which determines the male sex.

The results of that experiment showed that, in competition for the female's preference, the XYY chromosome fish won out 88% of the time, not because the XY fish was not trying, but because the super-male emerged victorious in almost all cases of physical combat with the normal male. The killifish carrying the XYY chromosome always showed greater homosexual activity, and its aggressiveness greatly impressed observers. The purpose was to demonstrate that in the animal kingdom, a human being carrying an extra Y chromosome could also be affected in his behavior, becoming potentially anti-social.

In this regard, perhaps one of the most powerful arguments is the report, produced in 1967, at a public hospital for delinquents with mental problems, in Scotland, about people bearing the XYY set. The IQ ox examinees varied from 60 to 80. They had been sentenced at a lower age than their companions bearing XY chromosomes and presented severe disturbances to their personalities. They frequently behaved themselves in a violent and aggressive manner, but it was not possible to determine the level of influence of the environment in which they had previously lived.

Robert Stock concluded his work calling attention to the serious social and ethical consequences created by the so-called *double Y syndrome,* among other things noting that out of every three hundred men, at least one will probably have an XYY chromosome makeup.

In Europe, there has been concern over the issue, especially during recent years, when governments and specialized entities have begun planning studies and research to precisely verify if men carrying the XYY genotype are really more inclined to criminal acts than those possessing a normal constitution. The article recently published by French geneticist Jean Médioni evidences such a concern.[35]

Besides conclusions drawn from isolated cases, as occurred with French delinquent Daniel Hugo, a carrier of the XYY chromosome, who in 1965 killed a prostitute in a Paris hotel,[36] other experiments have been performed on groups of individuals giving evidence of aggressive and even violent impulses.

Eva Zeuthen, Johannes Nielsen, Mariann Hansen and Anne-Lise Christensen were responsible for important research in Denmark, carried out in psychiatric hospitals, prisons and establishments where large number of people commonly coexisted. The most commented upon of those studies was exactly one with men recruited for Danish military service.

From a total of 3,840 citizens, 1,115 were chosen for a chromosome exam. It was found that five of them possessed the XYY, and because of that they were submitted to highly specialized physical, psychiatric and psychological examinations.

The total IQ scale, on average, and the cultural level of the five men were significantly low. In fact, three had to attend special classes in special schools for children with adaptation problems. All five had been raised in good environments, but had been restless, temperamental and impulsive since childhood. Two of the five had criminal backgrounds: one for theft and the other for theft and damages. Submitted to psychological tests, all five revealed immaturity of a cognitive origin and lack of emotional adaptation, which did not allow them to control aggressive impulses. The researchers concluded that "the effects of extra Y on intelligence and behavior made it more difficult for these five men to have the same development that their brothers and their fathers had had."[37]

Other interesting experiments in this area were held between 1968 and 1972, in England, involving the study of 1,811 mentally ill men in 18 London hospitals, seeking to determine the prevalence of the XYY genotype, its clinical aspects and its psychiatric effects.

Of the 1.811 patients forwarded, fifteen (.08%) had an excessive number of Y chromosomes. Of those fifteen, twelve presented the XYY genotype, two had the XXYY formula and only one was XYYY.

The IQ of the twelve XYY patients reached a mark of 46, leading one to suppose that in men with a XYY genotype there is a tendency towards reduction of the IQ, at least in terms of standard deviations from those of other people. They had little discernment and acted aggressively. They did not have good relationships with their family members and all had only fair school performance.

The researchers, who were under the coordination of Dr. Henry Hunter, that the level of indolence in educational and social activities among male children who were carriers of the XYY genotype was more accentuated than in normal boys. They found slowness in development of the sex drive and saw that they are always distrustful, with some even being hostile.

Dr. Henry Hunter's team concluded the research "with the impression that the XYY group tends, with the passing years, towards a reduction of impulsiveness and anti-social, aggressive or violent behavior. A tense environment may cause behavior problems in persons with a XYY genotype, with appropriate social and therapeutic assistance being necessary for development of maturity and emotional control."[38]

Arthur Steinberg, professor of Human Genetics at the University of Cleveland and Alexander Bearn, head of the Department of Medicine at Cornell University in New York published an interesting work in 1974 dealing with questions linked to the male carrier of the XYY chromosome. This is a detailed report containing the conclusions of empirical research,[39] whose clientele were patients at the Carstairs Hospital, linked to the maximum security penal establishment in London destined for delinquents with accentuated inclinations for practicing anti-social acts.

In summary, the conclusions presented can be specified as follows:

a. Curiously, the research results led to a finding that individuals carrying the XYY karyotype who are involved in criminal proceedings are not always more aggressive, violent and impulsive, when compared with the XY chromosome control groups in the same population;
b. Individuals with the XYY control, when thus identified, began to be indiscriminately stigmatized, isolated or rejected even by other patients, even when the violating behavior of those individuals is no different from that of citizens with the XY control;
c. Carriers of XYY, by a significant majority, showed better adjustment in relation to carriers of the XY control, during the phases in which the exams in penal establishment were being carried out, thus once again refuting the reasoning that an extra Y always means a predisposition to aggressive or violent behavior;
d. For the researchers, an adverse family environment and social instability were, at a high scale, notable in families of persons examined who had chromosome abnormalities, since to a large degree they came from families with disturbed relationships, where the parents' behavior model was learned and became active in the maladjusted behavior of the children;
e. As a preventive measure, it is prudent to offer whenever possible to carriers of chromosomal aberrations a program of genetic counseling and a healthy socio-family environment, structured together with prophylactic pedagogy;
f. Having XYY does not mean being mentally ill, since there are reports of people considered normal having that constitution, although, in certain patients, the chromosomal anomaly may be associated to mental disorder or irregular behaviors, without that meaning that the XYY karyotype, alone, is the determining factor;
g. The occurrence of an XYY constitution was not shown to be associated with chromosomal formation in the parents, be they young or old, nor to IQ equivalency among examinees;

h. Finally, the researchers stated that they had not found a characteristic pattern, either from the psychological, the psychiatric or the behavioral point of view that can obviously distinguishes the personality of XYY carriers. Regarding the physical aspect, only height offered an exception, since, from the cases analyzed, it was clear that an extra Y chromosome tends to increase the height of the carrier.

Reflection on the conditions enumerated above, one may imagine the serious issues of a legal, constitutional and public order nature that might be raised if accused or convicted persons were, against their will, forced to submit to a karyotype examination of their chromosomes. We understand that such a requirement would be unjustified, because up till now, no one has presented plausible reasons for basing criminal decisions exclusively with support from chromosome constitution, as being different from phenotypic manifestations that a person may present. To illustrate, Steinberg and Bearn mention in their previously cited book an appeal made to the Maryland Court of Special Appeals, which upheld the judge's decision,[40] of a case in which the accused, a carrier of the XYY chromosome makeup, appealed his conviction, seeking to overturn the decision through alleging defense by virtue of "insanity, based on the XYY genetic disorder, at the time the crime was committed."

Another criticism to be considered is that normally, in order to understand the relationship of the extra Y chromosome with aggressive or violent behavior, researchers seek out institutionalized groups, serving sentences in prisons or handed over to psychiatric treatment establishments. If the hypothesis to be tested is that the XYY constitution contributes to criminality, it seems logical then, that the ideal thing would be to determine, through analyzing different situations and environments, the circumstances in which XYY carriers are more impulsive that the XY control groups. Trying to make that comparison only through criminal records and histories means only to compare differences in crime rates in special groups, at the risk of increasing stigmas and apprehensions of the examinees, besides providing dangerous publicity done through mass communications media, which has facilitated public incomprehension regarding the XYY karyotype.

Based on those deductions, the majority of studies carried out so far on psychological, psychiatric and behavioral characteristics of XYY carriers, have not been able to present firm definitions in evaluating the different variables obtained.[41] They do not make clear, for example, when the extra Y chromosome is related directly with impulsiveness and aggression or if those implications are derived from a series of environmental variables. The uncertainty thus continues, regarding the precise measure in which the influence of the extra Y chromosome is detected, and the degree to which it is exacerbated or interacts with phenotypic heterogeneity factors.

What is consolidated in the overall understanding is the extraordinary power of the environmental bases in structuring the personality and developing the human character. Not even the staunchest supporters of biological sciences, concerned with unraveling the enigmas of somatic mechanisms, will dare deny that affirmation.[42]

If the deficiencies caused by the XYY genotype can be overcome with the efficient employment of therapeutic and educational measures, there is no reason to speak of criminal-genetic predisposition or specificity, since a series of other factors can influence the conduct of any person, dragging him or her towards antisocial attitudes. There are individuals who have genetic dysmorphias and never behave aggressively or violently against their social environments.

Genetic dysmorphias may even reduce resistance to the practice of wrongdoing, but even if they act in that way, they will always be associated to other stimuli that facilitate a reduction of resistance, so that the individual will commit wrongdoing, perhaps even with touches of perversion, vileness or wickedness. It must be clarified, however, that perversity or wickedness characterize only one substrate of the individual's personality and must not be considered in isolation, because every act entangled with touches of perversity, in itself is something so abstract that it must have a cause or condition from the biomesological point of view.

One of the most eminent specialists on this issue in Brazil, the late professor Hilário Veiga de Carvalho, underlined in his work a synthesis of the ideas of Carrel, Pende, Anile and Rostand, regarding the idea that "heredity transmits only genetic factors and does not transmit the characters, strictly speaking. That means saying that heredity only transmits tendencies for forming characters, tendencies that will develop or not according to the favorable or unfavorable co-participation of environmental factors."[43]

There seems to be no denying the assertion that exogenous mechanism forces intervene, from the earliest childhood, modifying the influence of the endogenous mechanism. All of this is inherent to human conduct, which is a result of hereditary and environmental factors.

The same lesson is found in Alexander Lowen, who states:

> We are thus led to consider the genetic factures in the development of character structure, but analysis of this character does not depend on the purity of type, or on the dominant pattern of behavior. The growth of the organism both physically and psychosocially is a continuous process.[44]

Therefore, an extreme case of dogmatizing anti-social behavior cannot be accepted by a group of citizens with a higher sense of civic duty, but on the other hand, can be benefitted with the justification of inimputability of divergent behavior or by the mentality that the social environment demands in the cases of vengeance, of "saving one's honor" or things of that sort. We must consider that an extremely aggressive temperament, perhaps even wickedness, if it were polarized into a useful direction, instead of revealing criminal dynamism could make a person have a spectacularly well-developed capacity for getting things accomplished.

NOTES

1. DARWIN, Charles. *L'origine des espèces.* Paris. Schleicher Frères, s.d., p. 14.
2. JOHANN MENDEL, an Augustinian monk, was born in Heinzerndorf in 1822, and died in Brünn, in 1884. In the latter city he was a professor and observed the transmission of hereditary characteristics among plants and bees. He published the results of his studies in 1865, in a booklet entitled "Experiments with hybrid plants" (*Versuche Über Pflanzenhybriden*). In 1869 he published another work: "On some herbaceous bastards achieved by artificial fecundation" (Über einige aus künstlicher Befruchtung gewonnene Hieracium-Bastarde).

MENDEL's contemporaries did not know how to assess the results of his conscientious and patient labor. But at the beginning of the Twentieth Century some botanists (DE VRIES, TSCHERMACK, CORRENS) rediscovered the laws, and named them "Mendel's Laws."

MENDEL sent his works to forty scientific academies. Not one took the trouble of responding. The great naturalist and professor at the University of Munich Karl Wilhelm von Nägeli disdained MENDEL'a work with the written observation: "HASTY CONCLUSIONS."

Just as the recessive characters that he told us about, MENDEL remained hidden until other scientists brought to light his "recessive" discovery. As would be said by geneticists today, he "Mendelized," meaning that he reappeared in the next generation.

An excellent critical study on the biogenesis thesis formulated by MENDEL can be found in a paper published in France by: VERNET. J. *Chromosomes et criminalité.* Paris, Études, 1968, pl. 207-17.

3. See that experiment in PIERANTONI. Umberto. *Compêndio de biologia.* Barcelona. Labor, 1940, p. 208.
4. BATESON, H. La vida. In: *Collection moderna de conocimentos universales.* New York. W.M. Jackson, 1958, p. 183.
5. All of those examples illustrate what JEAN TAVLITZHI, professor of Molecular Genetics at the University of Paris VII, summarizes as "unity and diversity of the genetic program responsible for the development and functioning of organisms." Consult: TAVLITZHI, Jean. À la génétique moleculaire. La Recherche. Paris, 5 (155): 591-93, mai 1984.
6. MENDEL's Laws are also presented in five propositions:

a. *Law of dominance.* In crossing two pure races, if there are antagonistic characteristics, one of them predominates and is the only one appearing in the offspring. It is thus called dominant;

b. *Law of recessiveness.* The dominated characteristic stays hidden in the following generation and is thus called recessive. However, it reappears in subsequent generations;

c. *Law of segregation.* In the descendants of the first hybrid generation a separation of characteristics is produced, with the return of some descendants in the primitive form and the permanence of others in crossed forms;

d. *Law of proportion of recessives.* In the following generation the recessive characteristics appear as pure in 1/4 of the offspring;

e. *Law of proportion of dominants.* In the second generation, the dominant characters appear as pure in 1/4 and mixed with recessives in 1/2 of the descendants.

Regarding those laws, see also the work of MINHAN, Júlio. *Mistérios da biologia.* Rio de Janeiro. Ateneu, 1957, p. 66-84.

7. This is not the appropriate place for describing the phenomenon of *mitosis or karyokinesis,* found in any compendium of biology.

8. For more details, consult: KAHN, Fritz. *O livro da natureza,* 2. ed. São Paulo. Melhoramentos, 1965, 2v., v. 1. p. 345.

9. For more information on this very interesting subject, consult: GUYÉNOT. E. *L'heredité.* Paris. Recueil Sirey. 1924, p. 324-9 and PIERANTONI, *op. cit.* p. 216-8.

10. JENNINGS, H. S. *Heredity, variation and evolution in Protozoa.* New York, Harper, 1909. p. 52-3.

11. KAHN, *op. cit.* p. 340.

12. See also the work by: KAHN, *ibid* p. 342.

13. German psychiatric literature cites two classic cases: that of the poet FRIEDRICH HÖLDERLIN, who described the transformations he himself underwent during the time in which the recessive gene for schizophrenia was becoming dominant, and that of the philosopher FRIEDRICH NIETZSCHE, whose path towards madness was accompanied by observant friends.

There is a very modern work by PHILIP REILLY with a profound approach in cases involving the genetic component and human behavior. See: REILLY, Philip. *Genetics, law, social policy.* Harvard, University Press, 1977. p. 152-89 passim.

14. Regarding this, see: BARBA, Francisco Esteve. *Historia de la cultura.* Barcelona, Salvat, 1955. 4 v., v. 4. p. 1742-8.

15. The Swedish biologist MÜNTZIG, artificially obtained several new species in 1930. The American MÜLLER demonstrated that genes have their structure modified by ultraviolet, Roentgen (X-ray) and gamma short waves. THOMAS MORGAN and his disciples verified that if when splitting, chromosomes tear, they lose substances. Still other causes of mutation have been discovered.

From 1935 to 1948, a controversy raged in the Soviet Union regarding genetic theories.

TROFIM DENISOVICH LYSENKO took a position against Mendelianism. Based on the experience of IVAN VLADMIROVICH MICHURIN, who had proclaimed the transmissibility of acquired characteristics, he affirmed that MENDEL's theory presupposed the existence of mysterious forces, whose existence was incompatible with Marxist materialism. LYSENKO returned to the Lamarckian concept and defended the causal force of the environment. The success he obtained in developing varieties of cotton and barley drew the attention of Soviet leaders and he was raised to the presidency of the Academy of Agriculture and directorship of the Genetics Institute, a position he occupied for twenty-five years. But LYSENKO's entire theory was based on a materialist preconception and preconception is the primordial enemy of science. The facts give the lie to those who defraud them; scientist continued to observe reality, and beginning in 1952 LYSENKO's star began to fall. In 1956 we was fired as president of the Academy of Agriculture and in 1965 as director of the Genetics Institute.

16. Obstinacy in wanting to change the genetic characteristics of persons led, during the Second World War, to one of the darkest chapters in the Nazi regime. The Head of the Medical Department at the AUSCHWITZ Concentration Camp, in Poland, JOSEF MENGELE became notorious for the experiments he carried out on children, twins, dwarfs and pregnant women, in the name of a delirious scientific obsession. He tried to change hair color and injected ink to turn eye color into blue. He applied injections of cement in women's uteruses and loved castrating young Jews. He performed operations without anesthesia and treatments using gasoline, phenol and acid. The objective: to reproduce the Aryan race (predominantly blond and blue-eyed in the laboratory, because being superior to all others, only it deserved the gift of life. MENGELE the "Angel of Death," was accused of practicing crimes against humanity, determined the mutilation and death of around 400,000 persons), but, curiously, strolled daily around the AUSCHWITZ signing and whistling WAGNER and MOZART.

Regarding AUSCHWITZ, the main Nazi center for exterminating prisoners, consult: MANVELL, Rober & FRAENKEL, Heinrich. *Le crime absolu.* Paris, Stock, 1968, p. 143-245.

17. Regarding the bases for genetic manipulation, see: FLETCHER, J. *The ethics of genetic control.* New York, Anchor Press, 1974. p. 116-9 e REICK, Wilhelm. *Analisis del carater*, 5. ed. Buenos Aires, Paidos, 1975, p. 201.

18. The human body produces natural interferon, which acts in defense against flu, hepatitis and other viruses. However, extracting it, besides being difficult, is expensive. Fortunately, Genetic engineering has proved that this antibody produced by cultured microbes in a culture can be as good as what is produced by human beings, and also much cheaper. Microbes are also being used in laboratories to make insulin for diabetics and growth hormone for dwarves, which even today are still extracted from pituitary glands in cadavers.

19. Previously, when cases of pathogenic genes were found, there was an attempt to segregate the individuals so that they would not transmit harmful genes or dangerous chromosomal aberrations. During epidemics, notification and quarantine were imposed by law. During the period of the so-called "euphoric eugenics," several countries legislated on compulsory sterilization of the retarded, epileptics and other

supposed carriers of manias. The development of genetic development of populations has demonstrated, however, that such measures are inadequate, since, with such an extreme violence, an entire family generation would always run the risk of being unjustifiably harmed. The focus of the problem was thus shifted: because it was not shocking and they have the family's greater interest prevail, medicine has encouraged the development of genetic counseling to substitute the eugenic campaigns. Compare in: FROTA-PESSOA *et alii*. *Genética clínica*. São Paulo, Alves, 1975, p. 229-235.

20. Consult: CARAKUSHANSKY, G. *Doenças genéticas na infância.* Rio de Janeiro. Guanabara Koogan, 1979, p. 483-484.

21. For more details, see: YAMASHIRO, Robert *et alii.* Diagnóstico ultrassonográfico em obstetrícia e ginecologia. *In: Clínica Geral.* São Paulo. Abaeté, 1977, p. 27-29.

22. The principal benefit of *fetoscopy* consists in the fact that it can save around 75% of fetuses, which, if it were not for this method, would be miscarried. However, just as with amniocentesis, a fetoscopy is an exceptionally delicate surgical method. The patients are submitted to local anesthesia beginning with the fifteenth or twentieth week of pregnancy. Doctors explore the patient's belly with sound waves to locate the fetus, umbilical cord and placenta. After making a small incision in the abdomen, they introduce into the abdomen a probe about as thick as a pencil equipped with an endoscope containing bundles of optic fibers that transmit light. This allows them to see the more sensitive areas of the fetus (it is even possible to count the fingers), remove samples of skin and blood for whatever exams they need. Some doctors make impressive forecasts. They believe that medicine can make use of fetoscopy to administer medicines directly to the fetus and even to perform intra and extra-uterine surgeries.

In that sense, treatment of fetuses at the University of California has developed a very successful experiment. The monkey 19999, in December, 1981, was removed from its mother's uterus at 96 days of gestation (half-term), underwent surgery for hydrocephaly and was placed back in the womb, to be born later normally at term. Today the monkey lives at the Primate Research Center and, thanks to the experiment performed on it, many other babies—this time humans—began to be saved from terrible diseases even before birth. Fetal has ceased being merely diagnostic and preventive to become effectively corrective and therapeutic.

23. Regarding this: BOUÉ. J. *et alii.* Diagnóstico pré-natal das doenças metabólicas hereditárias. *La Nouvelle Presse Medicale.* Rio de Janeiro. *1* (4): 268-9. jun. 1982.

24. One of the greatest achievements in the history of atomic science occurred on August 20, 1978, in Geneva, when physicists at the European Center for Nuclear Research, headed by the Italian professor GUIDO PETRUCCI, announced an unprecedented accomplishment: they were able, in the Initial Cooling Experiment (ICE) apparatus, to generate antiprotons and maintain them for 85 hours in an intense magnetic field, after which they were annihilated upon coming in contact with common antimatter particles. Antimatter was thus, for the first time, imprisoned by humans, a marvelous result for obtaining answers to many questions about the enigmas of the Universe. Regarding this, see: DAVID, Catherine, Ces enfants qu'on nous fabrique. *Le Nouvel Observateur.* Paris, 83 (970): 35. jun. 1983.

25. As was widely publicized, the birth of LOUISE BROWN, occurring in London in 1978, was the result of pioneering fertilization provoked under special conditions, outside of the mother´s uterus. Not only in England, but in other developed countries, such as the United States, Sweden, France, Australia and South Africa, there are sperm banks where spermatozoids are kept under storage in climatized conditions for future artificial insemination in a woman. See also: DAVID *ibid.* p. 36.

26. KAHN. *op. cit.* p. 349.

27. Derived from research developed in the field of Child Psychology, Genetic Psychology seeks to understand and explain changes in behavior throughout someone's existence, in other words, the behavioral transformations that occur due to age, environmental influence and the various aspects of individual variations.

Very useful explanations about those objectives are found in SCHELL, Robert & HALL, Elizabeth. *Psychologie Génétique.* Montreal, Renouveau Pédagogique, 1980, p. 7-9.

28. Some criminologists, such as LOPEZ-REY ARROJO, go farther and question the value of conclusions reached by MORGAN and his school, with respect to humans: "It will always seem inadmissible to us to intend to submit man to the generalizations that one obtains experimenting with Drosophila or in another more or less similar animal." Examine: ARROJO, Lopez-Rey, *Introduction al estudio de la criminologia.* Buenos Aires, El Ateneo, 1945, p. 119-20.

29. EXNER, F. *Kriminologie.* 3. ed. Berlim, Krepper, 1949, p. 28.

30. MIDDENDORFF, Wolf. *Teoria e prática de la prognosis criminal.* Madrid, Espasa Calpe, 1970, p. 136.

31. MEZGER, Edmundo. *Verbrechen als Schicksal.* Munich. Bavarian Academy of Sciences, 1957, f. 7, p. 5.

32. See what is said by: SUTHERLAND, Edwin & CRESSEY, Donald. *Criminology,* 4. ed. Chicago, University Press, 1960, p. 103-4.

33. Read about MAY in: MIDDENDORFF, *op. cit.* p. 139.

34. STOCK, Robert W. *The XYY and The Criminal.* New York, Times Magazine, 1968, p. 29.

35 MÉDIONI, Jean. *La Transmission des comportements.* La Recherche, Paris, *5* (155): 706-08.mai.1984.

36. STOCK, *op. cit.* p. 30.

37. ZEUTHEN, Eva, *et al ii. A psychiatric psychological study of XYY males found in general population.* New York, Institute of Living-Hartford, 1975, p. 161.

38. HUNTER, Henry. *Some clinical and psychiatric aspects deriving from survey of 1811 males in hospitals for the mentally handicapped.* New York, Institute of Living-Hartford, 1975. p. 68.

39. STEINBERG, Arthur & BEARN, Alexander. *Progress in medical genetics.* New York, Grune and Stratton, 1974, p. 201-5.

40. STEINBERG & BEARN, *ibid* p. 196.

41. Many scholars support this viewpoint. Among them, we note the reflections of: MONTAGU, Ashley. *A natureza da agressividade humana.* Rio de Janeiro, Zahar, 1978, p. 194.

42. In this regard see: SCHELL & HALL, *op. cit.* p. 59-60.

43. CARVALHO, Hilário Veiga de. *Compêndio de criminologia.* São Paulo, Bushatsky, 1973, p. 176.

44. LOWEN, Alexander. *O corpo em terapia:* a abordagem energética. São Paulo, Summus, 1977, p. 171.

Chapter Thirteen

The Delinquent by Tendency

Edmundo Oliveira

A human being does not live alone. The figure of Robinson Crusoe on the desert island is a theme of fiction, certainly interesting, but unachievable. We must coexist with others and that is how we grow, perfect ourselves and achieve our major goals. And, exactly because we must coexist with others, we must regulate that coexistence so as to make it orderly and harmonic. That discipline in social life has always been the task of the jurist, from the most rudimentary forms in primitive societies until the modern, complex and sophisticated social-judicial structure. In this often primordial task, the person of Law, the scientist, the practitioner, the judge, and in general the preparer and applier of judicial norms has been perfecting humanity, doing the work of a jeweler. One can summarize this task by saying that the goal is to term man as defined by Hobbes, *Homo homini lupus*, into Rousseau's man, naturally good and lover of the good; in going from a state of war to a state of peace.

The jurist has fought slavery, suppressed ordeals, proscribed dueling, feuds, the *Mangeld* (price of a man); refined humans, civilized them and purified customs.

Nonetheless, jurists have not been able to eradicate crime, harm to goods and violation of laws. With admonitions, warnings and impositions (precepts), the jurist is able to avoid many evils, but is not able to eliminate all offences to Law (crimes). Thus there is the need to threaten the possible offenders of laws with the promise of inflicting evil on them (penalty) and of really carrying it out (condemnation) if the threat does not hold back the evil-doer's arm. That, reduced to the simplest expression, is the origin of Criminal

Law, of the set of norms (precepts and sanctions) that have the purpose of preventing and repressing crime.

But Criminal Law is not arbitrary; it does not arise in the human mind at the mercy of *a priori* concepts. To the contrary, it is the fruit of refined observation and careful experience. It is nourished by the conclusions of the various branches of science that study crime as a phenomenon, as a happening, as a fact, that is, not as an abstraction, but as something concrete, existential, historic.

Of those sciences, some look at the criminal individually: Anthropology and Psychology; others consider humans as a group: Sociology and Statistics. Additionally, there is in entire range of other auxiliary sciences.

Criminology is ontological, studying criminals as they are; the Science of Criminal Law is axiological, examining the value of persons and of their actions. The first is naturalistic, concerning itself with *being*; the second is normative and tells what *should be.* Thus, for example, homicide, prostitution, blasphemy, polygamy, incest are facts that Criminology examines under their natural aspect; however, Law views them from a cultural point of view. Thus, for Law, the value of homicide is not the same when it is practiced for vengeance or following provocation or in strict fulfillment of a legal duty. Sacred or hospitable prostitution, in some ancient peoples, is assessed differently from what is practiced today in the civilized world. Blasphemy, which in other periods was held to be a crime, today may be considered a sin, but is a colorless act for Criminal Law. Incest, which was the law in Hawaii up until two centuries ago, today is punishable in various countries. Similar examples could be multiplied to infinity.

Criminal Law and Criminology for a long time were separate watertight compartments. Currently, thanks to the studies of Augusto Balloni, Baumann, Emilio C. Viano, Denis Szabo, Douglas Durán Chavarria, Exner, Georges Keltens, Georges Picca, Göppinger, Hans von Henting, Hurwitz, Jescheck, Jorge Figueiredo Dias, Kaiser, Kern, Lackner, Lange, Lenckner, Luiz Rodriguez Manzaneira, Mannheim, Marc Ancel, Maurach, Mezger, Mireille Delmas Marty, Peters, Pierre Henri Bolle, Triedemann, Reiss, Schmidhäuser, Schmidt, Schönke, Schöder, Severin Versele, Stéphan Parmentier, Stratenwerth, Welzel and many others, the two branches are linked to the same trunk, which is crime as defined by penal law, the concept of natural wrongdoing having been abandoned.

Additionally, the concept of *social defense* has evolved in recent decades so as to harmonize Penology and Criminology, with the work of Gramatica, Marc Ancel, Pinatel and others being very important.

From this activity a question emerged, first raised, then discarded and later brought up again for review: *is anyone born with a tendency towards crime?*

Lombroso affirmed the existence of born criminals and described their morphological characteristics. However, later studies have refuted his ideas. When he did, Gemelli dedicated a book to him: *I Funerali di un uomo e di una Dottrina*. Better, perhaps would be: "The funeral of a *genius* and a *mistake*," as geniuses also can relax their guard (*quandoque bonus dormitat Homerus,* says Horace in *Ars Poetica,* verse 359).

But the idea of a tendency towards crime was not buried with Lombroso. Or if it was, it was later exhumed by the Italian *Codice Penale* of 1930 (Rocco Code), in articles 108 and 109.

Studies carried out in Italy in condemned persons as delinquents by tendency led criminologists and penalists to again raise questions about the existence of such a type. The question, one of distinction, is polemical and impassioned. This gave rise to the idea of examining it from its various angles and offering the result of research that is not merely bookish, but which has gone to the field, to the living reality of penitentiary establishments. That is the input that we now appreciate with hopes that the difficulties and pioneering character of the research will be taken into account.

ORIGIN AND BACKGROUND OF THE TENDENCY TO COMMIT WRONGDOING: THE INITIAL CONCEPTION

The tendency towards wrongdoing, considered as a special inclination towards committing crimes does not present, in our days, the same orientation followed in the Nineteenth Century, when the Positive School began the movement to enshrine that figure so as to specifically indicate the born delinquent. We find the most remote precedent, suggesting the judicial classification of criminal due to congenital tendency, in the work of Enrico Ferri,[1] titled *Archivio di Psichiatria,* published in Turin in the year 1880.

The Italian code of 1889 made no allusion to a criminal due to tendency. In Italy, when it was being prepared, the Preliminary Project for the Penal Code for Criminal Offenses, known as the Ferri Positivist Project,[2] spoke in article 2.1, number 3, of "abnormal organic and psychic conditions, which can reveal criminal tendencies." Article 33 also made mention of the "delinquent who, without being alienated, was in a state of chronic intoxication by alcohol or other venomous substance, or was found in a state of grave psychic anomaly." In such a situation, "the criminal should be segregated into special work colonies." This provision, however, did not apply when the psychic anomaly consisted exclusively or principally of a congenital or acquired tendency towards criminal offense.

Criminological positivism substantially valued individualizing the classification of delinquent due to congenital tendency or natural-born delinquent. Congenital tendency meant natural inclination, innate disposition towards crime, instinctive need for committing it, and, in the individual, is an abnormality of an ethical and social nature, which determines the specific manner of reaction to environmental stimuli.

In this sense, Ferri (1929, p. 189) argued that "among men, delinquent or not, in certain cases there exists a biosocial type in whom congenital or acquired characteristics prevail and lead that individual to be more or less disposed, because of his physio-psychical constitution, towards a certain activity or profession. Thus, there is also a purely biological or anthropological type of delinquent in whom criminal tendencies are congenital and manifest themselves from the early years on, accompanied by profound anatomical, physiognomic and also psychic characteristics, which may not be explained as having been produced in the individual solely due to life habits, nor yet by social conditions in general."[3]

It was in his famous *Sociologia Criminale* that Enrico Ferri presented, for the first time, the distinction between habitual delinquent and delinquent by tendency, delineated in his Preliminary Project, later enshrined in the Penal Code of 1930 and received in the Italian criminal military laws of 1941.

Ferri was not isolated in his studies. His doctrine received the support of renowned criminologists who at the time defended the validity of the thesis of transmission of degenerative characteristics as an effect of the laws of heredity. Garofalo (1916, p. 119) was one of those supporting "the conception that criminal tendencies and predispositions are especially transmitted by hereditary factors."[4]

THE FORMULA OF THE ITALIAN PENAL CODE OF 1930

With the advent of the work to prepare the Italian Penal Code of 1930, known as the Rocco Code, a new aspect was attributed to the figure of the criminal due to tendency, as may be seen in the marked divergences between article 104 of the Preliminary Project of 1927,[5] and the definitive wording that was adopted in article 108 of that Penal Code, which is still in effect.

The words of professor Agostin Gemelli translate the philosophy adopted by the Italian legislators of 1930:

> The divergence was not only one of wording, but of concept. In the Project care was taken in defining a type of delinquent by instinctive tendency; in the

> Penal Code, the special inclination towards wrongdoing of the delinquent by tendency finds its cause in the particularly perverse natural disposition, which is revealed in some offences due to the existence of some objective and subjective circumstances.[6]

In light of the argumentation presented by the followers of the Positive School, when they affirmed that the tendency to commit wrongdoing adopted by the Ferri Project represented recognition of the doctrine that they defended, the "Consultative Commissions" responsible for the long debates surrounding adoption of the Rocco Code decided to abandon the primitive formula and admit a category that would identify with the logical conclusion that there are conducts which, with a certain ease, have an inclination towards repeating criminal actions.

The terms of article 108 of the Criminal Code, in effect in Italy since 1930, thus define the tendency towards wrongdoing:

> A delinquent due to tendency shall be considered as one who, although not recidivist, habitual or professional, practices a non-negligent wrong against life or individual integrity, although not provided for in title twelve of the second book of this code, and that, singly and jointly with the circumstances indicated in the paragraph of article 133, reveals a special inclination towards wrongdoing, an inclination having origin in the particularly evil natural disposition of the guilty party.
>
> The rule of this article shall not apply if the inclination towards wrongdoing should have its origin in infirmity, as provided articles 88 and 89.

With regard to specific treatment, according to article 109, the accentuated social risk posed by such violent delinquents induced the Italian legislature to formulate a judicial declaration on the tendency towards delinquency, with the purpose of consequently applying appropriate security measures.

The heading of criminal due to tendency in the current Italian positive Law, despite its more restricted contents, along general lines presents a biopsychic and social characterization along the same lines of the thesis previously put forth by defenders of criminological positivism. Besides the definitions found in the body of article 108, it should be noted that, while for the Positive School there were no limitations established on the concept of imputability (enshrining the principle of legal or social liability), on the contrary, for the Italian Penal Code, there is no imputability for those who lack "the capacity to understand and to desire." On the other hand, the concept of tendency adopted in the Italian Code means that such an imputability will remain, but with a broader concept involving a certain approximation with the positivist principle of legal or social liability.

Regarding the issue, the jurist Raoul Alberto Frosali says that "article 108 does not impede an abnormality of moral consciousness from accompanying or of being a cause or an effect, in confrontation with a physio-psychic state, in which one may recognize a given infirmity that will produce a generic incapacity for understanding, or wanting (furthermore, it is purely an ethical-social assessment of the behavior itself), provided for by article 85 and connected sections as non-imputability."[7]

The characteristic elements of the delinquent according to tendency defined by the Italian legal document of 1930, insofar as a rational social defense are concern, did not distance it from the category of incapacity, since the Code imposed treatment as a security measure reserved for the various categories of incapacitated persons. It is understood that article 108 does not provide for a declaration of tendency to be the result of an inclination found in incapacitated or semi-incapacitated delinquents, who are respectively dealt with in articles 88 and 89. The same reasoning is directed towards acts committed in a state of chronic intoxication produced by alcohol or stupefacient substances, as provided for in article 95 of the statute being examined.

The dogmatic concept of a criminal due to tendency instituted by Italian law as being one revealing a notable inclination towards wrongdoing due to a particularly perverse natural disposition, was rapidly able to achieve undeniable international projection in the field of specific research and debates, which decisively contributed to the inclusion of that category in penal legislation in numerous countries.

That was one of the notable merits of Italian judicial culture; it opened doors for later scholarly work, with so many points to be questioned regarding the efficacy of the concept of the criminal due to tendency, in the domain of typology for delinquents employed by Positive Law.

THE CRIMINAL TYPE OF THE DELINQUENT BY TENDENCY

Although scholars in the field have tried at different times to remove doubts concerning the judicial structuring of the delinquent by tendency, some aspects still require a more accurate analysis, since there have been countless consequences of the appearance of this classification for progressive speculation by the sciences concerned with the criminal phenomenon.

The scientific requests that stimulate us to establish, with such precision as possible, the convergent and divergent points of the so-called tendential delinquency, do not exclude the possibility of omitting important points in this work, considering that we are faced with a controversial theme, which is thus subject to formulation of various interpretive hypotheses.

THE CRIMINOLOGICAL CHARACTER OF THE TENDENCY TO DELINQUENCY

In Italy, The Ministerial Report on the Definitive Project for the Italian Penal Code of 1930 made a point of leaving it clear that the provisions of article 108 of the Rocco Code had nothing to do with employment of the expression "delinquent due to instinctive tendency" adopted by the first draft of the Project.

In summary, the Ministerial Report clarified that:

> Instinctive tendency meant no more than a natural inclination, disposition towards delinquency, with its own nature; one might say an abnormality in the moral and social sense of the agent. Normality in the moral sense is a concept quite distinct from normality of intelligence and of will. The Project based itself on imputability; that is, the capacity for understanding or for desiring, but in no case does it require of the agent the consciousness of moral and social principles.
>
> The abnormal, as long as this does not include those with sickness of the intellect or the will, is also imputable. To avoid any doubt that might arise as to the meaning of the word 'instinctive,' the same has been eliminated from the article.[8]

This was an opportune clarification, because it demonstrated the exclusion of the hypotheses of total or partial defect of the mind and showed that a particular inclination for transgression could in no way be based upon diseases of the intellect or of the will.

Following up on this understanding, Manzini (1959, pp. 263-264) inserted in his treatise that the Italian Penal Code, in withdrawing the expression "delinquent due to instinctive tendency," leaving only "delinquent due to tendency," avoiding the mistake of affirming that the project wished to allude to the natural-born delinquent or any other person impelled towards transgression by psychopathological forces. Delinquents due to tendency are individuals who, despite having a lucid intellect and perfect will, lack only an ethical and social sense.[9]

This philosophy of the Rocco Code was what projected internationally the figure of the delinquent due to tendency and offered conditions for analyzing and estimating the concrete ends desired by Italian law.

In Brazil, the authoritative voice of Professor Benjamin Moraes thus justified adoption of the type in an examination, in the revoked legislation of 1969:

> The Penal Code of 1969, in abandoning the thesis of recidivism as the tonic of the 1940 Code, should adopt another thesis. Recidivism would only be really important in the case of a habitual criminal, who, as has been provided for in the new Code, deserves a new treatment.

> Regarding the delinquent by tendency, the doctrine that comes to us from the Italian Code understands that the seriousness of the crime, although practiced for the first type, here demands a totally special treatment, similar to what was given to the habitual criminal. Even though founded on a psychological reason, the doctrine provides for a very objective form for analysis and conclusion: the horror of the crime practiced.[10]

In the same vein, Professor José Beleza dos Santos, one of the greatest scholars in Portuguese Criminal Law, has pointed out:

> In mentioning the delinquent by tendency the law did not have in view a certain criminal type, made up of morphological data and by a precise set of characteristics from the psychic point of view. It merely started from a verified fact: the existence of persons who practice crimes due to movies or circumstances which, on the one hand reveal a lack of pity for the other's suffering or even the pleasure in seeking it, and on the other, denounce a danger of recidivism in serious crimes.[11]

From those positions, we see that judicial classification of the delinquent by tendency is considered to such a degree as not to allow confusing it with the type known as born delinquent. For the legislative codes that follow the Rocco Code, what is interesting is a verified fact in which there is a predominance of indifference, lack of compassion faced with the sufferings of one's neighbor, a strange pleasure in practicing criminal acts colored with extreme revulsion.

The *Merit of Cesare Lombroso*. One correctly remembers the positive side of balanced criticisms directed at the postulates of Lombrosian theory, but it would be unjust not to recognize the undeniable value of Lombroso's studies. We all know that, together with Enrico Ferri (*Sociologia Criminale*) and Rafaele Garofalo (*Criminologia*), the celebrated author of *L'uomo Delinquente* form the trio of principals of the Positive School.

Regarding Lombroso, professor Edmund Mezger wrote:

> Notwithstanding the fact that one cannot demonstrate that the born delinquent is a genuine human species, Lombroso's theory is also important in our days, have been the first to clearly and definitively promoted and attempted scientific-causal consideration of wrongdoing and a political-criminal treatment of the delinquency problem, supported by that consideration. We cannot forgo such a scientific-natural complement of the judicial side of that problem. Precisely if we highlight with great precision and clarity the judicial-positive nature of the concept of wrongdoing and the historic-positive delimitation, and finally, changed due to circumstances of time and place as to what is considered delinquent, we will need to demand, on the one hand, an exact scientific-experimental investigation of that phenomenological scope, which, as previously enunciated, was the

> object of normative delimitation. For without the knowledge of the object on which the norm will apply, it is not possible to generically apply a normative function that is appropriated to the nature of the object and in harmony with its reality.[12]

Professor Gerardo Vasconcelos, in his splendid considerations regarding Criminological Legal Medicine, broadened the scope of recognition for the work of Lombroso:

> Lombroso's merit was this—of having reached this more modern and scientific conclusion, of proceeding in agreement with the virtuous mean, abandoning the petrified positions of intransigent antagonism—always erroneous in that position of dogmatic rigidity—to move towards a terrain that is more realistic and agreeable to human truth, in which people must be duly appreciated and, as persons, carefully examined in terms of the influences that they may have experienced from the environment and from their own constitution.[13]

For having evaluated criminals carrying a bloodthirsty instinct, related to atavistic regression, Cesare Lombroso endured various reproofs. But he never ceased to recognize the relevance of sociological data in the notion of crime, so much so that he attached great importance to crime prevention, noting, for this purpose, the need for education and instruction.

Professor Roberto Lyra, after noting that Gabriel Tarde asked Lombroso for his indulgence, expressed himself in this manner:

> There is no need for tolerance for someone who, as Lombroso did, was self-critical before he was critical. Love for science—always austere, solid, fertile—inspired him towards probity in making retractions and towards an eagerness for overcoming errors. When he authorized the 5th edition of the *Experimental Treatise on the Delinquent Man,* Lombroso wrote: "The more I ascend along the path, as someone who, higher up, sees farther, I see ever more clearly the gaps." That is why he recognized that the first idea, as imperfect, as improvised as it is, is modified and transformed.[14]

Upon Lombroso's death, Enrico Ferri, founder of Criminal Sociology, paid a fair homage to his revolutionary feat, expressing himself with the following words that Leonídio Ribeiro transcribed in his book:

> Lombroso's discovery pointed out the possibilities of fertile action by Social Hygiene, as a recourse for preventing crime, substituting the tardy means of repression that are savage and negative. In countries that are more civilized and have greater practical sense, free of the prejudices of academic tradition, such as England and the two Americas, a series of reforms in penal legislation has shined a spotlight on the truth of Lombrosian doctrine in its practical application, such

> as asylums for the criminally insane, indeterminate segregation for habitual offenders, agricultural work that substitutes the monumental penitentiaries, special treatment for criminal minors. Lombroso created a new Science and a School of Criminal Anthropology, born in Italy and now spread throughout the civilized world, teaching us to seek, in an individual's organic constitution, in the family and the social environment, the causes and roots of wrongdoing, knowledge of which will enable us to discover effective remedies.[15]

It is easy to conclude that the sense of the legislator was to build a legal type without the characteristics of an individual destined for crime by his or her constitution, but nonetheless having a sort of vocation for crime, responsible for his or her acts, and therefore punishable. However, the extremely obscure contours that are inherent to the profile of a classification exam, lead to a diversity of positions related to criminality by tendency, as can be perceived in the doctrinal focalizations adopted by specialists in the subject.

THE ISSUE OF TERMINOLOGY

Some authors have opposed the term *tendency* to signify the formula suggested by legislators when linking that word to the idea of "torpidity, perversion or cruelty."

Dirceu de Mello, a member of the Public Prosecution Service of the State of São Paulo, has taken this position:

> There seems to be a consensus to say that, in preparing legal text, the legislator should above all else pay attention to the precise meaning of the words. Formulated *erga omnes*, in fact, one cannot understand in a law the expression of a meaning that is discordant from the current understanding given in the language to be used to express such a law.
>
> Tendency (from the Latin *tendentia*—a force that determines the movement of a body), according to that which is recorded without discrepancy in the lexicons, is inclination, leaning, vocation, propensity, disposition.[16]

Dirceu de Mello refers to the fact that Nelson Hungria always calls attention to the grammatical method, as an important piece that the legislator needs for duly translating his or her thought. That is why Dirceu de Mello thought it strange that Nelson Hungria, in his Draft Legislation, linked the concept of criminal tendency to concepts of torpidity, perversion or cruelty.

Following the same line of reasoning, Professor Hilário Veiga de Carvalho pointed out:

> According to the lexicography, torpidity is the quality of that which is torpid, meaning dishonest, repugnant, infamous, disgusting, ignoble. Perversion, for its part, is the act of perverting, that is, making perverse, which means having a very bad disposition, ferine, treacherous. Cruelty, finally is the quality of one who is cruel, who practices cruel acts.
>
> Obviously, the expression "tendency" does not adjust well as a synonym for torpidity, perversion or cruelty. And neither do those characteristics cover all of the processes through which certain antisocial agents act in their delinquent activities, e.g., those with cupidity, lubricity, cynicism, etc. And for these one also intends to recognize a tendency.[17]

Professor Hilário Veiga de Carvalho wished to show that employing the expressions "by tendency," "accentuated inclination," "bad disposition," was defective. For him, using the terms "perversion" "cruelty" or "torpidity," means using expressions that in themselves do not properly reveal the origin of a type of behavior.

In reality, either the word "tendency" has a special significance, with purely judicial foundations, or the nomenclature use has to do with the intended description of that type of criminal. If "perversion," "torpidity" or "cruelty" are capable of revealing a tendency towards crime, it is undeniable that the symptoms of any of those qualities may be present in individuals whose criminal behavior is not characterized by such traits. One who is not torpid, perverse or cruel, from the legal point of view cannot be declared a criminal by tendency. Nevertheless, no justice system can label as a criminal by tendency someone who, albeit recognizably torpid, cruel or perverse, does not present a tendency towards crime.

One may then readily raise an objection to the expression "tendency," without wishing to propose to substitute it by terms such as aptitude, predisposition, disposition, inclination or any other. In our view, none of those expressions express the perfect idea of what the legislator intended to express in structuring the delinquent by tendency.

It must be said that the aforementioned terms have meanings outside of criminology that have nothing to do with what interests us here. One cannot say, furthermore, that there are exact equivalences to those expressions in other languages, given the enormous extent of the psycho-cultural content that each language contains.

"Tendency" or "disposition" presupposes a biological foundation, with major genetic potentiality. It can mean, on the one hand, a series of specific biological potentialities being developed, and, from another angle, others of the same nature that may develop. It thus has a double aspect: one that is active, already manifest or being manifested, and another that is latent, which may or may not reach the point of manifesting itself. There is no rigid or clearly established limit between the two zones.

The tendency is not precisely a quality or characteristic, even though it can give rise to them. Nor does it consist of an absolute manner of being, although it influences the way one acts. It is a set of acting and not acting possibilities, which vary according to the complex nature of each personality and its respective dynamization in the surrounding world. Each person, even if coming from the same parents as others, has its own distinct disposition, there being a negligible possibility of two children being genotypically equal, as even with twins, their identity is not absolutely the same.

It is not a question, therefore, of conceiving of a tendency or disposition as something acquired, fixed in a definitive form for the same person, but instead as something variable, evolving, the consequence of a series of powers that constitute the natural disposition, and of the forces of the surrounding world acting upon them.

The external characteristics of a person, by virtue of various interactions and co-actions, may not correspond exactly to the genotypic powers, given that, because those are in principle a series of probabilities and possibilities, they may or may not manifest themselves completely, and even if they do manifest themselves, they are subject to the configuring action of other powers of the human constitution, or even that of characteristics acquired by the organism's adapting to the surrounding world, leading to a different result than what they might produce, by themselves.

THE INDIVIDUALIZATION OF THE DELINQUENT BY TENDENCY IN THE GALLERY OF CRIMINOLOGICAL TYPES

In this topic we will focus on the serious disagreements in conceptions related to the complex figure of the delinquents being studied, when, in our days, the validity of classifying criminals in penal statues is still being questioned.

Analyzing the insertion of the criminal by tendency in the Sá Pereira Project (revised), Professor Roberto Lyra showed why he was against including that figure in the 1940 Code, in effect in the country.

The great professor inquired:

> What is the tendency to act delinquently? How do we define and determine it?
>
> As for the doctrine, it retains essential controversies and offers no formula for the judges. It revives the old anthropological concept of types, or constitutions, as if crime were not above and before everything, a social phenomenon. In my

view, there are no biological predispositions for practicing acts even in future level characterization and extending to men of the highest biological purity.[18]

More than forty years later, professor Roberto Lyra maintains his intransigent conviction:

> Born criminal, in 1975, under the undefined euphemism.
>
> Tendency! What one is questioning now is something less vague and indistinct, incompatible with the constitutional rule of individualization. What is tendency? Tendency towards what crime? And what of the motives, the ends, the means? The individual dangerous state, by habits and tendencies, comes from conserving, not aggravating its causes. There are no criminals, there are men.[19]

In the opinion of Edmund Mezger "every human being possesses a substrate of impure, low and malignant or criminal thinking and tendencies, which can be manifested at any time. The inclination towards criminal acts is not circumscribed to a given species of men in the sense of the Lombrosian doctrine of born delinquent, but exists as instinctive criminality, patent in every man, including the minor.[20]

For Giuseppe Maggiore the atrophy of the moral sense, which characterizes the delinquent by tendency, is also found in habitual and professional delinquents, with the failing in those being due almost always to environmental and social causes, while in the delinquent by tendency it is principally derived from endocrine coefficients. The delinquent by tendency, although amoral, cruel and dangerous, conserves all of the requisites pertaining to imputability, and is consequently responsible for his acts."[21]

Inner excitation, as a stimulus for revealing conduct with a tendency towards crime has also been pointed to by Luiz Jiménez de Asúa[22] and Enrico Altavilla.[23] The excellent explanation by Vicenzo Manzini, considering the delinquent by tendency as one in whom the defect in the moral sense is not associated to any pathological perturbation in the intellectual and volitional sphere, we have already situated in the chapter destined for analyzing the guidelines for the tendency towards delinquency in the Brazilian Penal Code of 1969, precisely when we deal with the judicial presuppositions that configure that tendency.

Accompanying the conceptualizations of Benjamin Moraes and José Beleza dos Santos, also examined in earlier pages in this chapter, Professor José Frederico Marques highlights the fact that the delinquent by tendency "is not a criminal type made up of morphological factors, because the law simply began with a verified fact, which is the existence of individuals who practice crimes, on the one hand revealing indifference to the suffering of the other or even evident sadism, and on the other hand evidencing undeniable danger of reiterating the practice of serious crimes."[24]

The problem surrounding the difficulty in separating delinquent from non-delinquent, as a fundamental difference in constitution and disposition, was surveyed by Magalhães Noronha, who understands that "it is difficult the fit into models the infinite number of criminals, each one presenting their own and undefined peculiarities, suffering the influence of the most diverse factors, reacting to entirely distinct causes. Finally, we believe that the value of classifying delinquents is quite relative, in light of the complexity of the human soul, or if one wishes, in light of the personality of the creature. We believe that it is problematic to catalogue the thousands and thousands of delinquents who crowd the jails and prisons, in four or five categories."[25]

The words of Professor Magalhães Noronha are entirely appropriate, when one considers that in the Nineteenth Century the major argument against the thesis of a born criminal was the finding of degenerate individuals who had never committed any crime. The doubt regarding the existence of the delinquent by tendency type, because of the lack of a solid prognosis as to the scientific bases of that classification, was one of the strongest reasons that led some authors, among them Agostino Gemelli,[26] in Italy and Everardo da Cunha Luna[27] in Brazil, to incisively defend the removal of the type from the gallery of classifications of criminals found in penal laws.

For his part, Professor Manuel Pimentel dealt with a relevant aspect of the problem, considering the classification of criminal by tendency to be a "dangerous innovation in light of the Brazilian reality, due to the absence of resources for unprotected children, the moral abandonment of many youths, illiteracy, factors that lead a man to a typical state of life for which he cannot be entirely held liable, but for which society is also responsible."[28]

Sharing similar thinking, Virgilio Donici believes that "the criminological discussions regarding the criminal by tendency do not reach a definitive conclusion, if such a person is mentally infirm or a natural delinquent by tendency, as the Brazilian reality does not know criminals by tendency in a sufficient number for a criminal classification."[29]

Another serious criticism has to do with the existence of a type of tendency with a characterization that is visibly of a more judicial than criminological nature. Regarding the matter, the analysis by Alcides Munhoz Netto deserves attention:

> This does not mean that Criminal Law has divorced itself from Criminology, in classifying such types of author. It means, to the contrary, that Positive Law has stratified into legislative definition the characteristics that the criminological sciences attribute to those species of delinquents. And it has done so in order for the recognition of habitual action or of tendency, with serious reflexes in

> the measure of penal response, not to vary according to personal conceptions of who would be a habitual criminal or a criminal by tendency.[30]

Professor Alcides Munhoz Netto wished to show that when Criminal Law specifies the requirements, conditions or circumstances of criminal types, it does so for the purpose of limiting judicial discretion, in favor of the guarantees resulting from the principle of legal reservation, That does not mean that the legislator has created a purely legal type, because there are evident criminological implications in the identification of the delinquent by tendency. As we have shown in the previous chapter of this book, the close relation between the purposes practiced by Criminology and those of Criminal Law, legitimate the criminological characteristic of the orientation followed by legislation, which seeks to individualize the criminal by tendency, by means of a special inclination towards horrendous, perverse or cruel crime.

IMPORTANCE OF PSYCHOPATHOLOGY FOR STUDIES PERTAINING TO THE DELINQUENT BY TENDENCY

The great usefulness of the topic that we will now examine resides in the verification of the probable identity existing in the judicial qualification of the delinquent by tendency and a given type of psychopathic personality recognized by a large number of clinical specialists.

There is no psychic anomaly with which a doctor comes so often in contact, like that of psychopathic personalities, above all those that, instead of being clearly revealed, hide behind the most varied organic elements.

With Psychopathology being defined as the discipline that has the objective of knowing about the abnormalities of mental life, it is appropriate to at least briefly define what is understood as mental abnormality and establish how it is different from normality.

The predominant thesis seems to be that normality is everything that corresponds to a pattern that we take to be the norm, the measure. For our activities we have the establishment of two types of norms: the average norm and the ideal norm. If we adopt the first, we shall call abnormal that which diverges from the common, the habitual, the average. If we utilize the second, we shall call abnormal that which opposes creation of the ideal, the model of human personality that we take as the norm.[31]

Clearly, the norm established as the sense of ideal value depends absolutely on the criterion for appreciation in each person, as it will vary from individual to individual, according to personal opinions and convictions. The ideal of perfection will be, for some persons, represented for example in the poetic talent of Goethe, for others in the humility of Saint Francis of Assisi, and even for some, in the coldness of Hitler.

In his Psychiatry Course, Honório Delgado reminds us that "we cannot utilize the ideal norm, but only the median norm to establish an assessment of the value of each individual."[32] Even though it may be vague and not expressible by numbers, all of us have a notion of what is an average individual. By this paradigm of norm, the poet, the saint or the criminal are equally abnormal, given that any of those individuals diverges from the average level.

The numerous discussion that this issue has raised show how difficult it is to explain that the median norm is really the most effective, chiefly because it does not derive from the free assessment of each person. It may be complicated to understand, even exemplifying that according to the purposes of the norm of averageness, Goethe must be classified as an abnormal personality, simply because the majority of earthlings do not possess his talent and his prestige.

Despite the criticism that it may deserve, it seems more convenient to define abnormal personalities as variations that distance themselves from the average standard. One cannot affirm, nevertheless, that such personalities are clearly separated from the norms, although there is no individual who can guarantee that he or she does not possess one or several of the attributes of abnormal personalities.

The *Psychopathic Personalities.* The concept of psychopathic personality is often employed exactly with the same broad meaning of abnormal personalities. To avoid certain confusions, the renowned Professor Kurt Schneider of Heidelberg University maintained that "it is more convenient, because it better corresponds to the needs of the doctor, to isolate, from within the very vast field of abnormal personalities, those that suffer or make society suffer due to that abnormality and apply only to them the designation of psychopathic personalities."[33] Bearers of psychopathic disturbances are individuals who, despite generally having an average or high intellectual level, exteriorize disturbances of an ethical or antisocial nature, with difficulties in learning the norms of sociability and good sense.

It is important also to make it clear that abnormality does not have the broad meaning of disease.

Kurt Schneider teaches us that "the concept of infirmity, principally in Psychiatry, in the proper sense, exists only in the somatic sphere, and we may only call psychic anomalies 'morbid' when they can be connected to morbid organic processes. To call 'morbid,' manifestations that are psychic or purely social, without that foundation is only an image, and thus does not possess any scientific value."[34]

Since the Nineteenth Century, the specialists have sought to unravel the possible causes for psychiatric deviations. Disagreements still exist today between those who argue that such deviations originate from a certain constitutional disposition, those who claim to find the origin in functional deficiencies in the brain and those who believe they can define the cause of the deviations in a possible rejection suffered by the child during the first years of life. What all scholars can agree on is in recognizing that the psychopathic personality syndrome is distinct from other deficiencies related to psychosis and neurosis, even though there is a marked similarity between the psycopathy with other neurotic disturbances and certain modes of psychosis, considering that, in the final analysis, both neurotics as well as psychotics and psychopaths are maladapted personalities.

As for the possibility of recovery psychopaths, Albrecht Langelüddeke considers that treatment of those individuals is "not a very gratifying task, because it has not been easy for medical science to make psycopathy susceptible to a cure."[35] As Honório Delgado has also pointed out "the childhood period is the most appropriate one for combating such anomalies, especially because in that phase, the treatment has a positive influence from the environmental factors that stimulate good formation of the character."[36]

Of the various typologies of psychopathic personalities, Kurt Schneider's proposal enjoys the greatest acceptance among students of the subject.[37] This is doubtless due to the precision of his lineaments and the comprehensive gallery of all the ten groups that is well structured and has precise differences.

The groups defined by Schneider are composed in the following manner: hyperthymics, depressive, insecure, fanatics, ostentatious, inconstant, explosive, insensitive, abullic and asthenic. The asthenic psychopaths are divided into three subgroups; sensitive asthenics, persons with a feeling of incapacity and persons easily subject to perturbation of their organic functions.

Schneider did not forget to highlight the possible combination of different traits, as well as the possibility of signs appearing in individuals who were declaredly provided with a normal personality. He also recommends that "one should not confuse determination of a type with a medical diagnosis. In diagnosis we are working with nosographic entities, concepts that are perfectly delimitated and defined. The types, on the contrary, are only schematic standards, through which we try to measure and compare them; in the diagnosis we affirm that an individual has or does not have a given disease. In classifying a type, the affirmation cannot be so peremptory and we limit ourselves to noting that an individual comes more or less close to this or that type.[38]

One cannot deny the real validity of the observation above, because, when we say, for example, that a certain individual is despotic, we do not employ that designation in the sense of a diagnosis, It is not appropriate to draw a line between despotics and other individuals that will absolutely separate them. There are individuals who correspond completely to the despotic type we have idealized, while others only come close, and still others present only a few of their characteristics.

The ten types that we have just cited can be found combined in different manners. One frequently encounters explosive fanatics, insecure depressives, abullic asthenics and insensitive hyperthymics with characteristics of the ostentatious types. It is impossible to intend, Schneider affirms "for one who is insecure to be at the same time insensitive."[39]

One should also note, according to this specialist, the viability of frequent combinations of psychopathic personalities with the different degrees of mental weakness, as is the case of the hyperthymic who is mentally weak and has the traits of an insensitive individual. With the exception of the insecure, who are almost always intelligent individuals, all of the other psychopathic personalities may be accompanied by mental weakness.[40]

It appears that psychiatry still has difficulties in identifying the relations between psychopathic personalities and psychoses, a situation that generates serious doctrinal controversies involving the complete study of psychopathic problems. Knowing whether we should class certain hyperthymic and depressive types as permanent cases of cyclothymia (manic-depressive madness); seeking to establish the relations that unite the inconstant types to epilepsy and cyclothymia: situating the relations of certain fanatics and certain insensitive to schizophrenia are only some of the many problems that involve that complex part of medical science.

Another aspect that does not offer us conditions for precise numbers is the question of the number and types of psychopathic personalities. The ten groups gathered by Kurt Schneider have been tested and today are almost unanimously accepted by other students of the subject, but in no passage of his work did Schneider ever assert that he had exhausted the possible hypotheses and other factors relative the problem of characterizing and prognosticating the psychopathic symptoms. The way in which we should designate those personalities depends on the choice of each interested party, with professor Benigno Di Tullio having name the insensitive type a "soulless psychopath."[41]

Highlight on the Insensitive Type. It is exactly this category that now receives special attention in our work. It would be very interesting to comment with more depth on all of the psychopathic groups, but to plunge into all the formulas could cause the effect of causing us to dilute ourselves in details whose explanations would be removed from the appropriate purpose of this work.

Considerations regarding the insensitive type point out the significant importance that studies in psychopathology provide in forming a conclusive reasoning about the delinquent tendency. However insignificant our thinking may be, reflection has led us to consider that the characteristic traits utilized by Positive Law to qualify *de lege* the delinquent by tendency are extremely similar to the attributes of the insensitive psychopathic personality described by Schneider.

As we have noted previously, in conceiving of the delinquent by tendency class based on psychological reasons and as a pragmatic reason for social defense, the legislator employed an objective formula to punish someone demonstrating a special delinquent capacity in practicing a crime with a high degree of torpidity, perversion or cruelty. It is therefore appropriate to specify, so as to have a precise understanding of this item of the work, that the legal sense of criminal by tendency requires configuration of a human fact, where there is visible indifference to another's suffering, by means of commission of a crime with horrible features, which will provide the conviction that the agent is capable of practicing other offences with aspects just as cruel.

When he characterize the insensitive psychopaths, Schneider "referred to individuals devoid or almost devoid of compassion, shame, feelings of honor and remorse. They are frequently somber, introspective and morose individuals. *In their actions the show themselves impulsive, brutal, cruel. Regarding the criminal insensitive, one must not forget the existence of insensitive who are entirely sociable, with a nature of steel, capable of marching over cadavers.*[42]

In light of the identification above, the similarity of characteristics between the insensitive psychopath and construction of the figure of delinquent by tendency is genuinely undeniable. This irrefutable evidence seems to supply us with the necessary data for placing the tendential criminal on the scale of psychopaths, and consequently, deserve the treatment dispensed to those who are semi-imputable.

Even if this is not the most viable positioning for the correct scientific placement of the delinquent by tendency type, we can inquire if the individual's psychic structure, capable of revealing a special inclination towards crime with perversion, torpidity or cruelty is not contaminated by another sort of disturbance with a prognosis that is not yet known to science.

There is no doubt that the question is extremely complex, especially because it involves profound secrets of the human body and soul. What one must not do, at least, is intend to hurriedly classify delinquents, using as a basis only models that present symptoms reflected in conduct incompatible with social dictates. We must not forget that the origins of crime always conjugate endogenous and exogenous factors, many of which are still unknown by the authorities who investigate this enigmatic phenomenon.

It is non-scientific to determine objectively that perversity of disposition, supposedly displayed in a criminal act, will justify employing the label of criminal tendency, without having a solid diagnosis about a given behavior. Although the individual may have the capacity to understand and to want, due to various reasons, he or she may be psychically abnormal.

We want to emphatically specify the care that is needed when one speaks of tendency towards crime. We see no relevance in placing the label of tendency in one situation or the other, since the important thing is to know what, in this or that case, is the formative core of that which is externally presented with characteristics of a tendency. Thus, it is necessary to distinguish as much as possible, what are the elements that reduce resistance to the practice of an antisocial action, meaning, that can supplant the ethical core of the individual, and that being overcome, facilitate or bring about the criminal action.

It does not seem easy to scientifically prove the objective classification of criminal by tendency, even faced with an enumerated series of conditions of biological disposition or mesological disposition, which can alter a person's behavior. Here lies the crux of the matter, towards which we must focus all the light of our intelligence, to verify to what point, how and how much any of the biological or mesological factors, in its expression or in each hypothesis, can have an action over a human personality with influence to reduce the resistance to practicing a crime.

Let it be clearly stated that this is not the case of pointing to any factor that will specifically impel towards crime. To wish to palpably show such an idea is nonsense, a totally non-scientific position, since we have the greatest variety of hypotheses in crime, and consequently, we would need to have another countless number of hypotheses with specificity for each one of those criminal conditions. So that, to speak of specificity of factors, such as the crimogenetics, is a lovely example to present at an academic gathering, but in our view, lacks any scientific value.

While searching in the doctrine for some position that might, perchance, at least approach the present supporting arguments, it was with great pleasure that we located in the work of Professor Veiga de Carvalho, the same conception summarized in the following example:

A hyperthyroidal person, stimulated by this endocrine disorder, may be a great artist, capable of marvelous accomplishments; many have been. He may be an efficient captain of industry, lively and with a large and penetrating vision, full of successes; many have also been. But he may be—within the same endocrine status—a criminal, also touched by the *ébranlement* that the excess of thyroidal activity determines.[43]

The thesis of reduction in resistance to committing crimes also finds support in the thought of Professor Benigno Di Tullio, when he speaks so expressively of *crimino-impellent factors.*[44] This seems very well formulated to us, because it is not reducible to a symptomatology that defines the individual as necessarily a criminal.

In light of this panorama, in which for a long time answers will be sought for so many scientific inquiries, raised by the progress of criminological knowledge, we will never be able to discard the need for careful analyses that will allow us to appreciate a certain dangerous behavior, detect the causes and choose the measures capable of neutralizing, or even suppressing, the factors that participate in the complex mechanism of the criminal act.

The obscure contours of the human personality, which often reveal shocking criminal actions, will lead us to necessarily deposit our hopes in the growing success of investigations in criminology, whether in the fact itself, or in the biological, psychological and social aspects inherent to the personality of the agent. Only with these complete exams can we achieve precise clarification, or even positive data that will favor broader use of studies and research in treating problems that present themselves in each individualized situation.

Specialized techniques and services will have the task of pointing out, always precisely, the causes of syndromes and behaviors, many of them with judicial-social implications. The admirable knowledge of the human interior undoubtedly leaves the margin of incurability progressively smaller. Nevertheless, all this fantastic advance must never extinguish the awareness of our earthly limitations.

VIOLENCE AND AGGRESSIVENESS IN CONTEMPORARY LIFE

There seems to be a well-defined modern orientation not to label criminal personalities with the same naturalistic spirit employed for the purposes of botanical, zoological or mineralogical classification.

The typology of delinquents must correspond to a practical requirement imposed by the needs of the treatment. The classificatory requirements must rely on scientific acquisitions and not only on the circumstantial orientation that Positive Law wishes to attribute through legislative regulation of the subject, principally when there is a need for formulating a diagnosis that will reveal the origin of the anti-social behavior.

In proposing one of the most influential theories on the causation of delinquency, according to which crime is the product of learning and group relations, Edward Sutherland in 1930 spoke of "the great diversity in criminal behavior and the multiplicity of influences on criminal conduct."[45]

The theory of differential association and learning put forth by Sutherland has suffered criticism, especially for having relegated biological and psychological factors, but its appearance to investigate the socio-cultural aspects of criminality, besides providing for the appearance of promising concepts in this area,[46] has ratified the principle that criminality, related to the social structure context, is an inherent phenomenon in the functioning of society.

With crime being a human fact, it is obvious that social and biological factors are part of it. The sociocultural influences for forming a human's personality or social accomplishment, acting on biological individualization, do not allow us to define human behavior in terms of deterministic causality but through probabilistic conditioning, which is why we understand that in criminal conduct the sociological dimension complements the biological, psychological and culturological dimensions.

The most characteristic trait in societies is undoubtedly their cultural base. Even those who study the natural sciences accept that conclusion, as Gilberto de Macedo remembered in commenting on the thought of Theodosius Dobshanki, summarizing that "insect societies are founded on genetically instinctive behavior, while those of humans are founded on culture that the individuals learn, instead of inheriting from their gens."[47]

It is clear, then, that human behavior is the product of two roots: biological nature and social nature. Through the first it receives its constitution and its biopsychological development. Through the second, it achieves structural fullness, that is, the social evolution obtained through acculturation.

In the biological foundations of human conduct it is essential to distinguish the phenotype and genotype constitutions. The phenotype, the external characteristic, changes continuously over the years as development proceeds. The changes in manifestation of the phenotype's heredity contrast with the relative interior stability of the genotype. The phenotypical plasticity of our behavior is due to the socialization process, and although originally determined by gene reproduction, the extent of its development is directly linked to cultural structure and not to the foundations of biological laws, without, however, being contrary to those laws.

Based on this reasoning, one reaches the conclusion that criminal behavior is directly or indirectly linked to the patterns of life in society, which explains the sociological understanding of crime as a preponderantly social phenomenon. In that regard, adjustment of the personality can either lead us to a life according to the degree of average morality in a collectivity, or follow in the direction of a contrary pattern, when, for example the adaptive reaction necessary to social coexistence goes beyond those bounds, moving towards pathological aggressiveness that is harmful to society, generated by the pressures of modern life, emotional tensions, states of anxiety, anguish, insecurity and affective needs.

The synthesis of criminal behavior is thus demonstrated as an expression of a socio-culturally conditioned biological unity.

Since childhood we have learned the style of the society to which we belong, and according to the interiorization of social norms, we will give a model to the assumed behavior. The delinquential syndrome constantly results from the conflict of values due to the lack of sublimation of feelings, from the lack of preparation to overcome anxiety, insecurity and fear.[48] As the outside world takes its place in a person's life, concomitant changes progressively occur in actions, perception, volition and way of feeling. If those changes do not find, in the family environment and the community environment itself, healthy stimuli to accompany modifications in character, there may be a sad result in which the individual is subjected to the rules of maladjustment or even delinquency.

French professor Jean Chazal has written a work on the details if this theme, where he notes states in a certain passage "the temperamental or characterological change that a child suffers from having had a more or less direct relation during its development with some concrete irregular conduct. Occasions are not few in which, inquiring into the life of some adult delinquent, we find ourselves before an emotional, sentimental and often intellectual maladjustment, brought about by lack of interest of the parents or by ignorance regarding the mutation carried out in the minor."[49]

In those conditions, it is logical to find interference of socio-cultural factors in forming the aggressive behavior, and, consequently, the criminal conduct, given that the criminal phenomenon is linked to individual, family and environmental interactions.[50]

Culture as a whole, provides for members of the collectivity and indispensable guide in all of the fields of life. The existence of cultural standards is crucial both for any society to function and to efficiently conserve it.

In this sense, the words of Felte Bezerra are resonant:

> It seems essentially important to know the conception that each people have of their values. The interlinking that is established among individuals, each and every one, is the cultural whole, constituting a closed cycle in a relation of reciprocity. The interaction between the individual and the culture is thus so complex and intimate, almost in a process of amalgamation, that it would be difficult to point to the predominance of one component over the other, since there is no prevalence, but interdependence among all.[51]

Through conscious learning, the child assimilates the culture in which it is situated, carrying out the interiorization process. If a youth comes from a family or group in a cultural conflict, his or her adaptive aggressiveness leads to life with other people in order to have protection and compensate for the insecurity and anxiety that result from affective needs and lack of educational support. Adjustment for such people will become even more difficult, if they are more engaged in violent subcultures. The heavier the degree of integration of an individual in some subcultures, the higher will be the possibility of the person's behavior becoming aggressive and brutal.[52]

Criminality often has its roots in childhood. It is not possible to win the fight against delinquency, if we do not take into account the different facets of the phenomenon and its causes linked to individuals and the environment in which they live.

The child's soul is not born perverse, equipped with animalized instincts, nor is it exclusively led to purity and goodness. In every child, notes Richard Lewontin, there are always egotistical dispositions, which are gradually attenuated and transformed into a moral sense, through the process of evolution of its personality, and above all, under the influence of education and instruction.[53]

All educational activity must be based on knowledge of the personality, through its static and dynamic, somatic and psychological aspects, in order for us to have conditions to combat the maleficent origins of existing situations and adopt the appropriate prophylactic and re-educational means.

In our time, the adaptation of the structural reality of each problem is becoming even more difficult, given the lack of social and psychological planning in the economically less favored communities.

On the other hand, overpopulation in large urban centers is undoubtedly a major factor in determining violence. In the megalopolis there is an invasion of personal space, which causes disharmony and increasingly maladjusted reactions. With daily life disturbed by countless factors, one cannot accept the aggravation of anxiety, which leads to predisposed people being affected by a neurosis and those who are not predisposed to be involved by a form of stress. The exaggerated mechanization of people leads to an empty existence, without affective significant, and it is as maleficent to the values of life as are the tensions coming from the growing misery of the oppressed.

Life in society today is not so easy. The first step of the socially needy individual is to kill for survival. The marginalization process for those social classes leads people to become ever more aggressive and emotionally prepared for crime.

The moral values of the marginalized classes are exactly the opposite of what we defend as being the best for the current society. We are living in a genuine social crisis, where the solutions in effect seem to be bankrupt before the success of the vicious cycle of egotism, hate and violence. Terrorism, for example, is reaching the dimensions of a crime against humanity, with proportions never seen before and the stain of barbarianism that is marking our society.

Regarding these problems, the precise meditation of Miguel Reale Junior deserves reflection:

> We are the heirs of victories for human rights, and nonetheless, we live in a world where aggressiveness and egotism prevail. We relive past violence, in new and ancient forms of criminality, such as piracy, the wars in Ireland and the Middle East, terrorism and police arbitrariness in the streets of Paris, Rome, etc. The great metropolitan complexes cause a rupture in the balance of community life, through the destruction of ancient forms of coexistence, the disappearance of natural bonds, the disintegration of the family, the juxtaposition of humans in anguish as they seek social recognition and participation in a consumer society.[54]

The severe crises open in the prophylactic undertakings and prison systems, with negative pedagogical effects, are removing fundamental stimuli that can guarantee a happy result for reforms in the area of penal execution. The traditional system of repression and retribution is left increasingly reeling, and is a true factor in the rise of crime and deformation of personalities. Public opinion has already been stirred with the lack of respect for the dignity and the fundamental rights of individuals in prisons, where an inferior social status conditions the prisoner to always feel persecuted by the inefficient police-judicial-administrative complex. It is an indisputable fact that the empirical incompatibility between punishing and rehabilitating, continues to be an open question.

Regarding all of these considerations, Professor Heleno Fragoso authoritatively denounced that

> the administration of justice, in criminal matters, constitutes the most dramatic aspect of the inequality of justice, with the principle of equality before the law being purely formal and totally illusory. The identification of the criminal with the marginalized persons results from the fact that justice above all strikes at the poor and disfavored, who fill the prisons and constitute the system's clientele. They constitute only the "apparent criminality," incomparably smaller that hidden criminality, together with that which is known, but not denounced, and what is denounced, but not subject to prosecution.[55]

The disquiet of contemporary criminality, even with the consumption of horror and suffering, must be assumed by all of us. In the current scenario, we should not feel ourselves to be only participants, but responsible in part in the sense of seeking and guaranteeing that our mentality and our customs are guided by a strong moral consciousness.

The goodness of everyone's ideas and works needs to be more active in our world, so that we may all be spared the tragic and unjust results that only lead to fear and to general consternation.

NOTES

1. FERRI, Enrico. *Archivio di psichiatria.* Turim, Ed. Bocca, 1880, v. 1.°, p. 474.

2. The Preliminary Project for the Penal Code for Wrongdoing was organized by a Royal Commission to reform Italian criminal laws, according to a Royal Decree on September 14, 1919. The Commission had as president Enrico Ferri and the members, besides him were: R. Garofalo, E. de Nicola, A. Berenini, A. Setti, R. de Notaristefani, P. Alberici, R. Maietti, A. Lusting, E. Florian, S. de Sanctis, S. Ottolenghi, G. Ferrari. Acting as Secretaries were: F. Grispigni, G. Ricci, U. Aloise, A. Spallanzani, A. Santoro and M. Piacetini.

3. FERRI, Enrico. *Sociologia Criminale.* Turim, Editore Utet, 1929, v. 1, p. 189.

4. GAROFALO, Rafaele. *Criminologia.* Trans. by Julio de Mattos. Lisboa, Livraria Clássica Editora, 1916, p. 119.

5. Article 104 of the Preliminary Project for the Italian Penal Code, dated from October 1927, established: "Delinquente per Tendenza—Chiunque, ancorchè non recidivo o delinquente abituale e profissionale, commete un delitto, non collposo, che, di per se, o unitamente ad alcuna delle circostanze indicate nell'ultimo capoverso dell'articolo 134, riveli nel colpevole una instintiva tendenza a delinquere, è dichiarato delinqüente per tendenza. Se la pena da infliggere per il delitto commesso sia la reclusione superiore a quindici anni, è sostituita l'ergastolo—Le altre pena sono raddopiate, esclusi gli aumenti di pena stabiliti per la recidiva."

For its part, article 105 of the Project provided guidelines for the hypothesis of a criminal by tendency who committed another type of crime, thus establishing: "Qualora il delinquente per tendenza commetta un altro delitto, non colposo, la pena da infliggere per il nuovo delitto é sostituita o aumentata secondo la disposizione dell'articolo precedente. Non si fa luogo, tuttavia, all'applicazione della pena di morte a norma della prima parte, dell'articolo 73, quando la pena dell'ergastolo sia inflitta soltanto pereffetto della sostituzione stabilita nel precedente articolo."

6. GEMELLI, Agostino. *La personalità del delinquente; nei suoi fondamenti biologici e psicologici.* Milão, Dott. A. Giuffrè Editore, 1948, 2. ed., p. 311-2.

7. FROSALI, Raoul Alberto—Il delinquente per tendenza nel diritto positivo. In: *Studi in Memoria di Arturo Rocco.* Milão, Dott, A. Guiffrè—Editore, 1952, v. 1, p. 450.

8. *Relazione Ministeriale al Progetto definitivo del Codice Penale.* Roma, Tipografia Ufficiale, 1929, t. 1, p. 156.

9. MANZINI, Vincenzo. *Tratatto di diritto penale italiano.* Turim, Unione Tipografico Editrice Torinese, 1959, v. 3, p. 263-4.

10. MORAES, Benjamin. *A Parte geral do futuro Código Penal.* Belém, S.E., 1977, p. 9 (Conferência proferida no Ciclo de Estudos de Direito Penal, em homena-

gem ao professor Aldebaro Klautau, promovido pelo Instituto de Criminologia do Pará, em 23.05.1977).

11. SANTOS, José Beleza dos. *Os tribunais de execução das penas em Portugal.* Coimbra, Editora Coimbra, 1953, p. 32.

12. MEZGER, Edmundo. *Criminologia.* Trans. by José Arturo Rodrigues Muñoz. Madrid, Editorial Revista de Derecho Privado, 1950, 2. ed., p. 35.

13. VASCONCELOS, Gerardo. *Lições de medicina legal.* Rio de Janeiro, Editora Forense, 1976, 2. ed., revisada e atualizada, pl. 437-8.

14. LYRA, Roberto. *Direito penal normativo.* Rio de Janeiro, José Konfino—Editor, 1977, 2. ed., p. 25.

15. RIBEIRO, Leonídio. *Criminologia.* Rio de Janeiro, Editorial Sul-Americana. 1957, v. 1, p. 46.

16. MELLO, Dirceu de. Criminoso by tendency. In: *Revista dos Tribunais.* São Paulo, Editora Revista dos Tribunais, 6 (444): p. 264, out., 1972.

17. CARVALHO, Hilário Veiga de. *O Novo Código Pena: Comentários médico-legais, médico-sociais e criminológicos.* Bauru, Instituto Toledo de Ensino, 1971, p. 38.

18. LYRA, Roberto. *Direito Penal;* parte geral. Rio de Janeiro, Livraria Jacyntho Editora, 1936, p. 552-3.

19. LYRA, Roberto. *Direito penal normativo.* Rio de janeiro, José Konfino, Editor, 1977, p. 132.

20. MEZGER, Edmundo. *Criminologia.* Trans. by José Arturo Rodriguez Muñoz. Madrid, Editorial Revista de Derecho Privado, 1950, 2. ed., p. 252.

21. MAGGIORE, Giuseppe. *Diritto penale.* Bolonha, Nicola Zanichelli Editore, 1958, v.2, 5ª edizione accrescinta e aggiornata, p. 649.

22. ASÚA, Luiz Jiménez de. *La ley and el delito.* Caracas, Editorial Andrés Bello, 1945, p. 683.

23. ALTAVILLA, Enrico. *O Delinqüente e a lei penal.* Trans. by Fernando de Miranda. Coimbra, Editora Coimbra, 1964, p. 286.

24. MARQUES, José Frederico. *Curso de direito penal.* São Paulo, Edição Saraiva, 1956, v. 3, p. 59.

25. NORONHA, Magalhães. A classificação de delinqüente no novo direito penal. In: *Revista Brasileira de Criminologia e Direito Penal.* Rio de Janeiro. Instituto de Criminalogia da Universidade do Estado da Guanabara, 4 (14): p. 99, jul./set., 1966.

26. LUNA, Everardo da Cunha. Das penas e sua execução. In: *Fondamenti biologici e psicologici.* Milão, Dott. A Giuffré—Editore, 1948, p. 320.

27. LUNA, Everardo da Cunha. Das penas e sua execução. In: *Ciência Penal.* São Paulo (s. ed.), 2 (2): p.37, ago., 1975.

28. PIMENTEL, Manuel Pedro. A reforma penal. In:*Estudos e Pareceres de Direito Penal.* São Paulo, Editora Revista dos Tribunais, 1972, p. 79.

29. DONNICI, Virgílio. Aspectos criminológicos do novo Código Penal. In: *Revista de Informação Legislativa.* Brasília, Serviço Gráfico do Senado Federal, 7 (27), p. 133, jul./set., 1970.

30. MUNHOZ NETTO, Alcides. Criminosos habituais e por tendência. In: *Revista de Direito Penal,* 9 (15/16), p.24, jul./ten., 1974

31. Regarding this subject, we recommend the modern work by SAIZ, Ignacio Lopes e CODON, José Maria. *Psiquiatria jurídica penal and civil.* Burgos, Ediciones Aldecoa, 1969, t. 2, 3. ed., p. 563-7.

32. DELGADO, Honorio. *Curso de psiquiatria; psicopatologia-psiquiatria especial.* Barcelona, Editorial Científico-Médica, 1978, p. 17.

33. SCHNEIDER, Kurt. *Psicopatologia clínica.* Trans. by Emanuel Carneiro Leão. São Paulo, Editora Mestre Jou, p. 43.

34. SCHNEIDER, Kurt. *Psicopatologia clínica.* Trans. by Emanuel Carneiro Leão. São Paulo, Editora Mestre Jou, 1976, p. 29-30.

35. LANGELÜDDEKE, Albrecht. *Psiquiatria forense.* Trans. by Luis Beneytez Merino, Madrid, Editorial Espasa-Calpe, 1972, p. 508-9.

36. DELGADO, Honório. *La personalidad y caracter.* Barcelon Editorial Científico-Médica, 1966, p. 132.

37. That affirmation, contained in several studies on psychopathology, is highlighted in the work of Hans Göppinger, one of the greatest names in current Criminology. Consult: GÖPPINGER, Hans. *Criminologia.* Trans. by Maria Luiza Schwarch e Ignácio Luzarraga Castro. Madrid, Instituto Editorial Reus, 1975, p. 133.

38. SCHNEIDER, Kurt. *Lições de psiquiatria para médicos.* Trans. by Fernando Ferreira São Paulo, Editora Livraria Acadêmica Saraiva, 1936, p. 38.

39. SCHNEIDER, Kurt. *Lições de psiquiatria para médicos.* Trans. by Fernando Ferreira. São Paulo, Editora Livraria Acadêmica Saraiva, 1936, p. 52.

40. SCHNEIDER, Kurt. *Psicopatologia clínica.* Trans. by Emanuel Carneiro Leão. São Paulo, Editora Mestre Jou, 1976, p. 63-74.

41. TULLIO, Benigno Di. *Principi di criminologia clinica e di psichiatria forense.* Roma, Instituto de Medicina Sociale, 1958, p. 131.

42. SCHNEIDER, Kurt. *Lições de psiquiatria para médicos.* Trans. by Fernando Ferreira. São Paulo, Editora Livraria Acadêmica Saraiva, 1936, p. 46.

43. Besides that passage, the explanations presented by Professor Hilário Veiga de Carvalho are in harmony with our position. Regarding aspects of the hypothesis situated here, consult: CARVALHO, Hilário Veiga de. *Compêndio de criminologia.* São Paulo, José Bushatsky, Editor, 1973, p. 80-1.

44. TULLIO, Benigno Di. Le Problème de la constitution delinquentielle par rapport à l'état dangereux. In: *Conferénces du II Cours International de Criminologie.* Paris, Imprimerie Administrative, 1953, p. 73-94.

Observation: In supporting the formulation of "crimino-impellent" or "crimino-repellent" factors, we do not wish with this to defend the theory of delinquent constitution, which indicates a state of predisposition towards wrongdoing and was proposed by Benigno Di Tullio.

The thesis of delinquent constitution is one of the most debated principles established by the modern Italian anthropological school. Many authors understand that to admit the delinquent personality essentially means reviving the failed concept of congenital criminal. In this regard, the criticism seems to have grounds, for if a delinquent constitution is identified in an individual and should that person, without any other motive, at least apparently, commit a crime, how will one substantially separate the Di Tullio theory from the ancient Lombrosian concept?

If, on the other hand, we accept the reasoning of the possibility that the delinquent constitution can receive the influence or collaboration of another cause, it will obviously be necessary to investigate the degree of participation by this other source. The pluri-dimensional analysis of the individual who fits into this situation will corroborate the thesis, which we have embraced, that there is no single specificity for practicing crimes, but the possibility of reducing individual resistance.

If since childhood we are oriented towards distinguishing good from evil, that is because the will exists in a human being as a fundamental characteristic, and, consequently, the practice of evil does not depend on a delinquent constitution but on human nature itself. The factors that may perchance act on the will of an individual do not lead to contradiction or doctrinal accommodation, but to a timely conciliation, seeing that humans can suffer a reduction of their will due to biological contingencies of their own nature or of the environment in which they have lived, live now, act, react and operate.

45. SUTHERLAND, Edwin. *Principles of criminology*. Philadelphia, Ed. Lippincott, 1947, p. 6-7.

46. One of the most interesting theories on the social causes of criminality is known as the "Differential Opportunity Theory" of RICHARD CLOWARD and LLOYD OHLIN who maintained the existence of three types of differentiated delinquent subculture: criminal subculture, subculture of conflict and escapist subculture. Criminal subculture refers to development of the "gang," which can be devoted to theft, extortion or other means for gaining unlawful advantages. The subculture of conflict, on the other hand, finds its expression in the group that manipulates violence as a means of gaining status. As for the escapist subculture, it is evidenced through the dramas of drug traffic and consumption. Regarding the Differential Opportunity Theory, examine: CLOWARD, Richard & OHLIN, Lloyd. *A Theory of delinquent gangs*. New York, Free Press, 1960, p. 150.

47. MACEDO, Gilberto de. Crime, sociedade, cultura. In: *Revista de Direito Penal*. Rio de Janeiro, Editor Borsoi, (6), p. 98, abr./jun., 1972.

48. Regarding this sociological concept, see the work of: BEKER, H. Y BOSKE, A. *Modern Sociological Theory in Continuity and Change*. New York, Ed. University, 1967, p. 16-7.

49. CHAZAL, Jeran. *L'Enfance delinquente*. Paris, Editora Puf, 1953, p. 88.

50. Regarding the linked of the criminal phenomenon to the cultural bases of the individual, we recommend two interesting works:

a. SOLIS QUIROGA, Hector. *Sociologia Criminal*. México, Editorial Porrúa S.A., 1977, 2ed., p. 210.

b. CARDOSO, Fernando Henrique & IANNI, Octávio. *Homem e sociedade*. São Paulo, Companhia Editora Nacional, 1971, 7. ed., p. 98 9.

51. BEZERRA, Felte. *Antropologia sócio-cultural*. Brasília, Coordenada-Editora, 1973, p. 203.

52. An excellent work on violence and aggressiveness has been produced by Franco Ferracuti and Marvin Wolfgang. In that work, aggressive and violent behaviors, more precisely in cases of homicide, are examined with a certain depth, examining the bio-sociological aspect. See: FERRACUTI, Franco & WOLFGANG,

Marvin. Il Comportamento aggressivo violento come fenomeno sócio-psicologico. In: *Appunti di criminologia.* Roma, Bulzoni Editora, 1970, p. 217-21.

53. LEWONTIN, C. Richard. Adaptation. In: *Scientific American.* Nova Iorque, Ed. University, 239 (3), p. 166, set., 1978.

54. JÚNIOR, Miguel Reale. *Antijuridicidade concreta.* São Paulo, José Bushatsky, Editor, 1973, p. 137.

55. FRAGOSO, Heleno. *Direito penal e direitos humanos.* Rio de Janeiro, Editora Forense, 1977, p. 28.

Chapter Fourteen

Importance and Usefulness of the Criminological Exam

Edmundo Oliveira

The identification of human conduct bearing a tendency towards crime makes it necessary to have an overall assessment of the highly personal conditions of each criminal, addressing authentic practice and real case studies that will provide guidance to be followed in the treatment indicated, among the options offered by the penitentiary policy existing in the system.

With the concrete purpose of examining every hypothesis as to criminal type, no work can do without an important role for the scientific evolution of criminological investigation methods. Thus, having in mind our precise objectives, the overall picture of a criminal personality that has a special inclination towards crime will never be dictated with positive certain without the legal performance of a holomorphic exam.

Investigating anomalies, whatever they may be, through analysis of endogenous and exogenous factors is a primordial function of modern clinical Criminology and solidifies the ever growing alliance between Criminal Law and the other sciences concerned with the discovery of so many enigmas directly or indirectly linked to human life.

ORIGIN AND EVOLUTION

Although the pioneers of criminology were already considering the possibility of carrying out an exhaustive exam of prognostics on the somatic, psychic and moral disturbances of criminals, Judge Álvaro Mayrink da Costa reminds us that historically, "their necessity was affirmed for the first time by Lombroso at the International Penitentiary Congress in Saint Petersburg, in 1890, with the social *enquête* being praised at the same time by Garofalo, who noted that in the Anglo-Saxon countries and in the context of the Probation system, the practice of the social *enquête* had already been practiced for a long time."[1]

By the 1940s, specialists in penal and extrapenal sciences had begun to dedicate decisive support to the improvement of mechanisms destined to the most effective investigation of the delinquent's personality. By way of illustration, the issue received special attention at the following international congresses:

I International Congress on Social Defense (Liège, 1949);
II International Congress on Criminology (Paris, 1950);
VI International Congress on Criminal Law (Rome, 1953);
III International Congress on Criminology (London, 1955);
I French Congress on Criminology (Lyon, 1960);
XI International Congress of Criminal Law (Budapest);
V Congress of the United Nations for the Prevention of Crime and Treatment of Offenders (Geneva, 1975).

Praise is also due for the useful work that the International Society for Criminal Law and the International Society of Criminology have been developing in this sector, either by organizing courses or by cooperating with the UN and with governments interested in implanting penal and penitentiary policy in each nation, according to conveniences and possibilities.

LEGITIMACY AND APPROPRIATENESS OF THE EXAM

The exam, which appears in French legislation with the name of *Examen Medical Psychologique,* is forbidden in the Italian Code. Those two orientations derive exactly from the existence of favorable and unfavorable arguments, as we will present below.

There are those who maintain that the criminological exam is illegitimate, while others defend their use because of the need for investigating the personality in order to be able to efficiently measure the criminal's dangerousness.

When the *Convegno Nazionale de Alcune Fra Lê Più Urgenti Riforme della Procedura Penale* was held in Italy, on November 28, 1953 and presided over by Enrico Nicola, the issue of the scientific exam of the delinquent's personality came up for debate. In that session, two scholars highly regarded by judicial science in Italy questioned aspects of the problem in depth. On the one hand, Frei Agostino Gemelli brought arguments against the criminological exam, and on the other, Professor Pietro Nuvolone defended the thesis of the legitimacy and appropriateness of the examination.

Frei Gemelli brought reasons against the criminological exam that we will now present.

First, he maintained that before sentencing, the defendant has not yet been condemned, and may even be innocent, and thus, no one, not even the State, has the right to violate his or her intimacy, to want to penetrate his or her soul. State power, even when criminally prosecuting someone, does not reach the defendant's intimacy.

Second, he argued that the criminological exam would violate the guarantees given to the accused in interrogation. The Criminal Proceedings Code declares that the accused is not obliged to respond to questions asked during the interrogation. It also gives the defendant the freedom even to lei and not allow the judge to use mechanical means such as the Lie Detector, or psychic means such as hypnotism, or chemical means such as truth serum and brainwashing. The Code philosophy then, is not to violate the defendant's intimacy and avoid the inconsistency of prohibiting constraint at one point and later on allow constraint of the defendant by the judge.

Now, said Gemelli, if all of those guarantees are given to the accused and later they are allowed to be submitted to a criminological exam, that means annulling those guarantees, since the law contradicts itself, when at one point it keeps the accused from being constrained and at the other allows the deepest corners of the human soul to be dug up.

The able Italian scholar further said that, for the criminological exam to be effective, it would be necessary to examine the defendants in their normal daily habitat, their customary life. If we place a delinquent in a prison, hospital or clinic, isolation makes the environment totally artificial and does not allow us to know how he or she is or how he or she will react to society. All of this would make the criminological exam very precarious.

Finally, for Gemelli the very fact of someone being prosecuted and know the risk of a condemnation already alters the individual's personality. Any one of us, who enjoys the concept of being a normal person, a good person, is not free from being prosecuted, even unjustly. The simple threat provokes inside of us a natural reaction to the possibility of becoming a defendant in a criminal suit; so it is easy to understand that the fact of a person being *sub judice* is already sufficient to alter one's personality. The criminological examination thus cannot achieve its objective, since it is very difficult to get someone to behave naturally when the precious value of liberty is at stake.

Many authors took a position in favor of the criminological exam, notably Pietro Nuvolone, who at the *Convegno Nazionale* of 1953, laid the foundations for justifying the appropriateness of a scientific investigation into the delinquent's personality.

Nuvolone's main reasons for defending the criminological analysis were the following:

He first affirmed that the legislators, in limiting the exam to verifying the capacity to understand the unlawful nature of the fact and to decide according to that understanding, ignored the fact that the action is indissolubly linked to the defendant's entire personality and not only to intelligence and the will. The crime, Nuvolone continued, is an episode in a soap opera, which can only be understood in connection with the life of its practitioner. That means it is not enough to confirm that the person practiced that fact; it is necessary to link that fact to all of the rest of the agent's life, in order to be able to form an overall judgment of his or her personality.

Secondly, Nuvolone maintained that the law itself, when it distinguished the categories of criminal: habitual, professional and by tendency, did so with the purpose of allowing a specialist to opine regarding the qualification of the criminal. That specialist is not a judge, who is not obliged to be a specialist in Criminology. But the criminal judge needs enlightened advice given by a doctor, psychologist, sociologist, anthropologist, social worker and other technicians who will say if the defendant has or not the tendency to wrongdoing, if he or she is or is not perverse, if the fact practiced was an isolated act in the person's life.

Nuvolone's third point is based on the idea that it is not enough to examine the conscious, when the influence of the unconscious is obvious. It is thus necessary to make use of scientific processes for analyzing the mind, in order for the judge to have precise information regarding what is in the defendant's unconscious. Obtaining those data requires great effort, given that it depends on a certain dose of goodwill from the defendant, and, furthermore, few countries are prepared to precisely investigate the defendant's inner world.

In the fourth place, Nuvolone says that the auxiliary sciences for Criminal Law, among them psychology, sociology, anthropology and psychiatry, acting like true lenses, have created methods of observation that have made it possible to increase the vision of human actions. Even at the interrogation, when before the accused, the judge does not see many things that at that moment are going unperceived. Such details would certainly not escape the attention of an anthropologist, a psychologist, a sociologist. Thus, it is appropriate for the judge to be enlightened, when necessary, and always be able to count on the decisive collaboration of specialists of interest.

The fifth argument has to do with the law's inconsistency, in, on the one hand, gives guarantees to the defendant and on the other, allows investigation of his or her intimate life. Nuvolone teaches that the inconsistency exists in countries that allow a criminological exam in a minor and do not permit the same exam in someone of legal age. Now, if a code determines the investigation of a minor by sociologists, social workers and psychologists, there is an even stronger reason for allowing the person of age to be the focus of the same exam.

Regarding the violation of intimacy, the notable scholar taught that it can be avoided by establishing norms that limit the exam to given points.

To override the inconvenient points of the criminological exam, Pietro Nuvolone proposed a formula supported on two basic points:

1. that the experts only examine the accused if he or she consents and upon authorization by the judge;
2. that the exam be attended by the judge.

One cannot deny, after this succinct analyses of the pros and cons, that the criminological investigation has both advantages and inconvenient points.

Nuvolone's final formula tends to restrict the exam for two reasons. First, because it is very improbable that the defendant will want to be exposed and consent to investigation. Second, because in no part of the world are there judges in sufficient numbers, with availability to accompany, in each situation, an entire process that by its very nature is complex and demands time for interning the accused, assessing the results, and for all of the possible eventualities inherent to the particularities that such cases reveal.

As to legitimacy, we believe that the criminological exam should be admitted, as long as it is surrounded by precautions to safeguard human dignity. It is inconsistent to want to ignore that the investigation will penetrate human intimacy and can even shake the person's psychic structure, but it is also absurd to speak of a typology of delinquents, without having a series of exams prepared for each type so as to identify their characteristics and recommend the appropriate treatment.

Regarding the appropriateness of the exam, we only make the proviso that one should pay attention to the real possibilities of each country. In Brazil, for example, the Draft Project for the Penal Proceeding Code of 1970[2] ordered that the exam be performed whenever there was the suspicion that the defendant was a criminal by habit, by tendency and so on. Now, this would be absolutely impossible in the hinterland of the country, where there are almost no material and human conditions to carry out scientific activities for investigating the personality.

It is not prudent to place in law a precept that will obligate the judge. It is better to leave to judge, in his or her fair conscience, the attitude of determining examination in delinquents or not. Fortunately, the formula that finally prevailed in the Code Project in Brazilian procedural legislation was that which determines the exam only when it is possible to realize it.

THE USEFULNESS OF THE EXAM

At present, inquiries as to the personality of the accused have formally acquired an interdisciplinary and integrated character, demanding that the impulses of Criminology stimulate planning and structuring of centers specializing in scientific investigations, of use both to the examinee and to society.

The Importance of the Exam for the Accused. That importance will be apparent due to the reasons we will analyze as follows.

First of all, it aids in setting an appropriate sentence, so that certain circumstances in favor of the defendant can be taken into account that would otherwise go unnoticed by the judge. The delinquent sometimes has motives, some of them unconscious, which, if they did not lead to the crime, at least collaborated in the criminal act. Those details can only be identified by specialists committed towards aiding the judge as may be necessary.

In the second place, the exam is of interest to the defendant in that it provides the judge with conditions for ruling on dangerousness. It is not enough for the law to point out the items that the one judging should take into account, since it is crucial to have a reliable investigation to clarify the judge's doubts.

Third, for treatment in prison or in a mental facility. Because the treatment must be specific to the defendant, it is the criminological exam that will enable the employment of appropriate measures for a true personalization of the sanctions and the treatment indicated.

One of the major goals in the current scientific period of penal execution is to have knowledge of psychobiological and social indexes on recuperating criminals and determining them based on congruent foundations with a view towards individualization. In reality, recuperation indexes cannot be those resulting from a simple administrative criterion or the exclusive domain of penitentiary regulations. Quite to the contrary, they must be exclusively technical, derived from knowledge of the complete personality of the delinquents, and must only be determined through bio-typological investigation.

Administrative discretion alone can only be supported by witnessing the prisoner's behavior, but that indicator is decidedly unreliable, as in the great majority of cases it is falsified by considering that good conduct manifested by the delinquent results only from an objective view of behavior that has been compelled to be expressed in that manner in the prison environment.

The fourth argument considers the criminological exam as indispensable for the assistance to be given to the convicts after they are freed. After serving the sentence, the departing prisoner, generally feeling discouraged and resentful, without assistance from an efficient supervisory agent, leaves the prison convinced that daily life will be a series of unfortunate events. That is one of the serious problems with penal execution, since the State has the judicial duty of seeing to it that departing prisoners leave prison completely cured of their anomalies, or at least with a treatment underway that will give them hope of being freed from their ills. To this end, the defendant should be guaranteed the right to a complete criminological exam, that will make it possible to carry on the treatment, even if it lasts for his or her entire life.

The Importance of the Exam for Society. For society the criminological exam is absolutely necessary for establishing a general prevention policy. To put it into effect we need to know the environment in which people live, the crimes that are most often committed, the most common propensities, in order to carry out the appropriate measures. That is one of the most relevant tasks in common Justice, meaning, to determine as the case may be, the appropriate punishment that will allow safe protection of society and the social and moral rehabilitation of the delinquent.

To fulfill this sacred duty, a new orientation within Criminal law was established with the *Social Defense* movement, begun by Filippo Gramatica, when in 1945 he founded the International Center for Social Defense, in Genoa. In France, the movement begun by Gramatica was later enriched with new principles and led by Marc Ancel, who called it *New Social Defense.*

Gramatica's proposals for substituting sentences with preventive, educational and curative measures, for the establishment of those measures related to subjective anti-sociability are the clear differences between the positions of Filippo Gramatica and Marc Ancel.[3]

The *New Social Defense* vigorously opposed the doctrines that intended to suppress Criminal Law as a judicial system. The considerations commended by Marc Ancel defend a criminal policy directed towards improving Law and the ever growing adaptation of anti-criminal reaction to the combined needs of the individual and of society, the objects and subjects of protection.[4]

THE ESSENCE OF THE EXAM

The criminological exam consists of research into the concomitant factors of crime and the defendant's personal and family background, examining physio-psychic, psychological and socio-environmental aspects, to obtain data that will reveal a person's personality and state of dangerousness.

TECHNIQUES FOR EVALUATING CRIMINAL BEHAVIOR

The personality, because it derives from a series of factors that come together to form a whole, should deserve a multidimensional observation that will allow one to form an image of the person.

Bio-psycho-crimogenetic observation is as important as the dynamics of human behavior and the corresponding social engagement. In order to judge appropriately, the criminal judge needs to know about the defendant's family, professional and friendship relations, in order to construct an idea about his or her sociability and anti-sociability background.

Besides the collaboration of pedagogues, social workers, sociologists and anthropologists, the participation of a psychologist is extremely important, since in order to analyze the several elements that make up the personality, it is not enough for the psychologist to state the isolated characteristic of the emotional aspect, the intellectual aspect and the volitional aspect, but needs to specify how all those factors are processed and interconnect.

Making a comparison with chemistry, we could conclude that a personality is a compound, as is sulfuric acid. It is composed of hydrogen, sulfur and oxygen, and it is thus erroneous to attempt to proved that only one of those elements is sulfuric acid itself (H_2SO_4). When we combine two parts of hydrogen, one of sulfur and four of oxygen, we obtain a new body that is not any of its components. To analyze that new body, we need to verify all of its components, which result in a synthesis, in the same way as happens with the personality.

To evaluate the personality, psychologists generally divide the existing techniques into three classes: subjective, objective and projective.

Among the subjective techniques are all forms of self-description, through self-evaluation, autobiography, diary, letters and literary composition.[5]

The objective techniques include both physiological measures and behavior observed in a laboratory or in daily situations, assessments made by third parties and other scientific experiments.[6]

Projective techniques are of three types: expressive-motor (gestures and letters), structural-perceptive (interpretation of figures) and dynamic-perceptive (use of narration or dissertation).[7]

Subjective Techniques. Among the personal documents, the process of self-evaluation allows the person to make an examination of conscience and give a deposition regarding his or her defects and qualities. The examiner needs to exercise the greatest caution, since there are people who falsify or cover up the truth, often displaying a certain propensity, such as overestimating themselves of assuming a "victimized"[8] role.

When dealing with autobiography, it is also necessary to pay attention to the purpose that the author has in writing it. It may reveal only a passage about the author's life, which will not allow one to reach an overall conclusion on his or her character. It is thus necessary to always verify the examinee's inclination when analyzing the documents, which are always in the first person, since the author generally will seek not to reveal anything that will testify against him or her, or does not speak of some happening whose episodes might be important in analyzing the personality.

The diary has an advantage over the autobiography, for in it the person really says what he or she thinks and feels, and because it is something reserved, that is not meant for any person to read. Its disadvantage is that the banal things in life, even those with a certain importance for analysis, do not normally appear in this contents. The ordinary, routine facts easily go unperceived by the author, who is more directed towards notable or extraordinary occurrences.

Letters also have their importance, but since they are directed towards someone, they have the same defect as the autobiography. In them it is important to pay attention to the purpose intended by the author, as well as to the important details that say much about the temperament and about other characteristic traits of the personality of the one who is writing them. Here are people, for example, who like to write letters and publish them only with a desire for exhibition, while others easily reveal clues that they have an aggressive temperament.

Objective Techniques. The objective psychological tests, prepared to reveal scientific data on human behavior, may be classified into two major groups: intelligence tests and character tests.

Intelligence tests are divided into those for children and those for adults. To measure intelligence in children there is the *Binet-Simon* test, and for adults the *Wechsler-Bellevue* scale of intelligence is employed.

In the *Binet-Simon* test[9] a child age five to six should be capable of making a picture identical to the one shown to it; at seven it should recognize four colors exhibited, show its right hand, left ear and describe a simple engraving; if the child is 10 years old, it should know how to organize five boxes of the same appearance and volume by weight, and should critique absurd phrases; at twelve, the child should be able to say sixty words in three minutes.

The *Wechsler-Bellevue* test,[10] for adults, also allows us to establish an intellectual quotient, whose value is strictly quantitative. The interpretation of those results must be prudent, and take into account the individual's biological characteristics and those of the social group in which he or she is situated. The intelligence tests are completed with particular tests, which, together with school tests, show evidence of intelligence functions (comprehension, memory, imagination, verbal adaptation), as well as of their depth and orientation (concrete or abstract, objective or subjective).

For their part, character tests have been applied in the United States for several years, in the form of questionnaires, objective tests and professional orientation.

Among the questionnaire-type tests, we can cite: *Woodworth-Matheus*, *Cornell Index* and the *Minnesota Multiphasic Personality Inventory (M.M.P.I)*,[11] which have the advantage of posing apparently insignificant questions so as not to arouse the suspicions of the examinee, and thus, to obtain the intended result.

Among the objective-type tests is the Hartshorn and May ethical sense method, which delimits the moral level and the honest or dishonest character of the person.[12]

The professional orientation exam essentially consists of the study of certain intellectual attitudes (vocabulary, calculation, attention) the sensory functions, the skill level and professional interests. One of the great advantages of this test, quite often used in Europe, by the way, consists in indicating the degree of average morality exhibited by the individual in all of his or her ethical attitudes. Sinoir reminds us that, from the social point of view, those tests are very important, considering that "frequently there are individuals who enter the path of crime because they ignore their intimate vocation."[13]

Projective Techniques. In the study of those techniques, a very important element in evaluating the personality, which is being emphasized by psychology, is the expressive behavior.

In the psychological examination, psychomotor assessment is done through the word and the gesture. From gesticulation we can know if an individual is tranquil or agitated. Gestures are a form of language, especially for the great orators and for those who abundantly employ this method in the theater, to perform their roles.

Modern psychologists, among them Allport and Vernon, maintain that the way in which we practice the act is much more important than the act practiced, for the purposes of reaching a conclusion about the examinee's personality. A witness, when giving a declaration in court, can say the same thing in different manners, but even so it will be possible for the judge to observe if he or she is being sincere or not, or is hiding something or not. The way in which a witness behaves is thus highly important, since the manner of speaking, gesticulating, walking, reveals much regarding the person.

In children, expressive behavior is normally spontaneous, since the child does not know how to hide its intentions, while adults police themselves and have the conditions to deliberate before practicing an act, to weigh the pros and cons and to finally decide whether or not to practice it. All of those decisions are conscious and directed towards a goal, but the way in which one practices the act is the product of habits, reflexes and unconscious facts. In that way, expressive behavior, the manner of acting is much more important for evaluating the personality that the action itself. That which we do may be controlled, but the way in which we do it is uncontrollable.

There is a very curious experiment by psychologist M. Krout demonstrative that gestures translate what is inside a person, what he or she would like to say or would not know how to say. Krout[14] performed his experiment on several persons, reaching the conclusion that, for each type of response, all of the people revealed what they would be capable of doing with hand gestures. Many affirmed that they would not be capable of practicing a homicide, but their hand gestures denounced the opposite.[15]

To evaluate structural-perceptive elements there are the *Rosenzweig* test, that of *Rorschach,* the *Szondi* test and the *Mira* or *P.M.K* test.

The *Rosenzweig* test, also known as the "picture frustration test,"[16] consists of showing several persons the same figure, so as to project their visual stimuli and reveal traits of their behavior, as they evaluate the frustrating scene presented to them.

The *Rorschach* test, also known as the "*Rorschach* blots,"[17] is the most used instrument for perceptive techniques and consists of presenting the examinee with ten inkblots, five black, two in white and purpose and three in multiple colors. The observer's predisposition will lead him or her to say what he or she sees in the blots presented. An assessment of that test will reveal certain mental infirmities and generally enable discovery of characteristics of aggressiveness and need for affection.

For its part, the *Szondi* test uses the technique of showing the examinee a series of photos that depict a homosexual, a sadist, a hysteric, an epileptic, a schizophrenic, a paranoiac, a depressive and an maniac. In those situations, the subject is asked to choose, in each series, the two most agreeable and disagreeable types. The choice reveals what situations are approved or reproved, or the ones that evinced indifference from the examinee. *Szondi*[18] wished to show with his test, that the choices made by the individual denounce the satisfied or unsatisfied instinctive needs and the reactions linked to instinctive unsatisfied inclinations.

The *Mira* test or *P.M.K* (Myokinetic Psychodiagnosis of Delinquent Dangerousness) was prepared by *Mira y Lopez*[19] for the purpose of more precisely evaluating the degree of latent aggressiveness in a person. It is a simple and rapid technique that requires a pencil, paper, a special table and a chronograph. Evaluation involves the measurement of the variations in the examinee's hands, after performing a series of drawings in two separate sessions, if possible, after a one-week interval. The examinee draws six figures with the right hand with the visual stimulus, and later draws six figures with the left hand without visual control. The analysis of deviations in the two hands is done more precisely by comparing the last figure produced under control by sight and the last done with blindfolded eyes.

After several experiments, Mira y Lopez sought to find a series of signals in the traits of delinquent's hands whose frequency was statistically significant and as such could characterize the group. The *Mira* psycho-diagnosis is capable of indicating the existence of a dangerous state, through associating the examinee's super median aggressiveness with a certain degree of his or her excitation.

Initially presented by Mira y Lopez at the Royal Society of Medicine in October 1939 in London, this method has been widely applied by various specialists who employ it together with the *Rorschach* and *T.A.T* test, which we will describe below. The use of those three test simultaneously has made it possible to precisely identify those elements that make up the core of the delinquent's personality.

To evaluate the dynamic-apperceptive elements, we have the *T.A.T* psychological test (Thematic Apperception Test) of American psychiatrist Henry Murray. It consists of submitting to the subject a series of photographs, so that he or she can tell a story about each one of them. As the stories are being narrated, it is possible to verify: the degree of affectivity; if this is a tranquil person; egocentric or aggressive; if he or she manifests over-esteem; strong sensitivity or emotion and other behavioral manifestations.[20]

The examinee's capacity for intellectual provisioning is measured by using the *T.A.T.* test, since it enables the person to project his or her preoccupations, needs, fantasies, fears and hopes in the pictures. The resulting story says more about the person than about the photograph.

Leibniz employed the expression *apperception* in psychology to mean intellectual provisioning. Many times, we look but do not apperceive, and because of that soon forget what we have seen. When we incorporate something, we are apperceiving. Every learning activity is a work of incorporation that which will become part of a person's intellectual assets.

As the perceive apperceives new knowledge, it combines or clashes with what is already known. In the first case, there is only an increase in the general knowledge of what has been apperceived. In the second, that is in the case of a conflict between the new knowledge and the old idea, an intellectual process of critique, decantation and synthesis arises. One example will serve to illustrate what has just been said. Until the Nineteenth Century, some naturalists, among them Agassiz, Cuvier, Jussieu and Linnaeus maintained the theory of species fixedness, based on the argument that one cannot scientifically prove the unequivocal transformation of one species into another.

With Lamarck, who published *Zoological Philosophy* in 1809, the theory of transformism began to appear. Lamarck maintained that the action of the environment, habit and necessity little by little transform some species (plants or animals) into others.

In the middle of the Nineteenth Century, Charles Darwin began a long research voyage and later, in his book *The Voyage of the Beagle* made a critical appreciation of the theory of transformism, in which he corroborated Lamarck's thesis. Upon publishing his famous work *On the Origin of Species* in 1859, defending the thesis of human evolutionism, Darwin was strongly attacked at the outset because he clashed with official science and, *apparently*, with the teachings of the Bible. Gradually, however, those who apperceived the new ideas and began to look at them without prejudice, were able to reconcile them with old ideas, in a harmonious thesis in which fixism partly gave in and evolutionism yielded somewhat.[21]

Besides Murray's *T.A.T,* modern psychologists have lately been attributing special importance to the technique of psychoanalysis, which sees humans as dynamic systems of living energies acting at the conscious and unconscious levels.

The psychoanalytic technique, begun by Sigmund Freud, has the characteristic of indissolubly associating treatment and investigation with the objective of shining light on unconscious conflicts. Originally reserved for neurotics, and for hysterical and obsessive persons, psychoanalysis today is extended to the minor problems, such as inhibitions and certain character difficulties.[22]

The psychoanalyst must be capable of situation not only what the subjects consciously project outside themselves, but also that which they do not project, which are at their core and that interior censure does not allow to surface. It must be a reliable and meticulous work in order to retrieve from the depths of a person's soul that which is bothering them, be it a repression, a frustration, a complex, which many times dates from the first years of life.

Although it is a valid method for analyzing the personality of a delinquent, psychoanalysis in this field has its difficulties.

It is a lengthy method, which is normally developed over a two-year period, at the rate of three to five weekly sessions of an hour each. When the individual treatment intends to reach a global reformulation of the personality, it is relatively expensive and extends for five years, on average. Besides being a very lengthy test, psychoanalysis only produces effects when the patient is relaxed, and it is not for nothing that the examiners first of all see to it that the patient relaxes the body, because if it is tense, very rarely will the problem be discovered because it will not surface.

Now, in the criminological exam, the patient is under coercion, under criminal prosecution. That situation contributes decisively towards the examinee relaxing, and consequently complicates the exam. The scenario will be even more delicate if the patient is under arrest, because experience has shown that there is a barrier between the ideas exposed by the patient during psychoanalysis sessions and the stigmatizing stimulus of the jail environment. The jailed individually is generally a stigmatized person, who even after serving the sentence, as Erving Goffman teaches "will pay the high psychological price of covering up whenever possible, his or her personal identification, as social prejudice against the effects of criminal conviction is still terrible."[23]

The difficulties in applying individual therapies, including the high cost, have led psychoanalysts and psychologist to imagine a group treatment with special characteristic. Already in 1905, in treating tuberculosis patients in France, Pratt was utilizing what is now called *group therapy*,[24] which has the purpose of discussing, in a circle or meeting, the origins of participants' problems. The group observes the reactions and behavior of its members, comparing the lack of consistency of those reactions with reality. In an effective and empathic climate among the group members, the educator and the person chosen to be analyzed, there is an effort to determine the extent of the states of anguish, aggressiveness timidity or other conflict dominating the individual. Collective explanations have the advantage of showing the examinee that his or her case is not unique and that many identical problems have already been eliminated.

During the last world war, group therapy experiments were carried out in military prison establishments in the United States. After the war, numerous penitentiary systems have experimented with applying Group Therapy, and in the United States today this method is frequently used.

The inclusion of the dramatic movement in group psychotherapy, to give more emphasis to emotional and intellectual participation, is currently known as psychodrama.[25] Psychodrama begins where group psychotherapy ends. Its creator was the Austrian doctor Jacob Levy Moreno, who staged productions with his patients in a theater he owned in Vienna.

For Jacob Moreno, the perceptive aspects of the *I* of an individual appear in the spontaneous acting of a role, that is, a cultural unit of conduct: the role of father, of employer, of employee, etc. Individuals perform their roles in given situations, since the role precedes the *I* in importance, and thus, the individual always tries to live more intensely, within a personal world, when performing on a stage.

The treatment in psychodrama comprehends the stage (space for movement) and groups of eight to fifteen persons who act in sessions of approximately two hours. The examinee is expected to be faithful to him or herself, contrary to a real act in which the *I* itself may be sacrificed. The director's role is to select the episodes and modify the scene, according to the hypothesis for each moment.

When the changes in reactions of the individual, through employing the psychodramatic tests seek to integrate that person into a new situation of different social relations, we move from *psychodrama* to the method of *sociodrama*.[26]

Over the last few years, in the context of methods employed in treating social maladjustments, we have seen great development in the *reflexology sessions*, a new technique utilized for the first time by the Russian Ivan Pavlov, who performed his primitive experiments on dogs.[27]

In reflexology, besides electro-sleep, hypnosis is frequently used, because the examiners believe that hypnotism reinforces the positive data that please the patient, as well as those that are negatively disturbing. In many countries, the reflexologists are recommending their method for prophylaxis in painless childbirth.

The Interrogation of the Accused. All of these techniques that we have just seen, destined for examining the personality in the field of criminology and Criminal Law, should be accepted as having relative value and it is not proper to consider each one in isolation, since it is necessary, when possible, to perform the highest number of tests, in order to bring an exact and complete judgment regarding the personality of the delinquent.

One should also emphasize that employment of these techniques can never serve to depreciate the significant value of the interrogation. On the importance of this highly personal act of procedural finding of facts, here is the worthy explanation of Professor Hélio Torgnaghi:

> The interrogatory is the great opportunity that the judge has to, in a direct contact with the accused, to form a judgment as to their personality, the sincerity in their excuses or confession, of the present state of their soul, of the malice or negligence with which they acted, of their coldness and perversity or of their high and noble state; it is the moment to study their reactions, to see in a first observation if they understand the criminal character of the fact and to verify everything else that is linked to the psyche and to moral formation.[28]

The illustrious Professor of Criminal Procedure Law, Judge Jorge Alberto Romeiro, wisely adds:

> Considered thus, the judge, during the act of interrogation, will not clash with the defendant's instinct for conservation, contradicting him or her with impertinent questions in search of truth. The judge will simply hear the defense of the accused, sincere or not, conducting the interview only with that purpose, to later on confront the allegations made with other evidence uncovered in the proceedings and investigate the same, reaching a conclusion of judicial truth.[29]

It is especially because of the judicial value of the interrogation that, in holding it, all invasive methods must be avoided, because Justice does not have the right to rummage in the corners of the unconscious, or the power to probe the depths of the defendant's soul. The minimum of dignity cannot be affected, which is why it is not recommended to employ methods such as the *association* our *constellatory diagnosis,* the *lie detector,* the *Lúria process for motor expression, truth serum, narcoanalysis, hypnosis* and the well-known *brainwashing procedures*.

Synthesis of Processes for Evaluating Answers. The associative method or constellatory diagnosis (the best know are those of Bleuler-Jung and Abraham Rosanoff-Jung) consist in suggesting to the person being interrogated a series of words, some related to the crime and others without any link to it, so that the person can say what reaction they inspire.

Enrico Altavilla says that "the defendant's responses will linked, in the constellatory diagnosis, not only to the stimulus of the word suggested, but to the ones with which it associates (constellation of ideas)."[30] Experiences of that type have revealed that answers not linked in the mind of the subject being questioned with the idea of his or her guilt require considerably less time that those linked with responsibility. Thus, an innocent subject answers to critical words as quickly as to the indifferent ones, while the guilty one takes much more time to say what the key-words inspire, sometimes with disconnected or absurd responses.

The *lie detector*, also called *polygraph,* is a device invented by J.A. Larson, of the Police school in Berkley, United States, and perfected in recent years by various researchers, especially A. Wollmer, a professor of Criminology at the University of Chicago. Its function is to register physiological changes that follow a person's emotional reaction when lying, especially reactions in the skin.[31]

Justification for applying the method lies in the philosophical concept that considers the truth as an act of intelligence, practice without effort, without demanding an effort of the will, while for lying a person needs to make an effort. Every guilty person experiences some emotion when there is a need to cover up his or her own guilt, and that emotion, as with all special emotions, is accompanied by physiological alteration, be it in terms of pulse, temperature, perspiration, blood pressure or respiration, that suffer the influence of the psychic state.

The *lie detector* is a device composed of a type of wrist bracelet or handcuff, by a mechanism for measuring arterial pressure, by a flexible tube placed around the chest to reveal the course and movement of respiration, by electrodes connected to the hands to measure the action of the sweat glands, and by a tremograph on the arm or leg to flag involuntary movements. In the interrogation, direct or combined with the associative method, all of the reactions are recorded by a needle and the *lie detector* proceeds to reveal the truth of lie of the answers.

One should not attribute great confidence to this apparatus, since an innocent person, dominated by pressures from the accusers, fearfully, ashamed because of submission and the guarantees of an impartial procedure, may become involved by the same reactions that the effort of lying produces in a guilty person.

The Luria motor expression, created by Russian psychologist R. Luria is another process for assessing the veracity of answers.

It consists of the following: the examinee should beat with one or even two hands on the membrane of a drum each time that he or she answers a question. The pressure exerted on the drum membrane will make it curve, and the curve is always the same for each person, even though there may be a variation in the intensity of the trait or in the height of the maximum and minimum points. The curve is equal and only the scale is diversified, with the effort to repress a compromising response causing an alteration in the record of the curve of the motor expression, due to the appearance of an affective shock caused by the stimulus words. The *Luria* method, so well described by *Mira y Lopez,*[32] represents a great progress in analysis to confirm the sincerity or insincerity of the examinee.

Truth serum is a process employed by using barbiturates, ethyl alcohol and other chemical agents to remove the psychic brakes and induce speech. Regarding this method, there was the famous experiment by Dr. House when, in 1918 in Texas, he employed a chemical solution of two centigrams of morphine chlorhydrate and one milligram of scopolamine bromide to be used as a subcutaneous injection.

For its part, *narcoanalysis*, a modality for applying truth serum, consists of placing the examinee into a light sleep or semi-sleep, through a synthetic chemical substance administered in the body. *Pentothal* (sulfobarbituate) is widely used in an intravenous injection, done slowly until the point of semi consciousness necessary to elicit truth from the subject.

The usefulness of narcoanalysis for diagnosis and therapeutics in hospitals and psychiatric clinics has not generally been the same in criminal proceedings, because it is an instrument for violating the intimacy of the accused, as well as reducing the power of their minds, which does not allow a precise criminological diagnosis.[33]

As for employment of *hypnosis*, the results in criminal investigations also have not been satisfactory. Many times, deep sleep is not achieved, or if it is reached, the answers almost always have the content suggested by the hypnotist. Additionally, the examinee, if he or she can control the capacity for censure, faced with the threat of criminal proceedings and to hide the truth uses astuteness, cunning, simulation or dissimulation and is able to impede the hypnotist's work, frustrating investigation into his or her sincerity.[34]

Brainwashing, also known as surgery of the soil is one the most savage among existing processes to achieve ideologically false confessions and change, insofar as possible, the personality of the accused.

In consists of neutralizing part of the brain or the nervous system or in directing its functioning to a certain degree. This method, which has the characteristic of having its use almost always shrouded in the greatest secrecy possible (the Nazis and Chinese used it on a large scale), owes its functioning to achievements by Pavlov and his successors in the field of cortical-visceral medicine, particularly with regard to conditioned reflexes.

According to reconstructed history,[35] brainwashing begins with the dramatic arrest of the accused, generally at night or in the early hours of the morning, who is then taken, blindfolded and with hands tied to a cell, where he is stripped of everything and receives pajamas, whose pants have no cord and need to be constantly held. The prisoner is generally immediately submitted to interrogation, usually under a very bright light, which causes tension and fatigue to the eyes, so that he will be frightened and confused, and feel overloaded and emotionally frustrated from a physiological perspective.

The prisoner's cell allows not the slightest communication and only a small opening allows air to be renewed. Lighting is now very strong, now very weak, firm or flickering, white or colored. No news of relatives or contact with friends. The accentuated fatigue and tension lead to patient to gradually lose the notion of hours and outside time, not knowing if it is day or night, rain or shine.

For several weeks and even months the savagery continues, with the prisoner disfigured through the intensification of cruelties such as hearing voices, images appearing projected on the walls, flies or rats in the cell and one very precarious daily meal. Sleep at times is not permitted the tortured subject, everything with the purpose of making him lose the concept of things and not know how to distinguish values.

In the midst of this martyrdom, the jailers again take the condemned to other interrogations. Crude threats, slaps, electric shocks and horrifying screams leave the human wreck incapable of even the slighted reaction. The result is the inhibition of his usual habits and beliefs. The only means of assuaging his suffering is to admit his guilt in the accusation, confessing everything his torturers wish.

The partial rest periods between interrogations serve to disorient even more the poor wretch's habit systems. The interrogations impel him to confess, confess and confess. It becomes excessively painful to maintain the difference between patterns of truth and lies, justice and injustice, because the human body is overcome by the action of the forces of weakness, dependence and feat, that destroy any resistance.

If the prisoner is to strong and is able to resist all those barbarities, the inquisitors resort to electrical shocks, injections of insulin to burn the body's glucose and affect the brain, which then begins to accept everything that is suggested to it. As a result, the personality falls apart. After the physical and psychological collapse, the individual, like a robot, is directed by his pitiless torturers.

Finally, there is the use of the *Third Degree*, which is similar to brainwashing and became quite famous in the United States. It consists of the maximum employment of physical brutality or of any other form of cruelty in order to obtain confessions of involuntary adherences. We were pleased to hear the news that the *Third Degree* has been banned by section 38 of the American Law Institute Code of Criminal Procedure. The inadmissibility of the confession obtained by the police, as evidence in a criminal trial, is one of the serious consequences caused by use of the *Third Degree* method. Already in 1932, Edwin M. Borchard[36] pointed out in the United States sixty-five judicial errors, many of them resulting from confessions extorted through application of such an infamous procedure.

Aleksander Solzhenitsyn in *The Gulag Archipelago*,[37] impressively relates the painful consequences imposed on all Russian citizens, who, after establishment of revolutionary power in 1917, in the Soviet Union, dared to combat the regime or belong to any party but that of the *Bolsheviks*. The blacklists sent by the Party directors at the slightest suspect, a report from a secret agent or even an anonymous tip were enough to lead to prison and to inevitable accusation with threats and all manner of tortures.

Solzhenitsyn recalls automobile headlights to "illuminate" the accused; air condition that alternately put out cold and fetid air, tickling a prisoner's nose with a feather, the act of putting out cigarettes on the prisoner's skin, strong electric light in a small cubicle with white walls, sleep deprivation, instruments that smashed nails, the female investigator who performed a strip-tease during interrogations to embarrass the accused, the dungeons where an imprisoned man, naked or only in his underwear was enfeebled by hunger and cold (Solzhenitsyn, 1973, pp. 107-124).

To sum it up, all of the perverse methods we have just described, leaves us to meditate, appalled, upon the tragic paths traveled because of human cruelty and insensateness. Besides offending human physical integrity and dignity, they degrade the sense and majesty of justice, through the inspiration of implacable and contagious feelings of hatred and revenge.

The Human Rights Charter, approved on December 10, 1948 by the United Nations, is one of the most glorious titles that any person, regardless of nationality, has available to see to it that, before the universal testimony of consciences, no violation in fact will impede recognition of that person's inalienable rights.

It is the duty of all of us, regardless of race, age, gender and religion, to work for human dignity, indefatigably seeking to have the cries of anguish heard, and protecting the weak from the violence of the strong, whatever its source may be.

NOTES

1. COSTA, Álvaro Mayrink da. *Exame criminológico.* São Paulo, Editora Jurídica e Universitária, 1972, p. 115.

2. The Draft Project of the Penal Proceeding Code was authored by Professor José Frederico Marques on the revising subcommittee were the jurist himself and Professors José Carlos Moreira Alves, Benjamin Moraes Filho and José Salgado Martins. For its part, the committee that gave the definitive form to the project was composed of Professors José Frederico Marques, Hélio Bastos Tornaghi, Benjamin Moraes Filho and José Carlos Moreira Alves. The material in the project that is pertinent to the criminological exam is contained in articles. 391 and 395.

3. GRAMATICA, Fillippo. *Princípios de defesa social.* Trans. by Juan del Rosal and Victor Conde. Madrid, Editorial Montecorvo, 1974, p. 61-2.

4. ANCEL, Marc. *La Défense sociale nouvelle; un mouvement de politique criminelle humaniste.* Paris, Editions Cujas, 1971, p. 127-8.

5. Regarding the subjective techniques, see: Allport, Gordon Willard. The Use of Personal Documents. *In: Psychological Science.* New York, Ed. Bull, 1942, p. 39.

6. With respect to objective techniques, examine: Allen, R. M. *Personality Assessment Procedures.* New York, Ed. Harper, 1958, p. 498.

7. On projective techniques, consult: Frank, L. K. *Projective Methods for the Study of Personality.* New York, Ed. J. Psychol, 1939, p. 389.

8. Nowadays, the most perfunctory exams made on the limits of victimology allow us to consider in the fields of analysis not only the victim of the criminal action but the victim in general, in other words, any person who feels harmed by an injury or destruction of property. The feeling of the victim determines, to a large degree, the future conduct of the "victimized," phenomenon that is subconsciously accepted, desired and even provoked, almost always because the person feels unjustly treated in his or her environment. Cultivation of this psychic conditioning provides an inversion of concepts, such as the feeling of minimizing the criminal acts practiced, destruction of legally protected values and discredit in systems for executing the sentence. See: Mendelsohn, Benjamin. La Victimologie: Science Actuelle. *In: Revue de Droit Penal et de Criminologie.* Brussels, Veuve Larcier Editeur (2), p. 825, abr., 1959.

9. See regarding this test: Jampolsky. P. *L'Examen Psychologique en Neuropsychiatrie Infantile.* In: Revue de Neuropsychiatrie Infantile. Paris. Ed. de Groupement Français d'Etudes de Neuropsycho-Pathologie Infantile (3), p. 576-82,set./out.1955.

10. More information about this test: Moor, L.—Comparaison des Resultats Obtenus au Test de Terman et à l'Fchelle de Wechsler—Bellevue. *In: Revue de Neuro-*

psychiatrie Infantille et d'Hygiène Mentele de l'Enfance. Paris, Ed. De Groupement Français d'Études de Neuropsycho-Pathologie Infantile (2), p. 271-5,mai./jun.1957.

11. To cite a specific source on the issue: Palem, R. M. Le Clinicien Devant le M. M. P. I. *In: Annales Medico-Psychologiques*. Paris, Ed. de la Societé Medico-Psychologique, 1966, p. 35-8.

12. Regarding Hartshorne and May, consult what was said by: Lopez, Emilio Myra and. *Manual de Psicologia Jurídica*. Trans. by Elso Arruda. São Paulo, Editora Mestre Jou, 1967, 4. ed., p. 84-5.

13. Sinor, G. *L'Orientation Professionnelle*. Paris, Éditions Puf, 1955, p. 120.

14. Allport speaks with great precision about Krout's experiment. See: Allport, Gordon Willard. *Personalidade; Padrões e desenvolvimento*. Trans. by Dante Moreira Leite, São Paulo, Ed. da Universidade de São Paulo, 1974, 3a reimpressão, p. 577-8.

15. The language of gestures, of mimicry, is basically universal. In the mother's arms, it is the first language one learns, and throughout life that language is naturally used to express ideas emphatically and clearly. In Brazil two interesting works have been published on the issue: 1. Well, Pierre & Roland, Tompakow. *O Corpo Fala*. Petrópolis, Editora Vozes Ltda., 1976, 6. ed., p. 7-8; 2. Oates, Eugênio. *Linguagem das Mãos*. Rio de Janeiro, Gráfica Editora Livro, 1969, pp. 9-11.

16. Regarding the *Rosenzweig* method, one may cite: Cattel, Raymond B. *Análise Científica da Personalidade*. Trans. by Eugênia de Andrade. São Paulo, Editora Ibrasa, 1975, p. 136-8.

17. Greater details abou the *Rorschach* test in: 1. Bohm, E. *Traité du Psycholdiagnostic de Rorschach*. Paris, Editions Puf, 1955, p. 585; 2. Traunberg, Nina Rausch de. *A Prática do Rorschach*. Trans. by Álvaro Cabral. São Paulo, Editora Cultrix, 1975, p. 13-20.

18. Szondi. L. *Diagnostic Experimental des Pulsions*. Paris, Éditions Puf, 1952, p. 319.

19. Lopez, Emilio Myra y. *Manual de Psicologia Jurídica*. Trans. by Elso Arruda. São Paulo, Editora Mestre Jou, 1967, 4. ed., p. 222-30.

20. In relation to the Murray Test: Shentoub, C. Le Thematic Apperception Test. *In: Revue de Neuropsychiatrie Infantile et d'Hygiène Mentale de l'Enfance*. Paris, Ed. de Groupement Français d'Études de Neuropsychs. Pathologie Infantile (3), p. 588,set./out., 1955.

21. There is a vast bibliography on this issue. To cite only one among many authors who have written on fixism, transformism and evolutionism: Lahr, C. *Manual de Filosofia*. Porto, edição da Livraria Apostolado da Imprensa, 1958, 7. ed. p. 714-17.

22. Broader considerations on employment of the psychoanalytical technique are found in: Lagache, D. L'Examen Psychanalytique en Criminologie. *In:* Conférences du 1.er Cours International de Criminologie. Paris, Ed., Imprimerie Administrative, 1953, p. 488-501.

23. Goffman, Erving. *Estigma: Notas sobre a manipulação da identidade deteriorada*. Trans. by Márcia Bandeira de Mello Leite Nunes. Rio de Janeiro, Zahar Editores, 1978, 2. ed., p. 98.

24. There is an ample bibliography on the subject. For an overview, we can cite: Turns, Danielle. *Entretiens de Groupe ou Cours de l'Instruction Pénale.* Lyon, Editions Bosc, 1963, p. 31.

25. An interesting work regarding gthe psychodramatic technique comes from: Anzieu, M. D. *Lê Psychodrame Analytique Chez l'Enfant.* Paris, Éditions Puf, 1956, p. 175-6.

26. See, with respect to sociodrama: Ferracuti, Franco. Il Trattamento della Criminalità Sotto-culturale. Roma, Pubblicazione del Ministero de Grazia e Giustizia; 1966, p. 153-64.

27. Precise information on reflexology in: Cattell, Raymond B. *Análise Científica da Personalidade.* Trans. by Eugênia de Andrade. São Paulo, Ed. Ibrasa, 1975, p. 20-1.

28. Tornaghi, Hélio. *Instituições de Processo Penal.* São Paulo: Saraiva, 1978, 2. ed., revista e atualizada, v. 4, p. 12.

29. Romeiro, Jorge Alberto. *Elementos de Direito Penal e Processual Penal.* São Paulo: Saraiva, 1978, p. 110.

30. Altavilla, Enrico. *Psicologia Giudiziaria.* Turim, Ed. Utet, 1956, 6.1. p. 216.

31. An interesting study on the lie detector is offered in: Sasini, J. *Lie Detector Tests and Freedom of the Will.* New York, Journal of Criminal Law, 1957, p. 570-4.

32. Lopez, Emílio Mira and. *Manual de Psicologia Jurídica.* Trans. by Elso Arruda. São Paulo, Editora Mestre Jou, 1967, 4. ed., p. 204-9.

33. An essay on narcoanalysis was published by Schmidt, A. La Narco-Analyse et son Application Pratique. *In: Revue Internacionale de Criminologie et de Police Techanique*, Genebra, Edition Emprimerie Atar (1), p. 64-75, jan./mar. 1956.

34. Regarding the ways for producing hypnotism, consult: Delgado, Honório. *Curso de Psiquiatria.* Barcelona, Editorial Científico-Médica, 1978, 6. ed. p. 415-6.

35. A detailed report on the use of brainwashing in found in: Lipton, R. J., Thought Reform of Western Civilians in Chinese Communist Prisions. *In: Review of Psychiatry Wiley.* New York (19), p. 173-85, Mar. 1975.

36. Borchard, Edwin, *Convicting the Innocent:; Sixty-Five Actual Errors of Criminal Justice.* New York, Ed. Univ. Press., 1932. p. 14.

37. Soljenitzyn, Aleksandr. *Arquipélago Gulag.* Trans. by Francisco A. Ferreira, Maria Llisto & José Seabra. São Paulo, Editora Círculo do Livro, 1973, p. 107-124.

Chapter Fifteen

The Scientific Character of Criminology

Edmundo Oliveira

Having been the target of so many studies and research over the years, involving its multiple and varied aspects, Criminology has earned the title of an autonomous science, robed with handsome scientific production and having a peculiar methodological character.

Scholars in general consider the first work of weight in the criminological field to have been the book by Rafaelle Garofalo, published in Turin in 1885, with the name *Criminologia,* in which he presented a broad study on crime and on the theory of repression.[1]

Some specialists, more specifically those who are dedicated to criminal Anthropology, also wish to consider that Cesare Lombroso, well-known author of the theory of "congenital criminal due to physiognomic characters and traits" is the true father of Criminology.

In fact, the consequences of the Lombrosian theories, despite their exaggerations, were fantastic for the period. When publishing *L'Uomo Delinqüente* in 1876, Lombroso was a physiognomist at heart, so much that in Criminal Policy his doctrine enabled the appearance of the concept of dangerousness. But Garofalo, besides being the forerunner in adopting the term "Criminology." Was the first person willing to define an offence from a criminological point of view (for him, a "natural offence"), characterized as being an "offence against the fundamental altruistic sentiments of piety and probity, as possessed in average measure by a given social group."[2] The practical results of Garofalo's propositions, although defending the theory of criminal predispositions, transmitted especially by hereditary factors, were not the target of such heated criticisms as those leveled at Lombroso, thus giving him the benefit of strong sympathy that greatly contributed to consideration of his work as having the most substance published up till then in the domains of Criminology.

When one speaks of Garofalo and Lombroso, one naturally remembers the work carried out in the Criminology area by Enrico Ferri, a disciple of Lombroso, who became famous as the creator of Criminal Sociology, after publishing in Turin in 1881 his book *Nuovi Orizonte Sul Diritto e Sulla Procedura Penale,* which in later editions was published with the title of *Sociologia Criminale.* Ferri, who, together with Garofalo and Lombroso, forms the trio of coryphants in the embryonic stage of criminology, had the merit of being the first to distinguish, among the causal classifications of crime, the social causes (environment in society) and physical causes (the cosmo-telluric environment), although he recognized the predominance of biological causes (inheritance and constitution).[3]

EVOLUTION OF CRIMINOLOGY

The years went by and publications in the *genre* multiplied. In Paris in 1901, the publication of Raoul de la Braserie's work *Des Principe Sociologiques de la Criminologie,* prefaced by Lombroso achieved success. Later on, the Spanish professor Quintino Saldaña published in Paris in 1929 a work that gained notice with the title of *La Nouvelle Criminolgie,* although Saldaña had previously shown his aptitudes in the criminological field by launching in 1914 the work *Las Origens de la Criminologia.* One should also point out *Criminology,* by M. Parmelee, published in New York in 1918 and the excellent study *Criminology* by Edwin Sutherland (Philadelphia, 1924), reissued in 1934, with the title, still in reprint, of *Principles of Criminology.*

Worthy of attention in Latin America we have the very distinctive book by Mariano Ruiz Funes, published in Madrid, *Endocrinologia y Criminalidad.* Ruiz Funes was the great student in our America in the field of Criminal Endocrinology, which flourished in Italy thanks to the rich contributions of Benigno di Tullio. With justice, we also remember the sociological studies of Manuel Lopez-Rey Arroyo, in publishing in Buenos Aires in 1945 a work with the title of *Introdución al Estudio de la Criminologia,* a book that made him deservedly famous on out continent. In the same year, the Argentine professor Luiz Jimenéz de Asúa released *Ley y el Delito,* which contained a serious study about the endogenous and exogenous reasons that lead a personality to crime.

Shortly before, in 1934, Benigno di Tullio founded in Italy the Societá Internazionale di Criminologia and in 1938 in Rome organized the First International Congress of Criminology, which, because of its success, laid the foundations for the First Panamerican Conference on Criminology, held in Rio de Janeiro in 1947 and for the II International Congress on Criminology, held in Paris in 1950. These last two meetings were extremely important for the future of Criminology, especially because it was they who made it possible to organize all of the fruitful work undertaken by scholars in criminological science, a work that ran the risk of being dissipated during the fever of World War II.

Without the intention of exhausting the subject, three other great authors have a guaranteed place in any listing of the rich criminological studies: first, German professor Edmund Mezger, profound in the field of Criminal Policy, with his *Kriminal Politik Auf Kriminologisccher Grandlage* (Munich, 1933); second, in the field of Criminal Biology, the also German Franz Exner, with his work *Kriminalbiologie Ihren Grundzügen* (Hamburg, 1939); and third, in the area of Criminal Psychology, Italian professor Agostino Gemelli, immortal through his *Personalitá Del Delinqüente: Ney Suoi Fondamenti Biologici e Psicologici* (Milan, 1946).

THE CONCEPT OF CRIMINOLOGY

In ancient, traditional and especially in the more modern studies, we have observed that the definitions of criminology vary substantially from author to author, exactly because criminologists in general bring in their experiences from other specific fields such as Criminal law, Legal Medicine, Sociology, Biology, Psychiatry, Anthropology, etc., where they have already labored and given proof of their genuine scientific value.

Since the II International Congress of Criminology (Paris, 1950), Criminology has had the established task of seeking to find a new object to offer for applying the various sciences that compose it; establish a coordinating link between them, gather and summarize the ties obtained and hierarchically order their values for the purpose of developing a consistent and secure doctrine. Following the tendency of that congress, today the prevailing reasoning is to call Criminology "the set of disciplines that study the causes or factors of crime, in the individual and in society."[4]

The logic of characterizing Criminology as a complex science is thus established, supported by the thought that the specialist, before becoming a student of Criminology, already has a curriculum that will guarantee the prominence achieved. Consequently, it becomes difficult to conceive of monopolizing Criminology in favor of a single specialty, chiefly because criminologists seek to highlight those aspects of crime that are more closely related to their personal and professional training. Sellin summarizes the question very well: "the criminologist-sociologist must be first a sociologist and only then a criminologist."[5]

Certain unilateral positions have generated, in some cases, an attachment to the concept that Criminology is simply one chapter in a given fundamental science. Such an understanding has greater appeal among authors who see Criminology as "the systematic study of wrongdoing and of criminality, not in the legal aspect, but in relation to the processes that lead to social or anti-social behavior."[6]

In keeping with those deductions, some scholars, inspired by the principle that there are no basic differences between delinquents and non-delinquents, understand Criminology to be "the complete science of human beings." These are exactly the ones who broaden criminological investigations to the multiple problems of human life to then say that Criminology is directed to the "complete and integral study of humans with a constant concern for better learning the causes and the remedies for anti-social activities." Two authors have become noted for defending this position: Jean Graven and Fillipo Gramatica. Graven considers Criminology as "the science of the sciences of humans"[7] and Gramatica, who even proposed that Criminology be called "social phenomenology,"[8] says that it is "the science that evaluates the anti-social phenomenon as a human manifestation," a concept that is perfectly molded to the postulates of the Social Defense Movement, which excludes any criminal aspect in the investigation of someone who commits an antisocial act.

There has also been support for the idea of considering Criminology as part of an encyclopedic conception, given the ease with which it invades the field of other sciences. This thinking found major support within the Austrian School of Criminology, where it was defended by Kinberg, Seeling and Grassberger, as was explained by Hurwitz[9] in his work *Criminology*. In Latin America, the vision of Encyclopedic Criminology enjoys considerable support, as there are many scholars for whom the term *Criminology* is reduced to the expression of a set of disciplines involved with the criminal phenomenon.[10]

For his part, Constant[11] distinguishes a *strictu sensu* Criminology as an experimental science, directed towards the social and individual causes of criminality, a *lato senso* Criminology, encompassing theoretical Criminology and practical Criminology. That being the case, within the first category we would have Criminal Anthropology, Criminal Psychology, Criminal Sociology and Penology. In the second set we would find Criminal Prophylaxis and Criminalistics, also called Scientific Police Work.

One extremely interesting conception of Criminology, considered by many as being original, considering that what was in fact the first attempt to prepare a *general theory of criminology,* was what H. Bianchi maintained in his work *Position and Subject Matter of Criminology,* in which he conceived of Criminology as the Metascience of Criminal Law, because he directed his concerns towards Criminal Law. Professor Michelangelo Peláez, in maintaining Bianchi's originality, affirmed that considering Criminology the "metascience" of Criminal Law does not mean the loss of autonomy for Criminal Law, even though it does acquire lesser importance due to its positive-legal character.

NOTES

1. Before the Nineteenth Century, two important works deserve note as precursors to the scientific development of themes related to crime and to the criminal. In this first place is *Utopia* by Thomas Mores, published in 1516, in which Mores grounds criminality in economic and social causes, due to a relaxing of the moral order, resulting from the irritating and demoralizing ostentation of the higher classes. The second study was *Dei Delite e Delle Pene* by Cesare Bonesana, Marquis of Beccaria, published in 1764, which contains a serious protest against the unjust, cruel and arbitrary procedures of criminal Justice in his time.

2. Garofalo, Rafaelle. *Criminologia.* Trans. by Júlio de Mattos, Lisboa, Livraria clássica Editora, 1916, p. 119-20.

3. Feri, Enrico. *Sociologia Criminale.* Turim, Editore Utet, 1929, vol. 1. p. 189.

4. Fragoso, Heleno Cláudio. *Lições de Direito Penal.* São Paulo, José Buschatsky Editor, 1976, p. 19.

5. Sellin, Throsten. *Le Sociologue et le Probleme du Crime.* Paris, Rev. Intern de Defense Sociale. 1950. p. 527.

6. Mezger, Edmundo. *Criminologia.* Trans. by José Arturo Rodriguez Muñoz. Madrid, Editorial Revista de Derecho Privado, 1950, p. 20.

7. Graven, Jean. *La Criminologie et la Fontion Pénal.* Paris, 1950, p. 165.

8. Gramatica, Fillipo. *Le Point de vue de la Societé Internationale de Defense Sociale.* Paris, Rev. de Criminologie et de Police Technique, Genebra, Editions. Em primerie Atar (4), 1955, p. 679.

9. Hurwitz, Stephan. *Criminologia.* Barcelona, Ediciones Ariel, 1956, p. 25-27.

10. See: Asua, Jimenez. *Tratado de Derecho Penal.* Buenos Aires, Editorial Losada, t.1. 1960, p. 70.

11. Regarding the Constant's Theory see: Peláez, Michelangelo. *Introdução ao Estudo da Criminologia.* Coimbra Editora, 1974, p. 31-32.

Chapter Sixteen

Criminology and Criminal Policy

Edmundo Oliveira

The comparative study of positive criminal law in its functional aspect, reveals the importance of criminal policy concepts in each system being considered, because it is exactly criminal policy that confers on systems of law and criminal justice their own spirit and coloring, enabling them the be explained in detail.

The methodology of field research in criminal policy in itself presents a peculiar characteristic. This method consists, according to the comparative process, of studying the evolution, the current state and the future of systems for anti-criminal reaction as a result of their purpose, the means employed and the results obtained. It is not a case of abstract science or theoretical speculation, but of rigorous observation of the realities of criminal law and of penal justice as they effectively function.

However, a prior question presents itself and can be formulated in very simple terms: when we speak of criminal policy, exactly what are speaking of or do we want to speak? What do we have in our spirit and what do we intend to do? And how can we concretely and yet systematically consider research in the field? Only after clarifying those preliminary points will it be possible to precisely establish a consistent work program.

To be useful, such an examination must be primarily focused on a concrete level. One should void purely academic debates as to the exact definition or historical origin of criminal policy, as well as purely methodological, axiological or epistemological controversies, even though such concerns are in fashion. In the same way, we should not lose ourselves in frequent doctrinal squabbles regarding the fundamental bases of criminal policy according to the different schools (classical, positivist, eclectic, social defense, modern neoclassical). We certainly do not deny the eminent interest of those different problems at both the methodological and the comparative dogmatic systematization levels; but at the moment, when asking ourselves about the usefulness and possibility of *autonomous* criminal policy research, the first question seems to be clearly the appropriate delimitation of the field established by our investigation. In order to better specify our thinking, we shall endeavor to present below a general overview of the various problems which, in our view, should be studied within the perspective of the scenario we have just mentioned.

THE APPROPRIATE FIELD FOR CRIMINAL POLICY RESEARCH

The fundamental problem consists of determining the object of this research and the exact extent of the objective. Everyone seems to agree to consider that criminal policy, above all and indisputably has the objective of repressing crime through the means and procedures of criminal law (or more broadly, of the penal system) in force. Every system of criminal law, meaning every systematic state organization of a legal regime for incrimination and penalties is necessarily endowed with a criminal policy, be it embryonic, implicit or nor yet well developed in terms of penal philosophy. But, on the other hand, one may only in fact properly speak of a criminal policy, when the system for repression is organized according to harmonious guidelines. That is certainly the case of modern penal codifications, when they are methodically prepared. The research will consist, then, of extracting and defining those guidelines for repression, starting from positive criminal law. That aspect is indisputable; however, we should immediately ask if it is necessary to also understand this reach as an extrapolation of the repression regime *strictu sensu*.

The first possible area for extension is that of the criminal proceeding considered not in itself, but with a view towards the organization and perfecting of techniques for employing the repression system (which encompasses in part the judicial organization to the extent in which it is an instrument for criminal policy). That point of view has been contested by some scholars, who are concerned only with the penal dogmatics of legal incrimination and intend to distance their studies from questions of a procedural nature. However, if such an attitude can be understood in the field of pure science in terms of offenses and sentences, it cannot be justified in the terrain of criminal policy, which is the terrain of the system in action, considering that the criminal proceeding is precisely where the system of criminal law itself is put into place. That being the case, in a systematic study of criminal policy in action it will be necessary to include the problems of applied penal proceedings. For identical, or at least parallel reasons, one must also include in this overall plane of research the procedures and measures for penitentiary action, oriented towards satisfying the purposes of criminal policy (which differentiates this specific investigation from a study of penitentiary science as such).[1]

Another more complex and controversial question is that of knowing if the research should extend both to prevention and to repression of crime. Here is where the doctrines oppose each other and there is a considerable literature in this regard. This is not the moment to debate this question, since, to repeat, we do not intend at the moment to take a position on the definition, the notion and the methodology of the criminal policy being considered. It is merely a question of delimiting a field of study in which to usefully support systematic research. On this issue, we will limit ourselves to three very simple observations.

Initially, modern doctrine and especially French doctrine clearly tend to include at the same time both the problems of prevention and the repression system in criminal policy.[2] That position seems even more justified when we consider that contemporary criminal science is making an effort not to separate repression and prevention.[3]

The issues of minor offenders and juvenile delinquents are dominated by curative or preventive concerns, meaning preventive and not repressive, without, however, any punishment point of view being removed from them; well, is that not one of the fields that modern criminal policy has chosen? The issue of security, which is also an institution, or at least certainly a manifestation of that criminal policy, likewise situates itself on the boundary between repressive and preventive. Prison itself, a classic sanction of the repressive system, seeks to be curative or re-educational and every "treatment" policy in the modern penological sense of the term, effectively depends on the level of social reintegration of the condemned person. It therefore seems impossible to exclude the problems and methods of crime prevention from the field of systematic research in criminal policy.

However, the question arises of knowing how the far a "preventive criminal policy" extends, or can be extended. Since their first appearance a century ago, criminology and especially criminal sociology have emphasized the social causes of delinquency and the effectiveness in this regard of a policy that is not repressive but preventive.[4] And so, it is important to integrate the entire criminal policy, considered as an object of its own research, with social policy, which, for its part depends on the general policy that the State defines or at least adopts and pursues, in a given moment.

At any rate, if we wish to consider the concrete field of criminal policy, we can never forget that it is situated at three different and complementary levels: the *legislative* level, where the decisive options are determined; the *executive* level that normally puts into practice the legislator's choices according to the technical resources that "executors" have; and the *judiciary* level, through which the system enforces legal imperatives. The existence and the actions of those different levels constitute an important field for criminal policy as an object of research, as well as the reactions or attitudes of Public Prosecutors, lawyers, police and services that carry out the sentences. It will be equally necessary to consider the interaction between the different subsystems in light of the consistency or lack of consistency of the various forms in action, of the disparities or the opposition that may be expressed by those involved in theory and in practice, between the criminal policy that is declared—or officially proclaimed—and that which is concretely performed at the three principal levels we have just indicated. The appropriate field for criminal policy, as an open field for research, is essentially the field of positive realities in social life, and thus is eminently complex. Delimitation of the appropriate field for scientific research in terms of criminal policy thus demands as we have just seen, some prior explanations. The observations that we have just made about this subject necessarily lead us to raise the issue of the relations of criminal policy with related disciplines. At this point, we again run into theoretical discussions and methodological disputes, which, we will nonetheless not address. It is timely merely to rapidly determine some basic points, seeking only to rationally organize a program of criminal policy *research.*

RELATION WITH SIMILAR DISCIPLINES

The problem is quite current, because day by day we note the growing involvement of criminal policy in topics that depend, in principle, on action by other disciplines. This was seen, particularly at the congresses and colloquia especially organized by the International Association of Penal Law and the International Society for Criminology, or by the International Penal and Penitentiary Foundation. The same phenomenon can also be seen both in the work of the United Nations Social Defense Division and that of the European Committee on Crime Problems of the Council of Europe.

Without insisting on those different manifestations, we will limit ourselves to remembering that, at its Vienna Session in 1972, the International Penal and Penitentiary Foundation examined two questions—deviance and social reaction—which essentially highlight problems in criminal policy. At the Belgrade Congress of 1973, the International Society for Criminology dealt with evaluating different systems from the point of view of criminal policy. At that moment, among the numerous tendencies that were manifested (general criminology and clinical criminology, bio-psychological criminology or criminology with a sociological orientation), a tendency of a more recent origin known as "organizational" was, above all, concerned with the perspectives of criminal policy. The International Association of Penal Law, for its part, at its September 1974 congress in Budapest put on its program the examination of methods and means of criminal law. The presentation of the subject, as well as the discussions at the preparatory colloquium on that theme in Varna showed that this was above all a criminal policy approach to the enormous problem being spotlighted. The broad debates maintained by the September 1974 Budapest congress confirmed that orientation, and it was in that sense that the resolutions for the first section were prepared and adopted by the plenary assembly, which essentially consist of resolutions on criminal policy.

A few months later, two important scientific manifestations clearly revealed the ascendancy of political-criminal concerns. In the first place was the International Study Meeting, organized in Rome in February 1974, by M. Mario Zagari, Minister of Justice in Italy, with support from the United Nations Social Defense Research Institute (UNSDRI), whose theme was "A differentiated strategy for social defense against crime." In the second place were the First Workshops on Social Defense in Latin America gathered in August in Caracas to study "Planning out of social defense in developing countries." In both cases the problems were examined within the perspectives of an evolutionary criminal policy. Let us remember that in 1973, the Intra-Associations Colloquium of Bellagio (bringing together the International Association of Penal Law, the International Penal and Penitentiary foundation the International Society of Criminology and the International Society of Social Defense) had the central theme of the decriminalization movement studied mainly in its criminal policy aspects. It should also be recorded that the main concern of the International Congresses for Social Defense (of San Remo in 1974 and Paris in 1971) was always the rational organization of social reaction against delinquency. That happy union of all of the organizations specialized in criminal policy concerns obliges us to formulate the question as to the relations between the discipline that concerns us and that are equally linked to the criminal phenomenon and the fight against criminality.[5]

If we intend to move away from the arguments over theoretical definitions or the purely methodological discussions, to focus on delimiting the field of useful research in positive criminal policy, we will soon observe that from that viewpoint, the problem of relations with similar disciplines exists essentially on the one hand, with what concerns criminology, and on the other, with regard to the historical or comparative approach of anti-criminal social reaction.

There are evident and necessary relations between criminal policy and criminology. For some, criminal policy would constitute only one part of criminology; for others, the essential object of criminal policy would consist of integrating into the penal system the data and teachings of criminology. Our purpose, however, it merely to determine what criminal policy research presents related to criminological research, properly speaking.

The contribution given by criminological research to criminal policy raises some difficulties for which the criminal policy research needs to be prepared.

First of all, there is the reserve and resistance on the part of defenders of pure science or of fundamental research towards a discipline that openly seeks the practical utilization of data or scientific investigations. That will be the opinion of those for whom science (criminological or otherwise) is compromised—some will even say prostituted—contributing towards strengthening or improving the legal system in effect, accepting *a priori* the legitimacy of the State's legal order. Without going too far, and aside from any preoccupation, or any ulterior motives in contesting, that would be the fundamental difference in the vision of the criminologist and the jurists looking at the normative system taken as an object of study. It is only necessary to observe that, at that point (which would deserve a more exact examination), the criminal policy researcher, under any aspect, is much closer to the jurist than to the sociologist.

Finally, if the criminologists at times tend to refuse the judicial rule or institution because they seem artificial or weakened, the criminal policy researchers, for their part, are inclined to sometimes reprove the variations and uncertainties of criminological research. Criminal policy attempted, from 1880 to 1950, to extract from the work of criminologists the notions of dangerous states and of neutralizing security measures; later, in the 1950s, research looked to research into methods of institutional treatment. More recent criminology questions all of those notions, at any rate, the results obtained from the positions maintained by criminological science do not correspond to the innovators' expectations. Only let us remember at the moment that the important thing is to promote an acceptable coexistence between the two disciplines with a view to future cooperation, without the one depending on the other.[6]

Along the same line, criminal policy should view the institutions that it studies simultaneously in time and space. Historical research is frequently indispensable in order to understand those institutions within the perspectives of criminal policy, meaning, to examine the conditions of their birth, their development, their transformations and, should it happen, their disappearance. Comparative research is also very important, since we may speak of a "geography of criminal policy" in the same way that we currently speak of "judicial geography." The legislative, judicial or penitentiary experiences that are the most characteristic expressions of the modern criminal policy movement must be examined in the national or regional system in which they manifest themselves, and in the general context of the system being considered. In that regard, the method said to be *functional,* adopted and recognized today by many comparative specialists, is proving to be particularly effective.[7] As simple examples we may mention the treatment methods in Scandinavian countries, corrective work to substitute prison sentences in Western European countries and *white collar crime* as it is understood in the United States of America.

Thus, from the point of view of criminal policy, historical research and comparative research are frequently complementary, but it is important not to confuse them and even more important not to transform these three orders of scientific investigation into one. It is equally important in proceeding with such research not to intend only to draw from them the history of institutions or a systematic comparison of positive legislations. The exact difference between those respective fields can at times be somewhat difficult to establish precisely. The real criterion of that difference resides in the object of the research itself (which will be, by nature, specifically on criminal policy, history or comparative law) and on the means of approaching it (historical, comparative or political-criminal).

That critical exam of the appropriate domain of criminal policy research and on the relation between those studies and research in related disciplines makes evident the double nature or the double orientation of the research in question:

- On the one hand (specifically scientific orientations), the study consists, in principle, observing the criminal as it is (or was) effectively practiced in the various countries with a concern for studying as a social fact. Criminal policy research thus assumes the character of a *science of observation.*
- On the other hand (functional and prospective aspect), after considering the data and the teachings of observation, the research tends to extract the best conditions of a rational organization of social protection against crime. Criminal policy can then be considered more as an art than as a science, or, as the term preferred nowadays has it, as a methodical *strategy* for anti-criminal reaction.

It is necessary not to confuse—which, nonetheless has been done frequently, either intentionally or without our fully perceiving it—those two aspects of criminal policy research. It must be asked of those two distinct orientations are necessary, that is imposed by the nature of things, if they should be entirely disassociated, if they should be viewed as complementary, or if instead they are incompatible with one another or even contradictory. That problem of a methodological character will not be analyzed here, but it is necessary to understand that the research may not, at a given moment, stop questioning as to whether the scientific orientation does not run the risk, under certain aspects, of finding itself compromised by the search for a plan for positive reform or by the establishment of concrete suggestions with a practical reach.

As to the appropriate position of criminal policy in relation to similar or competing disciplines, a final observation is necessary, which is to highlight the specificities of criminal policy research. It should not be considered criminal law research, or even applied or comparative criminal law research, even though those refer to the structure and normative positions of the different systems. It is also not research of a criminological order dealing with social perception, the individual and collective repercussions of the criminal phenomenon and its essential manifestations. Even less should one consider research tending to expose or detail the doctrines of different schools of criminal law, criminology or penitentiary science in confronting the evolution of criminality. The originality of criminal-political research lies precisely in being separate from the research that those other disciplines investigate. Its exact value thus consists of isolating, from those particular and specialized investigations, that which has not yet been characterized as constituting the organized and deliberate reaction of collectivity against unlawful, deviant or antisocial activities that threaten its cohesion or its harmonious development. That essential specificity of criminal policy will, in our view, certainly manifest itself in the examination of two principle aspects of research in that area, to the extent in which it is a case of observing the anti-unlawfulness reaction as it really is, or in trying to define it as it should be.[8]

CRIMINAL POLICY CONSIDERED AS A SCIENCE OF OBSERVATION

In terms of this vast topic, we will limit ourselves to providing some explanations about three essential problems. To begin with, as we are talking about observation, how should one conceive of and proceed with that observation in the field that concerns us? In the second place, what is the field of exploration toward which it should be directed, that is, in terms of learning a concrete reality, what are the phenomena that will form its object? Finally, with those phenomena or those orders of phenomena having been established, would it not be opportune to attempt, always on the positive plane, to propose an explanation (the *why* and the *how* of the evolving facts) and an assessment (the results)?

The observation, as we understand it, in other words, the objective study of the facts, may be seen in two different ways.

1. *Horizontally,* it may take as its field of study criminal policy considered in a certain was as *global* as it is understood and practiced in one or several countries or in a group of countries in which an effort will be made to establish the essential options within the organization of the system for reacting against delinquency. It is quite common, in this context, to hear of the criminal policy in Scandinavian countries, or of the policy of socialist or capitalist countries.[9]
2. *Vertically,* the observation will not be dedicated to studying the general configuration or the essential orientations of comparative systems, but the positions taken separately in the different systems on:
   a. certain problems that bring to the attention of those responsible or whom we could call the agents of criminal policy, unlawful behaviors or criminogenous situations that deserve special care. One only needs to cite, for example, the problems with violence, with drugs, with modern economic delinquency (which is no longer that of financial criminal law of 1930, or that of war times and of the 1950s, but *white collar crime*, without forgetting the financial frauds). To this one may add the constant concerns with the so-called "classic infractions" such as traffic violations on roads, uttering worthless checks, shoplifting or abortion. It would be instructive to compare the problems of criminal policy for the years of 1885-90, 1925-30, 1945-50 and inquire as to the meaning of those variations in point of view as to orientation of the criminal policy in action;
   b. certain *institutions*, at least to the extent that they can be considered as being of "criminal policy." This is particularly the case of the halfway house, the interdiction of rights, personality examinations and the attributions of Penal Execution Justice itself.[10]

The object of the research in the field of criminal policy, or, in other language, in its field of observation, is broad and significant.

Criminal policy research should devote special attention to the General Principles of Criminal Law, to Special Criminal law, and above all, to the evolution of those disciplines in judicial science. The nomenclature or catalogue of infractions, in that respect, is of the highest interest and the variations of those infractions are particularly significant. Let us remember, for example that every modern movement for decriminalization manifests itself mainly in relation to the qualification, repression or non-repression of particular infractions. Besides, to be precise or more exactly to explain the exact reality of the anti-criminal reaction phenomenon, the researcher should be concerned with the police and judicial statistics and verify to what extent the facts qualified by law as crimes are still effectively treated as such by criminal justice.

In the positive penal law system, the object for observing criminal policy, it is also necessary to include the procedural structures. In that regard one should not forget from a political-criminal point of view the particular phenomenon represented by citizen participation in the public reaction against crime.

In effect, it is not a question of taking as an object of study the criminal law system discussed to a certain degree in a static manner even in its essential structures, but of restricting oneself to the effective functioning of that system. It is in those practical, daily and even routine workings that criminal policy in action manifests itself. As we have just mentioned, and without it being necessary to insist on the subject, special attention needs to be given to the effective organization and action of the different agencies of criminal justice, even outside of the judicial agencies considered in their own activity, and to the real powers and methods of police practice and the various agents who carry out the sentences.

The workings of the penal system, a privileged them in positive political-criminal research, should not remain isolated in the concrete environment where they manifest themselves, that is, the political-economic-social context that at the same time causes and suffers criminal policy action. It is not a question now of the state apparatus through which this criminal policy now manifests itself, but of all of the components of the sociological order that act upon human existence. We must remember, for example, occurrences in the economic and social orders, insofar as they reveal problems of criminal policy: the strikes, the invasions, the expulsions of squatters, the implantation of large stores or "supermarkets" (which give rise, in fact, to occasions or openings for delinquency), the advances of urbanization (the problem of large housing complexes) and industrialization (from environmental pollution to alienating conditioning of the human being).[11]

CRIMINAL POLICY AS THE ART OF ORGANIZING THE FIGHT AGAINST CRIME

We have just explained that the observation of facts, in other words, of criminal policy in action, of the experiences undertaken and the results obtained, was the prior and necessary condition for preparing every effective strategy for reacting against delinquency. It is equally true, from our explanations, that every reaction against crime, and more especially, against certain forms of delinquency does not in itself necessarily constitute a criminal policy deserving to be recognized as such. The policy of "an eye for an eye," the law of pure circumstance called to give immediate satisfaction apart from public opinion, "panic legislation" constantly intended for serving as an alibi for incompetency in prevention and for the failings in common protection of citizens, do not constitute a criminal policy but reveal, to the contrary, to the careful observer the absence of any legitimate criminal policy. If policy is, as Marc Ancel reminds us, the art of governing a State, criminal policy for its part can be consider the art of driving the resistance that the entire society should provide against crime considering that every art presupposes the employment of certain means to achieve previously established objectives.[12] Determining what those means are, and next, the use that can be made of them, seems to us to constitute the two essential poles of research into criminal policy taken as an "art" or as a "strategy."[13]

The search for and success in a rational and progressive criminal policy presuppose bringing together—or creating—several conditions. We many classify them into three essential items.

First, it seems necessary to assure adequate *preparation* for those who will determine and put into effective practice the reforms or new measures. This is especially the case with the judge, the members of the Public Prosecution Service, the lawyers, the administrators and the employees in related services. The lack of success with many innovations and the lack of success as well with some of the experiments are normally due to the fact that those who are supposed to apply them or seek them do not understand their extent and innovative character very well, or are disturbed by thought habits and professional routines that are not very compatible with those experiences, or finally, clash with stronger external resistance. We have seen that political-criminal observation must discern and measure those resistances; the art of criminal policy must have the objective of prevailing over them or making them disappear and research should serve exactly to determine the means of achieving that objective.

From that point of view it is appropriate for criminal policy to dedicate itself particularly to training for the judge, logically the first person to be called on to translate the abstract or general modifications of existing legislation into individual decisions. Some problems exist in this regard: Will it be necessary to include specialization for a penal judge? Does that specialization, on the contrary, not run the risk of locking the judge into a technical horizon that, under certain aspects or at certain moments will make him or her less available to accept necessary modifications? In order to favor the effective application of reforms, will it be necessary to associate the judge with some technicians or allow him to appeal more broadly to specialists in the human sciences or simply to those in social work? Will it likewise be necessary to consider recycling judicial personnel, lawyers, judges and prosecutors? Then how shall we insert that recycling into the organization, and, should conditions allow it, into the judicial hierarchy? How do we keep technological training and periodic recycling from becoming the elements of or present the threat of becoming a conditioning that is incompatible with the true function and necessary independence of a judge? How do we assure that the faults or gaps of the system in effect, denounced by observation of facts, will be effectively corrected within the perspectives of an authentic criminal policy? In those interrogations, there are several precautions to be taken and technical proceedings to be clarified. We do not intend here to propose a concrete proposal, but will limit ourselves to indicating the various points that will inform political-criminal research when it goes about determining the conditions for a strategy to fight criminality.[14]

Alongside, and perhaps even before training of persons called to concretely interpret the evolving criminal policy, it is necessary to place the information that must precede and accompany political-criminal action. Therein lies what is undeniably one of the essential means for carrying out that action. Initially, the action will naturally be directed towards those who have the initiative or the responsibility for carrying out reform, since it is essential to enlighten legislators and governments regarding the exact conditions of the problem and the consequences that may result from the intended solutions (experience will reveal that some measures are inapplicable or criminogenous). It is equally appropriate to inform the appropriate commissions or committees especially set up to study and prepare reforms, under conditions of scientific rigor that will precisely assure organized and systematic research into criminal policy. It is also necessary for those entrusted with applying the reform to be fully informed of its exact meaning and its possibilities for development.

It will be necessary, finally, to insist upon *critical and precise* information for the community. The criminal policy strategy must b e concerned with that information as a means for enlightening public opinion so as to lead the public to ask for or accept reforms scientifically recognized as necessary.[15]

A third condition for efficacy in an anti-criminal strategy seems to be a *prospective* vision of criminal policy itself. We have just finished underlining the need for forecasting and studying, in this perspective of development, the consequences of the options intended for extracting the best means of transposing them to the institutional level.[16] The deliberate utilization of a positive experience as a test of objective reforms is an effective process for clarifying a reflected action against criminality. The vision of the future allows one at the same time to organize the experience in the present and to orient it in light of the needs and the predictable necessities. It also allows us to discern the experiences and the concrete studies that need to be undertaken, as well as the hypotheses in which, to the contrary and with full knowledge of the issue, it is appropriate to suspend or stop experiences or attempts that do not correspond to the needs of tomorrow. In all of those issue research of a scientific character and level is unique in its conditions for supplying useful indications for determining an anti-criminal strategy.

The utilization of the means that have just been mentioned constitutes, to tell the truth, criminal policy in itself, to the extent to which it is organized and effective. Insofar as it is driven to act, it is the result of systematic studies regarding which we out to give an explanation. The research here will be based, on the one hand, on the objectives chosen for that utilization, and, on the other hand, on the concrete problems that it is supposed to resolve.

That being the case, every legitimate criminal policy is first addressed to a deliberate purpose end and it is exactly that purpose that distinguishes and defines it. In an authentic political-criminal perspective, that purpose seems to present two essential characteristics: it should constitute a systematization of the whole and should carry out an updating of the system.

The *systematization of the whole* is the characteristic through which the criminal policy opposes indiscriminate reactions.[17] Each reform should be part of a system or at least a movement in which it constitutes only one element, and the reform in itself should not be disturbing, nor should it be isolated or unusual in the general system. That demand is constantly forgotten by promoters of reform, who are anxious above all, when they can, to enact an immediate change. The result is the practical ineffectiveness of many innovations that although justifiable in themselves, remain useless because it was not possible to place them in the appropriate judicial context for receiving them. It is useless to multiply the provisions intended to prevent abuses in detention before judgment as long as a police and judiciary system subsists in which provisional detention is the rule and not the exception.

At any rate, an authentic criminal policy will only realize its objective through an *updating* of the system to which it applies. It must correspond to the conditions, the necessities, the aspirations and the scale of values in modern society,[18] and thus, from that angle it is perfectly conceivable to characterize the criminal policy by saying that its principle is the mission of promoting an updating of the penal system.

If those are effectively the objectives of the criminal policy, what is left is to see how they will be reached, that is, what are the concrete problems faced as to clarification of the anticrime strategy. At this stage of our exam, we can be content with indications that are almost schematic.

It is, first of all, a case of taking sides on a system of fundamental values and that from a double point of view: First on the basic values which the anticrime strategy intends to defend (this leads us to seek how to determine and appreciate those values and to go beyond the narrow scene of criminal law considered as a judicial technique); next, on the ways of evaluating the different criminal policy processes or regimes that observation of the facts and comparative analysis have been able to extract.

In the second place, it is a question of determining what acts or behaviors the anticrime reaction should arouse and the forms or structures that will be given to that action. Therein, evidently, lies the essential problem of utilizing the proper data and means for realizing the social protection strategy. Since we cannot provide here the necessary development for this issue, we will restrict ourselves to two brief recommendations.

As to acts and behaviors, we face the particularly current problem of the distinction (for which it will be necessary to research the reality, legitimacy and exact definition) between criminality and the problem of decriminalization within a rational system of modern criminal policy.

As to the determination of positive means of action, it will be useful to especially consider, among other things, the modern dichotomy that tends to distinguish two essential varieties of antisocial behaviors, presenting each one in a distinct manner of reaction: major criminality that demands a policy for neutralization or "maximum security" and delinquency with a smaller social impact depending above all on a prevention policy and one for recuperating delinquents. It is the general problem of what we call today the problem of "stratification" or of "differential stratification" and where the issue is not longer the question of criminalization or decriminalization, but eventually, the problem of de-penalization, meaning the types of reaction we can have in mind outside of the purely repressive domain or in place of the ancient penalties, especially privation of liberty.[19]

LIMITS OF CRIMINAL POLICY

We have already observed that criminal policy, above all as a strategy of combating criminality, goes beyond the strict bounds of criminal law, occupying a broad space at the general policy level. Some complementary explanations are needed regarding what one would call the natural boundaries of criminal policy, remembering that the problem can be successively viewed from an extensive or restricted point of view.

From the point of view of extent, we must first avoid locking criminal policy into a very restrictive concept or even definition. Von Liszt defined it as an adaptation of the penal system in the form of anticrime reaction to the personality of the delinquent.[20] It is appropriate to go beyond those restricted limits to see inside criminal policy the adaptation of the social reaction system to the particular conditions of delinquency and the general needs of society, because criminal policy is the science that observes how the different countries truly organize the fight against crime, in other worlds, the art or the strategy with a view to making this reaction more effective against criminality. That are or that strategies implies a series of options, of rational choices between different solutions or even attitudes.

It is not possible to separate crime prevention and repression from governmental programs related to education, health, food, transportation, leisure and labor. Some forms of economic development have criminogenous consequences, witness the identification of a specific "third world delinquency" exemplified by the proliferation of marginalized groups substantially composed of poor and discriminated persons.[21] Criminal policy research should not go beyond its restricted scope to reveal and denounce those factors of criminality, those noxious germs arising from an economic or social policy that is unthinking or indifferent to the dramas of the people.

Thus, some infractions, some antisocial or deviant behaviors, some states of social danger find their explanation not in the individual dangerousness of the subjects, but in their living conditions and their social conditioning, so that a criminal policy of "prevention of crime and treatment of delinquents" will not have legitimate significance and effect if it does not seek to at the same time, or firstly, to remedy those social conditions and that criminogenous environment. The anticrime reaction thus involves an action that must be situated, at least on a large scale, at the general policy level. Criminal policy research, or even simply a concern for it, tends to a natural and necessary attitude of going well beyond its initial boundaries.

To the contrary, however, the possibilities for extension and even expansion of criminal policy can be quite reduced or limited in some cases or as a consequence of some circumstances. It is enough to evoke two very different varieties with similar limits.

1. Initially, we should not forget that every authentic criminal policy, meaning one innovative in its efforts at keeping updated, arouses several resistances. Some come from traditionalists or followers of immobilism. Others come from skeptical spirits who doubt, by *a priori* determination, the usefulness or even the possibility of any change. Even others come

from jurists uneasy with any incursion outside of their habitual discipline, or those who mistrust an excessive "criminalization" of criminal law and criminal justice. It is important to know and measure all of those resistances and that should equally be the role of criminal policy research. That research (at the information stage) or that action (at the strategy stage) should never be timid, but instead, should demonstrate circumspection and believe in the force of criminal policy in taking on the attitudes to be employed for solving conflicts.

2. A second and even more important limitation, comes from the consideration and the respect that must be dispensed towards human rights and dignity, even if the anticrime reaction presupposes the use of some authority over the individual. In that way, research in the field of criminal policy finds in the social context, its notable role in the sense of contributing towards the efficacy of a fairer and more egalitarian justice, reducing the distance between the ideals of laws and judicial administration in penal subjects.

CRIMINAL POLICY AND CRIME PREVENTION

Penal Codes are generally centered on ideals of individualizing the sentence and on social reinsertion of the delinquents, which, actually, already was the tonic of the classical penal schools directed towards the traditional concept of general prevention characterized by intimidation with rigid penalties established in criminal sentences considered to be exemplary.

The effect of general prevention even in our days is exerted through simple social reproof of the fact translated into its incrimination. That is to say, the simple reason for the criminal law to express a judgment of reproof for certain conducts would act on the social collectivity, leading its members not to adopt it. One would speak in this sense of the moralizing influence of the penal laws, affirming, for example, that the legislation of one generation may become the morals of the next generation.

General prevention is thus one of the purposes of the sentence, for which reason the criminal laws, along with prison, which today is so discredited, include the considerations of being able to opt for non-detention measures that have the conditions to promote the effectiveness of the sentence dictated by the judge, although the sentences in which the political sense of general prevention have a decisive influence of the sentence applied are rare. Such considerations when mentioned in the sentence, which does not always happen, are always counted as one of the elements that the judge has in mind in establishing the sentence, and are always alluded to in vague and generic terms.

The sense of general prevention thus sacrifices the notion of special prevention, identified particularly with the goal of social and moral reinsertion for the delinquent. That disillusionment is notoriously found in serving a sentence that deprives one of liberty, where, in practice, the pedagogical notion of special prevention of delinquency is being systematically substituted by the idea of neutralizing or incapacitating the criminal: people are locked up in jail so that for the time in which they remain there, they cannot disturb the social order.

Because the measures taken in the sense of reducing the weight of criminogenous circumstances are not producing great results, private prevention techniques with accentuated use of techniques and precautions that make crime difficult have begun to prosper. Private police services, iron bars, sophisticated locks, alarm systems, bulletproof windows and so on are now in fashion. That new conception in terms of social defense has become an open challenge to the State's capacity to promote collective well-being with an efficient public safety policy.

On the other hand, it is good to emphasize that the extent of the general and special preventive policy has been seriously compromised by virtue of a penal system that is inadequate for the objective of readjusting the personality of the condemned to the standards demanded by the community.

If we try to concisely characterize our convict population—especially those who are incarcerated—we will see that it is a population with little education, with weak or nonexistent professional qualifications, mostly responsible for crimes committed against property, most of which are not particularly serious. The incrimination of such conduct, in practice, is circumscribed to the domain of common crime, which in principle is closer to the life experience of the poor classes.

In that perspective, the elaboration of a criminal policy truly appropriate for our reality will first of all require that we de-dramatize the problem of criminality and destroy the stereotype of the delinquent, which is usually identified with the thief.

To do that, it will be necessary to make it clear to public opinion that the individuals who are in the jails are not necessarily—maybe not even in cases in general—those who have the most damaging behaviors for society. They are merely the most vulnerable.

It is important to remember that the delinquents are not necessarily "marginal," as they are often termed, as if they were always predisposed to reject the values and forms of life that are dominant in society. They are only, and generally, people who do not have, in their concrete existence, lawful means of achieving such means of living.

In our understanding, one ignores that reality when one proposes, en masse, the idea of "treatment" of the delinquent, invoking the legitimacy of imposing certain forms of life—the ones that are dominant in society—on those who wish to refuse them.

This way of seeing things confuses marginality freely chosen and assumed—which should, in principle, be respected, so long as it does not harm others—with the marginality imposed by society. Setting aside certain borderline cases, the so-called "marginals," if they could, would most probably wish to have a bourgeois life in society: to have a house, money, an automobile, comfort, employment, affection and other privileges.

One should also not hide the fact that, regarding individuals who are agents of more serious and violent criminal behaviors, those that we could more appropriately designate as marginal, society has a responsibility for producing such situations. No one is born delinquent or chooses at a given point in life to become a delinquent, if other worthwhile forms of life are within reach.

There is a delinquency that is born in ramshackle slums, in need, in social inequality, in the lack of opportunities, in rejection. For that reason, society may not sit on the sidelines of the problem, calling for applying mere measures for neutralization and even for vengeance on the delinquents.

From the facts pointed out one may easily conclude that a criminal policy that has as its tenor social support for delinquents is more consentaneous with our criminal reality, not in its real configuration, but in how it is presented in the courts and in prisons.

Such a policy should be concretely put into practice towards those who have been the objects of condemnation, with special support measures that signify a positive discrimination, namely in terms of achieving housing, employment, health, education, and resolution of personal, family or social conflict resolution.

A policy if this type, to be put into practice, will demand active participation by the community, so that those who have been condemned will not be systematically rejected from the social circle.

To this end, it is essential that there be a community social solidarity effort, which through human warmth and supported by modern re-socializing techniques represents, in our opinion, the main banner in the victory over the agonizing challenge made to the weakened condition of execution of sentences and security measures. In that perspective, community participation is much richer than the long toil of reinforcing locks, installing alarm systems, hiring private police and paying closer attention to one's wallet.

THE INTEGRATION OF CRITICAL CRIMINOLOGY IN THE DYNAMICS OF CRIMINAL POLICY

1. The term "critical criminology" is applied to a vast and heterogeneous domain in contemporary criminological and sociological-judicial thought, encompassing discourses that are characterized by a new form of defining the object and the terms of the criminal issue itself, and in this way is distinct from "traditional" criminology.

In the etiological aspect, criminology is the science of the causes of criminality, and this has remained true, since its positivist origin at the end of the Nineteenth Century, including "traditional" criminology and encompassing more modern currents.

The etiological aspect presupposes an ontological notion of criminality, prior to definitions of its consequences, excluding judicial and social norms from the object of reflection, as well as the action at official levels and mechanisms that define certain behaviors and individuals as "criminal."

From the epistemological point of view the intention of traditional criminology to offer a theory of the conditions (or causes) of criminality is not appropriate.

The reification of criminality, produced by etiological criminology leads to the construction of the theory of criminality being acquired through the simple observation of a part of the phenomena being studied.

The labeling approach, under the influence of phenomenological currents, determines in contemporary criminology a greater emphasis on the mechanisms for definition and social reaction, thus creating an alternative to etiology, which is called exactly the paradigm of "social reaction" or "paradigm of definition." This, in practice brings about a displacement of the causes of criminal behavior in the direction of the conditions, establishing the process of criminalization.

The labeling approach has suffered criticism "from the left," denouncing three possible mystifying effects, to wit: a) the emphasis on definition may hide situations that are socially negative and involve real sufferings; b) deriving from the stigmatizing effects of the sentence the thesis of "radical non-intervention" may frustrate socially appropriate and fair interventions; c) attention to certain sectors may contribute towards the stereotype of criminality as a normal behavior of those groups and ignore the negative behavior of the "white-collar" workers and the mighty.

The discussion verified inside Marxism shows that even a materialist theory, if it is not dogmatic in relation to Marx, may broaden the paradigm of the labeling approach without falling into idealist mystifications.

2. One should not confuse technological reason, which is above all a point of arrival for practice with critical reason, which is above all a starting point for the theory. It is not a norm for action, but a norm for thought, and at the same time, the law and logic of the real. Since the real, meaning social reality is a movement, its logic is not static (logic of non-contradiction) but dynamic (logic of contradiction), that is to say, dialectic. One of the main achievements of modern thought, dialectic, is at the same time *ratio essendi* and *ratio cognoscendi* of reality.

From that viewpoint, the distance between the declared principles and the real functioning of the penal system is not attributed to error and imperfection, but that proposed ideal image has the statute of an ideology, and the functioning of the system is carried out not despite, but through that contradiction.

Judicial mediation between the relations of production and social relations in modern capitalist society (equal law) is ideological; it does not serve to produce equality but to produce and maintain inequality. It serves to assure, reproduce and even legitimate relations of inequality that characterize our society. And besides reflecting the unequal distribution of power and resources in society, it serves to reproduce relations of subordination and exploitation.

To resolve the contradictions of the system, technological reason positions itself differently from critical reason. In effect, the first is not able to act except inside the same system, seeking to advance and improve the current criminal policy, from a humanitarian point of view. The other assumes judicial ideology as the object of knowledge and seeks a perspective of criminal policy outside of it; it is not a perspective of rationalization, but a rational perspective for overcoming the system.

3. From that there arise two different models of social science and criminology. Traditional criminology, with its etiological paradigm, proposes a reformist-type policy. It is a level of the system, not a scientific theory about it, and thus contributes towards legitimating it. Even in its more updated versions, its function is immediately and directly auxiliary in relation to the official system.

For critical criminology, the positive system and official practice are not the addressees, but the object of its object. It is not its place to provide prescriptions, but to scientifically examine the genesis of the system, its structure and functions. Its action, therefore, cannot be the immediatism of traditional proposals, and the transformation that it inspires could only be realized in a relatively short time either if there were a social transformation where the interest of the subordinate classes could be really determinant, or, in another hypothesis, if the historic delay of the left and the worker movement were recovered through an alternative consciousness and culture for the subordinate classes.

It is not a question, therefore, of weakness, but to the contrary, of the force of critical criminology in the perspective of reform.

This will certainly perform an important role, which the legislators and the higher levels of authority cannot look down upon, but that is with the condition of avoiding, in any radical reform, any sectarian attitude of global opposition to the State and to "power," as if these were the monopoly of traditional or conservative movements.

For etiological criminology, the presupposition is that there is a natural environment for behaviors and individuals, which is distinct from the others: that would be criminality, which, because it is an ontological entity, would have possible causes to discover, in the interest of a practice for combating it. And such a concept is so rooted in common sense that to move away from it would represent a risk of appearing to be a renunciation of combating socially negative situations and actions. That is the case of critical criminology, which first of all, seems to challenge common sense. But in that case the contradiction between the theory and common sense is only apparent. And the arguments trying to prove the contrary are absurd, when they affirm that for critical criminology, criminality does not exist or have causes, excluding the possibility of combating criminality and its causes, and consequently, the hypothesis of a preventive criminal policy.

Affirming the "objective" existence of socially negative situations and actions does not depend upon the accepted paradigm and may become integrated into the more general process of defining and constructing social problems.

Discarding the return to the naturalist notion or that of the natural law of objectivity, one may examine the hypothesis that utilizes the combined elements of: a) a theory of construction of social problems; b) a theory of necessities; c) a theory of "free communication of power."

The official definitions and common sense may be considered as the result of an ideological communication, for reproducing existing relations of power. In that sense, "free communication of power" does not indicate a reality in fact, but a principle of emancipation and autonomy, inside the subordinate classes, for consciousness and political action by those classes, seeking the transformation of relations of hegemony in society.

Antagonistic constructions are those that adopt that point of view, in competition with ideological constructions, to define the problems to be resolved. One should not that "criminality" and "deviance" do not denote natural means but cultural means. Arguing, therefore, that the principal real function of the penal system coincides with the declared function of combating criminality is equivalent to admitting that the real function of the system reproduces the social relations of inequality and subordination.

History, especially that of socialism, shows that the exaggerated use of notions of criminality and deviance is not compatible with the ideal of a society of free and equal individuals, "under whose banner the proletariat set forth to take the Winter Palace." And that is not equivalent to a conception of deviancy as entirely positive.

The perspective of radical reform in critical criminology starts with the recognition of the unequal distribution of the "negative asset" of criminality, and constitutes, according to E. Resta, the "awareness of inequality."

Inequality does not mean only unequal distribution of the stature of criminal among individuals, but also means unequal response to negative situations and homologous social problems. This conception is formed equally by men and women on the street and the mass media.

The relativization of the penal moment as a technique for construction and resolving social problems means, first of all, their integration in a more complex extra-penal perspective of reconstruction of problems, assuming new integrated models, with new social tasks, through which—in the words of D. Pulitano—"criminal law can travel in search of a new face."

The natural function of the penal system is to conserve and reproduce existing social reality. A policy of transforming that reality cannot consider criminal law as one of its most advanced forces, as a driving instrument. To the contrary, criminal law remains a line of defense, at a triple level.

1. Defense *of criminal law* from attacks directed against liberal guarantees that are conferred by the States of Law.
2. Defense *faced with criminal law,* in a movement for reducing traditional intervention and the negative effects and social costs, above all in the weaker and more marginalized zones of the proletariat who have contributed to dividing and weakening it materially and politically.
3. Defense *through criminal law,* to the extent that it can still be considered a legitimate response to social problems.

Nonetheless, the regulatory idea of an alternative criminal policy continues to be one of overcoming the penal system. Adopting it does not mean renouncing possible reforms, but choosing and evaluating reforms on the basis of their possibility for radically transforming the system in the interests of the subordinate classes. This overcoming may amount to a "concrete utopia," but it does not impose the delay of any possible reform in the present as one awaits the advent, certainly far off (or perhaps even impossible?) of a society that knows how to do without sentencing.

What Gustave Radbruch wrote in this respect is still valid, to wit, that "the best reform of criminal law is not substituting it with a better criminal law, but substituting it with something better."

NOTES

1. Marc Ancel called attention to that question when he launched his thesis on *The New Social Defense* in 1954. Consult: Ancel, Marc. *La Défense Sociale Nouvelle.* 3.ed. Paris, Éditions Cujas, 1981. p. 203 and following.

2. Sacotte, Jacqueline. Trent Ans de Politique Criminelle en Matière Penitentiaire. *In: Archives de Politique Criminelle.* Paris, Édition du Centre de Recherches de Politique Crimininelle, (3), p. 75 e s., 1978.

3. The UN itself, has since 1955, when it approved the *Minimum Rules for Treatment of Delinquents Delinqüentes,* been establishing a movement in criminal policy based on uniting the concepts of "prevention of crime and treatment of the delinquent."

4. See the comments by: Bouzat, Pierre. Le Centenaire d'Enrico Ferri. *In: Revue de Science Criminelle et de Droit Pénal Comparée.* Paris, Édition du Centre François de Droit Compareé, (1), janvier-mars. p.1 e s., 1957.

5. See the considerations that Jacqueline Bernat de Celis presents in commenting on the last 25 years of social defense movements: Celis, Jacqueline Bernat de. La Politique Criminelle à la Recherche d'elle—Méme. *In: Archives de Politique Criminelle.* Paris, Édition du Centre de Recherches de Politique Criminelle, (2), 46 e s., 1977.

6. In this regard, consult the comments of: Baratta, Alessandro. Criminologia Crítica e Política Penal Alternativa. *In: Revista de Direito Penal.* Rio de Janeiro, órgão oficial do Instituto de Ciências Penais do Rio de Janeiro, (23), p. 7 and following 1978.

7. That conclusion was considered by participants at the 3rd International Colloquim on Criminal Policy, organized in Paris on May 4 and 5, 1979, by the Centre de Recherches de Politique Criminelle. The debates and conclusions of that colloquium are included in nº 4 of the *Archives de Politique Criminelle*, published in Paris by the Centre de Recherches itself.

8. In that respect, see the notes of: Szabo, Denis. Criminologie et Politique Criminelle. Paris, Librairie Vrin, 1978. p. 106 and following.

9. Mireille Delmas-Marty, set out very well the differentiations between the dynamics of criminal policy in state organizations. Consult: Delmas-Marty, Mireille. *Modèles et Mouvements de Politique Criminelle.* Paris, Édition Economica, 1963, p. 56 and following.

10. See the disciplining of those institutions in the current Law of Penal Execution (Lei nº 7.210 de 11.07.1984)

11. An excellent book was published in France about those problmes in contemporary society. See: Coing, Henri J. Meunier. Christine. *Insécurité Urbaine? Une*

Arme pour le Pouvoir. Paris, Éditions Anthropos, 1980; especially as pages 77 and following.

12. Ancel, Marc. *La Défense Sociale Nouvelle*, 3ème édition. Paris, Édition Cujas, 1981. p. 123 and following.

13. We will take up this topic again more broadly when we look, later on, at the *Limits of Criminal Policy*.

14. An interesting approach to the role of the criminal judge in light of advances in criminology and criminal policy was presented by: Vouré H, Catherine. Une Application Socio-Educative du Controle Judiciaire. *In: Archives de Politique Criminelle*. Paris, Éditions du Centre de Recherches de Politique Criminelle (2), p. 107 and following 1977.

15. Jacques Verin has shown the importance of participation by the public in criminal policy activities in analyzing the English experience in: Verin, Jacques. Le Succès du Community Service Anglais. *In: Revue de Science Criminelle et de Droit Pénal Comparée*. Paris, Éditions du Centre Français de Droit Comparé, (3), juillet-septembre, p. 636 and following 1979.

16. Let us remember that in Brazil we are currently beginning to live under new experiences arising from implantation of the New Law of Penal Execution (Lei nº 7.210/84), such as, for example, employment of the halfway house regime and installation of the Community Councils.

17. The *Lex Talionis*, for example, enunciated by the classic expression "eye for an eye," although it represented the first limitation to punishment in the history of sentencing, today would be censured in light of current standards of penal justice.

18. Delmas-Marty, Mireille. *Modèles et Mouvements de Politique Criminelle*. Ob. cit. p. 177 and following.

19. Read the panoramic overview regarding the situation in Europe presented by: Sacotte, Jacqueline. Le Mouvement de Dépenalisation. La Limitation et la Privation de Liberté dans les Pays de l'Europe Occidentale. *In: Archives de Politique Criminelle*. Paris, Édition du Centre de Recherches de Politique Criminelle, (5), p. 61 and following 1981.

20. Hans Goppinger presents, in his book, a definition in the same sense: "Criminal Policy is the science that concerns itself with a policy for reform of Criminal Law (in the broad sense) and of carrying out the fight against crime by means of Criminal Law." Consult, Goppinger, Hans. Criminologia. Trans. by Maria Luisa Schwarck e Ignacio Luzarraga Castro, Madrid, Editorial Reus S.A., 1978. p. 19.

21. See the report by Fragoso, Heleno. *Direito Penal e Direitos Humanos*. Rio de Janeiro, Editora Forense, 1977. p. 4 and following.

Chapter Seventeen

Prison

Past, Present and Future

Edmundo Oliveira

IMAGE ACROSS THE CENTURIES

Prison is as old as human memory and, even with its afflictive nature, it continues to be the sentencing panacea appealed to all around the world.[1]

At the dawn of humanity, people were already being bound by the feet, by the hands, by the neck and so on. Humans and animals alike were tied, chained, manacled, fettered. From the zoological origins comes the use of the term "seize" or "lay hold of" (Latin *prehendere*). Caves, caverns, tombs, pits, towers, anything served to hold people. Voltaire, in *The Spirit of Laws* referred to the pits that the barbarians called prison.

The ancient Greeks and Romans emphasized chaining and segregation in establishments especially prepared for offenders. The Latin word *carcer* (which in English appears in "incarcerate") in the Ancient Age designated the place in a circus where horses awaiting the starting signal for a race. It later was used to designate prison, where slaves, delinquents and those vanquished in wars were placed.

During the Middle Ages, castles, fortresses and convents kept spaces as prisons. The Church, in its laws, admitted the use of a sentence that deprived one of liberty, and during this period the term "penitentiary" came into widespread use. The criminal (sinner) accepted and at time implored penitence as a grace. "Rehabilitation" came as a result of inner acceptance of purifying suffering.

Prison as a penalty that serves as a means of reeducation[2] was inaugurated in the Netherlands at the end of the Sixteenth Century, with the creation of correctional houses in Amsterdam in 1595 and 1597, respectively for men and women. Those two prisons, destined in principle to be a sort of "presidium" for vagrants, beggars and prostitutes, were later transformed into penitentiaries. Later on, houses with the same purpose appeared in Bremen (1609), Lübeck (1609), Hamburg (1622) and so on, until their use became generalized. One should note that the pioneering element in the aforementioned Amsterdam penitentiaries consisted in their adopting a philosophy of directing the establishments towards specific serving of a sentence with an educational character, which previously did not exist.[3]

The Seventeenth Century saw the dawn of the Humanitarian Period in prisons—not because they became truly humane, but because the public was exposed to the truths that everyone felt and whispered about related to the abuses, atrocities and injustices against people subjected over the centuries to imprisonment. This led to a sequence of reform movements that lasted in Europe during the Eighteenth and Nineteenth Centuries, combating the harshness of prisons, the complication of investigatory processes, delays in the judicial apparatus and the fitness of prisons as a place to serve resocializing sentences.[4]

It is curious to note that, in the midst of movements for reforming the prison regime, the French Revolution appeared. And what one then saw was the people of Paris storming the Bastille, for them the symbol of oppression. The Bastille was an ancient fortress build in Paris in 1370 by King Charles V. In the Seventeenth Century during the Government of Cardinal Armand Richelieu, the Bastille was transformed into a prison to incarcerate, among others, those who displeased the King or his Court. When the French Revolution began, the first thing the people did was attack and destroy the Bastille, on July 14, 1789.

Of all the prisons in France, the Bastille was the one that held the most distinguished people and the one where the treatment was the most appropriate. Citing the *Legendes et Archives de la Bastille*, written by Funck-Brentano (Paris, 1898), Adolphe Prins comments that in that "State" prison, "le traitement fut doux, le logis passable, la table soingnée, la surveillance complaisante." What predisposed public opinion against the Bastille was not so much the treatment dispensed there to prisoner, but the arbitrary way in which they were sent there. The Bastille was, above all, the figure, the image of despotism in the Ancien Regime. For that very reason, the demolition of such a bastion of capricious absolutism represents a landmark the humanity's struggle against prepotency.

In the Twentieth Century, the so-called Scientific Period of penal and criminological studies, it is not yet possible to tranquilly affirm that someday humanity will reach a perfection that will allow it to abolish prison.

At any rate, the fact is that today we cannot get along without it. Someone who intends to break the law needs to be offered a counter-stimulus, a reason not to do so.

The great tragedy at the end of the century is that prison continues to present a depressing spectacle that affects more than the individual offender: it makes orphan children of a living father, widows of wife of the disheartened husband; harms the creditor of the prisoner who becomes insolvent, ill-adapts the incarcerated for society; leads to serious sexual conflicts, burdens the State, piles humans into dirty humid cages where they vegetate in Olympian promiscuity.[5]

THERE IS NO HAPPY PRISON

Truth be told, there is no happy prison, since no one chooses a prison as a dream house, especially because deprivation of liberty does not allow any balance between body and spirit, in an environment with an intense negative charge, where people are always showing and reflecting pain or suffering, in the daily battle for survival. That is why the rehabilitation intended by penal legislation, in every place around the world, has in practice laid bare discouragement, affliction and definitive rebellion against a society that shuts its doors to the freed prisoner when the time comes for *le lendemain de la peine,* as the French elegantly phrase it. Prison thus continues in search of a new future capable of enabling practical measures for penal execution that correspond to the longings for social and moral reinsertion.

So many difficulties indicate that there must be a vital effort to work on executing sentences, reserving prison for those cases in which the offender represents a concrete and continuous threat to social tranquility. Outside of that circumstance, if there is no need for a sentence that is so qualitatively serious, it is crucial that prison be substituted not only by the ancient formula of fines, but also by other options with a real educational meaning, that will enable the offender to return to collectivity, without burdening the taxpayer so much.

But the question does not reside simply in reducing the mass of prisoners, given that emptying the prisons should pay the high price of loosening repression. Harmonizing the ideal of a human jail with the need to assure repression of wrongdoing is not an easily performed task. Equally difficult is the undertaking of offering prisoners everything that they need in terms of assistance, creative culture, occupation with productive work, respect for religious convictions, relations with family and society, and recognition of those rights not affected by the criminal sentence.

Those difficulties are attested to by the existential rawness of the prisons, which is why it is indispensable to perfect penal legislation and reengineer the structure of the Judicial Power, in order to enable prison to be reserved to cases in which the offender presents a concrete physical danger to society, making it possible, on the other hand, for the sanctions that substitute *imprisonment*[6] to reduce the pressure on the financial resources demanded to maintain a prison, opening up space for the rational occupation of those establishments, besides allowing the condemned to serve the sentence near their families and the communities where they live.

CANONS FOR IMPLEMENTING SENTENCES

The greatest purpose should be banishing promiscuity,[7] so that the prisoners will have support to feed love for their own dignity, preparing a future in which, once free, they can honorably and autonomously provide for their own subsistence. If people go to prison and there face a machine that destroys their personality, how can the feel the sensation that they will be useful to society tomorrow? Without conditions for exercising their potential, without the therapy of work, the prisoner will never be assured of success in a harmonious reintegration with society.

That is why it is constantly stated that prison:

a. does do what it says it does;
b. neutralizes the formation or development of values;
c. stigmatizes human beings;
d. functions as a machine for reproducing a career in crime;
e. introduces in the personality the prisonalization of the nefarious jailhouse culture;
f. stimulates the process of depersonalization;
g. legitimates disrespect for human rights.

To the contrary, in order to fully achieve its ends, the sentence must be:

a. proportional to the seriousness of the crime and the agent's culpability;
b. effective in defending society;
c. reparative of the damage caused;
d. exemplary for everyone;
e. tranquilizing for men and women of good will;
f. medicinal for the delinquents themselves;
g. foundational for exercising citizenship.

Those who deal with criminals know the residues of morality that they present. It can be verified daily that many have a feeling of their own reprobate status; that they frequently feel themselves to be despicable; that they long for forgiveness from their relatives for the faults committed; that they recognize the justice of the sentence imposed; that they accept it with pain, nonetheless, with resignation. It is nor even rare to have cases of criminals who turn themselves in spontaneously to Justice or even commit suicide to free themselves from the remorse that shames them.[8]

The starting point for a just and efficient criminal policy, therefore, is that the sentence, far more than having an afflictive basis, must be the basis for personal restructuring.

And that is not all. Consisting of deprivation of a judicial asset of the criminal, the penal sanction must not strike at certain rights that are sacred and inalienable to all people. It must be proportional to the damage caused by the crime and the degree of culpability, which is the reproachability of the criminal. Here also one applies the physics principle of action and reaction: every action provokes a reaction of equal intensity and in a contrary sense. The sentence that exceeds that measure is iniquitous and counterproductive. Intending to reestablish equilibrium, it compromises it and throwing too much weight on one side of the scales. The sentence that is set under or over the fair level, fails in its purpose of allowing the State to sensibly demand accountability from any imprisoned person.[9]

These considerations bring up a serious problem: is a just sentence[10] achievable in "practical" terms? It is easy to theorize; putting it into effect is difficult. But we should not content ourselves to see justice reigning at unachievable heights. If, on the one hand, it is vain to intend to carry out Criminal Law from Olympic heights, on the other hand, we cannot renounce the search for a reasonable solution and one that comes as close as possible to the ideal. In other words, we must act as is done in Mathematics: by approximations. That is why we must confront the illicit profit sought by the depraved will of the offender through the sacrifice that the punishment will impose on him or her.

What would be the use, for example, of inflicting a shameful penalty on someone who has degraded his or her own name in the paths of addiction?

To summarize, the solution to the problems that affect the penitentiary system, on all continents, will only be obtained if it is based on the conviction that this is not an isolated, watertight issue. Quite to contrary, it needs to be understood as a true system with communicating vessels,[11] founded on four points: social justice, the police system, the judicial system and the penitentiary system. Furthermore, it demands a broad discussion involving all social segments, whose components must not continue to be contaminated and immobilized by prejudice and indifference.

Both the Government and public opinion need to prepare themselves with effective policies to face the penitentiary issue as a relevant component of scientific and technological progress, considering that a just, equitable, educated and economically expressive society must be able to face this problem seriously, determinedly and competently. In that manner, it is possible to firmly confront the strong rejections of the failed traditional prison model that is waiting for a new approach, be it through an innovative concept of prison standards, be it through alternative mechanisms, which, without ceasing to punish the fault, can reeducate the offender in the exercise of responsible citizenship, so as to respect the rights of others and be willing to assume the solidarity and the sacrifices demanded by the commonweal.[12]

In all cases, we must consider that the criminal act represents the choice of a deviated nature in relation to the normal standards of human conduct, because all of the social structure, all of the messages of civilization, all of the appeals of human coexistence, all ethical principles, all of the strength of the educational process, all of the proposals of religion and philosophy, all of this inclines humans toward the good.[13] But if, despite all of this immense torrent dragging them towards virtue, someone steps onto the path of crime, strange and hidden forces will begin building up in the lowest depths of his or her being, to, at a certain moment, neutralize the grandeur or rightness and unbalance the normal routine of a personality.

It has thus become indispensable, for the guidelines of a solid policy in social sanitation, to investigate the multiple paths in the domains of sentences, which can be served in a free environment, without being limited to the pragmatic sense of a mere counterblow against injury, meaning, less violent for the delinquents and avoiding violence against the non-delinquents.

In the modern movement known as the *Penal Counter-Reformation*,[14] the idea has arisen, over the last few years and followed by some exponents, of calling for the abolition of prison.

Is such a logic possible?

At the institutional level we do not see how such a phenomenon can become a concrete reality.

It is true that the administration of Criminal Justice is selective and has its operating capacity limit considering the filters of symbolic delinquency generally represented by the poor who fill the prisons and constitute the system's clientele, which is why the "abolitionists" say that the suppression of jail time punishment is already in operation for "subterranean criminality," practiced by those who count on having immunity because of prestige, privilege or influence.

Now impunity has to do with a problem of applying justice in the sphere of legal and judicial jurisdictions for a value judgment on the criminal act.

Consequently, the question is not to jail everyone, but to provide effectiveness to alternative Criminal Law to follow the principle of minimum intervention in certain situations, to be nonexistent in others and act more rigorously, but with the necessary gradation, at appropriate moments. Prison must always be the last of the solutions.[15]

Prudence and wisdom must inform the legislator in choosing the sentences that are transformed into law, which must not be of only one type, nor should multiply excessively.[16] Furthermore, the penalty imposed in the condemnatory sentence must not remain immutable. To the contrary, it must be made ductile and malleable in the execution phase, so that it may adapt to the changes presented by the offenders during the dynamics of their re-education.

We thus are encouraged by the conviction that the criminal sentence can fulfill its pedagogical mission with prestige, effectiveness and desirable fruits at the dawn of the third millennium.[17]

NOTES

1. ANCEL, Marc. *La Defense Sociale Nouvelle,* Paris, Edition Cujas, 1986, pp. 256-285.
2. BERISTAIN, Antonio. *La Pena Retribución and las Actuales Concepciones Crimino-lógicas*, Buenos Aires, Depalma, 1982, pp. 91-107.
3. CALON, Eugenio Cuello. *La Moderna Penologia*, Barcelona, Bosch Casa Editorial, 1973, pp. 626-657.
4. CARRARA, Francesco. *Programma del Corso di Diritto Criminale,* Firenze, Casa Editrice Fratelli Cammelli, 1902, Parte Generale, vol. 1, pp. 559-594.
5. DEL OLMO, Rosa. *Ruptura Criminológica,* Caracas, Universidad Central de Venezuela, 1979, pp. 31-48.
6. DIAS, Jorge de Figueiredo e ANDRADE, Manuel da Costa. *Criminologia. O Homem Delinqüente e a Sociedade Criminógena,* Coimbra, Coimbra Ed., 1984, pp. 373-395.
7. FAVARD, Jean. *Le Labyrinthe Pénitentiaire*, Paris, Éditions Centurion, 1981, pp. 151-174.
8. GARRAUD, R. *Droit Pénal Français*, Paris, Librairie des Lois et das Arrêts, 1898, vol.1, pp. 603-623.
9. HULSMAN, Louk e CELIS, Jacqueline Bernat. *Peines Perdues. Le Système Pénal en question*, Paris, Éditions Centurion, 1982, pp. 55-81.
10. TRANSLATION NOTE: FOOTNOTE LEFT BLANK
11. JESCHECK, Hans Heirinch. *Tratado de Derecho Penal*, tradução de S. Mir Puig e F. Muñoz Conde, Barcelona, Bosch, 1981, pp. 1187-1205.
12. KAUFMANN, Hilde. *Criminologia, Ejecución Penal and Terapia Social,* Buenos Aires, Ediciones Depalma, 1979, pp. 69-78.

13. PICCA, Georges. *La Criminologie*, Paris, Presses Universitaires de France, 1983, pp. 108-114.

14. ROTMAN, Edgardo. *Beyond Punishment. A New View on the Rehabilitation of Criminal Offenders*, New York, Greenwood Press, 1990, pp. 154-171.

15. SOMMER, Robert. *The End of Imprisonment,* New York, Oxford University Press, 1976, pp. 171-195.

16. SZABO, Denis. *Criminologie et Politique Criminelle*, Paris, Édition Vrin, 1978, pp. 236-241.

17. ZAFFARONI, Eugenio Raúl. *En Busca de las Penas Perdidas*, Buenos Aires, AFA Editores Importadores, 1989, pp. 79-125.

Chapter Eighteen

Justification for Punishment in Judicial Organization

Edmundo Oliveira

GOVERNMENT REACTION

The recourses that the governmental reaction can take towards crime are determined in number, efficacy, selection and category by the action of state Criminal Law, in which the common platform for application is wrongdoing committed by someone who, being liable, falls into the sphere of judgment as to capability.

In each opportunity in which it seeks to modify the punitive system, the State must assume the primordial obligation of sufficiently justifying use of the sentence, a powerful coercive recourse that it has to limit individual rights for the purpose of assuring peaceful coexistence. That legitimization should be carried out, from the point of view of its practical effects, with both the delinquent, individually, and before the judicial community.

The State has to resort to the penalty to reinforce prohibitions, indicate what is allowed and show the citizens that observance of legal commandments is absolutely necessary for avoiding as much as possible actions or omissions that strike at the bases of social coexistence.

If, despite the promise of punishment, someone violates the precept and practices a crime, it is necessary to apply the promised sentence; otherwise, the threat would be a sham, a fantasy. It is thus necessary to punish, meaning to "retribute" the crime with a sentence. This "retributive character" of the execution does not result, therefore, from genuine considerations of a moral order, but from the nature itself of the mechanism used by the state to repudiate criminality in all of its colors. Up till now no other mechanism has been invented, among other things, because no new Pasteur has discovered vaccine against crime, even though a large part of the work of criminologists consists of identifying the causes of criminality and pointing to therapeutics for crimes. Nonetheless, if, despite everything, there will always been the possibility of wrongdoing, then one must make use of the penal threat to avoid crime and execute that threat if crime is not avoided, so that sentencing is not demoralized as a lyrical promise that is not fulfilled.

There must be punishment. However, so that the penalty is not applied to someone who did not commit an offence, and so that it is only dealt out in the appropriate measure to wrongdoers, one must investigate facts, hear persons, examine documents, investigate, weigh and judge in the procedural context, with all of the guarantees that make criminal proceedings the skilful instrument for reaching a just solution.

The sentence, in any legislative structure in the contemporary world, goes beyond the purpose of retribution for the unjust act, as no one may ignore the major relevance of the preventive scope of reintegrating the condemned person to society, intimidating potential wrongdoers and strengthening the judicial consciousness of all members of the social group. That is why we must combat the practice of transforming penal punishment onto a terror apparatus, as if it were the only proclaimed end needing to be met.

In aligning a penal execution oriented towards the consequences set forth in the preceding paragraph, it is necessary to make use of realistic alternatives that renounce the application of more serious reactions, which can be easily substituted by recourses that satisfy the objectives of social relations and that strengthen Criminal Law.

PILLARS OF MODERN CRIMINAL POLICY

That being the case, there are three pillars in modern criminal policy: sentences, safety measures and the mechanisms employed to limit application of the sentence. That means that employing a sanction should be reduced as much as possible, and whenever possible avoided, without the absence of reaction to wrongdoing bringing discredit to Criminal Law.

Up till the first half of the Twentieth Century, Criminal Law was basically grounded on sentences that deprived wrongdoers of liberty. Criminal policy, as it was preponderantly understood, trusted in the resocializing force of executing a sentence that removed liberty, as if it were capable of producing a positive effect during the period of reclusion. This immemorial "ideal of rehabilitation" ended up completely losing its worth, when people ceased to believe in the possibility of successfully resocializing someone through the traditional prison regime, especially in overcrowded jails. Faced with extreme positions that called, on the one hand, for a return to pure retribution, and on the other hand, for a major increase in the efforts of Criminal Justice administration in the struggle against criminality, voices in the middle were raised calling for a criminal policy without ideological prejudices, in which the incriminatory penal norm would be an indispensable tool for protecting the legal order. In that regard, it is worth noting that Criminal Law serves to simultaneously limit the power of governmental intervention and to effectively combat crime. It thus protects the individual from unlimited repression by the State, but at the same defends society and its members from abuses that a member of the social group may commit.

There is no doubt that, in certain concrete situations, there is a clear need to reinforce the general prevention function attributed to the penal system, particularly with respect to cases of serious offences that arouse a profound and pernicious feeling of insecurity. If there is no appropriate response to such shocking crimes, which cause pain and affliction, one runs the risk of a return of the days of "taking the law into one's hands" or "lynch laws, without the constraints of legal judgment." Certainly, the violation of certain rights can bring about, in the victims, their families or in public opinion, vehement needs for retribution that can only be assuaged with the certainty of punishment appropriate to the degree of culpability. By knowing how to assess such effects in the ideal application of the penalty to the offender, Criminal Law can grow in the cultural structure of a people, as a regulator of socially appropriate conduct, strengthening citizen faithfulness to its norms.

Any proposal that includes exceptions or limits to the government's attitudes towards wrongdoing must be carefully evaluated, because an excessively permissive system that does not impose and does not seriously affirm its laws, displaces or devalues other sectors of social control, favoring the appearance of private justice, which will end up imposing its own norms, sanctions and procedures.

But Criminal Law is not arbitrary; it does not arise from the human mind by means of *a priori* sentiments. To the contrary, it is made through scrupulous observation and careful experience, which is why general prevention functions not only through deciding sentences, but also through imposing and executing them. Of what use is it for the law to impose very strict sentences, if certain delinquents have very good reasons for thinking that they will not suffer them? To reiterate: the intimidating strength of sentences provided for by law resides in the certainty of punishment. That is the only means for providing the punishments called for in penal norms with the intimidating character that one wishes the law to have, with its purpose of reducing criminality.

Thus, penal execution takes place so that the admonition of law will be a genuine threat. The dynamics of the sentence imposed serve precisely to reinforce the effectiveness of the legal threat, because, without it, the threat will be in vain and ineffective. If it does not know how to perform this juxtaposition, the State will be despising the healthy guarantee of judicial organization, and consequently, every future murderer can rest on the fact of non-punishment of others, and in the same way, have reasons to take the risk, judging crime pays and escaping the penalty.

The principles of the punitive judicial system that limit criminal policy are characterized by their mission of formalizing social judicial-penal control, freeing it from surprise, opportunism and subjectivity. Thus, the points out in writing, to everyone, with the greatest possible precision what constitutes existence of conduct labeled as deviation, in what form the sentence will be imposed, who will be the authority with jurisdiction to apply it and what are the guarantees for applicable appeals. The process through which the sanction is imposed is public, but it is also protected from pressures that can be placed on it by public opinion.

Finally, although it is an arduous undertaking, albeit one with great significance, judicial-penal control must always seek full conditions for exercising citizenship, with balance and responsible authority, without sacrificing public well-being.

WORKS CITED

ANIYAR, Lolita. *Democracia y Justicia Penal*, Caracas, Ediciones del Congresso de la República, 1992, pp. 59-72.

FONDATION Internationale Penale et Pénitentiaire Publication. "Régles Minima pour la Mise à Exécution des Sanctions et des Mesures non Carcérales Comportant une Restriction de Liberté," Deventer, Kluwer, 1988, pp. 49-73.

FOXIN, Claus. *Problemas Básicos of criminal law,* Madrid, Reus, 1976, pp. 55-57.

GINBERNAT, Enrique Ordeig. *Tine Futuro la Dogmatica Jurídico Penal*? Bogotá, Temis, 1983, pp. 12-13.

HASSEMER, Winfried. *Fundamentos of criminal law,* Barcelona, Bosch, 1984, pp. 33-35.

MAURACH, Reinhart. *Derecho Penal,* tradução de Córdoba Roda, Barcelona, Ariel, 1962, pp. 483-489.

OLIVEIRA, Edmundo. *Comentários ao Código Penal. Parte Geral,* Rio de Janeiro, Ed. Forense, 1994, pp. 119-125.

ROTMAN, Edgardo. "Do Criminal Offenders Have a Constitutional Right to Rehabilitation?" *in: The Journal of Criminal Law and Criminology*. Northwestern, vol. 77, n. 4, University School of Law, 1986, pp. 1.053-1.068.

SCHNEIDER, Hans Joachim. *Kriminologie*, Berlin, Walter de Gruyter, 1987, pp. 858-861.

Chapter Nineteen

Penitentiary Consensualism

Edmundo Oliveira

With the firm desire to contribute towards a new Renaissance in the field of Criminal Law, *Penitentiary Consensualism* made its appearance. We recall that among the trademarks in the Enlightenment of the Eighteenth Century was implantation of the Humanitarian Period in Criminal Law, an extraordinary movement of ideals and concepts in the sphere of defining crimes and establishing sentences, inaugurated in 1764, in Italy, by Cesare Beccaria with his work *On Crimes and on Penalties*, a revolt against continuing tortures and degrading prisons, which were irreconcilable with the purpose of recovering delinquents.

Penitentiary Consensualism is a remarkable criminal technical method, built upon scientific experiments, which was examined by the International Penal and Penitentiary Foundation (FIPP), an agency created by the General Assembly of the UN with headquarters in Berne (Switzerland). Gathered in Lisbon (Portugal), from May 21 to 25, 1999, the FIPP Council members recommended the beginning of a new and unusual route towards transforming prisons in the third millennium, beginning with engagement in a project for changes, in line with the affirmation and internationalization of Human Rights.

That transformation must begin with a conceptual valuation. According to the FIPP Council Members, one should no longer speak exclusively of *Penitentiary Consensualism,* in situations where one can establish the reason of *Penitentiary Consensualism*. Let us examine what that means.

THE PATH OF CONSENSUS IN VIEW OF THE HUMAN PROBLEMS AND THE PROCESS OF VICTIMIZING THE PRISONER

Consensualism seeks to offer conditions for converting the routine of the penitentiary apparatus in an appropriate location, eliminate defects and institutional and individual paradoxes related to the feelings of injustice that are feed in prison life, as well as feelings of insecurity absorbed by the population in community life. To summarize, it it's a prison policy built on a scale of ethical, moral and normative values, integrated in the State's social policy system, which still maintains privation of freedom operating as the heart of the system of penal sanctions, in a permanent diagnosis with a triple disadvantage;

a. disadvantage of a utilitarian order: prison is expensive, both at the construction stage and in maintaining its administrative structure, without a compensating return;
b. disadvantage of a moral order: prison, as means of neutralization, is pure punishment and to remove a person's liberty only as a punishment, has become intolerable;
c. disadvantage of a social order: prison, as it always has been and continues to be, will not be able to perform the ideal of its resocializing role at the level of the hopes, efforts and investments implemented.

The feelings of injustice that are fed by prison life, have to do with absorption of human problems that are peculiar to the population contingent that forms the closed society in prison,

In the process of *prisonization*—cited by José Maria Rico as the "adoption, at a greater or lesser scale, of the uses, customs, tradition and general culture of the penitentiary"—are found the human problems of the prisoner:

a. insecurity;
b. brutalization;
c. solitude;
d. idleness;
e. abandonment by family;
f. sexual maladjustment;
g. uncertainties about a free future.

To the problems that predate the prison experience, others are progressively added, leading the convict to gradually become brutalized, perverted and rendered insensitive. His or her suffering is dominated by the fixed idea that the authorities do not care about him or her. Convicts consider themselves socially marginalized. Because they have no way of demanding adequate treatment, prisoners feel unsafe and involved in the *marginalization subculture*. The prison syndrome, discouragement, revolts, rebellions and attempted escapes are the results of the impossibility of making convictions, sentences that deprive one of freedom and detention security measures viable under the aegis of legality and humanity. The prisoners are aware that if their social conditions were different, they would certainly not be in prison, as normally the most prosperous are not.

Regarding the family's attitude, either they assume a position of reproving the prisoner, abandoning him or her to fate, given the feeling of repulsion, aversion to prison life, or then, the family, when the prisoner has one, assumes the sufferings of the condemned and exposes itself to the moral and material consequences of misery. Reality has shown that normally, visits at the beginning are frequent and full of promises, but over time become farther apart until they are totally abandoned.

With abandonment by family and friends, solitude becomes the most complete companion for the prisoner. Sometimes we even ask to be alone to encourage and cultivate our inner worlds, but imposed solitude is terrible and cruel. No prisoner can easily bear the complete lack of human warmth, the total absence of a little love.

Idleness or even work that does not attend to differences in the age, health and culture of the prisoner invalidate the purposes of evasion and occupation, since because of its unsuitability, it causes natural deviations in productivity and enterprise. The State does not have the right to deprive the prisoner of productive, specialized and remunerated work. Adequate work is an elemental factor in a person's reentry, under favorable conditions, into the social environment which he or she had left.

Aggravated by idleness, the sexual issue in prisons has defied humanists in the century in which we live. We do not view optimistically any solution proposed as viable for the dignity and normality of sexual life in prison. Without any means for closing the question, we admit the possibility of a visit home, at least to minimally fulfill the *debitum conjugale*. That position, also defended by Roberto Lyra, is better justified by citing the words of that notable Teacher:

> Should it be impossible to break down the iron bars, the walls and the barriers between couples, which desperately open their arms to the purity of the legal hiding place, we admit a home visit as a duty-right of women and men who are imprisoned or interned, couples or companions. The evils that we are studying will be at least attenuated. The visit of a prisoner or internee, man or woman, to

> the home, will attenuate the iniquity, if not the morality of the sexual pasturage into which women serve or are coerced, giving rise to abortions, infanticides and homicides against the newborn or those being born.
>
> From these legal and moral visits by the prisoner and also internees, except for in exceptions of good sense, one would not see a pregnancy kept hidden, propitious for the use of means destined to provoke abortion or avoid contraception. It would be the "intimate visit," with its impossible modesty and lack of absolute privacy that would lead to an apparently illicit pregnancy. The secret is also a condition of discipline, tranquility and security. There is more. Experience has revealed even the official exploitation of prostitution through the entry of prostitutes as false wives and companions, brought in by intermediaries on the outside and inside. This has led to cases of venereal contagion in the 'tolerance rooms' installed and exploited in public buildings utterly lacking respectability.

Furthermore, there have been confirmed cases of prisoners refusing to receive their wives or companions for an intimate visit, since they understood that they would be shaming them or placing them in a humiliating situation. A penitentiary system, in adopting the intimate visit formula, should keep it as an option, along with periodic licenses for home visits, without distinction of marital status.

The perversion of intimacy reaches its peak without guaranteeing the exercise of this right to all persons. Repressed affectivity gives rise to the need for compensation, and thus masturbation, homosexuality and other aberrations that, in the prison subculture, encourage aggressiveness and an increase in the impulsive instinct. Without the moral practice of sex, it is impossible to reintegrate humans and have them reencounter themselves. If an animal, during rut, moves to a blind and determined finalism, guided by its instincts, the prisoner, in identical conditions, will act exactly like an animal. When the impulse of the instinct manifests itself, the prisoner will be compelled to satisfy it, even using physical violence to overcome obstacles.

All of these disquieting problems last until the end of the sentence. Near to the day of freedom, if the prisoners feel the joy and enthusiasm of knowing that free life is approaching, on the other hand, they fear reintegration into their own families, if they still exist, and know of the risk of perpetuating in their own soul the convict stigma which, besides influencing the family environment, will extend to a society that is still not prepared to receive them.

The distinctive traces of human problems in prisoners have led Victimology to formulate the theory of the *Prison Victimization Syndrome*.

In fact, for many offenders subject to a prison regime, society is like a victimizing whole, before the conscious or unconscious fixation in his or her *self*, which conditions a retributive feeling of high hetero-aggressiveness whose origin is explained by the validity of compensation.

Once there is a consciousness of victimization, the prisoner behaves as one who has an immense credit in relation to society. Sometimes prisoners feel that they have an immense credit in relation to society, and feel that they have powers to exercise their rights even through the use of physical violence because they have not established a cause and effect flow between their crime and the loss of liberty. The sensation of being victimized removes motivation for personal rehabilitation. Duly or unduly, the prisoner, even with a reasonable personality structure, seeks to undervalue the significance of the crime practiced, by virtue of the formation of a structure that does not find means to adapt to the needy conditions offered by the system.

In the prison environment there is an entire process of growing reduction in then anti-ethical value of crime, whenever there is an attempt to establish a comparison with the effects of the prison sentence imposed on the condemned person. For those who have stolen, the right to property of their victims does not equal their greater loss of the value of liberty. Homicides, even admitting the proportionality of values, given the ineffectiveness of penal execution, also acquire a position of being victimized, which is stereotyped in their attitudes and behaviors.

From the sum of human problems of the prisoner come new characteristics of conduct that may lead both to practicing crime and to victimization, exactly because they are personal characteristics that are common to the delinquents and victims, an issue of enormous emphasis in victimology.

Let us observe the visualization of Figure 19.1.

Still within the focal points dealt with in terms of *Penitentiary Consensualism*, one should not the concern with the aspects of linking the principle of *normative equality* (example: simple homicide, minimum of 6 and maximum of 20 years of reclusion) to the principal of *judicial proportionality*. A sentence pronounced that begins to be carried out should be altered as convenient by the Judge, not because of the priority of the scale or punishments, but by the priority recommended by a reading of the concrete case, within a scrupulous respect for the freedom of coexistence of prisoners, with observance of their other fundamental rights.

For *Penitentiary Consensualism,* in the panorama of the modern view of criminal policy, the success of consensual prison depends on cultural conjugation of three desires: the first being the desire (of the condemned person); the second being the need to act well (the State); the third, which accepts and trusts (society).

The conjugation of those three desires thus fundamentally implies moralization of the life of the prisoner who, while safeguarding the principle of individuality, voluntarily cultivates socialization or resocialization of responsibility during the time the sentence is being carried out. In this context,

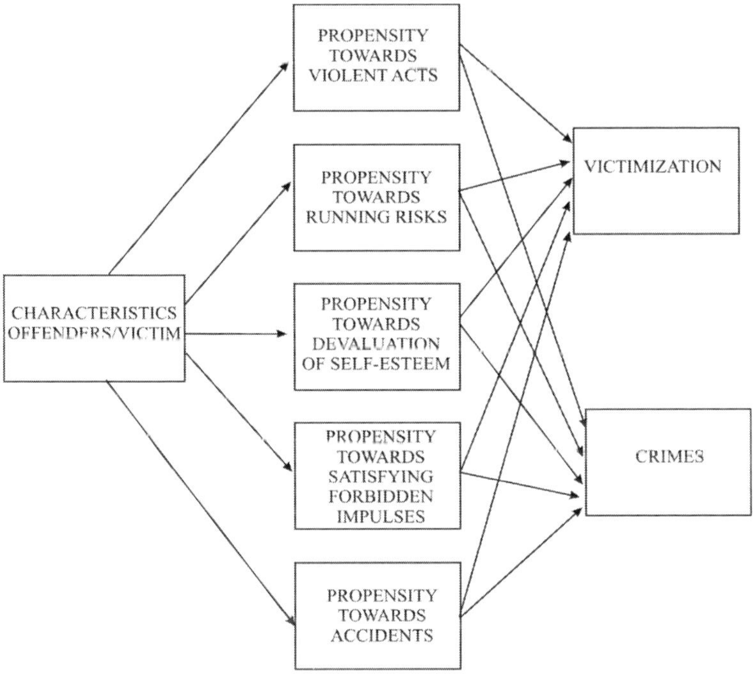

Figure 19.1. Propulsion to crime or propulsion to victimization in the closed society of a prison: common characteristics of conduct among offenders and victims.

the offer of any treatment program by the State will not mean imposition or violation of the will, nor, on the other hand, will it be transformed into authoritarianism for prisoners who do not accept such treatment.

Thus, offering a treatment program to prisoners means encouraging them to follow the administration of a progressive process, in which they themselves will choose and explore the services and activities that they have chosen in understanding with the authorities responsible for prison administration.

One thus perceives that *Penitentiary Consensualism* is unique in three distinct aspects:

a. it took a different position from the concept of punishment launched in the Eighteenth Century during the Humanitarian Period of the Criminal Code of Cesare Beccaria, who rebelled against excessive arbitrariness in incrimination and against the odious application of sentences.
b. it should not be confused with the therapeutic treatment model of the Positive School inaugurated in the Nineteenth Century by Cesare Lombroso;

c. it has gone beyond the model of therapeutic treatment in the progressive regimes of Classical Penitentiary Systems (Pennsylvania, Progressive, Irish Progressive, Elmira, Montesinos and Borstal) that appeared in the Nineteenth Century.

One concludes then, that the marked peculiarity of *Consensualism* is the theme of a policy of socialization or resocialization, in the domains of penal execution, with the reinforcement of an ethical and healthy culture founded on awareness, consent, adherence and acquisition or conservation of a sense of responsibility in the condemned, on participatory prison life in common, in which, in the dynamics of personal restoration with a constant search for solutions of human problems of the prisoner. This should be seen as an indissoluble portion of society, where the condemned person will leave a free life in the future, without being deprived of acceptance and support from the community.

Safeguarding and promoting Human Rights are essential functions of *Consensualism,* considering that it is essential not to lose sight of the need to find a balance point between the imperatives of security in the fight against crime and the efficacy of consensual treatment under the auspices of the jurisdictional power and of a judicial statute that respects the prisoner's freedom of conscience.

Consensualism points out that acting so that the prisoner will not be dissocialized implies in the positive realization of his or her fundamental rights, which is why it is essential to have wise social intervention by the State in planning and carrying out penal execution without the incompatibilities of the traditional model of a dissocializing prison.

In Europe, experiments are beginning inspired on the concept of *Consensualism* with the substitution of the traditional "*forced treatment*" by the responsibility of "*contractual treatment.*"

The purpose is not only to adapt *Consensualism* to more flexible penitentiary regimes without coercive treatment, but also to adapt it in the field of alternatives to imprisonment, with the condemned person having the advantage of choosing what is most effective among the options offered in pedagogical programs in the *society-sentence relation*, such as, for example, the choice of the most appropriate work as community service.

In England, the term *Penitentiary Synallagma* is applied to the increased flexibility of penitentiary organization through the concession of progressive benefits stipulated in a *contract,* without limiting itself to recognition of rights and without ignoring the disciplinary aspect. The *synallagmatic prison model* establishes a scale to measure the rate of socialization or resocialization by the values corresponding to the evolution of the condemned person's behavior.

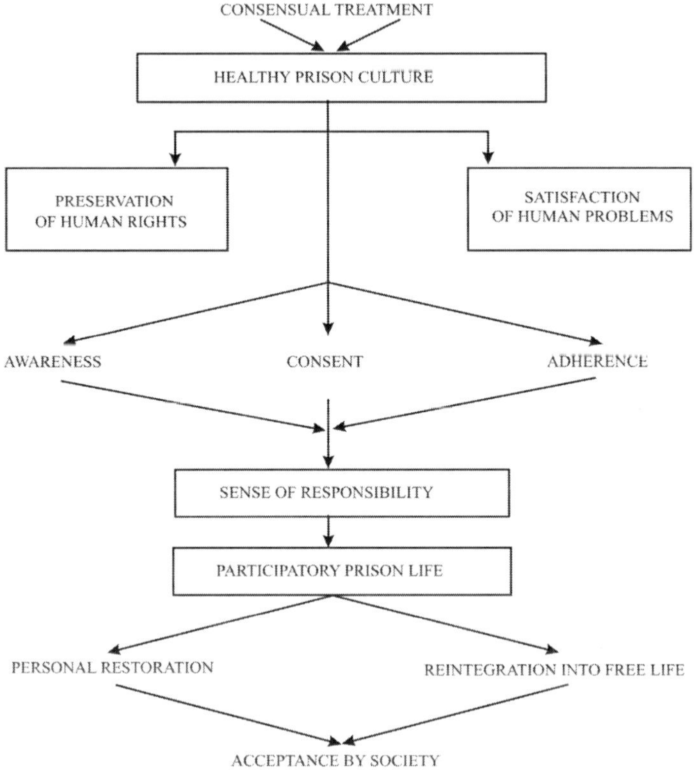

Figure 19.2. Steps towards rehabilitation.

In this regard, there are reports in England of the success of the Open Prison at *Latchmere House.* There, execution of the sentence is based on a prior contract, signed by the condemned party, by the Judge and by the Prison Administrator, in which objectives for a certain period of time are established. During fulfillment of the contract, the prisoner, with autonomy and responsibility, improves his or her behavior within the social environment. Failure to fulfill the objectives means that the condemned party will be sent to a closed prison.

THE PATH OF CONSENSUS

A healthy prison culture is one that does not violate the human rights that are not affected by the Criminal Sentence, with conditions to extend to the methods for creating awareness in the prison to, in the next step, obtain proof of good will regarding consent and adherence to the penitentiary regime.

Photo 1. Loneliness and uncertainties as to a free future are among the painful human problems added to prison life. Source: *Unesco Library, Paris, France*.

Photo 2 and Photo 3. Suicide in prisons: a consequence of the lack of satisfaction for the prisoner's human problems. Source: *Unesco Library, Paris, France.*

Made aware and having adhered to the exercise of values in prison life, the prisoner, in a responsible manner may experience forms of participation among the modalities of executing the sentence decided by the Penal Judge, together with the administrative authorities of prison management.

An opening is then created for the prisoner to take responsibility, which is indispensable for personal restoration, in the process of reintegration to free life, which is capable of enabling exercise of citizenship, with the acceptance and support of society, to the benefit of public well-being.

WORKS CITED

BOLLE, Pierre–Henri. *Consensualisme en Prison. In: Nouvelles Orientations du Régime Pénitentiaire,* Lisboa, FIPP, 2000, pp. 199-201.

FONDATION International Pénale et Pénitentiaire. *Nouvelles Orientations du Régime Pénitentiaire. In: Actes des Journées Internationales de Lisbonne*—Portugal, pp. 193-201, 21-25 mai. 1999.

LYRA, Roberto. *As Execuções Penais no Brasil.* Rio de Janeiro, Editora Forense, p. 30.

NEUMAN, Elias. *Victimología. El Rol de la Victima en los Delitos Convencionales.* Buenos Aires, Edición de la Universidad, 1994, pp. 5355.

RICO, José Maria. *Sanções Penais.* Trans. by Sérgio Fragoso. Rio de Janeiro, Liber Juris Editora, 1978, p. 97.

RODRIGUES, Anabela Miranda. *Consensualisme et Prison. In*: *Nouvelles Orientations du Régime Pénitentiaire,* Lisboa, FIPP, 2000, pp. 147-171.

Chapter Twenty

Prison and Human Rights

Edmundo Oliveira

In the historical evolution of human civilization, the violation of human rights has always exposed the notable reference of three connected lines of difficulties:

a. the discriminatory and stigmatizing effects of a criminal sentence;
b. insubordination of the condemned against the chaotic conditions in the prisons;
c. rejection of the prisoner by society in light of disappointment with the use of a sentence that deprives him or her of freedom.

During the thematic discussions, at the General Assembly of the United Nations in New York related to the process for approving the *Universal Declaration of Human Rights (UDHD),* proclaimed by the United Nations in 1948, one notable point was the recognition that prison, throughout history has always been the most emblematic synthesis of humiliating punishments, with lies, frauds and corrupting conveniences, which unmistakably fuel the weakening of the state apparatus.

That is the origin of the basic norm of the prohibition: "No one shall be subjected to torture or to cruel, inhuman or degrading treatment or punishment." (Article 5 of the UDHD).

Because of the great significance of this ethical commandment, the *First UN Conference on the Prevention of Crime and Treatment of Offenders*, held in Geneva in 1955, enunciated the *Standard Minimum Rules for the Treatment of Prisoners.* It was noted, in the *Exposition of Motives for those Minimum*

Rules: that "what is essential is not only to describe the detailed form of a model penitentiary system, but, above all, to guarantee that its organization is in fulfillment to the concept that every person, deprived of his freedom, should be treated with humanity and respect for the inherent dignity in each person, in order to achieve the principal objective of moral reformation and rehabilitation of the prisoners."

In its history, since 1948, the UN has tried to demonstrate is disagreement with the low standard of contemporary penitentiary systems, which explains the successive denunciations of concentration of violent acts in States that claim to be democratic but are not, because the practices of their Governments and agents do not respect the rules of democracy, are not able to monitor access to all fundamental rights and frequently violate human rights, many times counting on the privilege of impunity.

THE INTERNATIONAL LAW OF PENAL EXECUTIONS

As one may see, relevant instruments with global reach and others of a regional extent, at the European or Inter-American level have already been produced to assure the formation of *International Law for Penal Executions*, containing norms for impeding and controlling harm to human rights in the execution of penalties applied by the administration of Criminal Justice. That being the case, *International Law for Penal Executions* is the branch of the international judicial system that consists of employing principles and strategies that are multilateral or universal in scope, in order to achieve the respect and cooperation of Governments, Institutions and Social Segments in terms of the objectives for preventing crime through mechanisms for rehabilitation of offenders.

Experience has shown the need for measures for international protection, especially of a preventive nature, in the sense of seeking greater prestige for executing sentences with the transformation of deteriorated structures and with better quality of treatment for persons condemned by any system inherent to the power—duty of punishment.

The instruments of *International Law for Penal Executions* are situated along six channels:

a. Principles of the United Nations Organization (UN);
b. Principles of the Organization of American States (OAS);
c. Principles of the European Union (EU);
d. Principles of the Organization of African Unity (OAU);
e. Principles of the League of Arab States (LAS);
f. Principles of the Union of Asian States (UAS).

PRINCIPLES OF THE UNITED NATIONS ORGANIZATION (UN)

The guidelines for building an international system for protection of legitimate treatment of persons under arrest, in all Member States of the UN, are in the norms of International Law expressed in the following chronological order of Principles:

Universal Declaration of Human Rights, of 1948;
Convention Related to Treatment due to Prisoners of War, of 1949;
Minimum Rules for Treatment of Prisoners, of 1955;
International Covenant on Civil and Political Rights, of 1966;
Optional Protocol to the International Covenant on Civil and Political Rights, of 1966;
Declaration on the Protection of All Persons from Being Subjected to Torture and Other Cruel, Inhuman or Degrading Treatment or Punishment, of 1975;
Code of Conduct for Law Enforcement Officials, of 1979;
Principles of Medical Ethics relevant to the Role of Health Personnel, particularly Physicians, in the Protection of Prisoners and Detainees against Torture and Other Cruel, Inhuman or Degrading Treatment or Punishment, of 1982;
Convention Against Torture and other Cruel, Inhuman or Degrading Treatment or Punishment, of 1984;
Safeguards Guaranteeing Protection of the Rights of Those Facing the Death Penalty, of 1984;
Basic Principles on the Independence of the Judiciary, of 1985;
Model Agreement on the Transfer of Foreign Prisoners and Recommendations on the Treatment of Foreign Prisoners, of 1985;
Standard Minimum Rules for the Administration of Juvenile Justice, of 1985;
Declaration of Basic Principles of Justice for Victims of Crime and Abuse of Power, of 1985;
Principles on the Effective Prevention and Investigation of Extra-legal, Arbitrary and Summary Executions, of 1989;
Second Optional Protocol to the International Covenant on Civil and Political Rights, aiming at the abolition of the death penalty, of 1989;
Rules for the Protection of Juveniles Deprived of their Liberty, of 1990;
Standard Minimum Rules for Non-custodial Measures, of 1990;
Guidelines on the Role of Judges, of 1990;
Basic Principles on the Role of Lawyers, of 1990;
Basic Principles on the Use of Force and Firearms by Law Enforcement Officials, of 1990;

Model Treaty on the Transfer of Supervision of Offenders Conditionally Sentenced or Conditionally Released, of 1990;
Model Treaty on the Transfer of Proceedings in Criminal Matters, of 1990;
Declaration on the Protection of all Persons from Enforced Disappearance, of 1992;
Declaration and Program of Action Adopted by the World Conference on Human Rights, of 1993.

PRINCIPLES OF THE ORGANIZATION OF AMERICAN STATES (OAS)

Along the same dogmatic line as the UN, in 1969, the Organization of American States (OAS) approved the *American Convention on Human Rights,* known as the *San José Covenant*, which provided the following for all Member-States:

> *No one shall be subjected to torture or to cruel, inhuman, or degrading punishment or treatment. All persons deprived of their liberty shall be treated with respect for the inherent dignity of the human person.* (Article 5, Chapter 2 of the ACDH)

Reaffirming the purposes of the 1969 Convention, the Organization of American States (OAS), gathered in Cartagena de Indias, Colombia, in 1985, returned to the unresolved issue of the human rights of an imprisoned person. There, the *Inter-American Convention to Prevent and Punish Torture* was signed, in which it was declared that:

> *The States Parties shall take measures so that, in the training of police officers and other public officials responsible for the custody of persons temporarily or definitively deprived of their freedom, special emphasis shall be put on the prohibition of the use of torture in interrogation, detention, or arrest.* (article 7 of the ICPPT)

PRINCIPLES OF THE EUROPEAN UNION (EU)

In Europe several initiatives have directed their efforts at creating and assuring a more human execution of penal sanctions. Among those initiatives, several are especially noteworthy:

Declaration of the Rights of Man and of the Citizen, of 1789;
European Declaration for the Protection of Human Rights and Fundamental Freedoms, of 1950;

European Convention for the Prevention of Torture and Inhuman or Degrading Treatment or Punishment, of 1987;
Treaty of the European Union, of 1992;
Protocols for the European Convention for the Protection of Human Rights and Fundamental Freedoms, of 1994.

PRINCIPLES OF THE ORGANIZATION OF AFRICAN UNITY (OAU)

In the African Community, with an emphasis on regional distinctions and the cultural values of the various Nations of Africa, as well as the relationship between individuals, groups of individuals and the State, the convention in effect is the:

African Charter on Human and People's Rights, of 1986.

PRINCIPLES OF THE LEAGUE OF ARAB STATES (LAS)

In the evolution of initiatives for cooperation in the field of human rights, the League of Arab States has sought to put into practice measures for protecting individuals in their respective social groups and territories, in conformity with the norms set out by *Islam.*

In 1968, the League created the Permanent Arab Commission on Human Rights that prepared and approved the:

Arab Charter on Human Rights, of 1994.

PRINCIPLES OF THE UNION OF ASIAN STATES (UAS)

The Asian Human Rights Commission was founded in 1986. It has the task of disseminating and guiding, among the Asian peoples, the effective exercise of fundamental rights, not only inserted in regional laws and in the Constitutions, but also with regard to recommendations by international instruments, especially the Resolution of the UN Economic and Social Council, approved in 1993, for the Promotion and Protection of Human Rights in Asia and the Pacific Region. In Asian Countries, the orientations in effect are from the:

Asian Charter on Human Rights, of 1998.

THE BRAZILIAN CONSTITUTION

Supported by the worldwide tendency inspired by the judicial postulates established in International Law, the Constitution of the Federative Republic of Brazil brings together the development of specific values:

no one shall be submitted to torture or to inhuman or degrading treatment (article 5, III of the Constitution of Brazil);

no punishment shall go beyond the person of the convict . . . (article 5, XLV, of the Constitution of Brazil);

the sentence shall be served in separate establishments, according to the nature of the offense, the age and the sex of the convict. (article 5, XLVIII, of the Constitution of Brazil);

no one shall be deprived of freedom or of his assets without the due process of law (article 5, LIV, of the Constitution of Brazil);

no one shall be arrested unless in flagrante delicto or by a written and justified order of a competent judicial authority, save in the cases of military transgression or specific military crime, as defined in law (article 5, LXI, of the Constitution of Brazil);

the arrest of any person as well as the place where he is being held shall be immediately informed to the competent judge and to the family of the person arrested or to the person indicated by him (article 5, LXII, of the Constitution of Brazil);

the arrested person shall be informed of his rights, among which the right to remain silent, and he shall be ensured of assistance by his family and a lawyer (article 5, LXIII, of the Constitution of Brazil);

the arrested person is entitled to identification of those responsible for his arrest or for his police questioning (article 5, LXIV, of the Constitution of Brazil);

the illegal arrest shall be immediately remitted by the judicial authority (article 5, LXV, of the Constitution of Brazil);

no one shall be taken to prison or held therein, when the law admits release on own recognizance, subject or not to bail (article 5, LXVI, of the Constitution of Brazil);

there shall be no civil imprisonment for indebtedness except in the case of a person responsible for voluntary and inexcusable default of alimony obligation and in the case of an unfaithful trustee (article 5, LXVII, of the Constitution of Brazil);

habeas corpus shall be granted whenever a person suffers or is in danger of suffering violence or coercion against his freedom of locomotion, on account of illegal actions or abuse of power (article 5, LXVIII, of the Constitution of Brazil);

One may ask: in the dialectic of penal executions in Brazil, have the Constituted Powers assumed the relevant mission of fulfilling International Law and the Constitution of Brazil?

In practice, the dynamics of power in the Brazilian Penal System have always been proven incompatible with the ideology of human rights enshrined in the set of constitutional rights that are molded according to international norms for protection.

The constant commotion in the standards of Criminal Justice is sharply revealed in the current reality of prison establishments, which is typically criminalizing, for both those being tried and those already convicted. This is in the context of the prison chaos of an archaic system that is propitious for internationalizing the rotten values of prison life, which day by day promotes the evils that in theoretically proposes to avoid.

As a result, the efficacy of the judicial universe of criminal legislation—Penal Code, Penal Procedure Code and Law for Penal Execution—is completely compromised in terms of mechanisms for imposing duties regarding the rights, guarantees and advantages directed toward individualizing the sentence adapted to the profile of the condemned.

Can there be respect for human rights of prisoners, if the State does not provide them conditions for enjoying the benefits of a penal execution that is the product of observing constitutional and legal commandments.

The answer is obviously no. It would be like looking to the night sky and trying to count the stars. That is the reason for the fragility and the lack of prestige of the Penal Execution Law, when, caught up in a vicious routine, it does not appropriately guard the goods and values essential for healthy living by incarcerated persons. Without knowing how to valuate the effects of certainty of punishment and a just placement of a sentence, the Penal Execution Law will never be able to grow in the cultural structure of the community to become the regulator of conduct in the institutional dialogue between the prisoner and the State.

In practice, the legality imprinted on the penal system has ceased to be the most appropriate instrument for change, for transformation and acquisition of a new individual and social posture and has become simply the instrument for a security policy. That tendency disfigures the Penal Execution Law, whose legitimization implies a relationship of conformity with the principles of *legality, equality* and *humanity* honored in the Constitution of the Republic.

Another aspect deserves special reflection.

The way forward, in the sense of providing differentiated policy skills for alternative sentences, has always demanded, in any Country, implementation on harmony with the institutional representatives: *Legislators, Police, Prosecutors, Judges, Employees in the Penal System and Representatives of Community Entities.* These have much to offer towards the success of substitutes for prison, in an intelligent and creative manner, with conditions for going forward along a glowing path of protection and guarantee of human rights, without the stigmas that complicate or impede the social reinsertion of the condemned person into the community.

What will be the social profit of a new law issuing alternative sentences in Brazil, if the State does not provide the technical and administrative conditions for carrying them out?

The question is not simply to utilize the exactness of Mathematical Science in the technique of de-penalization (removing the punishment form the domain of Criminal Law) or the technique of de-judicialization (removing the actions from the jurisdiction of the Judicial Penal Power, considering the expediency of placing them in the civil or administrative sphere). It is not simply that. Effectiveness in a policy for alternatives to prison involves the engineering of knowing how to precisely dose who really needs to go to jail, by virtue of his or her complex and polymorphic human nature, for acting against the norms that protect rights, disrespect for which fundamentally strikes at principles of social cohesion, going beyond the limits of tolerance.

WORKS CITED

BALIBAR, Etienne. *Les Frontières de la Démocratie.* Paris, Édition La Découverte, 1992, pp. 134-136.

BERCIS, Pierre. *Pour de Nouveau Droits de l'Homme.* Paris, Éditons lattès, 1985, pp. 122-123.

CARRIÓ, Genaro. *Human rights and su Protection.* Buenos Aires, Editorial Abeledo-Perrot, 1990, pp. 41-48.

HAARSCHER, Guy. *Philosophie des Droits de l'Homme.* Bruxelles, Édition de l'Université de Bruxelles, 1991, pp. 11-13.

MADIOT, Yves. *Droits de l'Homme et Libertés Publiques.* Paris, Éditions Masson, 1976, pp. 209-212.

NINO, Carlos. *Ética and Derechos Humanos.* Buenos Aires, Editorial Paidós, 1984, pp. 23-27.

TRINDADE, Antonio Cançado. *A Proteção Internacional dos Direitos Humanos.* São Paulo, Editora Saraiva, 1991, pp. 631-632.

Chapter Twenty-One

Technological Progress and Penal Reform

Edmundo Oliveira

THE NEW WORLD WITHOUT FRONTIERS

Never has the slogan, the fetish of the visionary novel by renowned writer George Orwell, titled "Nineteen Eighty-Four," been so relevant as today, since its publication in London in 1949. Inspired by horror of the Stalinist and Nazi regimes, the common basis for all totalitarian power, Orwell's celebrated counter-utopia anticipated the extraordinary development of surveillance technologies, which more and more seem to bring nearer the fearsome horizon of absolute social control over humans.

The new world without frontiers is showing up with accelerated tendencies in the modern world, for which reason one hardly hears today the poetic lament from other times about the sinuous absences in the avenues of imagination. It is the coming together of technological enterprises which, in terms of telecommunications such as access to Internet, leaves us all more and more perplexed every day in the frenzy of globalized business, production and alternative commerce, in a market that is full of surprises and risks.

Through the force of technical progress and the inexorable proliferation of computer technology, what was merely science fiction half a century ago has now become tangible reality. Machines are so connected to people's lives that one does not perceive their presence day to day. It is not a case merely of automatic doors, elevators and escalators, synchronized traffic lights, domestic robots or the subway. Every day, Lawrence Lessing comments in his interesting essay "The Architecture of Privacy," "electronic mechanisms watch over, scrutinized, control, watch, . . . for better . . . or for worse . . ."[2]

Intended, in principle, to prevent assaults on persons and goods, the video monitor is present on streets, highways, in parking lots, inside large stores, in stadiums and in prisons. Telematic systems connected to central alarm systems protect apartments and cities. Devices allow distanced monitoring of houses of elderly people who, in case of emergency can activate a signal going to a rapid assistance service, reinforcing protection for more vulnerable individuals. Thanks to the network of cellular telephones, a mother can control her children's route to school, as long as she pays a specific fee: any detour from the programmed itinerary is automatically transmitted to her. A location signaler utilizing the Global Positioning System (GPS) mounted on the chassis on an automobile or truck makes it easier to locate a stolen vehicle. And thus, by producing an illusory feeling of safety, electronic control seems to tranquilize people. However, unless someone moves to an isolated desert island, deprived of any concession to modernity, nothing and no one can escape the impetuous vigilance dictated by technological progress.[3]

Because of its usefulness in terms of security, the Criminal Justice system is opening up to the technique of electronic monitoring by land telephone line and its variants that operate the tracking system around the world via internet and by the satellite surveillance map equipped with the Global Positioning System (GPS). The novelty does not lie in the possibility of controlling movement of the body (prisons have always performed the main role in retaining individuals in a confined universe), but in technology today permitting a systematic and potentially unlimited role over facts and gestures and, who knows, tomorrow over the thoughts of people being monitored.

SEDIMENTATION OF CREATIVE STRATEGIES IN PENAL EXECUTION

In the contemporary context of overcrowded prisons, every new penal policy demands a readjustment in carrying out sentences, with alternatives or combinations of alternations directed towards incarceration that seeks the social and moral reinsertion of the delinquent, as well as preventing recidivism.[4] The requirement of a fixed residence under electronic monitoring fits perfectly into the dialectic that counterpoints security and freedom. Taking advantage of the innovations and advances in the new millennium in such varied domains—including electronics, telecommunications, video, telephone wiretapping, lie detectors and biotechnology—the installation of electronic monitoring or satellite surveillance improves the dusty and anachronistic image of Justice, to the benefit of "high-tech" Justice, which is abreast of the evolutions occurring in contemporary society.[5]

Beginning with the first experiences in North America in the early 1980s, until its operationalization in Europe in the mid-1990s, electronic monitoring has been praised because of its singular properties in individualizing the sentence.[6] It avoids the nefarious effects of desocialization through imprisonment—mainly for first offenders—and facilitates maintenance of family bonds and the exercise of a professional activity. That system also makes it possible to reduce the occupancy rate in penitentiary establishments, by dealing with defendants and persons convicted of lesser offenses at a much lower cost. House arrest under electronic monitoring removes its beneficiaries from the promiscuity and poor hygiene conditions, the idleness and irresponsibility found in so many prisons. It is a type of punishment that does not bring with it the stigma associated with incarceration, and assures the continuation of a "normal" in the eyes of the employer and together with the family.[7]

Such a modality for controlling persons placed under the guidance of Justice thus constitutes a modern and effective means for administering sentences. Modern, because it enables an "intelligent" application of the penal sanction under a household regime, while at the same time its organization reconciles in space and time the best way to punish and guarantee social insertion. Effective, because electronic monitoring, automated and systematized by information technology has proven to be a control for open regimes that is less costly and not inclined to be a random practice. Furthermore, electronic monitoring, in its connective operations produces flexibility in the boundary between the public and the private space.[8] This measure touches on the traditional points of reference between the notion of prison associated to the absence of private life and the notion of household, contrarily associated with the sanctuary of private life and liberty. In this way, the virtual universe offers a new path for mitigating the depressing spectacle of traditional penal sentencing with the new horizon of improving the establishment of social peace in procedures that are capable of providing appropriate answers to the difficulties of human coexistence. Therefore, the law is applied, but without compromising the perspectives for rehabilitation and the imperatives of public protection.

Livingston is correct when he cautions that any political regime, in order to improve itself in the light of the principles and rules of legitimacy, will only be able to project its international prestige if it consolidates the task of firmly cultivate the responsibility of each citizen in seeking coordinated actions, which will germinate as the pendulum in the process of dialogue between the community and the Public Power.[9]

This being the case, harmonizing the ideal of efficiently avoiding commitment of criminal infractions under the auspices of full respect for the transparent exercise of citizenship is no easy task. It will require imposing on those in power the task of developing creative strategies, providing the best option for harmonious coexistence, above all in light of the challenge to adopt procedures capable of giving an appropriate response to specific problems in regions of delinquency, especially of criminal networks and organizations, which are always ready to give rise, in conflictive or threatening situations, to a profound and pernicious feeling of security, alongside the obstinate hope for better days.

All of the adjustments in favor of social peace, as Professor Edgardo Rotman appropriately clarifies, need to be managed with successful experiences, in which society sees, in the movements reacting to crime and violence, an example of respect for conciliating all of the values of the individual and society.[10] The establishment of that equilibrium needs to be understood as a true system of communicating channels, founded on the dynamics of three essential components: the police apparatus, judicial administration and the penitentiary system.

Both the government and public opinion, in safeguarding the Institutions, need to continue coordinating efforts directed at implementing the means and measures that will face, determinedly and competently, strong rejections from the failed punishment model, pushed through the filter of symbolic delinquency, represented by the poor who fill the prisons and constitute the system's clientele.[11]

In harmony with the worthy purpose of doing justice, a penal sanction, in any legislative structure, goes beyond the purpose of retribution for an unjust act, since none may turn their backs on the high relevance of the preventive scope of reintegrating the condemned person into society, intimidating potential wrongdoers and strengthening the judicial consciousness of all members of the social group. That is why one must combat the practice of transforming the punishment of the sentence into a horror apparatus, as if that were the only proclaimed purpose to be fulfilled.

TELE-DETECTION APPLIED IN CRIMINAL JUSTICE

The birth of electronic monitoring followed technological progress in tele-surveillance. It is justified by the need of Criminal Justice to develop alternatives to incarceration, thus reducing the recidivism rate at a much lower cost than entailed by prisons.

One should note that controlled household arrest is not something new. Professor Cristophe Cardet records that household arrest was already applied during investigative criminal proceedings in effect in the ancient Roman Empire.[12] The so called free custody enabled a person to be designated as a tutor,

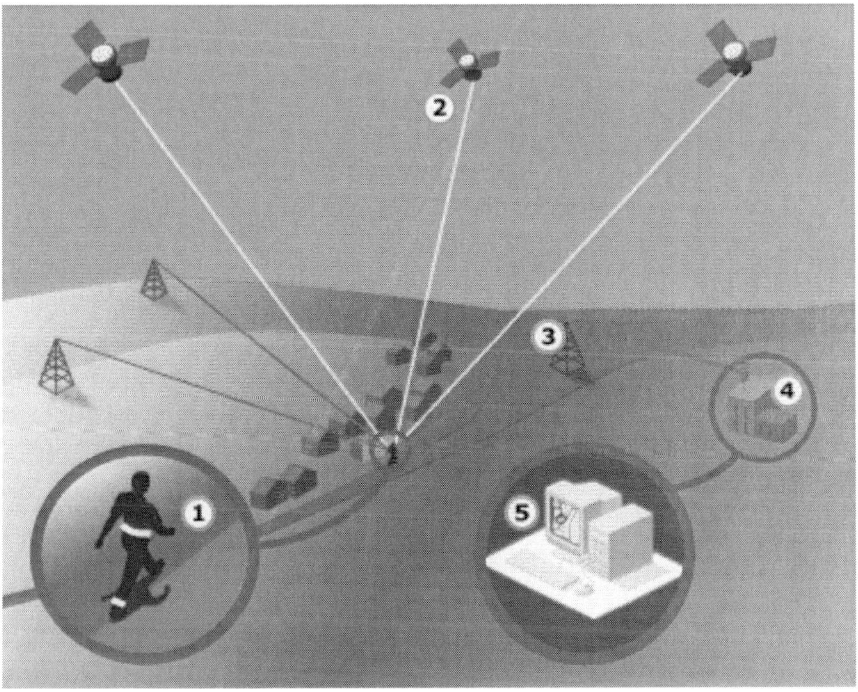

Figure 21.1. The progress of science and technology is fantastic in terms of tele-detection, which opens the horizons of Criminal Justice for tracking conduct by the wrongdoer through the satellite surveillance map and by means of internet access.

guaranteeing the representation of the defendant before the Courts, or authorizing the person to remain at home under guard by soldiers. Due to the difficulty of transforming a household into a fortress and actions by tutors who active in an excessively coercive manner towards the persons and their goods, the judges always used household arrest very prudently. The main barrier blocking the development of that type of practice, both in the pre-sentencing phase (before pronouncement of penalty) and in carrying out the sentence, was the absence of security from a supplementary guarantee, such as payment of a bond. As a measure of confidence, remaining in a household can only work if the interested party agrees to submit to the rules. At any moment, the individual in household arrest may elude the control of Justice, as long as he or she is not under careful surveillance. The result of technological advances in terms of tele-detection applied in the field of Criminal justice, electronic monitoring has arisen in a supporting role in providing secure enforcement of household arrest.[13]

Important persons deserve recognition in the sequence of advances in Physics in the area of tele-detection.

The Dutch physicist, Christiaan Huygens, in 1678, had the intuition of the ondulatory theory of light. Later on, the work of Frenchman Augustin Fresnel in 1819, on vibration and length of waves, and of another Frenchman, André-Marie Ampère, in 1820 about electromagnetism, and of the Englishman Michael Faraday, in 1830 on electromagnetic induction, allowed the American Joseph Henry, Professor at Princeton University, to carry out the first experiment in transmitting an electromagnetic signal. And in 1831, Joseph Henry was able to make a magnet spin at a distance of 1,609 meters and ring a bell.[14]

This research was enormously useful for expanding the set of devices and techniques employed in transmitting information over long distances, instantaneously, leading to what is today called tele-detection, or telecommunications systems. One should highlight here the association of innovations carried forward in the Nineteenth Century, the invention of the telephone, in 1876, attributed to the Scotsman Alexander Graham Bell, as well as the invention in 1897 of wireless telegraphy, and the progress of radio diffusion through the efforts of Italian physicist Guglielmo Marconi.[15]

Beginning in 1919, the United States Army began to employ radio signals to discover and follow ships and aircraft thanks to the effects of reflection of electromagnetic waves produced by the passage of large objects. In 1935, the first magnetometers, installed aboard the transatlantic steamers Oregon and Normandie facilitated iceberg detection. During the Second World War, some more evolved devices using artesian waves were used to locate, identify and follow targets in motion in the air and on the ground. All of those systems could be equipped with a fixed energy source: an electric battery. The invention of the transistor, in 1948 in the United States by John Bardeen, William Shockley and Walter Brattain, made it possible to accelerate direct experimentation with tele-detection or telecommunication in living beings.

The fertile paths traveled by Medicine and Physics certainly favored concrete development of the ideals of controlling lawbreakers involved in delinquency through monitoring.[16]

It is known that in Ancient Egypt doctors were already focusing their attention on the meaning of pulsing blood vessels, because, as the Ebers papyrus expressively relates, by placing one's fingers on various parts of the body, one can verify that the heart "speaks" through the vessels. However, the appropriate definition of pressure in the arteries was only begun in the Seventeenth Century, with the dedication of Italian doctor Santorio Santorio, to whom is attributed the first attempt to register the pulse through a Pulsiologium, a device that he launched in 1620, to measure pulse frequency and variation. Some have attributed invention of the Thermometer to Galileo Galilei, but it was Santorio Santorio who gave clinical applicability to both the Pulsiologium and the Thermometer, which he presented in 1612 to measure the body's temperature.[17]

The first attempt to numerically quantify the arterial pulse in a non-invasive manner was made by the Frenchmen J. Hérrison, physician, and P. Gernier, engineer, in 1834. This was a device similar to a thermometer and was called a Sphygmomanometer. Later on, other medical researchers created their Sphygmomanometers with clinical methods for assessing human arterial pressure, notably the technique designed in 1733 by the English doctor Stephen Hales and the invention of the Italian Scipione Riva-Rocci in 1896. Scipione Riva-Rocci's Sphygmomanometer even today, is universally used as an accurate instrument for measuring arterial pressure.

In May 1941, Harry Weiss published in the London Journal of Laboratory and Clinical Medicine, an article describing his oscillometric ausculatory method for automatically registering and codifying arterial pressure. Up till then, there was no device that would enable automatic, continuous and simultaneous recording of systolic and diastolic pressures, as well as the pulse pressure and cardiac frequency.

In 1960, Americans Allen Hinman and Maurice Sokolow, in California were the pioneers in developing non-invasive ambulatory methods for measuring arterial pressure. Those authors, with the use of the Remler Recorder, introduced an initial version of a voluminous system that needed manual inflation in order to operate. The same authors, in 1964, published a paper describing the application of the Remler Monitor in patients with high blood pressure and showed the great variability of arterial pressure during the day. Their paper also demonstrated that, in most patients, measurements of casual or office visit arterial pressures were higher than ambulatory pressure measurements.[18]

An essay published by Maurice Sokolow, in 1966 in the noted journal Circulation, demonstrated for the first time that ambulatory measures were better correlated with lesions in target organs than casual pressure measurements.

Allen Hinman became known as the father of the Portable Monitor, called the Portometer, which also became know by the name of its manufacturer Remler M Z000, which began utilizing the ausculatory method and the semi-automatic noninvasive technique (without harming the human body) to check arterial pressure.

The Riva-Rocci Sphigmomanometer today is still universally utilized, although other inventions have been tested, such as the Zero-Muddler Sphygmomanometer in 1963 and the Randon-Zero Sphygmomanometer in 1970.[19] Medicine in this area is fascinating and does not stop, but a succession of research activities on oscillographic monitors continues in search of the highest reliability in examining body temperature and blood pressure in humans, with studies carried out, among other places, in the laboratories of the National Aeronautics and Space Administration (NASA) laboratories in the United States, to determine arterial pressure and cardiovascular risks in their astronauts (consult: http://www.nasa.gov/about/research/index).

All this fantastic trajectory in Science and Technology made possible the construction, in 1970 in the United States, of the Theory of H. Swan and C. Gang, with a view to launching Invasive Hemodynamic Monitoring through the use of the Swan-Gang Catheter. This has become an important clinical procedure in Medicine for treating patients under critical circumstances. Connected to a computer, the Swan-Gang does a reading and recording of hemodynamic parameters in the pulmonary artery for treating states of shock, infarct of the myocardium, acute respiratory insufficiency, septic conditions and other severe complications that require intensive treatment in an ICU, even though its use is limited due to its high cost.[20]

In 1962, research with the Cooperative Shark Tagging Program headquartered in Rhode Island, in the United States, obtained information about sharks in the Atlantic Ocean by means of devices fixed on their dorsal fins. Later on, more sophisticated equipment, signalers, and the Argos satellite (from the name of the Greek mythological hero with multiple eyes) were applied with other marine animals (whales, turtles, killer whales), land animals (bears, wolves, caribou) and migratory birds so as to follow their movements. Thanks to biosensors, miniature data acquisition systems began to supply information about the body temperature and depth of dives of sea-lions or seabirds. Using the same principle, it became possible to follow fishing boats, recover shipwrecked sailors or locate a lost tourist, as long as such people have a GPS (Global Positioning System) signaler.

The applications of such distanced localization systems has developed rapidly, but the use of electronic monitoring, in the area of Criminal Justice has required much more time and effort, perhaps because of the lack of security with the first devices, and certainly also because of prudence in judicial circles regarding what were perceived to be simple electronic gadgets.[21]

TECHNICAL OPTIONS FOR ELECTRONIC MONITORING

Currently, there are four technical options for electronic monitoring of offenders:

a. adaptation of a bracelet;
b. adaptation of an ankle bracelet;

c. adaptation of a belt;
d. adaptation of a microchip implanted in the human body (now being tested on volunteers in the United States and the United Kingdom).

Those devices send signals to a transmitter placed in the Monitoring Control Center. It has been absolutely necessary to have technical support from a landline fiber optic telephone, installed in the offender's house, to stimulate signal transmission. Cellular telephony has so far proved ineffective, but advanced experiments are underway.

The transmitter connected to a satellite makes it possible to know the exact location of the offender. Efficiency has increased due to processing information processing achieved through the advanced GPS integrated circuit technology.

GPS has the advantage of calculating the longitude, latitude, direction and speed of the device-wearer at all times. It is also highly useful for alerting the Monitoring Control Center when, for example, the offender penetrates an

Photo 4. Technical option for electronic monitoring of an offender with adaptation of a bracelet. In this model of technological device, the Monitoring Device needs to be close to the bracelet, otherwise an alarm will be sounded, notifying the Monitoring Control Center.

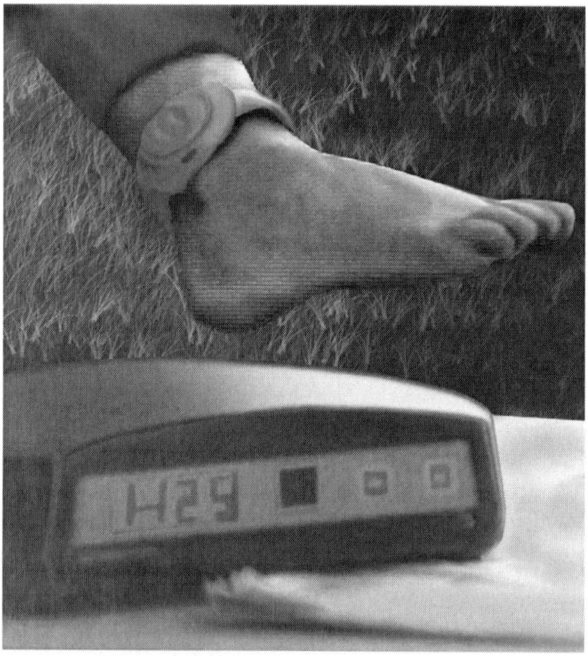

Photo 5. Technical option for electronic monitoring of an offender with adaptation of an ankle bracelet. The Receiver, installed in the offender's residence, transmits the connecting signals between the ankle bracelet and surveillance via satellite.

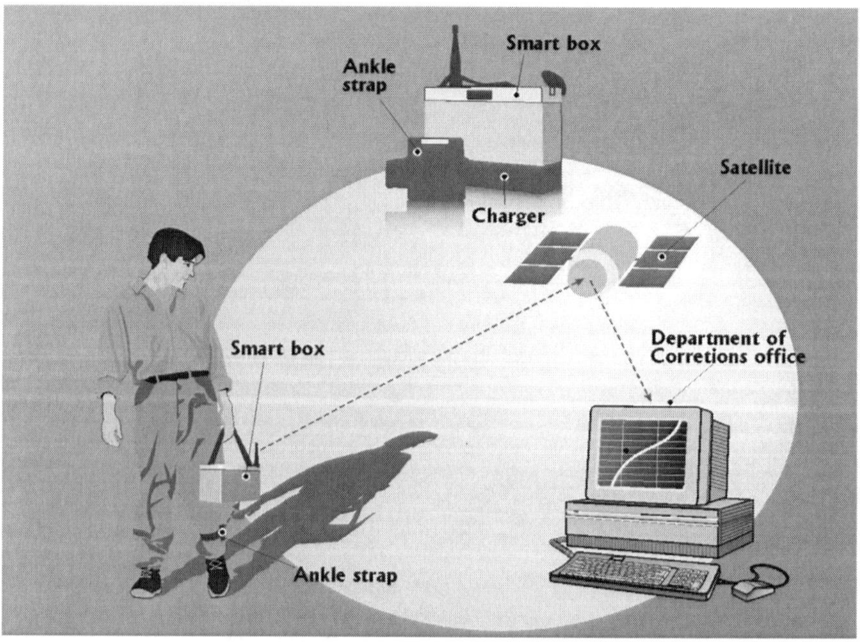

Photo 6. Technical option for electronic monitoring of an offender with adaptation of a Receiver-Belt connected to the satellite system.

Photo 7. Technical option for electronic monitoring of an offender with adaptation of a microchip in the subcutaneous level of the human body, inserted in the arm, between the dermis and epidermis, without affecting the blood vessels.

exclusion area, such as schools, malls, hospitals and public parks, as determined by the Judge.

It is interesting to note that the GPS can also serve as a means to prove the offender's innocence, in circumstances where there has been prejudgment brought through a false or unfair accusation.

NOTES

1. HEINER, Robert. Criminology: A Cross-Cultural Perspective. St. Paul, West Edition, 1996, p. 197.
2. LESSIG, Lawrence. "The Architecture of Privacy," in Vanderbilt University Journal of Entertainment Law & Practice, Nashville, no 56, p. 13-14, 1999.
3. HEINER, Robert. Social Problems: An Introduction to Critical Constructionism, Oxford, Oxford University Press, 2006, p. 147-148.
4. BOLLE, Pierre-Henri. "Consensualisme en Prison," in Nouvelles Orientations du Régime Péitentiaire, Lisbonne, Actes des Journées de la Fondation Internationale Pénale et Pénitentiaire, p. 119-200, 2000.
5. BONNEMAISON, G. "La Modernisation du Service Public Pénitentiaire," in Rapport au Garde de Sceaux et au Premier Ministre, Paris, p. 31, 1989.

6. LAVIELLE, Bruno & LAMEYRE, Xavier. Le Guide des Peines, Paris, Éditions Dalloz, 2003, p. 370-374 e 371-372.

7. VAUGHN, Joseph. Planning for Change: The Use of Electronic Monitoring as a Correctional Alternative, Warrensbourg, Central Missouri State University, 1997, p. 161-162.

8. FROMENT, J. C. "La Surveillance Électronique à Domicile: Une Nouvelle Économie du Pouvoir de Punir?" in Cahiers de la Sécurité Intérieure, Paris, no 34, p. 149-151, 1998.

9. LIVINGSTON, Jay. Crime and Criminology, New Jersey, Simon and Schuster, 1996, p. 123.

10. ROTMAN, Edgardo. Beyond Punishment: A New View on the Rehabilitation of Criminal Offenders, New York, Greenwood Press, 1990, p. 156-158.

11. BURKE, Roger Hopkins. An Introduction to Criminological Theory, Portland, Willan Publishing, 2001, p. 130-135.

12. CARDET, Christophe. Le Placement Sous Surveillance Électronique, Paris, Édition L'Harmattan, 2003, p. 28-76.

13. BLACK, M. & SMITH, R. G. "Electronic Monitoring in the Criminal Justice System," in Trends & Issues in Crime and Criminal Justice, Sydney, Edition of Australian Institute of Criminology, no 254, p. 6-7, 2003.

14. YOUNG, Hugh D. & FREEDMAN, Roger. University Physics, Massachusetts, Addison–Wesley, 1995, p. 423-431.

15. GIANCOLI, Douglas C. Physics: Principles with Application, New Jersey, Prentice Hall, 1998, p. 308-317.

16. ABADINSKY, Howard. Probation and Parole: Theory and Practice, New Jersey, Prentice Hall, 1994, p. 398.

17. METTLER, C. & METTLER, F. History of Medicine, Philadelphia, Edition Blakiston, 1947, p. 139-146.

18. ELLIOT, H. "Arterial Blood Pressure Monitoring," in Annals of Second International Nifedipine GITS Simposium, Paris, p. 17-20, 1994.

19. DOMINGUEZ, R. & MICHELI, A. "Evolución de la Esfigmomanometria," in Archivo Mexicano de Cardiologia, México, vol. 34, p. 315-323, 1994.

20. ASKEY, J. M. "History of Medicine: The Auscultatory Gap in Sphigmomanometry," in Archives of Internal Medicine, Chicago, no 80, p. 93-98, 1974.

21. JOHANSSON, Linda. "La Prison Électronique," in Le Courrier de l'Unesco, Paris, 51e année, p. 13-14, 1998.

Chapter Twenty-Two

Globalization, Cyberspace and Organized Crime via the Internet

Edmundo Oliveira

The Twenty-First Century has been characterized by the continued emergence and growing strength and influence of transnational crime and by the globalization of crime groups that take advantage of today's advanced technology as much as of the convenience of border-free international travel and trade to carry out their activities at a level and speed unknown before.

As a result of globalization and the spread of technology,[1] there have been changes happening in the nature and extent of organized crime. Indeed, there has been a strong tendency towards the diversification of the illegal activities commissioned by organized groups as well as an accentuated rise in the number of countries affected by them. There has also been an enlargement of organized crime activities in areas such as kidnapping people for ransom, trafficking in humans, human organs, counterfeit money, goods, arms, works of art, diamonds, stolen cars, natural resources, cultural objects, viruses, bacteria, ozone layer-depleting substances, hazardous waste, endangered wild flora and fauna and last but certainly even more disturbing, sex commerce related to the corruption of minors and child pornography.[2]

The advances in communication technology have opened new perspectives to highly sophisticated criminal activities. In this regard, it has been observed that there has been an increase in the number of fraudulent practices done via the internet, which as a matter of fact has become an instrument widely used by criminals. What is more, communication technology has made criminal organizations more flexible and dynamic—the electronic mail has become an essential tool that eliminates problems concerning time and space. Law adaptation to these new tendencies has been slow, whereas organized crime tends to quickly adapt and adopt the fruits of technological progress, which is no wonder, given the high profitability criminals can have by using it for their illicit activities.

The opening of new markets and the advance of communication technology have also been feeding the growth of organized crime in developing countries; that is explained by the diversity of activities involved in criminal operations. Transition-economy countries or countries affected by conflicts are particularly vulnerable to the growth of organized crime. In such cases, organized crime poses a real threat to reforms in police forces, customs services and judiciary institutions as these sectors can engage in criminal or corrupt practices, which represents a serious obstacle to the stability and prosperity in these societies.[3]

Organized crime and corruption are related; corruption facilitates illicit activities and stands in the way of law enforcement. The struggle against corruption is, therefore, an integral part of the combat against organized crime. Furthermore, there has been a connection between organized crime, corruption and terrorism. Some terrorist groups rely, for instance, on organized crime to finance their activities. For this reason, the adoption of appropriate legislation, law enforcement procedures and the promotion of international cooperation to battle against organized crime and corruption reinforces the ability to fight against the widespread network of crime strategies involving mafia and terrorist groups.

International organized crime has globalized its activities for the same reasons legitimate multinational companies did so. Just as multinational companies open branches throughout the world in order to take advantage of attractive labor or raw materials, the same is true of illegal businesses. Moreover, international businesses, legal or illegal, also create over the world all the necessary infrastructure for production, marketing and distribution requirements. Illegal enterprises can expand geographically in order to capitalize on economic conditions, thanks to revolution in communication and in international transportation systems.[4] In addition to the aforementioned benefits which international crime as a whole has gained from globalization, for terrorists it also offers opportunities such as overseas recruitment, access to more affluent communities, and the possibility of being in close proximity to diaspora communities which in turn can help them logistically and financially.

The end of the cold war had a great influence on the rising of transnational crime. The termination of confrontation between the superpowers resulted in big scale reduction of conflict potential, nevertheless, from the end of the 1980s there has been a huge increase in the number of regional struggles. Unfortunately, the weapons and the people involved in these conflicts are very often linked to transnational criminal activities. It is important to note here, the flourishing of a big service industry that provides for the needs of all kinds of transnational criminals. That includes suppliers of false documents, credit card counterfeiting, fabrication of materials used in mass destruction weapons used by terrorist groups, not to mention the juridical, financial and accountancy services provided by high-level professionals for money launders who use fake companies in their home countries or abroad in order to disguise their illicit activities.

The growth of illegal transnational activities has been greatly favored by big technological advances from the post second war period. The increase of commercial air traffic, the improvement in telecommunications (including telephone, fax and speedy communications through the Internet) and the growth of international trade have made it easier for the circulation of goods and people.[5] The anonymity of chat-rooms on the Internet along with other computer generated communication technologies are used by criminals and terrorists to plan and carry out their activities. The terrorists responsible for the heinous attacks of September 11, 2001, used public access computers to send messages and to buy plane tickets. Likewise, drug traffickers from Colombia use cryptographed e-messages to plan and accomplish their commercial activities.

Globalization walks alongside free markets, free commerce ideologies and the decrease of government intervention. As globalization advocates say, the reduction of regulations and international barriers to commercial trade and to investment will increase commerce and development. Nevertheless, the same conditions which enable a globalized environment are also fundamental to the proliferation of crime. Traffickers and terrorists have exploited the significant decline in regulations, the slackening of borders control and the resulting bigger freedom to widen their activities across borders and in new places in the world.[6] Contact between criminal groups has become more frequent and faster. While the growth of legal commerce is regulated by adherence to border control policies, to customs service control, and to bureaucratic systems, transnational criminal groups freely exploit loopholes in governments law systems in order to increase their range of activities. Thus, they travel to places where they cannot be extradited, set up their operations in countries where the law is feebly and corruptly upheld and take their money to nations where there is bank secrecy or little efficient controls. As they segmentalize their operations, criminals and terrorists reap the benefits from globalization and at the same time reduce operational risks.

From the second half of the Twentieth Century, global commerce began to have a remarkable growth. However, the enormous flow of legitimate products started sharing space with a rise in the number of illegal products.

Telling what is legal from what is not has become a real challenge. Just a small percentage of container ships have their loads checked, thereby facilitating the circulation of drugs, arms and contraband. Thus, drugs can easily be transported on fishing boats without being detected, and a honey business may very well be used for money movement and to generate profits to traffickers and terrorists alike.

The last two decades of the previous century have witnessed the rising of a great variety of globalized crime. Drug trading was the first illegal segment to maximize its profits in a globalized world. Criminals have obtained huge profits from drug trafficking, and many terrorist groups have made narcotrafficking their main source of financing, showing how the well-structured machinery of what has become known as industrialized crime is not just about generating money but about fueling and reaching well-defined purposes in the dark areas of human criminal behavior.[7]

Traffickers and terrorists cannot continue with their activities without any fear of being prosecuted or convicted, for this reason, the present time calls for the creation of preventive policy models in which civil societies may have an actual participation, as exemplified by the measures that have been put into effect by the United Nations Conventions, which bring advances and recommendations concerning new criminal practices and international cooperation procedures for police patrol across borders,[8] as well as procedures for confiscating money obtained from corruption and money laundering, responsible for fostering trafficking and terrorism.

Socio-economic globalization has enabled the globalization of crime. However, judicial globalization has yet to occur so that judicial systems in different countries will be provided with appropriate measures and means to suppress crime and effectively and pedagogically punish those who must be penalized for their criminal activities whether by serving imprisonment sentences or by receiving alternative punishments.[9]

Creative sanctions are and will always be welcome, for instance, the use of task forces that consist of the setting up of multidisciplinary units to work on prevention, control and repression of globalized crime. Such attempts will only be effective if there is a strengthening of police forces and judicial systems, as much as the adoption of concrete actions on the part of public and private sectors, and a real involvement of society as a whole.

It is utterly important today that there be a coordination of policies and harmonious international public strategies so as to allow all nations to receive unequivocal quality gains in their commitment to ensure conflict pacification and a reliable promotion of justice and respect for human rights, hence it is necessary that the goal of crime and violence reduction be equated with increase in assistance, in education, in productive work, as well as in the interaction of individuals within their families and their communities.

Each individual country must seek progressive improvements through planning that is effective enough to change risk management conceptions pertaining to globalized public security.[10] The prospect of useful investments is always the driving force responsible for speeding up the changes that are necessary for combating indicators of underdevelopment in infrastructures in need of new scientific and technological improvements. Such is the target of a healthy millennium capable of rescuing the benefits brought out by globalization.

THE WORLD RISK SOCIETY

The feelings of uncertainty derived from public policies failure to meet the needs of supportive human coexistence have brought about a global scale fragmentation of citizenship, thereby giving rise to the contemporary characterization of the world risk society, especially in poorer countries where the desired goal of integration and homogenization, as the focal point of globalization, has progressively become compromised due to the existence of complex social and economic inequality issues.[11] Such factors have been extremely harmful not only to the trust placed on institutions' values but also to the preservation of ethical interactions in people's relationships within families and communities.

Thus, the world risk society with its inherent two-fold issues, namely social exclusion and the dangerous and progressive influence of social insecurity have proved to be deeply worrisome. The world risk society has already presented itself as a human degradation phenomenon involving dangerous sequences of contemporary tensions that share the same level of aggravation: public insecurity, ecological degradation, financial crises, nuclear disasters, slave labor, hunger, disorderly migration, criminality, prejudice and different ways of discrimination.[12]

In view of that, the question to be asked is: how interrelated is the growing notion of the world risk society and crime globalization?

Firstly, as crime has become more internationally oriented and taken advantage of less restrictive cross-borders controls, it has also become more violent in all continents. Secondly, the lone offender became a much rarer occurrence as opposed to group crime whose schemes are orchestrated by gangs, by criminal networks or by criminal organizations.[13] Group crime has outdone lone criminal practices because it is easier for individuals involved in the former to set up mechanisms that generate wealth inasmuch as it is established in the obscure world of national and international financial systems, where the line separating territorial from extraterritorial zones is not always clearly seen. Some examples of such money generating mechanisms are the expansion of offshore enterprises, bank transactions in tax havens and on-line commercial practices.[14] Money flow is directly linked to the rise of globalised transnational crime in any of its varied types of procedures or connections; an instance of this is the link between trafficking and terrorism.[15]

Wherever there is economic power, there is also the intensification and strengthening of gangs, criminal networks and criminal organizations, which sometimes can even count on having the complicity of government officials to enable them to have easy transit within the public and private administrative spheres. For instance, in international financial and banking systems, the

annual transactions of about 20 billion dollars are derived from laundered money obtained from illegal drug dealing. According to the United Nations Organization,[16] such amount of money has the equivalence of 3% to 5% of the world's gross domestic product.

Present day political policies do not need to be in search of miracles or lyrical promises which cannot be fulfilled. What is needed is simply the wisdom of promoting trust in institutions, hopefully bringing positive results for the collective good and for human rights as well.[17] It is hoped that the goals set forth for the millennium in the year 2000 by the United Nations will be successfully achieved, given the expectations for lasting solutions to the problems besetting millions of people worldwide, in the restless scenario of globalization.

CRIME, COMPUTER AND INTERNET TECHNOLOGY

There is no doubt as to the fact that computer and internet-related technology has attained an almost ubiquitous-like nature and impacted the way we work, buy and sell, share information, or interact with people inside and outside of our communities. It is precisely because of its large dissemination and ample use in so many aspects of our lives, that cyber technology requires special attention as to the safety it offers to users.

Our confidence in technology, as well as our appetite for it, has turned us into avid users of the many options it brings us. However, while pleasurable and informative, technology is rapidly being transformed into a source of cybernetic victimization.

Inevitably, there are those who find ways to use their technological skills to take advantage of more vulnerable individuals, notably the young, the immature, the gullible and the greedy. As a result, cyberspace technology is rapidly becoming a tool for exploitation, harassment, threats and manipulation of an increasing number of people. One may even assert that the dual component: callousness of a cybernetic predator and cyberspace anonymity, make cybernetic victimization not only easy, but even virtually effortless.[18]

Furthermore, cyberspace is the new arena not only for solitary activities, but also, on a larger scale, for collective activities conducted by a network of criminal organizations specialized in transnational operations which include: money laundering, evasion of funds and terrorism. As already noted, criminals have been much more agile in adapting to this technological new world, and gained tremendous advantages in carrying out their goals across continents, swiftly, undetected and with their secrets well hidden.

Responses on the part of governments and international agencies have been, as a rule, slow, insufficient and for the most part not very reactive.

Special attention must be paid to the use of computers and internet-related technology in carrying out warlike and terrorist actions. There are common intersecting points between the real and virtual worlds that may and will be used as targets by a new form of cyber threat, namely cyber terrorism. Also known as infrastructural war, cyber terrorism is a differentiated manner of conducting conflicts, at a regional and worldwide level, and will probably be the dominant form of warfare in the Twenty-First Century. It poses a serious threat to the networked systems of countries and international institutions—cyber terrorism attacks can wreak havoc to computer networks and disable electrical facilities, Internet service, computer systems of airport control towers; disrupt phone services and corrupt or prevent access to data of banking systems, thereby causing generalized panic and bringing a country's critical infrastructure to a halt.

FORMS OF CYBERNETIC OR COMPUTER CRIMES

Is cyber crime a modality of crime exclusively created by the advent of computer technology, or is it a traditional crime that has been transformed by computer use?

There are several forms of crime linked to the information technology market:

- cloning of technology;
- threats;
- espionage;
- trafficking in password;
- invasion of data or privacy;
- extortion;
- cybernetic stalking;
- nuisance electronic mail;
- fraudulent transactions;
- copyright violation;
- undue appropriation of values;
- dissemination of false information or concepts;
- offenses to honor;
- piracy;
- drugs;
- money laundering;
- illegal immigration and trafficking in persons;
- weapons and animals trade;

- incitement and planning of terrorism;
- creation and propagation of viruses;
- pedophilia;
- prostitution;
- obscene publications.

When immersed in the vast cyberspace network, an individual's behavior tends to be less inhibited than in their normal off-line lives. In fact, the environment provided by the interconnected cyberworld, where one can enjoy the benefits of interaction with others while being physically distant, is conducive to attitudes some individuals would probably refrain from displaying were they interacting face-to-face with people in the real world. Unfortunately, this loss of inhibition coupled with a certain level of naïveté may lead some to share personal information and respond to apparently harmless requests or offers from certain sites or webfriends, and by so doing, placing themselves in very vulnerable positions.

Cyber predators rely on anonymity and physical distance to evade the immediate consequences of their actions. The impersonal nature of the connection and the distance from the intended target facilitate the criminal's task, through the process of desensitization.[19]

Information, reminders, commercial announcements, chat rooms and instantaneous message programs can all put people in the line of danger, especially children, who may become victims of predatory activity, and also obtain access to material from erotic sites. In fact, children and teenagers make up the majority of victims—predators frequently pass themselves off as one of them in order to make contact, and after having established a relationship of trust and common interests, proceed to influence their victims into deviant behavior associated with pornography. Rebellious or problematic youths, seeking to liberate themselves from parental authority and control, are especially susceptible to fall prey to these criminals. Equally susceptible are the elderly, who have become common targets of virtual swindlers.[20]

Ironically, despite being a facilitator of criminal activities, the electronic media, has proven to be the best enabling instrument for detection and prosecution of cyber criminals.[21] Just as criminals have become deft users of technology, authorities across the globe use computer expertise, software and electronic devices to track down and prosecute on-line criminals—computer forensic investigators use sophisticated software to track on-line criminals down through their digital trail, uncover evidence, restore deleted files and e-mails, decode encryptions and complex passwords in order to find hidden files, and in some cases, authorities can even intercept on-line communication in real time. However, most computer detection techniques are time consuming and costly, as they require expensive up-to-date equipment and continuous training of cybercrime agents. Not all governments have fully realized the extensive impact e-crimes have upon the public and private sectors of their countries, and, therefore, some are reluctant to allocate necessary funds to equip and train law enforcement agents.

THE NATURE OF COMPUTER CRIME

It should be pointed out that, so far, there is no universally accepted definition of the term computer crime. Internationally there is an ongoing discussion concerning what can be specifically construed as criminal behavior in the area of information technology.[22] The Council of Europe Convention on Cybernet Crime includes a variety of different violations related to computer crime in its substantial Criminal Law clauses. By way of illustration, a section that deals with computer-related offences is subdivided into articles on computer-related forgery and computer-related fraud.[23]

The difficulty in defining what computer crime is occurs partly due to the various roles in which computers may serve for achieving criminal intents.[24] They can be the tool used in committing the crime, the target of criminal action, or merely incidental to the crime. Additionally, a good number of criminal conduct, among the long list of computerized crimes, are in fact traditional offenses, familiar in the history of Criminal Law, that are now being committed in a high-tech fashion.[25] Perpetrators, victims and motives may also vary widely in computer crimes. For example, a transgressor may be a young hacker determined to exhibit his or her skills by invading a government agency or company security system. Or, the criminal may be a terrorist[26] invading the same system with the purpose of destroying or disabling a governmental or military agency.[27]

In light of that, one must not automatically presume that crimes committed in cyberspace[28] are an entirely novel phenomenon. Perpetrators may simply use cyberspace to carry out conduct long considered illegal. The advent of the telephone, radio and television, for example, enabled the rise of new and varied ways of carrying out frauds, but fraud in itself has been considered an illicit attitude for centuries. Some theorists argue that, since cyberspace is simply a means used in committing traditional crimes, there is absolutely no need to consider cybernet crimes as a separate category of crime nor of developing legislation exclusively for them.[29] They assert that the law does not differentiate types of crimes according to the method used in their perpetration. That is, regardless of the method used in a crime, in Criminal Law, the focus is on the harm resulting from specific conduct. Thus, there is no such thing as method-specific crimes such as, for example, homicide by stabbing, homicide by firearm, homicide by strangulation, homicide by stoning, etc.

It may be argued that what is currently described as cybernet crime represents more than the use of a specific method to perpetrate criminal offences long recognized by Criminal Law. The vast range of activities that can be associated with computer-related crimes, allows one, therefore, to conclude that the focus of attention must be on the criminal conduct, while considering the computer as merely the tool employed. In the United States, the Department of Justice seems to endorse such a crime policy approach.[30]

Opposed to this are specialists who believe that computer related practices need to be treated in a different manner. They make use, for example, of economic reasons to affirm that cyberspace is a unique medium, demanding a series of distinct rules in a changing world. That was an important theme discussed at the Twelfth United Nations Congress on Crime Prevention and Criminal Justice.[31]

In summary, the interpretation of federal legislation in the United States on crimes committed through the use of computer is of little aid in conciliating the differing views on this subject. In that country, there is legislation on computer-related frauds that establishes different types of conduct with regard to computers, as well as the possibility of punishment by both State and Federal Justice Systems for a wide range of actions. Among these are the use of a computer for harassment or espionage, unauthorized access of a government computer, interstate trafficking in passwords and extortion resulting from use of a computer. As an example, the United States Federal Law against cyberstalking establishes the following: *Whoever transmits in interstate or foreign commerce any communication containing any threat to kidnap any person or any threat to injure the person of another, shall be fined under this title or imprisoned not more than five years, or both.*

That law is based on intent. This being the case, the desire to cause harm must be proved in order to achieve a verdict of guilty. Such a concept was put to the test in the Baker Case, in which a young student at the University of Michigan posted a story describing the torture, rape and murder of a classmate. Baker was charged with five counts of transmitting threats of injury and kidnap of another person via e-mail messages, and in the end was found guilty

However, an examination of the guidelines in Statute 18 U.S.C.103 for determining prison sentences for the guilty reveals that for American legislation, the use of computers merely indicates the means employed in carrying out a traditional form of crime.

In addition to the Statute on computer-related fraud, Prosecutors in the United States also employ generic norms in prosecuting the perpetrators of cybernet crimes, especially with regard to acts of a public or private nature involving the attainment of advantage through fraud or developing a scheme to defraud. That is what has been occurring in investigations related to fraudulent use of computers at the level of corporate crimes, irregular communications services, copyright violations, illegal transport of stolen goods and conspiracy.

CYBERNET FRAUD

For the purposes of this chapter, we record here the definition of computer-related fraud utilized by the Convention of the Council of Europe for Cybernet Crimes.[32] This definition concentrates on the intentional causing of property loss with a view to unduly assuring economy benefits and advantages by means of any input, alteration, deletion or suppression of computer data or, additionally, any interference with the functioning of a computer system. Included in this definition is fraud related to Internet auctions, telemarketing fraud, illegal intentional access to sites for economic gain and the wrongful use of a computer for the purposes of achieving illegal economic advantage. Excluded from the definition is espionage because it is directed towards assuring political advantage. According to the European Convention, computer-related frauds may victimize not only individuals but also public or private corporate entities, making their perpetrators liable to both Civil and Criminal proceedings.

With regard to the real extent of cybernet fraud, observers note that both in Europe and in the United States, some institutions and companies are reluctant to divulge that they have been victims of cybercrime for fear of negative repercussions.[33] At individual level some people do not report to authorities partly because, apparently, they fail to detect that they have been victimized and partly because the losses they have had are small and probably not worth reporting. Nevertheless, the number of reported cases of e-crimes have increased in the past few years and keep growing every day—a clear sign that the number of frauds by internet is not a token figure and is rapidly rising. In recent years, the Federal Bureau of Investigations in the United States (FBI) has detected a series of worrisome on-line frauds such as Internet auction frauds, credit card frauds, bank frauds, investment frauds, impersonation/identity frauds, health insurance frauds and pyramid schemes, to name a few.[34] Although just a small sample of what people can fall prey to on the Web environment, the list of fraudulent activities that has been just mentioned is enough to show the level of ingenuity and sophistication of computer criminals. In fact, the level of sophistication with which cyber criminals have delved into is such that it has led Intelligence Services to seek non-stop updating, exactly like spies in secret missions. Indeed, the old form of espionage with disguises, false passports, wire taps, and hidden cameras has left the streets and entered the cybernetic environment.

In view of the multiple strategies put into effect by perpetrators of internet frauds, scientific studies were instrumental in providing concrete definitions for an array of unlawful practices that have become a constant reality in the technological scenario. What follows is a brief list of some criminal behaviors prevalent in the cybernetic world:

- Hacking: is broadly defined as an illegal intrusion into a computer system without the permission of the computer owner/user.
- Cracking: an illegal intrusion into a computer system or network so as to propagate viruses, change programs or appropriate data from sites and internet users.
- Phishing: the act of sending an e-mail to a user falsely claiming to be an established legitimate enterprise in an attempt to scam the user into surrendering private information that will be used for identity theft. The e-mail directs the user to visit a website where they are asked to update personal information, such as passwords, credit card, social security, and bank account numbers.
- Cyberstalking: the use of the internet or other electronic means to stalk or harass an individual, a group of individuals, or an organization. It may include false accusations, threatening or obscene e-mail, filling a victim's e-mail box with spam; leaving improper messages on message boards or guest books; sending electronic viruses; tracing another person's computer and Internet activity, and electronic identity theft.
- Virus dissemination: malicious software that attaches itself to other software (virus, worms, trojan horse, time bomb, logic bomb, rabbit, and bacterium are examples of malicious software that destroys the system of targeted victims).
- Pheaking: the act of breaking into telephone network illegally in order to steal calling card numbers, make free calls, have calls charged to a different account or acquire access illegally to communication devices.
- Denial of service: an attack on a network that floods it with so many additional requests that regular traffic is either slowed or completely interrupted, thereby preventing users from accessing e-mail websites or on-line services. An attacker can also flood someone's e-mail box with spam mail and deprive him or her from receiving legitimate messages.

THE EFFECTIVENESS OF INTERNATIONAL CRIMINAL LAW

The use of Criminal Law, as distinct from Civil Suits, depends largely on the adequacy of the punishment. An important point to be raised concerns the application of punitive measures against individuals who reside outside the country or countries toward which their criminal activities were directed. For example, if a country does not punish a given harmful cybernet activity, should the country affected use the coercive power of its legal apparatus to detain the individual who is outside the limits of its sovereignty?

Although the World Wide Web is global, Governments are not. Countries operate in the international community, may even participate in conventions, treaties, international agreements, and support other initiatives dealing with various global problems; however, all these types of mechanisms, encouraged by globalization, have not expanded effective application of Criminal Law in global terms, because countries have reservations as to the possibilities of yielding any portion of the sovereignty of their internal laws or jurisdiction over their citizens.

The reality, however, is that countries are not all consistent or unanimous in what they consider fraudulent conduct through the computer—a specific conduct on the Internet may be a normally accepted practice in one country while being prohibited and considered as fraud in others. Furthermore, even when there is some consensus among countries in considering a specific act as criminal, depending on the country dealing with the offense, such an act may receive very different treatment as to the way perpetrators are prosecuted and punished.

In view of the disparity of opinions existing among countries pertaining to various practices commissioned on the Internet, the inevitable question that does arise is: what community will set the standards for determining whether a conduct is in fact fraudulent? Will it be the country of residence of the perpetrator or of the victim's, or should there be a common definition agreed upon by all international communities?[35] There is obviously no quick or easy answer. The lack of a satisfactory answer makes it even more difficult for a country to impose punishment on persons who use the Internet to consciously engage in unlawful activities that will affect others within and outside of their countries?

One may take as an example the phenomenon of games of chance via the Internet. People residing in regions where games of chance are not legal, very often, have available to them through the Internet, an assortment of gambling options provided by the gaming industry located in regions where gambling is legal. Since the Internet was the medium through which the gambling services were made accessible, does that accessibility, in and of itself, provide sufficient jurisdiction for a suit? Should the gambling site operators be required to deny access to individuals trying to reach their site from areas where gambling is illegal?[36] Should the statutes regulating gaming in one country be used for prosecuting acts originating outside of that country? One may not exclude, in those cases, the hypothesis that imposing one country's legal standards on individuals from other countries may not be viewed favorably by international communities at large; reason why proper integrated cross-border criminal law procedures for cyber crimes, cannot, and should not, remain a subject exclusively relegated to the territory of debate among scholars and academics.

THE DILEMMA INTO THE PHENOMENON

Organized crime is hard to define in statistical or other accurate terms. This dilemma is reflected in much of the scientific and policy-related work aimed at gaining deeper insight into the phenomenon as well as at finding viable solutions to enhance its control, prevention and repression. More often than not, effective countermeasures seem to be seriously hampered by the lack of unanimity over definition of targets.[37]

The struggle against virtual criminality has left behind its connotation of a hermetic subject to become the object of strategies adopted by Governments seeking to assure a safer environment on the Internet for institutions, companies, consumers and Web users in general.

Organized crime can only be fought by means of technology, and for this to happen Criminal Law needs to be strengthened by the creation of appropriate legislation encompassing new definitions of crimes and fraudulent behaviors inherent to the cybernetic world. Many are the reasons for according cyber crime a differentiated treatment; some of them include: weakened credibility of technological evolution, loss of revenue, loss of time, loss of dignity and even loss of life. Moreover, cyber crime has the potential to simultaneously affect millions of people all over the world in a very short span of time, seen that it is not encumbered by physical restrictions such as roads, borders, airports, etc.—distinguishing it from traditional crimes which not only are limited by the physical world but also depend on it for its commission.

Another reason for differentiated treatment of cybernet crimes lies in the difficulties that the Police and Criminal Justice systems encounter in investigating and convicting the perpetrators of such acts,[38] given their difficulties in identifying on-line actors of unlawful practices and indirect liability.

The idea underlying the existence of specific legislation dealing with cybernet crime, is that it will highlight the disapproval with which society views using cyberspace as an instrument for crime. Such reaction might at least have an intimidating effect on some potential cybernet criminals.

It should be added that the issuance of international precepts regulating the principles and rules of criminal procedure at transnational level[39] would undoubtedly be important in reducing the difficulties of applying Domestic Law in light of the canons of International Law, because there is a need for an international police cooperation with independent operational capacities and structures.[40] Institutes or Agencies of the United Nations, such as the World Intellectual Property Organization or the Telecommunications International Union, might take the leadership in producing effective new Treaties and Conventions.

NOTES

1. FRANKO, Aas Katja. *Globalization and Crime*. Los Angeles, Sage Publications, 2007, pp. 145-150.

2. ANDREAS, Peter. "Smuggling Wars: Law Enforcement and Law Evasion in a Changing World," in *Transnational Crime in the Americas*. New York, Routledge Publications, 1999, pp. 86-87.

3. OLIVEIRA, Edmundo. *Co-operation and Law Enforcement to Counter Organized Crime in the Common Market Countries of South America*. Helsinki, HEUNI Edition, 2005, pp. 46-49.

4. DASQUE, Jean Michel. *Géopolitique du Crime International*. Paris, Ellipses edition, 2008, pp. 83-88.

5. VIANO, Emilio. "Cybercrime and Cybersecurity: The Post-September 11, 2001 Reality," in *Transnational Organized Crime*. Durham, North Carolina, Carolina Academic Press, 2003, pp. 174-178.

6. LEVI, Michael and GILMORE, William. "Terrorist Finance, Money Laundering and the Rise and Rise of Natural Evaluation: A New Paradigm for Crime Control?" in *Financing Terrorism*. Dordrecht, The Netherlands. Kluwer Academic Publishers, 2002, pp. 108-112.

7. EDWARDS, Adam and GILL, Peter. *Transnational Organized Crime: Perspectives on Global Security*. London, Routledge Edition, 2003, pp. 29-30.

8. ANDREAS, Peter and NADELMANN, Ethan. "Policing the Globe Criminalization and Crime Control," in *International Relations*. Oxford, Oxford University Press, 2006, pp. 11-15. See also at: http://www.interpol.int/public/icpo/legalmaterials/cooperation/ model.asp.

9. KLOCKARS, Carl B.; IVKOVIC, Sanja Kutnjak and HABERFELD, MAKI R. *Enhancing Police Integrity*. New York, Springer-Verlag Publishers, 2006, pp. 31-32.

10. LABORDE, Jean-Paul. *État de Droit et Crime Organisé*. Paris, Dalloz Édition, 2005, pp. 43-56.

11. SHEPTYCKI, James W. E. "Against Transnational Organized Crime," in *Critical Reflections on Transnational Organized Crime*. Toronto, Toronto University Press, 2003, pp. 126-134.

12. MADSEN, Frank G. *Transnational Organized Crime*. London and New York, Routledge Publications, 2009, pp. 80-83.

13. COCKAYNE, James. *Transnational Organized Crime: Multinational Responses to a Rising Threat*. New York, International Peace Academy, 2007, pp. 39-42.

14. ZINCANI, Vito. "Les Stratégies d' Opposition à la Criminalité Organisée," in *Les Organisations Criminelles*. Publication Institut National des Hautes tudes de Securit (INHES), Paris, Janvier-Mars, No. 7, 2009, pp. 79-84.

15. RAUSCH, Sharla LAFREE, Gary. "The Growing Importance of Criminology in the Study of Terrorism," in *The Criminologist: The Official Newsletter of the American Society of Criminology*. Columbus, Ohio, Publication Series Vol. 34, No. 4, November / December, 2007, pp. 2-4.

16. Consult: United Nations Office on Drugs and Crime (UNODC). *Compendium of United Nations Standards and Norms in Crime Prevention and Criminal Justice*. New York, United Nations, 2006, pp. 343-380.

17. STIGLITZ, Joseph E. *Globalization and its Discontents*. New York, London, W.W. Norton Company, 2002, pp. 214-222.

18. WALL, David S. *Cyberspace Crime*. Farnham, UK, Ashgate Dartmouth, 2003, pp. 11-21.

19. GRABOSKY, P. N. and SMITH, Russell G. "Digital Crime in the 21st Century," in *Journal of Information Ethics*, St. Cloud McFarland & Company, Inc. Publisher, 2001, pp. 8-26.

20. FINKELHOR, David, MITCHELL, Kimberly J. and WOLAK, Janis. *Online Victimization. A Report on the Nations Youth*. Arlington, VA, National Center for Missing and Exploited Children, 2000, pp. 09-13.

21. ELLISON, Louise and AKDENIZ, Yaman. "Cyberstalking: The Regulation of Harassment on the Internet," in *Criminal Law Review*, Special Edition, London, Sweet Maxwell, 1998, pp. 29-47.

22. NORRIE, Alan. "Dialogue and Debate: The Nature of Virtual Criminality," in *Social and Legal Studies*, 10, Sage Publications, London, Los Angeles, 2001, pp. 227-228.

23. PODGOR, Ellen S. "International Computer Fraud: A Paradigm for Limiting National Jurisdiction," in *Davis Law Review*, January, Davis, CA, 2002, pp. 273-274.

24. WALL, David S. "Cybercrimes; New Wine, No Bottles?" in *Invisible Crimes: Their Victims and Their Regulation*. London Macmillan, 1999, pp. 105-139.

25. CHANDLER, Amanda. "The Changing Definition and Image of Hackers in Popular Discourse," in *International Journal of the Sociology of Law*, 24, London, New York, 1996, pp. 229-251.

26. JORDAN, Tim and TAYLOR, Paul. "Sociology of Hackers," in *Sociological Review*, November, Keele University, UK, 1998, pp. 757-780.

27. DENNING, Dorothy E. *Cyberterrorism*. Washington, Georgetown University, 2000, pp. 29-37.

28. WILIAMS, Matthew. "Virtually Criminal: Discourse, Deviance and Anxiety within Virtual Communities," in *International Review of Law Computers and Technology*, 14, Routledge Publications, London, New York, 2000, pp. 95-104.

29. SPENCER, Jon. "Crime on the Internet: Its Presentation and Representation," in *Howard Law Journal*, Washington, DC, 38, 1999, pp. 241-51.

30. MANN, David and SUTTON, Mike. "Netcrime: More Change in the Organization of Thieving," in *British Journal of Criminology*, 38, Oxford University Press, Oxford, 1998, pp. 201-229.

31. Declaration of the Twelfth United Nations Congress on Crime Prevention and Criminal Justice. Salvador, Bahia, Brazil, 12-19 April 2010, p. 14. http://www.unodc.org.

32. JOHNSON, David R. and POST, David. "Law and Borders: The Rise of Law in Cyberspace," in *Stanford Law Review* 48, Stanford, CA, 1367, 1996, pp. 54-61.

33. Approved in Budapest, Hungary, on November 23, 2001.

34. There is a growing number of private companies who denounce, in collaboration with the Government, occurrences of security breaches in their businesses. See: http://www.fbi.gov. In this respect: *Cybercrime—Special Field Hearing before the Subcommittee On Technology, Terrorism, and Government.* Information of the Senate Committee on the Judiciary, 106th Congress, Washington, April 21, 200 and May 21, 2001.

35. In relation to this point: "FBI Cracks Down on Internet Fraud, National Investigation Nets Series of Charges," in *Cybercrime Law*. Report, June 4, New York, 2001, pp. 7-11. See also: http://www.fbi.gov and https://www.cia.gov.

36. STROSSEN, Nadine. "Cybercrimes v. Cyberliberties," in *International Review of Law Computers and Technology*, 14, Routledge Publications, London, New York, 2000, pp. 11-24.

37. PAKES, Francis. *Comparative Criminal Justice*. Devon, UK, Willan Publishing, 2004, PP. 141-143.

38. AROMAA, Kauko and VILJANEN, Terhi. "European Experiences in Preventing Organized Crime Field," in *Studies of Best Practices by a Council of Europe Expert Group*. European Institute of the United Nations for Crime Prevention and Control HEUNI, Helsinki, 2007, pp. 17-18.

39. TYLER, Tom R. "Compliance with Intellectual Property Laws: A Psychological Perspective," in *Journal of International Law and Politics*, 29, New York University, New York, 1996, pp. 222-223.

40. CASEY, John. *Policing the Word. The Practice of International and Transnational Policing*. Durham, NC, Carolina Academic Press, pp. 129-143.

Bibliography

ABADINSKY, Howard. (1981). *Organized Crime*. Boston.

———. (1929). *Sociologia Criminale.* Turim: Editore Utet. v.1, p. 189.

———. (1936). *Direito Penal: Parte Geral*. Rio de Janeiro, Livraria Jacyntho Editora. pp. 552-3.

———. (1954). *Psicología das multidoes.* Rio de Janeiro.

———. (1966). *La personalidad y caracter.* Barcelona, Editorial Científico-Médica. p. 132.

———. (1973). "Le Problème de la constitution delinquentielle par rapport à l'état dangereux," *Conferénces du II Cours International de Criminologie*, Paris, Imprimerie Administrative. pp. 73-94.

———. (1975). "Das penas e sua execução," *Ciência Penal*, São Paulo, 2, 2, ago., p. 37.

———. (1978). "Trent Ans de Politique Criminelle en Matière Penitentiaire," *Archives de Politique Criminelle*, Paris: Édition du Centre de Recherches de Politique Crimininelle. v. 3, p. 75.

———. (1980). *Lecciones sobre la filosofía de la historia universal.* Madrid, 1980, pp. 169, 177, 183, 215, 354, 596, 657.

———. (2006). *Social Problems: An Introduction to Critical Constructionism.* Oxford, Oxford University Press. pp. 147-148.

———. *Compêndio de criminologia.* (1973). São Paulo, José Bushatsky—Editor. pp. 80-1.

———. *L'uomo delincuente in rapporto all'antropologia, giurisprudenza e alle discipline carcerarie*: *delincuente nato e pazzo morale.* 3. ed. Torino. pp. 248-295.

———. (1974). *Personalidade: padrões e desenvolvimento.* Trans. by Dante Moreira Leite, São Paulo: Ed. da Universidade de São Paulo. pp. 577-8.

———. (1936). *Lições de psiquiatria para médicos.* Trans. by Fernando Ferreira São Paulo. Editora Livraria Acadêmica: Saraiva. pp. 38, 52, 46.

———. (1980). *Lecciones sobre la filosofía de la historia universal.* Madrid. pp. 169, 177, 183, 215, 354, 596, 657.

———. (1994). *Probation and Parole: Theory and Practice.* New Jersey: Edition Prentice–Hall, 1994, p. 398.

ABBAGNANO, N. (1973). *Historia de la filosofía.* Barcelona, II, p. 185.

ABBIATI-Agnoletto-Lazzati. (2003). *La stregoneria. Diavoli, streghe, inquisitori dal trecento al settecento.* Milano.

AGAMBEM, G. (2004). *Estados de Excepción.* Buenos Aires. Adriana Hidalgo.

———. (2007). *Il Regno e la Gloria.* Roma. Neri Poza.

AGIRREAZKUENAGA, Inaki. (1990). *La coacción administrativa directa.* Civitas. Madrid.

ALBANESE, Jay. (1985). *Organized Crime in America.* Cincinnati.

———. (1996). *Schmitt.* Editori Laterza. p. 7.

ALEXANDER, Franz and STAUB Hugo. (1929). *Der Verbrecher und seiner Richter.* Wien.

ALEXANDER, Jeffrey C. (1990). *Las teorías sociológicas desde la Segunda Guerra Mundial.* Barcelona.

ALLEN, R.M. (1958). *Personality Assessment Procedures.* New York: Ed. Harper. p. 498.

ALLER, G. (2006). *Co-responsabilidad social, sociedad de riesgo y derecho penal del enemigo.* Montevideo, B d F.

ALLIHER, John and JAMES. Cain (1974). "Citation Support for the Mafia Myth in Criminology Textbooks," *American Sociologist.*

ALLPORT, Gordon Willard. (1942). "The Use of Personal Documents," *Psychological Science*, New York, Ed. Bull. p. 39.

ALTAVILLA, Enrico. (1956). *Psicologia Giudiziaria.* Turim: Ed. Utet. p. 216.

———. Enrico. (1964). *O Delinqüente e a lei penal.* Trans. by Fernando de Miranda. Coimbra: Editora Coimbra. p. 286.

AMANDO, Jorge. (no date). *A.B.C. de Castro Alves.* São Paulo. p. 53.

AMBOS, K. (2005) *La Parte General del Derecho Penal Internacional; Bases para una construcción dogmatica.* Montevideo, B d F.

AMOROSO, Bruno. (1999). *L'apartheid globale. globalizzazione. marginalizzazione economica: destabilizzazione politica.* Roma.

———. "Globalización y las actuales orientaciones de la política criminal," *Nueva Doctrina Penal*, 1999/A, reproduced in Direito e Cidadania. Praia, República de Cabo Verde, 3, 8, November 1999, February 2000.

ANCEL, Marc. (1954). *La Défense Sociale Nouvelle.* 3.ed. Paris: Éditions Cujas. pp. 203, 123.

ANDERSON, Anneslise. (1979). *The Business of Organized Crime.* Stanford.

ANDRADE, Benito Mario. (1899). *Estudio de antropología criminal espiritualista.* Madrid. p. 203.

ANDREAS, Peter (1999). *Smuggling Wars: Law Enforcement to Counter Organized Crime in the Common Market Countries of South America.* New York, Routledge Publications, 1999, pp. 86-87.

ANDREAS, Peter and NADELMANN, Ethan (2006). *Policing the Globe: Criminalisation and Crime Control in International Relations.* London, Oxford University Press.

ANGELERGUES, R. (1975). *La Antipsiquiatría* siglo XXI. México.

ANIYAR, Lolita. (1992). *Democracia y Justicia Pena.* Caracas: Ediciones del Congresso de la República. pp. 59-72.

ANTÉBIS, Elizabeth. (1979). *I fabbricanti di pazzia.* Milano.

ANTONETTI, Guy. (1986). *Histoire contemporaine politique et sociale.* París. p. 239.

ANZIEU, M.D. (1956). *Lê Psychodrame Analytique Chez l'Enfant.* Paris: Éditions Puf. pp.175-6.

APDH. (1987). *La desaparición, crimen contra la humanidad.* Bs As.

APPLETON'S new English-Spanish Dictionary. (1916). New York. p. 115.

ARENAL, Concepción. (1985). "Las colonias penales de la Australia and la pena de deportación," *Obras Completas*, Madrid, 1895. Tomo X.

———. *ESTUDIOS Penitenciarios.* (1877). Madrid. p. 12.

ARICO, José. (1996). *El concepto de lo político.* Editori Laterza. p. 7.

ARROJO, Lopez-Rey. (1945). *Introduction al estudio de la criminologia.* Buenos Aires: El Ateneo, pp. 119-20.

ARROMAA, Kauko and VILJANEN, Terhi. (2007). "European Experiences in Preventing Organized Crime," *Studies of Best Practices by a Council of Europe Expert Group*, European Institute of the United Nations for Crime Prevention and Control. Helsinki, HEUNI.

ASCHAFFENBURG, G. (1903). *Das Verbrechen und seine Bekämpfung.* Heidelberg.

ASKWY, J.M. (1974). "History of Medicine: The Auscultatory Gap Sphigmomanometry," *Archives of Internal Medicine*, Chicago, 80, pp. 93-98.

ASUA, Jimenez. (1960). *Tratado de Derecho Penal.* Buenos Aires: Editorial Losada. t.1, p. 70.

———. (1935). *Psicoanálisis criminal.* Madrid.

———. (1929). *Libertad de amar y derecho a morir. ensayos de un criminalista sobre eugenesia, eutanasia, endocrinologia.* Santander.

———. (1945). *La ley and el delito.* Caracas: Editorial Andrés Bello. p. 683.

BAERT, Patrick (2001). *La teoría social en el siglo XX.* Madrid.

BALIBAR, Etienne. (1992). *Les Frontières de la Démocratie.* Paris: Édition La Découverte. pp. 134-136.

BARATA, Alessandro. (1982). *Criminologia Critica e Critica del Diritto Penale.* Bologna: Cedam.

———. (1978). "Criminologia Crítica e Política Penal Alternativa," *Revista de Direito Penal*, Rio de Janeiro: INSTITUTO de Ciências Penais do Rio de Janeiro, (23), p. 7.

———. "Criminologia e dogmatica penale. passato e futuro del modello integrato di scienza penalistica," *La questione criminale*, 2 p. 147.

———. (1982). *Criminología critica e critica del diritto penale.* Bologna p. 83.

BARBA, Francisco Esteve. (1955). *Historia de la cultura.* Barcelona: Salvat, 4 v., v. 4. pp. 1742-8.

BARBAROUX, C.O. (1957). *De la transportation*. París.

BARRETO, Tobias. (1926). *Obras Completas, V Direito, menores e loucos*. Sergipe. p. 151.

BARTOLOMEI, Maria Luisa Bartolomei. (1994). *Gross and massive violations of human rights in Argentina 1976-1983*. Lund.

BASAGLIA, Franco. (1972). La institución negada, informe de un hospital psiquiátrico. *Bs. As*.

BASSIOUNI, M. Cherif and VETERE, Eduardo. (1998) *Organized Crime. (A Compilation of U.N. Documents 1975-1998)*. New York.

BATESON, H. (1958). "La vida," *Collection moderna de conocimentos universals*, New York: W.M. Jackson. p. 183.

BATTISTA, Giovan. (1988). *Della fisonomia dell'uomo*. Parma.

BAUMAN, Zygmunt. (1999). *Globalizaçao:as conseqüências humanas*. Rio de Janeiro.

BECCARIA, Cesare (1955). *Opere diverse del Marchese Cesare Beccaria Bonesana, Patrizio milanese, Parte Prima, Prima* Edizione Napoletana, Napoli, 1770, I, p. 117; in *Dei delitti e delle pene, a cura di* FRANCO VENTURI, Einaudi, 1981, p. 89; Trans. by LAPLAZA, Buenos Aires, 1955, p. 188.

——. (1981). "Dei delitti e delle pene, con una raccolta di lettere e documenti relativi alla nascita dell'opera e alla sua fortuna nell'Europa del Settecento," *A cura di Venturi, Franco and Einaudi*, Giulio—Editore. p. 164.

——. (1770). *Patrizio milanese*. Napoli: Edizione Napoletana. I, p. 117.

BECK, Ulrich. (1999). *Che cosa è la globalizzazione, rischi e prospettive della società planetária*. Roma.

BEDAU, Hugo Adam. (1998). *The Death Penalty in America: Current Controversies*. New York. p. 189.

BEKER, H. and BOSKE, A. (1967). *Modern Sociological Theory in Continuity and Change*. New York: Ed. University. pp. 16-7.

BELL, Daniel. (1953). "Crime as an American Way of Life," *Antioch Review*, June.

BEMBO, Max. (1912). *La mala vida en Barcelona*. Barcelona.

BENDERKY, Joseph W. (1989). *Carl Schmitt teorico del Reich*. Bologna.

BENGOA, Fernando Bayardo. (1979). *Los Derechos del Hombre y la defensa de la Nación*. Montevideo.

BEQUAI, August. (1979). *Organized Crime: The Fifth State*. Lexington Books. pp. 2, 4, 7, 9, 34.

BERCIS, Pierre. (1985). *Pour de Nouveau Droits de l'Homme*. Paris: Éditons lattès. pp. 122-123.

BERISTAIN, Antonio. (1982). *La Pena Retribución and las Actuales Concepciones Crimino- lógicas*. Buenos Aires: Depalma, pp. 91-107.

BERNALDO DE QUIRÓS, Constancio. (1901). *La mala vida en Madrid: estudio psicosociológico con dibujos and fotografías al natural*. Madrid.

BERTILLON, Alphonse. (1888). "Sur le fonctionnement du service des signalements anthropométriques," *Archives de l'Anthropologie criminelle et des sciences pénales*. III. París p. 138.

——. (1886). *De l'identification par les signalements anthropométriques*. T. I. p. 193.

BETTIOL, Giuseppe. (1984). *Gli ultimi scritti 1980-1982 e la lezione di congedo 6. See 82. Padova:* CEDAM p. 13.

BEZERRA, Felte. (1973). *Antropologia sócio-cultural.* Brasília: Coordenada-Editora. p. 203.

BIANCHI, G. (1977). "Per quali ragioni fu soppresso Benito Mussolini," *La Seconda Guerra Mondiali nella prospettiva storica a trent'anni dall'epilogo.* Como, P. Cairoli.

BINSWANGER, Ludwig. (1072). *Tres formas de la existencia frustrada.* Buenos Aires. p. 127.

BISHOP, Norman. (1988). *Non-custodial alternatives in Europe.* Helsinski.

BLACK, E. (2003). *War against the weak; Eugenics and America's campaign to create a master race.* New York: Four Walls Eight Windows.

BLACK, M. and SMITH, R.G. (2003). "Electronic Monitoring in the Criminal Justice System," *Trends & Issues in crime and criminal justice.* Sydney: Edition of Australian Institute of Criminology, no. 254, pp. 6-7.

BOBBIO, Norberto. (1995). *Derecha e izquierda.* Madrid.

BODIN, Jean. (1587). *De la demonomanie de sorciers.* Paris. pp. 238-276.

BODIN, J. (1992). *Six Books of the Commonwealth.* London: Oxford Press.

BOFF, Leonardo. (2002). *Do Iceberg à Arca de Noé: O nascimento de uma ética planetária.* Rio de Janeiro: Sal Terrae.

———. (2003). *Civilização Planetária; Desafios à sociedade e ao Cristianismo.* Rio de Janeiro: Sextante.

BÖGEL, Marion. (1994). *Strukturen und Systemanalyse der organisierten Kriminalität in Deutschland.* Berlín.

BOHM, E. (1955). *Traité du Psycholdiagnostic de Rorschach.* Paris: Editions Puf. p. 585.

BOLLE, Pierre-Henri. (2000). Consensualisme en Prison. In: *Nouvelles Orientations du Régime Pénitentiaire.* Lisboa: FIPP. pp. 199-201.

BON, G. Le. (1895). *Psychologie des foules.* París.

———. (1912). *La psicología política and la defensa social.* Madrid.

BONESANA, Marchese Cesare Beccaria. (1770). *Patrizio milanese.* Napoli: Edizione Napoletana. I, p. 117.

BONNEMAISON, G. (1989). "La Modernisation du Service Public Pénitentiaire," *Rapport au Garde de Sceaux et au Premier Ministre*: Paris. p. 31.

BORCHARD, Edwin. (1932). *Convicting the Innocent: sixty-five actual errors of criminal justice.* New York: Ed. Univ. Press. p. 14.

BOUÉ. J. et al. (1982). "Diagnóstico pré-natal das doenças metabólicas hereditárias," *La Nouvelle Presse Medicale.* Rio de Janeiro, *1*,4, jun. pp. 268-9. Carakushansky, G. (1979). *Doenças genéticas na infância.* Rio de Janeiro: Guanabara Koogan. pp. 483-484.

BOURDET-PLÉVILLE, Michel. (1963). *Galeotes, forzados and penados.* Barcelona. p. 101.

BOUZAT, Pierre. (1957). "Le Centenaire d'Enrico Ferri," *Revue de Science Criminelle et de Droit Pénal Comparée.* Paris: Édition du Centre François de Droit Compareé, 1, janvier-mars, p. 1.

BRAS-CHOPARD, Armelle Lê. (2003). *El zoo de los filósofos. De la bestialización a la exclusión.* Taurus: Madrid.

BRÉHIER, Émile. *Historia de la filosofía.* Bs. As, t.2, p. 617.

BREULER, Eugen. (1960). *Demencia precoz, el grupo de las esquizofrenias.* Buenos Aires.

BRION DAVIS, D. (1964). *O problema da escravidão na cultura ocidental.* Rio de Janeiro, Ithaca.

BROWN, Norman O. (1986). *La vita contro la morte, Il significado psicoanalitico della storia.* Bompiani, p. 183.

BRUNDAGE, James A. (2000). *La ley, el sexo y la sociedad cristiana en la Europa Medieval.* México.

BRUNET, René. (1921). *La Constitution Allemande du 11 Aout 1919.* París.

BULMER, Martín. (1984). *The Chicago school of sociology.* Chicago: University Press.

BUNGER, Carlos Octavio. (1903). *Nuestra América.* Ensayo de psicología social. *Bs. As.*

BÜRGERSTRAFRECHT und Feindstrafrecht. (2004). *HRRS.* March.

BURKE, Roger Hopkins. (2003). *An Introduction to Criminological Theory.* Cullompton: Willan Publishing, pp. 130-135.

BURLEIGH, Michael and Wippermann. (1992). *Lo Stato razziale, Germania 1933-1945.* Rizzoli p. 158.

BYINGTON, Carlos Amadeu B. (1991). Preface to the Brazilian Edition of the Malleus Maleficarum. Rio de Janeiro: Ed. Rosa dos Tempos.

BYNUM, Timothy S. (1987). *Organized crime in America: concepts and controversies.* New York: T. S. Bynum. pp. 4, 6-8.

CALDART, Roseli Salete. (2000). *Pedagogía do movimento sem terra.* Petrópolis.

CALLZIGNA, Mario. (1988). *La malattia morale. alle origini della psichiatria moderna.* Venecia. pp. 30, 31.

CALON, Eugenio Cuello. (1973). *La Moderna Penologia.* Barcelona: Bosch Casa Editorial. pp. 626-657.

CALVERTON and SCHMALHAUSEN. (1930). *El sexo en la civilization.* Madrid.

CAMERA dei Deputati. (1998). *La lotta alla corruzione.* Bari.

CANCIO MELIÁ M. and GÓMEZ JARA C. (2006). *El Derecho Penal del enemigo y el discurso penal de la exclusión.*

CANOSA R. (2000). *Storia dell'Inquisizione Spagnola in Italia.* Roma, Sapere.

———. (2000). *Storia dell'Inquisizione in Italia dalla metà del cinquecento alla fine del settecento.* Roma, Sapere.

CAPEL, José Sáez Capel. (1999). *Pena de muerte, cuando el estado asesina.* Buenos Aires/Montevideo, B d F.

CARAVANTES, José Vicente. (1858). *Anales dramáticos del crimen, Causas célebres, españolas y extranjeras, estractadas de los originales and traducidas, bajo la dirección de . . .* , Madrid Trad. continued in the Twentieth Century: Roberts, HENRI (1924). *Les grands procés de l'histoire.* París.

CARDET, Christophe. (2003). *Le Placement Sous Surveillance Électronique.* Paris: Édition L'Harmattan. pp. 28-76.

CARDOSO, Fernando Henrique and IANNI, Octávio. (1971). *Homem e sociedade.* 7. ed. São Paulo: Companhia Editora Nacional, pp. 98-9.

CARLYLE, Thomas. (1931). *On heroes, hero-worship and the heroic in history.* N. Cork, 1931.

CARPENA, Fructuoso. (1909). *Antropología criminal.* Madrid. p. 15.

CARRANZA, Mora, Houed, Zaffaroni. (1983). *El preso sin condena en Latin America y el Caribe.* San José.

CARRARA, Francesco. (1902). *Programma del Corso di Diritto Criminale.* Firenze: Casa Editrice Fratelli Cammelli. Parte Generale, v. 1, pp. 559-594.

CARRIÓ, Genaro. (1990). *Derechos humanos y su protecíon.* Buenos Aires: Editorial Abeledo-Perrot, pp. 41-48.

CARVALHO, Hilário Veiga de. (1971). O *novo código penal*: *comentários médico-legais, médico-sociais e criminológicos.* Bauru: Instituto Toledo de Ensino. p. 38.

———. (1973). *Compêndio de criminologia.* São Paulo: Bushatsky. p. 176.

CASEY, John. (2009). *Policing the World: The Practice of International and Transnational Policing.* Durham, Carolina Academic Press.

CASOSA. Romano. (1979). *Storia del manicomio in Italia dall'unitá a oggi.* Milano.

CASTRO, Lola Aniyar de. (1985). *Derechos humanos, modelo integral de la ciencia penal, and sistema penal subterráneo* Rev. del Colegio de Abogados Penalistas del Valle. Cali. p. 301.

CATTANEO, Mario A. (1970). *Anselm Feuerbach, filosofo e giurista liberale.* Milano.

———. (1972). *Anti-Hobbes ovvero i limiti del potere supremo e il diritto coativo dei cittadini contro il sovrano.* Milano.

CATTEL, Raymond B. (1975). *Análise Científica da Personalidade.* (Trans. by Eugênia de Andrade). São Paulo: Editora Ibrasa. pp. 136, 20-1.

CELIS, Jacqueline Bernat. (1982). La Politique Criminelle à la Recherche d'elle–Méme. *Archives de Politique Criminelle.* Paris: Édition du Centre de Recherches de Politique Criminelle, pp. 2, 46.

CELS. (2003). *El Estado frente a la protesta social 1996-2002.* Buenos Aires.

CERCHIARI, G. Luigi. (1990). *Fisiognomia e mimica.* Milano.

CHALIAND, G. and TERNON, Y. (2002). *1915, Le génocide des Arméniens.* Paris, Seuil.

CHALHOUB, Sidney. (1996). *Cidade Febril cortiços e epidemias na Corte Imperial.* Sao Paulo. p. 20.

CHAMON JUNIOR, Lúcio Antônio. (2004). *Do giro finalista ao funcionalismo penal, embates de perspectivas dogmáticas decadentes.* Porto Alegre.

CHANDLER, Amanda. (1996). "The Changing Definition and Image of Hackers in Popular Discourse," *International Journal of the Sociology of Law*, 24. London and New York, pp. 29-47.

CHARDIN, Pierre Teilhard de. (1965). *El fenómeno humano.* Madrid. p. 277.

CHAZAL, Jeran. (1953). *L'Enfance delinquente.* Paris: Editora Puf. p. 88.

CHEVALIER, Jean and GEEVRABT, Alain. (1986). *Dizionario dei Simboli*, Bib. Univ. Rizzoli. p. 3545. Bonesana, Marchese Cesare Chicago: The University of Chicago Press. pp. 101-2.

CHOMSKY, Noam and DIETERICH, Heinz. (1996). *La sociedad global, educación, mercado y democracia.* Santiago de Chile.

———. (1998). *Habla de América Latina.* Buenos Aires.

CHOROVER, Stephan. (1986). Del Génesis al genocidio. Madrid. p. 70. Conde, Francisco Muñoz. Edmund Mezger y derecho criminal de su tiempo. *Estudios sobre drecho criminal en el nacionalsocialismo.* Valencia.

CHRISTIE, Nils. (1993). *Crime control as industry, towards gulags, western style.* p. 93.

CLOWARD, Richard and OHLIN, Lloyd. (1960). *A Theory of delinquent gangs.* New York: Free Press. p. 150.

COCCOLI, Paolo. (1999). *L'Inquisizione Santa.* Colognola ai Colli.

COCKAYNE, James. (2007). *Transnational Organized Crime: Multinational Responses to a Rising Threat.* New York, International Peace Academy, pp. 39-42.

CODE criminel de l'Empire du Brésil. (1834). (trans. by Fouchr, Victor). París.

CODE Pénal. Des 25 Septembre-6 Octobre. 1791.

COHEN, S. (1989). *Abolicionismo penal.* Buenos Aires, Ediar.

COHN, Norman. (1980). *Los demonios familiares de Europa.* Madrid.

———. (1983). *El mito de la conspiración mundial.* Madrid: Los Protocolos de los Sabios de Sión.

COING, Henri J. Meunier Christine. (1980). *Insécurité Urbaine?: une arme pour le pouvoir.* Paris, Éditions Anthropos. p. 77.

COLE, G.D.H. (1963). *Introducción a la historia economica.* Mexico, FCE.

COMBLIN, Joseph. (1977). *Le pouvoir militaire en Amerique Latine.* París.

———. (1979). *Dos ensayos sobre seguridad nacional.* Sgo. de Chile.

CONDE, Francisco Muñoz and MEZGER, Edmund. (2003). *Y derecho criminal de su tiempo. estudios sobre derecho criminal del nacionalsocialismo.* 4. ed. Valencia. pp. 85, 145, 193.

———. (2001). *Introduction a la criminologia.* Valencia. 2001.

CONGRESS of Criminal Anthropology. (1889). 2.

CONSTANCIO, Bernaldo de Quirós. (1901). *La mala vida en Madrid. Estudio psicosociológico con dibujos and fotografías al natural.* Madrid (reed. Madrid, 1998).

COPLESTON, Frederick. (1983). *Historia de la filosofía.* Barcelona. Vol. V, p. 122.

CORRE, A. (1889). *Le crime en pays créoles (Esquisse d'ethnographie criminelle).* París.

———. (s.d.). *L'Ethnographie criminelle.* París.

COSTA, Álvaro Mayrink da. (1972). *Exame criminológico.* São Paulo: Editora Jurídica e Universitária. p. 115.

COURTINE, Jean-Jacques & HAROCHE, Claudine. (1992). *Storia del viso. Esprimere e tacere le emozioni (XVI a XIX secolo).* Palermo.

COUSTÉ, Alberto. (1997). *Biografia do diabo, O diabo como a sombra de Deus na história.* Rio de Janeiro.

CRESSEY, Donald. (1969). *Theft of the Nation: the structure and operations of organized crime in America.* New York. p. 314.

CRIMINOLOGÍA. (s.d.). Revista de Derecho Privado. Madrid. p. 3-284.

CRISTIE, Nils. (1993). *Crime control as industry, towards gulags Western Style?* Roytledge.

DADRIANA, Vahakn N. (1997). *The History of the Armenian Genocide, Ethnic Conflict from the Balkans to Anatolia to the Caucasus.* Providence.

DAHRENDORF, Ralf. (1992). *O conflito social moderno.* Rio de Janeiro.

DALCKE. (1938). *Strafrecht und Strafverfahren. Eine Sammlung der wichstigsten Gesetze des Strafrechts und des Strafverfahrens mit Erläuterungen.* Berlin. p. 385.

DALMAU, Héctor Horacio. (1995). *El país de los ríos muertos.* Buenos Aires.

DANET, Amand. (1990). "L'inquisiteur e ses sorciéres," *Institoris*, Henry & Kraemer, Jacques Sprenger. *Le Marteau des Sorciérres. Malleus Maleficarum.* Paris. p. 53.

DAREST, F.R. Dareste. (1891). *Les constitutions modernes.* París.

DARMON, Pierre. (1991). *Médicos e assassinos na Belle Époque a medicalização do crime.* Rio de Janeiro.

DARWIN, Charles. (s.d.) *L'origine des espèces.* Paris: Schleicher Frères.

DASQUE, Jean Michel. (2008). *Géopolitique du Crime International.* Paris, Ellipses Edition, p. 83-88.

DAVID, Catherine. (1983). Ces enfants qu'on nous fabrique. *Le Nouvel Observateur,* Paris, 83, 970. pp. 35-36.

DAVID, Pedro R. (2001). Buenos Aires. 2001 p. 925.

DEBUYST, Christian. In: Debuyst and DIGNEFFE, Pires. (1988). *Histoire des savoirs sur le crime et la peine.* Montreal. II, p. 467, note 66.

DEL COL, A. (2006). *L'Inquisizione in Italia dal XII al XXI secolo.* Roma, Mondadori.

ELIACHEFF C. and SOULEZ LARIVIÈRE, D. (2007). *Les temps des victims.* Paris, Albin Michel.

DEL OLMO, Rosa. (1979). *Ruptura Criminológica.* Caracas: Universidad Central de Venezuela. pp. 31-48.

DELGADO, Honorio. (1978). *Curso de psiquiatria; psicopatologia-psiquiatria especial.* 6th ed. Barcelona: Editorial Científico-Médica. pp. 415, 416, 417.

DELLA PORTA, Giovan Battista. (1998). *Della fisonomia dell'uomo, con illustrazioni dell'edizione del 1610.*

DELMAS-MARTY, Mireille. (1963). *Modèles et Mouvements de Politique Criminelle.* Paris: Édition Economica. pp. 56, 177. Fragoso, Heleno. (1977). *Direito Penal e Direitos Humanos.* Rio de Janeiro, Editora Forense.

DENNING, Dorothy E. (2000). *Cyberterrorism.* Georgetown University, pp. 29-37.

DE RIVACOBA Y RIVAÇOBA, M. (1963). *Krausismo y Derecho.* Santa Fé, Castellvi.

DE VATTEL, E. (2004). *O Direito das Gentes.* Brasilia, Universidade de Brasília.

DEVOTO, F. and ROSOLI, G. (1985). *La inmigración italiana en la Argentina.* Buenos Aires.

DI TÚLIO, Benigno. *Manuale di antropología e psicología criminale applicata alla pedagogía emendativa, alla polizia ed al diritto penale e penitenciario* (Preface by Silvio Ottolenghi). Roma.

——. (1958). *Principi di criminologia clinica e di psichiatria forense.* Roma: Istituto de Medicina Sociale. p. 131.

DIAS, Jorge de Figueiredo and ANDRADE, Manuel da Costa. (1984). *Criminologia. O Homem Delinqüente e a Sociedade Criminógena,* Coimbra: Coimbra Editora. pp. 373-395.

DIC, Daniel. (1999). *Volti della degenerazione: una síndrome europea* 1848-1918. Firenze.

DIETERICH, Heinz. (2000). *Identidad nacional y globalization.* México.

DIREITO e Cidadania. Praia. República de Cabo Verde. 3, 8, November 1999/ February 2000.

DI TULLIO, Benito. (1950). *Tratado de* antropología *criminal.* Buenos Aires.

DOCUMENTO de Puebla. (1979). Buenos Aires. p. 67.

DOMÍNGUEZ, Carlos Horacio. (1980). *La nueva guerra y el nuevo derecho: ensayo para una estrategia jurídica antisubversiva.* Bs. As.

DOMINGUEZ, R. and MICHELI. A. (1994). "Evolución de la Esfigmomanometria," *Archivo Mexicano de Cardiologia.* México, 34, pp. 315-323.

DONNEDIEU de Verbras, H. (1938). *A Justiça penal hoje.* Sao Paulo. p. 102.

DONNICI, Virgílio. (1970). Aspectos criminológicos do novo Código Penal. *Revista de Informação Legislativa.* Brasília: Serviço Gráfico do Senado Federal, 7, 27, 1966, p. 133.

DRAGO, Luis Maria. (1988). *Los hombes de presa.* (2th. ed.) Buenos Aires.

DU BOYS, Albert. (1845). *Histoire du Droit Criminel des Peuples Anciens.* París, Joubert. p. 245.

DURKHEIN, Emile. (1897). *Le suicide.* París.

DUVIOLS, Pierre. (1977). *La destrucción de las religiones antiguas durante la conquista y la colonia,* México; Garibay, ANGEL M. and PORTILLA, Miguel Leon. (1961). *La visión de los vencidos,* México.

EBING, Krafft. (1875). *La responsabilité criminelle et la capacité civile dans les états de trouble intellectuel.* París.

ECO, Humberto. (1988). *Il pendolo di Foucault.* Milano: Bompiani.

EDWARDS, Adam and GILL, Peter. (2003). *Transnational Organised Crime: Perspectives on Global Security.* London, Routledge Edition, p. 29-30.

ELLIOT, H. (1994). "Arterial Blood Pressure Monitoring," *Annals of Second International Nifedipine GITS Simposium.* Paris. pp. 17-20.

ELLISON, Louise and AKDENIZ, Yaman. (1998). "Cyberstalking: The Regulation of Harassment on the Internet," *Criminal Law Review*, Special Edition. London, Sweet Maxwell, pp. 29-47.

ENZENBERGER, Hans Magnus. (1995). *Guerra civil.* São Paulo.

EQUIPO SELADOC. (1980). *Iglesia y seguridad nacional.* Salamanca.

ERIK. (1951). *Grosse Rechsdenker.* Tübingen. p. 543.

ESER, Albin and HASSEMER, Winfried. (2004). *La ciencia de la ley criminal ante el nuevo milenio.* Valencia, p. 472.

ESQUIROL, Jean-Etienne Dominique. (1838). *Des Maladies mentales considérées sous les rapports médical, hygiénique et médico-legal.* París.

ESER, Albin. (2004). *La ciencia del derecho criminal ante el nuevo milenio.* (Francisco Muñoz Conde, coordinador). Valencia. p. 472.

EVOLA, Julius. (178). *Il mito del sangue.*

EXNER, F. (1945). *Kriminologie.* 3. ed. Berlim: Krepper. p. 28.

———. (1957). *Biología criminal en sus rasgos fundamentales.* Barcelona. p. 80.

EYSENCK, Hans J. and GUDJONSSON, Gisli H. (1991). *The causes and cures of criminality.* New York.

FALK, Richard. (2002). *Globalization depredadora, una crítica.* Madrid.

FAVARD, Jean. (1981). *Le Labyrinthe Pénitentiaire.* Paris: Éditions Centurion. pp. 151-174.

FAVOREU, Louis. (1994). *Los tribunales constitucionales.* Barcelona.

Federal Criminal Code and Rules: as amended to February 1, 1993, St. Paul: West Publishing Co. p. 665.

FÉRÉ, Ch. (1903). *Degeneración y criminalidad.* trans. by Anselmo González. Madrid. 1903.

FERI, Enrico. (1916). *Sociologia Criminale.* Turim: Editore Utet. p. 189.

FERNANDEZ, Bernardo Mancano. (1999). *MST formação e territorialização em São Paulo.* Sao Paulo.

FERRACUTI, Franco and WOLFGANG, Marvin. (1970). "Il Comportamento aggressivo violento come fenomeno sócio-psicologico," *Appunti di criminologia.* Roma: Bulzoni Editora. pp. 217-21.

FERRACUTI, Franco. (1966). *Il Trattamento della Criminalità Sotto-culturale.* Roma: Pubblicazione del Ministero de Grazia e Giustizia. p. 153-64.

FERRAJOLI, Luigi; Diritto; Ragione. (1989). *Teoria del garantismo penale.* Laterza.

———. (1997). *La sovranità nel mondo moderno.* Roma.

FERREIRA, Raúl Gustavo. (2003). *La Constitución vulnerable. crisis argentina y tensión interpretativa*, Buenos Aires. p. 23.

FERRERO, Guglielmo and LOMBROSO, Cesare. (1915). *La donna delinquente, la prostituta e la donna normale.* Torino.

FERRI, Enrico. (1902). *Les criminels dans l'art et la littérature.* París.

———. (1880). *Archivio di psichiatria.* Turim: Ed. Bocca, p. 474.

FERRO, Marc. (1985). *La Gran Guerra (1914-1918).* Buenos Aires.

———. (2000). *La colonización, Una historia global.* Mexico, FCE.

———. (2005). *El libro negro del colonialismo, Siglos XVI a XXXI: Del extermínio al arrepentimiento.* Madrid, Esfera de los libros.

FEST, Joachim C. (1991). *Hitler, Il Führer e il nazismo.* Rizzoli. p. 46.

FEUERBACH, P.J.A. (1797). *Anti-Hobbes oder über die Grenzen der höchsten Gewalt und das Zwangsrecht der Bürger gegen den Oberherrn.* Giessen.

FICHTE, J.G. (1998). *Fondement du droit naturel selon les principes de la doctrine de la science (1796-1797).* París: PUF. pp. 269-293.

FINKELHHOR, David, MITCHELL, Kimberly J. and WOLAK, Janis. (2000). *Online Victimization: A Report on the Nation's Youth.* Arlington, National Center for Missing and Exploited Children, pp. 9-13.

FLETCHER, J. (1974). *The ethics of genetic control.* New York: Anchor Press. pp. 116-9.

FLORES, Marcelo and Mondadori. (2001). *Storia, verità e giustizia, I crimini del XX secolo*. Milano. pp. 222-226.

FLORES, Marcelo. (2006). *Il genocidio degli armeni.* Bologna, Il Mulino.

FONDATION INTERNATIONAL PENALE ET PENITENTIARE. (1999). *Nouvelles Orientations du Régime Pénitentiaire. Actes des Journées Internationales de Lisbonne,* Portugal, 21-25, pp. 193-201.

———. (1988). *Régles Minima pour la Mise à Exécution des Sanctions et des Mesures non Carcérales Comportant une Restriction de Liberté.* Deventer: Kluwer. pp. 49-73.

FORRESTER, Viviane. (1997). *El horror económico.* Buenos Aires.

FOUCAULT, Michel. (1980). *El saber y las formas jurídicas.* Barcelona.

———. (1975). *Surveiller et punir, Naissance de la prison.* París.

———. (2003). *Society Must be Defended.* London, Picador.

———. Michel. (2005). *El poder psiquiátrico.* curso en el collége de France, *Bs. As.*

FOXIN, Claus. (1976). *Problemas Básicos del derecho criminal,* Madrid: Reus. pp. 55-57.

FRAGOSO, Heleno Cláudio. (1976). *Lições de Direito Penal.* São Paulo: José Buschatsky Editor. p. 19.

———. (1977). *Direito penal e direitos humanos.* Rio de Janeiro: Editora Forense. p. 28.

FRANCISIANNI, Elizabeth Reuss Ianni. *A Family Business: Kinship and Social Control in Organized Crime*. New York. 1972.

FRANK, L.K. (1939). *Projective Methods for the Study of Personality.* New York: Ed. J. Psychol. p. 389.

FRANKO, Katja Franko. (2007). *Globalization and crime*. London.

FRÉGIER, H.A. (1840). *Des Classes dangereuses de la population dans les grandes villes et des moyens de les rendre meilleures. Ouvrage recompensé en 1838 par l'Institut de France* (Académie des Sciences Morales et Politiques).

FRENCH, N. Cork. (1914). *Les héros le culte des héros et l'héroïque dans l'histoire.* Paris.

FRIEDRICH von Spee, Malleus. (2004). *I processi contro le streghe*: *cautio criminalis*. Roma.

FREUD, Sigmund. (1974). "Totem und Tabu: Einige Übereinstimmungen im Seelenleben der Wilder und der Nuerotiker," *Kulturtheoretische Schriften.* Frankfurt, Fischer Verlag.

FROMENT, J.C. (1998). La Surveillance Électronique à Domicile: Une Nouvelle Économie du Pouvoir de Punir? *Cahiers de la Sécurité Intérieure.* Paris, 34, pp. 149-151.

FROMONT, Michel. (1996). *La justice constitutionelle dans le monde.* París.

FROSALI, Raoul Alberto. (1952). "Il delinquente per tendenza nel diritto positivo," *Studi in Memoria di Arturo Rocco.* Milão: Dott. A. Guiffrè—Editore, v.1, p. 450.

FROTA-PESSOA et al. (1968). *Genética clínica*. São Paulo: Alves. pp. 229-235.

FUNES, Mariano Ruiz. (1944). *Evolución del delito politico.* México, p. 18.

FURTADO, Celso Furtado. (1998). *O capitalismo global.* Rio de Janeiro.

GALEANO, Eduardo. (1989). *Patas arriba, La escuela del mundo al revés.* Montevideo.

GALZIGNA, Mario. (1988). *La malattia morale. Alle origini della psichiatria moderna.* Venezia. pp. 9, 11.

GARCIA, José Carlos. (1999). *De sem rosto a cidadão.* Rio de Janeiro.

GARGARELLA, Roberto. (2005). *El derecho de protesta, El primer derecho.* Buenos Aires. Raúl Gustavo Ferreira, *La Constitución vulnerable.*

GAROFALO, R. (1891). *La criminología.* (Trans. by Pedro Dorado Montero). Madrid. Editorial Italiana. pp. 7, 11, 14-15, 10, 97, 326 pp. 97, 133; p. 59 of the 2nd Italian ed. Torino. 1891.

———. (1916). *Criminologia.* Trans. by Julio de Mattos. Lisboa: Livraria Clássica Editora. pp. 10, 97, 102, 119. 133, 326.

GARRAUD, R. (1898). *Droit Pénal Français.* Paris: Librairie des Lois et das Arrêts. v. I.1, pp. 603-623.

GARRETT, Henry E. (1955). *General Psychology.* New York, p. 65.

GEMELLI, Agostino. (1948). *La personalità del delinquente; nei suoi fondamenti biologici e psicologici.* 2.ed. Milão: Dott. A. Giuffrè Editore, p. 311-2.

GENTILE, Emilio. (1996). *Le origine dell'ideologia fascista (1918-1925).* Bologna.

GETREVI, Paolo. (1991). *Le scritture del volto, fisiognomica e modelli culturali dal Medievo ad oggi.* Milano.

GIANCOLI, Douglas C. (1998). *Physics: principles with application.* New Jersey: Prentice Hall. pp. 308-317.

GINBERNAT, Enrique Ordeig. (1983). *Tiene Futuro la Dogmatica Jurídico Penal?* Bogotá: Temis. pp. 12-13.

GIRARD, R. and VATTIMO, G. (2006). *Verità o fede debole? Dialogo su cristianesimo e relativismo.* Torino, Transeuropa.

GIRARD, R. (1978). *Des choses cachées depuis da fondation du monde.* Paris, Le Livre de Poche.

———. (2005). *La violenza e dil sacro.* Milano, Il Mulino.

GIRARDIN, Èmile de. (1871). *Du droit de punir.* París: Henri Plon. pp. 3, 5, 6, 7, 8, 9, 10, 12, 13, 14, 12, 16, 19, 20, 114, 117, 440.

GIUFFREDI, Maurizio. (2001). *Fisiognomica, arte e psicologia tra Ottocento e Novecento. In appendice Suggio di fisiognomica di Rodolphe Töpffler.* Bologna.

GLUCKSMANN, André. (1978). *Los maestros pensadores*, Barcelona. p. 43.

GLUECK, Eleonore. (1971). *Nuove frontiere della criminología.* Milano.

GLUECK, Sheldon. (1952). *Crime and correction, selected papers.* Massachussets.

GÖBBELS, Hans. (1955) *Los asociales. esencia and concepto de la asocialidad.* Madrid.

GOFFMAN, Erving. (1978). *Estigma: Notas sobre a manipulação da identidade deteriorada.* 2. ed. (Trans. by Márcia Bandeira de Mello Leite Nunes). Rio de Janeir: Zahar Editores. p. 98.

GODDARD, Henry. (1920). *Human Efficiency and Levels of Intelligence (1920).* New York.

GÓMEZ, Eusébio. (1908). *La mala vida en Buenos Aires.* Buenos Aires.

GÖPPINGER, Hans. *Criminologia.* Trans. by Maria Luiza Schwarch and Ignácio Luzarraga Castro. Madrid: Instituto Editorial Reus, v. 5, p. 133.

GORING, Charles. (1972). *The English convict, a statistical study*. New Jersey.

GRABOSKY, P.N. and SMITH, Russell G. (2001). "Digital Crime in the 21st Century," *Journal of Information Ethics*, St. Cloud, McFarland & Company, Inc., pp. 8-26.

GRAMATICA, Fillipo. (1955). "Le Point de vue de la Societé Internationale de Defense Sociale." *Rev. de Criminologie et de Police Technique*, Genebra: Editions Emprimerie Atar, 4, p. 679.

———. (1974). *Princípios de defesa social.* (Trans. by Juan del Rosal and Victor Conde). Madrid: Editorial Montecorvo. pp. 61-2.

GRANDE, Elisabetta. (1993). *Accordo criminoso e "conspiracy". tipicitá e stretta legalitá nell'analisi comparata.* CEDAM.

GRAVEN, Jean. (1950). *La Criminologie et la Fontion Pénal.* Paris. p. 165.

GRISPIGNI, F. and MEZGER, E. (1942). *La riforma penale nazionalsocialista.* Milano, Giuffrè.

GUARNIERI, Luigi. (2000). *L'atlante criminale. Vita scriteriata di Cesare Lombroso.* Milano.

GUYÉNOT. E. (1924). *L'heredité.* Paris: Recueil Sirey. Pp. 324-9.

HAARSCHER, Guy. (1991). *Philosophie des Droits de l'Homme.* Brussels: Édition de l'Université de Bruxelles. pp. 11-13.

HÄBERLE, P. (1997). *Europäische Rechtskultur.* Frankfurt, Suhrkamp.

HAGAN, Frank. (1983). "The organized crime continuum: a further specification of a new conceptual model," *Criminal Justice Review*, Washington.

HARRIS, Marvin. (1983). *El desarrollo de la teoría antropológica. historia de las teorías de la cultura.* Madrid. p. 82.

HARRIS, Ruth. (1993). *Assassinato e loucura. medicina, leis e sociedade no "fin de siécle".* Rio de Janeiro. p. 81.

HART, Basil H. Liddell. (1999). *La prima guerra mondiale.* Milano.

HASSEMER, Winfried. (1993). "Características del moderno criminal law," *Actualidad Pena.* 43, Madrid.

HASSEMER, Winfried. (1984). *Fundamentos del derecho criminal.* Barcelona, Bosch. pp. 33-35.

HAUSER, Arnold. (1971). *Historia social de la literatura and el arte.* Madrid. pp. 64-66, 129.

HEGEL. (1985). *Filosofía del Derecho*, Trans. by Juan Garzón Bates, Mexico, pp. 31, 32, 35.

———. (1980). *Lecciones on the filosofía de la historia universal.* Madrid. pp. 171.

HEINER, Robert. (1996). *Criminology: A cross-cultural perspective*. St. Paul: West Edition. p. 197.

HERMAN, Arthur. (1998). *La idea de decadencia en la historia occidental.* Barcelona.

HERREN, Rudiger. (1973). *Freud und die Kriminologie, Einführung in die psychoanalytische Kriminologie* Stuttgart.

HERRNSTEIN, Richard. J. & MURRAY, Charles. (1994). *The Bell Curve: intelligence and class structure in American life*. New York.

HERZEN, Alexandre. (1879). *Physiologie de l'esprit, traduit de l'anglais*. París.

HILLMAN, J. (1991). *La vana fuga degli dei.* Milano, Adelphi.

HITLER, Adolf. (1939). *Mi lucha.* Sgo. de Chile. p. 126.

HOBBES, Thomas. (1997). *El Leviatan en la doctrina del Estado.* México.

HOBSBAWM, Eric J. (1995). *Il secolo breve, 1914-1991: l'era dei grandi cataclismi*. Roma, Mizzoli.

HOBSBAWM, Eric J. (2000). *Intervista sul nuovo secolo a cura di Antonio Polito.* Laterza.

HOEGEL, Hugo. (1904). *Geschichte des Österreichischen Strafrechtes in Verbindung einer Erleuterung seiner grundsätzlichen Bestimmungen.* Viena. p. 3.

HUET, A., KOERING-JOULINN, R. (1994). *Droit pénal international.* Paris, Puf.

HUGH, Thomas. (1998). *La trata de esclavos. Historia del tráfico de seres humanos de 1440 a 1870.* Barcelona, Planeta.

HUGHES, Robert. (1989). *La costa fatídica.* Barcelona.

HULSMAN, Louk and CELIS, Jacqueline Bernat. (1982). *Peines Perdues*: le Système pénal en question. Paris: Éditions Centurion. pp. 55-81.

HUNTER, Henry. (1975). *Some clinical and psychiatric aspects deriving from survey of 1811 males in hospitals for the mentally handicapped.* New York: Institute of Living-Hartford. p. 68.

HUNTINGTON, Samuel P. (1997). *El choque de civilizaciones y la reconfiguración del orden mundial.* Barcelona.

HURWITZ, Stephan. (1956). *Criminologia.* Barcelona, Ediciones Ariel. pp. 25-27.

HUSAK, Douglas N. (1992). *Drugs and rights.* Cambridge University Press.

I DELINQUENTI nell'arte ed altre conferenze e saggi di scienza ed arte. (1926). Torino.

IANNI, Octavio. (1997). *A era do globalismo.* Rio de Janeiro.

———. (1977). *Ideologia e doença mental, ensaios sobre a desumanizacao psiquiátrica do homem*. Rio de Janeiro.

ISRAEL, Giorgio and NASTASI, Pietro. (1998). *Scienza e razza nell'Italia fascista.* Bologna, Mulino.

IGNATIEFF, Michael. (1982). *Le origine del penitenziario.* Milano.

IHERING, R. von. (1877). *L'esprit du Droit Romain dans les diverses phases de son* développement. París. tomo I, p. 228.

INIKORI. Joseph E. (1981). *La trata negrega del siglo XV al XIX.* Barcelona.

INTERNATIONAL Colloquium on Criminal Policy, 3.1979. *Archives de Politique Criminelle.* Paris: Centre de Recherches de Politique Criminelle.

JACQUES-GUY, Petit. (1990). *La prison pénale en France, 1780-1875*; ces peines obscures. París.

JAKOBS, Günther & MELIÁ, Manuel Cancio. (2003). *Derecho penal del enemigo.* Madrid: Cuadernos Civitas. p. 65.

JAKOBS, Günther. (1999). *Norm, Person, Gesellschaft Vorüberlegunger zu einer Rechtsphilosophie.* Berlin, Duncker & Humblot.

JACOBY, Russell & GLAUBERMAN, Naomi. (1995). *The Bell Curve Debate.* New York Times Books.

JAMPOLSKY. P. (1955). "L'Examen Psychologique en Neuropsychiatrie Infantile," *Revue de Neuropsychiatrie Infantile.* Paris: Ed. de Groupement Français d'Etudes de Neuropsycho-Pathologie Infantile, 3, pp. 576-82.

JAULIN, Rober. (1976). *El etnocidio a través de las Américas.* México, FCE.

JENNINGS, H.S. (1909). *Heredity, variation and evolution in Protozoa.* New York: Harper. pp. 52-3.

———. (1981). *Tratado de Derecho Penal.* Trans. by S. Mir Puig and F. Muñoz Conde. Barcelona: Bosch. pp. 1187-1205.

JOHANSSON, Linda. (1998). "La Prison Électronique," *Le Courrier de l'Unesco.* Paris: 51e année. pp. 13-14.

JOHN, Landesco. (1929). *Organized Crime in Chicago.* Chicago: University Press.

JOHNSON, David R. and POST, David. (1996). "Law and Borders: The Rise of Law in Cyberspace," *Stanford Law Review*, 48, Stanford, 1367. pp. 54-61

JONAS, Friedrich. (1989). *Storia della sociologia.* Roma. 1989. p. 263.

JORDAN, Tim and TAYLOR, Paul. (1998). "Sociology of Hackers," *Sociological Review*, November. UK, Keele University, pp. 757-780.

JOSEPH, R. (no date). "El paso morágal: el proceso simbólico en las designaciones públicas de la desviación," *ESTIGMATIZACIÓN y Conducta Desviada*, (compiled by Rosa del Olmo). Universidad del Zulia. p. 73.

KAHN, Fritz. (1965). *O livro da natureza,* 2. ed. São Paulo. Melhoramentos, v.1. pp. 340, 342, 345, 349.

KAKU, Michio. (1998). *Visiones. cómo la ciencia revolucionará la materia, la vida y la mente en el Siglo XXI.* Madrid.

KAMEN, Henry. (1973). *La Inquisición española.* Madrid.

KANT, Imanuel. (1977). *Zum ewigen Frieden.* Berlin, Akademic Verlag.

KASSNER, Rudolf. (1957). *Fondamenti della fisiognomica, Il carattere delle cose.* Vicenza.

KAUFMANN, Hilde. (1979). *Criminologia, Ejecución Penal y Terapia Social.* Buenos Aires: Ediciones Depalma. pp. 69-78.

KAUFMANN, Matthias. (1989). *¿Derecho sin reglas?* Barcelona. p. 126.

KELSEN, Hans. (1995). *¿Quién debe ser el defensor de la constitución?* Madrid.

KEMP. *The death penalty in America.* p. 254.

KERSHAW, Ian. (2000). *Hitler 1889-1936.* Madrid. p. 489.

KING, Anthony. (1991). *Global Cities.* London.

KLOCKARS, Carl B., IVKOVIC, Sanja Kutnjak and HABERFELD, Maki R. (2006). *Enhancing Police Integrity.* New York, Springer-Verlag Publisher. pp. 31-32.

KNIGHT, Alan. (1996). *La Revolución Mexicana.* Mexico.

KOVALEVSKY, Paul. (1903). *La Psychologie criminelle.* París. p. 181.

KRAEMER, Heinrich & SPRENGER, Jacob. (1951). *Malleus Maleficarum.* Translated with an Introduction, Bibliography and Notes by the Rev. Montagne Summers, Londres, 1951. (Cited throughout the book from the Latin original and English, German, Italian, Spanish and Portuguese translations).

KRETSCHMER, Ernst. (1925). *Körperaubau und Charakter, Untersuchungen zum Konstitutionsproblem und zur Lehre von den Temperamenten.* Berlin.

KRIS, Ernst. (1993). *La smorfia della follia, i busti fisiognomici di Franz Xaver Messerschmidt.* Padova.

KÜNG, Hans. (2004). *Religiões do mundo, em busca dos pontos comuns.* Campinas, Editorial Unicamp.

LA CIENCIA de derecho penal ante las exigencias del presente. (trans. by Manso, Teresa). Porto. In *Revista Peruana de CIENCIAS PENALES.* año VII-VIII. Edición especial nº 12.

LA CIENCIA moderna de la persona humana. (1949). Buenos Aires.

LA DEFENSA de la Constitución. (1983). Madrid

LA PROBATIOS (Régime de la mise á l'épreuve) et les lemusres analogues. (1953). Imprenta Administrativa. Melón.

LABORDE, Jean Paul. (2005). *État de Droit et Crime Organisé.* Paris, Dalloz Edition. pp. 43-56.

LAGACHE, D. (1953). "L'Examen Psychanalytique en Criminologie," *Conférences du 1er Cours International de Criminologie.* Paris: Ed. Imprimerie Administrative. pp. 488-501.

LAHR, C. (1958). *Manual de Filosofia.* 7.ed. Porto: Livraria Apostolado da Imprensa, pp. 714-17.

LAING, R.D. and D.G. Cooper. (1976). *Razão e violencia.* Rio de Janeiro.

———. (1978). *O eu e os outros.* Rio de Janeiro.

———. (1978). *O EU dividido.* Rio de Janeiro.

LANDECHO, Carlos María. (2004). *La tipificación lombrosiana de delincuentes.* Madrid.

LANGE. (1929). *Verbrechen als Schicksal*:studien an kriminellen zwillingen.

LANGELUÜDDEKE, Albrecht. (1972). *Psiquiatria forense.* Trans. by Luis Beneytez Merino. Madrid: Editorial Espasa-Calpe, pp. 508-9.

LAQUEUR, Weimar Walter. (1996). *La Repubblica di Weimar, 1918-1930: I mali oscuri della democrazia europea.* Milano.

LA ROSA, A. (2003). *Jurisdictions pénales internacionales. La procédure et la preuve.* Paris. Puf.

LARRAURI, Elena. (1992). *La herencia de la criminología crítica.* Madrid.

LAVATER, Johann Caspar & Lichtenberg, Georg Christoph. (1991). *Lo specchio dell'anima*: pro e contro la fisiognomica. Padova.

LAVATER, Johann Caspar. *La physiognomonie ou l'art de connaitre les hommes d' apres les traits de leur.*

LAVIELLE, Bruno and LAMEYRE, Xavier. (1998). *Le Guide des Peines.* Paris: Éditions Dalloz. pp. 370-374.

LE BON, Gustavo. (1912). *La psicología política y defensa social.* Madrid.

———. (1954). *PSICOLOGÍA das multidoes.* Rio de Janeiro.

LECHAMPS, Hubert. (1971). *Storia della tratta dei negri.* Roma, Mondadori.

LEGRAIM, M. (1985). *Les dégénérés (état mental et síndromes épisodiques).* Paris.

LERMINIER, M.E. (1840). *Introducción General a la Historia de Derecho.* Barcelona, Gedisa.

LESSIG, Lawrence. (1999). "The architecture of privacy," *Vanderbilt University Journal of Entertainment Law & Practice*, Nashville, nº 56, pp. 13-14.

LEVIATHAN, 1, 8, 10, 13, 18, 2, 28.

LEVI, Michael and GILMORE, William. (2002). "Terrorist Finance, Money Laundering and the Rise and Rise of Natural Evaluation: a New Paradigm for Crime Control?" *Financing Terrorism.* Dordrecht, the Netherlands, Kluwer Academic Publishers, 2002. pp. 29-30.

LEWONTIN, C. Richard. (1978). "Adaptation," *Scientific American.* New York: Ed. University. 239, 3, set., p. 166.

LIPTON, R.J. (1975). "Thought Reform of Western Civilians in Chinese Communist Prisons," *Review of Psychiatry Wiley.* New York, 19, mar., pp. 173-85.

LISZT, von Franz. (1984). *La idea de fin en derecho criminal.* Valparaíso, p. 120.

LIVINGSTON, Jay. (1996). *Crime and Criminology.* New Jersey: Simon and Schuster. p. 123.

LOCKE, John. *Ensayo sobre el gobierno civil.* 2, 6.

LOMBARDIA, Francisco Sánchez. (s.d.). Valencia.

LOMBROSO, C. (1894). *Gli anarchici.* Torino.

———. (1892). *Le crime politique et les révolutions par rapport au droit, à l'antropologie criminelle et à la science du gouvernemente.* París.

———. (1884). *L'uomo delinquente rapporto all'antropologia, giurisprudenza e alle discipline carcerarie. Delincuente nato e pazzo morale.* Torino, Fratelli Bocca, p. 248.

———. (1894). *Gli anarchici.* Torino.

———. (1894). *L'uomo di genio in rapporto alla psichiatria, alla storia ed all'estetica.* Torino.

———. (1892). *Le crime politique et les revolutions.* París.

LOPEZ, Emilio Myra. (1967). *Manual de Psicologia Jurídica.* Trans. by Elso Arruda. São Paulo: Editora Mestre Jou, 1967, 4. ed., pp. 84-5, 204-9, 222-30.

LOPEZ, ERNESTO. (1998). *Globalización y democracia.* Buenos Aires.

LOWEN, Alexander. (1977). *O corpo em terapia: a abordagem energética.* São Paulo: Summus. p.171.

LUCAS, Charles. (1883). *La récidive et le projet de rélégation des récidivistes, extrait du compte-rendu de l'Académie des Sciences morales et politiques.* pp. 157, 160, 164, 173, 174, 191, 204, 206, 208, 216, 217, 220, 227, 226, 228, 235, 236, 241, 242, 244, 245, 246, 250, 251, 254, 255, 256-260, 261, 272, 275, 285, 280, 299, 318, 320, 322, 324, 326, 335.

LUKACS, Georg. (1983). *El asalto a la razón. La trayectoria del irracionalismo desde Schelling hasta Hitler.* México, p. 7.

LUNA, Everardo da Cunha. (1948). "Das penas e sua execução," *Fondamenti biologici e psicologici.* Milão: Dott. A Giuffré—Editore. p. 320.

LYRA, Roberto. (1977). *Direito penal normativo.* 2.ed. Rio de Janeiro: José Konfino—Editor. pp. 25, 132.

———. *As Execuções Penais no Brasil.* Rio de Janeiro: Editora Forense. p. 30.

MACEDO, Gilberto de. (1972). "Crime, sociedade, cultura," *Revista de Direito Penal.* Rio de Janeiro Editor Borsoi, 6, abr./jun., p. 98.
MACMILLAN. (1986). *Exploring criminology*. New York. p. 86.
MADIOT, Yves. (1976). *Droits de l'Homme et Libertés Publiques.* Paris: Éditions Masson. pp. 209-212.
MADSEN, Frank G. (2009). *Transnational Organized Crime.* London and New york, Routledge Publications, pp. 80-83.
MAGGIORE, Giuseppe. (1958). *Diritto penale.* Bolonha: Nicola Zanichelli Editore. v. 2, p. 649.
MAGLI, Patrizia. (1995). *Il volto e l'anima.* Milano.
MALINOWSKI, B. (1956). *Crimen y costumbre en la sociedad selvaje.* Barcelona, Planeta.
MALTZ, Michael. (1985). *Toward Defining Organized Crime: the politics and the economics of organized crime.* Lexington Books, p. 21.
MAMARELA, G. (1986). *L'America da Roosevelt a Reagan. Storia degli Stati Uniti dal 1939 a oggi.* Roma, Laterza.
MANUAL de derecho penal. (1977). Bs. As. pp. 446-448.
MANUEL théorique et pratique de Psychologie Médicale. (1927). París.
MANN, David and SUTTON, Mike. (1998). "Netcrime: More Change in the Organisation of Thieving," *British Journal of Criminology*, 38. Oxford, Oxford University Press, pp. 201-229.
MANZINI, Vincenzo. (1959). *Tratatto di diritto penale italiano.* Turim: Unione Tipografico Editrice Torinese, v. 3, pp. 263-4.
MARANÓN, Gregorio. (1930). *La evolución de la sexualidad y los estados intersexuales.* Madrid.
MARIN, CESAR Camargo. (1931). *El psicoanálisis en la doctrina y en la práctica judicial.* Madrid.
MARQUES, José Frederico. (1956). *Curso de direito penal.* São Paulo: Edição Saraiva. v. 3, p. 59.
MARTÍN, Luis Gracia. (2005). "Consideraciones críticas sobre el actualmente denominado 'derecho criminal del enemigo'," *Revista electrónica de Ciencia Penal y Criminología*, 7-2.
MARTINDALE, Don. (1960). *The Nature and types of sociological theory.* Boston. p. 162.
MARTINS, Hans-Peter and SCHUMANN, Harald. (1998). *A armadilha da globalizaçao, O assalto à democracia e ao bem-estar social.* Sao Paulo.
———. (1996). *Die Globalisierungsfalle.* Hamburg.
MATTEOTTI, Giacomo. (1910). *La recidiva, Saggio di revisione critica con dati statistici.* Milano. p. 240.
MAUDSLEY, H. (1879). *El crimen y la locura.*
MAUER, Marc. "The Fragility of criminal justice reform," *Social Justice*, 25 nº 3.
MAURACH, Reinhart. (1962). *Derecho Penal.* Translation by Córdoba Roda. Barcelona: Ariel. pp. 483-489.
MAYER, Otto. (1950). *Derecho administrativo alemán*, Buenos Aires. T. II, p. 3.

MÉDIONI, Jean. (1984). *La Transmission des comportements.* La Recherche, Paris, 5,155, mai, pp. 706-8.

MEJÍA, J.M. Ramos. (1912). *Las multitudes argentines*. Buenos Aires.

MELLO. (1972). Dirceu de. Criminoso por tendência. *Revista dos Tribunais.* São Paulo: Editora Revista dos Tribunais, 6, 444, out., p. 264.

MENDELSOHN, Benjamin. (1958). "La Victimologie," *Revue de Droit Penal et de Criminologie.* Brussels: Veuve Larcier Editeu, 2, p. 825.

MENEZES, Lená Medeiros de. (1996). *Os indesejáveis: desclassificados da Modernidade- protesto, crime e expulsao na Capital Federal* (1890-1930). Rio de Janeiro.

MERKL, A. *Teoría general del derecho administrativo*. México, p. 325.

MERTON, Robert. (1984). *Teoría y estructura sociales.* México.

MESSUTI, Ana. (2001). *El tiempo como pena*. Buenos Aires.

MESTRE J. (1995). *Cathari, Problema religioso, pretexto político.* Barcelona, Península.

METTLER, C. and METTLER, F. (1947). *History of Medicine.* Philadelphia: Edition Blakiston. pp. 139-146.

METTRAUX, G. (2005). *International Crimes and "ad hoc" Tribunals.* London, Oxford Press.

MEZGER, Edmundo. (1933). *Kriminalpolitik aus kriminologischer Grundlagen.*

MEZGER, E. (1944). *Rechtsirrtum und Rechtsblindheit.* In: Kohlrausch, F. (1944). *Probleme der strafrechtserneuerung*, fest. Berlin. pp. 180-198; pp. 197-198).

MEZGER, Edmund. (1942). *Criminología.*

——. (1944). "Rechtsirrtum und Rechtsblindheit," *Probleme der Strafrechtserneuerung, Fest. f. Kohlrausch*. Berlin. pp. 180-198.

——. (1950). *Criminologia.* 2. ed. Trans. by José Arturo Rodrigues Muñoz. Madrid: Editorial Revista de Derecho Privado. pp. 20, 35, 252.

——. (1957). *Verbrechen als Schicksal.* Munich: Bavarian Academy of Sciences. p. 5.

MIDDENDORFF, Wolf. (1970). *Teoria y prática de la prognosis criminal.* Madrid: Espasa Calpe. pp. 136, 139. Milano.

MINHAN, Júlio. (1957). *Mistérios da biologia.* Rio de Janeiro: Ateneu. pp. 66-84.

MISES, Ludwig von. (1981). *Epistemological problems of economics.* New York.

MOCCIA, Sergio. (1997). *La perenne emergenza, tendenzie autoritarie nel sistema penale.* Napoli.

MOLINARI, D. (1944). *La trata de negros. Datos para su estudio en el Rio de la Plata.* Buenos Aires, Uba.

MOLINER, Victor (1867). *La vie et les travaux de Jean Bodin sur sa démonomanie des sociers et sur les procés pour sorcellerie au seiziéme et au dix-septiéme siécle.* Montpellier. p. 21.

MOMMSEN, R. (1899). *Römisches Strafrecht.* (Trans. by Pedro de Castellana) Berlim.

MOMMSEN, Teodoro. *El derecho penal romano*. (Trans. by P. Dorado). Madrid. p. 63.

MONDADORI, Bruno. (2000). *El zoo de los filósofos*: de la bestialización a la exclusion. Madrid: Taurus.

MONIZ, Egas. (1940). *Confidencias de um investigador científico*. Lisboa.

MONTAGU, Ashley. (1978). *A natureza da agressividade humana*. Rio de Janeiro: Zahar. p. 194.

MONTEALEGRE, Hernán Montealegre. (1979). *La seguridad del Estado y derechos humanos*. Santiago de Chile.

MOOR, L. (1957). Comparaison des Resultats Obtenus au Test de Terman et à l'Fchelle de Wechsler–Bellevue. *Revue de Neuropsychiatrie Infantille et d'Hygiène Mentele de l'Enfance*. Paris: Ed.De Groupement Français d'Études de neuropsycho-Pathologie Infantile, 2, mai./jun., pp. 271-5.

MORAES, Benjamin. (1977). *A Parte geral do futuro Código Penal*. Belém: S.E. (Conferência proferida no Ciclo de Estudos de Direito Penal, em homenagem ao professor Aldebaro Klautau, promovido pelo Instituto de Criminologia do Pará, em 23.05.1977). p. 9.

MORALES, Ramiro Condarco. (1965). *Zárate, el temible Willka, Historia de la rebelión indígena de 1899*. La Paz.

MOREL, Bénédict, Augustin. (1860). *Traité des maladies mentales*. París.

MORRISON, W. (2006). *Criminology, Civilization and the New World Order*. New York, Oxon.

MOSSE, George L. (1992). *Il razzismo in Europa dalle origine all'olocausto*. Laterza, pp. 118, 127.

———. (1997). *L'immagine dell'uomo. Lo stereotipo maschile nell'epoca moderna*. Torino.

MUNHOZ NETTO, Alcides. (1974). Criminosos habituais e por tendência. *Revista de Direito Penal*, 9, 15-16, jul.-dez p. 24.

MURATGIA, C. (1984). *Director, Presidio y cárcel de reincidentes*: antecedentes, Bs. As., s.d., (1910 circa); also Ushuaia 1884-1984. cien años de una ciudad argentina. Tierra del Fuego: Municipalidad de Ushuaia.

MUSCO, Enzo. (1978). *La misura di sicurezza detentiva*: profili storici e costituzionali. Milano.

NAGLER, Michael N. (2005). *Per un futuro nonviolento*. Milano.

NAUCKE, W. (2000). *Über die Zerbrechlickeit des rechtstaatlichen Strafrechts*. Berlin, Nomos.

NEUMAN, Elias. (9940). *Victimología. El Rol de la Victima en los Delitos Convencionales*. Buenos Aires.

NICÉFORO, Alfredo and SIGHELE, Scipio. (1901). *La mala vida en Roma*. Madrid.

———. (1898). *Criminali e degenerati dell'Inferno. Dantesco*. Torino.

NICEFORO, Alfredo. (1952). *La fisiognomica nell'arte e nella scienza*. Firenze.

NICOLAI, Helmut. (1932). *Die rassengesetzliche Rechtslehre, Grundzüge e. nazionalsozialist. Rechtsphilosophie*. München.

NIEVEAU, Maurice. (1977). *Historia de los hechos económicos contemporáneos*. Barcelona.

NIETZSCHE, F. (1883). *Also sprach Zarathustra, II*. Berlin, Kart Müller Verlag.

NINO, Carlos. (1984). *Ética and Derechos Humanos.* Buenos Aires: Editorial Paidós. pp. 23-27.

NIVEAU, Maurice. (1977). *Historia de los hechos económicos contemporáneos.* Barcelona.

NORDAU, Max. (1902). *Degeneración.* Madrid.

NORONHA, Magalhães. (1966). A classificação de delinqüente no novo direito penal. *Revista Brasileira de Criminologia e Direito Penal.* Rio de Janeiro: Instituto de Criminalogia da Universidade do Estado da Guanabara, 4, 140, jul./set. p. 99.

NORRIE, Alan. (2001). "Dialogue and Debate: The Nature of Virtual Criminality, *Social and Legal Studies*, 10. London, Los Angeles, Sage Publications, pp. 227-228.

NÚÑEZ, A. Ricardo C. (1995). *El crimen organizado, una categoría frustrada.* Córdoba.

OATES, Eugênio. (1969). *Linguagem das Mãos.* Rio de Janeiro: Editora Livro. pp. 9-11.

OLIVEIRA, Edmundo. (1994). *Comentários ao Código Penal: Parte Geral,* Rio de Janeiro: Editora Forense. pp. 119-125.

———. (2005). *Co-operation and Law Enforcement to Counter Organized Crime in the Common Market Countries of South America.* Helsinki, HEUNI Edition, pp. 46-49.

OLMOS, Fray Andrés. (1990). *Tratado de hechicerías y sortilegios, 1553.* Mexico: UNAM, p. 47.

ORANO, Paolo Orano. (1939). *Inchiesta sulla razza.* Roma.

ORIGEN and evolución del discurso crítico en criminal law. (2004). Bs. As.

PAKES, Francis. (2004). *Comparative Criminal Justice.* Devon, UK, Willan Publishing, pp. 141-143.

PALEM, R. M. (1966). "Le Clinicien Devant le M. M. P. I," *Annales Medico-Psychologiques.* Paris: Ed. de la Societé Medico-Psychologique. pp. 35-8.

PASCUAL, Rossi. (1906). *Los sugestionadores and la muchedumbre.* Barcelona. p. 3.

PASTOREAU. M. (2006). *Una história simbólica de la Edad Media ocidental.* Buenos Aires, Katz.

PATRIZI, M. L. (1916). *Preliminari d'un indirizzo antropológico (bio-psicologico) nella critica e storia dell'arte figurativa,* en *Dopo Lombroso.* Milano.

PAVARINI, Massimo. (1980). *Introduzione a la crimnologia.* Firenze, Edizione Universitaria.

———. (1979). *Carcere e fabbrica, Alle origine del sistema penitenziario.* Bologna.

PECO, José. (1936). *La reforma penal en el Senado de 1933.* Buenos Aires.

PEDRO Dorado. (1916). *El derecho protector de los criminales.* Madrid.

PELÁEZ, Michelangelo. (1974). *Introdução ao Estudo da Criminologia.* Coimbra Editora. pp. 31-32.

PELLICIER, Pierre. (1985). *Emile de Girardin.* París.

PENA, Diego Manuel Luzon. (1994). "Control electrónico and sanciones alternativas a la prisión," *Jornadas Penitencias Andaluzas*, 8, Sevilla.

PENDE, Nicola. (1932). *Trabajos recientes sobre endocrinología y psicología criminal.* Madrid.

———. (1943). *Dizionario di Criminologia.* Milano. I. p. 400.
———. *¿A donde vas, hombre? Problemas humanos de nuestro tiempo.* Buenos Aires.
PESSOA, Mário Pessoa. (1971). *O direito da segurança nacional.* Rio de Janeiro.
PICCA, Georges. (1983). *La Criminologie*, Paris: Presses Universitaires de France, pp. 108-114.
PICK, Daniel Pick. (1999). *Volti della degenerazione, una síndrome europea 1848-1918.* Firenze.
PIERANTONI, Umberto. (1940). *Compêndio de biologia.* Barcelona: Labor. p. 208.
PIMENTEL, Manuel Pedro. (1972). "A reforma penal," *Estudos e Pareceres de Direito Penal.* São Paulo: Editora Revista dos Tribunais. p. 79.
PINEL, Sobre and KLAUS Dörner. (1974). *Ciudadanos y locos, Historia social de la Psiquiatría.* Madrid. p. 185.
PINTO, Julio & SCHMITT, Carl. (2000). *Reivindicación de la política.* La Plata. pp. 99, 179.
PLATÓN. (1967). Obras Completas, Bib. Ameba, Bs. As., T. IV. p. 95.
PODGOR, Ellen. (2002). "International Computer Fraud: A Paradigm for Limiting National Jurisdiction," *Davis Law Review*, Davis, CA, pp. 273-274.
POLIAKOV, León. (1989). *Historia del antisemitismo: raíces.* Buenos Aires.
———. (1999). *Il mito ariano. Saggio sulle origine del nazismo e dei nazionalismi.* Roma.
Política y dogmática jurídico penal. Directo e democracia. (2002). Canoas. 3, 2.
POLLARD, Charles. (1999). *Tolerancia cero ¿Y mañana qué.* Milenio: San Martín, 2, 3, p. 17.
PORTO, Teresa Manso. (2004). *Revista Peruana de Ciencias Penales.* March. (edición especial, nº 12), Spanish, pp. 7-8.
POSTEL, Jacques Postel and QUÉTEL, Claude. (2000). *Nueva historia de la psiquiatria.* México. p. 608.
PRATT. J. (2006). *Castigo y civiliaación. Una lectgura crítica sobre plas prisiones y los regímenes carcelarios.* Barcelona, Gedisa.
PRESA, José Octavio López. (Coord.) (1998). *Corrupción y cambio.* México.
PRICE, Richard. (1981). *Sociedades cimarronas, comunidades esclavas rebeldes en las Américas.* México.
PROTÁGORAS, Platón. (1967). *Las Leyes.* (Obras Completas). Bib. Ameba. p. 95.
RAFFIN, M. (2006). *La experiencia del horror.* Buenos Aires, Del Puerto.
RAMMONET, Ignacio. (1997). *Un mundo sin rumbo, crisis de fin de siglo.* Madrid.
RAMOS, J.M. (1912). "Mejía, Las multitudes argentinas," *General, on criminalization of multitudes.* Buenos Aires.
RAUSCH, Sharla and LAFREE, Gary. (2007). "The Growing Importance of Criminology in the Study of Terrorism," *The Criminologist. The Official Newsletter of the American Society of Criminology.* Columbus, Ohio. Publication Series Vol. 34, No. 4, November/December, pp. 2-4.
REALE JÚNIOR, Miguel. (s.d.). *Antijuridicidade concreta.* São Paulo: José Bushatsky Editor. p. 137.
REICHARDT, M. (1958). *Psiquiatria General y Especial.* Madrid, Gredos.
REICK, Wilhelm. (1975). *Analisis del carater.* 5. ed. Buenos Aires: Paidos. p. 201.

REIK, Theodor. (1932). *Der unbekannte Mörder, Von der Tat zum Täter.*

REILLY, Philip. (1977). *Genetics, law, social policy.* Harvard: University Press. pp. 152-89.

Relazione Ministeriale al Progetto definitivo del Codice Penale. (1929). Roma: Tipografia Ufficiale. t.1, p. 156.

RENON, Louis. (1907). *Les maladies populaires. Maladies vénériennes, alcoolisme, tuberculose.* París.

REPORT on the Task Force on Organized Crime. Washington: National Advisory Committee.

REUTER, Peter. (1983). *Disorganized Crime*: the economics of the visible hand. St. Paul: The Mit Press. pp. 3-5, 7-10.

RHODES, Anthony. (1993). *Propaganda. The Art of persuasion*: World War II. Pennsylvania.

RIBEIRO, Darcy. (1987). *O processo civilizatório,* estudos *de antropologia da civilização.* Petrópolis. p. 129.

RIBEIRO, Leonídio. (1957). *Criminologia.* Rio de Janeiro: Editorial Sul-Americana. p. 46.

RICKERT, H. (1965). *Ciencia cultural y ciencia natural.* Madrid, Calpe.

RICO, José Maria. *Sanções Penais.* (1978). Trans. by Sérgio Fragoso. Rio de Janeiro: Liber Juris Editora.

RIFKIN, Jeremy. (1997). *El fin del trabajo, nuevas tecnologías contra puestos de trabajo, el nacimiento de una nueva era.* Buenos Aires.

RITZER, George. (1998). *Teoría sociológica contemporânea.* México.

RIVALTA, Valentino. (1886). *Storia e sistema del diritto dei teatri secondo l'etica e i principii delle leggi canoniche e civili.* Bologna.

ROBBINS, Rossell Hope. (1988). *Enciclopedia de la brujería and demonología.* Madrid.

ROBIN, M. (2005). *Escuadrones de la muerte. La escuela francesa.* Buenos Aires, Sudamericana.

ROBERT, K. and MERTON. (1980). "Teoría y estructura sociales: a spectrum based theory of enterprise," *Crime and Delinquency.* p. 358.

ROCCHINI, Piero. (1993). *La neurosis del poder.* Madrid.

RODLER, Lucia. (1991). *I silenzi mimici del volto. Studi sulla tradizione fisiognomica italiana tra Cinque e Seicento.* Pisa.

RODLER, Lucia. (2000). *Il corpo specchio dell'anima: teoria e storia della fisiognomica.*

RODNEY, Walter. (1982). *De cómo Europa subdesarrolló a África.* México, Siglo XXI.

RODRIGUES, Anabela Miranda. (2000). *Consensualisme et Prison. In*: *Nouvelles Orientations du Régime Pénitentiaire,* Lisboa: FIPP. pp. 147-171.

RODRIGUES, Raimundo Nina. (1932). *Os africanos no Brasil.* Sao Paulo.

ROMANO, Sergio. (1990). *Giovanni Gentile. La filosofia al potere.* Milano, Firenze.

ROMEIRO, Jorge Alberto. (1978). *Elementos de Direito Penal e Processual Penal.* São Paulo: Saraiva. p.110.

ROMEO, Giovanni. (1990). *Inquisitori, esorcisti e streghe nell'Italia della Controriforma.* Roma, Sansoni.

ROSENBERG, Alfred. (1976). *El mito of the Twentieth Century. Una valoración de las luchas anímico-espirituales de las formas de nuestro tiempo.* Buenos Aires.

ROSTAND, Jean. (1961). *La herencia humana.* Bs. As. pp. 52-53.

ROTMAN, Edgardo. (1986). "Do Criminal Offenders Have a Constitutional Right to Rehabilitation?" *The Journal of Criminal law and Criminology.* Northwestern: University School of Law. 77, 4, pp. 1.053-1.068.

ROTMAN, Edgardo. (1990). *Beyond Punishment: a new view on the rehabilitation of criminal offenders.* New York: Greenwood Press. pp. 154-171.

ROUSSEAU, Jean-Jacques. (1973). *El contrato social.* (Trans. by Consuelo Berges). Madrid. p. 13.

———. *Contrato social*, I, 2.

ROVERE, Richard. (1987). *El Senador Joe MacCarthy*, México: FCE.

ROZITCHNER, Leon La Cosa and la Cruz. (1997). *Cristianismo y capitalismo.* Bs. As.

RUGGIERO, Vincenzo. (1996). *Economie sporche, L'impresa criminale in Europa.* Torino.

———. (1999). *DELITTI dei deboli e dei potenti. Ezercizi di anticriminologia.*Torino.

RUIZ-FUNES, Mariano. (1948). *La peligrosidad y sus experiencias legales.* La Habana.

RUPING, H. (1991). *Grundriss der Strafrechtsgeschichte*, Manchen.

SACOTTE, Jacqueline. (1981). "Le Mouvement de Dépenalisation: la limitation et la privation de liberté dans les pays de l'Europe Occidentale," *Archives de Politique Criminelle.* Paris: Édition du Centre de Recherches de Politique Criminelle. v.5, p. 61.

SADER, Emir. (1995). *O mundo depois da queda.* Rio de Janeiro.

SAIZ, Ignacio Lopes & CODON, José Maria. (19690). *Psiquiatria jurídica penal and civil.* 3. ed. Burgos: Ediciones Aldecoa. t. 2, pp. 563-7.

SALDANA, Quintiliano. (1936). *Nueva Criminología.* Madrid. p. 248.

SALÉIS, Jorge. (1995). *Médicos, maleantes y maricas, higiene, criminología and homosexualidad en la construcción de la nación Argentina* (Buenos Aires: 1871-1914), Bs. As.

SALILLAS, Rafael. (1898). *El delincuente español, Hampa (Antropología picaresca).* Madrid.

SÁNCHEZ, Jesús-Maria Silva. (1999). *La expansión de derecho criminal, aspectos de la política criminal en las sociedades postindustriales.* Madrid.

SANTOS, José Beleza dos. (1953). *Os tribunais de execução das penas em Portugal.* Coimbra: Editora Coimbra, p. 32.

SANTOS, Marino Barbero. (1985). *Pena de muerte (El ocaso de un mito).* Buenos Aires. p. 179.

SAPELLI, Giulio. (1998). *Cleptocracia, El mecanismo único de corrupción entre economía y política.* Buenos Aires. Saraiva. pp. 631-632.

SAS, Thomas S. (1984). *Legge, libertá e psichiatria.* Milano.

SASINI, J. (1957). "Lie Detector Tests and Freedom of the Will," *Journal of Criminal Law*, New York. p. 570-4.

SAUZE, Alfred. (1862). *De l'imprisonnement cellulaire: de sa double influence sur la santé physique et santé physique et morale des détenus.*

———. (1862). *Études médico-psychologiques sur la folie*, Paris, 1862.

SCHAMA, S. (2002). *Auge y caíde del Imperio Britanico.* Madrid, Crítica.

SCHELL, Robert and HALL, Elizabeth. (1980). *Psychologie Génétique.* Montreal: Renouveau Pédagogique. pp. 7-9, 59-60.

SCHILLING, Heinz-Dieter. (1983). *Schwule und Faschismus.* Berlin.

SCHIRAGIAN, A. (2005). *Condanato a uccidere, Memorie di un patriota armeno.* Milano, Guerini.

SCHMIDT, A. (1956). La Narco-Analyse et son Application Pratique. *Revue Internacionale de Criminologie et de Police Techanique.* Genebra: Edition Emprimerie Atar, 1, jan./mar., pp. 64-75.

SCHMIDT, Eberhard. (1951). *Einführung in die Geschichte der deutshcen Strafrechtspflege.* Göttingen. p. 21.

SCHMITT, Carl. (1985). *El concepto de lo politico.* Ediciones Folios. México. pp. 23, 25, 30, 51, 61, 68, 111.

———. (1988). *Il custode della Costituzione.* Milano.

———. (1938). *Der Leviathan in der Staatslehre des Thomas Hobbes.* Berlin, Dunclker & Humboldt.

———. (1929). *Der Hüter der Verfassung.*

———. (1992). *Teoría de la Constitución.* Madrid. p. 37.

———. (2005). *Theorie des Partisanen. Schwischenbemerkung zum Begriff des Politischen.* Milano. p. 79.

———. (2005). *Teologia política.* Buenos Aires, Struhart.

———. (2006). *Risposte a Norimberga.* Roma, Laterza.

SCHNEIDER, Hans Joachim. (1987). *Kriminologie.* Berlin: Walter de Gruyter. pp. 858-861.

SCHNEIDER, Kurt. (1976). *Psicopatologia clínica.* Trans. by Emanuel Carneiro Leão. São Paulo, Editora Mestre Jou. pp. 29-30, 43, 63-74.

———. (1962). *Las personalidades psicopáticas.* Madrid.

SCHWARTZENBERG, Roger-Gérard. (1978). *O Estado espetáculo.* Rio de Janeiro.

SCIACCA, M. Federico. (1966). *Historia de la filosofía.* Barcelona. p. 335.

SCIASCIA, Leonardo. (1973). *Storie nere di fine secolo. La mala Itália.* Milano.

SCHMITT, Carl. (1933). *Staat, Bewegung, Volk*: die dreigliederung der politischen Einheit, Hamburg.

SEDGWICH, John. (1995). *The Bell Curve Debate: history, documents, opinions.* Washington Times Books, pp. 144, 162.

SEE, Claus Roxin. (1976). *Problemas Básicos de la ley criminal.* Madrid: Reus.

SELLIN, Throsten. (1950). "Le Sociologue et le Probleme du Crime," *Rev. Intern de Defense Sociale,* p. 527.

SERVERN, Hill. (1969). *The end of the roaring twenties, prohibition and repeal.* New York.

SEVA DÍAZ, A. (1979). *Psiquiatria Clínica.* Barcelona, Espax.

SHELDON, W.H. and STEVENS, S.S. (1951). *Les variétés du temperament. une psychologie des différences constitutionneles.* París.

SHELDON, W.H.; STEVENS, S.S.; TUCKER; W.B. (1950). *Les variétés de la constitution physique de l'homme.* Paris.

SHENTOUB, C. (1955). "Le Thematic Apperception Test," *Revue de Neuropsychiatrie Infantile et d'Hygiène Mentale de l'Enfance*. Paris: Ed. de Groupement Français d'Études de Neuropsychs. Pathologie Infantile 3, set./out., p. 588.

SHEPTYCKI, James W. (2003). *Against Transnational Organized Crime.* Toronto, Toronto University Press, pp. 126-134.

SICHERUNGSHAFT, Kohlrausch. "Eine Besinnung auf den Streitstand," *ZStW*, 44, pp. 21-34.

SIEGEL, Heinrich. (1886). *Deutsche Rechtsgeschichte.* Berlin, p. 13.

SIGHELE, Scipio. (1910). *I delitti della folla.* Torino.

SILVA, De Josino do Nascimento e. (1863). *Código criminal do império do Brasil.* Rio de Janeiro.

SILVA, Golbery do Couto. (1981). *Planejamento estratégico.* Brasilia.

SILVER, Lee M. (1998). *Vuelta al Edén, Más allá de la clonación en un mundo felíz.* Madrid.

SIMONETTI, José Maria. (1998). *El ocaso de la virtud.* Buenos Aires.

SINOR, G. (1955). *L'Orientation Professionnelle.* Paris: Éditions Puf. p. 120.

SKROTZKY, Nicolas. (1991). *Guerres: crimes écologiques.* París.

SMITH & HOGAN. (1992). *Criminal law.* London. 1992. p. 269.

SMITH, Dwight. (1980). "Paragons, pariahs and pirates: a spectrum based theory of enterprise," *Crime and Delinquency*, p. 358.

SMITH, James Frank. (1990). *Derecho Constitucional Comparado México-United States.* UNAM. México.

SOLIS QUIROGA, Hector. (1977). *Sociologia Criminal.* 2ed. México: Editorial Porrúa S.A. p. 210.

SOLJENITZYN, Aleksandr. (1973). *Arquipélago Gulag.* Trans. by Francisco A. Ferreira, Maria Llisto & José Seabra. São Paulo: Editora Círculo do Livro. pp. 107-124.

SOMMER, Robert. (1976). *The End of Imprisonment.* New York: Oxford University Press. pp. 171-195.

SORI, Ercole. (1985). "Las causas económicas de la inmigración italiana entre los siglos XIX y XX," Devoto-Rosoli, *La inmigración italiana en la Argentina*. Buenos Aires. p. 15.

SOROS, George. (1999). *La crisis del capitalismo global, la sociedad abierta en peligro.* Buenos Aires.

SPEE, F. (2003). *Cautio Criminalis.* Virginia, University of Virginia Press.

SPENCER, Herbert. (1983). *Principes de sociologie.* (trans. By Cazelles, M.). París.

SPENCER, Jon. (1999). "Crime on the Internet: Its Presentation and Representation," *Howard Law Journal*, Washington, 38, pp. 241-251.

SQUELLA, Agustín Squella. (1977). "Ihering y la lucha por el derecho," *Revista de Ciencias Sociales*, Universidad de Chile. Valparaíso.

STEINBERG, Allen. (1989). *The Transformation of Criminal Justice*. North Carolina: University of North Carolina.

STEINBERG, Arthur & BEARN, Alexander. (1974). *Progress in medical genetics.* New York: Grune and Stratton. pp. 196, 201-5.

STEPHEN, Holmes. (1993). *The anatomy of antiliberalism.* London: Harvard University Press. p. 14.

STIGLITZ, Joseph E. (2002). *Globalization and its Discontents.* New York, London, W.W. Norton Company, pp. 214-222.

STOCK, Robert W. (1968). "The XYY and The Criminal." *New York Times Magazine*. pp. 29-30.

STODDARD, Lothrop. (1923). *The Revolt against civilization: The menace of the under-man.* London.

STOOSS, von Carl. (1893). *Avant-Projet de Code Pénal Suisse: partie générale. (Traduit par mission du Département Fédéral de Justice et Police par Alfred Gautier)*, Basel und Genf, Georg, Verlag von & Co. pp. 10-11.

STORY, José. (1863). *El Poder Judicial de los Estados Unidos: Su organización y atribuciones.* Buenos Aires.

STROSSEN, Nadine. "Cybercrimes v. Cyberliberties," *International Review of Law, Computers and Technology*. London and New York, Routledge Publications, pp. 11-24.

STUMPFL, F. (1936). *Die Ursprünge des Vebrechens.*

SUTHERLAND, Edwin & CRESSEY, Donald. (1960). *Criminology,* 4. ed. Chicago: University Press. pp. 103-4.

SUTHERLAND, Edwin H. (1978). *Criminology*. Lippincott. p. 270.

———. (1947). *Principles of criminology.* Philadelphia: Ed. Lippincott. pp. 6-7.

SYKES, G. and MATZA, D. (1957). "Techniques of neutralization: a theory of delinquency," *American Sociological Review* 22 (6).

SZABO, Denis. (1989). *Criminologie et Politique Criminelle.* Paris: Édition Vrin. pp. 6, 236, 241.

SZONDI. L. (1952). *Diagnostic Experimental des Pulsions.* Paris: Éditions Puf. p. 319.

TAÍNE, H. (1878). *Les origines de la France contemporaine*, La Révolution. tomo I París.

TARDE, G. (1900). *Essais et mélanges sociologiques*. París.

TAVLITZHI, Jean. (1984). À la génétique moleculaire. *La Recherche*, Paris. 5, 155, mai, pp. 591-93.

TAYLOY, Ian and WALTON, Paul; Young, Jock. (1973). *The new criminology, for a social theory of deviance.* Londres.

TEISSEIRE, Édouard. (1893). *La transporation pénale et la relegation d'apres les Lois de 30.* Mai 1854-27.mai., París.

TELLA, María José Falcón. (2000). *La desobediencia civil.* Madrid.

TERNON, Yves. (1995). *L'État criminel. las génocides au XXe. siècle*, París, Seuil.

THESING, Josef and HOFMEISTER, Wilhelm. (1995). *Medios de comunicación, democracia y poder.* Buenos Aires.

THOMSON, Basil. (1937). *La historia de Scotland Yard,* Madrid.

THOREAU, Henry D. (1994). *Desobediencia civil y otros escritos.* Madrid.

THORWALD, Jürgen. (1966). *El siglo de la investigación criminal.* Barcelona.

THUROW, Lester. (1993). *Cabeça a cabeça, a batalha econômica entre Japao, Europa e United States.* Rio de Janeiro.

TONNIES, Ferdinand. (1947). *Comunidad y sociedad.* Buenos Aires.

TORNAGHI, Hélio. (1978). *Instituições de Processo Penal.* 2. ed. São Paulo: Saraiva. v. 4, p.12.

TRAUNBERG, Nina Rausch de. (1975). *A Prática do Rorschach.* (Trans. by Álvaro Cabral). São Paulo: Editora Cultrix. pp. 13-20.

TRAVESSO, G.B. and VERDE, A. (1981). *Criminologia critica. Delinquenza e controllo sociale nel modo di produzione capitalistico.* Padova.

TRINDADE, Antonio Cançado. (1991). *A Proteção Internacional dos Direitos Humanos.* São Paulo: Saraiva. pp. 631-632.

TURNS, Danielle. (1963). *Entretiens de Groupe ou Cours de l'Instruction Pénale.* Lyon: Editions Bosc. p. 31.

TUSELL, Javier. (1997). *La revolution posdemocrática.* Oviedo.

TYLER, Gus. (1962). *Organized crime in America.* Michigan: The University of Michigan Press.

TYLER, Tom R. (1996). "Compliance with Intellectual Property Laws: A Psychological Perspective," *Journal of International Law and Politics*, 29, New York University, New York, pp. 222-223.

UGARTE, Augusto Pinochet. (1984). *Geopolítica.* Santiago de Chile.

UNAM. (1985). *Constitución Política of the United States Mexicanos Comentada*, Rectoría, Instituto de Investigaciones Jurídicas. México.

URRY, Scott Lash-John. (1987). *The end of organized capitalism.* Madison.

V. INTERNATIONAL COMMISSION OF JURISTS. (1983). *States of Emergency, Their Impact on Human Rights*,

VAHAKN, D. (1997). *The History of the Armenian Genocide: Ethnic Conflict from the Balkans to Anatolia to the Caucasus.* London, Bergham Books.

VALADÉS, José C. (1987). *El Porfirismo, historia de un régimen.* Mexico: UNAM.

VALCÁRCEL, Daniel. (1965). *La rebelión de Túpac Amaru.* México.

VAN GINNEKEN, Jaap. (1989). *Folla, psicologia e politica.* Roma.

VAN KALMTHOUSE, Anton M. and TAK, Peter J.P. (1988). *Sanctions-Systems in the member-States of the Council of Europe.*

VASCONCELOS, Gerardo. (1976). *Lições de medicina legal.* 2.ed. Rio de Janeiro: Editora Forense. pp. 437-8.

VATTIMO, G. (1999). *Credere di credere.* Milano, Garzanti.

VAUGHN, Joseph. (1997). *Planning for Change: the use of electronic monitoring as a Correctional alternative*, Warrensburg. Central Missouri State University. pp. 161-162.

VERDIN, Jean-Denis. (1995). *O Caso Dreyfus.* Sao Paulo.

VERDROSS, Alfred Verdross. (1962). *La filosofía del derecho del mundo occidental, visión panorámica de sus fundamentos y principales problemas.* México. pp. 35, 179.

VERIN, Jacques. (1979). "Le Succès du Community Service Anglais," *Revue de Science Criminelle et de Droit Pénal Comparée*. Pari: Éditions du Centre Français de Droit Comparé, 3, juillet-septembre, p. 636.

VERNET. J. (1968). *Chromosomes et criminalité.* Paris: Études. pp. 207-17, 216-8.

VEYGA, Francisco De Veyga. (1938). *Degeneración y degenerados. Miseria, vicio y delito.* Buenos Aires.

VEZETTI, Hugo. (1983). *La locura en la Argentina*. Buenos Aires.

VIANO, Emilio. (2003). "Cybercrime and Cybersecurity: The Post-September 11, 2001 Reality," *Transnational Organized Crime*. Durham, Carolina Academic Press, pp. 174-178.

VILLA, Renzo. (1985). *Il deviante e i suoi segni. Lombroso e la nascita dell'antropologia criminale.* Milano.

VILLAFAÑE, B. (1936). *La Ley Suicida.* Buenos Aires, El Ateneo.

———. (1937). *Chusmocracia.* Buenos Aires, Ediar.

VIÑAS, David. (1982). *Indios, ejército y frontera.* México.

VOLD, George B.; BERNARD, Thomas J.; SNIPES, Jeffrey B. (1998). *Theoretical criminology.* New York. p. 219.

VON IHERING, R. (1877). *L'Esprit du Droit Romain dans les diverse phases de son développment.* Paris, Maresccq.

———. (1881). *La lucha por el derecho.* Trans. by Adolfo Posada and Biesca. Madrid.

VON LISZT, Frank. (1891). *Lehrbuch des Deutschen Strafrechts*. Berlín. p. 216.

VON SOEE, Friedrich. (1986). *Cautio Criminales ovvero Dei Processi contro le streghe.* Roma.

VOUGLANNS, Pierre-François Muyard de. (1957). *Institutes au Droit Criminel, ou Principes Géneraux sur ces matieres, suivant le droit civil, canonique, et la jurisprudence du Royaume: avec un traité particulier des crimes.* París.

VOURÉ, H. Catherine. (1977). "Application Socio-Educative du Controle Judiciaire," *Archives de Politique Criminelle*. Paris: Éditions du Centre de Recherches de Politique Criminelle, 2, p. 7.

WALL, David S. (1999). "Cybercrimes: New Wine, No Bottles?" *Invisible Crimes: Their Victims and their Regulation.* London, Macmillan, pp. 105-139.

WALL, David S. (2003). *Cyberspace Crime.* Farnham, UK, Ashgate Dartmouth, pp. 11-21.

WALLERSTEIN, Immanuel. (1998). *Utopística o las opciones históricas del siglo XXI.* México.

WALTER, Martín. (2001). *Historia de la Inquisición Española.* Madrid.

WEBER, Max. (2004). *Ética protestante.* Bueno Aires.

WEBSTER'S Encyclopedic Unabridged Dictionary of the English Language. (1989). New York. p. 321.

WEISCHEDEL, W. (1977). *Zum ewigen Frieden*, en *Werkausgabe, herausgegeben.* Frankfurt. T. XI, p. 203.

WEITEKAMP and HERBERGER. (1995). *Kriminalpolitik.*

———. (1995). "Amerikanische strafrechtspolitik auf dem weg in die catastrophe," *Neue Kriminalpolitik.* book 2.

WERKAUSGABe VIII, *Die Metaphysik der Sitten*, p. 756.

WELL, Pierre and TOMPAKOW, Roland. (1976). *O Corpo Fala.* Petrópolis: Editora Vozes Ltda, 6. ed., pp.7-8; 2.

WERLE, G. (2005). *Tratado de Derecho Penal Internacional.* Valencia, Tirant.

WIER, Iean. (1569). *Cinq livres de l'imposture et de la tromperie des diables: des enchantements et sorcelleries.* Paris.

WILLIAM, J. & CHAMBLISS. (1976). "Functional and conflict theories of crime," *Whose Law, What Order*, edited by Chambliss–Mankoff. New York. p. 8.

WILLIAMS, Matthew. (2000). "Virtually Criminal: Discourse, Deviance and Anxiety within Virtual Communities," *International Review of Law, Computers and Technology*, 14. Routledge Publications, London, New York, pp. 95-104.

WILSON, James Q. and HERRNSTEIN, Richard J. (1985). *Crime and human Nature.* New York.

WINDELBAND, Wilhelm. (1948). *Historia de la filosofía*: *l*a filosofía del iluminismo. México. p. 60.

WOLF, Erik. (1951). *Grosse Rechsdenker.* Tübingen. p. 543.

YAMASHIRO, Robert et al. (1977). "Diagnóstico ultrassonográfico em obstetrícia e ginecologia," *Clínica Geral.* São Paulo: Abaeté. pp. 27-29.

YOUNG, Hugh D. and FREEDMAN, Roger. (1995). *A University Physics.* Massachusetts: Addison–Wesley. pp. 423-431.

ZAFFARONI, E.R. (1989). *En Busca de las Penas Perdidas.* Buenos Aires: AFA Editores Importadores. pp. 79-125.

———. (1993). *La rinascita del diritto penale liberale o la Croce Rossa giudiziaria.* In GIANFORMAGGIO, Letizia, "Le ragioni del garantismo. Discutindo con Luigi Ferrajoli." Torino, Giappicheli.

———. (2001) *La criminología como curso*, en "Política criminal, Derechos Humanos y sistemas jurídicos en el siglo XXI", vol. de hom. al Prof. Dr. Pedro R. David, Buenos Aires.

———. (2004). "Las clases peligrosas: el fracaso de un discurso policial prepositivista," *El penalista liberal, Homenaje a Manuel de Rivacoba y Rivacoba.* Buenos Aires.

———. (2006). *El enemigo en el Derecho Penal.* Buenos Aires, Ediar.

ZAFFARONI, E.R., ALAGIA, A., SLOKAR, A. (2002). *Derecho Penal Parte General.* Buenos Aires, Ediar.

ZALDIVAR, Carlos Alonso. (1996). *Variaciones sobre un mundo en cambio.* Madrid.

ZASLAVSKY, Victor. *La memoria storica nella Russia postsovietica: il bisogno di dimenticare e lo sforzo di ricordare.* In: AA.VSee

ZEA, Leopoldo. (1984). *El positivismo en México*: nacimiento, apogeo y decadência. Mexico.

ZEUTHEN, Eva, et al. (1975). *A psychiatric psychological study of XYY males found in general population.* New York: Institute of Living-Hartford. p. 161.

ZINCANI, Vito. (2009). "Les Stratégies d'Opposition à La Criminalité Organisée," *Les Organizations Criminelles.* Publication Institut National des Hautes Études de Securité (INHES). Paris, Janvier-Mars, No. 7, pp. 79-84.

Index

About the Authors

Eugenio Raúl Zaffaroni, Professor Emeritus of the Universidad de Buenos Aires. Vice-president of the International Association for Criminal Law. Judge of the Supreme Court of the Argentine Republic. Former General Director of ILANUD (Latin American Institute for the Prevention of Crime and Treatment of Offenders, San José, Costa Rica). Doctor in Judicial and Social Sciences. Doctor *Honoris Causa* from the Universities of Castilla-La Mancha (Spain), Macerata (Italy), Rio de Janeiro (Brazil) and several other Universities in Latin America and Europe. Author of general books on Criminal Law, monograph books, and three hundred twelve articles in specialized reviews. Member of the Eminent Jurist Panel of the ICJ (International Jurists Commission) for studying the impact of antiterrorist legislation on Human Rights. He received the Stockholm Prize in Criminology 2009 awarded for the explanation of genocide on the basis of criminological theory for the prevention of any mass killings through state power and for a critique of a purely retributive response.

Edmundo Oliveira, Full Professor in Criminal Law at the University of Amazonia, Amazon region, Brazil. Senior Jurist and Doctor with a Post-Doctorate from the Université La Sorbonne, Paris, France. Member of the International Penal and Penitentiary Foundation created by the General Assembly of the United Nations, headquartered in Berne, Switzerland. Vice President of the International Society of Criminology, Consultative Agency of the United Nations and the Council of Europe, headquarters in Paris, France. Member of the American Society of Criminology, headquartered in Columbus, Ohio,

United States. General Rapporteur of the Permanent Committee for Latin America for Revision of Minimum Rules of the United Nations for Treatment of Prisoners. Former President of the National Council for Criminal and Penitentiary Policy of Brazil. Scientific Consultant of the European Institute of the United Nations for Prevention and Control of Crime. Researcher in Comparative Criminal Law at the Institute of Public Safety of Lake County, Florida, United States. Developed the judicial theory, published in several languages, on the dogmatic conception of crime precipitated or programmed by the victim.